SIXGUNS by ELMER KEITH
1961 EDITION

SIXGUNS
ELMER KEITH

•

1961 EDITION
THE STANDARD REFERENCE WORK

Publisher Warning: Given changes in gun technology since this work was originally published, some suggestions in the following pages may no longer be relevant or safe. This work should be treated as a historical document. The reader assumes full responsibility for any actual loading or firing of firearms.

Published in 2016 by Silver Rock Publishing

Original Copyright © 1955

Sixguns
ISBN: 978-1-62654-570-0 (paperback)
978-1-62654-571-7 (casebound)
978-1-62654-572-4 (spiralbound)

Cover image: Revolver by Roberto A Sanchez,
Courtesy of iStock by Getty Images

Cover design by Justine McFarland
Studio Justine

REPRODUCTION OF AN ORIGINAL OIL PAINTING BY THE RENOWNED ARTIST

CHARLES MARION RUSSELL (1864-1926)

OUTSTANDING DELINEATOR OF THE OLD WEST

Courtesy of Naegele Printing Company, Helena, Montana

Dedicated To My Wife

LORRAINE KATHERINE KEITH

The lady who has shared the vicissitudes of life with me for the past 30 years and helped to make this book possible.

Foreword

I am prejudiced in favor of Elmer Keith. We have been friends for more than a quarter of a century. We have traveled rough trails together. We share a postdated, old West type of tough mindedness. As a friend and as a gun expert no one knows him as well as I do.

Keith has exceptional mental equipment. He would have been outstanding in any science or profession upon which he had cared to focus it. It happened that he had no choice. He brought the idea of guns into the world with him when he was born. Guns have been his obsession since he could toddle.

His life began in the heart of the Civil War guerrilla country. His father and uncles knew the notorious characters personally. He listened to tales of the old gun battles in his cradle. During his sixth year the family moved to western Montana. His boyhood mentors were the Indian fighters, Vigilantes, lawmen and gunfighters of the passing frontier.

Keith's old-time teachers are dust. Their deeds are history and legend. Their philosophies and Draconian codes live in him today. He uses a typewriter, drives a car and prefers to travel by air, but he is, anachronistically, in his innermost being, a part of the decade Charley Russell painted.

On the background of gun lore given him by his early associates, who survived because they did not make mistakes, Keith has grafted the knowledge, the improved techniques and advancements in gun know-how of the last thirty years. Out of all this a great pistol book has been born. It is a unique book. No one but Keith could have written it. Each passing day makes it more impossible for anything like it to be written. The old professors of "gunology" are as much a part of yesterday as are the knights who rode in the crusades.

John Slaughter or Pat Garrett would have traded a hundred steers for a book like this and called it a bargain. What John Wesley Hardin or Doc Holliday might have been willing to do for a copy is best left to the imagination.

But this is not a book just for gunfighters. It is an all-around pistol book for target shooters, hunters, sportsmen, for everyone who loves a good hand gun. It just happens to be scented with the pungence of sage brush campfires, cold for more than half a century.

DON MARTIN
Salmon, Idaho

Preface

Over half a century has passed since I cut my teeth on an old .36 Navy Colt. For 40 years I have almost never been out of easy reach of a good sixgun. Thirty years I spent in the saddle, packing, punching cows and breaking saddle broncs. The sixgun was worn just as regularly as my pants and many times was much more important to my existence. It pulled me out of several tight scrapes with wild horses, wilder cattle and some big game. Though I have witnessed several gun fights, have had guns pulled on me and have been shot at several times, I have never had to use my gun on a man. Several times it was touch-and-go and perhaps only the current knowledge that I was both fast and accurate with a sixgun that saved me from being embroiled.

Though I do not recommend a sixgun for big game, nineteen head of big game have fallen to mine, including elk, bear, deer, cougar, mountain goat and javalina. I have also trailed up a great many big game animals of various species that were wounded by sportsmen and then I finished them off. No record was kept of these or the many coyotes, bobcats and lesser game, or the livestock I have had to kill.

Thirty years have passed since J. H. Fitzgerald and I demonstrated quick-draw work in the W.M.C.A. tent at Camp Perry. My first pistol articles were published then and through the years many thousands of letters on pistols and revolvers have been received and answered. They came from all over the world except Russia. In the aggregate they covered the field—everything from target and game shooting to gun fighting. They taught me a great deal, not only of the guns and loads, but of the psychology of the men who use guns. They wrote and still write in utter frankness, giving one a first hand knowledge, from the classroom of Old Professor Experience. For twenty years I custom-loaded pistol ammunition and shipped it all over the world and had many reports on its use on both man and game.

In addition to these unnumbered correspondents, all of whom taught me something, I am deeply indebted to and can never repay the following good friends—members of the sixgun fraternity, many of whom have since passed on. They were my coaches and instructors: Chauncey Thomas, John Newman, J. D. O'Meara, Pink Simms, Ashley A. Haines, Harold Croft, J. E. Berns, Ed McGivern, Col. D. B. Wesson, Maj. Gen. J. S. Hatcher, Carl Hellstrom, Frank Kahrs, Lt. Col. and Maj. Charles Askins, Finn Garrett, Judge Don Martin, J. Bushnell Smith, J. R. Mattern, Jesse Thompson, Col. Bill Tewes, Gus Peret, Capt. A. H. Hardy, Sam Russell, J. H. Fitzgerald, Maj. R. E. Stratton, Bill O'Connell, Capt. W. R. Strong, Waldo P. Abbott, Samuel H. Fletcher, Dick Tinker, James E. Serven and a great many others.

All were, or are strong characters, experts in some phase of the game, and as interested in clear thinking as in accurate shooting. I also wish to take this opportunity to thank my many friends in the arms and ammunition companies and loading tool companies for their great help and contributions to the game. I wish to thank Jack Martin, the S. D. Myres and the Geo. Lawrence Companies for their fine gun rigs. Whether this book is good or bad, only the reader can judge, certainly if bad it is not from lack of experience.

ELMER KEITH,
Salmon, Idaho

Table of Contents

Dedication vii

Foreword..ix

Preface xi

CHAPTER I	History of the Sixgun	1
CHAPTER II	Selecting the Handgun	57
CHAPTER III	Learning to Shoot	87
CHAPTER IV	Sixgun Sights	101
CHAPTER V	Long Range Shooting	109
CHAPTER VI	Game Shooting	119
CHAPTER VII	Double Action Shooting	137
CHAPTER VIII	Gun Rigs and Holsters	147
CHAPTER IX	Quick Draw and Hip Shooting	161
CHAPTER X	Gun Fighting	177
CHAPTER XI	Revolver Versus Auto Pistol	191
CHAPTER XII	Aerial and Trick Shooting	197
CHAPTER XIII	Slip Shooting, Fanning, Cavalry Guns	205
CHAPTER XIV	Loading and Management of Cap and Ball Sixguns	209
CHAPTER XV	Repairs, Remodeling, Resighting	215
CHAPTER XVI	A Bullet Chapter	227
CHAPTER XVII	Cartridge Reloading	241
CHAPTER XVIII	Selection of Gun Cartridges	275
CHAPTER XIX	Ornamentation	291
CHAPTER XX	Care and Cleaning	306

Chapter I

History of the Sixgun

IN A SENSE revolvers are not new, as several were made in flint lock times, probably the most notable being the old Collier. As early as the Revolution, over-under rifles were made in the flint persuasion and the barrels were revolved for firing. It was not until Samuel Colt's revolving pistol in 1836 and the advent of the percussion cap, that revolvers really came into their own. Prior to that time the single shot or double-barreled muzzle loading pistol supplemented by the sword or Bowie knife were the commonly accepted sidearms. Sam Colt's new pistol, however, revolutionized weapons of self defense. The Patterson Colt manufactured by the Patterson Arms Mfg. Co. at Patterson, N. J. under Sam Colt's Patent No. 138, granted February 25, 1836 was first known as a revolving pistol.

It was so superior to the flint lock Collier revolver with the No. 9 percussion cap, in its ignition system, that it soon overshadowed that excellent arm. The four and six-barreled revolving pepperboxes that soon came out after the Colt invention gave young Sam Colt his greatest competition. They were woefully inaccurate compared to the Colt and sold for a much lower price, but never attained much popularity among real gunmen.

Mark Twain on an early trip to California, spoke of one of the passengers trying out his pepperbox revolver from the stage coach. "He aimed at the bole of a live oak tree, but fetched the nigh mule," of the hitch.

The Colt Patterson revolver early became popular, especially with horsemen. Texas was then having trouble with both wild Indians and their fight for independence with Mexico. The Colt Patterson pistol became very popular and brought enormous prices. While not many of these early Colts were in usage, they proved their superiority over all other belt guns. The fact that the owner could obtain an extra cylinder and carry it loaded, greatly facilitated quick recharging of the arm. All that was necessary to make the change from an empty gun to a loaded one was to drive out the key, pull the barrel off the base pin, then slip on the loaded cylinder and replace the barrel and key, and a man had another five rounds at his disposal. Extra cylinders could be cleaned and reloaded at camp or at home, and when in a fight this interchangeability of cylinders made the early Colt a priceless weapon to men who sorely needed the best. Colt's design was even better than he realized. His five shot pistols made one man the equal of five armed with swords or bowie knives. His pistols were well proven in the many sanguinary conflicts between the settlers of Texas and the Indians as well as in their war with Mexico.

Sam Colt's Revolver

The history of the revolver really starts with the Patterson Colt revolving pistol. The navy of the Republic of Texas probably used them first in organized combat with the Mexican navy. Captain Moore, later Commodore Moore of the Texas navy, was a close friend of Sam Colt, and Colt later engraved the

A picture of the Derringer Pistol with which President Lincoln was assassinated by Booth, the gun now in the custody of the Judge Advocate General's Office, War Department.

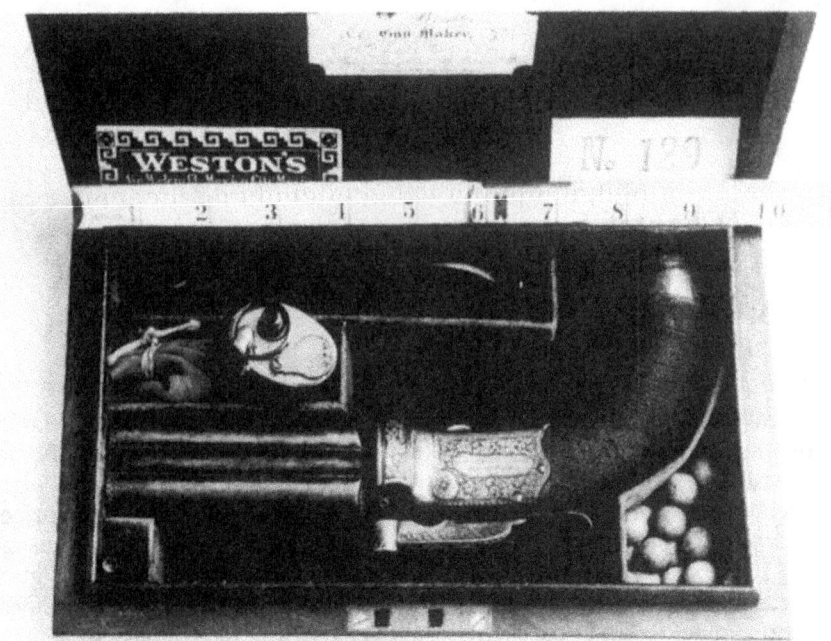

English four barrel folding trigger percussion pepperbox revolver marked, "Improved Revolving Pistol, J. Beattie, 223 Regent Street, London."

Rare Flint Revolver.

cylinders of many of his army and navy sixguns with the famous old Ormsby engraving of the fight between the Texas and Mexican navies, May 16, 1843. The Texas navy used these Patterson Colts from about 1839 and later furnished them to the Texas rangers and they in turn used them with telling effect on the Comanches. Capt. Jack Hays commanding a troop of the Texas Rangers, some 15 in number, more than once routed many times their number of Indians in close cavalry fighting, due to the rapidity with which they could deliver accurately aimed fire from the Patterson Colts.

The five-shot Patterson Colts were used in the Florida Indian wars, the Texas war with Mexico and in innumerable battles with the plains Indians. The U. S. Government bought some Patterson carbines as early as 1841, and both pistols and carbines in 1845.

Only about 350 arms were sold to the Government at this time, however, and the lack of government orders, combined with poor business accounting and management, finally led to the complete failure of the Patent Arms Mfg. Co. in 1843. Dudley Selden first managed it and later, after disagreement with Colt, resigned, and John Ehlers took over management of the plant. Colt and Ehlers in turn did not get along, and though Colt had assigned his patents to the Company, litigation started in 1841 when he tied up the records of the Company, demanding a thorough accounting which finally led to the complete failure in 1843.

Right to left: 1. Thuer Derringer, second type, .41 R.F. 2. Thuer Derringer, first type, .41 cal. R.F. 3. National Derringer, .41 cal. R.F. 4. National Derringer, .41 cal. R.F.

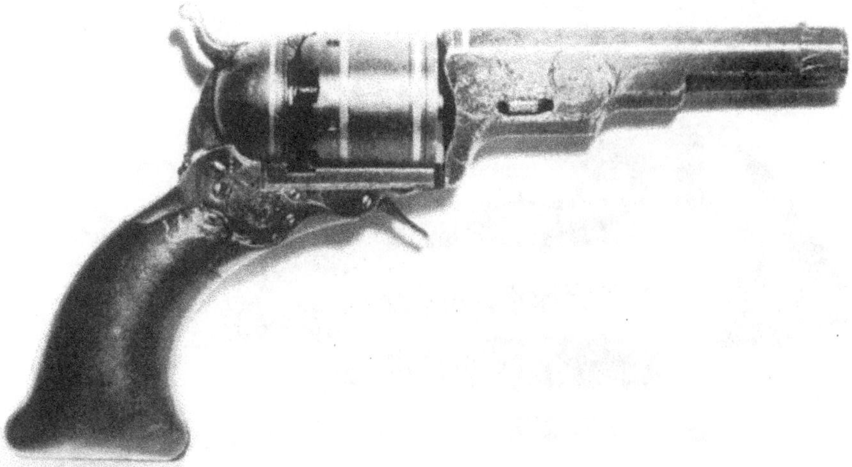

Very finely engraved heavy Paterson Colt.

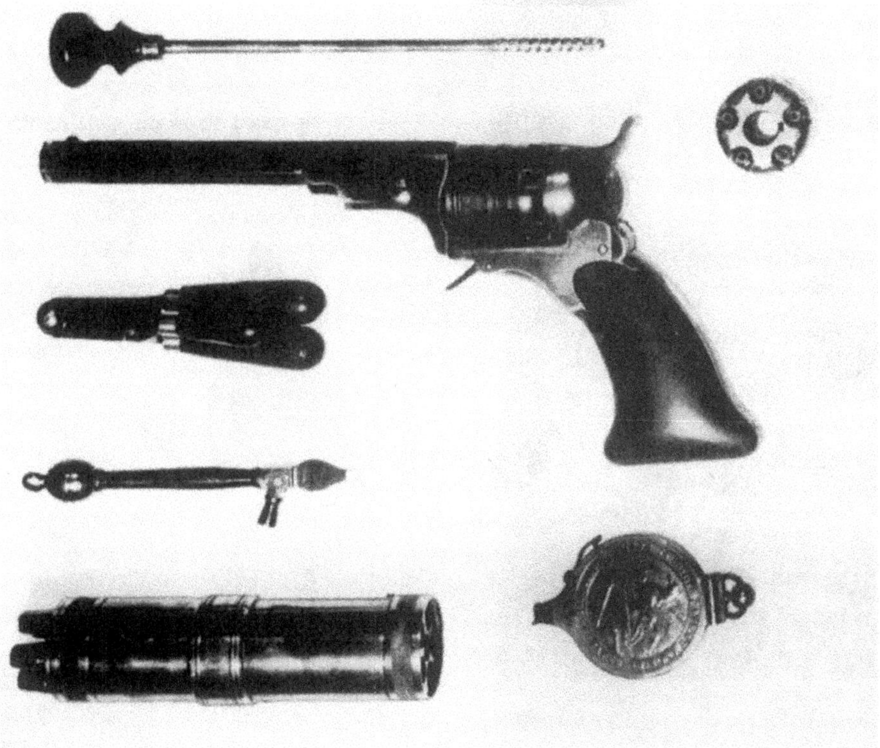

Fine Paterson Colt complete with all accessories.

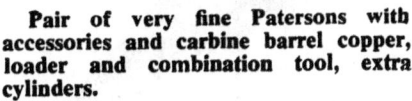

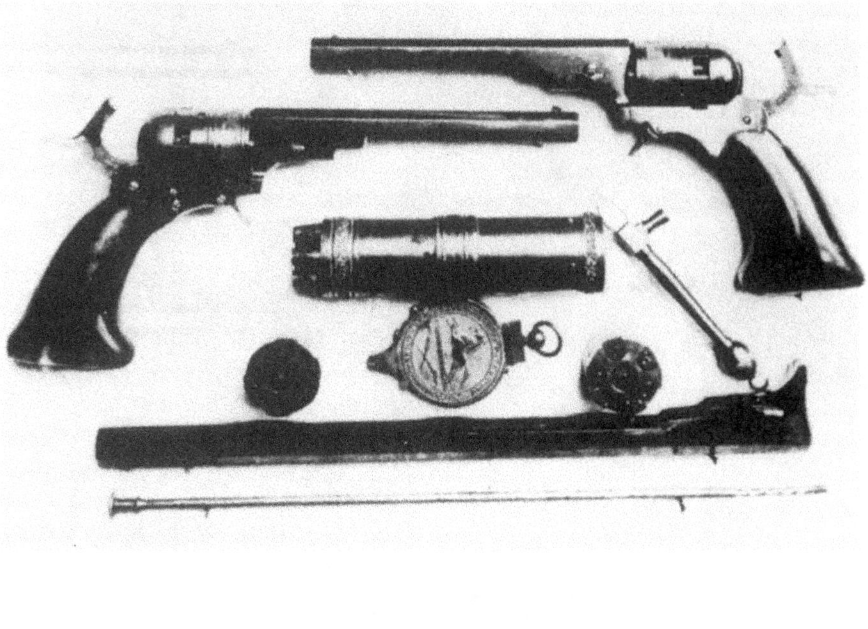

Pair of very fine Patersons with accessories and carbine barrel copper, loader and combination tool, extra cylinders.

Fine cased Paterson Colt outfit.

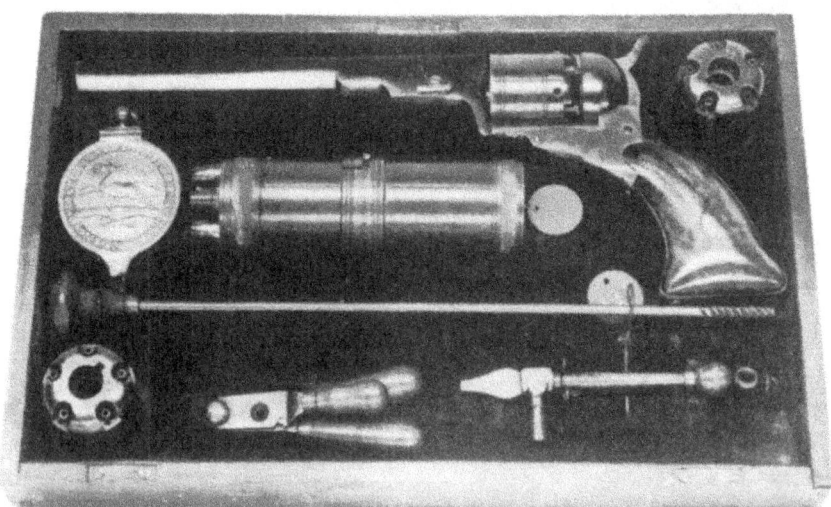

Cased Texas Paterson.

Courtesy of Phillips.
A pair of fine Texas Patersons.

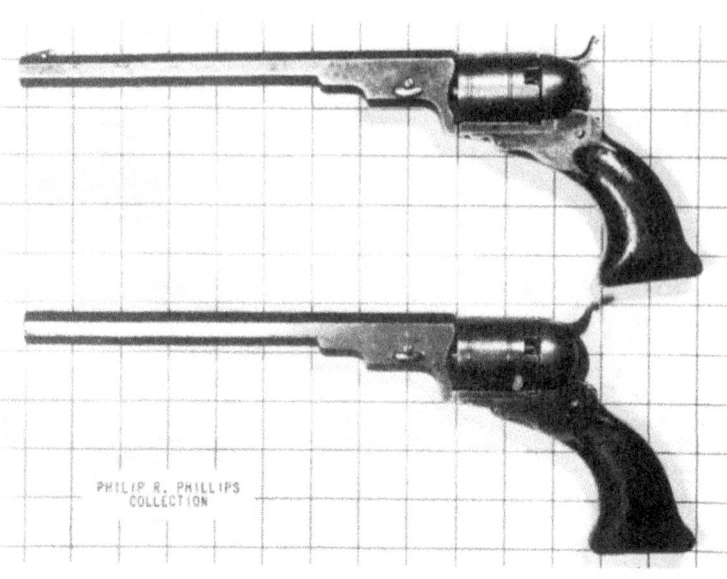

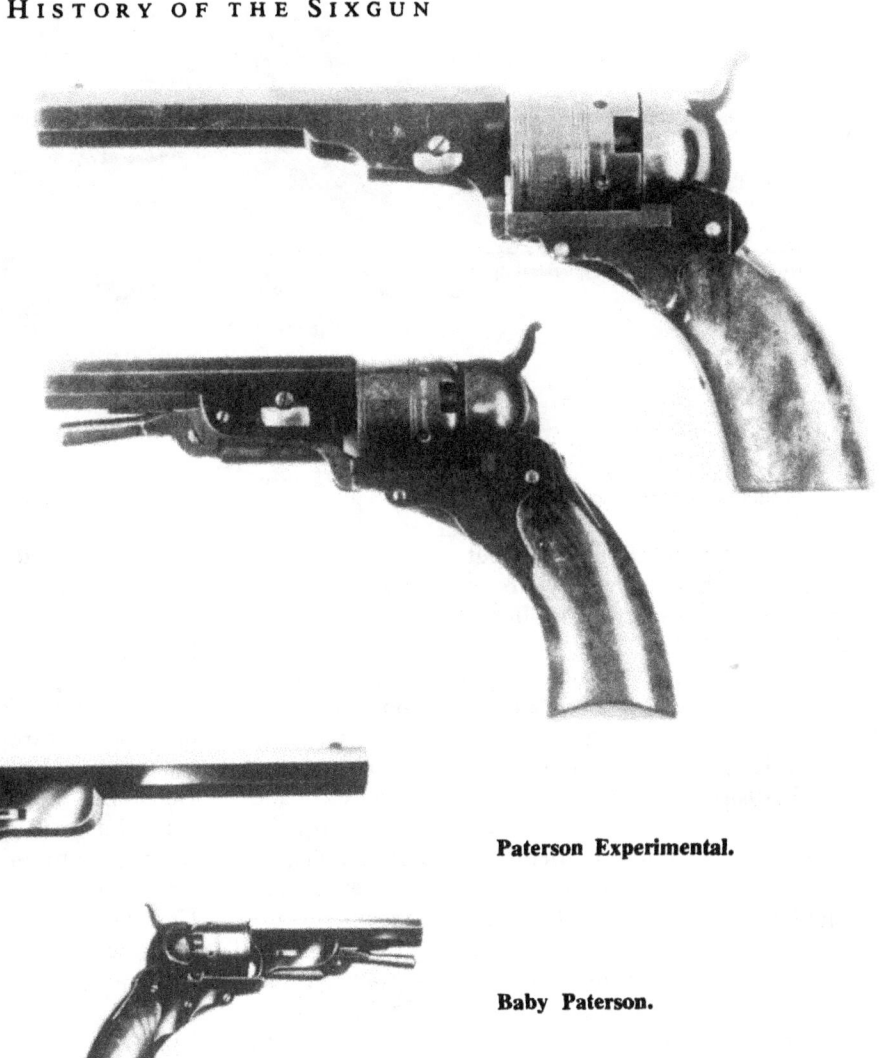

Belt Paterson.
Pocket or Baby Paterson.

Paterson Experimental.

Baby Paterson.

Texas Paterson.

Colt Paterson rifle, first improvement 1836.

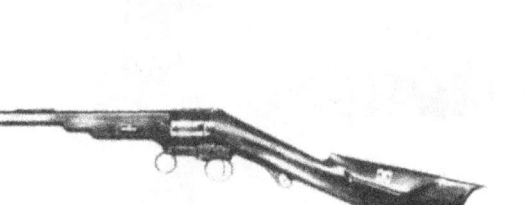

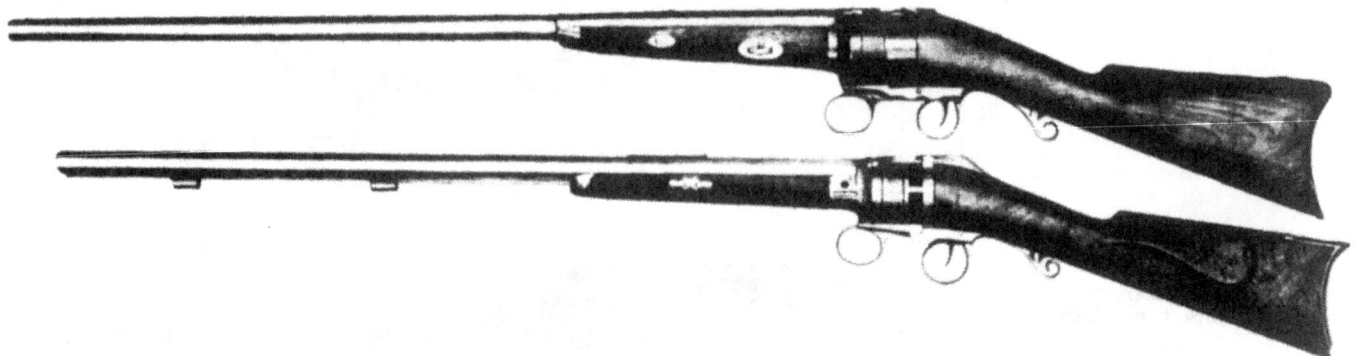

Top: Colt Paterson rifle, 10 shot, military arm 1836, first model. Bottom: Colt Paterson rifle, second model 1836 experimental.

Colt was smart enough to put a clause in his contract with the company to the effect that all patent rights would revert to him in event of failure of the Company.

Colt next spent five years in other manufacturing ventures and made money on telegraph wire and developed underwater mines and the marine telegraph cable. With the coming of the Mexican war, the gold rush to California, the Crimean war and the Mormon migration, the demand for Colt's revolving pistols reached unprecedented proportions. Those in existence sold for enormous prices. Texas was admitted to the Union in 1845 and the Mexican war followed soon afterward. The Texas Rangers were then taken into the regular U.S. Army. Rangers like Capt. Samuel H. Walker, Capt. Jack Hays and Ben McCulloch, who had used the big Paterson Colts with such telling effect in many forays against both Mexicans and Indians, wanted their commands armed with a pair of Colt revolvers. They fully realized their worth and pushed their demands until Capt. Walker was commissioned to go North to try to induce Samuel Colt to again take up the manufacture of his revolvers and to bring out a much larger, better designed, and more powerful arm suited to cavalry needs.

Dragoons

The Paterson Colt was fragile with a folding trigger and no rammer on the early models. Capt. Walker helped Colt design the first Colt Dragoon, the famous 1847 Walker Colt. General Zachary Taylor of Texas asked the governor for 5,000 volunteers and the war with Mexico was on. Captain Walker hunted up his old friend Samuel Colt who then had no facilities whatever for manufacturing the big revolvers. Though Colt had tried for years for a government contract for his Paterson pistols, he was in no position to furnish them when he received a Government order for 1,000 improved six-shot revolvers. In December 1846 Sam Colt hunted up Eli Whitney who did have the manufacturing facilities and they entered into a contract for the first 1,000 Colt Dragoons, model 1847, as designed by Colt and Captain Walker. Colt even obtained many of his old workmen from Paterson, N. J. and his old friend Commodore Moore loaned him a Paterson Colt to help in the design work. Whitney assigned Thomas Warner to oversee the work. A subcontract was let to Slate & Brown of Hartford for the barrels and cylinders. Colt arranged for the forgings for those 1,000 holster pistols to be completed in five weeks.

The new pistol was a six-shot, caliber .45 though called a .44, and weighed over four pounds with a 9 inch barrel and a 2½ inch cylinder. A strong rammer with a spring latch underneath the barrel was added, also a sturdy square backed trigger guard and possibly the finest grip ever devised for a big sixgun. The Colt Walker was the best known of all early six-shooters and really led to the name six-shooter or the later term sixgun. Government inspectors are said to have turned down about 12% of the arms submitted and the actual number made is still a con-

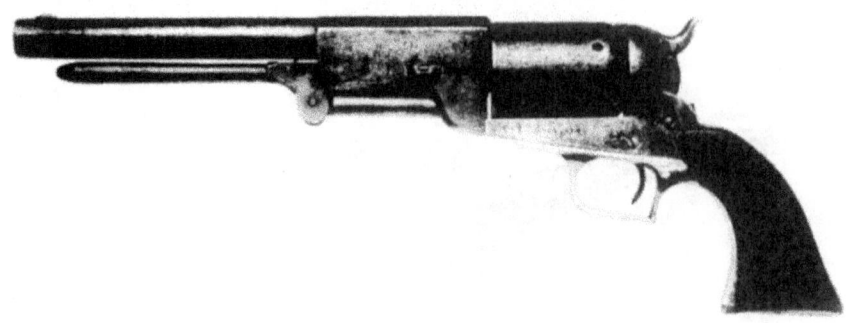

B Company Number 26 Colt Walker.

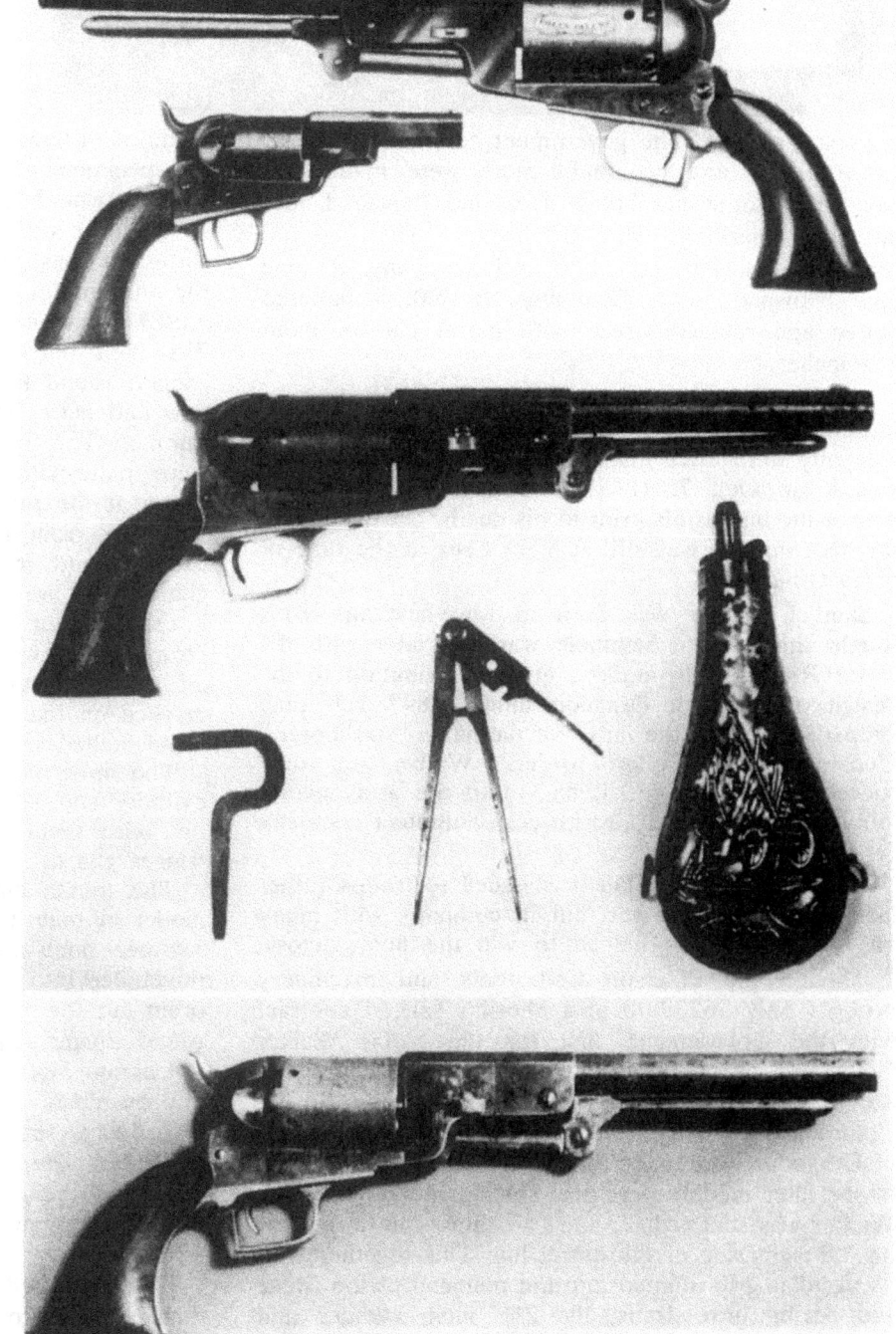

Whitneyville Walker Colt.

Whitneyville Walker.

Pocket 1848 or Baby Dragoon.

Colt Walker with accessories

Colt Walker or first Dragoon.

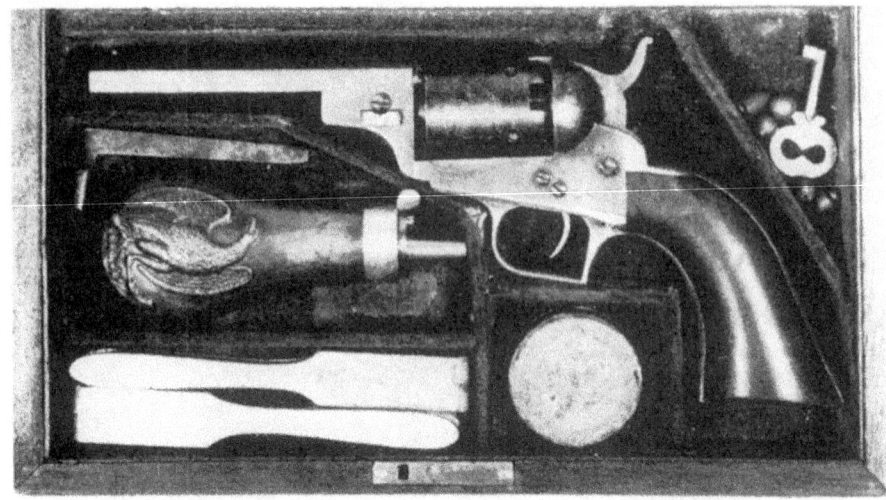

Rare cased 1848 Pocket Colt.

troversial subject. The government contract called for 1,000 pistols and no doubt more were made. We have seen some numbered over one thousand, but the usual markings were the maker's lettering and very low serials as issued to each company. At one time I owned an A Company No. 90, a battered buffed and reblued wreck with barrel cut to about 6½ inches.

Captain Walker commanded C. Company but his shipment of Walker Colts did not arrive for his company until after his death from a Mexican lance wound on Oct. 7, 1847. Colt had sent Walker a pair of the big pistols prior to his death, but the supply for his company was still at Vera Cruz at the time of his last charge.

Samuel Walker was born in Maryland in 1817, fought through the Seminole war and later with the Texas Rangers. He made a great contribution to the design of the Colt Dragoon model 1847 and may properly be called the father of the name "sixshooter." Under General Taylor's orders, Walker not only succeeded in getting Colt back into the arms manufacturing business but also raised a volunteer company for the Mexican war.

The 1847 Colt Walker was issued to troops rather late in the Mexican war, but in company with many old Paterson Colts, helped to win the final victory.

Though the Paterson Colt tools and machinery brought only $6209.00 at a Sheriff's sale, a contract with the Government, first for the 1,000 Walker Colts, and later contracts for the later model Dragoon six-shooters soon put Colt back in the arms business. Counting the Walker Colts the first, in all, four models of Dragoons were made for the Government and many of the later models were also sold to individuals. The Walker was stamped U. S. 1847 above the barrel key on the right side of the barrel lug. This together with its peculiar grip inletted into the rear end of the frame and flaring grip straps, the 2½ inch cylinder and 9 inch barrel, and the peculiar rammer handle hook underneath the barrel easily identify the first Colt Model Dragoon. Many false copies have since been made of this rare old arm and before being purchased all specimens should be given very careful scrutiny by men who know Colts.

We have seen but one that was cased with accessories. It was numbered serially over 1,000 and is the only one of its kind we have heard of. The second model Dragoon was made with a 2¼ inch cylinder, 7½ inch barrel, square back guard, short curved trigger, round bolt stops like the Walker and with a new and better rammer latch at the front end of the rammer. The first few of this second model Dragoon were made with Walker type stocks inletted into the frame at the rear end, an indication that parts were left over from the Walker contract. Also the very early second model guns have rather wide trigger guards and are much heavier than later productions. I have one of the only two of these second model Dragoons known to be in existence today, cased with all original accessories, its serial number is 5842, and marked on the cylinder is "U.S. Dragoons," with the usual etched scenes, and silver plated stock straps.

The third model Dragoon had the same dimension cylinder and barrel also with a short curved trigger, but with rectangular bolt stops and a square back trigger guard.

The fourth and last model differs from the third model in that it has a long trigger, and a still later rammer latch and usually a three leaf rear sight dovetailed into the rear end of the barrel. It was very often cut for a shoulder stock. Also distinctive is its round trigger guard.

Captain William A. Thornton, is credited with the improvements from the Walker 1847 model to the less bulky, shorter second, third and fourth model Dragoons. He ·was also the inspection officer who examined the guns before they were turned over to the Government. Thornton died a Major General in 1866.

Colt furnished the War Department with the 1,000 Colt Walkers together with a powder flask for each pair of guns for just $28 each. Today any good Walker Colt will bring $3,000. We know of one cased Walker that brought $10,000.

A second contract for another 1,000 revolvers at the same price enabled Colt to move to Hartford and establish an arms plant there. Colt started his Hartford plant in 1847 and made some more Dragoons there at that time, the first of the second model probably having the Walker type straps and stock. Only around 1,100 sixguns were made at the Whitney Armory. Colt soon established himself at Hartford and delivered the second 1,000 Dragoons to the Government in 1848. He also brought out the little 1848 Pocket model at that time, with a square back guard, short curved trigger, oval stops, full octagon barrel and no loading rammer. He also sold and delivered some private orders during the last of the year.

Colts Dragoons sold for as high as $500 each in the gold fields of California and often went for $150 and upwards along the Mexican border and in the Indian country in 1850. One experimental model made up by Colt but never put in production had a hinged top strap and a base pin or spindle extending only part way through the cylinder and had no wedge key. This was never manufactured in quantity but a beautiful pair are on exhibition at the Smithsonian Museum in Washington, D. C. Cylinder markings differed. Some had "U.S. Dragoons," some "U.S.M.R.," meaning U.S. Mounted Rifles and some were marked "U.S.M.I." for Mounted Infantry.

W. L. Ormsby designed the engraving for the Colt Dragoon cylinders—U.S. troops pursuing mounted Indians. These scenes were rolled on the cylinder. Some of the last model were fitted with three leaf rear sights and many with carbine stocks, some also having a canteen inside the stock. Some of these were also made with 8 inch barrels. These big six-shooters proved invaluable in the early Indian fighting and were also often used to run buffalo. They would drive a ball or the conical slug through the lungs of a buffalo at close range.

Civilian Demand

The Gold Rush to California and later the Mormon migration contributed to the demand for the sixgun. The Plains Indians were some of the finest wild cavalrymen the sun has ever shone on, and for this close range fast cavalry fighting, the heavy sixgun was far superior to any saber or single-shot rifle. The latter was usually a muzzle loader. Carried in pairs in saddle holsters or singly on the hip, they gave their owner a vast advantage over the Indian armed with a buffalo lance or a bow and arrow, or a white man armed with single shot pistols and rifles. Colt's future as an arms manufacturer was now assured.

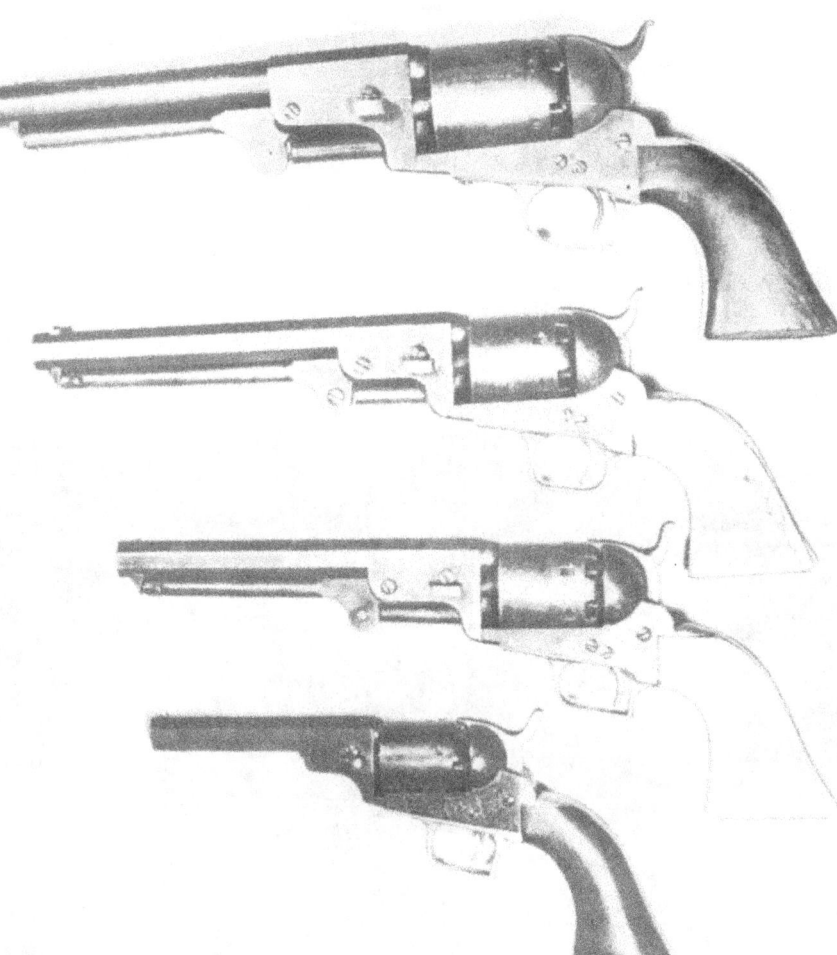

Author's Collection

Top—1848 Second Dragoon.

Second—Major R. E. Strattons .36 Navy.

Third—Rare 6½ inch square back guard Navy.

Bottom—1848 Pocket Colt.

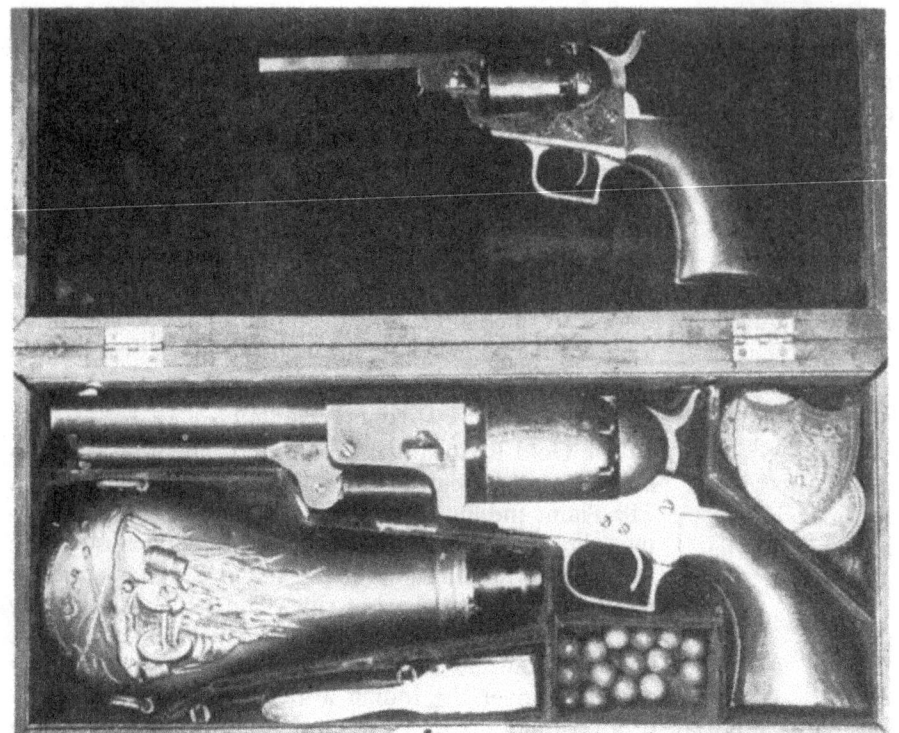

Author's Collection

Top—1848 engraved Pocket.

Bottom—Colt Dragoon cased with all original accessories. One of two such known in existence.

Pocket Pistol, "Little Dragoon", 6 inch barrel, .31 caliber, 1848 Model.

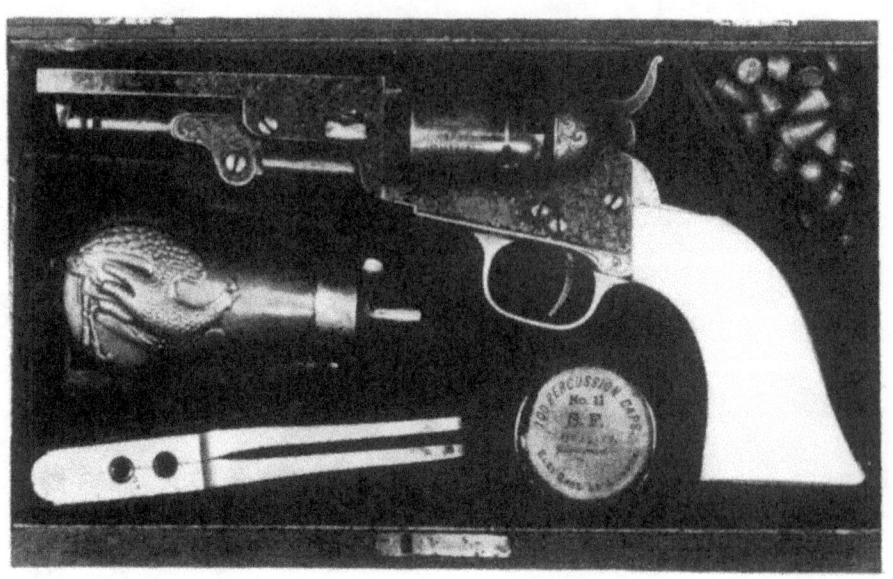

Very fine presentation cased 1849 pocket Colt.

The Santa Fe trail was opened up as early as 1822 but the Oregon trail was not pioneered and really in use until 1843. It ran from Independence, Missouri, to the Williamette Valley in Oregon. The Mormom migration rolled over it to about Fort Hall, Idaho, and thence into the Salt Lake Valley and a further trail led from Salt Lake on to the California gold fields. Probably in the entire history of man, no similar migration on so vast a scale has been accomplished.

Government troops were soon needed to fight hostile Indians, and to keep the trails open for the immigrants who were settling a vast area. Forts sprang up all along the various routes and vast amounts of supplies had to be freighted to these forts and trading posts along the routes.

The firm of Russell, Majors and Waddell, with headquarters at Leavenworth, Kansas, were pioneers in between Independence, Missouri, and Santa Fe, New Mexico. In 1858 John Butterfield started his over-land stage from St. Louis, to El Paso, Yuma and on to Los Angeles, California, covering some 2,759 miles in around 25 days and at a cost of $100 per passenger. He employed 750 men with a total of 100 Concord stages.

Ben Holliday next started a network of stage lines that at one time covered most of the Western territory, and operated as many as five hundred coaches. In 1866 he sold out to Wells, Fargo & Co. Wells Fargo had started in San Francisco in 1851. While many stage lines were knocked out by the Civil War, Wells Fargo continued to operate. As late as 1859 news took about a month to reach the West Coast from the East by stage routes.

The Pony Epress was inaugurated in 1860, and

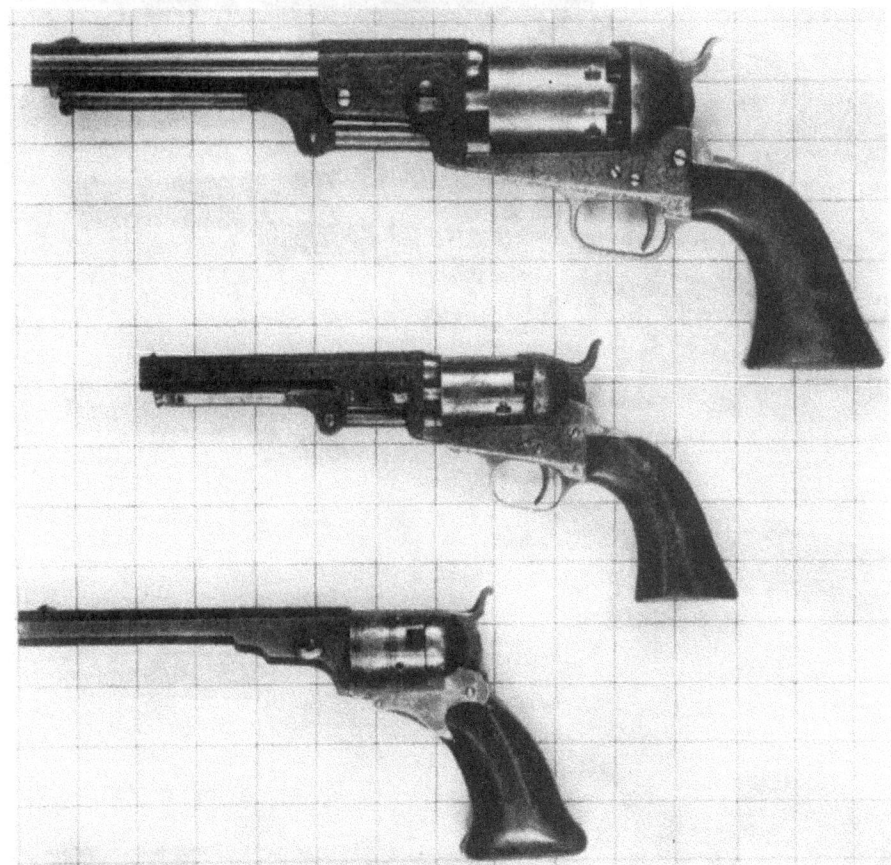

Third Model Dragoon 1849 Pocket Colt Paterson.

the freighting business supplying these outposts of civilization scattered through hostile Indian country. At one time they used as many as 75,000 oxen and employed well over 6,000 men in their freighting business.

Many went around the horn in ships to California and Oregon and still others went by ship to the Isthmus of Panama, by cart or horse across the Isthmus and again by ship to California or Oregon. In addition to the rich placers of California, the great Comstock, or Mother Lode of California and Nevada, drew still another great migration of fortune hunters.

As early as 1850 a stage coach line was inaugurated continued through 1862. Colonel Majors established the Pony Express line with 190 relay stations, 500 horses and 80 specially picked, lightweight riders. At first each carried two six-shooters and a carbine but they soon dispensed with the carbine and second sixgun, carrying but one extra loaded and capped cylinder. The Eastern telegraph reached to St. Joseph, Missouri, and the Pony Express ran from there to San Francisco—some 2,000 miles. They established the first fast mail service between the two points. All this early Westward migration and its attendant activities created an enormous demand for sixguns for protection. Colt developed the little Wells Fargo Colt

Cased Colt 1849 Pocket Presentation.

Colt shoulder stocked Dragoons, all third model. Bottom, rare canteen stock.

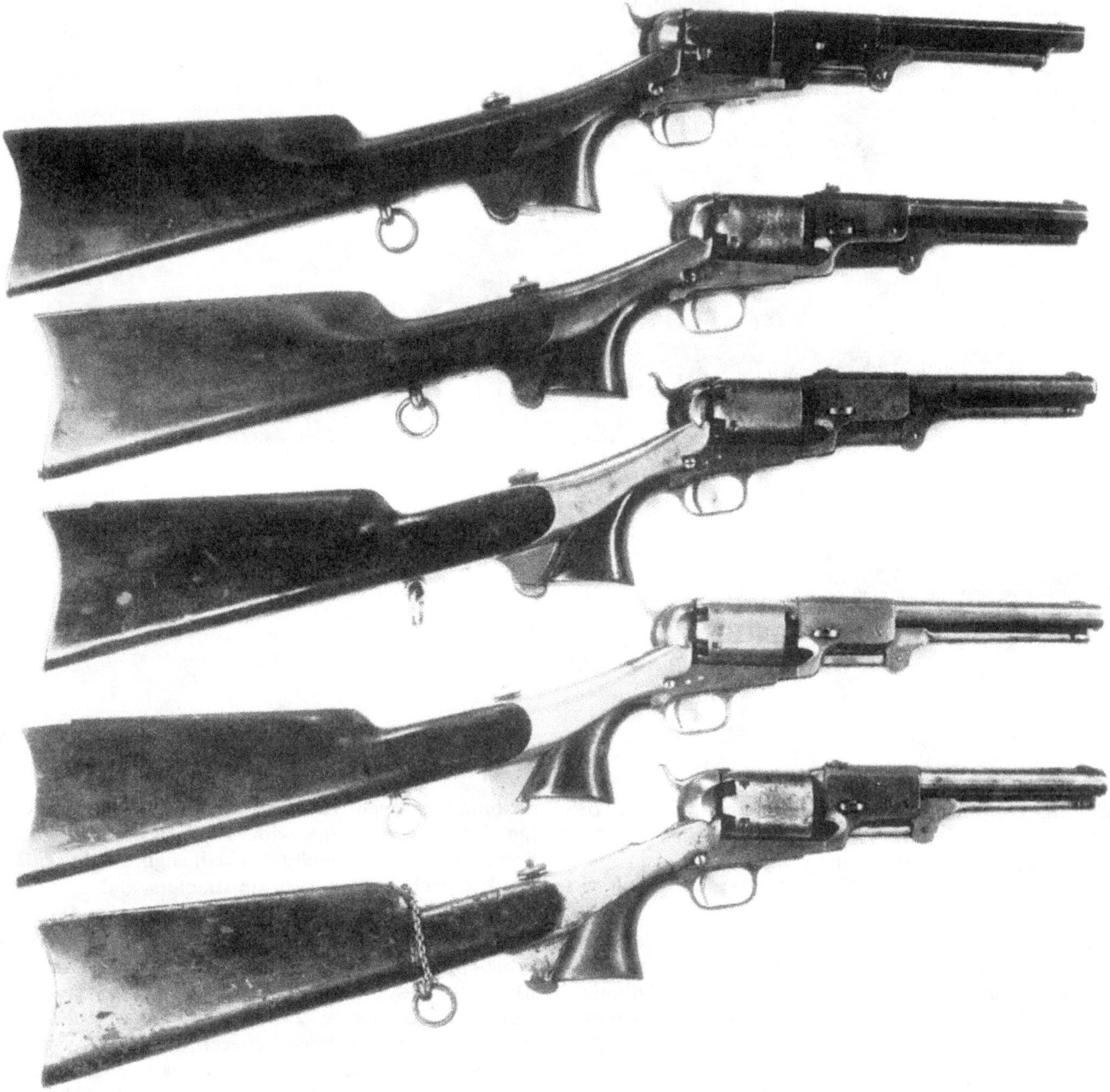

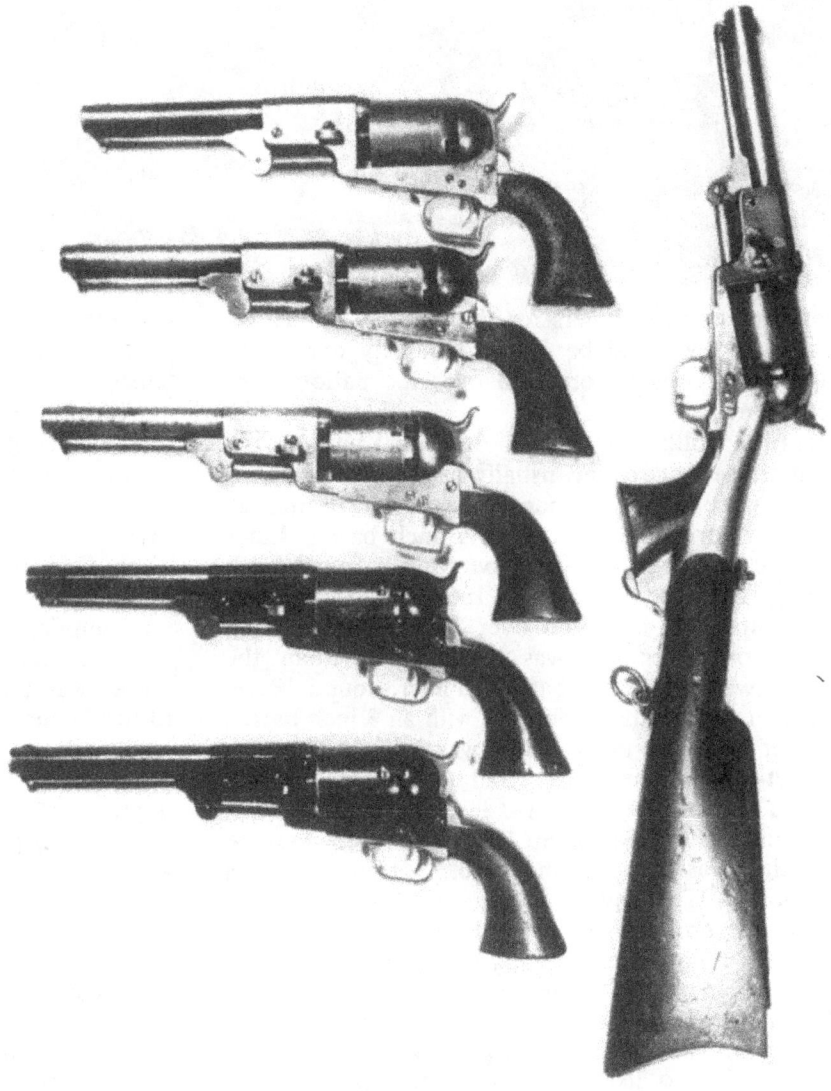

Dragoon Colts.
Top pair: First model after Walker.
Second Model.
Bottom pair: Third model and stocked gun, late third model.

with round trigger guard, long trigger, and no rammer. Very light weight, with the extra loaded and capped cylinder it formed the armament of many of the Pony Express riders.

Indian fights were numerous and stage holdups just as frequent, so that everyone went around armed to the teeth. The sixgun played a very important part in this early development of the West.

Fixed Cartridges

While the Western migration was in progress the Civil War broke out and this created an endless demand for six-shooters. Many firms sprang up to furnish revolvers, mostly for the federal forces but in the deep south some small factories also started making near copies of Colt arms for the Southern forces. Remington, Starr, Manhattan, Cooper, Savage and many others were made in percussion form. The firm of Smith & Wesson obtained a patent for a cylinder bored clear through to use fixed cartridges, and pioneered in American cartridge revolvers.

In this four year struggle everything was used, from the percussion sixgun, to the new Smith & Wesson in .22 and .32 rim fire calibers. The government let big contracts. Colt had by then developed his 1849 Pocket, his 1855 Root model side hammer, the famous 1851 model Navy .36 and also the 1860 model .44 Army. These in addition to the little Wells Fargo Colt. A great many of the heavy Dragoons were still in Service, so virtually everything that would shoot was used at one time or another on both sides in the great conflict. The ever increasing demand for faster loading in the Civil War spurred inventors and brought out many rim fire fixed cartridges such as the early Smith & Wesson and Volcanic types and the .44 Henry, the .56 Spencer and others. The great war also created a

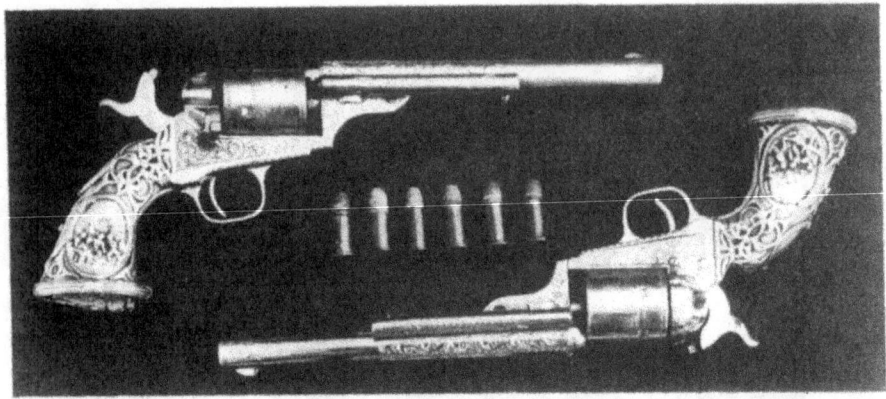

Pair of Super Presentation 1871-72 First Colt C.T.G. type revolvers (not a conversion).

demand for extra cylinders for the existing percussion sixguns so they could be changed quickly during an engagement. Arms factories all over the nation were humming at full speed.

The First Colt's Navy was in .36 caliber with square backed trigger guard and usually a 7½ inch octagon barrel, but some were made with shorter barrels as we have an original with only 6½ inch barrel. Later ones were in the same caliber but with a round back trigger guard. The .44 caliber 1860 Colt Army was very popular and it is said over 300,000 were made for the government. It was much lighter than the Dragoon with shorter, rebated cylinder, round barrel and rachet type loading lever, but with an 8 inch barrel. Still later the 1861 model Navy was brought out with a rachet-type loading lever and a 7½ inch round barrel. These arms were issued in pairs to cavalrymen and many of the Southern Cavalry carried four to six of them; as many as they could get and pack on their horses. The Indian fighting and the war with Mexico had proven the worth of the six-shooter over the sword or saber and cavalrymen were not slow in learning their use in battle.

Canteen stocks were also made in quantity for both the .44 Army and the .36 Navy guns and used by many outfits. Owing to its perfect balance, great accuracy and its record as a man killer, the .36 Navy became very popular both in the old octagon barrel model and the later round barrel model. Its grip was perfect for most men, and while smaller, it was much the same shape as the old Walker grip. In fact Colt pistols show little change in grip shape from the 1847 Walker on down to the Colt's S.A. Army, manufactured up to the second world war. No other grip will absorb the recoil of a heavily loaded revolver with less punishment to the hand, as it simply turns up in the hand in recoil, allowing the thumb to come up over the hammer for a quick repeat shot. This design was excellent for cavalrymen and both safe and fast when a recalcitrant horse had to be managed at the same time.

Army officers used everything and the little Smith & Wessons were very popular with them. Colts were thoroughly established and more of them were used in the Civil War than all other revolvers. They were also the standard issue to Federal troops. Officers and the C.S.A. used whatever pistol they could lay their hands on. The big heavy Starr was used extensively.

My old friend the late Samuel H. Fletcher, who served through the Civil War with the Second Illinois Cavalry, told me he emptied both .36 Navies in several cavalry fights and had to simply cut his way out with the saber. His company lost heavily on several occasions. One interesting anecdote he told me, happened as follows. In a fight with the Southern Cavalry, he had emptied a .36 Navy six-shooter and four shots from its mate before the fight was over. A Southern officer was turned over to him to be conducted back to headquarters to be turned over to the guard. On the way back to the Federal headquarters, he allowed the C.S.A. officer to retain his sidearms. They came on a group of Federal foragers, killing some hogs in a brushy hog pasture. The boys in blue asked Sam to kill one which ran out of the brush, which he did with his .36 Navy. Soon another hog broke cover and they yelled at him to get that one, which he also dropped with a ball back of the ear as it ran past his horse. He said when he tipped the sixgun up to blow through the barrel to moisten the powder residue he realized it was also empty. He told me many times he should have stopped right then and asked some of the infantry to guard the prisoner and his horse while he reloaded his sixguns, but as he had used but the one gun on the hogs, he doubted if the Southern officer knew his guns were empty, so he simply conducted him back to headquarters. There he showed him his two empty Colts. The Southern Officer said, "Suh, if I had known that, you would now be my prisoner and we would be well inside Confederate lines." "But," said he, "I saw you drop two running hogs, and as far as I knew both your Colts were still loaded. And, even though you allowed me to carry my saber and sixshooter, I knew you were a fine and fast sixgun shot, so I took no chances."

My old friend Maj. R. E. Stratton, now gone to his reward, carried a beautiful pair of fully engraved and carved ivory stocked 1851 model .36 Navy Colts through the Civil War where he served with the first Texas regiment with Lee in Virginia and elsewhere. Later he carried them for nine years of ranger service down along the Pecos, and later over much of the west. I bought one of them from him and when I asked him what became of the mate to it, he wrote me that he lost it, along with his left arm in a gun fight in Cheyenne, Wyoming and that I might possibly find it in or around Cheyenne somewhere.

He said the gun I now have had probably seen more service as a man killer than any Colt in existence. Maj. Stratton said that for a man stopper he preferred the round ball with a chamber full of F.F.G. to the pointed conical bullet. Sam Fletcher also told me he preferred a pure lead round ball in his Navy Colts with chamber full of black powder to the issued conical ball loads that came in little wooden boxes of six each. He claimed the round ball dropped enemy cavalrymen much better and took all the fight out of them, whereas the pointed bullet at times would only wound and leave them fighting. He stated, however, that when foraging and shooting cattle for meat, the pointed bullet was the best for body shots that had to be taken where penetration was needed, but that on all frontal shots on beef, the old round ball was plenty good and would reach the brain—even on bulls.

Major Stratton claimed that while the big Dragoon

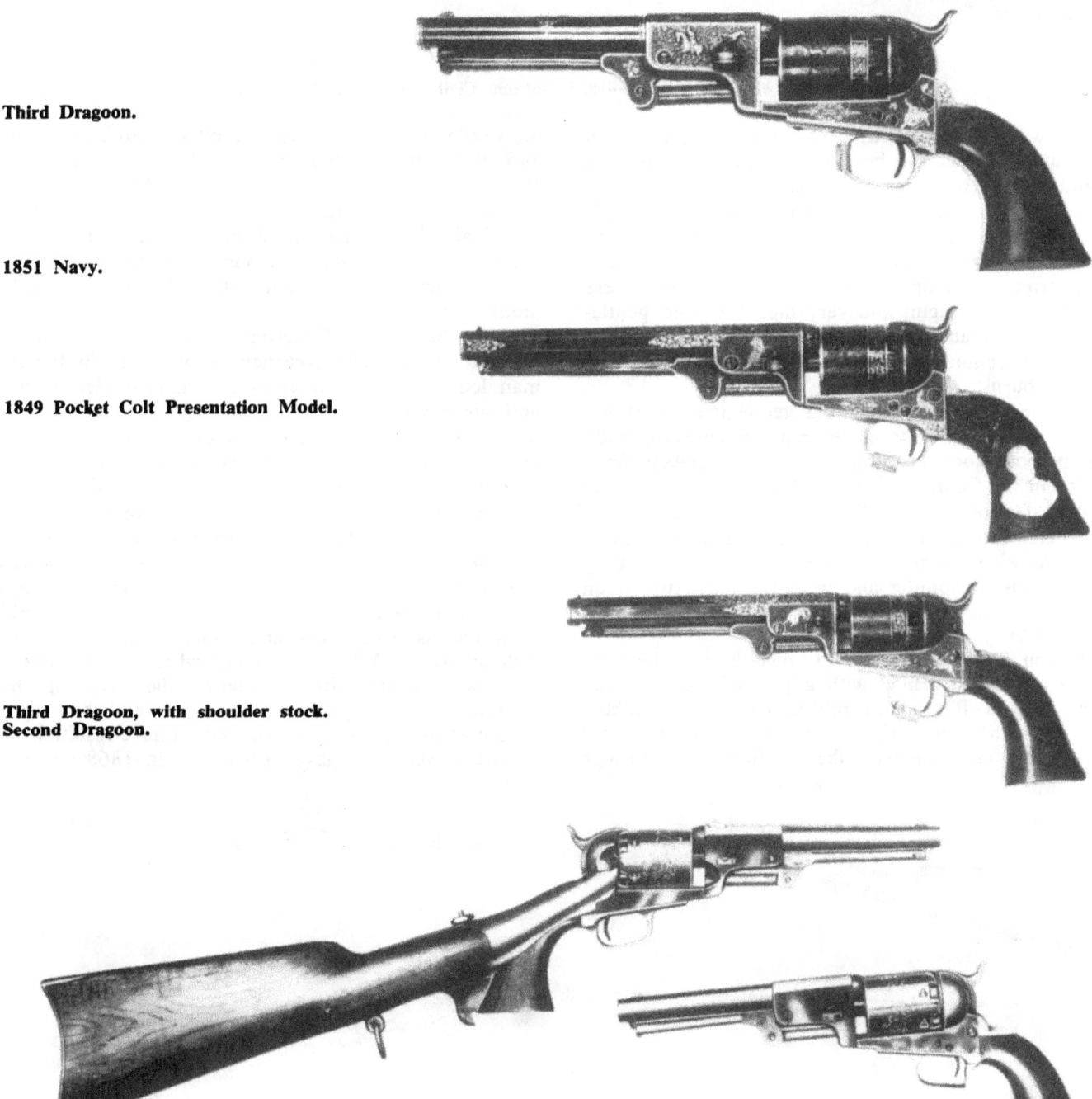

Third Dragoon.

1851 Navy.

1849 Pocket Colt Presentation Model.

Third Dragoon, with shoulder stock.
Second Dragoon.

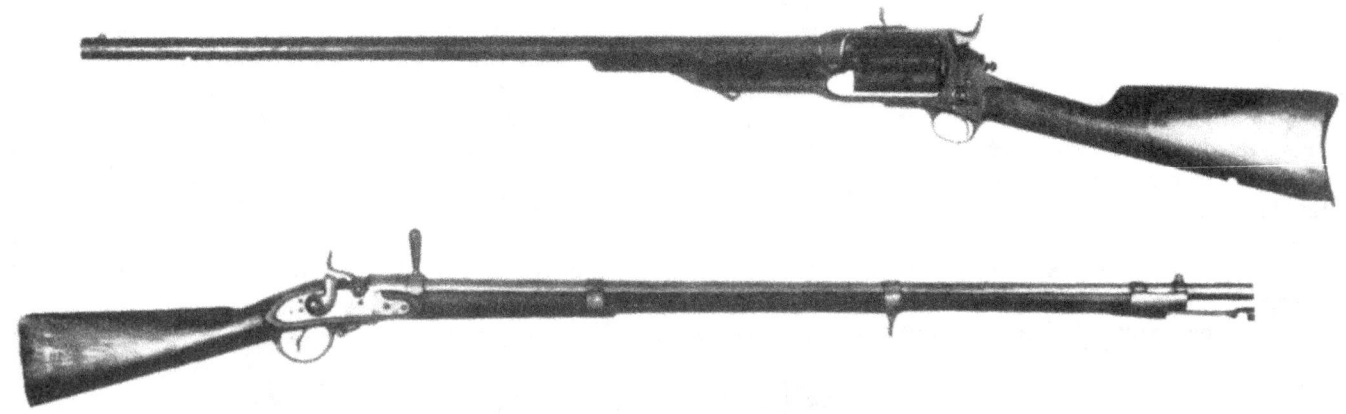

Top: Five shot elephant gun .70—1855. Bottom: Civil War single shot musket.

was slower for quick-draw work, once you had it in your hand it was the best cavalry pistol of all and would drop a horse as easily as a man with its .45 caliber round or conical ball and 50 grains of F.F.G. black powder. Those two old Civil War veterans, one fighting for the South and one for the North, saw an enormous amount of close infighting. Both were masters of the sixgun and very high class old gentlemen. I spent many happy months with Fletcher around Helena, Montana as a small boy recuperating from terrible burns.

Another very interesting old gentleman I met but briefly, and only had one evening to converse with, was Nelson Story. He was on a visit to Helena from his home in California and that evening he told me a great deal of his early life. He, with 30 Texas cowpunchers, brought the first trail herd of Texas longhorns to where Bozeman, Montana now stands. They came across Wyoming and were forbidden to go on by the commanding officer, Colonel Carrington of Fort Phil Kearney.

Nelson Story had some 30 cowboys on whom he could rely, each armed with a pair of cap and ball Colts and a Remington rolling block rifle, caliber .50-70, with plenty of ammunition. They disobeyed orders and came on over the Bozeman trail through the whole Sioux nation, fighting off Indians in daytime and moving the trail herd at night. They finally reached the site of Bozeman late in 1866. The Fetterman massacre occured later, on the old trail, and the fort was finally abandoned in 1868, but Nelson Story, an old Confederate veteran, brought the first trail herd into Montana and outfoxed and outfought the whole Sioux nation.

Later that fall the Fetterman massacre was to occur just out of Fort Phil Kearney, where Captain Fetterman led 81 men to their deaths against Red Cloud and his many braves. Though the Sioux claimed in later years to have killed most of the company with war clubs and arrows, the two frontier scouts who accompanied the little command certainly died fighting, for nearly 100 empty .44 rim fire cases were found by their bodies and there were blood clots on the snow. Around them were some 60 Sioux braves they had shot as well as a great many ponies. These two old frontiersmen, named Wheatly and Fisher, sold their lives as dearly as possible. The Sioux had planted 105 arrows in Wheatley's body when it was found. Both were armed with .44 Henry rifles. Had all the command been equally well armed, and had they fought as well, a different story would have resulted.

The Government gave up the fort in 1868 and the

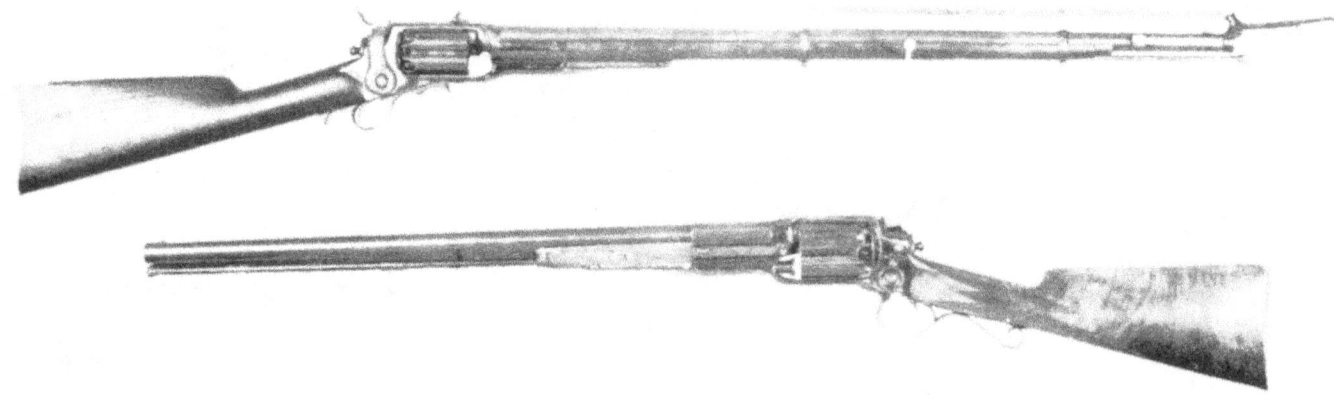

Top: Civil War revolving musket 1855 model. Bottom: Shot gun, revolving cylinder 1855 Model.

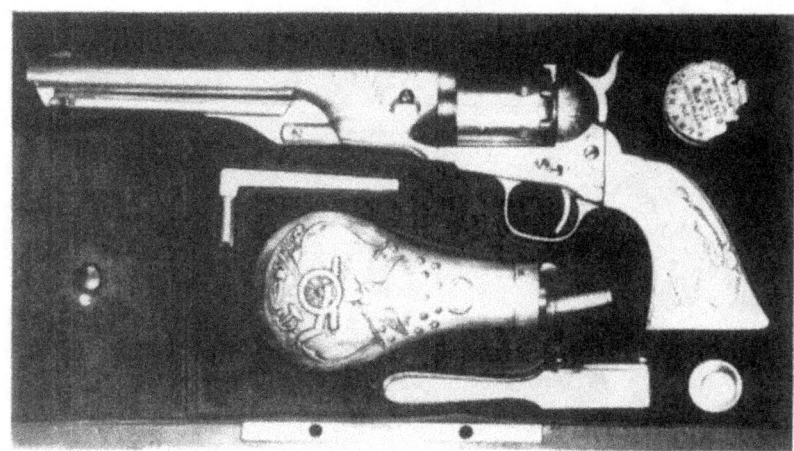

Beautiful Presentation 1861 Navy cased with accessories.

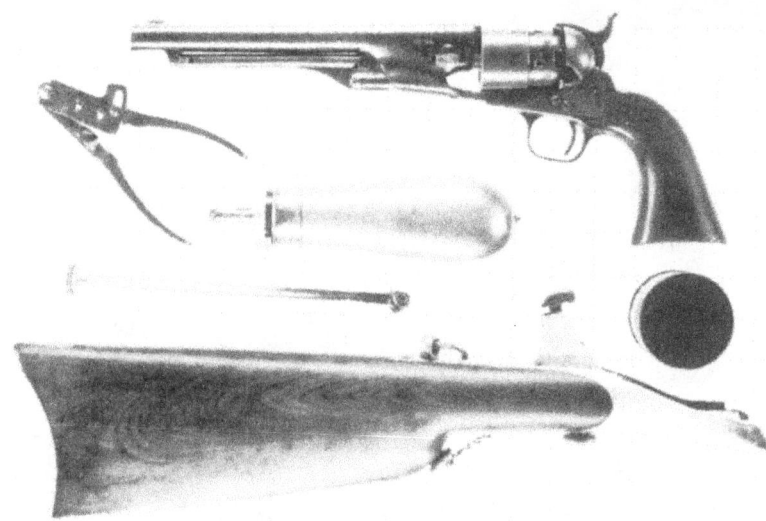

1860 .44 Army Colt outfit complete with shoulder stock.

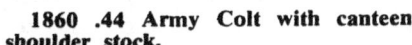
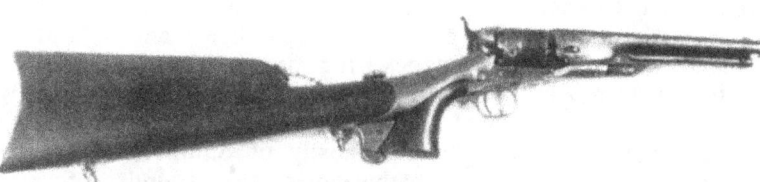

1860 .44 Army Colt with canteen shoulder stock.

Lightning Presentation Storekeeper's Model .38 Colt. It was originally silver plated.

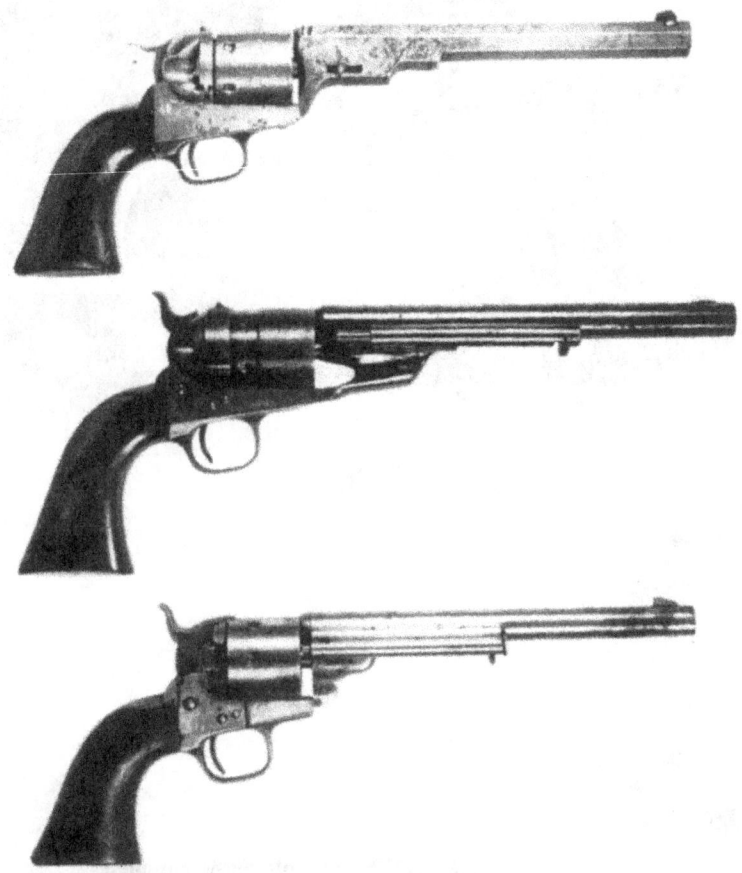

Alteration of 1851 Navy or Richards (not a conversion).

Conversion of 1860 Army.

Experimental stage gun—not a conversion.

Indians promptly burned it to the ground before the troops had marched a mile from it. General Carrington died in 1912 and Chief Red Cloud in 1910.

With the discovery of rich placer deposits in Bannock, Last Chance and Alder Gulch in Montana, another migration rushed off to these gold fields and founded the towns of Bannock, the first territorial capitol of Montana; Virginia City, the second, and Helena, the third and final capitol. These places were settled largely by war veterans, mostly of Southern extraction. All manner of highwaymen also found easy pickings among the miners and soon formed large gangs for organized robbery and horse stealing. Masons among the veterans formed a vigilante committee and began shooting and hanging the robbers. They did a most complete job and all through these early days in Montana the sixgun played an important role, both for and against the law abiding citizen.

The only law in Montana territory prior to the organization of the Vigilantes was the rifle and sixgun and nearly everyone wore a gun from necessity. Unlucky miners from California, came back to Nevada and Montana to each new strike, in hopes of making their fortunes. Others saw the opportunity for raising cattle. The trail herds from Texas that had been ending at the railroad in Kansas soon treked on north into Wyoming and Montana, and started the cattle industry. The great buffalo herds were exterminated in a few short years by the hide hunters, further pushing the Indians back and also opening the country for cattle raising.

The sixgun was as important a part of a cow-poke's outfit as his rope. Throughout the West the sixgun was responsible for most of the law, what little there was, and one of the main deterrents to wholesale outlawry.

Sixguns were in great demand everywhere and Colt began alterations to change their guns to cartridge forms, some of the most notable being the Richards conversion and also the Theurs conversion of the Colt .44 Army and .36 Navy guns. The Remington Percussion .36 Navy and .44 Army were also very popular. The pioneer work of Smith & Wesson with the fixed cartridge had created a demand. Remington and Colt also brought out single action cartridge revolvers. A great many of the percussion Army and Navy Colts were converted to rim or center fire, before the advent of the Single Action Army .45 Colt, the celebrated Peacemaker.

Remington made many of their S.A. Frontiers in .44-40 caliber. Merwin & Hurlbert, and many other early revolver makers added to the list and Smith & Wesson brought out their big .44 American and Schofield and .44 Russian. Some of the .45 Smith & Wesson Schofields were issued to troops for trial and they were well favored in some quarters, but the

S.A. Army Colt was adopted as the army revolver.

Production of the Colt .45 S.A. Army began in 1873 when 200 were produced and the next year, 1874, 14,800 were manufactured. This grand old gun was made right up to World War II and probably reached its peak of production in 1902 when 18,000 were made. Other heavy production years for the old Peacemaker were 1883, with 17,000, and as late as 1907 some 16,000 were manufactured.

It became the standard arm of the frontier, both for troops and civilians, and was soon brought out in many calibers from the lowly .22 in the target models to the .455 and .476 British calibers. The .45 Colt and the .44-40 were the most popular along the frontier. The Peacemaker was also made in .44 rim fire, as the .44 Henry flat cartridge had long been popular on the frontier.

In the early 70's with the introduction of the model 1873 Winchester, Colt chambered their single actions for the same cartridges, the .32-20, .38-40 and the .44-40. While a great many sixguns of competitive makes were carried, the Colts were predominant and the Smith and Wesson next in popularity.

In the early 70's Custer led an expedition into the Black Hills of the Dakotas, the heart of the Sioux nation and gold was discovered. This in turn led to the Sioux war, culminating in the battles of the Rosebud and the Little Big Horn, where Custer and his men went down fighting a vastly superior force under able Indian commanders. Custer's troopers carried Colt .45 single action 7½ inch barrelled six-shooters and .45-70 trap-door Springfields, no sabers being used in the engagement. Each troop went down under a horde of mounted Indians, fighting on foot as the Indians stampeded the horses after killing the horse-holders. The Indians used everything from old muzzle loaders to the latest Winchester repeating rifles in model 1873 and all types of sixguns that they could get by trade or massacre of small wagon trains. The famous scout, Charley Reynolds went down fighting at the side of Surgeon Porter, under Reno's Command at the ford and a handful of empty .44 caliber Winchester cases were found by his headless body after the battle.

Colt 1855 model cased with accessories.

Some 321,000 Colt S.A. Army revolvers were made in center fire plus a trifle less than 2,000 for the .44 rim fire. Some 45,000 of the Bisley model, brought out in 1896, were also made. The S.A. Army was most popular in .45 Colt and secondly in .44-40, third in .38-40, fourth .32-20 and lastly the .41 Colt. The barrels on civilian models were made 4¾ inches long, just to end of extractor, 5½ inches on the Artillery model and 7½ inch length on the cavalry model.

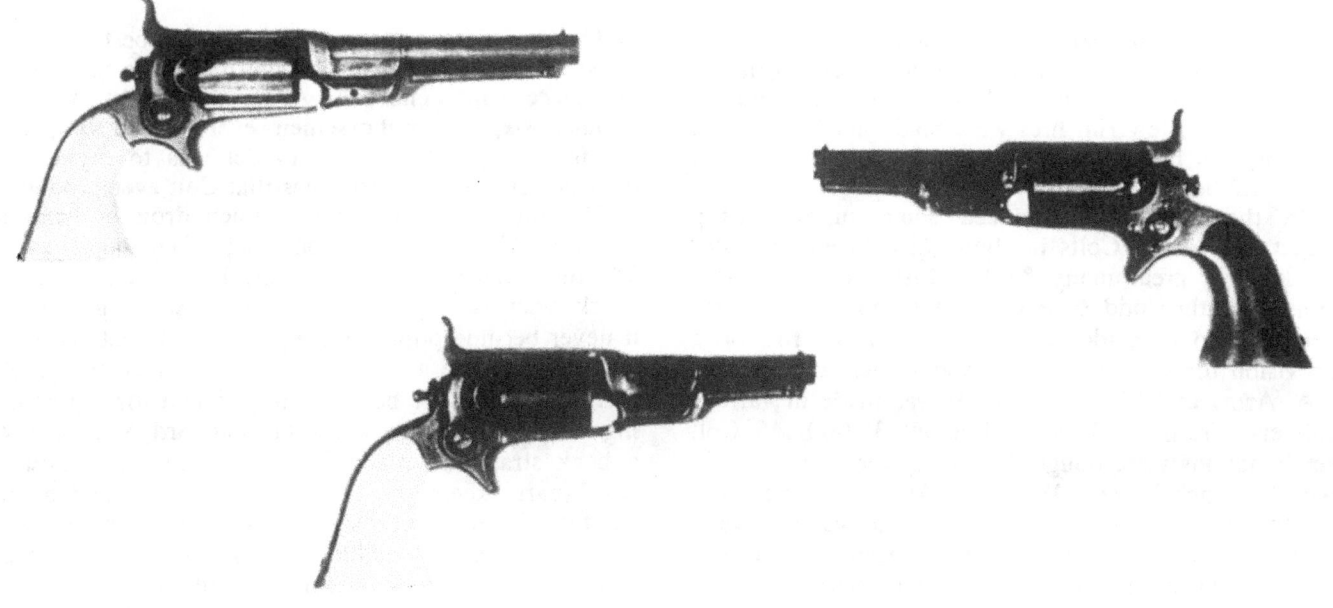

Colt Root side hammer revolvers.

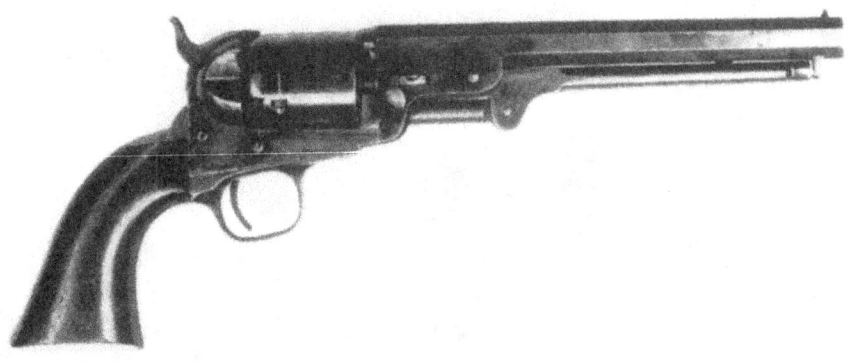

Colt Navy 1851.

Army Model of 1860.

.45/c Marine Model 1909.

Some few Buntline specials were made at the factory with very long barrels, some of which were 16 inches in length, and often fitted with a skeleton shoulder stock. A very few rim fires were made in .22, .32 and possibly .38 but most of the rim fire S.A. Colts were in .44 caliber.

In the 80's Colt produced some super flat-top target S.A. Army Colts in about all calibers and later produced a great many flat-top Bisley model Target guns. A rather odd Colt was the gambler's or storekeeper's model made without an extractor rod or a provision for same, in 3 inch and 4 inch and in both S.A. Army and Bisley models. It was made in various calibers. From 1873 to 1891 about 37,000 .45 Colt single actions were bought by the Government, mostly with 7½ inch barrels. While the Army had one piece walnut grips, commercial models usually carried black rubber grips, first with the eagle design, later just the rampant colt medallion, many with plain or carved pearl or ivory grips and some later guns with two piece checkered walnut.

The one-piece grips were by far the best in either wood or ivory. The Bisley model had to be made with two piece grips. The S.A. Army was easily the most popular sixgun for horsemen ever turned out, and the fine old flat-top target model was to my notion the best revolver for cartridges that Colt ever produced.

The Bisley model had too much drop or bend to the stock for instinctive pointing after dark or hip shooting and invariably it shot low when used for quick draw self defense work at close range. Hence it never became popular except among target shooters. The angle of the grip to frame was perfect on the old S.A. and is still the best pointing sixgun for hip shooting we know. Sights were the standard V in top of a back strap and blade front, increased in width in later years except the target model which had a fine flat top U notch back sight in a dovetail in the wide flat-top frame, adjustable for windage, with a bead front sight, in a split square topped lug or ramp. A very few single actions were made with a folding tangent rear sight on the order of the old tangent

History of the Sixgun

Conversion from hybrid parts basically 1849 parts.

Model of 1872—not a conversion. .44 R.F.

Richards conversion of 1849 Pocket.

Thuer conversion of 1860 Army.

carbine sights, but these are very scarce.

Frontiersmen and cavalrymen who were used to the old gun could make it interesting for any man caught in the open to 300 yards and to 600 yards for a man on a horse. Early loadings were rather light, but later loads for the old Peacemaker of 40 grains F.F.G. black powder and the 260 grain Government pointed bullet were lethal, and often went through 8 inch pine timbers. The old gun has killed every type big game on this continent at one time or another.

Fast Shooting

For quick draw work, no gun is any faster for the first shot, draw and hit from the hip, than the 4¾ inch .45 S.A. Army, and if the hit be on a man target, then a new target is needed for any further shots. After the first shot, a good Smith & Wesson double action is much faster for repeat shots. John Newman perfected the slip hammer, a low smooth and shorter hammer spur placed about half way down the back of the hammer and grasped with the base knuckle of the thumb. This slip hammer is slow for the first shot, draw and hit, when used without a trigger, or in comparison to a regular trigger gun, but is faster after the first shot by men trained in its use. It is very fast if used with both hands, one to hold the gun, the other to slip the hammer. Very accurate slip shooting can also be done with the Newman type hammer, but it requires training and when trained for the slip hammer

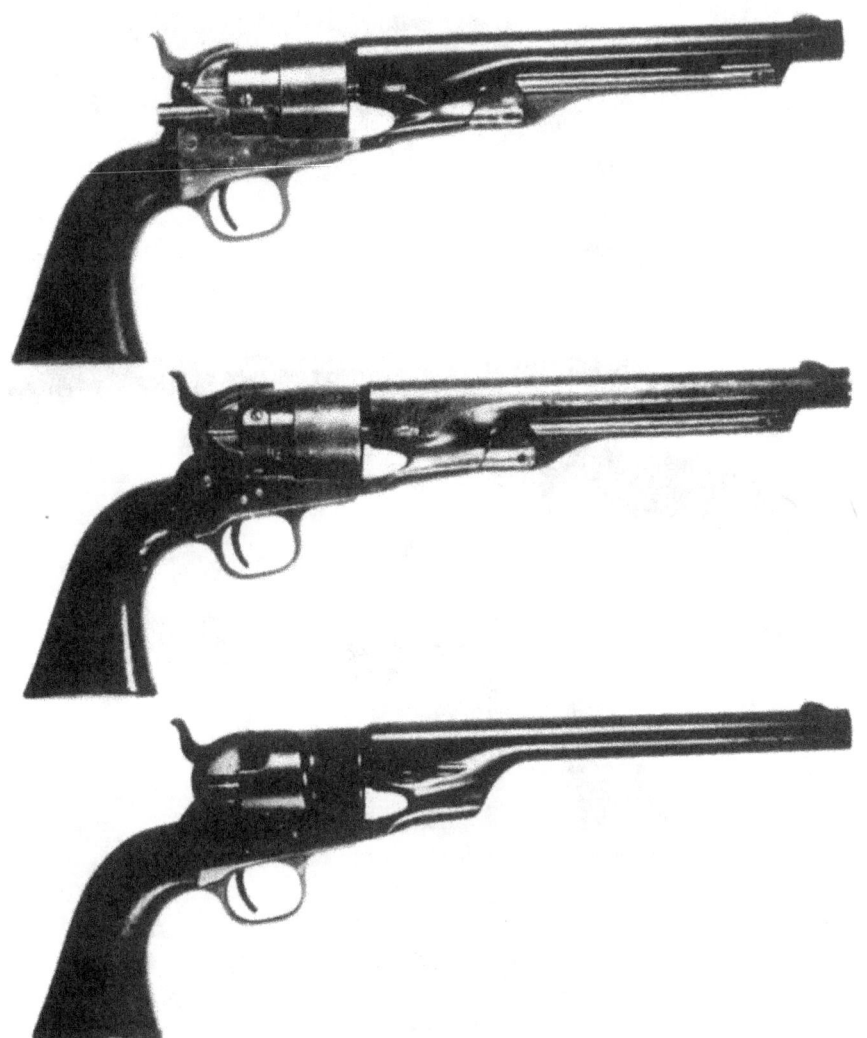

1860 Army Metallic conversion.

one must unlearn, so to speak, all he has learned of trigger shooting.

The old model 1851 Navy and the model 1860 Colt .44 Army formed the basis for the later model 1873 Peacemaker. First the Richards conversions of the .44 Army guns and later the Colt 1872 model made from 1860 Army parts, with the addition of a new cartridge cylinder and hammer was a new model. Throughout the long span of manufacture, the basic parts of the single action Colt are practically the same from the 1847 Walker and 1848 Pocket to the latest Colt single action Army made in 1940. Only the main spring of the Walker and 1848 Dragoons were basically different in shape, as hand, hand spring bolt and bolt spring were much the same, also hammer and trigger, cylinder rachet, etc.

While Elisha Collier developed the best flint lock revolver between 1800 and 1817, it was not until the percussion cap was developed, probably about 1816 and later in most countries, that multiple discharge was completely eliminated. Just prior to and during the Civil War, as well as for some years thereafter, revolver manufacturers were legion in this country. We will name but a few of them, though most of them were more or less successful in their operation and a great many makes were used through the Civil War. Some were of peculiar design, like the Savage-North, whose cylinder was revolved and the arm cocked by a small ring below the trigger and inside the huge guard that covered everything from the frame to butt of stock.

Here are some of the different makes: Remington, Starr, Butterfield, Springfield, Leavitt, Warner, Cochran, Manhattan, Cooper, Allen and Wheelock, Whitney, Rogers and Spencer, Whitney-Beals, Phoenix, Tranter, Adams, and Joslyn. Colts, however, were the predominant arm and it is claimed that by the close of the Civil War, Colt had manufactured 850,000 arms, both revolvers and long arms as against some 250,000 arms by all the competetive arms makers in this country.

Cartridge Revolvers

Probably the one best percussion revolver other than the Colt, was the Remington and great quantities of these were made and used. It never became as popular as the Colt but was in many ways superior, especially as to strength of the frame with its top strap. Neither did the Colt Side Hammer Root model ever become popular, though it also had a strong frame with top strap. Just as Colt pioneered in the production and development of the percussion revolver in this country and also made a great many more in his London and Belgian factories, so did the firm of Smith & Wesson pioneer in the development and production of the cartridge revolver with internal cap. In 1856 the S. & W. firm bought Rollin White's patent to bore the chamber clear through the cylinder. In 1856, at Springfield, Mass. they started manufacture of the first cartridge revolvers. They also made the Volcanic repeating pistol, but soon sold this industry to the Volcanic Arms Co. and concentrated on the manufacture of cartridge revolvers. Daniel B. Wesson and Horace Smith became partners in 1849 and this fine old firm has continued ever since and is today the best equipped and most modern revolver factory in the world. For a great many years after Mr. Smith left the firm in 1874, the company was managed by some member of the Wesson family. Today it is ably managed by one of the best business heads in the Arms industry, Carl Hellstrom. He has moved the business into a new, complete, large and very modern arms plant that he designed and built for the firm. Every part of a Smith & Wesson revolver is made in the plant, from the first rough forgings to the smallest screw or stock escutcheon.

The invention of the internally primed rim fire cartridge case made the early Smith & Wesson revolvers possible and their patents gave the firm a lead over competitors for many years in the production of cartridge revolvers. The Theurs patent Colt conversion was Colt's answer for many years as the Theurs cartridge loaded from the front of the cylinder.

Pauli, a Paris gunsmith, made the first successful brass cartridge case in 1812, 40 years before the rest of the world was ready for the development, but his center fire primers leaked gas.

However, in 1839, Pottet produced a successful metallic cartridge with a gas proof primer. Then

Thuer conversion of Pocket of 1849.

.38 R.M. conversion of Pocket Pistol of Navy caliber.

.38 R.M. conversion of Pocket Pistol of Navy caliber.

1855 Root sidehammer metallic conversion.

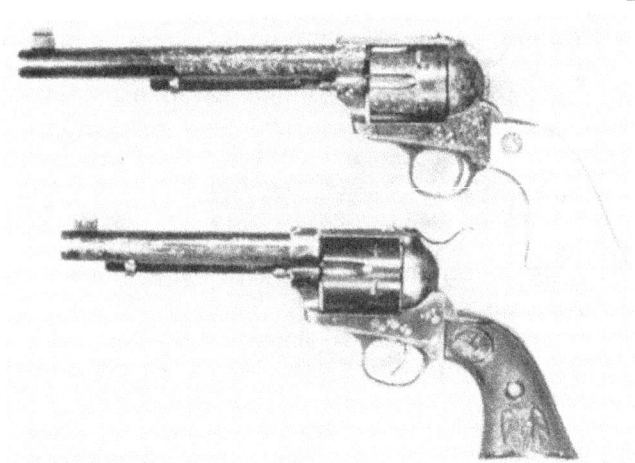

Colt Flat-Top S.A. Army. Top, 7½ inch barrel, bottom, 5½ inch barrel.

5½ inch Flat-Top S.A. Army Colt.

Houiller perfected the pin fire in 1846. In this country, work was started on hollow base bullets containing the powder charge and also a primer to ignite the same. Hanson & Golden of England did the pioneer work with fulminate of mercury, loaded into hollow base bullets to both ignite and propel the slug. Some years later Stephen Taylor, another Briton, further improved the system and did some work on a magazine arm to fire it. The patent was granted in 1847. Lewis Jennings was next to take up the idea and further perfect it and was granted a U.S. Patent in 1849. These hollow base projectiles contained the powder and a Maynard tape primer lock was used to fire them. The Jennings arms were made by Robbins & Lawrence of Windsor, Vt. Next B. Tyler Henry took up where Jennings left off. Henry went to Horace Smith and the latter patented a magazine firearm in 1851 with tubular magazine to use these hollow base powder-containing projectiles. Smith soon exhausted his capital and then went into partnership with Daniel B. Wesson. Wesson's older brother, Edwin Wesson, was the inventor of the Wesson-Leavitt hand turned cylinder revolver. On the death of the elder Wesson in 1850, young Daniel B. Wesson and other heirs inherited a patent application for a revolver with mechanically operated cylinder. The Massachusetts Arms Co. was formed and manufacture of a revolver with hinged frame was started. The barrel tipped up for easy and quick cylinder removal. This in turn brought on a lawsuit with Colt, as he claimed it infringed on his patents. Colt won the lawsuit and the Mass. Arms Co. was stopped by the court from making more such revolvers.

With only a few years for Colt's patent rights to run, Horace Smith, D. B. Wesson and Tyler Henry turned their attention to the manufacture of a rifle, while waiting for the Colt patents to run out so they could again go into the manufacture of revolvers. The firm of Smith & Wesson obtained a patent on a magazine firearm in 1854. Henry remained a silent partner.

The new firm of Smith & Wesson went into production of their repeating rifles and pistols which had a tubular magazine and used hollow base bullets propelled and ignited by fulminate of mercury contained in the hollow base of the bullet. No cartridge was used or needed as the fulminate fired and propelled the slug and left the chamber empty for the carrier to bring up the next round from the magazine. Tyler Henry was made plant superintendent, and from the very start, the new Smith & Wesson arms became very popular, as they were very carefully made and fitted, as well as perfectly finished. They maintained the highest possible standard of quality and throughout the entire history of the firm the name of Smith & Wesson has stood for highest quality.

These first Smith & Wessons were made in calibers, .31, .36 and .44. The very nature of their propellant, however, forced them to use only light charges in both rifle and pistol.

By steady experiment, Daniel Wesson developed the first fixed cartridge with internal primer and bullet, suitable for repeating pistol or revolver use, but it conflicted with the old Pottet patents, so his original ideas were not patented, though he proved they would work. Finally, by adding a lubricating disc, they were able to convince the Patent Office that they had something new. Next they sold the patents to Oliver Winchester on their repeating rifles and pistols, as well as all pending patents on fixed ammunition of their design. The machinery was moved to New Haven and the Volcanic Arms Co. headed by O. P. Winchester and Tyler Henry was formed. This started the firm that was later to become the famous Winchester Repeating Arms Co. and gave Smith & Wesson cash to go into a further venture. Smith & Wesson agreed verbally never to manufacture rifles and Winchester agreed never to manufacture revolvers. This gentleman's agreement has been kept to this day between the two firms.

At one time Winchester did make a few single action revolvers closely resembling the Colt .45 S.A. Army, but Colt also agreed to make no more rifles if Winchester would in turn make no revolvers, so the Winchester single actions were never put on the market and only a few exist in the Winchester museum.

Wesson continued to experiment with a fixed revolver cartridge and a revolver or sixgun to handle it as the Colt Patent was due to expire in 1857. Finally he succeeded in developing the first rim fire cartridge case with the fulminate put in the head of the case, then the powder, after which they were compressed with the bullet and its crimp.

Young Rollin White, who held the patent on cylinders bored clear through, interviewed Colonel Colt but Colt turned down his patents as being impractical and dangerous. Smith & Wesson bought up the White patents with White retaining the right to make arms himself, but few were ever made. He did, however, perfect the White Sewing machine and later the White Steamer automobile.

While Smith & Wesson were tooling up for revolver manufacture, Remington was doing likewise for the old percussion Remington made under the Beal patent. Smith & Wesson took the lead, however, and in November of 1857, had their first batch of cartridge revolvers and cartridges for them for sale. These first Smith & Wessons were in .22 caliber. Even today little change in the .22 Short rim fire from the first ones produced by S. & W. has occurred, except in better shell cases and better priming mixtures and better bullets. The basic design remains the same.

This little seven shot .22 Short, Smith & Wesson was manufactured up to 1869. In 1861 Smith & Wesson brought out the next model, their Model 1½, chambered for a .32 rim fire cartridge, the largest they had perfected owing to the difficulties of drawing and annealing copper so that it would stand the pressure of heavier powder charges. Smith & Wesson had to put on a night shift to keep up with the demand from Army officers for the new .32 rim fire revolver throwing a 90 grain bullet and propelled by 13 grains of fine black powder. Some 76,502 of this model were produced up to the last in 1874. My uncle owned and carried one of these in Civil War days. Smith & Wessons played no important role in the Civil War. These guns were carried chiefly by army officers and owing to their small caliber, were little used.

In 1861 Daniel Moore obtained a patent on a cartridge revolver. The barrel and cylinder hinged on front of the frame and could be rotated to the side for removal of spent cases by a sliding extractor rod and insertion of live rounds. This was the first side-swing gun even though the barrel also swung to the side along with the cylinder. It was made in .32 and later in .38 caliber. Merwin & Bray of N.Y.C. handled them.

Another cartridge revolver of Civil War days that was superior to the Smith & Wesson was the Prescott sixshooter of .38 caliber produced at Worcester, Mass. It and many other firms started manufacturing cartridge revolvers during the Civil War, and just after, in direct violation of the Rollin White patents, until Smith and Wesson had their patent attorneys get

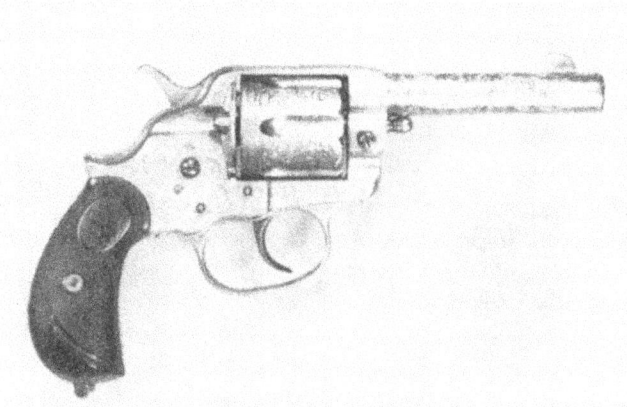

Rare D.A. Frontier Storekeeper's Colt without extractor.

after them. Infringement suits stopped most of these competitors. Although this left Smith & Wesson with a clear field and the problem of making larger rim fire cartridges and arms to handle them, it was not until they had obtained the patents of W. C. Dodge controlling the hinging of the barrel and cylinder on the front of the frame, and those of C. A. King covering the simultaneous ejection of all fired cases, together with a good latch at the rear end of the top strap, that the firm brought out a really powerful sixgun.

The first of the S. & W. .44 American guns were turned out late in 1869 or early in 1870. The new cartridge was center fired and used 25 grains of black powder and a 218 grain bullet. Velocity was 650 feet, and this was the first S. & W. sixgun to be powerful enough to play an important role in the development of the West. Prior to the advent of the S. & W. American, the heavy Colt cap and ball guns with their powerful charges were much preferred. Colt conversions also came into the picture, especially the Richards conversion of the .44 Army and their later 1872 model with new cylinder, and the model 1873 Peacemaker soon took the lead as the most popular gun of the time. Tests by the War Department gave the new S. & W. American second place in their trials and one regiment of cavalry was equipped with them. The new arm was made in large quantities and shipped to all points in the west, where it soon became quite popular on account of its fine accuracy and dependability. It carried a ribbed 8 inch barrel. The .44 American center fire cartridge was developed from the .42 Berdan brought out by General Berdan, with outside primer cup and the anvil being contained in the bottom of the primer pocket.

A Succession of Revolvers

The next Smith & Wesson was the Russian model and the firm received an order for 200,000 of these improved revolvers just after Mr. Smith had quit the firm in 1870. The new S. & W. Russian carried a

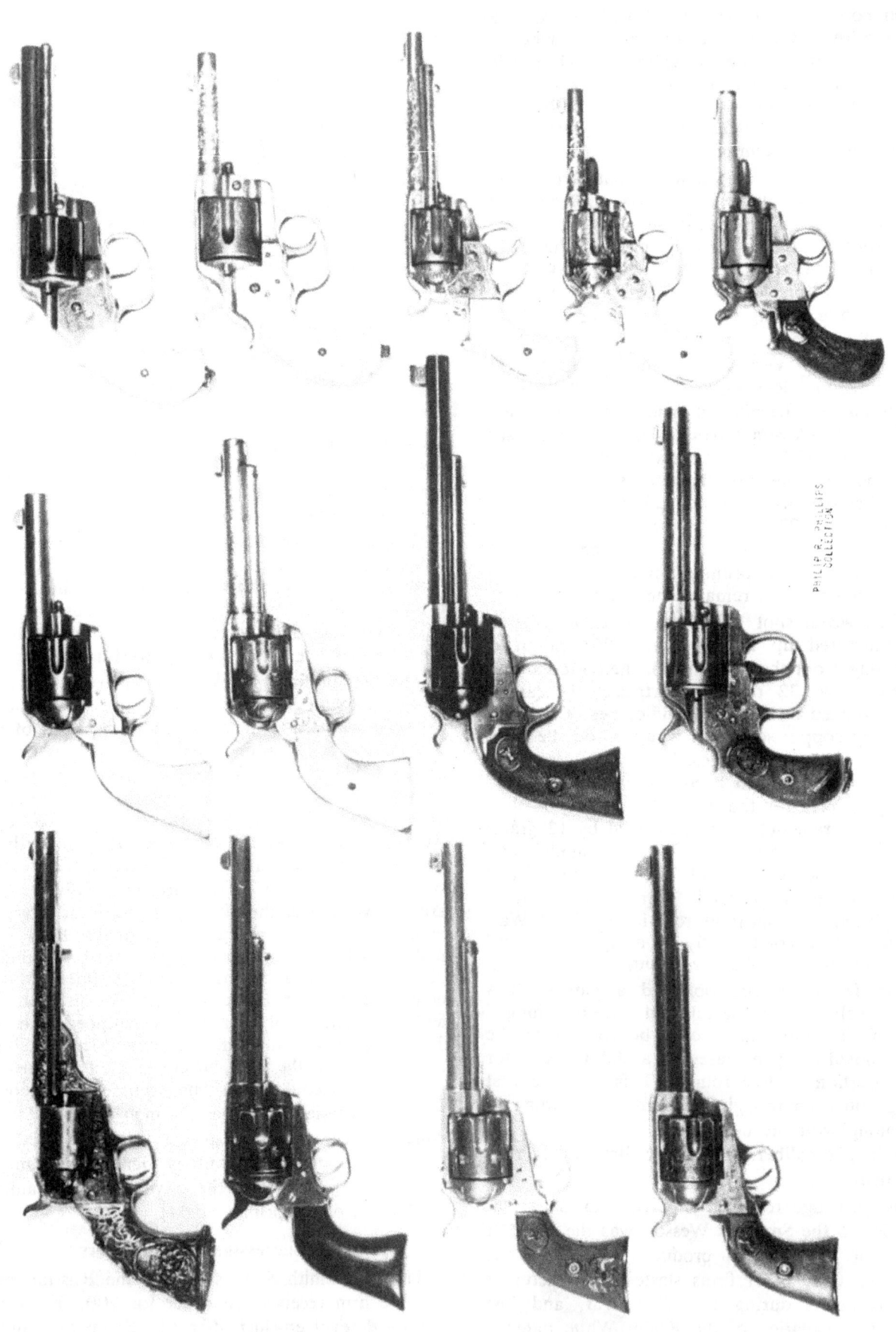

Collection of Colt single actions and Bisley Lightning and Frontier double actions.

6½ inch barrel and quite a few external changes, but the most important change was in the ammunition, as it was chambered and bored for the .44 Russian designed by some unknown Muskovite and carried a case larger than the groove diameter, allowing the groove diameter bullet to be seated down in the case and properly crimped in a groove and also allowing inside lubrication of the bullet instead of outside lubrication. The new .44 Russian S. & W. guns proved much more accurate and more powerful than the .44 American and used a charge of 246 grain bullet propelled by 23 grains of black powder at 750 feet per second, due no doubt to the full size bullet sealing off the pushing gas in the chamber mouth and barrel throat. The old S. & W. American .44, being a heel type bullet with a small base to crimp the case on, lost considerable gas at barrel and cylinder junction, so the new .44 Russian round was much superior, not only in power and ease of carrying but also in accuracy. The revolvers were made at the rate of 175 per day until a total of 215,704 were made, but as most went to Russia, very few are in American collections today.

During the war between Russia and Turkey, the Turks ordered a shipment of revolvers from Smith & Wesson and a total of 5,461 were made, chambered for a Turkish .44 rim fire cartridge similar to the American .44 Henry.

In the West, however, the Smith & Wesson did not early become popular, because its hinge was a weak point and while one could bend a Colt single action over some hombre's head, oft times without damage to the gun, such treatment would usually ruin a fine finished and fitted S. & W. gun due to the weakness of its hinge joint, in comparison with the solid framed S. A. Colt. While the S. & W. was no doubt the most accurate of the two guns in their earlier days, the Colt was by far the most popular.

Next Daniel Wesson designed a smaller cartridge on the lines of the excellent .44 Russian but in .36 caliber, called the .38 Smith & Wesson and carrying a 146 to 150 grain bullet propelled by 14 grains of black powder. The firm next built a gun to handle it. It was a break top with 3¼ inch barrel and fluted five shot cylinder in a single action model. In spite of its crude blade front sight and just a notch in the rear hinge stud, it was a wonderfully accurate little gun. We had one of them in blued finish with a square back trigger guard and it accounted for a great deal of small game—grouse, cottontails, ground squirrels, chucks, etc. That little gun was so accurate I have made many kills on the Columbia ground squirrel at a measured 60 yards, by holding all the front blade up in the rear notch, using both hands on the gun and perching the squirrel on top the front sight. Trajectory was high but the little gun would lob its bullet onto the squirrel with a dull plunk when the slug struck. While in the Montana National Guard, I

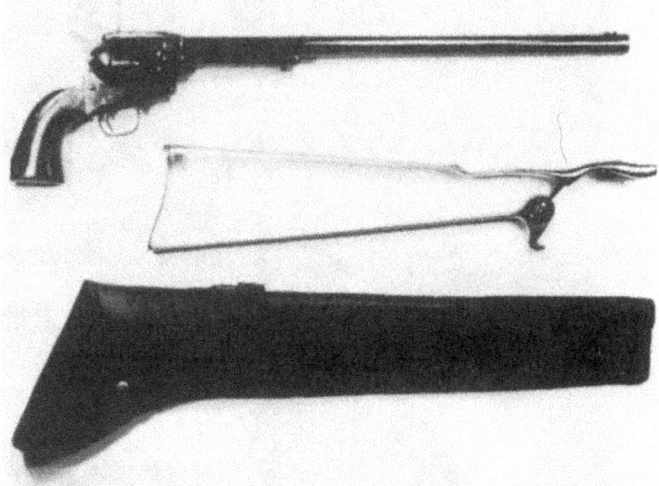

Courtesy of John duMont.
The very rare Buntline Special S.A. Colt outfit, tangent rear sight.

managed to hold my own with every pistol shot they had at that time including a regular army sergeant detailed to instruct us, I using the little pocket S. & W. and he and the others, the Army .45 model 1911 and the Colt and Smith & Wesson 1917 revolvers. I could not beat the sergeant at 50 yards, neither could he beat me with the larger guns when shooting them against my little pocket gun.

Many a tough old gun fighter died with his boots on, watching his opponent's big belt gun, while the latter plugged him full of holes from one of these little hidden S. & W. .38s. As a man killer, this little S. & W. saw a lot of service and was produced from March of 1876 through 1880. Some 24,633 were made up to 1880, then a slight improvement was effected and production continued on the second model. By 1891 a total of 108,255 had been produced.

The next Smith & Wesson of note was the .45 Schofield, with improvements in latch and extractor designed by Major Schofield of the U. S. Army. Repeated trials were conducted by the army, and Smith & Wesson was given a contract for 6,000 of these .45 caliber arms by the Government. The gun was patented by S. & W. in 1871 and the new arm came out with a seven instead of 6½ inch barrel as the Russian model. The cartridge was designed by Smith and Wesson and was shorter and far less powerful than the .45 Colt. The new S. & W. cartridge carried a 230 grain conical bullet backed by 28 grains of powder against the old .45 Colt load of a 255 grain bullet backed by 40 grains of black powder.

While many soldiers and cavalrymen could shoot the S. & W. better on account of its much lighter recoil, the S. & W. cartridge was never as good for knocking over a running Indian pony, and the gun never became as popular with cavalrymen, as the Colt Single action, with its much more powerful load and solid frame construction. The S. & W. 45 would work in the .45 Colt, but the .45 long Colt

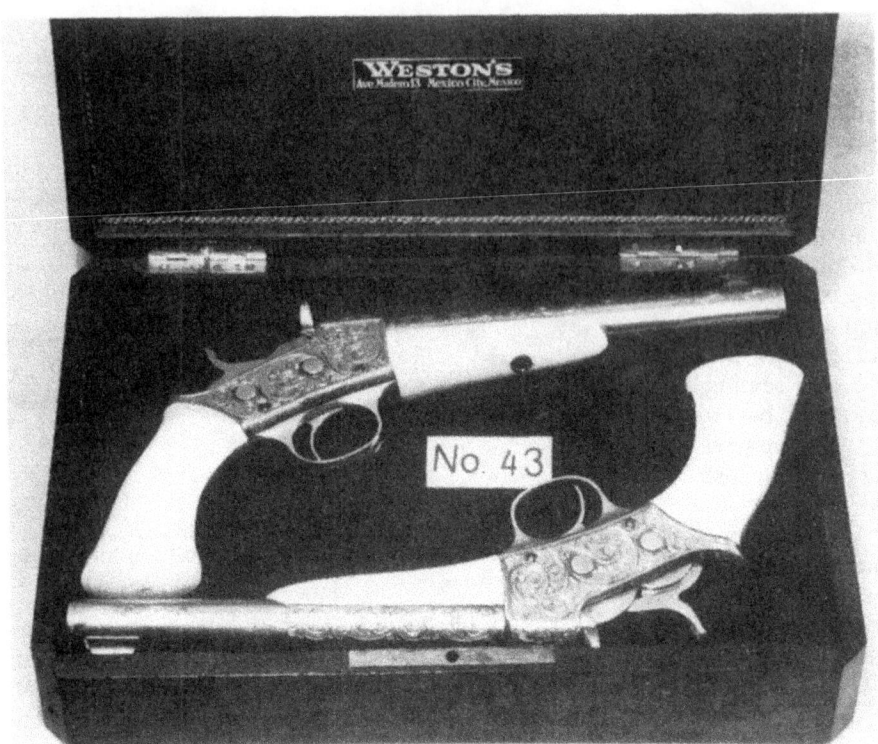

Pair of Remington Army Model of 1863, caliber .50 Navy single shot pistols, in presentation style.

cartridges were too long for the S. & W. cylinder. The government loaded short .45's that would interchange in both guns until the .45 was replaced by the Colt .38 in 1892.

Schofield .45s became popular with many civilians and were also used by Wells Fargo & Co. Jesse James carried a .45 Schofield S. & W. in one holster and a Colt single action .45 in the other, and he was probably one of the fastest gunmen of the times. Major Schofield designed a good gun, but it never became as popular with the Service as the Colt, and in December 1882, Major Schofield took his own life with one of these guns which probably was the reason the arm was not further perfected. He was then serving at old Fort Apache, Arizona. It is said that despondency over inventions was the ultimate cause of his suicide.

In 1877, Smith & Wesson produced their first break top .32 caliber to compete with the Colt line of small revolvers. It was brought out about 1875. The Colt .32 short and long were outside lubricated with heel type bullets, but Smith & Wesson improved the round by using an inside lubricated 85 grain bullet backed by 9 grains of black powder. This ammunition could be carried in the pocket without danger of rubbing off the lubricant, or having it contaminated with dirt and grit to scratch the bores.

In 1879 Smith & Wesson perfected and brought out a New Model .44, designed and improved from the Russian and Schofield models. It was with this arm that Ira Paine established his many records and shot exhibitions all over Europe as well as in America.

This new Smith & Wesson single action .44 proved

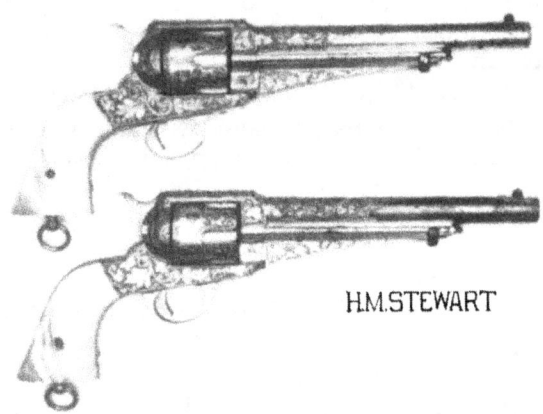

Courtesy of H. M. Stewart, Jr.
.44 Remington Frontiers.

one of the finest target arms of the day and did much to start the sport of revolver target shooting in this country. The National Rifle Association inaugurated a revolver match in their program in 1886. Ira Paine and W. W. Bennett, as well as Fred Bennett, were some of the top revolver shots of the day, and in a big match of 100 shots per day for six straight days, Fred Bennett was finally crowned Champion Revolver Shot of America with a score of 5,093. During the match, W. W. Bennett ran up one score for 100 shots of 914 and Ira Paine ran one for 100 shots of 904. When this 50 yard shooting was done with black powder, cleaning was allowed between five shot strings or by running a brush through the bore after each shot, and it is exceptionally fine shooting even today. Paine used for a time his new .38/44 made by S. & W. on the .44 Frame but with a long .38 case with the bullet held completely inside the case, but he went back to the .44 as the better arm. This New Model .44 S. & W. was manufactured to the tune of 38,796 arms before being dropped from the S. & W. line.

In 1885 Smith & Wesson brought out the last of their big top break revolvers for the then popular .44-40 or .44 W.C.F. Winchester rifle cartridge. Colt had brought out their single action for this cartridge and also the Remington Frontier was brought out for the same round as well as the Merwin & Hulbert. Many men along the frontier wanted a rifle and sixgun which utilized the same cartridge, as the model 73 Winchester had become very popular. Thus most revolver makers brought out arms chambered for the same round. Only 2,072 of the .44-40 S. & W. Frontier revolvers were made and many were later rechambered for the .44 Russian cartridge. They never became popular in competition with the solid frame Colt and Remingtons. Even the Merwin & Hulbert seemed to be more popular along the Western frontier.

Smith & Wesson also made 1,023 of their .38/44 target revolvers on the .44 frame with a long case to completely enclose the bullet and these were very popular target arms of the day. They also made a .32-44 with the same type of long case and bullet completely enclosed in the case. We once tested such a target outfit with three barrels, .44 Russian, .38/44 and .32/44 with extra barrels and cylinders and a fine assortment of sights for each caliber. It was a superbly accurate outfit.

Extension stocks were furnished for the various .44 S. & W. arms and around 1870 Frank Wesson, a brother of Daniel, put out his .22, .25 Stevens and .32 rim fire pocket rifles. In 1880 Smith & Wesson put out a small game rifle on the S. & W. Russian revolver frame with barrels of 16, 18 and 20 inches for an improved .32 caliber cartridge with 100 grains of lead and 17 of powder. Fine sights including peep sights, were fitted to this arm with its detachable shoulder stock and a hard rubber fore end. It proved a very accurate arm for small game shooting and was accurate to at least 300 yards. Only 977 of these S. & W. rifles were made as the fact that considerable gas escaped at barrel and cylinder junction, and powder burning the coat or shirt sleeves made them unpopular, as compared with a more orthodox rifle. The cartridge, however, became popular as it was also used in the .32/44 revolver. It was beaten for power only by the advent of the .32-20 cartridge.

Double Action

Though plenty of percussion sixguns were made in double action during and after the Civil War, namely the Tranter and Adams from Europe, the Cooper, Remington, Rider, Starr and Pettingill, neither Colt nor Smith & Wesson brought out double action arms until much later. Colt came out with their lightning model in 1877 in .38 long and .41 center fire and

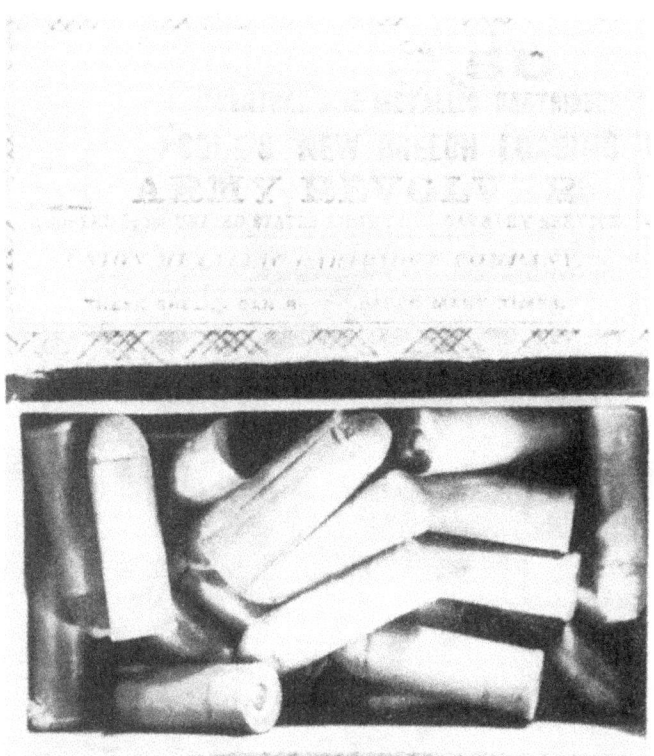

The old lavender colored U.M.C. box and .45 Colt ammo of the early days.

Smith & Wesson came out in 1880 with a .38 S. & W. double action arm. The Colts used the .38 short and long, and the .41 short and long outside lubricated loads, while S. & W. stuck to their good inside lubricated .38 S. & W. cartridge. The .38 S. & W. was much more accurate than the heel type bullets

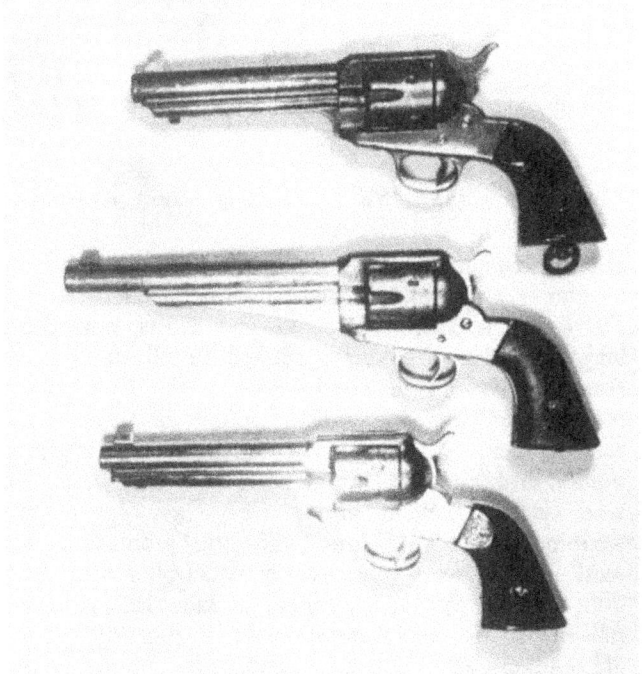

Three Remington cartridge revolvers from the Stewart collection.

.22 rim fire, Model No. 1, First Model, Smith & Wesson.

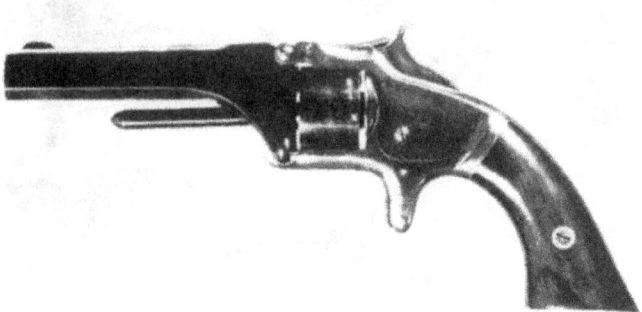

.22 rim fire, Model No. 1, 2nd Model, Smith & Wesson.

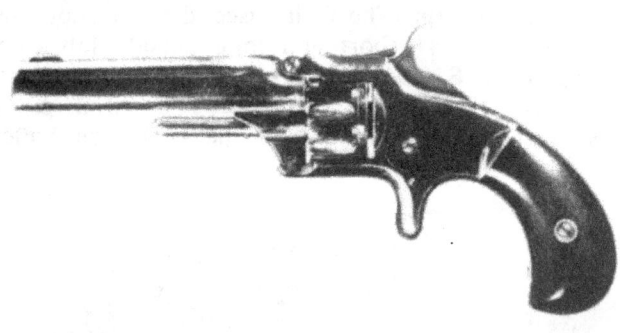

.22 rim fire, Model No. 1, 3rd Model, Smith & Wesson.

employed in the early .38 longs and .41 longs as well as shorts and did not give the fine accuracy of the .38 S. & W. The barrels of the Colts were bored large and depended on upsettage to fill the grooves. Again, however, the solid frame of the Colt with its rod ejector was the most popular and these Colt "self-cockers," as they were called, or the Lightning model, became very popular all over the west. They were well balanced and a very fast gun fighting weapon. In the .41 long with 200 grain slug, they were also a very effective man stopper, far better than the .38 Special of today, in fact. Billy, the Kid, real name W. H. Bonney, used a pair of them in .41 caliber, and, it is said, had killed up to 21 men at least before Pat Garret bumped him off, in Maxwell's bedroom, with a .45 single action Colt.

Two years ago a man in Butte, Montana wrote me about an old 6 inch barrel .41 rod ejector Colt he had. It was an old, dirty, rusty gun but when he scraped off the accumulation of years and removed the old hard rubber stocks, he found the name W. H. Bonney, New Mexico, and a date in 1880 carved inside one of the stocks.

One of my earliest recollections of Montana was in 1905 at Wolf Creek, when a cowboy dragged a mad fighting cow into a corral with his horse, then got down to try and get his rope off the critter without getting hurt himself. The cow had long horns, and, as he had taken most of the fight out of her by throwing her, he got down on foot and eased up to her and removed his rope, but before doing so he lifted the flap on his old laced leg chaps and turned the flap down inside, the better to have instant access to a .41 Colt Lightning he carried in that front chaps pocket.

We once returned a Lightning model in .38 long caliber to J. H. Fitzgerald of Colt, and had him make it into a .41 with barrel just to the end of the extractor. Colt did a beautiful job on it, but fitted to it what I will always believe to be an army Special barrel. At any rate the gun with barrel just to the end of the extractor made one of the fastest double actions of the old timer type I have seen and I carried it for years out of sight in my left chaps pocket. It was also quite accurate with the 200 grain .41 Long Colt load either inside or outside lubricated. I preferred the inside lubricated 200 grain load. I later swapped it to an old gun fighter, Sam Russell, for a pair of .45, 4¾ inch barrelled, single actions with ox head carved pearl grips on each, together with belt and holsters. Sam simply would not let me keep that gun and was after it every time I rode in to Helena from the ranch. He finally got it.

The Colt Lightning was made from 1877 to 1910. A very few of these guns were made for the .32 long Colt cartridge. Still more rare are the few of them made with flat top frame and target sights, with long 7 inch barrel. The rare target Lightning was made in .32 caliber and possibly other calibers.

In 1878 Colt brought out their .45 self-cocker or bird head grip double action. This was an improvement over the smaller Colt Lightning for the gun was made with solid frame and grip straps and a side plate added to get at the mechanism, while the Lightning had detachable stock straps like the Colt single action. This big gun was called the .45 double action Frontier. Later it was also brought out in .44-40 and .38-40 calibers. Some were made with very large trigger guards for use with gloved hands and called the Alaskan model. Some were made in .32-20, but we have never seen one, and also in .450, .455 and .476 Ely British calibers. Some few were also made with flat top target frame and sights with 7½ inch barrels. A very few were called the house pistol and made without the extractor and rod—the same as was done with the Colt single action and Bisley models. The Lightning was made both with and without the extractor rod and more are to be found without than with it. The D. A. Army without extractor usually came in a 3½ inch barrel. The regular extractor gun carried barrels of 4¾ inches, to the end of the extractor, 5½ and 7½ inch barrels, and we have owned them in all lengths. Some of them in .44-40 were engraved on left side of barrel "Colt's Frontier Six Shooter."

Some of the early Lightning models had one piece rosewood and also ivory grips, but later models had two piece grips. The D. A. .45 had two piece rubber and some ivory and pearl grips. The first D. A. Colt .45 grips were of checkered walnut.

The greatest fault of these first double action Colts was the poor cylinder locking arrangement which soon became worn until the cylinder was not always locked in perfect alignment and then accuracy fell off and the guns would sometimes spit lead at the side through shaving of the bullet. In spite of this fault, they were quite popular all over the West. The Lightning short barrelled .41 became known as the "gambler's gun," as it was small, short, and fast to get into action and easily concealed. The Lightning had a loading gate like the single action, but the D. A. .45 carried a different loading gate with a short pin projecting back for the thumb nail to catch to open same. Both models were made in blued and nickel finish, the Lightnings with case-hardened frames and the D. A. .45 model with blued frame.

The Government ordered 5,000 of the Alaskan model of Colts in 1902 with 6 inch barrels. Although some collectors call the .45 Frontier, the Philippine model, my friend, Col. C. E. Stodter, who fought through the whole campaign, never saw one in use there and claimed when the side-swing Colt D. A. .38's proved entirely inadequate to stop the mad Moros, that Colt S. A. .45's were issued the troops. This 6 inch barrel army issue is called the 1902 model of the arm. In and around Helena as a boy, we saw many of them in use in a 4¾ inch barrel in both .44-40 and .45 Colt calibers.

Many of the Army Colts, both S. A. and D. A., bear the inspector's initials and R.A.C. appears on a great many of them for the Government inspector, Rinaldo A. Carr.

Army Revolvers

The next Colt of note was the Army and Navy model with swing-out cylinder, six-shot, calibre .38 long. It was made from 1889 to 1892, the first Government order being for 5,000 of these revolvers with 6 inch barrels. The cylinder rotated to the left and they had the same type weak locking system at the rear end of the cylinder as on the first model of these Army and Navy Colt .38's.

From 1892 to 1908 they were improved with a bolt stop on the outside of the cylinder instead of locking at the rear, and this was quite an improvement in the locking of the cylinder at the time of firing. The .38 long Colt round, carried first outside lubricated heel type bullets and later inside lubricated bullets enclosed in the case with hollow base to upset and fill the slightly oversize bores of these revolvers. These are the guns that went to the Philippines and proved so ineffective on the Moros. Many times a mad Moro tribesman would absorb a whole chamber full of these little .38 slungs in his chest, then come right on in and clip off the officer's head with one swing of his bolo. They proved totally ineffective for stopping mad fighting men, and the Army back-stepped and issued .45 single actions before that fracas was over. When a Moro collected a 250 grain .45 Colt slug in the chest he usually lost interest in all things earthly, then and there. In spite of the lessons learned in that conflict, many army men today, and most police departments, still insist on a 9 M/M or .38 Special caliber for military and police use.

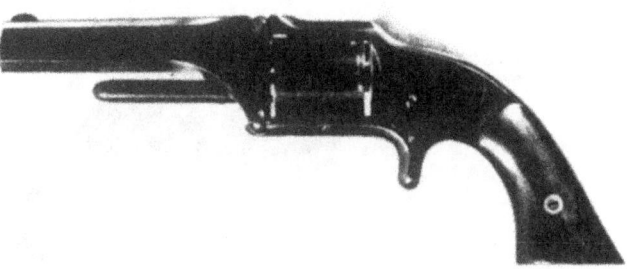

.32 rim fire, Model 1½, old Model, Smith & Wesson.

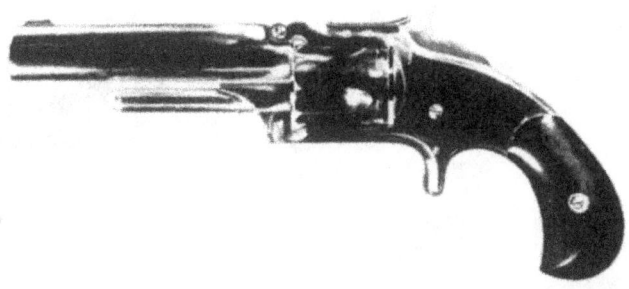

.32 rim fire, Model 1½, new model, Smith & Wesson.

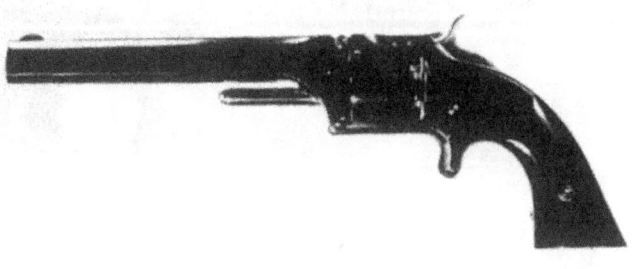

.32 rim fire, Model No. 2, old model, Smith & Wesson.

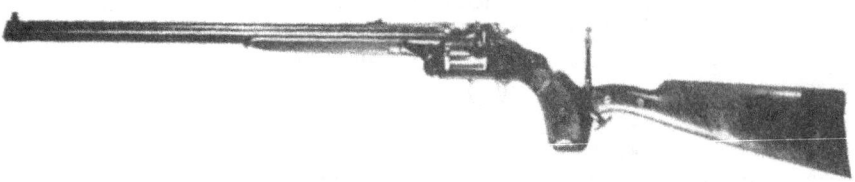

.320 Revolving Rifle, Smith & Wesson.

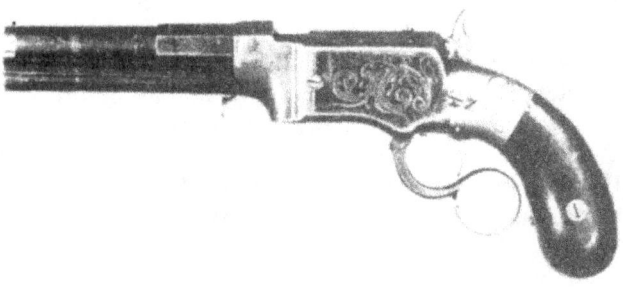

Volcanic, Smith & Wesson.

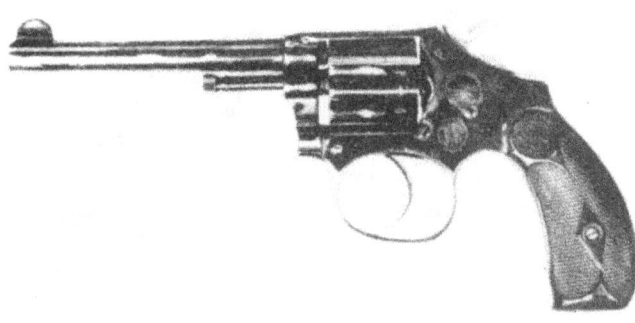

.22 Model "M" first issue, Smith & Wesson.

At close range, with men for targets, the old .36 Navy Colt and Remington cap and ball revolvers with their chamber nearly full of F.F.G. black and a soft lead round ball were much better stoppers, as they are really nearly .40 caliber, and with higher velocity and an almost flat ended round ball, they carry considerably more knock down shock than the pointed bullet of the .38 Long Colt and S. & W. or the .38 Special.

This first side-swing cylinder Colt in Army and Navy models was later made in a Marine Colt model. All of them were on the .41 frame and the arm later known as the Army Special was chambered for the .41 long Colt. This gun formed the basis of the later Colt Army Special and Officers model. The latter was made with flat top frame and fine target sights and became a very popular target gun, as well as a super-accurate revolver for any purpose, in the later caliber of .38 S. & W. Special and .38 Colt Special. In the .41 caliber the Army model became much more popular as a defense gun than in .38 caliber, as the big blunt nose 200 grain slug was an excellent man-stopper while the round nose .38 Special definitely was not.

.22 single shot, Model 1891, Smith & Wesson

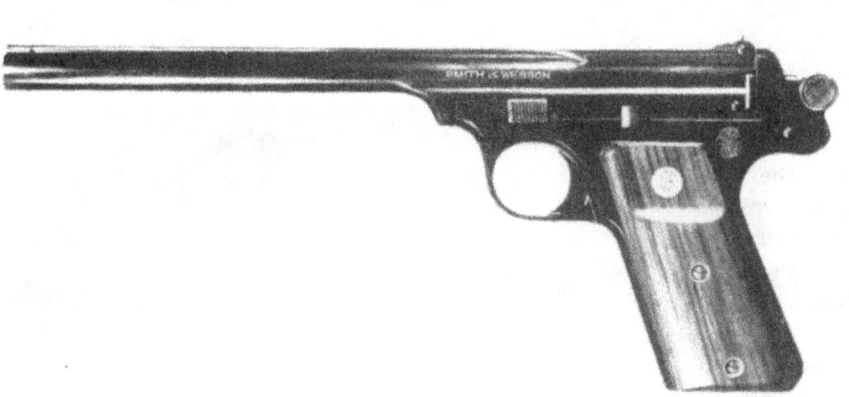

.22 single shot, Straightline, Smith & Wesson

Five thousand of the old Navy model swing-out cylinder were ordered from Colt by the Government in 1889. From then until 1892 little change was made. In 1892 the outside bolt stop was adopted with the result of a better locking of the cylinder. The army purchased a total of 68,500 of these guns from 1892 until 1903.

The Deluxe target edition of this arm was superbly fitted and finished in bright blue with checkered walnut stocks and usually with a carefully adjusted trigger pull.

The Colt Official Police and Officers Colts of today are further improvements of this model. The first models had the cylinders rotating to the left like S. & W. revolvers but this was changed to right hand rotation in later models. Today Colt builds their .357 on this same .41 frame.

Another army revolver that helped make history through the Civil War and right on through the Indian fighting and early frontier days up to the turn of the century, at least, was the famous Remington. It first came out in the Beals Army Revolver, then the first or old model 1861 Remington in .44 Army and .36 Navy calibers. It never became as popular as the Colt, but was superior in a great many ways. First the .44 carried an 8 inch octagon barrel and two inch cylinder with a solid frame with top strap and rear sight in the rear of the top strap. It also had a steel blade front sight and was more accurately sighted than the Colt which carried only a notch in the top of the hammer, and very often this did not line up with the barrel. The solid frame also made a much stronger weapon when empty and used as a club. Further, the hammer nose came down in a slit on the percussion cap through the recoil shield of the frame and did not allow broken and spent cap fragments to fall down in the works and gum up the gun, as was so common with Colts of that period. The gun was better designed in many ways than the Colt and with more strength where needed and better sights and a better frame and hammer arrangement. Grips were nearly as well shaped, and, had the Remington been out as long, it might well have given Colt more competition. The Whitney .36 Navy Revolver also closely resembled the Remington of the period.

The Remington was truly second only to the Colt in popularity and enjoyed nearly as wide a use in the Civil War and afterwards on the frontier. While Colt manufactured nearly 400,000 revolvers from 1861 through 1865 that were used on both sides, the Government purchased some 129,156 caliber .44 Army model 1860 Colts and some 2,056 of the 1851 Navy model. The Government also secured some 12,000 .44 Army and 2,500 Navy Colts of private dealers throughout the country early in the war. State troops were also supplied with Colts and Remingtons as well, of which no record exists. Except for the Colt factory fire they would, no doubt, have furnished many more.

.32 S. & W. Automatic Pistol, Smith & Wesson.

In comparison, the Government purchased 115,563 .44 Remingtons and 12,251 Remingtons in .36 Navy size, plus another 4000 of both sizes from private dealers. Army contracts for Remington six-shooters were filled from 1862 to 1865. Later the Army sold some 10,000 arms that had not been issued, of Remington make, and also exchanged 5,000 Remington cap and ball guns for a like number of the big Remington rolling block caliber .50 pistols.

While the first army contract price of .44 Colts was $25.00 each, competition with Remington soon brought the price down and the price was cut to $14.50 and later $14.00 for the Colt.

Remington's first sale to the Army brought $15.00, and the price was later lowered to $12.00, but, after the Colt fire, the price of Remingtons again was raised in 1864 to $15.50.

Among the Southern army, the Colts were much more widely used and probably there were five or six Colts used by the South to every revolver of other makes. The Johnny Rebs had a lot of Colts at the start of the war and captured a lot more from the Yanks.

The Remington was first converted to cartridge design under the Rollin & White Patent of April 3, 1855. These conversions appeared in 1869 and were made under a patent release from Rollin White and Smith & Wesson to the Government for army revolvers. The first Remington conversion was to a .46 caliber rim fire cartridge made by the old Union Metallic Cartridge Co.

Colt had some converted to the Theur cartridge but these were never popular and never used by the Army, and for some time Colt could not bore a cylinder clear through because of the White and S. & W. patents. This converted Remington .46 was no doubt one of the first cartridge revolvers issued to Cavalry troops and soon became very popular with them in the Indian fighting of the times.

The Indians also prized all Colt and Remington as well as S. & W. revolvers very highly and captured

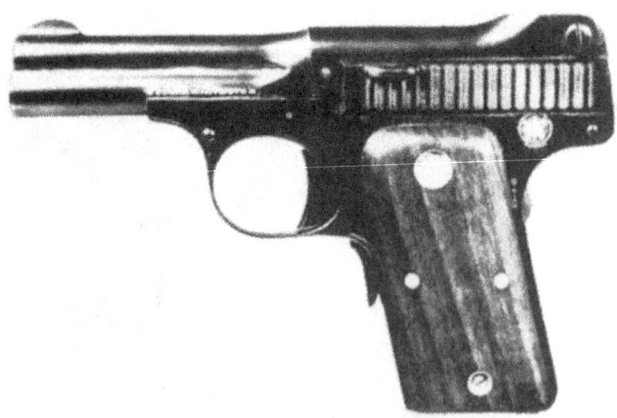

.35 S. & W. Automatic, Smith & Wesson.

a lot of them from the troops wiped out in the Fetterman massacre and later at the Custer fight. Neither the Fetterman disaster or the Custer debacle should ever be classed as a massacre however, for in both cases, cocky commanders with armed troops went out hunting for trouble against the orders of their superior officers, and died fighting vastly superior numbers of Sioux and Cheyenne warriors, who were better cavalrymen than the troops themselves. No better mounted fighters ever lived than the Sioux and Cheyenne warriors, and, when well armed, they always gave a good account of themselves in battle. Of 123 revolvers taken from Sioux and Cheyenne in 1877, 69 were Colts and of the balance, 41 were Remingtons, and, as these had largely been captured from troops and civilians of the period, it clearly indicates in about what proportion the two makes were used on the frontier.

In 1871 Remington brought out their improved .44 caliber cartridge revolver, another conversion, and also their big .50 caliber single shot Army and Navy pistol on the rolling block action. Both were issued to troops of cavalry. Smith & Wesson cartridge revolvers were purchased and used about the same time. In 1873, 1,529 of the big Remington single shot pistols were issued to troops along with 167,000 rounds of center fire ammunition. During the same period many Colt rim fire and center fire conversions were also issued to the troops along with both rim and center fire ammunition as well as the .44 American ammunition for the S. & W. .44 American revolver then also in service to some extent. Colt employed the Richards conversion and the later .44 Army conversion with new cylinder for the .44 center fire ammunition outside lubricated, and these were in use up to the advent of the Peacemaker .45 Colt model 1873, and were used among the troops for some time thereafter, until adequate supplies of the then new .45 Colt single action were on hand.

Custer's Command on the Little Big Horn was issued 18 rounds for their .45 single action Colts to be carried on the person. Each man also carried 50 rounds of .45-70 carbine ammunition, and 50 rounds more of carbine ammunition was carried on each horse. The Sioux all state that early in the fight they stampeded most of the horses, after killing the horse holders of Custer's five troops, and that the most of the cavalrymen went down firing their single action Colts at them in the close in-fighting. Chief Gall and Chief Crazy Horse massed mounted men under the brow of each hill on which a troop had made their dismounted last stand, then they simply rode over them and turned their attention to the next troop.

In 1875 Remington brought out their .44 Army revolver with a six-shot cylinder and 7½ inch round barrel, but they never saw service as a regular army issue as they did not stand up well to continued firing in dust and rust tests by the Army. Ten thousand of them were sold to the Egyptian government and many were sold commercially. They used a .44 outside lubricated cartridge. The Remington was also produced in an 1875 model for army tests in caliber .45 about 1877, but again the Remington did not come through the tests as well as the Colt model 1873 and was rejected for Army use. The later Remington .44-40 Frontier was a well-liked gun by all who owned it and those we tested were very accurate.

Small Revolvers and Pistols

With the advent of Smith & Wesson's fixed metallic cartridges and the heavy demand for sixguns and pistols of all kinds, a great many different firms sprang up and produced pistols and revolvers. Many of these were in small, easily concealed, sizes for pocket use.

Remington produced their share of these small pistols, but the one gun they produced that was destined to become popular and to last even to this day was their .41 caliber rim fire double barrelled Derringer. It was flat, easily concealed, carried nicely in the vest pockets and early became popular with gamblers and travelers. The main spring was so heavy and stiff that only strong women could cock it, so it never became much of a lady's gun. The stock was shaped much after the old Philadelphia Derringer with which Lincoln was killed, but the frame carried two superposed barrels and hinged upward at the rear top of the barrels. A swinging lever latch locked the barrels on the right side above the spur trigger. The .41 short cartridge did not have much authority and we have had its pointed bullet fail to go through a heavy tin can unless it struck square, but, nevertheless, it would penetrate into the middle of a man, carrying germs, dirt and lint with its greased pointed slug. He was then in need of surgery. Most gunmen would prefer to be hit with a .38 Special any day to that grease and dirt bearing .41 short that almost never went through a man and had to be dug out of him. Most real gunmen dreaded them.

Colt brought out many spur trigger small pistols in .22, .30, .32 and .38 rim fire and many of the smaller Colt pocket and percussion belt pistols were converted to handle rim fire ammunition. Colt made three models of Derringers for the .41 rim fire and many other firms produced these little pocket pistols, mostly in single shot. Remington also made single shot Derringers. Sharps produced, in addition to their well-known four barrelel model, a falling block single shot pistol that is very rare today.

Colt also brought out a four shot revolver called the clover leaf for the .41 rim fire and sold it as a house pistol. They also had a line of spur trigger police pistols. These small revolvers became widely used in the east by police, although they had little actual stopping power and never found favor in the West where a real gun was needed. Most of the Colt pocket models were made with the bird head grip while the police and house pistols by Colt invariably had square grips. Many very fancy ones were made; fancy cast metal stocks like some of the Tiffany model stocks produced for finely engraved Colt Percussion revolvers as well as fine woods, pearl and ivory and both engraved and plated models were produced. Service models of the police and house pistols or revolver, as they should be called, were usually fitted with hard rubber stocks, the police models with a cop struggling with a thug embossed on the side. While these little guns were produced in profusion, and many with loading gate and sliding rod ejector like the S.A. Colt, both in rim fire and center fire, they retained the spur trigger and were never popular as holster guns. Many companies brought out cheaper made counterparts of similar design. It would take a book to list them all. They never attained the popularity of the trigger guard models. All were single action.

The Colt Lightning double action brought out in 1877 soon became much more popular. Colt Derringers in single shot, and the House and Police pistols of their make, date from about 1870 and were made to about 1912 in some models. There were so many models and changes made in these small pistols and revolvers that collectors today have a very fertile field. Colt had plenty of competition in the Derringer field and the old Southerner was quite popular as well as the Marlin. The Philadelphia muzzle loading Derringers were still almost as popular, as the Derringer was a surprise weapon for close range only, and the percussion models usually actually carried more wallop than the early cartridge designs. Abraham Lincoln was killed with a Philadelphia muzzle-loading Derringer of medium size, .44 caliber.

Although arms listing of the times, 1870 to 1900, shows a great profusion of cheap, usually nickel plated small revolvers, they did little to make history and were purely for defense use, so that in a general history of the revolver, we need give them little further comment. The next heavy Colt revolver was the New Service model produced from about 1897 with various changes up to 1943.

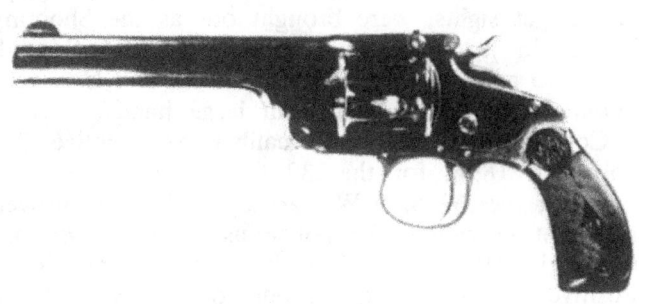

.38 single action, Smith & Wesson.

Heavy Duty

This, the largest of all Colt revolvers, came out in .45 long Colt caliber. The new service cylinder rotated to the right and the 1909 Army model was ordered by the Army, Navy and Marine Corps to the extent of nearly 14,000. The big gun was also brought out in a flat-top deluxe target model with fine target sights and checkered walnut grips. Service models usually were fitted with plain walnut grips and commercial models with wood or hard rubber grips. Most of these arms carried a lanyard swivel in the butt, except the fine New Service Target. The Target model was a very popular target arm and made high scoring possible. No more accurate revolver has been produced than this big gun in caliber .44 Special. It was also chambered for the .38-40, .44-40 and then, with our entrance into World War I in 1917, was chambered for the .45 auto cartridge to use the same ammunition as our model 1911 Service Colt Auto pistol. Later the arm was also chambered for the .38 Special and .357 Magnum and .44 Special. It was also made for English orders in calibers, .450, .455 and .476 Eley.

For men with extra large hands, the New Service Colt has always been very popular. It was made in 4½, 5½ and 7½ inch barrel lengths and with various changes in the cylinder latch.

In 1905 the Colt Positive safety device was added to the New Service revolver. The first lots of the 1917 were made with cylinders chambered straight through, necessitating the use of the three-shot clip to hold the head space of the .45 auto cartridge and to make ejection possible, but this was soon changed to a cylinder with proper chambering for the .45 auto cartridge so it would head-space with the front of the case on the shoulder in the chamber and could then be fired with or without the three-shot clips. Clips were still necessary, however, for simultaneous ejection until the .45 auto rim cartridge was brought out for the arm and its companion arm, the 1917 Smith & Wesson. Great numbers of these arms were used in the First World War and still are prevalent.

These big, heavy framed guns were very dependable and rugged and were widely used throughout the world. Later versions, with some refinements in grips and target sights, were brought out as the Shooting Master in .38 Special, .357 Magnum, .44 Special, .45 Auto and .45 Colt calibers. It was, and is, a very popular arm among men with large hands.

Colt brought out a .32 caliber New Police Revolver in 1896, for the .32 Colt New Police Cartridge or the .32 S. & W. cartridge. This arm proved too light in caliber for police use and was discontinued in 1905 when Colt brought out the Police Positive model. A target model of the New Police revolver was made in 1897.

Colt Police Positive revolvers were brought out in .22 L. R., .22 W. R. F., .32 Colt Long and Short, .32 Colt New Police, .32 S. & W., and .38 Colt New Police and .38 S. & W. Target models were also made. I once had a beautifully accurate Police Positive Target, chambered for the .32 S. & W. long cartridge.

Both standard and target models were discontinued in 1943. My old friend, Steven Camp, had one of these target revolvers in .22 W.R.F. and one spring he showed me the skulls of seven trapped bears he had killed with it—three grizzlies and four black skulls. He would wait until the bear lowered his head, biting at the trap and then usually from the side would drive one of those tiny pellets into the brain. Strange to say one skull showed where a .22 W.R.F. .45 grain slug went into the brain pan at the top and emerged on the other side and lodged under the skin in the muscles, and while it floored the bear, it did not kill him and he had to be shot again in the brain, lower down, to finish the job. Camp was an old woodsman and taxidermist and knew the exact location of the brain and just where to hit the bear's head. Barrel lengths were 2½, 4, 5, and 6 inches. I had the 6 inch in .32 S. & W. long caliber target. The little Banker's Special .22 caliber was made from this arm. Later models were made with a wider butt strap to afford a larger and better grip than earlier ones gave.

Colt's next arm was the Police Positive Special with a one-fourth inch longer cylinder and some changes to handle the .32-20 and .38 special cartridges. It was designed for police use. Barrels were 2, 4, 5, and 6 inches in length. The arm was also chambered for the .32 Colt and Smith & Wesson long cartridges. The two inch barrel version formed the basis of the later Detective Special and the present Colt Cobra is now made with either steel or aluminum alloy frame for extra light weight.

The Colt Army Special and Official Police was the last fixed-sighted version of the old Colt .38 Army and was made in calibers from .22 L.R. to .41 Long Colt. Its Target twin, the Officers Model, was made in .22 L.R. and .38 special and with the older models, in barrels up to 7½ inches. We once had a 7½ inch Officers model that had been fired so much that the lands were simply washed out. Lt. Syd Hines, later to become a General, borrowed this old gun at Camp Perry in 1925 for a trial, but it had lost its accuracy, and though he liked the long barrel, he found it useless for target work.

The latest .41 frame Colt guns are their new Officer's Model Special with heavy barrel and fine action and target sights, and their .357 Colt Trooper. Colt also made a single shot Camp Perry Model in Caliber .22 L.R. from 1926 to 1941 with the same .41 frame, but the barrel and cylinder were one piece and both swung out on the crane as the chamber portion was flat for one cartridge instead of the round revolving cylinder. It never became as popular as the Officer's Model. Some fine Officer's Models were made in .32 S. & W. long caliber.

The Colt Detective Special was made first in .38 Special caliber and after 1946 in .38 Colt and S. & W. and .32 Colt and S. & W. The little Banker's special .22 caliber was discontinued in 1945. This two inch barrel Colt pocket gun was also made in .38 Colt New Police and .38 S. & W. and later ones in .22 caliber with imbedded head cylinder.

The Colt Cobra with aluminum alloy frame is the last version of this arm and weighs but 15 ounces with rounded butt and can also be had with a hammer shroud to cover the hammer for double action pocket work. It may also be had with a square butt and 4 inch barrel when desired. The caliber is usually .38 Special, but also available are the .38 and .32 New Police. This about finishes our discussion of Colt revolvers, and while we have endeavored to touch most of the more important arms, space does not permit a treatise and description of all the many Colt arms.

Smith & Wesson

Although many double action percussion revolvers were used in the Civil War, Colt produced their first double action in 1877—their Colt Lightning. Smith & Wesson did not bring out a double action revolver until 1880, when they introduced their first for the .38 S. & W. cartridge. It early became very popular and great quantities were made and sold. Smith & Wesson maintained their fine finish and very close

.38 single action, sterling silver overlay by Tiffany, N. Y., Smith & Wesson.

careful fitting of parts. Twenty-five thousand were made first in .38 S. & W. caliber and then a smaller .32 S. & W. double action was added to the line late in 1880. After 25,000 replicas of the first model .38 were manufactured, the second model .38 double action was brought out and continued to serial No. 119,000.

Next, the third model, with improved single action trigger pull due to a change in the latch notch, also in .38 S. & W. caliber, was introduced and manufactured to serial number 322,700.

In 1882 the second model .32 was brought out and serials ran from 22,173 to 43,405. This arm has some changes and improvements over the first model, mostly in the type of cylinder stop or bolt.

With further slight changes in the trigger, covering the sear, the third model .32 D. A. was made from serial number 43,406 to 327,641 when discontinued in 1919. This was the greatest production of any single Smith & Wesson revolver.

In 1889 the fourth model D.A. .38 Smith & Wesson was introduced, with improvements in cylinder stop and with changes in the cylinder, and ran from serial number 322,701 to serial number 539,300. Next the fifth model .38 S. & W. ran from serial number 539,301 to 544,077. In this model, the front sight was forged intergral with the barrel and a new barrel catch, cam and spring, were added. This fifth model .38 D. A. Smith & Wesson was discontinued in 1911. It formed the basis of the .38 Perfected model.

In 1881 Smith & Wesson produced their first big .44 double action. This .44 D.A. S. & W. was on a large frame similar to the .44 Russian and was chambered for the .44 Russian cartridge but with a slightly shorter frame than the Russian model.

This arm was also made on special order for the then-popular .38-40 and .44-40 rifle cartridges. This was a sixgun instead of a five-shooter as were its smaller companions. This fine big gun was never popular in the West and while it became popular in some foreign countries, the popularity of the Colt single action was hard to overcome in the West, and only 54,668 of them were made in .44 Russian caliber and 15,340 for the .44-40 rifle cartridge. A few lighter ones numbered in the same series known as the Wesson Favorite were also made. These carried a rebated cylinder similar to the 1860 Colt .44 Army percussion revolver. The barrel diameter on these was reduced and a sighting groove added on top of a rib like the Schofield model had. Barrels of the .44 D.A. ran from 4 to 6½ inches and these fine arms were sold up to 1913, but the popular New Century, or so called Triple Lock, had by then taken over most of the sales for large caliber Smith & Wesson sixguns.

The famous Smith & Wesson Lemon Squeezer was brought out in 1887. Daniel B. Wesson designed the

.38 double action, Smith & Wesson.

.38 New Departure, safety hammerless, fifth model, Smith & Wesson.

new arm, the first hammerless Smith & Wesson. The first one was made in .38 S. & W. caliber and the next year the .32 S. & W. was produced. They contemplated the production of a .44 Russian on the same model for later production but it never saw the light of day. This little hammerless five shot revolver was made, either blued or nickeled, in 3¼, 4 and 5 inch barrels. It was purely a double action gun, with grip safety. The trigger could not be pulled back until the grip safety spring was depressed, making it one of the safest of all revolvers. It was especially good around very small children. We have seen many of them carried in grips, suitcases, the pocket or the war bag, fully loaded, and thrown in along with clothing. Many times, on hunting trips, we have seen sportsmen dig them out to shoot porcupines and pack rats around camp.

With no hammer to catch on the clothing the .38 S. & W. safety hammerless early became very popular with plain clothesmen, detectives and others for pocket use. Many gunmen carried it as a hide-out weapon, even when they wore a heavy belt gun. They used it left handed while their opponent watched for a move toward the big gun. It worked perfectly, either in or out of the pocket, and owing to the absence of hammer would not catch on clothing and could be fired through the pocket when necessary. A new coat was considered a low price to pay for one's life.

One hundred of the new arms were ordered with

.44 single action, American, first model, Smith & Wesson.

.44 single action American, second model, Smith & Wesson.

6 inch barrels for a test against 100 Colt Army models for possible cavalry use. The S. & W. won the machine rest test with its .357 inch caliber barrel and .357 inch square base bullet against the hollow base sub-caliber Colt bullet with its oversize .362 inch caliber barrel that depended on bullet upsettage to fill the grooves. In dust tests the S. & W. again came out ahead but in very severe rusting tests when the cylinders were almost rusted solid, the Colt came out on top. The close fitted S. & W. failed to operate and the Colt was adopted as the official Army side arm and used up to and until after the Philippine insurrection. The .32 is said to have reached in its first and second model a total production of 226,880 and was manufactured for some years more. Smith & Wesson next improved their single action and brought out their 1891 model in .38 S. & W. caliber. These were made from 1891 to 1911 to a total of some 28,107. Some 7,000 of these were a special so-called Mexican model, with spur trigger. The 1891 was also developed in a fine target single shot pistol for competition against the Lord Model Stevens and the Wurfflien pistols, first in .38 S. & W. caliber, next in .32 caliber and finally in the .22 long rifle cartridge. These guns had the revolver frame, but the barrel and lug to fill the frame latched at the top. It was without a revolving cylinder. They early became very famous as super-accurate target pistols. First made in 6 inch barrel in .38 S. & W., but in .22 caliber they were later fitted with a 10 inch barrel. They won many matches and were used by our Olympic teams for years, and became known as the Olympic model. Three thousand one hundred ninety-six were also made in a combination form in .38 S. & W. with a long single shot target barrel interchangable with a short pocket barrel and five-shot cylinder, giving the shooter both guns on the same frame. The second model was made from 1905 to 1909 and serials ran from 1 to 4,617.

In 1909 the Perfected Target Pistol was brought out in single shot only with improved lock work and speed of hammer fall and this arm became one of the standard slow fire target pistols.

The .38 Safety Hammerless New Departure ran through five models with serials from one to 190,064.

Smith & Wesson brought out their first solid frame hand ejector model in 1896, the first ones being in .32 caliber. These were six shot revolvers chambered for the center fire .32 Colt or S. & W. long cartridges. This was the first side-swing cylinder Smith & Wesson.

The War Department gave Smith & Wesson a contract for 3000 revolvers with swing-out cylinders, caliber .38 Long Colt during the war with Spain. Serials of the first model swing-out cylinder Smith & Wesson ran from one to 20,975. No doubt some of these first .38 long S. & W. guns were used in the Philippines along with the Colt .38 army. Both failed to stop the blood-thirsty Moros. This led Daniel B. Wesson to design the .38 S. & W. special cartridge with 21 grains of powder and a 158 grain bullet instead of 18 grains powder and 150 grain bullet of the .38 Long Colt. Colt then came out with a flat nosed bullet for the same cartridge and called it the .38 Colt Special.

Smith & Wesson next added the front cylinder latch in their 1902 model and serials started at 20,976 and ran to 33,803. More changes and improvements were made in this first model of the Military & Police and serials ran from 33,804 to 62,449. Beginning with serial 58,000 square butt grips were added.

In 1889 Smith & Wesson brought out their hand ejector M. & P. in .32 Winchester caliber or the so-called .32-20. The first model ran to serials 5,311 and the second model from 5,311 to 9,811 and the 1903 model serials ran to 18,125. With an improved cylinder stop, it ran to serial 22,436 and the improved 1905 model ran from 22,437 to 45,200. This model ran through third and fourth changes or models to serial number 191,161. In 1919 it was fitted with a heat treated cylinder. At serial number 191,161 it was fitted with a square-cut rear sight and square blade front sight, front and rear tangs grooved and trigger grooved. This gun formed the basis of the present K model and is still made in great quantities. In 1902 Smith & Wesson brought out their first side-swing cylinder solid frame .22 caliber with hand ejector. It had a seven shot cylinder and also the front cylinder latch. With the adoption of the front cylinder latch on all Smith & Wesson solid frame swing cylinder guns, the firm forged ahead of Colt and in this respect are today superior in their cylinder locking arrangement to double action swing-cylinder Colts.

The first model .22 hand ejector S. & W. did not have much of a sale as it was so very small, with barrels from 2 to 3½ inches. Its serials ran from one to 4,575. An improved second model was brought out in .22 L. R. caliber in 1906 and serials ran from 4,576 to 13,950. Barrels still ran to 3½ inches. Late in 1906 a third model was produced with barrel lengthened to 6 inches for target use. The rebounding and blocking hammer system was used together with target adjustable rear sight and a square butt grip. It was manufactured as late as 1915 and ran from 12,951 to 26,154.

In 1908 Phil Beakeart prevailed upon Smith & Wesson to bring out a larger frame .22 on the .32 caliber S. & W. frame for a real target revolver and ordered 1000 of them. These were produced around 1908 and greater production began in 1911. This Beakeart model had a heavier frame, target sights, separate firing pin, and square butt stock. These were numbered with the .32 hand ejector model and were very popular .22 caliber target revolvers. They were not made for high speed ammunition. These guns with match ammunition will group into 1½ inches at 50 yards.

Daniel B. Wesson, after fifty-two years of distinguished service, passed away in 1906. In 1907 Smith & Wesson brought out their Triple Lock, perhaps the finest revolver ever manufactured anywhere, at any time. Today no example of finer revolver making is to be had. The rear end of the barrel and the cylinder steel of the old triple lock are not as strong as in the present 1950 model Target S. & W. .44 calibers or the .357 S. & W. Magnum, but the old New Century was, and still is, one fine gun in any company.

They designed the .44 Special cartridge for this arm with 26 grains of black powder, instead of the 23 used in the .44 Russian cartridge. The .44 Special is simply a longer version of the .44 Russian and no more accurate sixgun load exists. It was made in both fixed military sight model and fine adjustable target sighted models. Barrel lengths ran from 4 to 7½ inches in length. Some 13,753 were made in .44 Special caliber and an additional 1,226 were produced for the .450 Eley Cartridge and another 21 for the .45 Colt Cartridge. Five thousand were also made for the British .450 Mark II during the first World War. The gun with 6½ inch barrel weighed 39 ounces. It was fitted with the first encased ejector rod. The frame followed the same lines as the Military & Police model but was much heavier and larger, affording a perfect grip for most men with average to large size hands. It was made in both nickel and blued finish. The third latch which led to its being called the Triple Lock was located at the front of the frame and certainly was a masterpiece of close

.44 single action, Model No. 3, New Model, Smith & Wesson.

.44 single action Russian, first model, Smith & Wesson.

fitting. We still consider it the finest job ever produced of locking a swing-cylinder gun.

With the start of World War I, the encased ejector lug was eliminated due to some army authorities claiming it would fill with mud. This second model started at serial 15,525 and a heat treated alloy cylinder was added at serial 16,600. Beginning with serial 15,525 the second model, without the triple locking feature and the encased ejector, became the famous .44 Military. The old grips came to the bottom of the frame and left the thin top of the frame grip to pound the hand in recoil. We exchanged many letters with Major D. B. Wesson urging that something be done about this bad feature as so many complained about the recoil of the S. & W. as compared with the Colt New Service. Doug Wesson's first answer to my prayers was a grip adapter that spread the grips too wide for most hands but did add a finger rest for the second finger. It made the grip too large and short for my hand and I early asked him to extend the grips on to the top corner of the frame. After considerable correspondence, and the remodeling of the grip adapter to one with far less material in back of the guard, Major Wesson finally adopted my idea and brought out the Magna stock that filled the web of the hand to the top of the grip on frame. This new stock eliminated the pounding of heavy loads and made the big gun comfortable to shoot with any load.

After serial No. 16,600 some 727 were made for the .45 Colt cartridge. These are the finest .45 Colt cartridge double action revolvers we have seen.

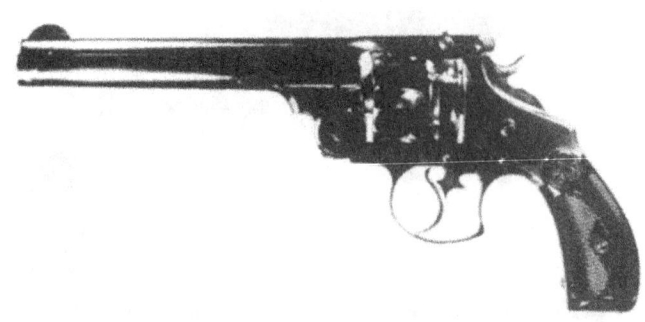

.44 double action, Smith & Wesson.

With the start of World War I, and the government's orders for both Colt and S. & W. revolvers to shoot the standard service .45 auto Cartridge, Smith & Wesson thought up the three cartridge clip idea and thus converted the gun to handle rimless cartridges. Another reason for the dropping of the famous old T. lock, Doug Wesson wrote me, was that British orders called for .455 caliber and that the gun had to be redesigned to allow about .1 of an inch greater distance from the center or axis of the cylinder to the center or axis of the charge hole for this big round. Then the British kicks on the encased ejector housing also had its bearing so that the gun was redesigned for the larger rounds and both the triple lock and the encased ejector eliminated. The encased ejector has always cost a lot more money to produce, machine and fit and in the rush of war orders, it was dropped. Some Triple Locks were still made to order rather late, however, and we remember one letter from Douglas Wesson in the late thirties stating that he had just filled an order to a South American gentleman for a pair of them. No doubt they were produced from parts on hand at the factory.

The .45 1917 S. & W. was the same as the second model .44 hand ejector in all but caliber, chambering, the 5½ inch barrel and the addition of a lanyard swivel in the butt. The blue finish was also changed to one easier to process though not as black and lasting as the old standard S. & W. blue. The checkered stocks were also changed to plain walnut.

The Smith & Wesson was bored .450 to .4517 inches groove diameter, one turn in 14.569 inches, number of lands six, and with right-hand turn. Smith & Wesson delivered 175,000 of these .45 caliber 1917 military revolvers to the U. S. Government. As compared with the rough finished Colt 1917, we much prefer the 1917 S. & W. It was, and still is, a very good combat and police weapon owing to the speed with which it can be reloaded with the aid of the clips.

Smith & Wesson also furnished Great Britain 73,650 of these big sixguns chambered for the .455 Mark II British service load. The first 5000 of these were made by reboring and rechambering the existing Triple Lock .44's and a total of 525 of these Triple Locks were thus turned out in .455 British caliber.

After the war, the 1917 was produced in a commercial model known as the .45 Army and with the fine commercial blue-black finish. The .45 auto rim cartridge was designed to eliminate the need of clips or the use of jacketed bullet ammunition. The new case holds more powder and can be loaded to equal the factory .45 Colt loads with proper bullet and powder charge. This will be discussed more fully later.

The Magna stocks were added in 1938 and those guns with serials above 175,000 are post war, commercially manufactured. The British .455 was made with a 6½ inch barrel.

We had a Canadian friend who went over with the Canadian forces and during one engagement was captured by three German soldiers in the night. They were conducting him back to their lines and, during some particularly heavy shelling, all four took refuge in a shell hole. He had an old .455 Triple Lock S. & W. inside his tunic, in a makeshift shoulder holster that the three Germans had missed when they disarmed him in the dark. Each time a flare shell went up he watched his captors, got them perfectly located, and then as the sky lighted again, he jerked the old .455 Triple Lock and killed all three before they could bring a rifle to bear on him, shooting fast and double action from his cramped position in the mud. He made his way back to the Canadian lines where he was gladly accepted on challenging the sentries.

Smith & Wesson ran into considerable competition with cheap arms made to closely resemble their break-top revolvers, but sold at a much lower price. They brought out their Perfected model with an extra latch and with coil springs and this sold in .38 S. & W. caliber to the number of 58,398. Smith & Wesson also brought out an auto loading pistol on the old Clement Belgian design. However, they made their gun in .35 S. & W. caliber to take a special cartridge with jacketed bullet tip and .008 inch larger diameter of bullet. This then being a proprietary cartridge with less power than the standard .32 Colt auto, never became popular. The .32 Colt auto ammunition could be used in the .35 S. & W. auto pistol but the .35 S. & W. ammunition was too large to chamber

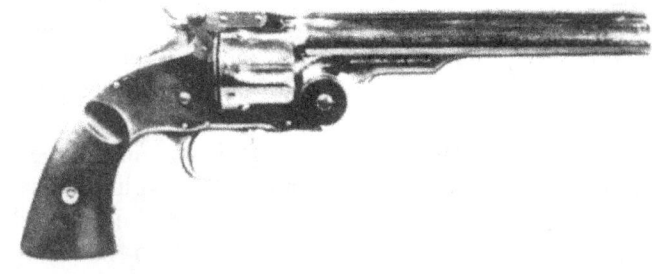

.45 single action, Schofield Model, Smith & Wesson.

in the various arms for the .32 Colt auto. All this aided in the gun's dying a natural death. Only 8,350 of them were made and they never offered serious competition to the Colt. J. Edgar Hoover's boys carried some of them for a time, but found they were lacking in stopping power.

After four years of making side-swing .32 calibers, Smith & Wesson brought out their .32 hand ejector for the .32 long S. & W. cartridge and it was made through 264,857 guns up through the sixth change in model. This, in the third model, became known as the Regulation Police model in 1917. Barrel lengths from 3½ to 6 inches and target models also were available. These were six shot, also with square butt stocks when desired. Smith & Wesson also brought out their .38 S. & W. Regulation Police revolver at the same time. It was built on the same frame and had five chambers. Later with a 2 inch barrel, it became known as the .38/32 and today the Little Terrier.

Smith & Wesson also brought out a new single shot .22 caliber target pistol called their Straight Line Model with a grip similar to most auto pistols. In spite of claims, this model never did become as popular as the old Olympic S. & W. Single shot and while some target experts did well with it, most of them went back to their old Olympic models. This model soon died a natural death. How many were made we do not know. A lot of money, time and thought went into the new arm for competition against the Colt Camp Perry model, but like the latter, it was soon discontinued.

Next Major D. B. Wesson brought out the first K-22 on the .38 Special M. & P. frame with encased cartridge heads and 6 inch barrel with a weight of 35 ounces. Early this became a very popular target arm and he sent the writer one of the first ones. It proved much easier and steadier to hold than the old Bekeart model .22/32 or the various S. & W. and Colt single shot pistols. It soon became a more or less standard target arm and was brought out to handle High Speed ammunition. Colt soon chambered their Official Police and Officer's models to meet the competition for the .22 L. R., also with imbedded case heads, and these revolvers are still going strong. Recently Smith & Wesson further improved their K model by adding a ribbed barrel and short action. It is still one of the very top .22 caliber target sixguns. It was also brought out in .38 Special and .32 S. & W. long. The first K models had no rib on the barrel but were fitted with fine target sights. They are continued today in both plain and target-sighted models and also the famous Combat Masterpiece with Baughman front sight, 4 inch barrel, the later full ribbed and with adjustable S. & W. micrometer click rear sight. No finer .38 Special sixguns have ever been produced. They are now made in .22 L. R., .32 S. & W. long and in .38 Special with ribbed barrels, the rib of various widths, so that matched sets can be offered the target shooter having the same weight for all three calibers. These are as fine target arms as human ingenuity and modern manufacturing methods have been able to produce to date. They will all three group in 1½ inches at 50 yards, which is very fine revolver accuracy. All the new models have the short action and the click micrometer target rear sight.

More Power

About 1930 due to armored vests and bullet proof glass for autos, the various big gangs over the country gave our police and law enforcement agencies a bad time. Colt answered the problem with their Super .38 auto on the good old model 1911 design. The new arm shot a 130 grain bullet at 1300 feet and proved an answer to the problem. J. Edgar Hoover's boys promptly adopted it for their side-arm. It would penetrate bullet proof vests, armored car bodies if not too heavy, and bullet proof glass.

Doug Wesson then brought out the Smith & Wesson Heavy Duty .38 Special on the time tried .45 frame and with the encased ejector again added, in a 5 inch barrel, with fixed sights of square design and an improved .38/44 cartridge loaded by Remington. This cartridge with a 158 grain metal tipped bullet at 1100 feet proved the answer and soon became a very popular arm with all peace officers. The gun had a very fine and fast double action pull.

Charles J. Koehler sent me one, along with 500 rounds of ammunition, asking that I practice and make a test to prove to them that Ed McGivern had really been able to get six hits on a gallon can tossed 18 to 20 feet in the air before it came back to the ground. I practiced all winter with that gun, tossing the gallon size cans up some 18 to 20 feet with the left hand while I simultaneously raised the Heavy Duty S. & W. with the right hand and started proceedings. Though I had written Koehler, I was sure in my own mind that Ed McGivern did everything he ever claimed to have done and many times before he even mentioned the fact, they still wanted me to conduct the experiment. By the expenditure of a lot of ammo and practicing all winter, I mastered the trick and finally threw my own cans with left hand and got six hits five times straight one morning before the cans reached the ground, shooting only double action. By throwing the cans up with right hand and then drawing the gun from a cross draw holster, I managed three hits nicely and a very few times got in four hits using the same hand for throwing the can and drawing and firing the gun.

About this time, my friend Major D. B. Wesson, or Doug as we call him, wanted to develop an even more powerful cartridge for the gun, and I started experimenting with the 173 grain bullet I had designed for the Lyman Gunsight Corp., with heavy charges of No. 80 powder. Mattern listed a load of 11 grains of No. 80 with a round nose 160 grain bullet at 1152 feet velocity. I used this load with the heavier 173 grain Keith bullet and put 1000 of them through the gun to see if I could blow it up. No Soap—the gun handled them perfectly, though this load with the 158 grain standard bullet had wrecked many a fine Officer's Colt. I sent a quantity to Col. Bill Tewes of the Peters Cartridge Co. for testing and he chronographed them at an average of 42,000 pounds pressure. The gun is still in good serviceable condition today and I, at that time, wrote Doug Wesson that the gun would safely handle a much more powerful load than the .38/44 Remington metal tipped Police load he had had Remington bring out for the .38/44 Heavy Duty. Doug wrote back that my experiments were the determining factor in his bringing out a gun to be called the .357 Magnum. We went to work. I had quantities of Keith bullets sent him, sized and lubricated and ready to load. Remington would not load them, so he went to Winchester and he and Mert Robinson started to work out the problem based on my experiments with the .38/44. They determined to bring out a longer case by one-tenth inch to prevent its use in standard .38 Special arms, but overlooked the old Colt .38 Long Army revolver, which will chamber them today and has been fired with them, though it is very apt to blow up the gun. This revolver was chambered straight through the cylinder and will accept the magnum load. It is a very dangerous load ever if overbored to .362 inches and with a .357 bullet.

They decided to redesign my bullet, retaining the square shoulder but changing the crimping groove to another narrow lubrication groove and crimping just over the front shoulder. I was opposed to this procedure as they practically eliminated the forward groove diameter band on my bullet and the new factory .357 Magnum was not as accurate as my original bullet loaded into the .38/44 case with proper crimping in the beveled crimping groove. At any rate, the .357 Magnum was brought out in this form and proved far superior in power and velocity to the .38/44 and with good accuracy. Smith & Wesson brought out the Magnum .357 with 8⅜ inch barrel. The .38/44 had used No. 1301 powder, and No. 2400 and was used for the .357 Magnum with a charge of 15.3 grains with the revised 158 grain Keith bullet. The new arm was, and still is, made of the very finest heat treated steels with recessed case heads and the encased ejector on the good .45 S.&W. frame. Doug sent me gun No. 0362 for testing and I gave it the works on jack rabbits and other pests, and wrote up the results in *The American Rifleman,* killing 125 jacks with it in three days at ranges from a few steps to one jack standing on his hindlegs at a measured 180 yards. Shooting was off-hand but using both hands.

Early in this work we soon found that the factory .357 Magnum load was not as accurate beyond 125 yards as our older Smith & Wesson Outdoorsman with a 6½ inch barrel and either the Remington factory .38/44 load or our hand load in the same cases with 13.5 grains of No. 2400 and the Keith hollow point (Lyman) 160 grain bullet crimped in its proper crimping groove and with my forward groove diameter band in front of the case.

We had made many kills on jack rabbits and chucks and one goshawk at a full 200 yards with that Outdoorsman and the above loads. Over 125 yards we could not do as well with the long ill-balanced Magnum, so we tried the .38/44 loads in the Magnum with the Keith bullet and 13.5 grains 2400. Long range accuracy picked up immediately. This is the load my old protégé, Dick Tinker, used in the Magnum 8⅜ inch S. & W. to shoot the long range targets published in Ed McGiverns most excellent book, Fast and Fancy Revolver Shooting. Next we returned our Magnum to the S. & W. factory and had the barrel cut to 6½ inches. It balanced much better and has since killed a lot of game, including some big game and two cougar, as well as innumerable bob cats, coyotes and eagles.

Major Wesson hunted big game and killed elk, antelope, moose and one grizzly with his 8⅜ inch .357 Magnum. Even when working with Major Wesson on the .357 Magnum, we wanted and held out for a Magnum in .44 Special caliber to use my heavy loads with Keith 250 grain solid bullet or 235 grain hollow point backed by 18.5 grains 2400 powder. We preferred this load for game or any long range work and still do. It produced about twice as great killing power on all game tried, as did the .357 Magnum. Neither load would outshoot that old Smith & Wesson .38/44 6½ inch barrel Outdoorsman at long range, but the .44 did throw up a lot more dust and dirt and hits were easier located when the .44 was used. While the .357 Magnum shot just as well with my reloads in .38/44 case, it did not beat that fine old Outdoorsman for accuracy and we doubt if any .357 caliber gun ever will.

The special agents of the F.B.I. early adopted the .357 Magnum as their main armament with the powerful factory load but in a short 3½ inch barrel gun. We still believe it was a mistake to cut the barrel of the .357 Magnum below 4 inches as about 38 feet velocity is lost for each inch of barrel removed from the 8⅜ inches downward. With so heavy and big a holster gun, nothing is gained by reducing the barrel length below 4 inches, and much is lost. With the 4 inch barrel it is just as fast on the draw as the 3½ inches and the half-inch longer sight radius does no harm in deliberate shooting.

The loading companies have ever been "charry" of using enough tin or antimony on their bullets to properly harden them for high velocity revolver loads. Short barrels have a tremendous muzzle blast and we believe some percentage of the bullets leave the muzzle with their base deformed from the muzzle blast when barrels are reduced below 4 inches in length. You can remove a revolver barrel and fire the gun with cylinder only and catch the slugs in soft snow or oiled sawdust or other soft material. You will find the bases are badly mushroomed from the powder gases, after leaving the front of the cylinder. We believe the same thing takes place with high velocity hot loads, such as the .357 Magnum in full loads, with barrels under 4 inches in length. We have received many reports of 3½ inch magnums shooting exceptionally well with .38 Special ammunition plain or .38/44 high speed, but when late issue .357 Magnum ammunition is used about 30% will keyhole on the target at 20 yards. We can see no reason for this other than a too soft bullet and a too short barrel.

The original .357 Magnum load came out with a 158 grain modified Keith bullet backed by 15.3 grains 2400 for 1510 feet velocity from the 8⅜ inch barrel, but during and just after World War II, we obtained some Western .357 magnum ammunition that was very soft, seemingly having no more velocity and power than the .38/44 ammunition and certainly not as accurate. Recently during the last year we have run onto some Western ball powder loads that are very hot and give more recoil and muzzle blast than any .357 Magnum loads we have seen to date. Fired in the darkened test range at the Smith & Wesson plant, they threw only a few red sparks from the muzzle in comparison with Remington .357 Magnum loads that created a big flash some six inches in diameter and a foot long. Needless to say, these hot new Western ball powder loads must burn most of the powder in the chamber and the first two inches of the barrel, but the recoil and muzzle blast was very objectionable, even to the hardened testing crew.

The .357 Magnum cartridge develops the highest pressures ever effectively used in a sixgun and the gun with the full length barrel weighed 47 ounces and 42 ounces even with the 3½ inch barrel as adopted by the F.B.I.

Colt produced their Shooting Master on the old New Service frame in .357 magnum caliber and also their fine old single action. Owing to the gradual slope of the S. A. Colt grip, it absorbs the recoil of this and other heavy revolver cartridges with less punishment to the hand than any other sixgun. The gun simply turns up in the hand in recoil. The first .357 S. & W. Magnums were punishing to the web of the hand until Doug Wesson brought out the Magna stocks that I had begged for for so long. It was then much more comfortable in recoil and that hump is not only needed but is a necessity at the top of the grip for fast double action shooting. For a single action arm, we have found no grip to be better than the old S. A. Army or a combination of the S. A. Army and Bisley models that Harold Croft and the writer worked out. For a double action arm we have found no grip the equal of the modern .45 frame S. & W. with Magna type stocks, but we do prefer the stocks to be slightly thinner than the factory version for our own use.

Jarvis engraving a gun at the Smith & Wesson factory.

Present and Future

After the fine old New Century or Triple Lock, Smith & Wesson produced the .44 Military without the encased ejector rod that all real sixgun men preferred. Then in 1926 they brought out their fine 1926 model again with the encased ejector rod in .44 Special caliber both in fixed sighted and 6½ inch target models. It was and is a very fine gun today and will handle the heavy 44 Special loads perfectly. It was made in 4, 5, and 6½ inch lengths. The latter length with target sights. This gun in .44 Special caliber became very popular with all real sixgun men. In the Target Sighted model, it would hold its own with any target arm for accuracy and was better for long range accuracy than most other arms with possible exception of the S. & W. Outdoorsman, the Colt Shooting Master and the .357 Magnum in both makes.

With the end of World War II, Colt dropped production of their New Service frame and also previously dropped manufacture of their fine old Single Action. Today only Smith & Wesson make a heavy .45 frame gun and since the war they brought out their fast, short-action, with shorter hammer fall and a wider shortened hammer spur. Contrary to popular opinion, the new short-action, once one gets used to it, is just as good for fast double action shooting as the old long action, and lock time is greatly speeded up.

Final inspection of guns at the Smith & Wesson factory.

Since the War, Smith & Wesson has brought out their 1950 Target with full ribbed barrel, short action, in .38/44 still known as the Outdoorsman, and the 1950 .44 Target for the .44 Special cartridge, also for the .45 auto and auto rim known as the .45 1950 Target. In the fixed sighted model it is still made in .38/44 heavy duty and .44 Special with 4, 5 and 6½ inch barrels and in the .45 auto rim with standard 5½ barrel, known as the .45 Army.

The short action has also been added to the .357 S. & W. Magnum. All are now produced with the fine encased ejector rod that not only offers protection to the extractor rod but greatly adds to the balance of the arm and also to its appearance. We firmly believe all S. & W. arms of present manufacture should incorporate the encased ejector rod and it should be a S. & W. trade mark. Its use greatly increases cost of manufacture but is well worth the cost.

The fine Smith & Wesson .357 Magnum is still made and sold at $110.00, representing their finest craftsmanship both in the high bright blue finish and also in the perfect fitting of the various parts. It is a superbly made arm, no better existing. We have long urged that the same fine Magnum be brought out in .44 Special caliber and have tried without success to have the various loading companies turn out a Magnum .44 Special with the Keith 250 grain bullet backed by 18.5 grains 2400, but so far to no avail. They are afraid of the old type case with protruding primer pocket and thin head which they could easily redesign and bring out in solid head. They are perhaps afraid of the old Triple Lock as being made of inferior steel, but we know of a great many of these fine old guns that have successfully digested my heavy loads for a great many years with no casualties. For years Smith & Wesson has had orders for many times the arms they can make, and as yet have been unable to go into this poblem of a Magnum .44 Special. One way it could be done, and would no doubt then have the sanction of the loading companies, would be to bring out the S. & W. Magnum in .44 Special with imbedded case heads, extending the cylinder back to the recoil shield, and also making the cylinder one-tenth inch longer on the front end, still leaving room enough for a gas ring. Then they could bring out a solid head .44 Special Magnum case one-tenth inch longer than the present standard and loaded with the Keith 250 grain bullet and 18.5 grains 2400 for 1200 feet. The extra case length would about equal the decreased inside capacity at the head of the case of the solid head over the old protruding primer pocket type. It would handle the same heavy Keith load and no doubt the cartridge companies would then be willing to play ball if enough such guns were produced.

Smith & Wesson has lately produced their Highway Patrolman in .357 Magnum caliber, made from straight Magnum steel parts and the same quality steels and inside mechanism, but with cheaper outside finish, the same as all their lower priced revolvers that sell at $85.00 with standard Magna stocks and $89.50 with their fine, big, full Target stock. This gun could also be well made in a Magnum .44 Special as above. The new Highway Patrolman is made in 4 and 6 inch barrels with Baughman front sight on the 4 inch and regular target blade on the 6 inch if desired.

The old S. & W. Target rear sight first used on the .357 Magnum would change its impact from recoil and many of the first Magnums would jar this sight out of adjustment. Smith & Wesson then developed their micrometer click rear sight, on the order of the well-known King sight and this has well withstood the test of time, and now is never jarred from its adjustment by recoil. The windage on the old sight tended to shift after a few guns full of .357 Magnum, which would loosen the screws, but ever since we had the new sight fitted to our Magnum, no change has occurred.

Since the War, S. & W. have improved their little .22/32 Kit gun, bringing it out in a 1953 model with the fine S. & W. micrometer click rear sight and Baughman one tenth inch front sight, with either two or four inch barrels, encased shell heads and coil main spring, with short action. It is today the finest light weight six-shot .22 caliber ever made, for the man or woman desiring a light, super accurate .22 caliber revolver for general practice and small game killing. The firm still makes their fine .22/32 Model 1953 Target, also with the improved short action and sights, and both this and the Kit gun, with ribbed barrel. Also they still make their .32 hand ejector and their little 2 inch barrel .38 S. & W. Terrier. These in addition to their fine K models, and their .32 and .38 Regulation Police models.

Smith & Wesson also make their Military & Police square butt .38 Special and in 2, 4, 5, and 6 inch barrel lengths. During World War II, they made a special rough finished combat weapon chambered for the .38 S. & W. and also the British .38-200 grain Service load for the British forces and .38 Special for our forces.

The Military & Police .38 Special is also made in a special round butt pocket edition often called the Detective Special.

In addition to these fine arms, the Company has also brought out two new and very interesting undercover arms for detectives and plain clothesmen and also to be carried as secondary hidden arms by peace officers and the F.B.I. One is the little Chief's Special with 2 inch barrel and five shots in caliber .38 Special having a weight in the steel frame of only 19 ounces, and in the aluminum alloy frame of only 10¾ ounces. The other is the Smith & Wesson Centennial model. This is a hammerless two inch barrel job, weighing 19 ounces in steel, and much lighter in the aluminum alloy frame but slightly heavier than the 10¾ ounce Chiefs Special. The little Chiefs Special has the new short action and the Centennial has an entirely new coil spring action, entirely double action. The Chiefs Special can be cocked and fired single action and is very accurate for its extremely light weight. Both arms are five-shot and both chambered for the .38 Special cartridge and while S. & W. do not advertise the fact, both guns will perfectly handle the .38/44 and other high speed ammunition in .38 Special. We recently made a test run of 500 rounds of this high speed ammunition through each of these guns with no ill effects we could detect either visually or by careful measurement of cylinders and rear ends of barrels.

One thing that adds greatly to the strength of these two little undercover arms is the fact they are five-shot, hence the bolt cut or stop in the cylinder comes between the charge holes, not over the center of them as is true of all six-shot arms. Another feature enabling them to handle such powerful ammunition is the fact that almost no barrel projects back through

Die sinker inletting dies for frame forging at Smith & Wesson factory.

Roll-burnishing cylinders at the Smith & Wesson factory.

the frame, barely enough to take for measurement is all that protrudes. Very little barrel to bell or crack is left unsupported by the frame.

The Centennial has a grip safety like the old New Departure safety hammerless in appearance. It can be blocked off by removing the stocks and slipping a small pin in place. This is the first swing-out cylinder, solid frame hammerless .38 Special. Today it is no doubt the finest true pocket gun ever made for close range defense work as it is absolutely safe in the pocket and cannot be fired unless the grip safety is pushed in and the double action actuated at the same time.

These two little guns along with the Kit gun, have already become very popular. The little guns sell at $60.00 blued and $66.00 with nickel finish in the Chief's Special, and $62.00, blued, and $68.00 nickeled, in the Centennial models.

Smith & Wesson has also recently designed and brought out a new 9mm. auto loading pistol in two models. One has to be cocked before the first shot, like the well known model 1911 Colt. The other is double action for the first shot like the P-38 Auto Pistol. These are small, light, compact and very well made pistols. Prices have not yet been announced but the double action model bids fair to become a very popular gun for lovers of the auto pistol and the fact that it can be drawn and fired double action for the first shot makes it a very fast defense gun.

The new manager and President of Smith & Wesson, Mr. Carl R. Hellstrom, picked the firm up by its boot straps, so to speak, and in the course of years, his very able management and supervision has put Smith & Wesson at the top of the list as revolver manufacturers. He bought a tract of land in the suburbs of Springfield, Massachusetts, and built a modern arms factory for the production of revolvers. Every part of a Smith & Wesson arm is built in that beautifully designed factory from the smallest stock escutcheon and medallion to the forgings from which each part is made. The factory is on a complete production line basis, from the huge forging hammers, through the trimmers, shapers and millers, to the barrel and cylinder boring, rifling and lapping machines.

The stocks are also machine checkered on special machines that do an even better job than hand work. All parts go through a magnaflux process to detect and discard any with flaws and each step is rigidly inspected. Each department has its own special job in the manufacture of and the careful handfitting of each part. The S. & W. handgun progresses from the rough forged parts at one end of the plant to the finest finished revolver imaginable at the other end. A crew of very fine engravers take care of special orders for finely finished arms. The stocking department is a small factory in itself. There is a repair department where all manner of S. & W. guns, old and new, are repaired and refinished. The blueing and plating departments are well supplied with the latest equipment as is the heat treating rooms. Many of the machines and developments to speed production of precision arms are the work of Carl Hellstrom. The great plant has been in full production for many years and still is unable to quite catch up on orders for any single model they produce.

Colt Products

Colt pioneered in the production of automatic pistols under the patents of John M. Browning. Colt produced the first commercially made automatic pistols that were wholly successful in their operation. The first model, a .38 automatic with six inch barrel, was produced in 1900. The first model had a rear sight safety that, when pushed down, prevented the hammer from striking the firing pin. Army Ordnance ordered 200 of these. This arm used a 130 grain bullet at 1260 feet and was found to give better penetration than the revolvers of the time. Less than 3000 of the first model were made prior to 1902. The 1902 or second model followed. This was made in both sporting and military styles with wood grips on the army and hard rubber grips on the commercial guns. Many small changes were inaugurated at the time. The sporting model numbered up to 10,999 and then the final run of these pistols was numbered from 30,000 to 30,190.

The 1902 Military model was changed somewhat in grip and shape of hammer spur and a lanyard ring added to the butt. The finger grip was first on the front of the slide and later on the rear of the slide. Numbering of these arms was very peculiar starting at 15,999 and receding with each pistol to the number 11,000. Later it was started with 30,000 and to a total serial of 43,266.

The 1900 model had a seven shot magazine, while the 1902 military model had an eight shot clip, and the grip was ⅜ of an inch longer. In 1903 Colt brought out a pocket edition of the .38 Military with 4½ inch barrel. It soon became very popular due to its flat shape and easy portability and its powerful cartridge. It was made from 1903 until 1927 and serials ran from 16001 to 42,226.

The next Colt automatic of note was their famous pocket pistol of .32 caliber, first produced before 1903 and later known as the 1903 model. These had a 4 inch barrel and eight shot magazine capacity. The .380 caliber was introduced in 1908 with a capacity of seven shots. They were furnished full blued or full nickeled and were one of the first successful hammerless automatic pistols. Pistols from one to 72,000 were made with 4 inch barrels and pistols from 72,000 upwards with 3¾ inch barrels, with barrel bushing and a larger extractor. The final lot of these pistols from serial 105,050 to serial 572,215 had a locking lug on the front end of barrel and no barrel bushing and had 3¾ inch barrels. Some few made in later years for military officers use had a parkerized finish. This was and still is a very popular pocket automatic, which is well attested by the tremendous number of them manufactured.

Colt produced their smallest version of the auto loading pistol, the tiny .25 caliber, in 1908. This little arm was made for vest pocket carrying and for ladies' use as a defense weapon. While it used a very small and impotent cartridge, it nevertheless managed to account for a lot of human lives. It was dropped from manufacture in 1946. This pistol was the work of A. C. Wright, as well as of John M. Browning. After serial 141,000 a safety disconnector was inaugurated. When the magazine was withdrawn, it broke all connection between trigger and sear until magazine was replaced. How many were made we do not know. It was never popular with real gunmen but did enjoy a tremendous sale from people who wanted a very light, concealed vest pocket gun, of the same type as the Remington Double Derringer a generation before.

The U. S. Army had learned its lesson in the Philippines regarding the necessary caliber for side arms. Not taken in by the .38 Auto Colt, they wanted a heavier caliber auto pistol for trial. Colt's answer was the Browning and they patented the .45 auto model of 1905. This arm came out with a 5 inch barrel and a grip set at a much better angle to the barrel and slide than the old .38 Military. Some 5000 of this model were made with various changes. Much experimenting was done and many small changes were made in the model 1905, leading to the final version—model 1911.

From all we can learn, approximately 5000 of the model 1905 were produced. The first ones had the rounded hammer, but later, about 1908, the spur type hammer was substituted. Two hundred experimental models were made, all told, in changing from the model 1905 to the final model 1911, in an effort to win Government contracts. Some 400 of the 1905 model were ordered from Colt by the Army in 1907.

These pistols are quite rare and valuable to collectors today. The rarest of all model 1905 Colt automatics being the one with detachable shoulder stock holster. The Colt Company advised me that less than 100 of these were ever made, and most of them for South American trade. The rear strap was grooved at the lower half of its length with a cross-cut at the bottom. The brass fitting at the end of the shoulder stock slides up and locks securely on this grooved rear strap of the pistol. The holster is made of good black leather over a steel frame. It is lined with buckskin and has a brass stud catch to the flap. Some were lined with tan grain leather. We have two model 1905 Colt autos, one very early serial number 136, in good serviceable condition, and the other, a nearly new original specimen, complete with the shoulder stock holster serial No. 883. Both have the rounded hammer. The shoulder stock holster has a small inadequate belt loop on the back and this in turn is fastened at the lower end by, of all things, a sort of overshoe buckle. The holster bears no serial number. These first model 1905 .45 pistols had very well finished checkered walnut stocks much like the fine stocks furnished on the early Officer's Model Colts.

With the adoption of the model 1911 Colt .45 auto as the official side arm for both the Army and

Smith & Wesson factory—fitting barrels for blueing tank.

the Navy, Colt production jumped. Just how many were made may never be known as it is confidential War Department information. Both civilian as well as military arms were produced. The civilian arms were marked with a "C" while the military weapons were marked with "United States Property." A few of these pistols were made at the Springfield Armory in 1912 under Colt patents. We have one of them, bought through the D.C.M., and the N.R.A., before World War I, by W. R. Strong, then Secretary of the Helena Rifle Club, for the sum of $14.25. Bill Strong, later Captain Strong, carried this gun in World War I and through the Chateau Thierry fighting. He told me he used several clips in one engagement and did not think he missed a shot. Bill Strong was shot and killed in a hunting accident while standing six feet in front of me on the south fork of the Flathead, October, 1919. The 150 grain .30-06 slug that took his life missed me by inches.

All parts for the model 1911 were made interchangeable and the arm is easily dismantled and taken down with the aid of very few tools. It was, and still is, in all probability, the finest of all automatic pistols, superior in design, durability, accuracy, and dependability. In .45 caliber, it is our personal choice of all automatics.

In the 1920's a checkered arched grip housing was added together with a shorter checkered curved trigger and a longer grip safety spur to keep the hammer from biting the web of the hand. These were very good improvements and greatly improved the feel and fit of the weapon as well as making it point higher and more in line with the extended shooting arm. Wider blade front sights with wider rear sight notches of Patridge type were also added. The frame just back of the trigger was hollowed out on each side, to give the trigger finger better access to the trigger. If carried cocked and with the side safety on, the gun can be gotten into action very fast, but it never was a good pointer and tends to shoot low in all fast, quick draw, hip shooting and only by constant practice can the gun be mastered for this work. While one of the hardest handguns to learn to shoot, it is very accurate and once mastered makes a dependable military arm. Its seven shot magazine with one round in the chamber gives the firer eight shots before reloading. The slide stays back and locked when the last shot is fired and on the insertion of a new magazine and the slide stop depressed the slide goes forward, loading the arm and leaving it cocked for the next seven shots. This makes for very fast reloading and continuous fire and it is doubtful if a better military pistol has ever been invented. The cartridge is a good one, either with the 200 grain or its variations at 900 feet, or the old service load of 230 grain at 800 feet plus.

During the last world war the model 1911 A-1 was brought out with parkerized finish and wider front sight of Baughman type. This is a superb shooting pistol. After testing many hundreds of them during the war and adjusting their trigger pulls and sights, I hold this pistol in very high regard.

The model 1911 .45 Colt Auto formed the basis of the National Match Target Pistol, also the Super .38, and the Colt Ace .22 caliber and the later Colt Commander pistol.

Colt could not supply the demand for these pistols to the Government during the two world wars and licensed the following firms to make them: Remington Arms Co.; Singer Sewing Machine Co.; Union Switch and Signal Co.; North American Arms Co., Ltd. of Quebec, Canada; Ithaca Gun Co., and Remington Rand Co. Imitations were also made in Belgium and Spain but of poor quality and workmanship throughout.

The .45 National Match Colt was brought out in 1933. It was fitted with target sights, a match grade barrel and carefully honed action parts. Trigger pulls were carefully adjusted. These fine pistols were marked on the left side "National Match Colt." This was and is, a very fine match .45 auto.

The Super .38 was made on the same frame and used the Super .38 cartridge with 130 grain jacketed bullet at 1300 feet. The Super .38 will handle the old .38 Colt auto cartridge but the new Super .38 cartridge is considered by Colt as being too powerful for use in the old .38 Military and Pocket models. The Super Match was a fine target sighted and selected Super .38, but is no longer made. It was brought out soon after the introduction of the National Match .45 Colt.

Conversion units for both the .45 and Super .38 were brought out to convert both arms to .22 L.R. These conversion units, however, will not fit the Colt Commander with its shorter slide and barrel. The Super .38 and its finer cousin, the Super Match, were very fine accurate arms and much flatter in their trajectory than the .45 auto and much better target arms. But they were never as good for either stopping power or game killing as the old, slower, heavy .45 slug. We purchased three of the Super .38's before we gave them up, using them extensively on game, along with the .45 auto. In all cases the old .45 auto was much the better killer and stopper. The Super .38 did have one advantage; it would penetrate the skull of a big bull better than the .45.

We consider the Super Match the better of the two for target work, because of lighter recoil and faster recovery of the arm in timed and rapid fire matches, but the .45 bullet holes are more easily spotted. As a man stopper, or for serious game shooting we would take the .45 every time.

The Colt Ace was brought out in 1931 with fine target adjustable rear sight and chambered for the .22 L.R. cartridge. The Service Ace was introduced later, about 1937. It was designed as an understudy to the .45, for army men. It was designed on the Williams floating chamber patent. The floating chamber of this Service Ace increased the recoil of the .22 some four times, thus simulating the recoil of the .45. The gun was a great help toward cheap practice for army men or shooters using the .45 auto in match work. The Service Ace was also fitted with interchangeable .45 target units so that the gun could be used either as a .22 or .45. The Stevens type adjustable rear sight was used on both. Though the Ace was made as a fine target arm, it never became popular—probably on account of the fine match Target Woodsmen models and other competitive .22 auto pistols. It was dropped from production in 1947.

The Colt Commander was first brought out in 1947 and is still in production. It is made in caliber .45 auto, super .38 and 9 mm. luger. The barrel is 4½ inches long and the magazine holds seven .45's or 9 Super .38's or 9 mm. luger rounds. The receiver and main spring housing are made of Coltalloy, a light weight metal of great strength. The shorter barrel and the small ring hammer, together with the lighter metal, bring the weight of the Commander down to 26½ ounces from the standard .45 weight of 39 ounces. The Commander is a fine light pocket or holster arm for the man wanting less weight in a powerful auto pistol, but recoil is heavier than with the regulation weight and the arm is not as powerful as the longer 5 inch barrel, nor as good as a target arm. In .45 caliber, it is a very effective defense gun.

The Colt .22 automatic was first brought out in 1915 and early became very popular with both target shooters and woodsmen. It came out with a 6½ inch barrel, and in 1933 a short version was brought out with a 4½ inch barrel. The latter became even more popular with woods loafers and trappers. It was not named the Woodsman until 1927. Pistols made before 1927 could be converted to handle high speed .22 L.R. by replacing the main spring, housing, and recoil spring and later type magazine which had been inaugurated in 1920.

First models carried a front sight of bead or Patridge type, adjustable for elevation, and the rear target sight adjustable for both windage and elevation. These little pistols were superbly accurate and soon established an enviable reputation. We have seen one fitted with a hollow tube over the barrel some 30 inches long on which was perched a front sight and a shoulder stock, with a rear peep sight. That little gun stayed consistently in a one inch circle, at 60 yards, all day at a turkey match. It won its full share of turkeys against heavy match rifles chambered for the .22 L.R., as well as many larger calibers.

The little Woodsman won many pistol matches and the demand steadily increased for a heavier target model, so that in 1938 Colt brought out their fine Match Target Woodsman. The new arm had a much heavier barrel and longer, fancy checkered walnut stocks extending down below the bottom of the old grip and magazine housing. The best of Target Patridge-type adjustable sights were fitted and owing to its weight, fine sights, fine trigger pull and exceptional accuracy, it early became the standard .22 L.R. target arm. Its weight of 36 ounces made it hold very steadily and the new stocks, set at an excellent angle to the frame, permitted very close holding for long strings. This Colt in turn led to the still finer Colt Match Target arms in the same caliber. These came

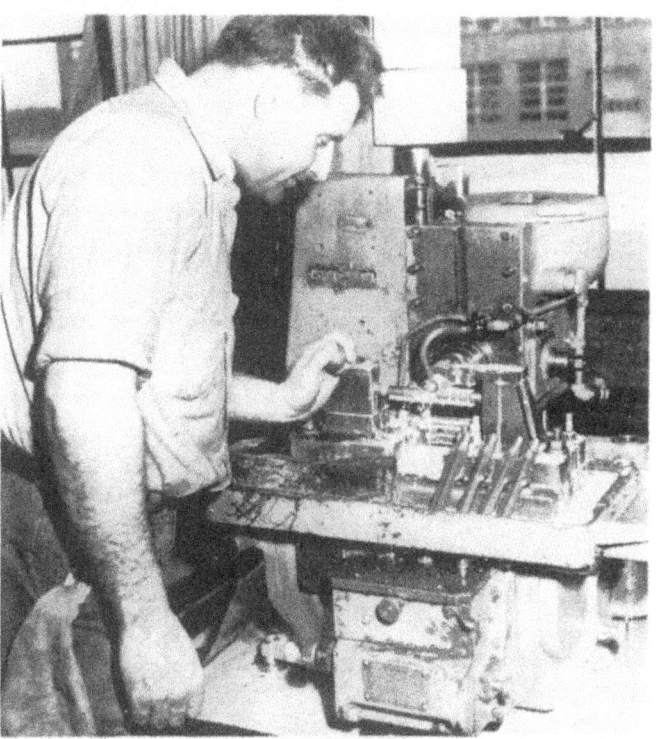

Smith & Wesson factory—milling bottom of barrel.

Mr. C. R. Hellstrom of Smith & Wesson.

The Smith & Wesson factory at Springfield.

Range-firing guns at the Smith & Wesson factory.

out with a still heavier flat top barrel for added muzzle weight and further improved grips with a longer magazine housing at a better angle. They also did away with the projecting wings of the walnut stock on the Match Target Woodsman, and were a great improvement in every way. Barrel lengths of the new arm were standardized at 6 inches and 4½ inches for the sport model. A ramp front sight with knife blade edge was introduced along with a fully adjustable rear sight. This arm is one of the top bracket standard .22 caliber target pistols and has won many tough .22 caliber matches.

The Woodsman Target and Sport models were increased in weight over the early .22 Colt Automatic by four ounces and fitted with the same fine target sights as the Match Target.

Colt also introduced a cheaper pistol, the Challenger, to compete with prices of Ruger and High Standard arms, in 1950. The Challenger does not have the fine adjustable sights of the Woodsman or Match Target or the arched grip housing, but is a very good low priced .22 auto pistol.

After World War II Colt discontinued their heavy frame revolvers and today the only heavy caliber they manufacture is the .45 auto. The Colt line now comprises the above mentioned automatic pistols, in .22 L.R., 9 mm., Super .38, and .45 Government auto. The little Colt Cobra in 2 inch and 4 inch barrel in calibers .38 Special and .32 New Police or .32 S. & W. long, with alloy frame, weighs but 15 ounces. A special hammer shroud may be had to completely cover the hammer, making it a double action pocket arm with no hammer spur to catch on the clothing or pocket. It may be had with either square or rounded butt, with wood checkered stocks, and in 4 inch barrel if desired.

It closely resembles the Detective Special made in two inch barrel, with steel frame and calibers .38 Special or .38 S. & W. or Colt New Police or .32 S. & W. These revolvers with the fine Officers model special and its later cousin just introduced, the Colt Trooper in .357 magnum caliber, comprise the Present Colt line. The Colt Official Police in .22 and .38 Special is also still in production.

The Colt Officer's Model Match is their very latest design of this justly famous old arm. It employs a heavy barrel with long target ramp front sight of Patridge type. It is made in both .22 L.R. and .38 Special and is one of the top target arms of today. A much longer, wider hammer spur has been added to the new arm, too long, in fact, for many shooters. Those with big hands that come to the top of the hump will have to grind off the rear of the hammer spur until it does not rest under the web of the hand. We tested one of the first ones that came out. It was superbly accurate and the easiest cocking single action of any revolver we tried and had less muzzle disturbance. But the hammer spur was so long we had to leave one finger under the butt of the gun to clear that hammer spur when it fell. The New Officer's Model Match has a fine, fully adjustable rear sight perched on the extreme rear end of the frame where it belongs, and is fitted with their latest checkered walnut grips of large size with a filler behind the trigger guard which comes down below the bottom stock strap. It is a big, very comfortable stock and points well, making for fine effortless target holding. The trigger pulls are light and clean, and altogether, this Officers Model Match—as it is now called—is one of the best target guns to be had. Milt Hicks, the sales manager of Colt, is responsible for much of its excellent design. The straps and trigger are checkered and the top of the frame stippled to prevent glare.

The new Colt Trooper utilizes the same frame as the Colt Officer's Model Match, but is made in 4 inch barrel and chambered for the .357 Magnum cartridge. It is on the same 41 Officer's model, or Official Police frame. It has the same superior adapter stocks as the Officer Model Match and a ramp type Baughman front sight, combined with a fine fully adjustable target rear sight on the rear end of the frame. It handles all .38 Special and .357 Magnum ammunition and is priced at $89.50. The New Colt Trooper also has a separate rebounding firing pin to better handle the .357 Magnum pressures. The new arm was designed to give peace officers a target grade Colt for the powerful .357 S. & W. Magnum cartridge for law enforcement work.

Colt still produces and fits new barrels and cylinders and does repair work and complete refinish jobs on their great old Single Action. It is to be regretted they ever dropped that fine and popular gun from their list. For over 20 years we urged them, both by letter and by articles, to modernize the old gun, with coil springs and improved base pin catch and go back to their original flat top frame design, further improve the bolt and bolt spring, fit the gun with target sights and keep it in production in all calibers. If they had done so, it would still outsell any other single model and make of sixgun today. We even offered to loan them our own single actions so they could study the improvements that Harold Croft and the writer designed and made, and thus bring out a truly modern single action Army. How true were our predictions is clearly shown today by the price of existing Colt single actions, also the current business of Christy Gun Works, of 875-57th St., Sacramento, California, who now make and furnish all parts but the frame and straps. The popularity of the old gun is also evident from the present sales and orders enjoyed by Bill Ruger for his modern new .22 Single Six. Colt sadly missed the boat when they dropped the grand old single action from their line. For years they did not advertise the gun, made no attempt to improve it, or its sights, so orders dropped to almost nothing and the machinery was accidentally scrapped during the second World War. We urged Bob Christy to manufacture frames and stock straps and bring out the complete arm, and he would have made money doing so. Colt collectors have today boosted the price to many times the original cost and we have seen new, in factory grease, S.A. Colt .45's, bringing as much as $300.00 in plain original finish and original boxes.

The High Standard Products

Colt enjoyed almost a monopoly on their .22 caliber automatic pistol brought out in 1915 later to be known as the Woodsman. Other firms of the time offered little competition. The Fiala pistol. while having the lines of a .22 automatic, was not an automatic at all, but a hand loader and the slide had to be retracted by hand for each new cartridge seated in the chamber. The Reising, however, was a real automatic and a good gun, but never gave Colt much competition. In fact it was not until the High Standard Manufacturing Co. came into being somewhere around 1928, that serious competition was offered. This enterprising Company early brought out a low priced .22 auto loader with small grip and light barrel intended only as a camper's plinging pistol. Sights were crude and it was a rather rough job. The materials used in some of the early ones were soft and soon became worn. The little gun sold for around $20.

After a decade of manufacturing this .22 auto, the Company decided to go into the manufacture of fine target .22 auto pistols and brought out completely new and improved designs with any weight barrel desired. These fine pistols first with internal hammers and later with an external hammer, are some of the best precision target .22 auto pistols ever produced. They were characterized by well designed frames and actions, perfect trigger pulls and excellent sights. They were soon winning matches. Barrel lengths ran from 4½ to 6¾ inches.

Grips of the new arms brought out in the 30's were longer and superior to the Colt line and soon became very popular. Grips were also set at an excellent angle to the frame and High Standard developed thumb rest grips and every conceivable improvement they could incorporate to give the target shooter the last possible point. The heavy barrel model E. with its fine target stocks became very popular.

About this time the company decided to bring out a .38 Special automatic target pistol dropped before World War II as impractical because of the great pressure variations in ammunition available. They made experimental models and promised me a gun but it never did arrive and was finally dropped before the second World War. They did, however, bring out a lemon in its stead, a .380 auto pistol on a heavy frame that would have been large and strong enough for the .45 auto but it was chambered for the low powered .380 Colt auto cartridge. Just how many were made we do not know. Some were sold but they were never popular and the Company soon kicked that model out of the corral for good. Early they made a few auto pistols in .22 short and also a few in smooth bore for .22 shot cartridges. They made models A, B, C, D, and E, and in addition those with hammers on the outside were designated as models H-D, H-E, etc. All models of A, B, and C were primarily light sport pistols, intended for plinking, informal target practice and small game work. The Models D and E were fitted with very heavy barrels and soon became prime favorites with top target shooters. These heavy barrel jobs early incorporated a long thumb rest, walnut stock, and, combined with perfect sights and trigger pull were just as accurate as any .22 pistol ever produced. Their excellent balance helped no end on the target range.

This company has continued to improve their product at every opportunity. The external hammer was dropped and they now have several new models. One is the little Flight King for .22 shorts only, with an ultra light aluminum alloy frame, a 4½ inch barrel and good fixed sights. The new models have a quickly detachable barrel, and barrels of various weights and lengths may be used interchangeably. Special alloy slide and frame make the Flight King one of the lightest .22 auto pistols. It is a very good small plinking pistol in either barrel length. This pistol was brought out in 1953 and their 1954 all steel Sport King is for the .22 L.R. cartridge.

The 1950 model Olympic is a top quality target arm for the .22 short cartridge. It is designed for special Olympic rapid fire matches, to give the least possible barrel movement off the target between shots. It comes with heavy weight barrels with either 4½ or 6¾ inch length and two sets of weights that slide on a dovetail at the bottom of the barrel for additional weight, if desired. It is a superlative target arm, capable of every point that is inherent in the .22 short cartridge. Recently some High Standard target arms have been further improved by cutting gas vents in the top sides of the barrel near the muzzle to act as muzzle breaks and make the barrel recoil straight to the rear and stay on the target rather than raise above the line of sight in rapid fire matches. Everything has been done to make these target arms tops in the field and today they are second to none in auto loading .22 caliber target arms.

The model 1950 Super-Matic is chambered for the .22 Long Rifle cartridge. It will be found in the largest matches and usually at or near the top in scores. It too, is fitted with either length detachable barrel and weights and is one of the finest target arms ever manufactured anywhere. We have yet to see one that came out with a poor trigger pull. All are perfect and ready for the range. Their barrel take-down system is strong and simple, yet locks the barrels to the frame perfectly with no chance of movement. This facilitates cleaning and inspection from the breech. The big, comfortable, thumb rest grip, set at correct angle to the frame, fits the average shooter's

Smith & Wesson factory—stocking job, sawing blanks.

hand. These guns come from the factory ready for the firing line. The sights are excellent, easily adjusted, and stay put when adjusted. The two sets of barrel weights come in two ounce and three ounce units giving the shooter just about any desired weight of barrel and balance with the two barrel lengths. With 6¾ inch barrel, this arm weighs 42 ounces. Some shooters prefer the 4½ inch barrel since the sights are more nearly in the same focal plane; others do their best work with the 6¾ inch barrel. This pistol will give anyone every point he can hold for, and is second to none in the field today.

This enterprising firm has a very nice modern factory at Hamden, Conn., situated, they claim, on the site of the old Eli Whitney factory of 1847 Walker Colt days. Just recently they added their latest pistol to their long line of .22 auto loaders. The new arm with choice of 6½ inch or 4½ inch barrel is chambered for the .22 L.R. cartridge and is designed for a general plinking gun to sell at the low price of $37.50. We suspect the new gun was brought out to compete with the well-known Ruger .22 auto loader selling for the same amount.

Sturm, Ruger .22 Automatics

Another firm that has offered the larger companies keen competition in the .22 auto loading field is Sturm, Ruger & Co. of Southport, Conn. Headed by Bill Ruger, a very enterprising youngster in the field of arms manufacturers, it first produced an entirely new .22 auto loader on the general lines of the well-known Luger parabellum pistol. The Luger has always been known as one of the best pointing auto pistols ever made. The Ruger has exactly the same angle of grip in relation to the barrel, and the same feel. The weight of the Ruger lies in the hand, the same as the Luger. It points easily and naturally. The Ruger is a wide departure from other .22 auto loading pistols in that the receiver is tubular and solidly attached to barrel. The breech block moves inside of this tubular receiver, allowing the rear sight to remain in one fixed position during firing. This makes for accuracy. The Ruger is made from stampings and electrically welded frame but with a very accurate, well rifled barrel, and excellent sights combined with perfect trigger pull. It sells at the low price of $37.50. Ruger reasoned wisely that more people would be able to buy a low priced pistol than a high priced one. His sales and orders have proven this to be correct. Since he started manufacturing this excellent pistol he has never been able to completely fill his orders. The Ruger Sport model has a 4¾ inch barrel and a weight of 36 ounces. The Mark 1, or Target model, carries a 6⅞ inch barrel and weighs 42 ounces. Both have become very popular and the Mark 1 has now run off with some of the most important .22 caliber pistol matches this country has to offer. This speaks well for the accuracy of the Ruger .22 automatic. Bill Ruger has a small, well-equipped factory and keeps it humming—but never seems to quite catch up with orders.

After Colt dropped their excellent, time-tried S.A. Army, Ruger noted the terrific demand and decided to do something about it. He made a trip west to interview several of us on the old gun. He told me he read all my old articles on the S.A. Colt in back issues of *The Rifleman* and other magazines, and then set to work to re-design and modernize the old gun. The two piece stock straps he designed to be cast in a single unit from an aluminum alloy of great strength. The flat breakable springs be redesigned and used coiled springs in their stead. He redesigned the bolt and bolt spring and eliminated the old cam on the hammer. He fitted a trigger return spring and plunger directly behind the trigger. He designed the frame to be cast. Thus he greatly improved the action of the old Peacemaker. While he designed the frame with a flat top, he erred sadly here and bevelled off the corners and set the movable rear sight much too far forward. He fitted the new frame with a rebounding firing pin, better suited to the firing of rim fire cartridges. In the loading gate, he again erred by not fitting it with a more adequate flange for the thumbnail. Also, in the rod ejector housing he left a square shoulder at the rear end of its travel into which the ejector rod would lock. And the thumb and finger button at the forward end of the extractor rod was too small to be grasped readily with thumb or forefinger. In all other respects he designed a better gun than the original Colt S.A.

The new Ruger came out as the Single Six and with a much smaller frame, barrel, and cylinder than the original Colt. Essentially a smaller version, it was designed for the .22 L.R. cartridge. Demand for the new Ruger Single Six far exceeded his wildest expectations and he now has over a half-million dollars worth of orders. The new gun, a smaller improved replica of the famous old Peacemaker, is destined to become very popular. Ruger contemplates a target model with adjustable target sights, a true flat-top frame with a rear sight on the extreme rear end of the frame, and many more refinements and improvements as soon as production of the first model will allow him to bring it out. He also expects to turn out a further improved full size model for all the popular big revolver loads. The Single Six has a 5½ inch barrel and a fixed front sight with a movable target-type rear which is adjustable by driving to either side for windage.

The cylinder is recessed for the case heads and the arm is big enough to be brought out in 25 Stevens. We have long urged that he do this as it would make a much better small game gun. It could be done quite easily by adding slightly to the length of the cylinder and chambering and boring for that most excellent cartridge with a 60 grain bullet at 1300 to 1500 feet velocity and with the bullet completely enclosed in the case except the ogive. This would give the hunter a cartridge he could carry loose in his pocket without having the bullet collect dirt and sand which injures the barrel. Due to the coil main spring, Ruger has achieved one of the easiest and fastest cocking single actions we have seen. We played with the pilot model for some time and found it very accurate; then Ruger sent us No. 15 of regular production and Judge Don Martin another low serial number. Both proved very accurate little arms. Stocks are furnished either in checkered black plastic or good, well-seasoned elephant ivory at the extra cost of $16.00. The current price of the Single Six is $63.50.

We believe this little arm will become one of the most popular .22 revolvers ever produced in America. Now that Colt collectors have placed the price of the original Colt Single Actions beyond the shooting value and beyond the reach of most men, we believe the new

Smith & Wesson factory—stocking job, profiler.

Ruger with its target sights and larger caliber models to follow, will in time fill the demand for the old Single Action, at least from the shooter's standpoint. If Ruger can ever catch up on production enough to allow him to introduce new and improved models, the full size Ruger single action will probably be brought out in .38 Special, .357 S. & W. Magnum, .44 Special and .45 Colt. His orders for the Single Six well justify our claims that a modern single action Colt would have outsold all other commercial models of hand guns. Military arms and orders, of course, would necessarily outnumber commercial demand for any single model of sixgun or auto pistol.

In this chapter we have endeavored to cover the high-lights in revolver and auto pistol production in America, covering only the more generally used and important arms. A bible would be necessary to cover all the arms made in this country alone. We have not covered the famous British Webley revolvers nor many European models of both revolver and auto pistols, nor many makes of the more inexpensive American arms.

To the collectors of Colt revolvers, we can recommend *The Colt Revolver* by Belden & Haven, as well as the work of James E. Serven of Santa Ana, California—*Colts from 1836 to 1954*. Collectors of Smith & Wessons will find a wealth of material in the book, *Smith & Wesson Handguns* by McHenry and Roper. Firearms students and sixgun cranks will find a wealth of excellent material in the following books: *Pistols and Revolvers* by Maj. Gen. J. S. Hatcher. For the arms technician and criminologist—*Textbook of Firearms Investigation, Identification and Evidence*, by General Hatcher. For those interested in learning trick and aerial and double action shooting we would recomend *Fast and Fancy Revolver Shooting* by Ed McGivern. For the all-around shot and the person interested in becoming a top notch match pistol shooter, the works of Lt. Col. Charles Askins are tops: *The Art of Handgun Shooting*, and his latest book, *The Pistol Shooters Book*. Charley Askins has won about every worthwhile award offered in competition in this country and well knows his subject. Two older, but most excellent books are *Shooting*, by the late J. H. Fitzgerald of Colt, and *American Pistol Shooting* by Maj. W. D. Frazer. *Double Action Shooting* by Bob Nichols is also an excellent treatise on this phase of the game.

Since writing this chapter, we have had the opportunity to test an entirely new single action revolver, patterned exactly after the old S.A. Colt Army. This new weapon is being manufactured by the Great Western Arms Co. of Los Angles, California. It is made in all calibers from .22 to .45 Colt and includes

Smith & Wesson factory—stocking job, checkering.

the .357 magnum, and the .357 atomic. The gun we tested was in .357 magnum caliber. It was almost a duplicate of the old Colt S.A. except the trigger and hammer screws were cut with different threads, the frame was about one sixteenth inch longer and the hand, bolt and trigger were made from beryllium copper instead of steel. These arms are being offered in barrel lengths from 3½ inches without extractor (known as the Sheriffs model), to 4¾, 5½ and 7½ inches. The prices range from $97.50 to $127.50 for the plain guns, and fancy plated or engraved and stocked arms run as high as you wish to go.

The gun we tested was very poorly timed, fitted, and showed a total lack of final inspection. The hand was a trifle short, the bolt spring did not have enough bend to lock the bolt with any certainty, the main spring was twice as strong as necessary and the trigger pull about three times as heavy as needed. The rear end of the barrel could have stood a bit more chamfering. In spite of all these minor faults the gun seemed to be made of excellent materials throughout. As received, it certainly was neither safe, nor in shape to have been put on the market, but only a few hours of careful gun smithing were needed to make a first class single action of it. The gun was accurate if you indexed it by hand, and the barrel appeared well bored and rifled but the chambering of the cylinder was rough and a trifle over size.

These guns are being offered with the standard old S.A. Colt type front sight and grooved top strap, and at $20. extra with Micro target sights.

It is to be regretted, that this Company did not contact someone who really knew single actions, and incorporate all the improvements possible instead of trying to make an exact copy of the old Colt. The new gun could have been greatly improved over the Colt but this has not been done. Any new Arms Company is bound to run into plenty of trouble at the start with a new production. All this company now needs is some good gunsmiths to assemble and time these arms and some competent inspectors to test and inspect them before they are shipped. There is no earthly reason why this new single action could not be just as good as the famous old Colt, but it will have to have a lot of re-design work to ever make it superior. The Beryllium copper hand, trigger and bolt are supposed to be far more shock resistant than steel, and this would be an improvement. The design is the same, however, and why they did not incorporate coil instead of flat springs in the new arm is beyond me.

The firing pin is rebounding and separate from the hammer. It was first designed and brought out by Herb Bradley of this town over 20 years ago and later produced in quantity by the Christy Gun Works. In this respect the new arm is superior to the old Colt. This new rebounding firing pin will also handle higher pressures without pierced primers and escaping gas than will the old Colt firing pin. The new gun should outfit the Movie industry well, but until I see some of them that are carefully fitted and inspected and come out the equal of the old Colt S.A. Army production, I cannot recommend them as finished arms.

Smith & Wesson factory—polishing frame.

Smith & Wesson factory, bluing room.

Chapter II

Selecting the Handgun

MORE TIME IS REQUIRED to master the handgun than any other type of firearm. To become an expert sixgun shot, one must live with the gun. Only by constant use and practice can one acquire a thorough mastery of the shortgun. You must work and play with it, eat with it, sleep with it and shoot it every day—until it becomes a part of you and you handle it surely and easily as you would your fork and knife at the table. Muscles and nerves must be trained for the job in hand.

Selection of the proper gun to start with is of utmost importance. Target shooting is just one phase of the game; trick shooting another. Game and defense shooting require different guns and techniques. Guns are expensive and ammunition much more so. For the beginner, nothing is as good as the .22 caliber. First you must decide whether you are going into match target work or game shooting, trick shooting or want a gun for social purposes. In any case the .22 is the gun to start with. Ammunition is cheaper for it than the big guns; it is just as accurate, has very mild recoil and report, and you can best learn to aim, hold and shoot the lowly .22. It is soon enough to graduate to a larger caliber after you master the .22 and can do first class work with it. Even then the change should be gradual, first going to the .38 Special and later to heavier guns. This is to accustom your muscles to holding first the .22 and then the .38, and finally the .44 or .45 caliber. The heavy loads come last.

Men and women vary greatly in temperament; some have no nerves, others are nervous and easily upset. It is of utmost importance to first establish good safe gun handling form and acquire accuracy with the small caliber. When this is done, one has no trouble graduating to the larger calibers. Recoil and report, slight in the .22, is disturbing to some people in the heavier calibers, and tends to cause flinching. This must be avoided at all costs. So, start with the .22 caliber, but get the best. You get about what you pay for in this world, be it guns, autos, whiskey or clothes. Start with the best gun you can afford.

It is well to decide what phase of sixgun shooting you are most interested in, and whether you prefer the revolver or the automatic pistol. Both have their good points. If you are going into match target work, decide if you wish to shoot sixguns or automatic pistols and make your purchase accordingly. Assuming the target game is to be your choice, the top guns made in this country in the auto-pistol are the High-Standard Super Match and Olympic, the Colt Match Target, and the Target Model Ruger. If you decide to shoot automatics, one of the above should be your choice. Graduate later to the 9 mm. Smith & Wesson, the Super .38 Colt and the .45 Government model Colt.

If you prefer revolvers (they are easier to master than automatic pistols for most people) your choice lies between the K model Masterpiece Smith & Wesson and the Colt Officer's Model Match in .22. For men and women, ordinarily these are the best .22 caliber handguns to start match target work. Select the gun that best fits your hand and also your trigger finger reach, and the one you can cock easiest and with the least disturbance to the arm. When you have mastered this arm in .22 caliber and are shooting in the eighties or better on the standard American target, it is time to graduate to a heavier caliber. In the Smith & Wesson line you can get a matched set of .22, .32 and .38 Special all in the K model masterpiece, that weighs exactly the same for all three calibers. No better guns are made. In the Colt line you can get the .38 Special in the same Officer's Model Match and no more accurate guns are to be had. In the Smith & Wesson line, if you like a heavy gun and find it advantageous to your holding after you become proficient with the K models, you can graduate to the Outdoorsman made on the .45 frame in .38 Special. Colt no longer makes a .44 or .45, so when you go in for large caliber target shooting you will be obliged to use the .44 Special or .45 auto rim model 1950 Target S. & W. Many of the old Colt Shooting Masters and New Service Targets are still around, in perfect condition, and these also are excellent. Also many of the old Triple Lock and 1926 Target models S. & W. are to be found in excellent shape, and better target guns are not made. The short action of the model K and S model S. & W. guns is, however, beneficial to rapid cocking of the arm in timed and rapid fire matches. Their short broad target type hammers with sharp checkering greatly facilitate rapid and effortless cocking of the arm be-

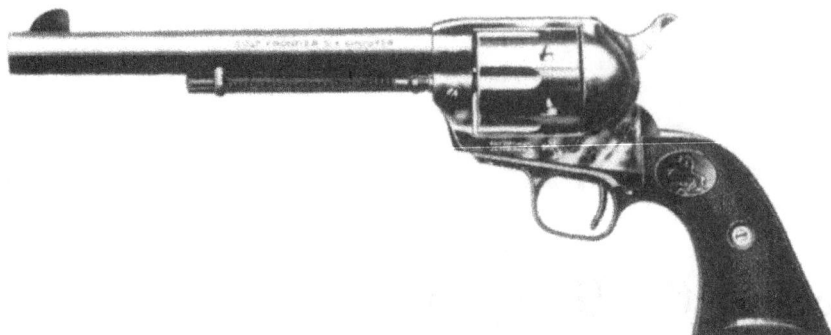

Colt Frontier six-shooter.

Detective Special .38.

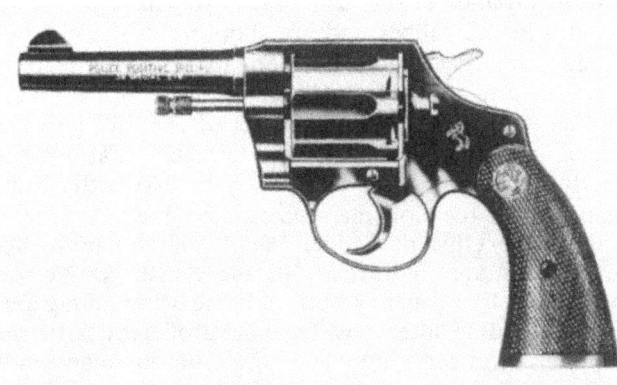

PP. .38 Special.

tween shots. In this respect the modern short action Smith & Wessons in K model, and the big S model on a .45 frame are superior to the older guns, and the same is true of the Colts. Their new Officer's Model Match is a much faster and easier gun to cock than the older models, but regretably no longer made in .44 or .45 caliber.

Target Shooting

For good scores you want the best adjustable target sights, so that you can quickly bring your point of aim and point of impact together at any range and hold as you wish on the target. With fixed sights you can seldom do this. Any change in ammunition causes a change in point of impact and that cannot be tolerated if you are to get anywhere in the target game. Many fine old Single action Colts are still in existence, and when fitted with wide checkered Bisley type hammer spur and Pachmayer, or other short action, as the King Gunsight Co. used to fit them, they are also excellent target arms and just as accurate as their double action cousins. Colt, during the eighties, made a splendid target arm in their flat-top Target S. A. Army. It is still a fine target arm if you can find one or have one made up from a standard single action Colt. The latter process is very expensive.

For straight slow-fire work we much prefer the revolver to the automatic pistol. It is easier to shoot and easier to learn and seems to balance better for most people. However, most modern pistol matches incorporate timed and rapid-fire matches. The National Match course covers timed and rapid-fire matches and these are where the auto pistol has its inning. With the automatic you simply recover from recoil and bring the arm back on the target for the next shot. With all sixguns you must also cock the arm while it is in recoil and then bring it back on the target. This requires much more practice for the sixgun shooter than does the automatic. So one must decide whether he will take the time to master fast effortless cocking of the sixgun in timed and rapid-fire matches or turn to the auto pistol with its faster action and self cocking facilities.

As to accuracy, there is little difference. Theoretically the automatic should be the most accurate with its chamber and barrel in one unit, but Smith & Wesson and Colt Target revolvers are so perfectly lined up as to barrel and chamber that they will nearly all do 1½ inch groups at 50 yards. The auto pistols are usually chambered looser than the revolver to assure perfect functioning. In accuracy there is little difference between the two types. What one gains in having barrel and chamber in one unit is made up by the closer chambering of the other. Choose your weapons with regard to which type best fits your hand and trigger finger, and with which you, as an individual, can do your best work. It is well for anyone entering the target game to practice enough with both types of arm to make their own decision on a personal preference basis.

Pistol shots are not born. They get that way by constant hard work and steady practice, studying each and every move and perfecting their technique with the type of arm that best fits them and their temperament. The angle of the grip to the barrel and frame should be studied. The eyes should be closed and the arm pointed at the target naturally and then the eyes opened and a check made to see if the gun points in line or not, and this continued until you find the type of arm that best suits your hold, either automatic or revolver. The sights should be studied and those selected that best suit your eyes and that show up on the target with a minimum of effort. This is important in long strings. Trigger pulls must be heavy enough to conform with the rules of the match. There is no "hoss sense" in practicing with a very light trigger pull, then having to switch to one of regulation weight when you start a match. Stick to allowed trigger pulls from first to last, and master them.

The stocks themselves on target pistols must come in for close scrutiny. Almost any type of thumb rest and hand fitting grips are permitted in many matches. In some only the straight Service pistol grips are allowed. We believe this business of hand fitting grips can be overdone. On the other hand they offer genuine help to some shooters. Study your hand. The grip that best fits it should be employed so that the arm can be held on the target with the least possible effort. If you find a thumb rest helps, use it. If more flare of the back strap at the bottom is needed to bring your gun muzzle in perfect alignment with a natural hold, use it, and have it incorporated in your grips. If you have very long fingers you may need a filler over the back strap and also a filler back of the trigger guard excepting the Colt Single Action, which has the perfect grip in this respect. *Homo sapiens* is an adaptable cuss and you will find you can become accustomed to almost any grip in time, but you will get along much faster if the pistol or sixgun grip fits your hand. Length of trigger finger must be studied. Those of us who were endowed with short fingers may have a hard time reaching the trigger on some auto pistols and for this reason will find the sixgun our best bet.

Many of the finest pistol shots in this country try to contact only the trigger with their trigger finger and this means either a long finger or a short reach from back strap to the face of the trigger. For this reason men and women with long fingers usually find the auto pistol right down their alley while shooters with short fingers usually prefer the revolver. Perfect fit between trigger and back strap are of utmost importance as it enables the shooter to place the finger on the trigger alone and not have to squeeze against the side of the frame or trigger guard to reach the

Cobra .38 Special.

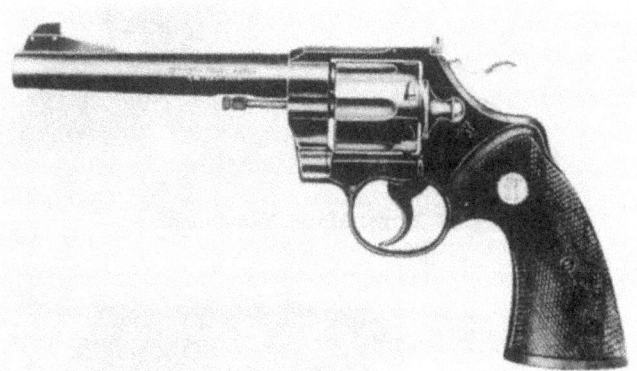

Officer's Model Match .38 Special.

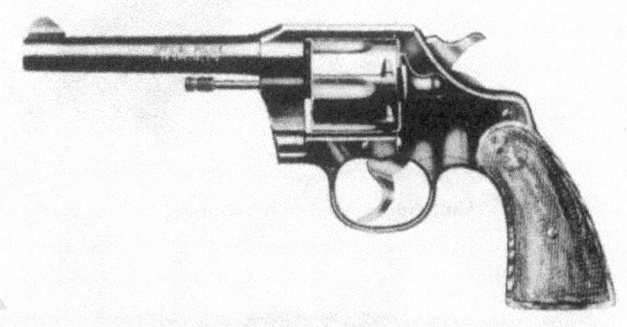

Official Police .38 Special.

trigger (which can cause the gun to shoot to the side). One must finger the heavy calibers as uniformly as a violin, or they will shoot to different points of impact. Perfect and uniform grip on the gun from shot to shot makes small groups. A uniform even grip of the gun is a must if high scores are ever to be attained. Remember all this in selecting your target guns and select the type that best fits you as an in-

Colt Trooper .38 Special.

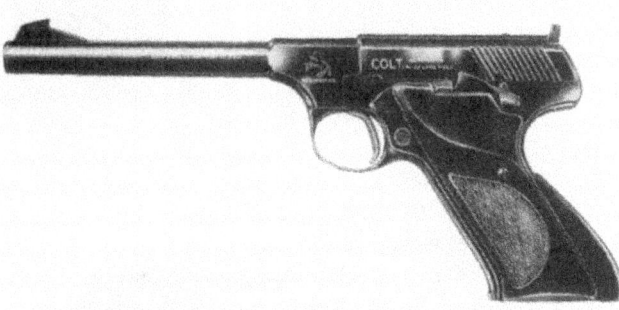
Colt Target Model Woodsman.

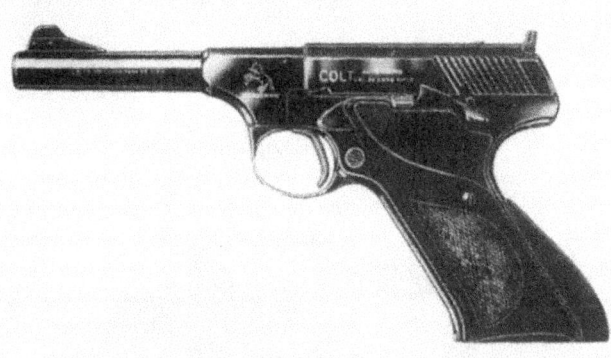
Colt Sport Model Woodsman.

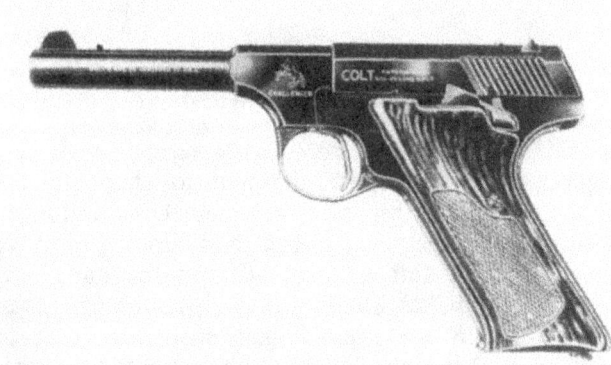
Colt Challenger, 4½ inch barrel.

dividual. Large hands are usually best fitted with large framed guns and small hands with small framed guns. In this respect the shooter with short fingers is usually better fitted with the large .45 frame Smith & Wesson or Colt Single Action than with the huge Colt New Service frame. The New Service, however, is the gun for the person with large hands. In this respect the Smith & Wesson K models will fit the people with small hands much better than will the larger 41 frame and stocks of the Colt Officer's Model Match.

Thus we see we have three sizes of frame and grips for different size hands in the large caliber revolvers, .32 to .45 caliber. As an illustration, I have a rather large but short fingered hand. Of all revolvers, the Colt Single action and the heavy S frame Smith & Wesson best fit my mitt. Nearly all automatic pistols are a bit long in reach for my short trigger finger. The K model Smith & Wesson grip is a trifle small for my hand but the big .45 frame S. & W., and this takes in the .38 Special Outdoorsman, the .357 Magnum and the .44 and .45 calibers in this make, give me a perfect fit when cocked for slow, timed or rapid-fire work. The New Service is large for our hand and thus is slower to cock. All these things must be considered when selecting the target gun if you want to reach the top in the game. Any good pistol shot will do good work with practice with any good accurate gun, but he will go much further in the game if he studies all elements of gun fit and uses the arm that best suits his physical requirements. Barrel length and muzzle weight are also things to consider. Some folks do best with a muzzle-heavy weapon, others like the weight to lie in their hand. Most .22 caliber auto pistols of best quality are heavy and can be made even heavier at the muzzle if desired. This cuts down uplift of the barrel in recoil as well as giving a different balance to the arm. It also aids in recovering from recoil and getting back on the target in the least possible time. In the .22 caliber target guns the High Standard Super-matic has additional weights to give the shooter about any desired amount of muzzle heaviness, while the Colt Match Target is made with a heavy weight barrel. The High Standard Olympic may also be had with muzzle brake vents that make it recoil straight to the rear without so much barrel flip and which aid in keeping the muzzle down and the sights in line with the target in rapid fire.

The Ruger gives one a pistol with the weight in the hand and less muzzle heaviness and it points more like the German Luger. Many fine shooters prefer this feel and balance to the muzzle-heavy makes of Colt and High Standard. Again the Colt and High Standard pistols may be had with 4½ inch barrels for less muzzle heaviness and the weight more on the balance point of the hand. The weight of the gun should rest on the second finger where possible, and this it does with many of these fine arms and the Colt Single Action as well. This can be accomplished in double action revolvers by a very slight filler to the stocks back of the trigger guard. Some will prefer, and find the thumb rest advantageous, while others do as well or better without it.

The distance between sights is also an important problem. Youngsters with good eyesight accommodation can see the sights in perfect relation, even on very long barrels, while oldsters may well find that shorter barrels bring their sights more closely in focus and they will do better shooting with the shorter sight radius. Theoretically, the longer the sight radius, the more accurate the aim, but it will often be found in match shooting that the older person, with less accommodation, will see both sights in better focus if they are closer together and will do more accurate shooting with a shorter barrel. The Colt Match Target .22 Auto pistol may be had with either a 6 inch barrel or the 4½ inch, and the High Standard with 6¾ or 4½ inch barrels interchangeable on the same gun, which can be ordered with both length barrels. The Ruger Target may be had in 6⅞ or 5¼ inch heavyweight barrels. The Smith & Wesson K Model .22 may be had in the standard 6 inch barrel or in the Combat Masterpiece with 4 inch barrel. Remember, in revolvers you have the length of the cylinder as well as the barrel proper. The Colt Officer's Model Match .22 now comes only in 6 inch but we believe they will also bring it out in a shorter barrel and in .38 or .357 caliber; it is to be had in the Trooper or .357 with a 4 inch barrel. Of course long barrel guns can also be cut off and a new front sight fitted to any desired length to give the shooter exactly the sight radius he thinks desirable.

Whichever type arm you select, start with the .22 caliber and practice with it until you master it, then change to a heavier caliber gradually and become accustomed to its louder report and greater recoil and thus avoid any tendency to flinch. If you do show any such tendency, then drop the big gun and go back to the .22 caliber again until you are over it.

The novice starting with a heavy caliber will often develop the flinching habit and the best way to break it is to get a .22 and start over again and if possible have someone else load the gun, giving you some loads and some empty cases so that you never know when the gun will fire or snap. This is the best check in the world on whether you flinch or not, this and also your ability to call your shots. If you call them, you see them, and you do not flinch, and if you do not perfectly call them then you are not seeing them and may be flinching. Flinching is fatal to good scores, hence the reason it is mandatory to start with a small light caliber of little recoil and report.

The fit and spread of the stock in your hand makes a lot of difference in perceptible recoil. With a perfectly fitting stock, recoil of even heavy loads will not be so noticeable.

If you choose the .45 auto pistol for your armament,

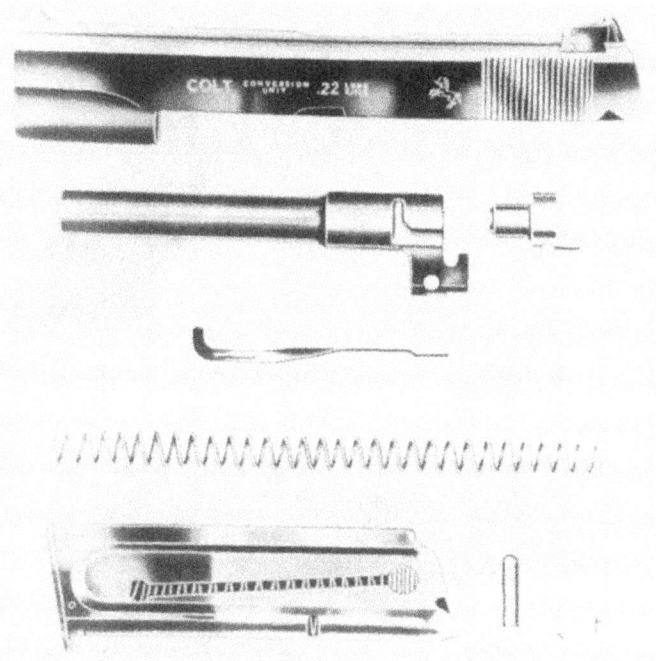

Colt Conversion .22.

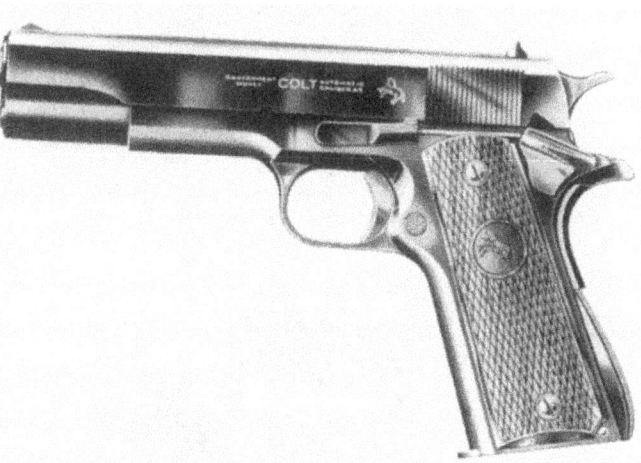

Colt Government .45.

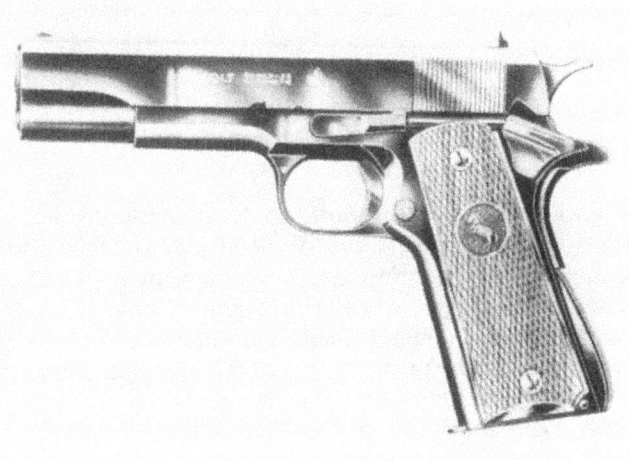

Colt Super. .38 automatic.

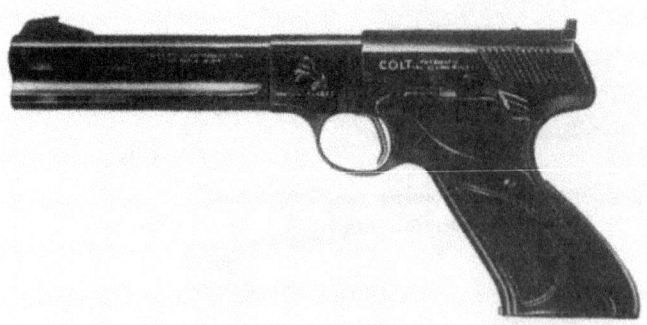

Colt Match Target Woodsman, 6 in. barrel.

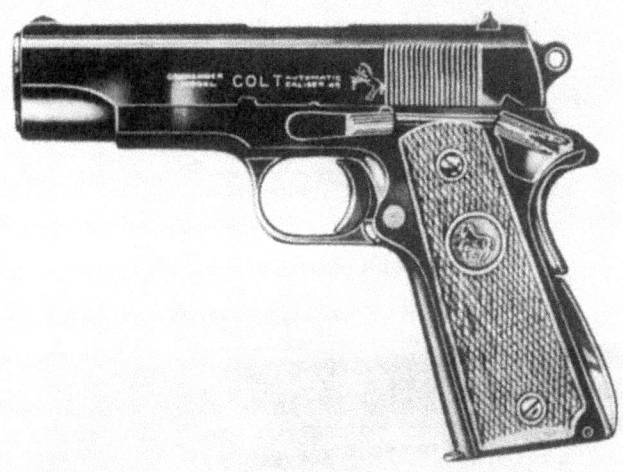

Colt .45 Commander. Super .38 and 9 mm. caliber.

.38 Colt Marshall.

you will have a lot of work to do in mastering it. It is perhaps the hardest gun of all to manage, but once mastered, fine shooting can be done with it at either slow or rapid-fire. A good firm grip is necessary. In many matches, lighter loads are allowed and many shooters reload for these matches, but this requires a worked-over gun that has a lighter recoil spring. Then when they turn to full loads and heavier recoil, their scores often suffer. It is best to shoot the big gun with full loads, or factory match loads, and get accustomed to it. The Colt Conversion Units and the Colt Ace are fine understudies for the big gun, but you will have to shoot the .45 with full loads plenty to get the best of it. Men with heavy, fleshy hands will find that the hammer spur pinches the web of the hand against the top of the grip housing, the longer spur grip is better, but even then some will still have trouble. It is then best to grind off the rear end of the hammer spur until it does not pinch the web of the hand when the slide brings the hammer back to full cock in recoil. The Smith & Wesson 1950 Target is a much more comfortable gun to use, as is the big Colt Shooting Master or New Service Target, but again you have to learn fast cocking in rapid fire.

The Gun For Trick Shooting

So much for selection of the target arm, next let us turn to selection of the gun for trick shooting. For many phases of trick shooting the .22 target arms are excellent and the automatic and the revolver are equally good. Shooting with the aid of a mirror, shooting swinging targets, long range shooting, and for almost any slow-fire trick, shots are best taken with a good target arm. Fast trick shooting is something else again, especially aerial work. For single shots at thrown aerial targets, any good accurate target arm is fine but for fast repeat shots on one target, or more than one target thrown up at once, i.e. where rapidity of aimed fire is involved, it is very doubtful if anything is as good as the double action revolver fired double action. The single actions are all slow to cock for this very fast phase of trick shooting and the automatics hop all around and you cannot pull them back on the target like you can with a smooth double action pull. When it comes to a fine fast double action pull, the Smith & Wesson is in a class by itself. An Ed McGivern can shoot both makes double action with speed and certainty of placing his shots, but most men will, in older guns, find that the Smith & Wesson double action trigger is superior in character to that of the older Colts. A smooth double action pull actuates while the gun is in recoil in fast aerial shooting, and in time one seems to pull the muzzle back and down in alignment with the falling target much faster with a double action than with any other type of arm. For very fast aerial double action shooting, long barrels are not necessary and one seems to do as well with a four or five inch barrel as with a longer one. Good sights are a necessity, but a heavy sixgun is best suited to this work, as the double action seems lighter with a heavy gun than with a light gun. We have done our best work with a .38/44 Heavy Duty S. & W. with target sights in .38 Special caliber for such speedy fast shooting. The K model S. & W. guns are also excellent. The larger the caliber, the more time required to recover from recoil and the less number of hits will be made. The .22 calibers are excellent but for some reason we never could shoot them quite as fast double action as the .45 frame Smith & Wesson in .38 Special caliber. For us, at least, that is the fastest of all double action guns. In automatics when used for this kind of shooting, the .22 is the best, having the least recoil, and is the quickest of all the autos to get back on the target.

The Smith & Wesson .357 magnum and the new Smith & Wesson Highway Patrolman, which is simply a plainer finished Magnum, are also tops for fast double action trick shooting, when the trigger pull has been smoothed up as much as possible. The fit and balance of these guns with 4 or 5 inch barrels, combined with their weight, well designed sights, and fast short action makes them an excellent choice. They should be used with .38 Specials or even .38 Short Colts for fast work such as putting six slugs through a gallon can tossed 18 to 20 feet in the air before it hits the ground.

The late Bob Nichols was an exponent of the old long action Smith & Wesson double action, claiming it best for double action shooting. It was very good for either aimed double action shooting or fast work, but we fail to see how it beat, or even qualified with the new short action. Many double action shots pull the trigger until the hammer comes back to about full cock, then squeeze off the shot exactly as in cocked hammer slow fire. This works well enough with long fingered gentry but is not so easily accomplished by men with shorter fingers. For fast double action work, the wrist should be squarely behind the gun. The double action pull is hard and fast with a firm grip and no hesitation in the pull.

The grip is like closing ones fist. The thumb should be down against the side of the frame and pointing toward the trigger finger. For really fast double action trick shooting, whether it be hitting a can tossed in the air or more than one aerial target, as McGivern did so often, or simply rolling a can down the road, we have failed to find any gun that is superior to the .357 Magnum, or its later cousin, the Highway Patrolman when used with .38 Special loads. The weights of these guns dampen recoil and make fast recovery possible, and the inertia of the heavy cylinder seems to help. In time one learns to function with the arm even as he is pulling it out of recoil and down on the target. These guns are the fastest of all for accurate fire. The automatics all recoil in a different manner and you cannot pull them down and out of recoil without firing them again if any pressure is exerted on the trigger in so doing.

John Newman used the slip gun exclusively. Uusually a .45, but he also had some bushed single actions for the .22 caliber. He made as many as five hits with the slip gun on a gallon can tossed up 20 feet before it reached the ground. The slip gun is fast, but not as fast as the double action. It is one of the most reliable of all arms in a gun fight, as there is little left in the gun to break or malfunction. If one masters

Colt Courier .32 Special.

Colt .357 Magnum.

Colt Python .357.

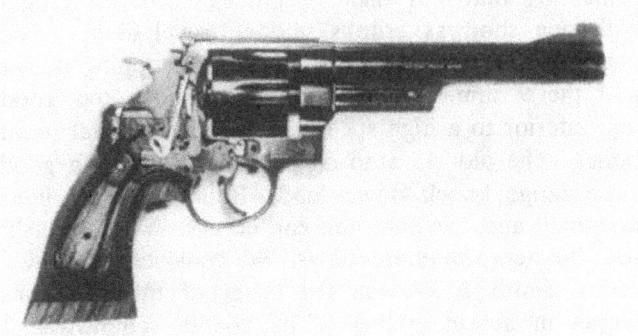

Smith & Wesson 1955 Target .45 with new and U-type main spring and wide trigger.

the slip gun, he must forget all he has learned of trigger shooting as its an entirely different technique. Men trained with the slip hammer become nearly as proficient as shooters using the trigger, either single or double action, but then they cannot do good work with trigger guns.

For trick shooting with a single action gun, the new Ruger Single Six is excellent, as it cocks very fast and easily and has a very smooth fast action. This is due to the new coil springs throughout. In the .22 caliber arms the Smith & Wesson Kit Gun is also excellent for folks with very small hands, and it too has a splendid double action pull. For most men and some women the best combination for fast double action trick shooting is the Combat Masterpiece Smith & Wesson in a matched pair of .22 and .38 Special calibers. These guns are about the best for folks with small to average size hands, who want matched guns in both calibers. Their 4 inch barrels with Baughman front and target rear sights make a perfect combination, both for aerial targets as well as all quick draw, fast double action hip shooting. For slow-fire trick shooting, one can do good work, with practice, with any good target-sighted pistol or revolver, but for the fast work, the arm that fits best and feels best and balances perfectly should be selected. Regardless of what the other fellow uses, get the gun that suits and fits *you* best.

Defensive Work

Next let us select the gun for defense use, be it military, peace officer, or just plain John Q. Citizen. In my opinion the caliber should never be less than .38 Special, 9 mm. Luger or Super .38 auto, and these only for hidden pocket guns. Detectives, plain clothesmen or citizens needing a small, compact, hideout gun for emergency use at close range will find these arms very good. They should be listed as a pocket gun and in this category we have many good guns to choose from. For those preferring the auto loader, the best we know of are the Colt Commander and the new, just released 9 mm. Smith & Wesson in the double action model. The Colt Commander can be had in either 9 mm. or .45 auto and is at its best in the latter caliber. For a defense gun, you want something that will take all the fight out of a man with one shot, as crooks seldom travel alone. The various .32's and .380's are lacking in stopping power and the 9 mm., for that matter, is none too good and inferior to a high speed .38 Special with flat point bullet. The old .45 auto on the other hand, is a good close range knock down load. Both makes of guns are small and compact and can be had in light weight with the new aluminum alloys. We consider the double action Smith & Wesson the faster of the two guns to get in action, owing to its double action trigger pull for the first shot. Both are very reliable auto loaders—the best to be had in any country. Automatics are never as reliable as revolvers, because they are totally dependent on perfect ammunition.

If a jam occurs—and it can and has happened many times—two hands are necessary to get that gun in operation again and you may have one hand or arm disabled or in use holding a criminal or yourself in some position. For that reason our preference goes to the sixgun every time for defense use. In speed of reloading, the auto pistol has its inning as you simply drop out the old clip and fit in a new one and you are ready to fire again, but for reliability the revolver is best. A faulty primer resulting in a snap with an automatic pistol and you must retract the slide with the other hand to get a fresh load under the firing pin, while with the revolver you simply pull the trigger or cock the gun to bring a fresh load under the firing pin.

For military purposes we can see the advantage of the automatic where sustained fire is often needed, but for individual combat give us the sixgun. The Smith & Wesson double action automatic and the P-38 are both fast owing to their double action trigger pulls, but after the first shot they are susceptible to the basic faults of the autoloader. They may jam or a cartridge may misfire. These two Colt and Smith & Wesson pocket autos are very compact, carry nicely and are easily concealed on the person, but both are so large that they must be carried in a hip or coat pocket.

In true pocket guns for defense use, the best we know of today are the Smith & Wesson Centennial and the Chief's Special and the Colt Cobra. The Smith & Wesson 2 inch barrel, round butt Military and Police model may be added to this list. These are true pocket guns—all capable of handling the various high speed and super police loads in .38 Special. The smallest and lightest of the lot is, of course, the Chief's Special with light alloy metal frame. Next come the Smith & Wesson Centennial and the Colt Cobra and lastly the detective specials in Smith & Wesson and Colt. For a true pocket gun the 2 inch barrel is about right. The safest of all pocket guns is the Centennial Smith & Wesson, but Colt also makes a hammer shroud covering the hammer of the Cobra, if desired.

For weight the Smith & Wesson Chief's Special with alloy frame can be had in a weight of 10¾ ounces and in a steel frame to weigh 19 ounces. The Centennial can be had in an alloy frame in a weight of 11¼ ounces and in a steel frame at 19 ounces. The Colt Cobra in alloy frame weighs just 15 ounces. The six shot S. & W. 2 inch barrel Detective Special on the M. & P. frame comes at 26 ounces with a steel frame and lighter of course with an alloy frame. The Colt Detective Special comes in a weight of 21 ounces. Both the Colt Cobra and the Colt Detective Special are six-shot weapons as is the M. & P. frame Smith & Wesson, but the Chief's Special and Centennial Smith & Wessons are five-shot revolvers. This five-shot feature of these little guns enables them to handle heavy loads because the bolt-cuts do not come over the center of a chamber as is true of all six-shot weapons. Rather, the bolt-cut, or indent, is between the charge-holes on these five-shot weapons. This feature allows full thickness of chamber metal over the cartridge case and the little guns will handle High Speed .38 Special ammunition perfectly in spite of their very light weight. Recoil, of course, is very severe from these loads in such extremely light weight guns, but the guns will take it and any man would rather have a sore hand than a slug through his middle. Another feature that adds greatly to the strength of the two little Smith & Wessons is the fact that their cylinders extend forward almost to the frame and leave very little of the rear end of the barrel projecting out of the frame unsupported. The springs are coil and almost unbreakable. They are very reliable little guns. The Chief's Special is very accurate for aimed single action fire, while the Centennial can only be used double action. On the other hand the Chief's Special has a hammer that can catch on the corner of a pocket or on the clothes while the Centennial is as clean as a hounds tooth.

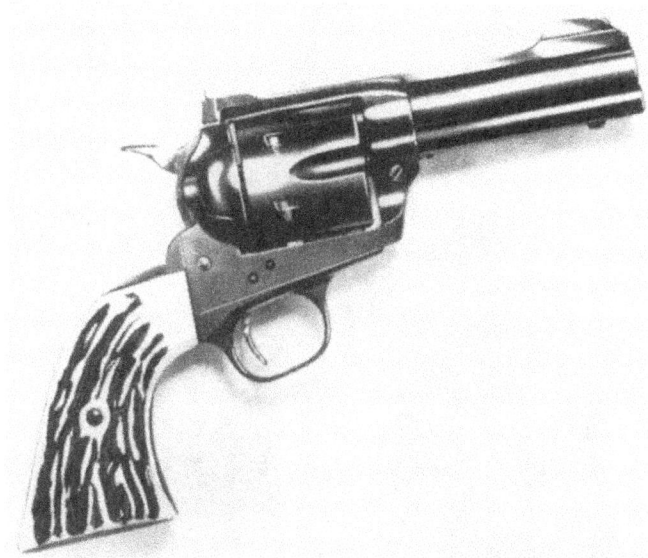

Great Western Deputy Caliber .357, 4 inch barrel.

The Centennial also has a grip safety in addition to the regular double action. You cannot fire the gun without pushing in the grip safety. It is impossible for any pressure exerted on the trigger alone to fire the gun in your pocket. It is the safest of all modern pocket revolvers and is on a par, in this respect, with the old Smith & Wesson New Departure safety hammerless. That gun was chambered for the .38 S. & W. cartridge which we do not consider powerful enough for serious defense use. The Chief's Special is also the lightest of the lot. Both guns can be had full nickeled in the steel models, as can the Colt and Smith & Wesson 2 inch barrel Detective Special six-shot revolvers. This is a feature for those living in very hot, humid or damp climates, where body perspiration will rust any blued finish gun except those with aluminum alloy frames. Guns with aluminum alloy frames can be had with nickeled barrels and cylinders making them rust proof also, as pocket guns, for hot, humid climates. The Centennial Smith & Wesson is the safest gun of all if left loaded around small children. Children should be taught at an early age to respect all guns and leave them alone, except when being coached in their use by their parents.

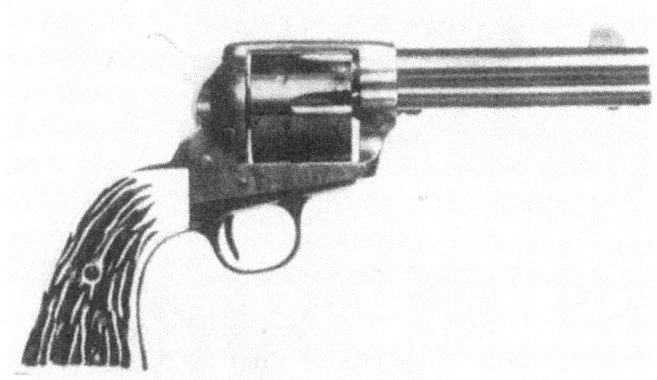

Great Western Single Action, 4¾ inch barrel.

For shooting through the coat pocket, the Centennial and the Colt Cobra with hammer shroud would be the safest bets—tough on a suit of clothes, but it might save your life. The Colt Detective Special may also be had with hammer shroud for such use.

In a factory cartridge, no doubt the most effective of all loads for those small guns would be the Super police 200 grain blunt point bullet load. The most effective hand load would be the Keith 160 grain hollow point backed by 5.3 grains Hercules Unique

Great Western Single Action, 5½ inch barrel.

powder or the Keith 173 grain solid backed by 5 grains of Unique powder.

These are pocket guns, pure and simple, and there is no reason to have them with longer than 2 inch barrels or using them in holsters. If you are going to employ a holster, you can just as easily carry a real sixgun as these small pocket guns and have something twice as effective when the chips are down.

Movie Actor John Wayne with Great Western Revolvers.

These pocket guns are also a valuable addition to the officer's armament when he does pack a heavy holster gun. He may lose it in a scrimmage and also may have some thug get the drop on him and disarm him. Then the little hidden pocket gun may prove a life-saver. We know some very good officers who carry a light weight Smith & Wesson Chief's Special hidden away for the left hand in addition to their holster gun. In the old days almost everything was used for pocket guns, in autos from the .25 Colt upwards through the .380's and the short hammer model .38 Colt auto; in revolvers from the .22 L.R. Banker's Special Colt through the .32's and .38's as well as .38 S. & W. Also the Remington .41 double barreled rim fire Derringer was used extensively. That Remington Double Derringer, while possessing little actual knock down shock, was a good branding iron, as anyone hit with it would be in serious need of immediate surgery, as the pointed slugs with their light charge of powder would drive to about the middle of a man and stay there along with their lubricant and what germs and dirt they picked up, and that unfortunate man would soon be in bad shape without surgery. Most old gunmen would far rather be hit with a .45 than a .41 Derringer for the above reasons.

Today with the fine Colt and S. & W. arms on the market in .38 Special caliber or 9 mm. and .45 in the automatics, there is no point in anyone going back to the older, less powerful arms for a good hidden pocket gun. The .38 Special and 9 mm. autos we believe small enough for serious police or defense use.

Next let us look into the heavy holster gun for serious use by peace officers, the military, or in personal defense. If you are going to carry a gun in a holster, it should be a powerful gun that will put a man down with any good hit between the pelvis bone and the top of the cranium. Thirty-eight Specials have proven inadequate in so many gun fights that there is no doubt as to their inferiority in comparison with larger and more powerful calibers. Crooks seldom travel singly, and the same can be said of enemy soldiers. For the holster gun, you need a fast, powerful and handy arm capable of digesting the most powerful loads. We realize more police are armed with .38 Specials than any other caliber and we also consider this a grave mistake. Each year it costs the lives of valuable officers, who would be alive and on duty today if they had been armed with an adequate gun. Our sympathy is all with the officer. If he is in uniform, he is easily spotted and marked and he cannot make a move with his gun until he is fired on or the criminal at least shows a gun. He may be alone and have to handle two or more criminals. He desperately needs a gun that will stop them with one hit.

We could fill this chapter with cases where criminals took from one to six shots from standard .38 Specials and stayed on their feet and kept fighting, often to the demise of the officer.

An accurate, powerful gun is simply life insurance to any soldier, peace officer, or civilian for that matter. The uniformed officer or soldier can pack any length he desires in plain sight, and the same is true of the Western peace officer when riding a horse, or the cow-puncher or packer. In the open where ranges may well be long, the long barreled guns are best, but for close in-fighting, shorter barrels are much to be preferred.

For the officer or civilian preferring an auto loading pistol, we consider the Colt Government model .45 in a class by itself. It is a better stopper than any smaller caliber. It is accurate and very reliable for an automatic, if kept clean and oiled in warm climates, and with dry graphite lubricant in extreme cold climates. It can be carried in any number of styles of holster or in the waist band of the trousers and held by pressure of the waist belt. For quick work and defense shooting it should be carried with hammer at full cock and the side safety on. This safety can be thrown off quickly as the gun is drawn. It points too low for any fast hip shooting or shooting after dark, and has the inherent faults of the automatic for defense use, but we consider it the best to be had in an autoloading arm. The 9 mm. calibers and even the more powerful Super .38 all lack stopping power in comparison to the .45 auto. It is a good military arm owing to the ease with which broken or damaged parts can be changed with a minimum of tools and the ease of loading with a clip, but we consider it far inferior to a heavy sixgun for defense use. Those wishing a light-weight holster gun in an automatic pistol can well choose the Colt Commander for the same .45 auto cartridge. The new Smith & Wesson is fast for the first shot, but we do not consider its 9 mm. cartridge nearly as effective as the .45 Colt at any range.

For the peace officer, special agents of the F.B.I., army officers and civilians packing a heavy holster weapon for defense, the best calibers are the .357 Smith & Wesson Magnum, the .38/40, .44-40, .44 Special, .45 Auto Rim and .45 Colt. For average size men riding in cars a great deal and carrying gun holster on the waist belt the 4 inch barrel is tops. Big men using the same waist belt holster and having longer hips and greater distance from their waist belt to the seat of their pants can carry a 5 inch barreled sixgun just as easily without having it poking against the chair or car seat and pushing up their belts. For most men, however, the 4 inch barrel revolver is the best length not only for ease of portability, but also for very fast quick draw work. When your life may be at stake, the best is none too good. We believe all defense sixguns should be fitted with good adjustable target sights. The front sight should of course be of the Baughman pattern so it cannot catch on clothes or holster in quick draw work. We also believe the front sight should not be less than one-eighth inch in width and even one-fourth inch width is satisfactory.

For the man who was raised on the Colt single action, nothing is faster for the first shot, draw and hit. Even the latest double action is no faster for that first shot. Single action men are best fitted by a 4¾ inch barrel S.A. Colt in .357 Magnum, .44 Special, .38/40, .44-40 or .45 Colt. Then for city and car use or close range gun fighting, the 4¾ inch balances the best and is the fastest of all lengths of single action. No gun points quite as well for fast hip shooting or for shooting in the dark of the night by feel of the gun alone. If these calibers are used, one hit is all that is necessary to put an adversary out of business. The old gun is still preferred and still carried by a great many peace officers and with good reason for their choice. With present factory loads the .357 Magnum with best high velocity loads and the .45 Colt are the best calibers, but when hand loaded the .44 Special is on top of the list and the .45 Colt second—a very close second however. During the late Thirties we had dinner with an F.B.I. special agent who wore an old Hopkins & Allen, Merlin & Hulbert patent, 4 inch barrel .44-40 single action as his sole armament. It was slow to reload, but a very effective, accurate and fast gun for six shots.

In double action guns we have the Colt New Serv-

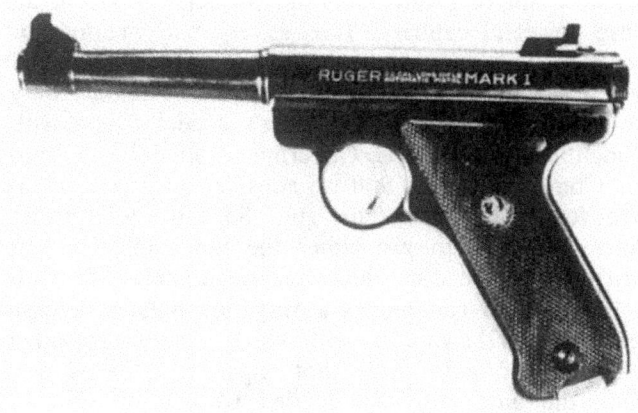

Ruger, best auto .22 Target Pistol.

Ruger Standard .22 auto.

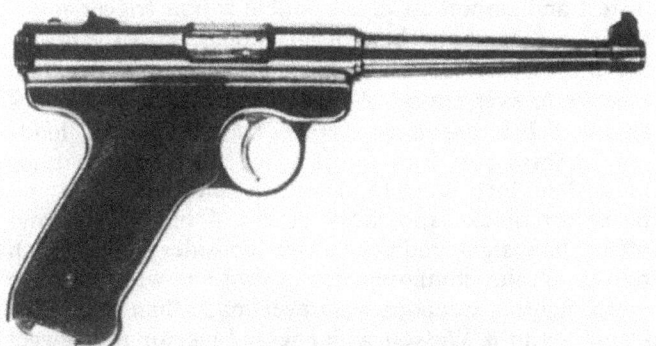

Ruger Low Price .22 auto.

Ruger Single Six, caliber .22 L.R.

ice, now out of production, but formerly made in all these powerful calibers. It is a very fine weapon for the men with extra large hands. These guns should be fitted with target sights. Today Colt makes only the new .357 on the .41 Officer's Model frame with 4 inch barrel, and the Government model .45 auto and Commander .45, that we consider adequate armament for the holster defense gun. So, those who prefer Colts will have to use either the new .357 Colt or turn back to the older New Service model. The Colt 1917 .45 auto rim makes a very fine holster defense gun owing to the rapidity with which it can be reloaded using the .45 auto three shot clips. It is at its best using the auto rim case loaded with Keith 240 or 250 grain flat point (Lyman) bullet backed by 7.5 grains Hercules Unique powder and with extra rounds carried in the three-shot clips in the .45 auto cases for quick reloading.

Smith & Wesson now have almost a monopoly on heavy caliber sixguns in double action. They still produce the .357 Magnum Smith & Wesson, one of the great guns of all time, and also the new Highway Patrolman, both to be had with 4 inch barrels, or longer if desired and the .357 Magnum in 3½ inch barrel, also the 1950 Target model in .44 Special and .45 auto rim. Both can be had to order with barrels cut to 4 inches or 5 inches and with Baughman type one-eighth inch target front sight. In addition we have the New Century Triple Lock, the 1926 Model Target, the .44 Military and 1917 .45 as well as the fixed sighted .45 Army. These sixguns have the fastest and smoothest of all double action trigger pulls, fit the average hand best of all double actions and use the most powerful loads available. We consider it a mistake to ever cut a holster gun barrel below 4 inches as the F.B.I. has done. High velocity factory loads may deform soft lead bullet bases from muzzle blast in a 3½ inch barrel. The 3½ inch barrel is no faster for quick draw work than a 4 inch barrel and offers less sight radius, so we consider the 4 inch barrel as the minimum for a holster weapon. No better fighting weapons were ever made than the heavy frame Smith & Wesson with encased ejector rod, target sights and a barrel of 4 to 5 inch length for all around combat use. Next to the Colt Single Action, they point best of all heavy caliber sixguns for hip shooting. The hump at top of grip is adequate to hold the hand in place in speedy double action shooting and they balance and handle perfectly for fastest sixgun work.

These guns in .357 magnum caliber give the shooter a very effective weapon combined with their ability to handle standard .38 Special ammunition for practice. However, we consider the larger calibers, the .44 Special and the .45 auto rim, better all-around guns for defense work when properly hand loaded. The 4 or 5 inch 1950 Target in .45 caliber when loaded with the Keith solid bullet in 240 or 250 grain and 7.5 grain of Unique in auto rim cases is a very much better man stopper than the .357 Magnum and the .44 Special when hand loaded with the Keith 250 grain bullet backed by 18.5 grain of Hercules 2400, the most powerful hand gun load in existance. It has almost double the actual stopping power on either man or game as has the .357 Magnum with any load. We have shot enough game and had enough reports on this load used on man targets to know whereof we speak.

The .45 Target S. & W. with Baughman front sight and 4 or 5 inch barrel makes a very fine peace officer's weapon due to its quick reloading feature with the .45 auto case in the S. & W. three-shot clips. The .44 Special hand loaded, as above mentioned, is more powerful and our own personal choice of a defense gun is the .44 Special 4 inch barrel 1950 Target with our heavy loads. The only thing that could be better would be a Smith & Wesson Magnum in .44 Special caliber having the same specifications. The .44 Special 1950 Smith & Wesson is our idea of absolute tops in a gun fighting weapon. It is lighter to carry than the 4 inch .357 Magnum. Like the Magnum, it will bust a motor block or shoot through car bodies or bullet proof glass with our heavy load. It will also drill to the brain of the biggest grizzly or bull moose or elk or domestic bull. We have had these slugs go through a big bull elk behind the shoulders and the big .44 caliber bullet of 250 grains weight tears a big wound channel all the way and has the necessary weight for either shock or penetration. If you want the most powerful sixgun that can be carried and in a short, handy, well balanced gun, I know of nothing better. The single action men can have the 4¾ inch .44 Special S.A. Colt equipped with Baughman type front sight and S. & W. micrometer rear target sight, wide trigger and Bisley type hammer and have the same thing in a single action gun.

The best stocks for a gun fighting weapon are first choice ivory, either plain, carved or checkered; second choice rosewood; and, third, hard dense walnut like Circassian. Heavy material, such as ivory, gives the weapon a better balance in the hand. They may be severely plain, or checkered or with raised carving on the palm side of the grip. The checkered and carved with raised carving, give a little firmer grasp to the hand.

On Single Action Colts I prefer one piece stocks, simply cut out for main spring and straps and made of one solid block of ivory or rosewood, with walnut as third choice. On the Smith & Wesson .44 1950 Target 4 inch barrel I prefer, first, ivory; second, rosewood. Third choice is walnut of the magna type that comes to the top of the hump of the back strap, but for my use I prefer them to be thinner than the standard magna stocks which are too full and too round to suit my hand.

The gun fighter's weapon should not have extra

large stocks, unless the man has an abnormally large hand. Thumb rests and finger grooves and extra length below the little finger are totally out of place on a gun fighting weapon. They are slower and do not make for accurate gun pointing from the hip, and much close-in gun fighting must be done from the hip, if the officer is to get his shot off first.

Avoid any abnormally large hand filling grips, or stocks that extend down below the butt of the gun unless your hand is large enough to really need them. Thumb rests will never do for fast double action shooting, and from the hip they will cause you to shoot to the side they are fastened to the grip.

The defense gun should be clean of any such gadgets and stocked to allow its fastest possible use. The defense gun should not be butchered, with hammer spur cut off, front of trigger guard cut away or finger grooves cut in the stocks. The trigger guard is part of the handle on any gun and you can carry it on the forefinger if necessary and with a single flip of the wrist have the gun in your hand and shooting. We never could see any horsesense in cutting out the front of the trigger guard. The trigger guard is on the gun to protect the trigger and a gun with the front of the guard cut out is much more likely to be fired accidentally than one with the trigger guard complete. Some men with long fingers claim they can find the trigger easier with the guard cut out and this may be true, but to our way of thinking the disadvantages of a butchered gun far outweigh the advantages. In the pocket the gun can be fired accidentally a lot easier than if the guard is complete. The shooting finger, if properly trained, knows exactly where the trigger lies on the gun and will find it without having half the guard cut away. The fastest double action shot this world has yet produced, Ed McGivern, never cuts away any trigger guards or alters the guns in any way beyond sighting equipment. We would do well to emulate him.

There is some excuse for cutting the top of the hammer from a pocket gun so it will not catch on the clothing. Hammer spurs have a habit of catching in the corner of the pocket when drawn hurriedly. I had two friends in Detroit, Michigan, who were practicing quick draw with a .45 S.A. Colt without a holster. One would place the gun in his front overalls pocket, make a break for the gun and draw and shoot, cocking the gun as it came from the pocket. The front sight caught on the top of the pants pocket spinning the gun forward out of his grasp while his finger pulled the trigger of the cocked .45. The 250 grain Western lubaloy slug hit him in the right side and passed completely through his body, missing the vertebrae and all vital organs, then hit his pal in the left forearm and penetrated up the arm and through the elbow, stopping under the skin on the back of the elbow. They had to cross some vacant lots and a railroad with barbed wire fences, but both managed

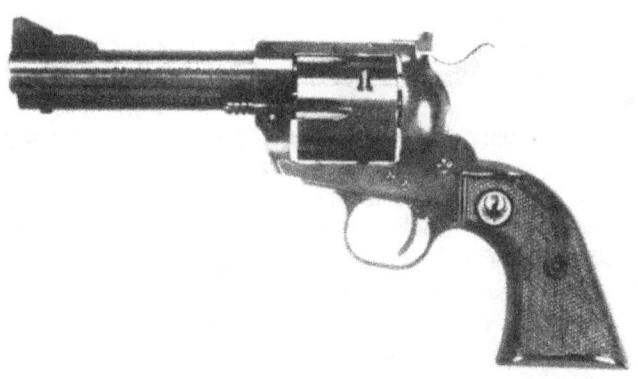

Ruger Magnum .357. Also to be made in other calibers and .44 Special.

Ruger .357 Magnum S.A. Other calibers to come: .44 Special, and .45 Colt.

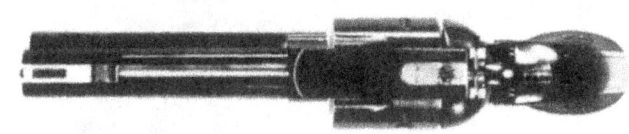

Ruger .357 Magnum Single Action.

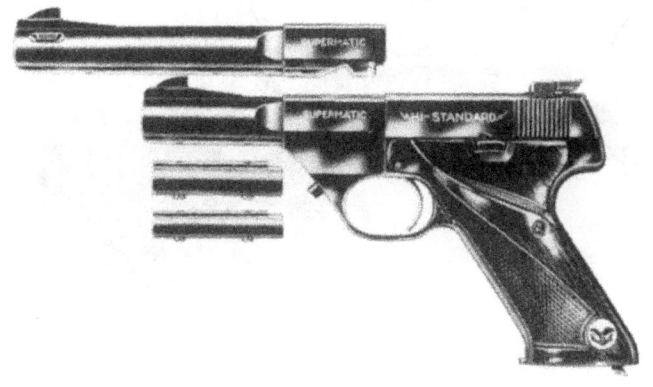

Hi-Standard Supermatic.

to make it to the hospital under their own power and both recovered.

Last spring when in Washington, I met three boys in the Smithsonian Museum while looking over the Arms Collection. Two of them informed me they had shot themselves about a week apart with Keith 250 grain slugs from their S.A. Colts while practicing quick draw. The third said he then decided to stop all quick draw practice. Each of these had let the hammer slip while pulling on the trigger as the gun was drawn and the heavy Keith slugs went almost the length of their right legs, even though they were light loads. Quick draw practice should be with empty guns until thoroughly mastered.

The S.A. Colt, when used as a defense gun, should have a wide, deeply checkered, Bisley-type hammer, as it affords a better grip for the ball of the thumb. Some folks use a different draw and merely wipe a crooked thumb up along the front of the holster until it contacts the hammer of the gun and cocks it. This is fast but not faster than the other method and has dangerous fumble possibilities. One must train the shooting hand to keep the finger off the trigger until the gun is drawn and poked toward the target.

The single action slip gun is the one gun that has a legitimate right to be altered, and this gun, when cut to pocket length, has no need of a trigger at all nor the trigger-half of the bolt spring. These can be removed and the hole in the trigger guard welded up solid. Just the same, the trigger guard is useful and needed and still a part of the gun grip. The very low slip-hammer will not catch on clothes as the thumb is hooked around it when drawn.

We have seen big holster guns with both the hammer spur and the front of the guard cut away, and see no reason for so ruining a fine gun. The hammer spur is necessary if single action aimed fire is called for, which is often the case in defense work. Any time you have to hit a distant target, be it man or automobile, you can do a better job by cocking the gun, taking deliberate aim and squeezing off the shot properly.

Only the small double action guns should ever have the hammer spur removed. If a true pocket gun is wanted, the Smith & Wesson Centennial or the Colt Detective Special with hammer shroud, are the best choice.

The Hunter's Sixgun

So much for defense guns. Now let us look at guns for the hills and for hunting. True, the rifle is the better hunting arm. However, there are many times when a rifle is an encumbrance and will be left at home, as when back packing, working green colts, or fishing in bear country. The prospector needs both hands most of the time when climbing through rough country and a rifle is in the way. At such times a good heavy sixgun carried on a belt or in a shoulder holster is much handier and will do the job nicely, both for defense and for acquiring game for the stew pot. The most powerful sixgun loads are far under ordinary rifle loads in actual killing power, so one should use the most powerful sixgun he can get if any big game is to be killed with the short gun. Hunting use of the sixgun demands the best in sights, as well as the best possible accuracy. For these reasons target sighted weapons are the best. Unless you inadvertently meet a bear, cougar, or other dangerous game at very close quarters, or step on a big rattler, quick draw is seldom needed in the hills, but the gun should be carried so it is instantly available in case one does meet with such an emergency. Long barrels give better and longer sighting radius and aid in placing the slug and also give higher velocity and more power with the same load. Target accuracy is what you want for game killing, whether it is knocking a big blue grouse out of a tall yellow pine or hitting a deer through the shoulders or spine for camp meat. You want a gun you can shoot very accurately and place your bullet exactly where you want it. The sixgun is your intimate personal weapon and one you can have with you at all times. A great many chances will then come for its use on game and at such close range that you can kill with it about as well as with a rifle.

Much deer hunting is done along the West Coast and in Alaska where any good sixgun shot is about as well off with a heavy pistol as with a rifle. He then has both hands free to part brush and to help move

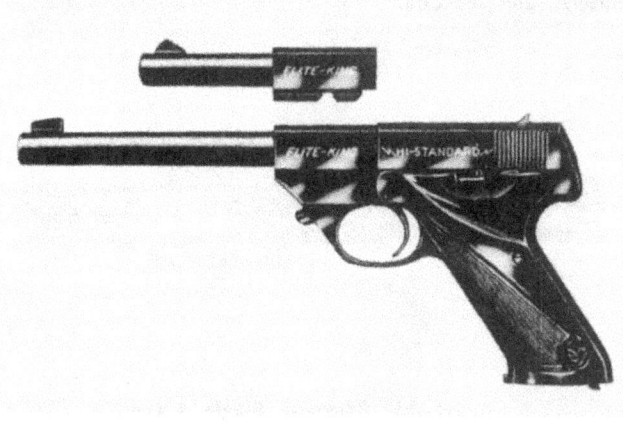

Hi-Standard Flite-King

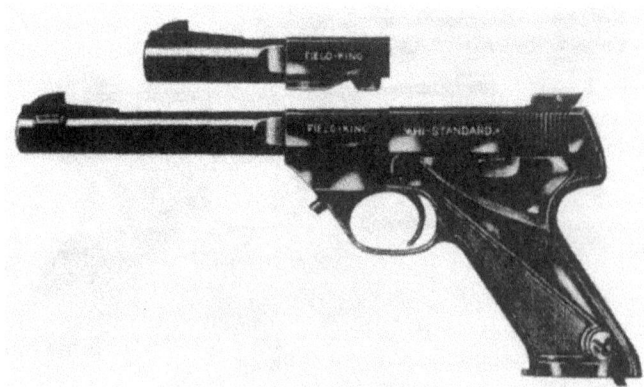

Hi-Standard Field-King.

through the forest with the least noise, yet has a gun that can be brought to play instantly when needed.

Many times in our four years of surveying in the high mountainous country of Montana the old sixgun supplied the whole crew with badly needed fresh meat, because we always had it with us. When game offered a sure shot at close range we collected. Sometimes it was a mess of grouse and sometimes it was a fat mule deer. They were eaten with just as much relish as if they had been killed with a rifle.

The standard .22 L.R. is not a very good killer, except on the very smallest of small game. It will do nicely on quail, doves, pigeons, bull frogs and turtles, but is not sure on big fox squirrels or the larger grouse unless high speed hollow point ammunition is used. With these cartridges, the .22 target guns make excellent small game hunting arms.

Even the .22 L.R. hollow point is none too large for jack rabbits, big blue grouse or sage hens and must be placed right for sure kills. In small game country the target .22 calibers, either automatics or revolvers, are excellent when used with high speed, hollow point ammunition. If you favor the auto pistol, the Colt, High Standard, or Ruger will fill the bill. If you prefer revolvers, the Colt Police Positive Target or Officer's Model is very good, or the Smith & Wesson Combat Masterpiece or K-22 is excellent. For the man or woman wanting a very light .22 revolver for small game to be carried with a rifle, there is nothing quite so good as the little Smith & Wesson Kit gun with a 4 inch barrel. It is superbly accurate, and, if properly loaded, it is deadly on small game and grouse, and weighs but 22½ ounces. This is one of the finest little companion guns ever made.

The new Ruger Single Six is also excellent but all that we have seen so far need a higher front sight to make them shoot right for the usual close range small game killing. All these .22 caliber revolvers would be better small game guns if they had been chambered for the .25 Stevens long cartridge. Then with the use of a hollow point bullet of about 65 grains, at velocities of 1200 feet or better, they would be adequate for big sage hens, jack rabbits, even close shots on coyotes and bobcats. With solid bullets they would not be too destructive for even fox or grey squirrels. The ammunition with its bullet encased in the neck of the cartridge case could be carried loose in the pocket and not pick up dirt and grit as do all outside lubricated .22 L.R. ammunition. For this reason the old .22 Special was a better small pistol cartridge for the hunter or woods loafer than our present outside lubricated bullet .22 L.R. ammunition, which to be kept grit free must be carried in a tight box of some sort.

Remember that .22 caliber pistols do not give standard rifle velocities with .22 L.R. ammunition. We consider this ammunition really suitable for only the smallest game even in high speed hollow point loads. We remember Doctor Wilson L. DuComb

Hi-Standard Sport-King.

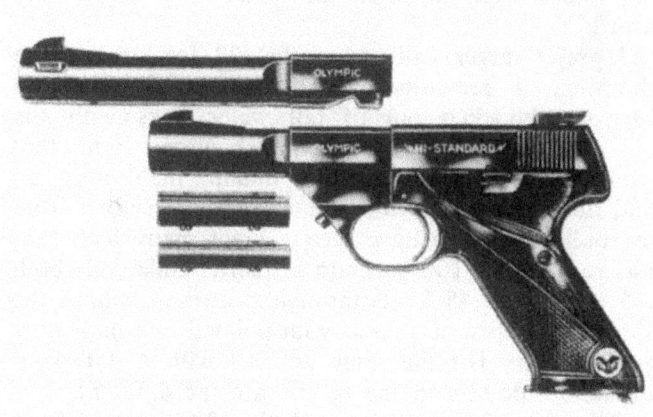

Hi-Standard Olympic.

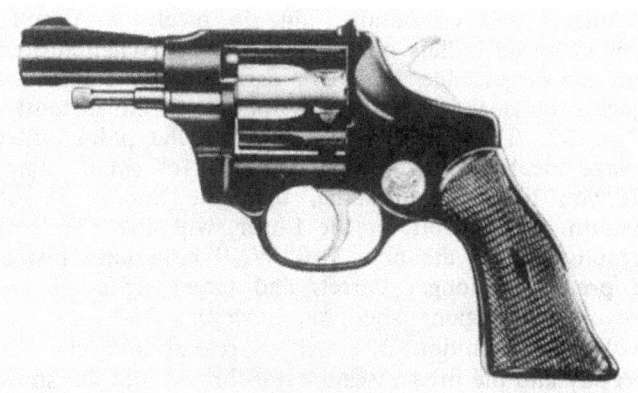

Hi-Standard Sentinel.

trying to kill a big Gila Monster down in Sonorra with his K-22 and Western solid copper coated high speed bullets. He emptied the gun, hitting that tough old lizard about the head, neck and shoulders with every shot and only made him hiss. All shots struck him on an angle and they simply made a smear on his tough hide and glanced off. Finally Doc walked around to get a square side shot at the head and then

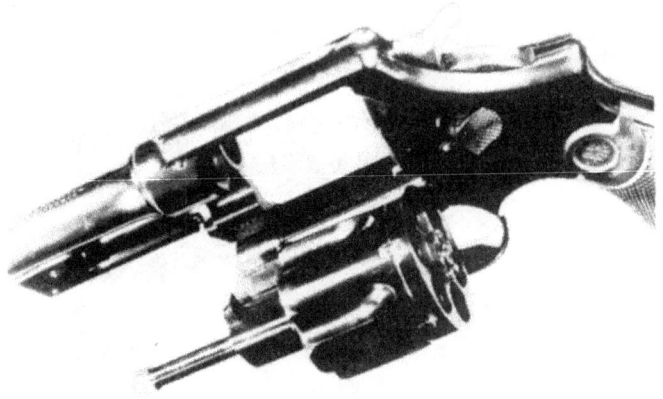

.44 Triple Lock or New Century Model.

the bullet went through and killed the tough little lizard.

I prefer larger calibers to the .22 for small game shooting. I remember tough old fox squirrels in Missouri knocked out of tall water oaks with the .45 auto and 1925 National match ammunition, that would hit the ground with a thump, then jump up and run into a hole with their entrails protruding from the bullet exit. We have seen a great many jack rabbits run from a 100 yards to a quarter mile with both .45 autos and .45 Colts through them and behind the shoulders. This, of course, with pointed or round nose ammunition. Hit the same animals with a flat point or hollow point and the results are far different.

The .32 S. & W. long and the .32-20 as well as the .38 Special with flat point or hollow point bullets make most excellent small game killers. With hollow points they are too destructive for the smaller grouse, squirrels and cottontails, but do nicely with solid round nosed bullets on this small game. When turned on the larger blue grouse or sage hens or tough old jack rabbits, the flat or hollow point will kill instantly. The .32-20 and the .38 Special with flat point bullet make ideal loads in target revolvers for small game. If you like an automatic, then the Super .38 or 9 mm. in the Colt, or the Luger, will give excellent results as will the new S. & W. 9 mm. auto pistol. I prefer the longer barrels and target sights of the revolver for game shooting, however. Also, the revolver ammunition is easier to reload and cheaper to buy and the fired cases are not thrown into the snow or underbrush where they are hard to recover.

The target-sighted Colt Single Action in .32-20 or .38 Special, the Colt Officer's Model in .38 Special, the Smith & Wesson K model in .38 Special and the Smith & Wesson Outdoorsman in .38 Special all make ideal small game guns.

When a boy, our best small game revolver was an old .36 Navy Colt 1851 model. It accounted for a great many grouse, sage hens and rabbits, both big Montana jacks and cottontails. Later I used a 7½ inch barrel .32-20 S. A. Colt with even better results for all small game revolver shooting. That flat point 115 grain bullet is a killer on all small game. The .38 Special with standard round nose ammunition was not as good, but when reloaded with a flat point bullet was even better than the .32-20. These fine guns all shoot very accurately when tuned up and are the best to be had for hunting small game with a sixgun.

For the person working or prospecting or fishing in big game country or bear country, the heaviest most powerful guns to be had are what is needed. Again we prefer target sights on all guns. Long barrels are also preferable for all game shooting but are not quite as handy as shorter barrels. There are no set target rules to be followed in game shooting, so one should use both hands to steady the gun and take advantage of any arm or shoulder rest that is available. The main desideratum is to place your slug where it will do the most good and any position that will best promote it is the one to use. We would suggest nothing smaller than the .357 magnum caliber for such use or the Super .38 Auto Government model Colt, and larger calibers are infinitely better. If you prefer to use an automatic, then the Government model .45 Colt auto is your best tool and the Super .38 and 9 mm. Luger and the S. & W. or P-38 are poor seconds.

In revolvers, the best are the single action Colt with target sights and the Smith & Wesson 1950 Target .44 Special or .45 auto rim or the older Smith & Wesson Target models in .44 Special and the big Colt New Service Target arms in .44 Special or .45 long Colt.

The .38-40 and .44-40 arms are very good if properly hand loaded but the .44 Specials or .45 Colts are still better. The .357 Magnum is also good but inferior in knockdown power to the .44 Special and .45 Colt with heavy hand loads. These big guns will, with round pointed normal loads, kill all small game nicely without mutilation, and with their heavy hand loads with flat pointed bullets, will kill any game on this continent at close range if properly placed.

.44 Hand Ejector Military Model.

1950 Army .45.

The big Smith & Wessons and the New Service Colts are the fastest to reload with their simultaneous ejection, but the old Colt Single Action has the best shaped grip of all for absorbing heavy recoil of powerful loads. The longer the barrel, the more velocity and power you have, and in hunting you usually employ both hands. The Single Action came in 4¾, 5½ and 7½ inch barrels, and the 7½ inch is the best game gun with the 5½ inch being the best compromise for both fast work and easy portability.

In the big Smith & Wessons, the standard target 6½ inch barrel is excellent for the hills and some of the earlier triple lock target guns came with 7½ inch barrels. These also are excellent guns for the mountain man. The 4¾ inch single actions are very handy guns to carry and give a good account of themselves. We have one old .45 S.A. in that length that has killed a lot of game, both wounded big game as well as some that we shot for meat. The 5½ inch length, however, has more power and greater sight radius. The big Colt and S. & W. guns can be cut down in barrel length but should never be cut under 4 inch barrels for any holster use and 5 inches is better for game shooting. The New Service Colt came in 4½, 5½ and 7½ inch barrels and also in the later Shooting Master in 6 inch barrels. The 5½ through 7½ are the best lengths for the woodsman. For the cowpuncher and packer, the long gun is just as easily carried on the gun belt as the shorter ones, and gives him more range and power on game or stock. The gun does not have to be concealed in the hills, so there is no reason for having it short enough to be hidden by the coat. It is better by far to have an accurate long barrel with which you can place your slug.

Frank Waterman, as a small boy in the early days of Wyoming, was given a 7½ inch .45 S.A. Colt by his father. Frank carried that nickel plated .45 all his life. It accounted for all species of game in that section except buffalo. He killed elk, moose, deer, antelope, black and brown bear and mountain sheep with it. He once loaned it to a guide who had to go back with pack string and bring out a bull elk one of his sportsmen had killed. The packer was on foot after a heavy snow storm, picking out the trail and leading the pack horses up a willow-covered stream-bed. As he neared the elk, the horses snorted and pulled away from him. Instantly a big grizzly rose to full height over the kill. The packer drew the .45 S.A. Colt and aimed just under the chin of the big grizzly and squeezed off a careful shot at 15 yards. The big bear went down like a sack of beans with his spine smashed where it joined the skull.

When I was a youngster in Montana, a couple of brothers named Waggoner had a ranch in the Yak Valley in the extreme Northwest corner of Montana. Coming out for mail and supplies over the long trail, one of them met three grizzlies, an old boar, an old sow and a two-year-old. The old male started blowing and chopping his teenth and Waggoner killed him with a single brain shot from his .45 S.A. loaded with 40 grain black powder loads. Then the female started for him, chopping her teeth in rage and he killed her with a single brain shot. The two-year-old ran and he planted the remaining three slugs in his gun in it before it got out of sight. He made the long trip back to the ranch, got his dogs to trail the young grizzly. That incident shows what can be done by a cool hand with a heavy sixgun when the chips are down. Doug Wesson killed elk, moose, antelope and one grizzly with his 8⅜ inch .357 Smith & Wesson Magnum, mostly clean one-shot kills.

I have killed eight mule deer, three elk, three black bear, one record cougar, one mountain goat billy, one whitetail buck and two Mexican Javalina with a sixgun, besides innumerable wounded big game animals that I trailed for others. I have never kept a record of the wounded animals I killed for other hunters.

Today only Smith & Wessons are made in suitable calibers for hunting other than small game, with the exception of the recent Colt 4 inch barrel .357 and the Colt automatic pistols in .45, Super .38 and 9mm., but the older Colts in single action and New Service models will be with us for many years to come. For the man wanting a new gun for the woods or mountains and for defense, camp meat, and hunting, the best to be had is the 1950 Target Smith &

.38/44 Outdoorsman, 1950 Model .44 Target, 1950 Model .45 Target.

.38/44 Heavy Duty, 1950 Model .44 Military.

Wesson in .44 Special, with the .45 auto rim as second choice, and the Smith & Wesson .357 magnum third choice.

The .357 Magnums are good guns and work well on small game with standard .38 Special loads but the .44s and .45s will do anything the Magnum will and do it better, with their 250 grain bullet loads at 1000 to 1200 feet per second velocity. The 250 grain slugs will cut a larger hole and allow more hemhorrage and the 250 grain .44 or .45 caliber slug has more shock than a 160 to 173 grain .38 even at higher velocity. We prefer the .44 Special and the .45 Colt to the .357. The .45 auto rim with 250 grain bullet and heavy load of Unique is also a better killer than the .357 Magnum. When it comes to strength of the gun and its ability to handle heavy loads, we place the Colt S.A. Army at the top and the Smith & Wesson heavy frame guns are about on a par except for the fact they have more of the rear end of the barrel projecting back through the frame, unsupported, than has the S.A. Army. We consider the big Smith & Wessons with their front cylinder lock and encased ejecter rods superior to the New Service Colt in this respect, but the latter is a mighty good gun. Its extremely large grip best fits men with extra large hands.

With factory loads the .357 Magnum, .44-40 and .45 Colt are all superior to the .45 auto rim and .44 Special in actual killing power but hand load them and the picture is greatly changed. The .44 Special is the cream of the crop.

Select the gun that suits you best, get a first class bench reloading tool and moulds for it and live with that gun until you master it and are capable of hitting small game out to 50 yards regularly. Then, and only then, are you ready to tackle hunting with a sixgun. Shoot only when you know you can place your shot, is a rule for all hunters and especially so for pistol hunters. There is no satisfaction in wounding and losing game.

In recent years Smith & Wesson has developed a large target grip for both their K and S model guns. This grip is usually of walnut or rosewood and incorporates a filler in back of the trigger guard as well as covering the front strap of the grip. No wood covers the back strap however, but the new grip comes up to the top of the frame, full and wide enough for the largest hands and it extends about three-eighths inch below the butt strap, making a full, large and very well shaped grip. The extreme lower edge of the grip flares out and the whole grip is modelled to fit the average large hand.

This new grip is an improvement over the standard Magna grip for all straight target shooting and is also excellent for hunting. Its large size makes the trigger pull feel lighter—either single action, or double action—and it is easier to cock the arm fast in timed and rapid fire matches with this grip. I would not, however, select it for use on a gun for fast work—especially quick draw—as it's a trifle large for my hand to give speed in the draw and is also large and bulky to carry as a defense gun. It is on the .45 frame size, a bit large for my hands for fast double action shooting, but is Smith & Wesson's answer to men with extra large hands. The filler in back of the guard also causes the weight of the gun to rest on

Centennial.

.38 Chief's Special (steel or Airweight).

the second finger leaving the trigger finger free for just one purpose—to press the trigger.

Since starting this book several worthwhile new guns have appeared. We have held back the press to cover them.

Ruger .357 Blackhawk

When Bill Ruger first mentioned bringing out his now famous Single Six, incorporating all coil springs and a new type rebounding firing pin, we urged him to bring out a larger version as to frame, barrel, and cylinder, for the most popular big cartridges, .357 mag., .44 Spl. and .45 Colt. We also criticized his .22 caliber Single Six, suggesting that the flat top be left a full flat top frame and the rear sight be fitted back at the extreme rear-end and adjustable for both windage and elevation. We recommended a sloping ramp-type front sight with its highest point near the muzzle to give maximum sight radius. We also asked for an improved thumb piece to the extractor rod, which we will get, and a wide Bisley-type hammer and wide trigger, not in view at this writing.

Ruger had his first two pilot models at Washington, D. C. at the N.R.A. annual meetings and later shipped them to me here for testing. Both proved very superior guns needing only some changes in heighth of front sight. Both were very accurate. They shot well with .38 Special handloads, with my bullet, and also with full factory .357 magnum and magnum reloads. Barrel length is 4¾ inches, just to the end of the extractor. The gun feels heavy but is perfectly balanced and is very well built to handle the heaviest safe sixgun pressures. The flat top is a beautiful job and a Micro rear target sight is set down flush with the top rear of the flat top frame, making a most pleasing outline as well as low sights.

A micro front is silver soldered to the barrel with a sloping ramp type front sight of one-eighth inch width. The coil main spring makes cocking the piece fast and easy and the trigger pull is excellent. We would still prefer a Bisley shaped, wide, checkered thumb piece, which we may get one of these days, and a wide trigger. Grip straps and trigger guard are one piece cast aluminum alloy, the same as on his .22 caliber Single Six. All coil spring construction makes it a very indestructible gun that will stand years of hard service. It is perfectly balanced and fast handling. The first production, against our wishes, is to be in .357 caliber and we expect it will be some time before he can get into production of larger calibers. For the shooter, be he plinker, peace officer, cow-poke or hunter, this new Ruger is a good, well-made arm. Colt collectors may prefer the original old peacemaker but any shooter who wants to have first class target sights combined in a really modern arm with all improvements including the rebounding separate firing pin will find the new Ruger Blackhawk the finest single action revolver manufactured

Terrier.

to date. Aside from the few minor improvements we have mentioned and which we will no doubt get in the final production run, it is the best commercially made gun we have yet tested in single action. There is no base pin bushing in the Ruger cylinder as on the Colt and Great Western, and we frankly do not yet know whether this will be an improvement or a detriment to the longevity of the cylinder. Base pin bushings are replaceable and for this reason the cylinder might well be fitted with a base pin bushing in these bix sixgun calibers to better take up the wear of the forward thrust on the cylinder when it is fired. The flat top is wide and heavy and adds considerably to the strength of the frame. The 4¾ inch barrel will suit most men as it is the best balanced of all single action lengths and the fastest for quick work combined with enough barrel for excellent accuracy and velocities. Grips are Ruger's standard plastic with Ruger medallion. No doubt ivory or walnut will also be optional at greater cost, as on the Single Six.

We do not yet know the price of this new gun, but it will be in full production, with a price tag attached before this book is on the shelves. We look for prices to be competitive at least. The frame of this new Ruger closely follows the design Harold Croft and myself dreamed up thirty years ago, except that the top strap is even thicker and heavier, and does not extend to the rear quite as far. The Ruger hammer fills the cut at the base of this flat top job, while we had the flat top extended slightly further to the rear and the top of the hammer cut off so it would go under the overhang. Instead of a Micro rear sight being dovetailed through the rear end or the S. & W. type blade fitted in the flat top, as we used to have them made, this Micro tang is set in from the rear of the frame, leaving the top flush with the flat top frame and making a very neat, practical rear sight installation and one that is also pleasing to the eye. The sight radius is maximum for the length of frame and considerably greater than the old Colt flat top S. A. Army of the eighties. The front Micro ramp fits right out flush with the muzzle of the gun. We would have preferred

.38 Regulation Police.

.32 Regulation Police.

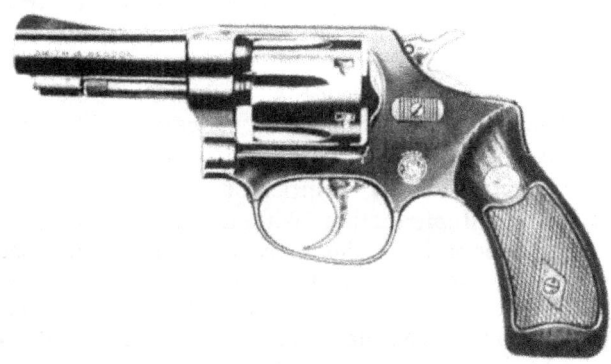

.32 Hand Ejector, 3 inch barrel.

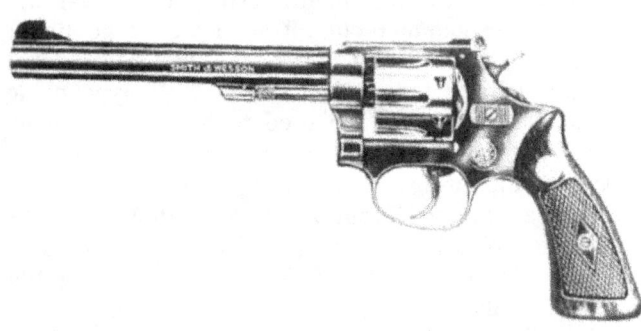

.22/32 Target.

a slightly larger frame and a cylinder a bit larger in diameter, especially for the .45 Colt cartridge, but this .357 Ruger is one honey of a gun and amply heavy for the .357 and .44 Special and will give standard chamber wall thickness if Bill ever chambers it for the .45 Colt.

A new improved flat top Single Action was the dream of Harold Croft and myself thirty years ago. We insistantly urged Colt to bring it out but with no success. We did all the necessary design work and had several fine models made-up. I understand that Colt will produce the standard single action model of 1872 again this fall, priced at $125.00. It will sell to collectors and to those who just want a genuine Colt Peacemaker, but for the shooter or gun crank, Bill Ruger has a far better single action than has ever came out of the Colt factory.

The new Black Hawk Ruger will handle all ammunition from the .38 Short and long Colt, to the .38 Specials as well as the .357 magnum. We believe it will become a very popular arm for all lovers of the single action. No other sixgun absorbs recoil so well as the grip of the S. A., as it simply turns up in the hand in recoil, thus cushioning the blow on the palm of the hand. We find the new gun a pleasant one to shoot with the heaviest magnum loads.

Nearly seventy years have passed since Colt made the fine flat top target model S. A. Colt, although they did produce some flat top Bisley models after that. Our hats are off to Bill Ruger for again bringing out a flat top target single action and a gun that is greatly improved as to springs and sights, and which incorporates much of the design Croft and myself worked out so long ago. If he will fit it with a wide Bisley hammer spur and wide trigger and an improved base pin catch such as we designed, it will be a perfect single action. The small rebounding firing pin makes the gun suitable for the heaviest sixgun pressure. It is a great improvement over the old Colt type of firing pin fitted into the hammer and of such large size that it in time, pounded out the recoil shield until primers from heavy loads would flow back into the recoil plate and tie up the gun. Finish of the new gun is plain satin blue for the frame, barrel and cylinder; the straps and guard are of anodized aluminum black finish the same as the Ruger Single Six.

The foregoing is based on the two pilot models we checked out. We do not expect the factory production to vary in any important detail.

Smith & Wesson 9mm. Double Action Automatic

This new pistol is made in both single and double action models for the first shot. We have been testing Serial No. 1153 in the double action model. The new arm is one of the most advanced of all auto pistol designs. The action is the locked breech, short recoil, with dropping barrel, on the well-known Colt-Browning design, but with improvements. In addition to guide rails on the sides, the frame also has a guide rod extending out through the front end of the barrel bushing to further slide alignment. The slide is of the best steel, the frame of aluminum alloy, and the grip incorporates an arched checkered housing with lanyard loop. Magazine capacity is 8 rounds of 9mm. Luger ammunition, which, with one in the chamber, makes it a nine-shot weapon. The barrel is 4⅛ inches long, overall gun length just 7¼ inches, and the weight is 28 ounces. The grip is full and man-sized and though it looks to be very straight with the frame, it actually points quite well from the hip.

The new weapon is reminiscent of both the 1911 model Colt Browning and the Walther P-38. The bottom front edge of the grip is flared forward to position of the fingers and improves the hold, while the rear top of grip is extended back over the web of the hand until the hammer cannot bite when the slide is in recoil, as is possible with the Colt .45 auto.

Trigger position for the double action is well forward in the trigger guard. The arm has a long, heavy double action pull, but it is perfectly adequate for fast work. The first shot can thus be fired double action on the draw, the same as with a double action revolver. After that first shot, the gun remains cocked and the trigger returns to a position in the extreme rear of the guard. This feature we particularly like, as most auto pistols have too long a reach from back of grip to trigger for short trigger fingers. The new Smith & Wesson automatic gives us the perfect position of a trigger for all automatic fire. Even with our short trigger finger the trigger is far enough to the rear that we can reach it as easily as a cocked double action revolver, allowing perfect finger placement for fine shooting. This double action feature is one of the most valuable improvements ever placed on an automatic intended for combat use. It allows emergency firing double action for the vital first shot that may spell life or death to the soldier or officer. We like it.

There is no grip safety on this weapon, but on the left side is a manual safety placed in about the same position as the manual safety on the Colt .45 auto. However, it works entirely differently being more like the Walther P-38 safety. In the upper position it leaves the arm ready for firing and when pushed down to the lower position it disconnects hammer and trigger and imposes a bar between hammer and striker. This side safety is also an added protection to the shooter in loading or unloading the weapon. The safety should be pushed down to load the arm. Then by pulling back the slide and engaging the slide stop, one can drop a round in the chamber and press the slide stop down, releasing the slide and loading the weapon. The hammer follows the slide forward with a click but does not fire the cartridge. Then the magazine may be inserted and locked, and after the arm is fully loaded the safety may be pushed upward to its firing position. The arm is then ready for a double action first shot, or can be manually cocked for the first shot. If fired

.22/32 Kit Gun, 2 inch barrel.

double action, the trigger is in the forward double action position, but if the arm is manually cocked for the shot the trigger swings back to the rear of the guard in the automatic position. The same procedure can be used to unload the weapon safely, as it cannot fire when the side safety is pushed down to the lower, or safe position. This feature eliminates all hazards of loading or unloading the pistol. The arm has a further safety feature in that it will not fire unless the magazine is in place and fully locked. This makes the pistol as fool proof as humanly possible.

This arm is the latest advanced design, with the hammer drilled through near the top and with the long spring extractor. Magazine release is on the left side in about the same position as the .45 Colt Auto model 1911. The stocks are of checkered walnut with S. & W. medallion. These stocks are anchored with two screws to each, and will not loosen on the gun as is so typical of the Luger. The finish is traditional Smith & Wesson high bright blue on the slide and highly polished jet black on the frame. The top of the slide has a dull parkerized black finish that will not reflect light or glare. The sights are excellent. The wide one-eighth inch ramp-type front sight is milled integrally with the top of the slide. There is no riveted

.22/32 Kit Gun, 4 inch barrel.

front sight to shake loose on this pistol. The rear sight is a flat top bar with adequate clearance, so a strip of light can be seen on each side of the front sight and is adjustable for windage. Elevation is controlled by a screw from inside the slide, which is set at the factory. These sights are nearly perfect for either target or defense use. Nothing to catch on clothes or holster in quick draw work, and yet it has perfect target sights.

All told, the new pistol is very short, light and compact to handle the 9mm. cartridge. It is also thin and flat and easily concealed in either the waist band or a holster. Its double action feature makes it one of the best of all automatics for combat use. At the same time the trigger position, when used single action and cocked for the first shot, is short enough in the reach for most women or men with short fingers. The slide travels not only on the guide rails on the frame, but also on the guide rod extending through the barrel bushing, making for utmost accuracy. Its single action trigger pull is perfect, firing at three pounds pull. The double action pull is but little heavier than a double action revolver. It is the easiest auto loading pistol to do fine shooting with we have yet seen in calibers larger than .32 L. R. and really handles and shoots like a fine target .22 auto pistol.

Judge Don Martin and the writer gave it the initial test with Winchester 115 grain full patched ammunition. My first shot was at a bullet hole in an old car body at about ten yards. I cut into that bullet hole, then handed the gun to the Judge and he proceeded to clip the handles off the doors. Both of us went right to work with the new gun, breaking bottles out to fifty yards—small ones at that. We then tried it across a gulch at junked car fenders, finding we could hit them with ease by holding up a little of the front sight in the rear notch. Since then I have tested it to a full 400 yards, finding it one of the most accurate auto pistols I have ever fired in large caliber. The old Luger is a traditionally accurate weapon, but we found the new Smith & Wesson even easier to shoot accurately and just as accurate as the Luger. There is no comparison whatever between a Luger trigger pull and that of the new arm.

Combat Masterpiece (.22 or .38).

K-.32, K-.38 Heavy Masterpiece.

We tried shooting at very small targets over water at a full 400 yards and found the new pistol as accurate as our .44 Special Smith & Wesson 1950 Target gun with 4 inch barrel. We used both Winchester ammunition with 115 grain full patch pointed bullet and also Peters ammunition with a 124 grain bullet, preferring the heavier bullet load. We also fired some old imported pointed hollow point ammunition. The arm functioned perfectly with both the Winchester and Peters ammunition but malfunctioned with the old stuff. All automatics are totally dependent on perfect ammunition and this ancient vintage stuff failed to eject or load at times, purely a fault of the ammo. All told, we have never seen a nicer handling or better shooting automatic pistol.

Years ago when the Colt Super .38 first came out, we purchased three of them and shot them continually for some years on all manner of small game and some game not so small. We found that while they gave excellent penetration for head shots on big game, they offered very little shock on body shots. Ammunition was all Western full patched solids. Chucks and jacks would often drop at the shot, then jump up and run off. One cougar absorbed a magazine full in the chest for a friend, and still sat on his limb in a big pine tree spitting and snarling for several minutes, then jumped out and tried to run but was too far gone to escape. We found the .45 auto cartridge was much the better killer on all game either large or small. It was much easier to hit game at unknown ranges with the flat shooting Super .38 or the 9mm. Luger than it was with the high trajectory .45 auto, but a chuck hit with the .45 would drop and his tail go up in the air to the vertical, then it would slowly fall back to the ground and stay there, very dead. When hit with the Super .38 or the 9mm. Luger he would often lay still a few seconds and then jump up and run into a hole. Both the Super .38 and the 9mm. Luger seemed to be about right for grouse and rabbit killing, with little meat mutilation but on Jacks and chucks they did not always make clean kills by any means. Porcupines are hard to kill if you do not hit brain or spine and these would often take a gun full of .38's or 9mm's. We have had the same thing happen with the .45 but it gave much the better over-all performance.

Most of Europe has gone to a 9mm. for a service pistol cartridge and the new Smith and Wesson was no doubt brought out with NATO in mind. We understand that our own clear thinking, hard headed, U. S. Army brass holds out for the .45 auto cartridge and with good reason. The .38 has proven inadequate for man stopping on too many battle fronts to need further comment here. It is very true that the soldier or peace officer has a much lighter weapon and ammunition to carry in this new Smith & Wesson 9mm. pistol, but two or three hits could be necessary for the same stopping effect on a mad enemy as one .45 slug. We see no good reason why the new Smith & Wesson could not be made to the same design in .45 auto caliber and it would then offer the very ultimate in a precision made super accurate military weapon. It is a great little gun just as it is. If made in .45 auto caliber, we would prefer it to any large caliber automatic pistols of either domestic or foreign manufacture.

The fact that the gun will not fire with magazine removed makes it a safe arm around the house where small children might pick it up. Small children would also find it about impossible to move the side safety from safe to firing position. Many accidents have occurred with our well-known .45 Colt auto, but we do not anticipate them happening with this new arm. Even though a loaded round is in the chamber, the gun cannot fire unless the magazine is also in place and locked. When the side safety is pushed down to the safe position, it cannot fire, regardless of the magazine, or whether it is fully loaded. It is a SAFE auto pistol.

New 1955 Smith & Wesson

Smith & Wesson has a 1955 model target revolver for the .45 auto and auto rim cartridge. The new gun is similar to the 1950 target model but incorporates a new U type main spring, making the arm easier and faster to cock. The new main spring eliminates the need for the trigger return spring and pin in the trigger return lever, and greatly improves the double action pull. The double action pull is softer and there is less

K-.22 Masterpiece, target hammer and target stocks.

.38 Military and Police, round butt, Airweight.

reaction when the sear lets go than with the conventional flat main spring. The faster, easier cocking helps materially in timed and rapid fire matches.

The new arm also has a forward balance, as many target shooters like a muzzle heavy weapon. This is accomplished by the use of a wide heavy top rib and a heavily encased ejector rod with a 6½ inch barrel. In addition to the U type main spring, the new arm also has a wide finger contouring trigger, fully grooved. It makes the trigger pull feel much lighter than it really is and gives the trigger finger a much wider surface contact, helping materially in fine target work. The gun is fitted with Smith & Wesson target stocks that incorporate a filler in front of the front strap and behind the trigger guard and which are over a quarter inch longer, giving the hand a better target grip with the weight of the gun resting on the second finger, thus allowing freer trigger finger movement. A wide hammer spur, a quarter of an inch longer than standard, aids materially in fast cocking of the arm. This long wide hammer spur is possible only with the target grips that force the hand lower than does the conventional magna type grip. Altogether the 1955 target adds up to one fine target arm for those who prefer to shoot the jacketed .45 auto ammunition in a revolver for match work instead of the .45 Auto Colt.

The new arm balances and holds very steadily on the target and its wide trigger promotes perfect trigger control. The heavy forward balance gives a very steady hang to the piece and the big full grip makes for comfort in long target strings. Very close groups have been made with the new Smith & Wesson and we expect more high scores to be run up with its continued use.

New Colt Python

Colt has two new arms scheduled for limited production, both to sell at $125.00. One is the standard

.38 Military and Police, round butt, 2 inch barrel.

.38 Military and Police, square butt, 4 inch barrel.

Single Action Army Colt and will be made today exactly like the old gun whose production was dropped at the start of the last war. Too bad that Colt could not see the writing on the wall. They would have a monopoly on S. A. Army revolver production if they had improved and modernized the old gun as Ruger and Great Western have done. The new production will be an exact duplicate of the old 1873 gun and needs no further comment here, except that its market will be limited to collectors and Romanticists with Ruger and Great Western selling target sighted S. A. pistols with greatly improved actions, to those who want a gun to shoot. The new Colt will come in .38 Special and .45 Colt calibers.

The other gun is Colt's supreme effort in a fine target arm on the famous old Officer's model .41 frame, but greatly refined as to weight, balance, sights, action and stocks. It carries a new type of barrel with a round lug full length underneath the barrel, encasing the extractor rod, for the first time in Colt history. This one feature alone is worthwhile but they should have added a latch to the front of the extractor rod or a yoke latch at the front of the frame. This lug adds considerably to the muzzle weight of the arm. The barrel is also fitted with a full length ventilated rib—something we do not care for on a sixgun as it adds three more places for dirt and rust to collect that are hard to clean. On top of this rib is a full length tapered ramp, leaving room for only a low front sight blade of excellent ramp type design. An Accro rear sight is fitted into the rear of the flat-top frame much the same as on the Ruger Black Hawk model.

It is adjustable for both elevation and windage. The barrel length is six inches. The hammer spur is long, wide and well checkered and may prove a bit long for hands which ride high on the grip. The stocks are full checkered walnut and cover the entire front strap and butt of the gun as well as adding a filler behind the trigger guard. They are very well shaped, large, and make a very fine target grip. The action is highly polished and both single and double action trigger pulls are exceptionally smooth and good. This gun, in fact, has the best D. A. pull we have seen on a Colt double action. The gun is very fast and easy to cock for timed and rapid fire matches. Finish is Colt royal blue, a very good, highly polished, blue job. All told the Colt Python, is the finest double action target revolver this company has produced. It weighs 44 ounces or exactly the same as a Smith & Wesson .357 Magnum with 6 inch barrel, but carries more weight at the muzzle and in front of balance for steady offhand target work.

It is made in both .38 Special and in .357 magnum, and is a truly fine target arm, but personally, we would still prefer a Smith & Wesson Outdoorsman or Magnum with their .45 caliber frames and less muzzle heaviness. Men wanting a heavy target .38 or the same in .357 magnum and who prefer a muzzle heavy arm will find the new Colt to their liking. It should become a very popular target arm. We found that it holds very steadily on the target and also cocks very easily and should be excellent for target or game shooting.

The High Standard Sentinel

One revolver, entirely new in design, has appeared over the horizon in recent months—the High Standard Sentinel. It is a low priced $34.75 nine shot revolver chambering the .22 L. R. Cartridge. This gun is made in 3 inch or 5 inch barrel and was designed by my friend, Harry Sefried. It is the first radical change in revolver frame design we have seen in a great many years. The frame is in two parts, namely the frame proper, and the grip and trigger guard. The grip is one piece with a through bolt and shaped much like the early Colt Cap and Ball actions in .31 and .36 caliber and has about the same angle to the frame. It is a double action revolver holding nine rounds. The cylinder has a drilled hole rachet and counter sunk shell heads cut out for the firing pin so it will not burr chamber rims. The cylinder latch is also an innovation and a complete change from existing models, yet it is a solid frame gun as only the crane swings out for ejection and reloading. It has simultaneous ejection, and a hardened cone shaped pin in the rear end of the base pin that fits into a tapered hole in the aluminum alloy frame. That is the main cylinder lock but an enlargement of the extractor rod also recesses into the frame cut to hold the front end of the base pin in alignment.

It is a very hard gun to disassemble or reassemble and this should be done only at the factory, as it is complicated. The barrel is simply pinned in the frame with a cross pin. Barrel and cylinder, crane and extractor rod are of steel as well as the hammer and trigger and internal parts. The grip is of plastic and in one piece. The rear sight can be driven either way for windage adjustment. The front sight is a ramp type fitted by a dovetail lengthwise of the barrel—the same as we recommended to Bill Ruger for his Single Six. It is anchored by an allan screw.

The sample tested, Serial No. 2775, with a 3 inch barrel, had excellent sights and trigger pull both single and double action. High Standard was a bit stingy with front sight material or their man who ground down the front sight was over-energetic, as the front sight is far too low making this specimen sighted for long range. Judge Martin, to whom it belongs, claimed it was a darn good 200 yard gun. The frame is given a non-glare gun metal finish and the steel parts, except the hammer and trigger, are blued. The finish is rough, not highly polished. Two pins and one stock screw seem to hold the whole assembly together.

The little gun seemed to shoot very accurately and was a very good gun for fast double action practice, either aimed fire or hip shooting. And the fact that it holds nine rounds is something to be appreciated in a .22 revolver. To open the cylinder, pull forward on the extractor rod and swing it out. This pulls the lug on the extractor rod forward out of engagement with its seat in the front of the frame and also the tapered pin at the rear of the base pin from its tapered seat in the recoil plate of the frame. It is a unique design. That it can be improved, we do not doubt. The front cylinder lock should have some study in our opinion. We would like to see High Standard bring this gun out in an all steel model and with higher finish and refinements even though cost would, of course, be doubled. The firing pin is integral with hammer. No malfunction or misfires occured throughout the tests. All told, it seems to be a good little gun for the price asked, and one that balances perfectly and has a remarkably well-shaped grip set at the correct angle to the frame. It is low enough behind the trigger guard so that the weight of the gun rests on the second finger, the same as the Colt, Ruger and G. W. Single actions do. This, and its excellent pointing from the hip make it a very fine understudy for the big caliber double action revolvers. It should prove a popular and practical gun for the fisherman or camper.

Great Western Single Actions

When we started this book we could not recommend the Great Western Single Action. The samples we had tested and which we had reports on all showed poor inspection, or none at all, and while they were made of best materials throughout and incorporated the new rebounding firing pin, they were not properly timed, the chambers did not always line up with the barrel and the main spring was twice as heavy as necessary. The trigger pulls were terrible. The gun needed several hours of expert gunsmithing before being fired.

Since then we are happy to report Great Western has really gotten on the ball and is now cooking on all four burners. They overhauled their design and inspection departments, put in some gunsmiths who know the score and are now turning out first class single actions. Their guns are a very close copy of the original Colt except that the frame is very slightly longer. Beryllium copper, more shock resistant than steel, is used in the hand, trigger and bolt. The first ones we tested were accurate but had such hard trigger pulls they were difficult to shoot accurately.

All the late manufacture Great Western single actions we have seen and tested are excellent arms: accurate, properly timed and adjusted and for the most part have good trigger pulls. The frames are case hardened in colors and the rest of the gun is given

Highway Patrolman, 6 inch barrel, target stocks.

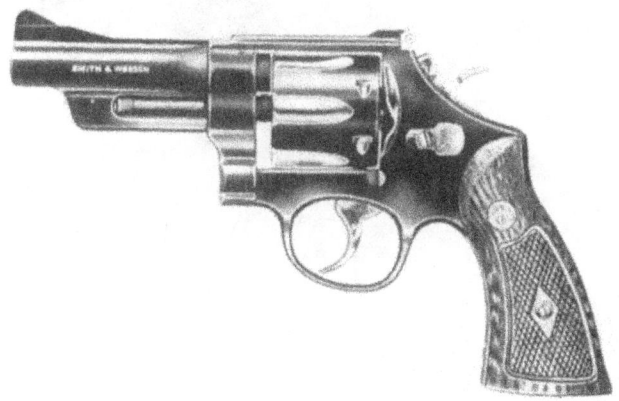

Highway Patrolman, 4 inch barrel.

a high, bright blue that is a better finish than we have ever observed on a factory Colt single action. Grips are a plastic imitation of stag. We would prefer ivory or wood but these grips are superior to the old Colt hard rubber type that warped and pulled out of shape in the sun until it was next to impossible to keep them tight on the gun. The sides of G. W. hammers are highly polished, the thumb piece and back blued. The straps and guard are of steel the same as the Colt. The firing pin was first a Christy, later redesigned into a larger and stronger firing pin of the separate type. The hammer was cut out on its face to fit over this firing pin and gave a poor appearance when at full cock. The hammer spur is too long for most men, as at full cock it comes down over the back strap too far, crowding the hand.

Standard sights, like those on the original Colt are furnished and also a target model with the frame flattened off on top and a Micro Target rear sight screwed to the top rear of the frame. This with a Micro ramp type front with one-eighth inch blade silver soldered to the barrel, completes the target model. We have one in 4¾ inch .44 Special and it is a very fine single action in every way, perfectly timed, sighted and very accurate. It has performed perfectly with factory loads and our heavy loads and is very accurate at extreme ranges, the real test of any sixgun.

We had considerable correspondence with Mr. William Wilson, President of Great Western Arms Company, both before and after testing this gun as to ways and means to further improve the gun along the lines of those designed by Croft and myself some thirty years ago. We are happy to report that Mr. Wilson is looking well ahead in arms design and now has introduced a new and entirely different model of the Great Western—the new DEPUTY. This gun, which will be in production soon, incorporates an entirely new design on the original frame and grip.

The hammer is a shorter Bisley type with wide

.357 Magnum, 8⅜ inch barrel.

.357 Magnum, 6½ inch barrel.

thumb piece and with improved notches. The trigger is wide with a sturdy sear instead of the old narrow one. A completely redesigned action eliminates the small easily broken parts of the old S.A. which often caused trouble. The flat type sear and bolt spring have been changed to coil springs and the split bolt has also been changed. Also, the handspring has been altered. The hammer nose has been cut off to go under the rear sight as on the models designed by Croft and myself. I believe they will also incorporate a new base pin latch which I designed long ago, or one very similar, before the gun comes into production. The sights are something new in that the entire sighting plane is one piece from muzzle to hammer. This is set down in the form of a rib in the frame and along the length of the barrel ending at the front in a ramp-type, blade front sight. Pilot models have the aiming portion of the front sight at least an inch too far to the rear for maximum sight radius and we have urged that they change this design to the sloping ramp type with the highest portion of the front sight flush with the muzzle of the gun to give maximum sight radius. The rear sight raises into a ramp with Smith & Wesson type adjustments of the sight blade for both windage and elevation. This rear sight blade is also set back for maximum length between sights, right over where the tip of the old obsolete hammer used to rest, yet leaves ample thumb clearance for cocking. This sighting system makes a very attractive gun with a full rib from rear sight to muzzle. It is the best of modern sixgun sights in design and adjustments. It also gives a fairly low sighting line. The whole gun has a beautiful outline and will be furnished in plain satin blue or high bright blue, with the frame either blued or case hardened in colors if desired. The case hardened frame will cost five dollars more. The new Deputy will be made in two lengths of barrel. The 4 inch is standard and a mighty fine length for the peace officer or gun fighter, and a handy length for any use. The Target model, also at five dollars greater cost, will have a six inch barrel.

Grips are plastic imitation stag, the same as the older models of Great Western single actions. In this new gun Great Western has departed from the old

1873 Colt design, and brought out a first class modern single action along the lines Croft and I, and many others, urged for thirty years. It follows our design very closely in all things except the top of the frame which we flat-topped. This new treatment with a full rib of Great Western design, reminiscent of the old King ribbed S.A. sight design, makes a very fine looking gun. The new Deputy has an improved floating firing pin. We hope it will be made to allow the carrying of six cartridges in the chambers safely. We like the hammer and trigger, they are the best yet turned out on a commercially made single action. The best of modern steels are used in this gun and it should stand up to a lifetime of use and be ideal for the heaviest safe loadings.

The Deputy will be made in .22 L.R. and .38 Special at $75.00 and in .357 magnum or, as they call their version of this cartridge, the .357 Atomic to sell at $98.95 and in .44 Special at $137.50. We believe they should bring it out in .45 Colt as many peace officers will prefer that load in factory loaded ammunition to the .357 or .44 Special. If restricted to factory loads we would prefer the .45 Colt for serious business.

High cost of production of single order items is the reason for the extra cost of the .357 and .44 Special calibers. If enough are ordered the price should come down on these calibers. The Great Western Deputy is a truly modern single action in every respect. In the four inch barrel it is an ideal gun for social purposes and for the peace officer. It is short enough to be easily concealed in a belt holster and to ride high enough to not punch a car seat or chair when the owner is seated.

The only criticism I have of the new arm is the shape of the front sight blade. I believe it should be changed to the sloping ramp-type and thus gain over an inch in sight radius. Sixgun cranks and shooters are going to prefer the Deputy of Great Western over the old standard model Great Western or the Colt Single action, as it and the new Ruger .357 are the first truly modern single actions as to design. I predict that both will enjoy a large sale. The Colt Company could not see a modern target single action, but both Bill Ruger and Bill Wilson are far sighted enough to see and meet the demand. Shooters will soon have two ultra modern, highly dependable, single actions in target models that will not fail from small parts breakage. These guns have far fewer moving parts than a double action, and with the new modern design of action and coil springs they become the most reliable handguns ever turned out. No gun is better suited to heavy loads, for so little of the rear end of the barrel projects through the frame and their solid frame makes for strength. They are just as fast on the draw as double action for the first shot, but after the first shot the double action is far speedier than any single action for accurately placed hits.

The single action is a fine gun for the horseman, the hunter or for the hills. In heavy calibers it is also a great defense gun as anyone hit with a heavy load is not going to shoot back accurately, which gives time to cock the weapon for another target. They are also ideal for the hand loader who wants to use heavy loads for game shooting.

We would not like to have the reader get a wrong impression from our comparisons of speed of fire between the double action and the single action revolver. The two guns are in a close tie for the first shot, with the double action running ahead from then on, but it is a matter of split seconds. With low powered cartridges and easy targets the double action would have a great advantage, with .45's and difficult targets the double action advantage would be considerably cut. In the end, it boils down to a question of proficiency. Speed and precision are more likely to be personal than mechanical.

New Great Western Derringers

Great Western has also redesigned the old Remington .41 caliber Double Derringer, popular for more than half a century. The new gun incorporates coil springs, and cocks so easily that any lady can handle it. The hinge has been greatly strengthened so it will not break easily as did the old Remington. They have also changed from a cast iron frame to the best of modern steel S.A.E. 4130 chrome moly. All flat springs have been eliminated and the caliber changed to .38 S. & W. center fire. This formerly popular little gun, now modernized, will sell at $49.50 in standard finish satin blue with black grips. High bright blue will be obtainable at special order; also nickel, silver or gold plating and pearl or ivory grips as well as three styles of engraving. This is, of course, at extra cost. Here is truly the gun for the ladies' hand bag. It is very small, as was the original Remington from which it was redesigned. It is also an excellent under cover gun for the peace officer or soldier for emer-

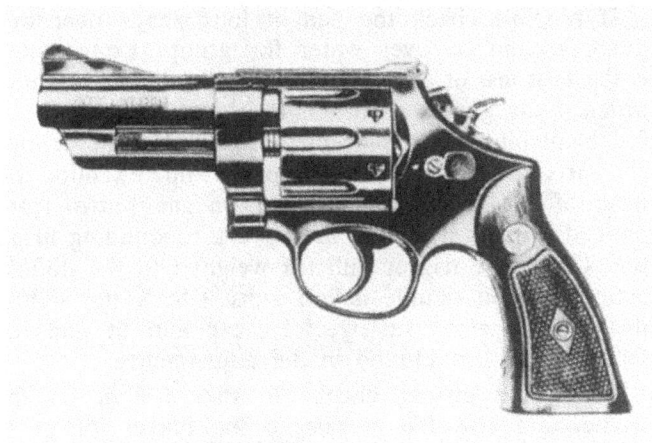

.357 Magnum, 3½ inch barrel.

gency use, or for anyone for a close range defense gun. The small cartridge is not the best for serious work but is far better than no gun at all and is quite effective at close range where such a gun would be used. This new gun should be in the gun stores by the time this is published.

It is possible we have crowded the line a trifle in our effort to keep this manuscript up to date. Great Western's history is mostly before it. Their production is not yet fully standardized. Our contacts with the Company induce us to think that they have gun-sense, can be taught by experience, and are genuinely interested in producing the best guns possible to make.

Check Used Guns

Many times excellent used sixguns or auto pistols are offered for sale. The buyer should give them a careful scrutiny before purchasing. Often they are in first class condition and can be purchased at a saving, but a secondhand gun may look good and be a lemon. A few cautions on what to look for may not be amiss. First, check the barrel for pits or worn throat and see if bottom of grooves ahead of the cylinder are clean and bright, or gas burnt from much shooting. It is well to upset a soft slug in the bore and push it through from the muzzle to check grove diameter. Next, check the cylinder for pitting around the muzzles of chambers. Check the gap between barrel and cylinder. It should not be excessive, and usually should have from .003 to .010 inch clearance. Upset a soft slug in chamber mouths and mike it. It should not be over .003 inches larger in .38 caliber and preferably not over .002. In a .44 or .45, we would prefer the chamber mouths within .003 inches of the groove diameter, but many run larger. We have seen old .45 Colt S. A. guns with .450 groove diameter, and chamber mouths .457 or larger. This is a dangerous combination with heavy loads, as the slug upsets to fill the chamber mouth before it hits the end of the barrel and then has to be swaged down to get into the barrel proper.

Next check the cylinder for alignment. With large caliber guns, a sheet of thin white paper may be placed over the recoil shield and with the morning or evening sun shining over your shoulder and down the barrel, you can see if the chambers line up perfectly with the bore when the arm is cocked.

Sometimes one can get a good light behind the gun and through the firing pin hole to determine whether the chambers line up, and sometimes a side light reflected in on a piece of white paper will tell the tale. Twenty-two calibers are hard to check because of the recessed cylinder heads and small bore. Next, see if the bolt-cuts in the cylinder are clean and sharp, and the bolt locks surely and with little cylinder looseness when the gun is cocked. Check to see if the hand is long enough by cocking the gun slowly. If the cylinder revolves fully to place, and locks securely, the timing and bolt are satisfactory. If the cylinder stops before reaching alignment with the barrel after cocking, and the cylinder can be turned with the fingers, the hand is too short, and the cylinder will only index if the gun is cocked fast, to flip it in place.

If a single action, check the safety and half-cock notches and the full-cock notch. This can be done by feel. Many old S. A. Colts have both safety and half-cock notch removed so they cannot break the sear off the top of the trigger if the hammer slips while cocking the arm. These will be slightly slower to load as you must hold the hammer at half-cock position with one hand while removing spent cases or reloading.

Check the muzzle for burrs and the general appearance of the gun. A gun may be worn bright from much carrying in the holster and still be clean and sound in every respect. If the gun shows abuse, better not buy it. If it has been dropped or nails have been driven with the butt, better pass it up. The straps may be sprung. A glance at the angle of stock to frame on the S. A. Colt or Lightning models will tell you if the stocks squarely abutt the frame and whether or not the straps have been bent or sprung by hitting some hombre over the head. Next look over the frame from the rear and also from the muzzle and see if the barrel appears to be in alignment. Many guns used in police work to club some adversary have their barrels bent up and out of alignment with chambers.

Check the screws and see if the heads are clean and true or if battered from too much use of an ill-fitting screw driver. Check the fit of the side plate on double action guns and see if it fits tightly and smoothly as it should or if it has been on and off so often that the edges are curled and rough. All these things indicate the use and care the gun has had.

Lastly, it is best to fire a dozen shots on a paper target squarely facing the shooter, both to check for accuracy and to see if all bullets print round and true without keyholing. If one or more chambers keyhole or tip the bullet, better reject the gun. Do this with standard ammunition, not wad-cutters as most wad-cutters tip at 50 yards.

If possible check the gun at long range over dry dusty ground or over water for group. Long range is the best test of any sixgun and will tell you in short order if the gun is accurate. It is also well to check for availability of replacement parts. If you cannot get parts and the gun is worn, pass it up. Examine the nose of the firing pin for pits or gas burns from pierced primers if it does not have a rebounding firing pin. Check the trigger pull for weight and the double action pull on double action guns. Check the sights, if they are target variety, for wear and fit and for looseness or lost motion in the adjustments.

With auto pistols, check the slide for fit on the frame, and also the muzzle of the barrel for fit in the barrel bushing. Check slide for battering of the cut in slide where the stop holds it when the last

9 mm. automatic pistol (single action).

cartridge is fired. Check the gun for looseness of slide on frame. If snug and tight and the bore is good, the chances are it is still a good gun, but a battered slide betokens much use and a loose gun is seldom accurate.

If an auto pistol has been fired extensively, the rear end of barrel just forward of the chamber will show a flattening of the lands. Invariably the grooves just ahead of the chamber will be gas burned and discolored, as hot gas escapes past the corners of hard bullet jackets and erodes the throat in all auto pistols shooting jacketed bullets. Twenty-two calibers are harder to check, but a careful scrutiny of the chamber and just in front of it, will tell if the bore is in good condition or not.

With all side-swing double action guns, check the locking of the crane and cylinder to the frame when the gun is closed. If the crane and cylinder are loose in their locking at the front end of cylinder and any side-play of the cylinder can be detected when the gun is closed, it is worn and can only grow worse with use. Colts are the worst offender in this respect as they have no forward cylinder lock. Check all cylinder guns by cocking them and then see if it is possible to revolve the cylinder either forward or backward with the fingers. If excessive movement is encountered, or if the cylinder can be moved from its locked position, you may be sure the bolt is worn or the bolt spring is weak, or that the bolt-cuts in the cylinder are rounded off at the corners. Reject any gun that does not lock tightly and securely when cocked or when the cylinder can be moved on its axis after cocking to any great extent. A gun with a worn bolt, or bolt-cuts, or a weak bolt spring, will allow the chamber to be fired when it does not quite line up with the barrel and this is fatal to accuracy.

Carefully check the rear end of the barrel for cracks with a good strong glass. The barrel should show no flaws at this, its weakest point, and the chambers should show no bulges under the bolt-cuts, indicative of the gun having been fired with excessively heavy loads.

Check the fired cases as they come from the chambers. Reject any gun that shows excessive expansion of the cases or hard extraction. When a case is hard to extract usually the chamber is bulged. Many revolvers will be found with one defective chamber, so should be rejected. Also check the condition of the recoil plate through which the firing pin passes when it strikes the primer. If the plate shows any cracks, either replace the plate or reject the gun. Check the position of the hammer at full cock on S. A. Colts. If it does not come back and engage the sear in the proper full cock position, you may be assured the full-cock notch has been torn out at some time and a new one has been filed in the hammer or the top of the sear has been broken off. If it is the sear, a new trigger will cure the damage. But if the hammer notches have been broken out and rebuilt, reject the gun or have a new hammer fitted. Check the base pin catch of S. A. Colts and see if it holds the pin securely during recoil of full loads. A careful check of used guns will save you money.

9 mm. automatic pistol (double action).

Chapter III

Learning To Shoot

IF POSSIBLE, get a good pistol shot for a coach when you take up pistol shooting. He will start you in proper position, teach you safe handling of your gun and many short cuts that will enable you to form good habits from the start. Start with the .22 caliber hand gun. Its light report and absence of recoil and extreme accuracy will give you confidence and teach you the rudiments of the art in much less time than if you start with a heavy gun. Practice safe handling of the gun from the start. Never point a gun at anything you do not want to shoot; never point the gun at anyone you do not want to kill. A sixgun or automatic pistol is a tool, and a deadly one; handle them as such. From the start, consider all guns as being loaded whether you know them to be empty or not. Treat them as loaded guns always and you will never have an accident. I am scared of empty guns and keep mine loaded at all times. The family knows the guns are loaded and treats them with respect. Loaded guns cause few accidents; "empty guns" kill people every year.

Hundreds of N.R.A. members come to my home each year to see my guns. When I tell them they are loaded, they then handle them with care. This not only makes for safety and a total absence of careless gun handling, but also saves the gun a lot of senseless snapping, with probable damage to the sears or firing pins. Show a person that a gun is loaded and they are far more apt to keep it pointed away from everyone and are not trying the trigger pull. The place to try a trigger pull is on targets with live ammunition.

So far we have never had a gun accident and mainly because we keep guns loaded and treat them as loaded guns. An empty gun is a dangerous gun, because it will then be handled carelessly and who knows when someone might have slipped a cartridge in the chamber or cylinder. Russian Roulette is not conducive to longevity. One never knows when he may need a gun, and if it is kept loaded, he knows he has a gun ready to use if necessary. Everyone, including himself, will treat the gun as loaded and handle it accordingly. Only last week the Sheriff called me in to investigate a case which illustrates the point. One man, crazy drunk, came at another with a knife. The sober citizen talked him out of using the knife, the while he backed to his bedroom and jerked a .45 New Service from its holster on the wall. He expected the gun to be loaded but his wife had unloaded it. When the knife man came for him, he snapped the gun three times before he realized it was empty, and then struck at the drunk's head with the barrel and dropped him to the floor. The drunk jumped up and received a blow which put him out cold. However, the gun weilder, had he not been very active and husky, could have gotten himself killed very easily by having an empty defense gun hanging on the wall. When you need a gun, you usually need it badly and have no time to load it, or look for cartridges. So my motto is keep them clean, oiled, loaded and ready for business. If all members of a family know a gun to be loaded, very few accidents will occur. It's the "empty gun" that accidentally kills people. The old excuse, "I did not know it was loaded," has never brought anyone back to life.

We are against the use of cap pistols. Youngsters should be taught early that guns are dangerous and only to be pointed at things you want to kill, never at friends and playmates. I never allowed a cap pistol on the premises and never allowed my youngsters to play with them or to point any arm at a human being. Kids are best trained from infancy in safe gun handling. When they are allowed to play cops and robbers and snap cap pistols at each other, they lose respect for a gun. Sooner or later they get their hands on the real thing and an accident may occur. Every time I see some youngster pointing a cap gun at a playmate or friend and popping off a cap, I feel like turning him over my knee and giving him the works. If everyone in this country would raise their children with due respect for firearms, there would be few accidents. Youngsters would grow into adults having due respect for safety and the proper handling of firearms.

When a child is old enough to shoot, he should

Bill Toney instructing U. S. Border Patrol.

then be taught how to use a real gun safely. Until he is old enough to be taught shooting, all guns should be kept out of his reach. As soon as children are old enough, we believe they should be taught to handle firearms and to hold them in respect. The cap pistol has no place whatever in this program.

When you start pistol shooting, first assume the correct position. Face the target squarely, then turn to about a 45 degree angle to the target. Extend the gun toward the target and see if it comes naturally and easily on the target. If not, shift the feet until it does. Usually the shooting arm should be extended toward the target at about a 45 degree angle to the way a person is facing. If you face the target too squarely when shooting with one hand, the groups are apt to be spread up and down. If you turn too much at right angles to the target, your groups will tend to have a lateral dispersion. This is caused by body sway. Individuals will require some difference in position, but select the one that allows the arm to be extended toward the target with the least body sway, either up and down or sideways, and is comfortable and relaxed. Put the non-shooting hand in the pocket of the trousers, or on the hip, or hook a thumb in the belt, but assume an easy relaxed position. Line the rear sight with the bead, or blade, held level with the top of the rear sight, bring the gun up on the target until the sights bear on the center of the bull, and start the trigger squeeze. You will not be able to hold steady—no one can. When the sights swing squarely on the bull, increase the pressure on the trigger; when they swing off the target, hold what pressure you have; when the sights come back, increase again until the gun is fired. You should know about when the gun will fire and try to finish the trigger squeeze with a careful increase in pressure just when the sights swing back on the bull. Watch the position of the sights carefully when the gun fires, for recoil will blot out the target. Call your shots where you saw the sights last. As long as you can call your shots you are not flinching. But, unless you have a clear sight picture in your mind and know where the sights were on the target when the gun was fired, you are flinching. Practice cuts down the amount of swing of your sights across the target and as muscles become trained, you will hold in a smaller circle and have more time to squeeze off the shot as the sights swing on the bull.

Adjust your sights until point of impact and point of aim coincide exactly. We do not believe in a six o'clock hold unless the gun has fixed sights and shoots high. The place to aim is where you want to hit.

With practice the trigger squeeze becomes much faster, until finally you can squeeze off a shot in a very short time interval with no jerk or flinch. If the arm gets tired, as it will at the start, lower the arm with the gun pointing at the ground, take a long breath, exhale part of it and start over again. Relax and rest between shots. In time you will learn to put most of the pressure necessary to fire the gun on the trigger as soon as the sights come on the target. This will allow you more time for aim and less time for the arm to become tired from holding. Never hold too long. If you cannot get the shot off in a decent time interval, lower the gun, rest, and try again. Strive to fire the gun the first time the sights bear correctly

Bill Toney, U. S. Border Patrol, awaiting signal to fire.

U. S. Border Patrol Pistol Team minus two members. Left to right: John C. Forman; Elmer W. Hilden; W. T. Toney Jr.; Harlon B. Carter; Jeff Fell; William C. Joyner; Presly O'Gren. This is the present Border Patrol Pistol Team minus Joe White and Andy Mosser.

on the bull. Nothing can be gained by holding too long and much is to be lost. The longer you hold, the more the eye will become fatigued and the sights fuzz up, or grow whiskers and the arm will become more tired, and less steady. Learn to put the initial pressure on the trigger as soon as the sights bear, and increase the pressure steadily, but surely, until the gun fires. If possible, fire the first time the sights cover the center of the bull.

Always take a high firm grip on the gun, but do not grip too hard and cause the muscles of the wrist to tremble. Try to keep the gun in a straight line with the forearm and the arm and gun in a straight line with the eye. The hand should always grip the gun high and with the wrist squarely behind it. Leave enough clearance so the hammer spur does not come down under or on the web of the hand between thumb and forefinger. The nearer you can get your hand squarely behind the gun, and the higher the grip, the more the gun recoils straight to the rear and the closer it will group. A different grip on the gun will make it shoot differently, so strive to always hold the gun exactly the same way. Many fine target shots take the gun in the left hand and place it squarely in the crotch of the shooting hand, then fit their fingers around the grip to insure exactly the same hold on the gun for each string of shots. This care pays dividends in close groups. The second finger and the thumb are really your grip on a sixgun and the second finger should come up against the frame in back of the trigger guard. The weight of a sixgun should rest on the second finger. On many double action guns some sort of filler back of the trigger guard is a help. The Colt S.A. Army, of all sixguns, has the best grip in this respect, as the weight of the gun rests squarely on that second finger. For folks with long fingers, the trigger should come nicely, either across the ball of the tip joint, or in the crotch of the first joint. Avoid having the trigger finger press against the frame at all costs. Keep that trigger finger as clear of the frame as its length will permit. Its job is to press the trigger, not to hold the gun. This, of course, is for single action shooting. Double action shooting requires an entirely different technique.

The thumb should be laid on the ball of the frame on single action Colts, or on the cylinder latch with double action Colts for slow fire, or projected upward at a 45 degree angle when using automatic pistols.

Billy Toney coaching U. S. Border Patrol.

Border Patrol Team in late 1930's. Left to right: Askins; P. K. Crosby; unknown; Tommy Box; Bobby Jackson.

Bill Toney instructing U. S. Border Patrol.

U. S. Border Patrol shotgun practice. Bill Toney throwing targets.

When shooting double action, the thumb should be pressed against the side of the frame and downward toward the tip of the trigger finger, not laid up on the cylinder latch. Many fine shots do not lay their thumb on the cylinder latch, but press it against the side of the frame below the latch. They seem to do just as well as those using thumb rests or using the latch of the cylinder for a thumb support. With guns of heavy recoil this is the better procedure as the latch recoils backward sharply and may batter the thumb nail. Men with large hands will usually find their best bet with Colt, Ruger and G. W. single action guns is to curl the little finger under and around the butt of the gun. It is then in the best position to aid in cocking the gun during recoil for the next shot. Keep that wrist in a straight line, with hand squarely behind the gun. From the muzzle of the gun to the elbow should be one straight line.

Place the feet about two feet apart—more for tall people than for short ones. Keep them apart and balance with a trifle more weight on the forward foot. This correct placing of the feet with relation to the target, at about a 45 degree angle and spread wide enough to offer maximum support of the body, is very important. Hold the head up in a natural relaxed position and bring the shooting arm and gun up into line with the eyes in a natural easy stance. Make no attempt to hold the gun down in recoil; let it raise naturally and easily. Grip the gun not hard but firmly and relax your whole body. A comfortable relaxed position is not tiring and will add many points in a long string. Maintain the gun and forearm as one shooting unit and let it raise naturally in recoil. Don't fight recoil. Relax and let the gun turn up in your hand as it recoils. With the old Colt single action, the gun naturally rolls in your hand as it fires and this in turn brings the thumb up ready to hook over the hammer spur for the next shot. With double action guns the hump at the top of the grip limits the amount of movement and these guns should not roll or turn up in the hand, but an even grip be retained from shot to shot and only the thumb moved

Courtesy of U. S. Border Patrol.
Colonel Askins instructing trainees at Border Patrol School.

Bill Toney instructing class of Border Patrolmen.

to cock the gun. Do not shift the grip on a double action gun when cocking it. Maintain that same firm even grip on the gun and as it raises in recoil, move only the thumb upward to cock the gun while you maintain the same exact grip on the stock. With the .45 and other large auto pistols, a firmer grip is necessary. This grip should be maintained so that you simply pull the gun and forearm down out of recoil and in line with the target for the next shot. However, a grip that will cause the wrist to tremble is fatal to accuracy. The revolver can be shot with a looser grip than the .45 auto. An even pressure on the gun is necessary to keep the group at the same elevation. The larger pistols are as sensitive to a change in grip pressure or position as the strings of a violin. Grip the same each time.

Never take a freak or strained position. Adjust your feet until the gun points naturally and do your shooting from the easiest, most relaxed position, you can find.

Both eyes should be kept open. With practice your shooting eye will become the master and it will see and align your sights while the other eye merely sees the target. Point your thumb at some object and close both eyes, then open them and see if your thumb does not stay on the object for one eye or the other. If it does, that is your master eye. If you are right handed and your right eye stays on the object with the thumb in line, then all is well, but if you find the left eye to be the master then considerable training is necessary. Align your gun on the target with both eyes closed, then open the right eye and then the left and if the sights stay glued to the target for your right eye, then you are all right, but if the sights shift when you open the left eye, then it's best to open the shooting eye fully and sort of squint the left or non-shooting eye, seeing as much as possible of the target without looking at the sights. By constant practice you can train either eye to become the master and then the other eye merely sees the target. Nearly

Bill Toney, winner of the National Pistol Championship, 1952, looking over one of his tight groups.

Bill Toney with class of Border Patrolmen ready to fire on man targets.

all of the best shots shoot with both eyes open, and you should, if possible.

Some folks are handicapped by having their master eye on the wrong side, that is, they may be left handed and have the right eye the master, or vice versa. But we believe with practice they can train the eye to become the master on whichever side they shoot. Constant practice with the thumb aimed at some object or other will greatly hasten the process, if one eye must be trained to become the master. Squinting of the non-shooting eye will also help, and in time it becomes automatic for one eye to see the sights on the target and the other to merely see the target.

Oldsters whose eyes are getting far-sighted, may find they see the sights in better relation on short barreled guns than on long barreled guns. Also the Merit iris shutter attachment for shooting glasses is a great boon for target shooting for many, as they can stop down the aperture until the sights show up sharp and clear. This is the best answer for target shooting with eyes that are far-sighted and it also helps near-sighted shooters.

Practice your breathing carefully. Take a full breath as you raise your gun on the target, then exhale about half of it and hold the rest until the shot is off. With practice this becomes automatic and the subconscious takes over so that you do these things naturally with no thought on your part.

Always start pistol practice at a big target at close range. After you can hit it regularly and easily, it is time enough to increase the range. Move the target back as your skill increases, until you are at the standard distance. It's well to start with a 20 inch target at ten yards and continue to shoot at this close range until you can stay in the black before moving the target farther away. A good coach is of inestimable value. He will soon spot your faults in technique and help you no end in overcoming them. After a string of five or six shots, its well to take the gun in the other hand and flex or relax the fingers and grip of the shooting hand. Then when you start the next string be sure and obtain exactly the same grip on the gun as for the former string. Rest the eyes also between strings and even between shots, in slow-fire, by looking off at other objects away from the target, or at the coat sleeve or hand. When you pick up the gun for the next string, bring the sights in alignment with the eye, with top of front sight level with top of the rear sight and an even strip of light on each side of the front sight. Raise the gun up on the target until it bears on the bull while you take up initial pressure on the trigger and finally, as the sights bear right, get the shot off as soon as possible. Nothing is gained by a long aim. It only gives the wobble gremlins a chance to get in with their skullduggery.

In rapid-fire shooting, keep the eyes glued on the target between shots and bring the gun back on the target and in correct relation with the sights and eyes without head movement. The gun will recoil upwards anyway and the sights will then be sadly out of alignment. Strive to do everything the same way each shot so that the gun and arm naturally come back on the target as they recover from the uplift of recoil.

Good shots are not born, they are made by careful conscientious training. The best shots practice daily. You can put up a target in your home and fill the gun with empty cases and practice several rounds of dry fire per day and greatly increase your ability in a short time. Always place empty cases in the gun to cushion the blow of the firing pin, so it is not broken from constant dry firing. Strive always for that sight picture. And you must know just where the sights were each time the gun fired, or you are flinching. Flinching is fatal to accurate shooting. Once this habit is acquired it is hard to break, and the best method is to have the coach load the gun, if a revolver, with some loads and some empties, not letting you know what is under the hammer until the gun snaps or fires. If you flinch on an empty case, it will be instantly apparent. Then is the time to fill the gun

1953 Winners N.R.A. Center-Fire Pistol Team Championship, U. S. Marine Corps (l. to r.) M/Sgt. Walter Fletcher; Lt. Col. Walter Walsh; Maj. Harwood, Team Captain; M/Sgt. Walter Devine; and M/Sgt. Fowler.

with empties and continue dry firing until you can see those sights squarely on the target each time the hammer falls and have a clear cut mental picture and call your shots.

Continue such dry firing until you do not flinch, then have the coach again load the gun, placing some loads along with the empties so that you never know if you are squeezing off on a dead primer, or a live one. In this way you can soon break the flinching habit, but it is a hard one to break alone and you need the assistance of a good coach, if flinching is ever started. This is another reason why all beginners should start with the .22 caliber. Recoil of heavy calibers is much more likely to cause the novice to flinch than is the lowly .22. Do not expect to become a good pistol shot overnight. It takes months and years of training both to train your muscles and to acquire proper shooting habits. Don't expect to do your best shooting on a full stomach, for you never will. One always shoots best on an empty stomach. If you take a drink occasionally, then take one if you want it. If you smoke, then continue to do so. Don't try to change your habits or reform yourself to become a pistol shot as it will usually work the other way. Excessive use of alcohol to the extent that it affects the eyes is bad and will ruin any man's shooting. On the other hand, many times I have seen match shooters who were jittery and had a tummy full of angle worms, so to speak. A drink of whiskey frequently took the springs out of their tummies and calmed them down until they were deadly accurate shots. To be a good shot, just be your normal self, do not eat to excess or drink to excess or smoke to excess. Maintain a calm even temperament as far as possible.

Left to right: Major Charles Askins, firearms editor of "Outdoor Life" magazine; Colonel Charles Askins, Jr., formerly Chief Instructor of Firearms, U. S. Border Patrol, and current National .22 Pistol Champion. Trophy shown in picture is to be presented to pistol shooters of Texas for annual competition.

Major General Julian S. Hatcher, U. S. Army Retd., Technical Director of *The American Rifleman*. A Very fine pistol shot and one of the greatest authorities on pistols and revolvers in the world.

Some match shooters have told me they did their best after being up late at night, but I do not believe it and think anyone who wants to get anywhere in the game is better off going to bed early and getting up early, then doing his shooting on a very light breakfast or just a cup of coffee, if he or she is a coffee drinker. Loss of sleep usually affects the eyesight, as does any stomach disorder, and should be avoided at all costs.

Heavy guns hold steadier, once the muscles are trained to them, than do light guns, and they swing more slowly on the target. For the start, a gun should be selected whose weight feels good and whose grip fits naturally. You will do your best work with an arm in which you have confidence and which fits you. After you have been trained with the .22 and can shoot 80 or better on the standard American target, then is time enough to try the heavier guns. The .38 Special is your next best bet. Practice should be continued with the .38 until you can do at least 80 on standard targets. Then is the time to tackle the big .44's and .45's. By this time the correct shooting habits you have formed from your work with the .22 and later with the .38 will take over and you will have no trouble graduating to the big gun. However, if you start practice with the big guns, you are likely to develop a flinching habit and your muscles, not being trained, will soon tire and your scores be bad enough to discourage you from further practice. So, start with the .22 and work with it for several months at least, then graduate to the .38 and lastly, when you are good with both the .22 and .38, take on the big guns. This procedure is just as necessary to become a good game or defense shot as it is to acquire a top rating among the target shooting clan.

Match nervousness is something that comes to everyone at one time or another. I have had it, and all other shooters have at one time or another. It can ruin the scores of a good shot very quickly. The best antidote is to relax, look over the other shooters and feel that you are just as good as they are, and that they do not look too big to beat. A cup of coffee or a drink of whiskey won't hurt you at all if you are used to them and it often helps let down the tension. Figure you are just as good as they are and that you don't give a hoot whether you win or not, but that you are just going up on the line and be your normal self, concentrating only on your target and placing each shot as near center as possible to the exclusion of everything and everyone around you. Just ignore and forget them all and figure out how close a group you can make on that target and just how accurate your gun and ammunition are, if you hold it carefully each shot. Such distractions of the mind often do wonders when the old Wandering Willies hit a match shooter. If you can get your mind off the match entirely, and think only of just making a nice neat small group on the target and concentrate every faculty on that one job, then you have match nervousness licked.

Hunters making their first shots on big game are not so different from a match shooter going up in a stiff match where all depends on a good score. Many times when guiding green hunters, after getting them in good range of a good head of big game, I have simply talked to them slowly, telling them to figure there is an old rusty tin can just back of the shoulder on the beast and to see if that little light patch back of the shoulder can be drilled right in the center just as if it were an old rusty can, and they have then calmed down, held steadily and placed their shot right where it should go.

Never practice too long in one day, as to do so will often form bad shooting habits. Do not shoot until the eyes and body are tired. Practice a limited amount each time, but do not shoot until you go stale. A little practice daily is far better than a lot in one day. Never get careless or hurry a shot; make them all as good as you possibly can. Master slow-fire first and then only, take up timed-fire. Master the latter before you take up rapid fire. Good shooting habits formed in slow-fire, will then carry you on through the timed and rapid-fire stages.

Timing is the essence of rapid and timed-fire. Very often shooters produce higher scores in timed and rapid-fire than they do in slow-fire, clearly showing that their first picture of the sights on the target is the clearest and if they get the shot off then, it is much more apt to be a ten than if they dwell on their aim until their eyes grow dim. It is well to learn to use less than the permitted time in all slow-fire and to finish timed and rapid-fire slightly ahead of the allotted time. The first time the sights swing on the target and bear right, the trigger should be pressed enough to fire the shot. It takes months of practice to teach the trigger finger to apply the initial pressure quickly, and confidence in rapid-fire work can only be gained through long practice. The old adage, "He who hesitates is lost," well applies to competitive pistol shooting. Learn to count your shots as you fire them, and know when the string is finished. It is always well to finish a second ahead of the turning of the targets. Rapid-fire practice will enable one to use up his full time in an even cadence and spacing of shots, allowing just so much time to pull the gun down out of recoil and just so much time to get the sights back on the bull. Target pistol shooting is a highly specialized and exacting game. I cannot overemphasize the importance of acquiring exactly the same grip on the gun at the start of each string of shots and in rapid or timed-fire, maintaining an even grip pressure on the gun through the entire string.

With the .45 auto, grip and finger pressure must be exactly the same or the group will shift its zero more with this gun and its short sight radius than any other handgun I know. If a slump occurs in one's .45 scores, he should immediately drop back to the Service Ace or the Conversion unit and practice with the .22 caliber for a time. Light loads for the .45 that cut down recoil and allow the big gun to settle back on the target in the least possible time, are useful until one has thoroughly mastered it.

Unless service ammunition is specified in the match, one will do better shooting, as a rule, with the lighter handloads. The big gun tends to twist and recoil to the side more than does a revolver and should be shot with a firm grip. Practice alone will teach one to pull it down out of recoil and on the bullseye in the least possible time, allowing a specified time to aim and squeeze off the next shot. A smooth, even timing of the shots will develop an even cadence and then the shooter is on the way toward success.

A uniform sight picture is an absolute essential to accurate grouping of shots on the target. Never change

An excellent Army pistol team: (l. to r.) Capt. Ben Curtis, Lt. Col. Thomas Sharpe, team captain Col. Perry D. Swindler, M/Sgt. Huelet L. Benner, and Maj. William Hancock.

The firing line at Tampa, Florida, scene of the National Midwinter Matches.

the sight picture on any hand gun. Always fill the rear notch level with the top of the front sight, so that the top of the front sight and the top of the rear notch make a straight horizontal line. Never cant the gun. Hold it level and keep the notch full of the front sight. One-eighth inch sights, we feel are better than one-tenth inch or any narrower sight. There must also be plenty of white showing on each side of the front sight in the rear notch, to insure precise centering.

Maintain a perfect sight picture at all costs. The head, the shooting arm and the gun should be held in a straight line, as one unit, with the sight picture perfect; then move the whole unit to line up with the bullseye. If the group goes high, shift the aiming point down rather than taking a finer sight. Hold at six o'clock if necessary. You are always shooting for the center of the bullseye. The sights should be adjusted to shoot there. If due to grip, light changes or temperature, the gun starts shooting high or to one side, shift the point of aim with relation to the center of the bull, but *never* change your sight picture. In all target shooting keep the sights smoked black. Employ the old carbide lamp or the new spray cans of prepared sight blacking, but keep those sights black. It is well to blacken the whole top of the gun to eliminate glare. With the .45 auto, high sights are an advantage as they keep the line of aim above the heat waves over the slide which are much more apparent with low sights in long strings.

The shooter will have to study out his own problems of vision. We have known pistol shooters like Dick Tinker who could not see a bullseye at 20 yards without his glasses, but was an excellent target shot. There were others who were equally good but farsighted. This ailment seems to be common to most of us as the years roll around. We can still see perfectly at a distance but the sights begin to fuzz up and grow whiskers.

Our friend Bill Mitchel of the Mitchel Optical Company has done considerable research on the problem of fitting shooting glasses to both rifle and pistol shooters. The eyes of the pistol shooter who can see the target perfectly and the sights dimly, due to farsightedness, can be corrected to bring his sights in sharp and perfectly clear, but then his target will haze. Many target shooters say they do their best work with sharp sights and a hazy bull. We have tried both methods but seem to shoot best with clear sight of the bull and some growth of whiskers on the sights. In fact our eyes are not yet farsighted enough in good light for glasses to be much help, but in dim lights and indoor ranges, the shooting glasses with correction of focal length to correspond to the sight picture seems to help a great deal.

One must maintain that sight picture at all costs, and if he cannot see well enough to maintain a true and clear sight picture, then correction is needed in his glasses.

One gadget we have found that will sharpen up the sight picture with plane lenses, is the little Merit Iris Shutter that can be fitted to the shooting glass lens by suction cup. You peer through a tiny aperture that is adjustable and can be stopped down to give you a perfect picture of both target and sights when the eyes are so bad as to make good scores impossible without the gadget. We recommend all who are having trouble with vision of the sights to try the Merit Iris Shutter disc on their shooting glasses. It will mean many points in a match. Target pistol shooting allows such aids to clear vision and the non-aiming eye will line you up on your target.

If any trouble occurs with maintaining a clear sight picture, we would first recommend a trial of this Merit Iris shutter on the shooting glasses stopped down until side lights are eliminated and the sights and target show clearly. Many shooters whose eyes are past the stage where they can maintain accurate aim of the sights, can be greatly helped with this little gadget on their glasses, and I feel that it is better than having the glasses corrected for either the sights or the target alone. Mitchell Optical Company now furnishes shooting glasses with their own adjustable aperture affixed to their glasses.

Never practice until the eyes and the muscles grow

tired. Fifty shots per day is plenty as a rule, and less is advisable at the start.

Learning to become a good practical game shot is not so difficult as learning the match target game. One should learn all the essentials of good one handed target shooting and be able to use the gun in one hand on game when the other hand is occupied, but when both hands are available for game shooting, they should be used. One can bring the gun on the target or game quicker with both hands than with one, and can also grip it better and squeeze off the shot more quickly with two hands, with less chance of moving the sight picture off the game as the trigger is pressed. Start at close range with big targets. Tin cans or bottles are excellent. Move back only as skill increases and in all game shooting, shoot only at ranges where you can be certain of making good killing hits, unless worthless vermin is being shot. Even then, the sporting thing is to make clean kills or not shoot.

Grip the gun normally in the shooting hand, whether right or left, then bring the other hand up loosely under the shooting hand to form a good steady rest for the shooting hand. Never grip the gun with both hands. It will shoot to a different point of impact if you do so. In two handed game shooting, face the game or target squarely with the body and feet well spread for easy balance and support. Maintain that same correct sight picture you first learned on the target range and then bring the sight picture to bear on your game animal and where you want to hit it and squeeze off the shot in the least possible time. Game will not always wait for a slow aim before it jumps or takes wing. With a sitting bull frog or a perched horned owl you may have all the time in the world, but a rabbit or squirrel or grouse may have seen about all of you it wants and is liable to move any time; so it is imperative to learn to shoot as quickly as consistent with accuracy.

Don't hesitate to rest the arms out a car window or over a log or the shoulder against a tree bole. Take advantage of any rest offered in game shooting. You are not then on a target range and its rules do not apply. You are interested only in killing your game cleanly and that means placing the shot right and in the least possible time. When shooting at a deer or other big game with a heavy sixgun, pick out the vital area first and concentrate only on that portion of the animal the same as if that vital point were a bullseye or a tin can or bottle and hold and aim for that point alone. Take advantage of the best position time will allow. If you can get a seated position with your back against a tree bole or stump and a head rest, so much the better, then draw up the knees and hold the gun loosely between the two knees, using both hands in the same identical relation to the gun you used when standing. This is a very steady and deadly position and one can shoot both fast and with extreme accuracy. It is also one of the best positions for gun and ammunition testing. This seated back and head rest position is also best for all long range pistol shooting. It permits the arms to be fully extended holding the gun forward enough to give one an excellent, clean and sharp sight picture. We will take up the change in sight picture for long range shooting under that chapter, but in this one we are interested only in learning to do good elementary game shooting.

Another excellent game shooting position, also a good combat position, is to drop to the ground with the feet extended toward the target, then pull up the knee on the side of the shooting hand and extend the gun and shooting hand out along the side of the leg, resting the arm and side of the hand along the leg. Be careful to keep the gun clear of the knee both in the aiming position and also when the gun recoils as the butt of a heavy caliber gun can strike the knee a very painful blow in recoil. The nonshooting hand and arm should be brought around back of the head to form a head rest. This position gives greatest of all distance from shooting eye to sights and allows a perfect sight picture on the game with greatest visual acuity of all positions. Both the Army and the Police teach prone position with head and arms extended toward the target. This gives a very low position of value in combat, but places the gun too close to the eyes for best sight picture and is a far more strained position than the back position which we favor at all times over the prone position for pistol shooting. In prone position, the elbows must support the gun or

Three prominent pistol shooters who fired at the 1955 National Midwinter Matches: William B. Blankenship, Jr., C.W.O. Oscar K. Weinmeister, and Capt. Lloyd Hummert.

The cap and ball revolver matches staged during the National Matches provide real shooting sport for those competitors who don't mind the smoke of black powder.

the nonshooting hand must do so, and in either case the elevation of the target must be greater than in one or the other of the two back positions.

With practice it is surprising how quickly one can fall to a back position, either with his back supported by stump, tree, boulder or log and the knees drawn up for a two handed rest position with gun and hands between knees or the reclining position with the shooting hand rested along side the drawn up leg and the other hand used for a head rest. Either position provides plenty of latitude for both elevation and horizontal swing of the arm to cover the game, which the prone position does not. In game shooting we are not interested in target procedure, nor time limits, etc., but only in placing our sixgun or pistol slug where we want it on the game. Any advantage we can acquire from the position of the body is acceptable.

One old mountain man we knew for years killed all his meat with a 9 mm. Luger. He used a sling on the butt of his pistol that formed a loop around his neck and when he extended the gun in both hands the sling pulled tight around the back of his neck. He shot very steadily from this position and could use this sling, with snap attached to the ring in the butt of his Luger, even in a fairly strong wind when off-hand standing pistol shooting would have been difficult by any other method from the standing position. Elmer Purcell is now dead, but he killed a lot of deer, elk, goat and sheep with the old Luger from the two handed position with a tightly pulled sling extending from his neck and shoulder to the snap on the butt of his Luger. He used head shots on big game at all times where possible.

Another aid to accurate off-hand double handed pistol shooting, especially on windy days, is to pick up a stick and hold it in the nonshooting hand against the shoulder exactly as if it were a rifle stock and grip the stick back in the hand while the fingers of the stick gripping hand also help support the gun hand. This gives you both hands and a stick or cane for a shoulder stock and is very steady. Either the stick method or the sling method are superior to the two extended arms alone on windy days or for long shots. Where possible to assume the reclining or back rest position, they are the best and most steady positions to be had, next the arms rest positions over a log or out a car window or with shoulder against a tree bole, next the stick or sling position, and then the straight standing two handed shooting position. Lastly, of course, in game shooting comes the one handed target stance. In this phase of sixgun shooting,

The range at Camp Perry, Ohio, scene of the National Rifle and Pistol Matches. Pistol shooters are on the firing line in the foreground while the high power rifle firing line is visible in the distance.

we are interested primarily in killing game and target rules do not apply. Anyone can learn to shoot a sixgun or auto pistol one handed in straight target shooting. If you are interested in a sixgun or auto pistol for game shooting, general plinking and defense work, these positions should be first mastered as they will enable you to hit game or an adversary far quicker than standard target pistol practice.

The police officer is confronted with still different problems. He never knows when or where he will need a gun. He should never touch his gun until he has to use it, then shoot to kill and with the least possible loss of time. Gun bluffing is very poor business and we believe firmly in leaving the gun in its holster, or wherever carried, until necessary to use it. The officer should learn not only standard target shooting and get all he can from it, but also to take cover, learn to shoot accurately from any position and also learn to assume the best gun platform he can with his body in the least possible time. To be thoroughly prepared against any eventuality, he should be able to shoot from any position and also to take any position that will give him maximum effectiveness for his weapon and do it instantly in whatever situation that may arise. In addition he must be able to do fast hip shooting and fast double action work in close range gun fights. In defensive shooting, it is only the shots that hit that count, and the man who can deliver hits first is the one who lives longest. The same applies to the soldier in battle. He must put his adversary out of commission before the adversary's bullet claims him as its victim. To do so, often requires fast thinking and equally fast action with a gun.

The soldier or peace officer must learn to take cover instantly when a fight starts, if any cover is to be had, and if not, to instantly drop down into a good shooting position from which he can deliver accurate aimed fire if the range is at all extended. If the range is close, on a street or highway or in a building, then speed counts first and the man who can land the first smashing slug on his adversary usually wins the fight. In addition to all we have covered in target and game shooting technique, he must master quick draw and hip shooting, which is really not hip shooting at all but instinctive throwing or pointing of the gun without the use of sights. The peace officer or soldier must also be able to do accurate shooting by feel of his gun in the dark when many gun fights occur. This means constant practice under simulated conditions of a night fight. Months and years of actual practice are required to make a really competent gun man in all phases of the game and we learn more each year. The more one learns of the game and the better he becomes with his gun under all conditions, the more proficient he will be and the better his chances of survival when the need for accurate shooting occurs.

In learning defense shooting, either close range hip shooting or the use of the gun on distant targets, be they man or speeding automobile, one should start with big targets at close range. First learn accuracy and then extend the range as skill increases. Fast hip shooting is needed only for close range work, and when the range is extended to over 20 yards the sights should be brought to bear whenever possible. Accuracy then becomes more important than speed. Smooth even timing of both draw, aim and shooting are then what counts. As the range increases the need for speed decreases and accuracy becomes paramount. Strive for accuracy of delivered fire first and speed will come with practice. It is a wise man who knows his own limitations and acts accordingly. The man who uses his head as well as his gun is usually the winner in combat. Hip shooting and long range shooting will be covered in separate chapters as will double action shooting, since each is a game in itself.

Chapter IV

Sixgun Sights

TIME WAS, when a bell-mouthed match lock, or flint lock pistol was aimed simply by pointing. Hits were obtained only by accident. Then the fine flint duelers were developed and eventually even army pistols were given something in the way of sights. By the time the revolver came into general use after 1836, sights were put on all pistols. The first sixgun sights were very crude and seldom did the gun shoot to them. Colts and many imitations and competitive arms carried a notch in the tip of the hammer to be used when at full cock in connection with a tiny brass bead front sight. Very often the hammer, when standing at full cock, was out of alignment with the barrel. Many sixgun shots of that era fitted a dovetail rear sight on the rear end of the barrel just ahead of the cylinder and thus put accurate sights on their arms. Soon blade dovetail front sights appeared due to these individuals wanting their sixguns accurately sighted. The Remingtons and many others carried a hog wallow with a rear notch in the top of the frame—a much more substantial and accurate rear sight than a cut in the tip of the hammer. The third model, sometimes called the fourth model, Colt Dragoon carried one of the first attempts at fitting a really good rear sight on a sixgun when they dovetailed a folding leaf rear sight on the rear end of the barrel. The 1855 Root Model sidehammer Colts, in both rifle and revolving pistols, had a groove rear sight in the top of the frame.

It was not until the advent of target shooting that much was accomplished in the way of sighting pistols except on the fine old sets of single shot dueling pistols. These were accurately sighted, even though they had low sights, and the Philadelphia Derringers were also accurately sighted. When target pistol shooting finally came into the picture, excellent target sights were fitted on the flat-top target Colt S. A. Army, Bisley and later double action models as well as on Smith & Wessons and the Stevens single shot target pistols.

With all the misinformation put out by the Western movies, and their impossible shots accomplished by the hero shooting blanks while a rifleman or two stand out of the picture to make the hits, the fact that people acquire erronious ideas is not to be wondered at. Single

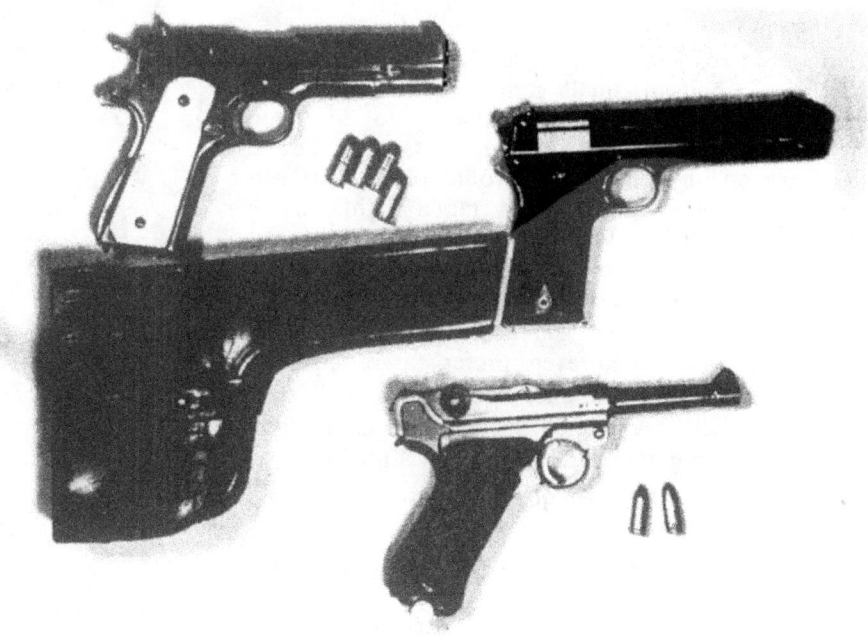

Author's Guns. Top: .45 auto 1919 King sights. Top right: Colt .45 auto with shoulder stock holster. Very rare. Bottom: 9 mm. Luger.

Guns from Author's Collection.

action "six-shooters" that may be shot fifty times without reloading, and hitting small objects from the hip at fifty yards, are common in horse opera but not elsewhere. Formerly, Captain A. H. Hardy and his daughter did much of the accurate shooting from *outside the picture*. Such hocus-pocus, permissible in pictures, unfortunately gives people many fallacious ideas of what can, and what cannot, be expected of a hand gun. Some take movie miracles at their face value, while others, among them the military, believe pistol accuracy is limited to twenty yards or less. The truth is found (as it usually is) between the two extremes.

Even the lad carrying a .22 pistol on his trap line soon learns that he has to carefully aim his little gun to kill trap-bait or small game. While target sights are not necessary on a gun used solely for hip shooting at close range, usually on human targets, they are necessary on any gun if you would place your shots at any but close range. Good target sights are infinitely better than any fixed sights, and to our notion all sixguns and auto pistols should be fitted with accurate adjustable sights if the barrels are 4 inches or more in length and the gun is intended for accurate aimed fire. We would even prefer target sights on small pocket guns, and once shot a two inch barrel M. & P. model S. & W. .38 Special with target sights. It was surprising how accurately that little gun shot.

For straight target shooting, almost any type of target sight can be used that gives a clean sight picture. For straight target punching, the sights can be any height or shape that best serves the purpose. The standard today is the well-known Patridge type with square rear notch and a square topped blade front.

It is doubtful if a better sight exists for target work. The front sight can have a square faced or a hawk billed Marine Corp type blade which when smoked black will give a perfect sight picture against the white background of the paper target. Young folks with sharp eyes can use a narrow front sight but the majority of good shots prefer a front sight not less than one-tenth inch in width and most of them want one-eighth inch. We have seen some use a front sight of a full quarter inch in width with good results. The

Author and Son's Guns. Top: Christy job. Son Ted's .44 Special single action. Bottom: King job. Author's .45 single action. Top gun has Micro rear. Bottom gun has King S. & W. type rear sight.

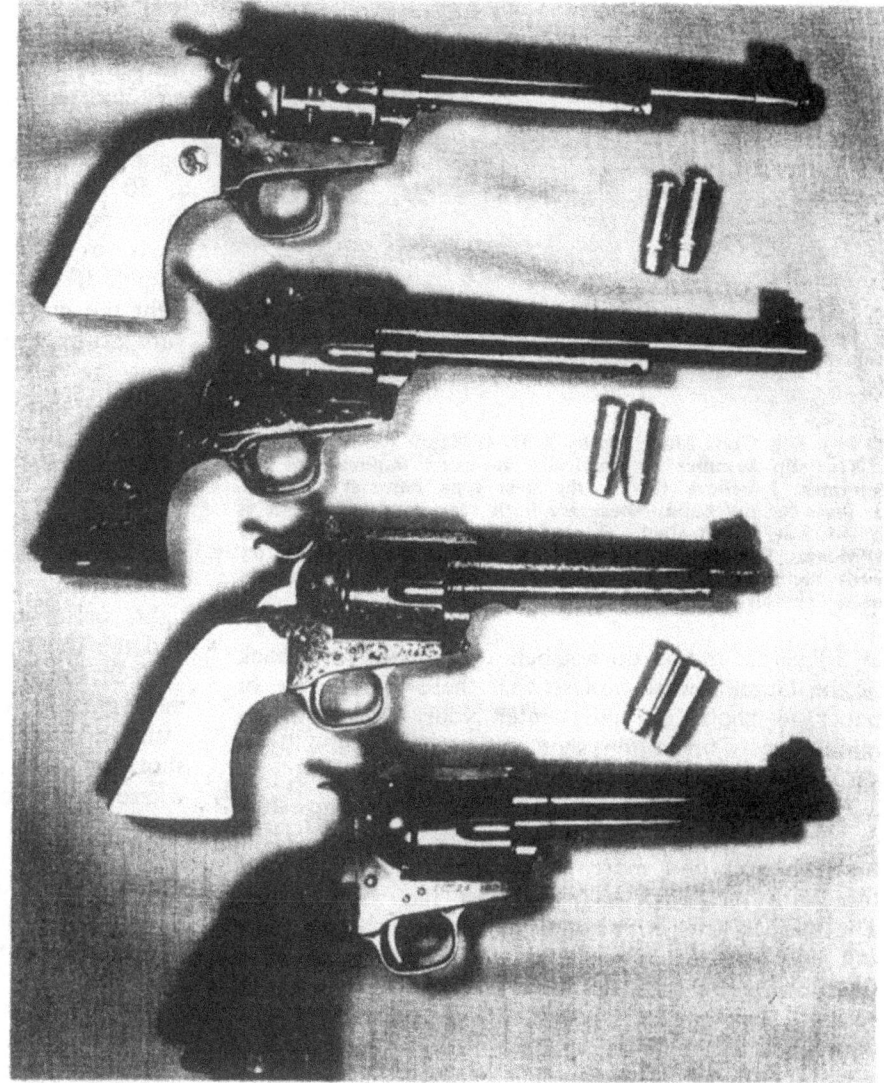

Author's Four .44 Special S. A. Colts.

King short action job, 7½ inch barrel.

Original flat-top target.

No. 5 S.A. Colt, converted by Sidgley to author and Harold Croft's design flat-top target.

Flat-top target by Hawkins. One-piece rosewood grips by Pachmayr. Keith long range sight. Keith three leaf rear sight.

front sight should be wide enough to be seen perfectly with no eye strain. The poorer the eyesight, the wider the front sight should be as a general rule. The rear sight notch should be square on the sides and *must* be wide enough to allow a strip of light to be clearly seen on each side of the front sight when the gun is held at arms length to be certain the front sight is centered in the rear notch. Many guns, both target and fixed sighted varieties, come from the factory with too narrow a rear sight cut to accommodate the front sight and still leave a strip of light on each side of it in the target shooting position. These must be opened up to give you that strip of light. Only then can you center the front sight, and any rear notch that does not allow a strip of light, makes perfect centering of the front sight impossible and will throw you for a loss at the target.

The top of the front sight must always be held level with the top of the rear sight for standard fixed target ranges. Move the point of aim at six o'clock or up in the center as you choose to make the gun group in the center of the bull, but maintain that perfect sight picture with the top of front sight level with top of the rear sight.

Many plinkers and hunters prefer round bead front sights and flat-top U rear sight notches. These will not hold elevation as well as a square flat-top post or blade front sight. All fixed rear sights of the hog wallow variety, just a groove down the top of frame with V, round U or square rear notch, will reflect side lights and shoot away from the light.

Some eyes prefer a red or gold insert in the tip of the front blade even for target shooting and like the contrast in color against the black bullseye. We prefer a front sight of one-eighth inch width that appears wider than the bullseye and then aim at the center when possible, leaving a half of the bullseye over top center of the front sight. This has always been our hold for long range .30 caliber military target shooting as well as pistol shooting. It is true that the black sights on a gun do not offer much contrast against a big bullseye at close range or even

Two Slip Guns Made Up by J. D. O'Meara for Newman.
The slip hammer is practically an exact duplicate of my hammer. I believe this is the best type hammer of all—at least for my hand. These are both very good guns. One is a .45, one a rebushed .22 made from an old .41 S.A. by O'Meara. The triggers were left in so that a novice can try both methods and compare scores. Top gun has extra .45 auto cylinder.

at 50 yards. If you do not believe this, turn the back of the target toward you so that there is a square of paper to shoot at, and center your sights on the middle of it for a ten shot string, and you will be surprised to find you shoot a much smaller group, as a rule, than if you were aiming at that skimpy bull in the center. The reason is simply that you get a much clearer and more easily maintained sight picture with the black sights against the white paper. The same is true with scope sight rifle shooting. You can and will do better shooting when aiming at a small white bullseye in the center of the black and seeing your cross hairs imposed over that white center than when trying to see their location perfectly against a black bullseye. A square bull of white in the center of a black bullseye that allows plenty of space for your cross hairs is the best scope target. That is the reason you will shoot smaller groups aiming at a square of white target paper than if you aim at a little bullseye in the center of a target.

We believe that all adjustments, both horizontal and vertical, should be in the rear sight. The front sight is more apt to get bumped and also moved in a holster or worn from the leather or get its adjustments changed. Of all target sixgun sights made today, we prefer the recent Smith & Wesson click micrometer type. Clicks should be close enough together to accurately sight in the gun for the center of the bull so you can hold exactly six o'clock or exactly center as you desire. Many shooters who use the center hold, like a red insert in the front blade right at the top to show in contrast against the black of the bullseye. Others prefer gold for the insert and still others prefer the Call-type with round gold bead set into the face or the square topped blade front. Our preference for a contrasting color or front sight is gold, either in a narrow bar across the top face of the front sight or the Call gold bead set in a square Patridge-type blade.

Red, with our eyes at least, tends to show up black in dim light. I believe in sighting all sixguns for 50 yards and holding lower for shorter ranges when necessary and holding more front sight up in the rear notch for longer ranges. Longer range is the only time the sight picture is changed. If the gun is sighted center at 50 yards it is usually about right with a slightly lower point of aim at 25 yards and some guns do not seem to require much change in hold for the two ranges. If your shooting is all at 25 yard targets, then sight the gun for that range, but if mixed 25 and 50 yard ranges I prefer to sight for 50 yards and hold to bring the center of the group in the center of the bull at 25 yards.

Side lights or a change in grip may make your group higher or lower or to one side. It is best to hold off for it rather than be continually meddling with the sights. If you know your gun is sighted for the ammunition being used, make no sight changes but hold off if it becomes necessary, due to adverse light, or other temporary conditions. Herb Bradley and the writer once fired a 12 shot group with a pair of Colt Dragoons. The guns were both new and far too valuable in their present state to ever think of fitting a rear sight, so we used the hammer notch. We shot both guns a couple of cylinders full, to know where to aim on the 20 yard target. One gun had to be held in the lower left hand corner and the other in the upper right hand corner of the target to center the groups in the bull. Our composite group of 12 shots clearly shows what can be done even with guns that are not correctly sighted by holding off the bull the same way for each shot.

The longer the barrel the greater the distance between sights and the greater the sight radius. This makes for more accurate aim. On the other hand some oldsters seem to do as well with shorter barrels that bring both sights more nearly in the same focal plane, as their eyesight does not accommodate as fast as the eyes of younger shooters. With the longer barrel, an error in sight alignment is more apparent than with the shorter barrel and shorter sight radius. Guns

A close inspection will show the clip which holds the Pachmayr "Sure Grip" adapter to the gun frame. When on the gun and in use, the adapter is a permanent part of the gun, but nevertheless, it can be installed or removed in just a few seconds time.

intended for hunting or for defense, where the quick draw may enter the picture, and where you may need a fast gun to save your life, should be equipped with the Baughman type sloping front sight, first brought out in 1927 and '28 by Harold Croft and the writer and also used by C. V. Schmitt. Such a front sight is better for fast holster use than a square back blade front sight. It wears the holster less and there is nothing that can catch on clothes or holster to fumble a fast draw. Baughman type front sights can be had with

John Newman's original slip hammer.

gold or red insert for better contrast against game or man if desired. The high Micro rear sight is excellent for straight target shooting but we do not like it for game or defense use as it is too high and requires too high a front sight on revolvers. It works wonderfully well on auto pistols. Our favorite in target rear sights for all revolvers is the S. & W. type click rear sight also furnished formerly by the King Gun Sight Company of San Francisco. This type sight weakens the frame of a revolver less by its installation than any other sight. It gives the longest possible sight radius by being in the rear position, just as does the Baughman front sight, by having its highest (aiming) point nearest the muzzle of the gun.

This is the best sight to have fitted to any fixed sighted revolver. King Gun Sight Company used to do a most perfect job of such sight installations. Any competent gunsmith can do it by milling out the hog wallow in the top of the frame and making the cross cut at the extreme rear of the frame for this type of target sight. C. H. McCashland, Box 57, Hinton, West Virginia, does a very good job of such sight installations. It requires a much lower front sight than does the micro. High sights are an advantage on auto pistols used for straight paper punching and long range shooting, but we prefer the lower sights on guns for all-around use. If we had our way, all sixguns and auto pistols would be made with adjustable target type sights for all purposes. When the Baughman front sight is used, target sights do not offer any handicap whatever for fast shooting, and are there if you need the gun for accurate aimed fire at longer ranges.

Target sights are best for aerial and trick shooting. One variety that is very good for aerial shooting is a wide angle English V rear sight with a platinum center line, and not over a 20 degree angle to the sides of the V. It should be quite shallow and extend from the center to the very edge of the rear sight which should always be full width of the top of the frame. This wide angle V back sight is fast with either a post or bead front sight. The post or bead should be tipped with red or gold. With a square topped Baughman-type front sight with a gold square or narrow gold band insert at the top, one should hold up just the gold portion of the front sight above the platinum center line in the rear sight. This makes a very fast combination, particularly for aerial double or single action shooting. We believe the front sight should be 1/8 inch in width for best results, so it can be seen clearly and quickly in any light. For those who prefer the round bead front sight of 1/16 or 1/10 of an inch, this makes an excellent combination and is the same the English have used for many generations on the big double rifles they favor for dangerous game.

We do not like any convex faced bead or blade front sight, as any sight of this shape will shoot away from side lights. The insert bead of either gold, silver or red material should always be flat faced and flush with the steel that surrounds it. If of metal, it can be smoked black when desired for target use, but if of some red material you should know whether or not it is susceptible to heat before any smoking operation.

Many shooters like a deep rear notch so they can hold a perfect square of the front sight level with the top of rear sight. We prefer a shallow rear sight

1917 S. & W. remodelled by C. R. McCashland, Hinton, W. Va. Short cylindered and very accurate.

notch of good width, rather than the deep square type. We are only interested in the top line of the front sight and the top of rear sight forming a perfect line, with a strip of light on each side, and care nothing about the bottom of the rear notch. Hence we prefer a shallow rear notch and less front sight. Whatever the sight picture used, it must be maintained, shot after shot, if you would shoot good groups.

Many years ago we designed a long-range front sight and it was put out for a time by the King Gun Sight Company and also furnished on some Smith & Wessons at the factory. This comprised a square topped, square backed blade of one-eighth inch width. On the face of the front sight were three gold bars—narrow ones that would just fill the wide but shallow rear sight for elevation when the top of the gold bar was held level with top of rear sight. The gold bars were evenly spaced down the face of the front sight. The upper bar was held level with the rear sight notch for point blank 50 yard range. Then the black space between it and the next lower bar could be used for a longer range and the second and lower gold bar for still longer range. Finally the next black space for a still longer range and the lower gold bar for maximum long range. This sight worked out very well, in fact has proven to be by far the best we have ever used in a front sight for long-range shooting. It can be fitted to either a standard target blade with square back or even to a Baughman type front sight and gives one definite aiming points for longer than point blank ranges. In practice you simply perch your target on the top center of the front sight. Holding up as much of the front sight as is necessary to lob your slug to the long-range target. This is the finest, most exacting kind of sixgun shooting and will soon separate the men from the boys. It is also the finest accuracy test known for either gun or ammunition. Many guns will shoot well at close ranges but are hopeless for any long range work. Likewise many pistol and revolver loads are good only at short range. Long range shooting really tells the tale and soon shows the inherent accuracy of both guns and ammunition.

Any time I find a gun that shoots well at long range, even though it may have a very high trajectory, I know it is accurate at short ranges. Long range shooting is the real test of any sixgun or auto pistol. Of course it can only be practiced where you have either dry dusty ground or water to shoot over, so the strike of the bullets can be picked up and correction made in the aim for the next shot.

The best of all rear sights for long range shooting would of course be a tangent rear sight as fitted on a few Colt single actions and many Winchester carbines. Such a sight could be graduated by 50 or 100 yard lines, with a certain load, and would give the shooter exactly the same sight for each shot by a sliding bar that could be moved up and set as desired. Three leaf rear sights are also good and we worked one out on a S. A. Colt with point blank for 50 yards, then a leaf for 100 yards and another for 200 yards. It worked mighty well when all leaves were filed down to exactly the right height for our heavy .44 Special load and we have done some excellent long range shooting with this gun. The Keith front sight will fill in when you do not have a three leaf or tangent rear sight for long range work. It can also be used to great advantage in conjunction with leaf or tangent rear sights, giving the shooter even greater range. One can burn up a lot of ammunition in this sport and we will cover it further in a chapter on long range shooting.

At one time we owned a small Stevens single shot pistol, in .22 caliber, with peep and globe sights. It was impossible to shoot it, with accuracy, in the orthodox manner. With arm extended one could not see through the tiny peep aperture. By holding the back of the shooting hand against the cheek bone and further steadying the barrel with the left hand, the peep and globe sights then showed up very well except the front sight was too close to the eye. In this position we killed many a squirrel, ruffed and blue grouse as well as frogs and snakes. It was not as practical as another Stevens we had with a very short barrel and conventional sights that could be used with one hand and the arm extended.

Telescope and peep sights have no place whatever on a sixgun or pistol of any kind.

About the worst possible type of pistol sights are the knife blade or Barleycorn front and small, narrow V rear sight. A thin blade front sight or a round bead will not hold elevations exactly and a narrow rear V notch, while it may accommodate the width of the front sight under perfect lighting conditions, will not do so in anything less.

When you fill the rear notch with front sight, you cannot tell if you are centered or not; too often you are not, and the shot goes to one side. The most accurate front sight possible is some form of a square blade; either standard target blade, Hawk billed Marine Corps type or the sloping Baughman type. Thin front sights tend to blur out in dim lights and

Newman's latest slip gun made up by O'Meara.

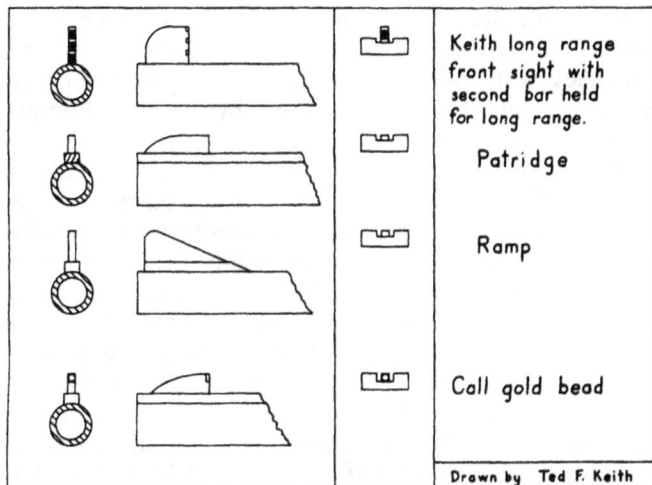
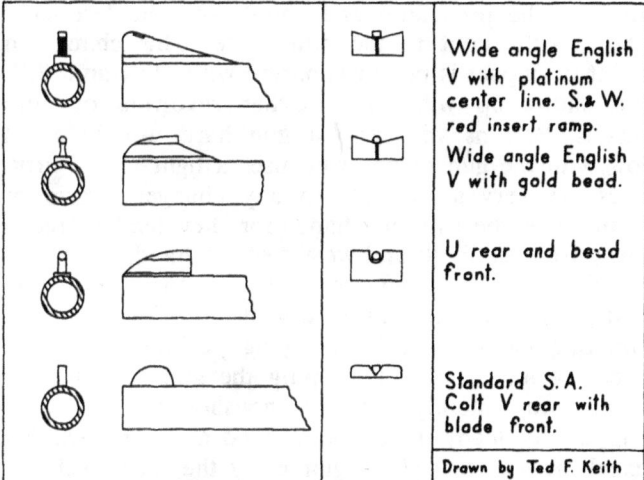

there is usually some aberration of the extreme tip if they run up to a point so that holding the top of them level with the top of the rear notch is an almost impossible chore. You can shoot only as well as you can see. Get the best sights obtainable for your individual eyesight. What suits one man may not suit another. It's you who will use the gun, so sight it to suit yourself.

Very often it will be found that two men shoot to different locations on the target. This may be due either to different grips on the gun or to variations in eyesight. Cheap glass spectacles sold at drug stores, are no bargain for pistol or rifle shooting. We have seen guns perfectly sighted in without glasses, shoot completely off the target when these beer bottle glasses were used. If you use or need glasses get the best prescription or plain ground lenses. Don't expect to do accurate shooting when gazing through the distorted fog of a set of cheap spectacles, however much they may cut down the glare of the sun or improve sight-target picture.

Telescope sights also are an abomination on any pistol, either target or for other purposes. We have seen them mounted on some long barreled sixguns and one that was mounted very high on a luger carbine. Unless the gun has an illegal shoulder stock, it is virtually impossible to use a telescope sight on it. The gun cannot be held steadily enough for accurate shooting while still keeping the ocular lens close enough to the eye for correct eye relief. On any heavy caliber gun it will either hit you in the eye or on the forehead in recoil. We remember an old cow-poke in Montana who was given to telling tall tales about his shooting. One day we asked him to demonstrate with our .45 S. A. Colt. He said he always laid the gun in the crook of his left arm and held it close to his face and could then shoot off chickens' heads. An old rooster was feeding in the bronc corral so we asked him to snip its head off. The gun was loaded with 300 grain .45-90 Winchester bullets sized down to .454 inches and backed by 35 grains of F.F.G. Black powder. At the shot, some feathers did fly from the rooster's neck, but the front sight of the gun turned up in recoil and cut a beautiful buttonhole in his forehead. The rooster ran off squawking, but the shooter lost more blood than the chicken.

Many so-called bellyguns, with barrels cut to two or three inches, have had the front sight completely removed in the process. While its true the sights are of no help to fast hip shooting in defense work at close range where you shoot by feel of the gun, nevertheless, there may come a time when you want to hit something at a distance; you are then better off with a front sight. We believe in accurate sighting of even 2 inch pocket guns and personally would prefer them with an adjustable target rear sight. Then if you have to hit a man or game at 25 to 50 yards, you can do so.

Many fixed sighted guns will shoot to one side or the other and if you examine them carefully you may well find that the barrel was turned into the frame a little too far or not quite far enough to properly line the front sight up with the frame. The best treatment, of course, is to have the barrel turned to place so the front sight stands vertically, but when that cannot be done, the front sight can be bent slightly at its base on some guns. Have a friend hold the gun with a square cornered block of hardwood under the very base of the front sight, and then with a block of hard type metal or lead you can, by using it as a drift and using a hammer, tap the drift a blow that will bend the whole front sight at its base and perfectly line it up yet not mar the sight or have it show any bend. We have corrected hundreds of old guns by this method. It is far better than to tolerate a gun that shoots to one side.

Usually left hand shooters take different lateral adjustment on a rear sixgun sight than do right hand shooters. A gun sighted for a right handed man will usually shoot to the right for a south paw, and vice versa. It is due to the bulk of the right handed person's hand being on the right side of the gun.

Reverse the procedure and shoot with the left hand and it will shoot to the other side. This change in point of impact is not so apparent with .22's and .38's but shows up with .45's, either revolvers or auto pistols. Persons who grip a gun hard usually shoot low with the gun of one who uses a light grip. Forty-fives are very susceptible to any change in grip or position of the shooting hand, for they tend to recoil away from the bulk and weight of the hand.

When sighting in your gun, it is best to use an arm rest if possible and also is well to bring the non-shooting hand up to a steadying position under the shooting hand but not gripping the gun or gun-hand in any way, merely using the nonshooting hand as a support to steady the shooting hand and gun. Another excellent way to sight a gun is by the back reclining position—with gun-hand and arm extended and resting alongside one drawn-up leg while the free hand supports the head. Still another, and the steadiest position of all, is the old back seated position with head and back rest, knees drawn up, the gun held between the knees and loosely supported by the nonshooting hand.

With revolvers, cylinder and barrel joint flash is hard on the trousers and will powder-blacken them, but it offers one of the steadiest possible positions for sighting in a gun and with the sights held well away from the eyes for sharp definition. After satisfying yourself the gun is sighted correctly, check it in the usual stance with one hand, on a target, and with both hands squarely facing the target. When the gun is properly sighted, if you maintain the same grip on it, it should shoot to the same point of aim from all positions. Practice with it until that sight picture becomes automatic with you and you have confidence in the gun.

Chapter V

Long Range Shooting

LONG RANGE SHOOTING is the real test of any revolver or pistol. True, some loads were never intended for any but short ranges, but in the main, long range shooting will prove both gun and load. Many shooters of experience with rifles do not realize that only a very short barrel is necessary to stabilize and accurately start a slug on its way to a distant target. Trajectory is necessarily very high, but accuracy of a good sixgun or auto pistol and a good load is surprising. Many guns and loads will do fairly well at close range but are absolutely hopeless for long range work, hence long range shooting is the real test of a gun or load.

Some 30 years ago a revolver club in Kentucky regularly held 300 yard revolver shoots. They used .38 and .44 caliber target guns, Smith & Wessons and Colts, and shot at the silhouette of a full size turkey. Several of those shooters were able to get from two to three hits out of five shots at 300 yards, shooting off hand. Of course they had their guns accurately sighted for the 300 yard range, and while the slugs described a high arc, they landed with regularity on that paper cut-out of a turkey. Today, few shooters realize the long range possibilities of a sixgun or auto pistol. We remember during the war the foreman of the Small Arms Shop at The Ogden Arsenal, and some of his best armorers, made the statement they would not be afraid to let me shoot at them all day at 100 yards with a .45 auto. We repaired to the range and behind the 200 yard target was a small snow drift not a fourth the size of the average man. By dropping down to the old back position, and holding the front sight far up above the notch in the rear sight of my .45 auto Colt, I perched the snow drift atop the front sight and fired. First shot was short, but a little more elevation of front sight until I could see a bit of the slide between sights did the trick and I pounded the rest of that clip into the snow drift, using this very steady position with right arm rested along the side of my drawn up right leg while I supported my head in a steady position with left hand. They had their eyes opened.

During the Indian campaigns on the plains, quite a few cavalry officers who had learned to shoot a sixgun during the Civil War became very expert at long range revolver shooting. Many a time with their horses shot out from under them, they were able to keep enemies out at long rifle range and completely out of bow shot with the old 7½ inch Peacemaker. A good revolver shot with a long barreled gun and accurate heavy ammunition, can, and they frequently did, make it hot for enemy horseman out to 400 or 500 yards. When the shooting was over dry, dusty plains or over water where the strike of the bullet could be located, they could hold accordingly and soon walk their shots onto the target.

Effective long range revolver shooting requires as much, perhaps more, practice than any other phase of the game. One must learn the trajectory of his pet load and how much front sight to hold up above the level of the rear sight notch to attain different ranges. With enough practice, one becomes proficient and can surprise the natives. We had the Zane Grey outfit here on a two months pack trip in 1931. One day the boys started shooting at a rock at 400 yards with their .30-06 model 1895 rifles. Grey had a weakness for finger lever guns. They were far from expert riflemen and we laid down with our back against a log for a perfect back and head rest and with a 7½ inch .44 Special S. A. Colt, with target sights, held with both hands between the drawn up knees, proceeded to hit the rock repeatedly. That was something new to Zane Grey and he used what he learned on that trip about long range pistol shooting in his novel, Thunder Mountain.

In 1928, S. Harold Croft of Philadelphia, with whom I had had considerable correspondence regarding sixguns and various loads, spent a month with us on the ranch at Durkee, Oregon. He brought a suitcase full of good sixguns, mostly .44 special or .45 Colt caliber and asked me to demonstrate some of the long range shooting I had been writing about. Seven hundred yards across a dry, dusty field I had a target four feet square. By laying on my back with my saddle used for a head and shoulder rest, and shooting with both hands held between my drawn up knees, I proceeded to lob slugs into that target. I hit it with every gun he brought along before the gun was empty except one 2 inch barreled .45 S. A. slip gun with a Newman hammer. It required eleven shots

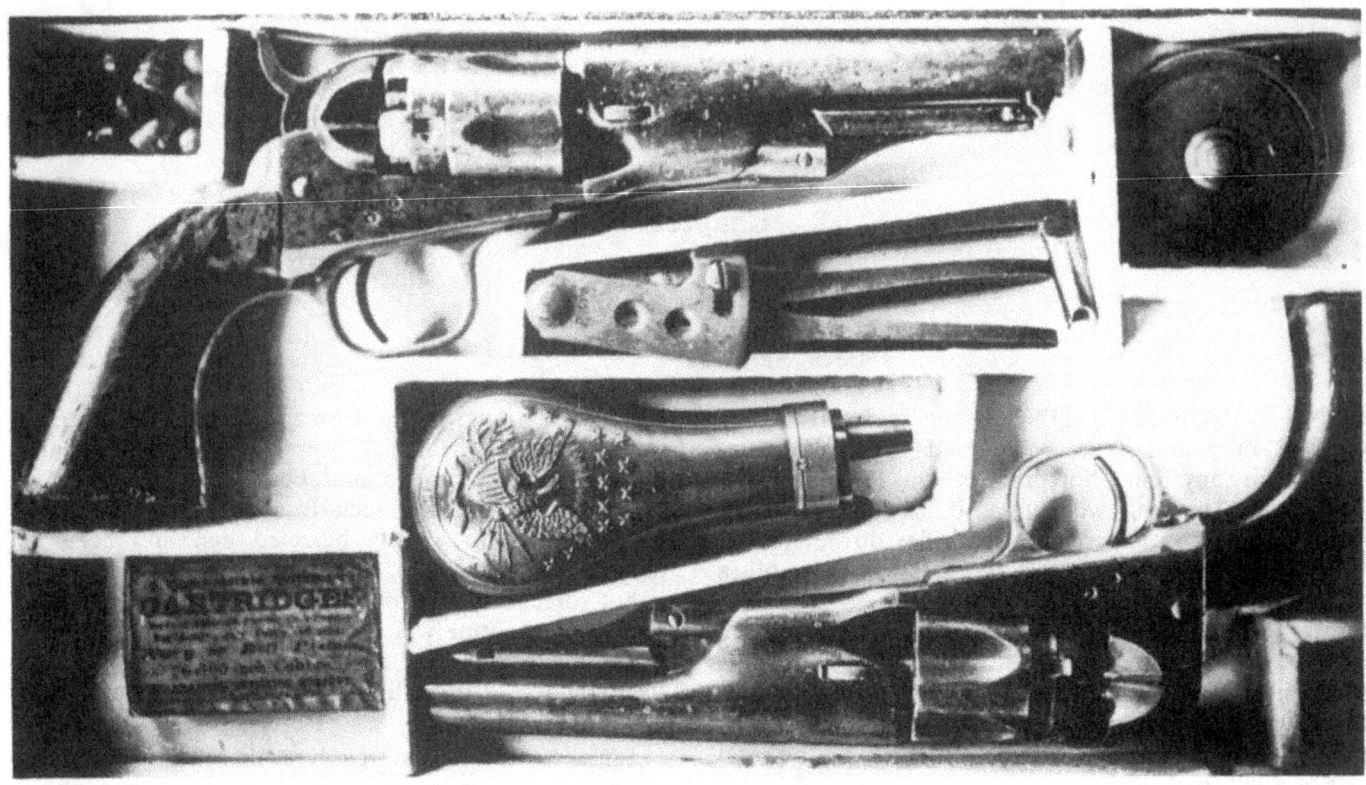

A pair of nice Colts.

to find the target with that short barreled gun and I was then aiming at a sage brush on top of a small mountain behind and a bit to one side of the target before I finally hit it. The short barrel was not burning the 40 grain black powder charge, and trajectory was hopelessly high. With the good .44 Special and .45 Colt guns with barrels of 4 to 7½ inches it was no trouble to find the target in a shot or two, and with some I hit the four foot target with three out of five shots. Croft was soon convinced I had been writing facts and not fiction, but was very skeptical before the shooting started. We experimented most of the month, and during that time I designed the first of my line of Ideal Keith bullets in caliber .44 Special Ideal No. 429421. When the new mould arrived I had to try it at long range and also on jack rabbits and one eagle to find out what it would do on game with powder used mostly at the time, Dupont No. 80. I worked up a load of 12 grains No. 80 with the 250 grain bullet and found I had the finest long range load I had ever used. Evenings were spent casting and sizing bullets and the days in shooting and riding around the cow range looking for animate targets. Jack rabbits were in profusion, with plenty of hawks, horned owls and some coyotes and eagles as well, so I had plenty of opportunities to try the guns and loads on small game. Croft left with a thorough knowledge and a much better appreciation of the possibilities of a sixgun for long range work. We killed numerous jack rabbits to a full 200 yards with some of the target sighted guns including a 1917 Smith & Wesson he gave me and some 1925 National Match .45 auto ammo I had on hand. Although extremely accurate, the .45 auto load was one of the poorest tried for long range shooting owing to its very high trajectory. One day we had a shot at a big golden eagle at 150 yards and I lobbed a slug through him. Another day a goshawk sat on a cliff at about the same range and I killed him. Both with a 7½ inch .44 Special Target sighted S. A. Colt and our home grown loads with the then new Keith bullet and 12 grains No. 80 powder.

Jack rabbits, however, were our best targets as they would often stay put for several shots until we found the range and also how much front sight to hold up. The dull sodden plunk would denote a hit and the jack would go down in a cloud of dust as he kicked his last. Sometimes when forced to, we shot off-hand using both hands and facing the target squarely but when terrain permitted we usually dropped to the back position with gun held along the drawn up right leg and head resting on the left hand. This position places the sights a maximum distance from the eyes and is best for long range work when a back rest cannot be found. When a suitable back rest could be had, it proved an even better long range position, using both hands on the gun held between the drawn up knees. My overalls usually were about burned through between the knees from cylinder-barrel flash. I did considerable writing on the subject at the time and today shooters are re-discovering some of the things I learned twenty-five years ago about long range revolver shooting.

As a boy in Montana I had done a lot of long range sixgun work. One summer my father purchased a band of sheep and put them on our cow range. The place was surrounded with cow ranches and I was hard put to keep those woolies from getting into our neighbors fields. We had no sheep dog and my cow dog was far too rough and would kill them as he had about the same opinion of sheep as I did. I would spend the evenings every day reloading .45 Colt ammunition with 250 grain slugs and 40 grains of black powder to throw in front of the leaders of that band of sheep the next day. Father would buy me black powder in 25 pound kegs and lead by the 200 pounds in five pound pigs. As I was shooting every day, I learned the trajectory of the old gun and how much front sight to hold up to make a hit on some distant rock in front of the sheep. I never learned to like sheep or be a competent sheep herder. I did learn long range sixgun shooting and it saved my horse many a weary mile that summer. It was a gala day for me when we sold the woolies and went back to cattle.

We also ran wild horses at times and many times I have turned a band of wild horses by throwing heavy sixgun slugs in front of them where they would kick up the dust and howl off into space. Only by such constant daily practice does a man really learn a sixgun and its possibilities. The gun became a part of me, a tool of the range and an extension of my right arm, so to speak. One fall while hauling a four horse load of baled hay to the ranch from the railroad siding, I jumped a coyote crossing a meadow. By the time I had turned the lines over to my partner, the sage wolf was going strong. I started shooting at him at about 300 yards as he ran broadside across the meadow. The gun used was a 5½ inch .38/40 S. A. Colt and my heavy hand loads with a 210 grain .40/65 Winchester bullet sized down to .403 inches and 40 grains of black powder. My first three shots were all behind him though I had the elevation fairly well, but out at 400 yards my fourth shot hit him in the shoulder and sent him somersaulting across the meadow. He got up and headed away from me on three legs and I missed my fifth and last shot before he went over a ridge. A neighbor hearing the shooting, headed toward our ranch and ran into the coyote and easily roped and killed him. The slug had broken the right shoulder but stayed under the skin on the off-side of his chest. That was straining a sixgun but illustrates what can be done with one along with good loads.

Another time at Durkee, Oregon, I jumped a coyote and fell off my horse for the shot, as he went up a dry gulch. I missed him the first three or four shots, although getting close, and plunked the last slug through him at around 400 yards. I trailed him over the ridge and found him dead on the other side with that .44 Special Ideal 250 grain slug through his lungs. Sure, hits at such crazy ranges are accidents, pure and simple, but if you do enough long range shooting with a sixgun and keep it up, you will have more "accidents" than the man who shoots only rarely.

One time a neighbor and I were driving to Salmon from North Fork and spotted a big goshawk eating a ring neck pheasant on a ditch bank across a field. We could plainly see the hawk but did not know what he was eating. I had a Smith & Wesson Outdoorsman and Remington .38/44 loads Doug Wesson had sent me. Rolling down the car window, I rested both hands out the window and held up enough front sight for 200 yards, perched the hawk on top that wide front sight and slowly squeezed the trigger. We heard the bullet plunk and the hawk rolled over. Jerry Ravndahl, my partner, stepped off the distance with his long legs at a full 200 yards. The hawk was dead and had almost devoured the Chinese pheasant.

One winter at Durkee, Oregon, we kept a strict account of the number of horned owls killed with my No. 5 S. A. Colt. That was after Harold Croft had had the gun rebuilt to my order by Sedgley and before it was engraved, as we felt it should have a real test before going to the expense of engraving it. I killed 32 great horned owls with that gun that winter while running my coyote trap line. Killing jack rabbits for trap bait, as well as crippled range horses for coyote bait, gave me plenty of daily practice with a sixgun.

Later when Smith & Wesson brought out the .357 Magnum on which Doug Wesson and I had done so much experimental work, we took it up to the Pahsimeroi Valley and shot jack rabbits for three days with it, killing, all told, 125. They were then such pests and in such great profusion they would eat around a haystack during the winter until it toppled over on them. We soon found the factory .357 Magnum load did not do as well as our handloads for the .38/44 Smith & Wesson and at ranges over 125 yards did most of the killing with the Keith 160 grain hollow point backed by 13.5 grains 2400 in Remington .38/44 cases in the 8⅜ inch Magnum gun. The longest kill recorded was a jack that ran part way across a field and stood up on his hind legs at a distance later measured by Julius Maelzer as 180 yards. A single shot dropped that jack in a heap. We killed many up to 125 yards with the factory magnum load, but over that range found our home grown load much more accurate.

Doug Wesson had fitted the gun with the Keith long range front sight which has three gold bars spaced uniformly down the blade, which helps on the first shot and enables the shooter to retain his elevation more accurately on succeeding shots. This load of 13.5 grains 2400 and the Keith 160 grain hollow point was used by the late Dick Tinker in

Good deer country for sixgun hunting.

shooting the long range targets published in Ed McGivern's great book, Fast and Fancy Revolver Shooting. I coached Dick Tinker for many years, as we grew up together in Montana, and although he had very poor eyesight necessitating the use of thick lens spectacles, he learned to be a very fine pistol shot.

Last spring while Clarence Negus and I were fishing for steelhead at the mouth of Deadwater below North Fork, Ben Dillon and two of his friends joined us. My old cow dog, Stub, began barking. We started looking. One of the strangers spotted a coyote running up a ridge across the river. I asked him to take my rod so I could work on the coyote, but he saw no gun in sight and did not know what I was about. Finally he took the rod and I jerked my 4 inch 1950 Target .44 Special Smith & Wesson from under my coat and holding up half of the front sight in the rear notch and with both hands, from a comfortable seated position, held the running coyote on top the *front sight and squeezed one off.* The slug landed on the little sage wolf with a plunk and down he went. He got up, however, and turned back down the mountain in high gear. I shot again leading him some 30 yards. He rolled over but I do not think I hit him again, as he crossed a gulch and went up the other side followed by two more of my heavy 250 grain slugs backed by 18.5 grains 2400, but they did not connect. The first hit was a good solid one and I think he rolled from the effects of it rather than any second hit. Ben said, "Keith usually does better than that, he usually kills them." Little did he know how lucky I was to land one slug at that range on a running coyote. Not long ago when approaching the same spot to fish for steelhead, Negus and I jumped another coyote across the river. It was raining and he ran a short distance and stopped. I dropped my fishing gear and got the short .44 Special in action. This shot was only about 80 yards as the coyote stopped on a sand bar across the river and I did not take time to estimate the distance and held up level with top of his shoulders. He went down at the shot, but I merely clipped some hair from the top of his withers and never got a second shot as he was on his feet and in the brush in a second.

Early last spring I had an experience that made my face very red. Wes Lowe and I were traveling down the Salmon River in his jeep in a snow storm when I spotted a big Golden Eagle perched on a dead snag across the river. I watched him through the small side window telling Wes when to stop. I shoved this same 4 inch barreled .44 Special S. & W. out the side of the jeep for an easy shot. Owing to the swirling snow I did not look down at the river to estimate the distance and supposed the eagle to be about 125 yards, the usual distance for such shots across the river on an angle. I held up level with the top of the big bird's shoulder and shot right over him. Seeing rock dust raise over his shoulders, he flapped toward us and soon was out of sight in the storm. I had overestimated the distance and overshot the big bird. When we kicked the jeep door open and looked over the range it was not over 40 yards.

A couple of years ago, Mrs. Keith, son Ted and I were driving along the Salmon River when we spotted another big golden eagle sitting on top of a small cliff some 50 yards from the road. The boy had his .22 rifle so I told him to poke it out the window, and when I stopped, to center that eagle's chest and shoot as quickly as possible. Ted did the job perfectly and feathers came out the old eagle's back, but he simply fell off the cliff, caught himself and turned down the road, soaring to catch the wind and gain elevation. As he swung back up the road in one of his circles, I was out of the car and had that short .44 Special S. & W. aimed on him and then moved the sights about four feet ahead of him as he swung directly towards us and shot. Feathers puffed out of the his back and we could plainly hear the heavy slug strike him. He turned in another circle down the river and catching a rising air current sailed back toward us and again I held on him and led him a bit more this time and again was unusually lucky for we heard the second slug strike and saw another big puff of feathers come out of his back. That was too much for him and he nose-dived into the river, a good eagle that will kill no more mountain sheep lambs. It was very lucky shooting as both shots were at around 125 yards.

Two years ago Rollin Westfall and I were fishing for steelhead at the mouth of Squaw Creek on the Salmon. Old Stub barked at something across the river. We had just seen three deer walking around a trail on the far side, so we started looking for the object of Stub's attention. Soon we saw a coyote come along the trail around the steep mountain side. He stopped on a hummock in the wet snow and I handed my rod to Rollin and drew the 4 inch .44 Special and got my sights lined up as quickly as possible using both hands and holding up about one-fourth of the front blade and perched the coyote on top of its center. At the shot he went down and then regained his feet and came back toward us in high gear but with his tail doing the old windmill act that always denotes a fatally hit coyote. He rolled into a clump of low brush and stayed there. The river was running mush ice and we had a hard time restraining old Stub from swimming across after him. He would have drowned in the slush.

I have recounted these experiences just as they happened and will recount several more in this chapter just to show what can and has been done with a sixgun if you always carry it with you and know the gun. Though I have many longer barreled .44 Special sixguns and one Magnum, all of which are better for long range sixgun work, this short 4 inch barrel .44 is handy. I carry it when working with the police department and the sheriff's office. It rides nicely on the waist belt, is easily concealed under a coat, and does not touch the car seat. It is the gun I pack most of the time.

Just after Remington brought out their new Match target .45 auto semi-wad cutter with 185 grain bullet, Vic Braucher, the Northwest Remington manager, visited here and brought a supply along with him. He asked me to try them for accuracy. I told him that long range was the real test of any sixgun or load, so waited to shoot the new ammunition until we had driven down the Salmon River to the mouth of the Middle Fork, seventy miles below home. Just across the main Salmon from the mouth of the Middle Fork the Forest Service has lined up a string of breast high logs. Looking up the Middle Fork there is a small rock projecting out of the water on the left side about 8 inches to a foot high depending on the stage of water, and some three to four feet wide. It is cone shaped with a small tip and a wide taper to the water on each side. Using my 1917 S. & W. with target sights of one-fourth inch width I proceeded to test the new ammunition. The range is a full 200 yards and I held up as much front sight as I thought would be required, set the rock on top of the wide front sight and using both hands and both arms rested over the breast-high log, fired. The strike was a few feet short of the rock so I tried again and held up more front sight. Too much this time and I went over the rock. I split the difference in amount of front sight held up and put the other four slugs on the rock, reloaded the gun and put all of the next six on the rock. That was test enough for me and I knew Remington had a good match load and Vic was amazed that a sixgun would shoot so accurately at a range of 200 yards.

Just after Harold Croft had had my No. 5 Single action .44 Special engraved and blued and I had been shooting it for some weeks, Mrs. Keith and I went down to Weiser, Idaho, for a visit with her folks. We were driving to town from the Randall ranch when a Chinese pheasant lifted his head up out of the grain stubble to the right of the road and raised his rusty voice. Dad Randall stopped the old Ford and asked if I could hit him with my new sixgun. The range looked a good 75 yards and only the cock's head could be seen above the grain stubble. I told him I would try if he would get the pheasant if I

Keith with the bronc that later turned out to be the best cow horse he ever broke, named him Satan. Dec. 1919, 20 below, and his breath did not help the picture.

connected. Resting both arms out the car window and with the motor dead and everyone holding their breath, I held a trifle of the front blade up above the rear sight notch, made sure I was centered and then perched the cock pheasant's head on top and started a slow gradual squeeze of the trigger. After the gun recoiled the pheasant went high in the air in a series of somersaults and finally only dust came up out of the stubble. Mr. Randall was as good as his word and not only crawled through the barbed wire and retrieved the pheasant but also paced the distance at 70 long steps.

Another time Harold Croft and I were driving from Durkee, Oregon, to the ranch in an old Model T. We had the windshield turned up so we could shoot at jacks in front of the car. A magpie was eating a dead rabbit and Harold asked me to try him, so we put on the brake and stopped the old flivver. Resting my hands over the windshield frame and using this same No. 5 .44 Special S. A. Colt with my 250 grain bullet and 12 grains No. 80, I held up a bit of front sight, perched the magpie on top and squeezed one off. The bird stayed right there dead as a mackerel and Harold stepped off the distance from the gun to the bird as 71 yards.

Late that fall Van Stull and I were getting out our winter's supply of wood on Lookout Mountain. Going up the mountain one morning we jumped some blue grouse. I crawled off the wagon and laid down at the side of the road with a perfect back and head rest against a boulder and pulling up my knees held that old No. 5 S. A. Colt between my knees with both hands and tried for the blue grouse. At my shot, down he came amid a cloud of feathers and Van, who is over six feet tall, and still living at Durkee, Oregon, got off the wagon and stepped the distance as 70 yards to the bottom of the fir tree.

Another time at Durkee, Oregon, Jay Keefer, another lad and I were gathering cattle in the fall. We were pushing a small bunch up a draw intending to cut over a low saddle into Manning Creek and thence on to the ranch. I rode on ahead to try for a mess of grouse or sage hens before it became too dark to shoot. Rounding a bend in the draw, I spotted a big cock sage grouse sitting on top of a small cliff, high and to the left of the draw. Slipping off my cow horse and dropping the reins, I tried for him with my old 1917 target sighted Smith & Wesson. Using both hands and 1925 National match ammunition, I fired at a range of around 50 yards hitting the big bird squarely in the center of the breast. He fell off the cliff, but caught himself before reaching the ground and came sailing down the gulch just about ten feet over my head. I hit him again, double action, as he sailed over me but too far back. One leg came down and he sailed on around the bend toward my partners and the little bunch of cattle. Just in front of the lead horse he folded his wings, and came down. The horse started pitching and threw his rider beside the dead sage hen. I got the devil for scaring the horse. Lorraine served us a mighty fine dinner next day. She baked that tough old sage grouse to perfection and filled it with oyster dressing. The first slug had taken off the top of his heart and the second had gone through one thigh and the intestines, yet he lived long enough to sail down the gulch for over 200 yards.

I established quite a reputation around Durkee, Oregon, with that 1917 Smith & Wesson and the No. 5 S. A. Colt, killing a lot of jack rabbits up to a full 200 yards before many witnesses, and still more at 100 to 150 yards. Van Stull, my brother and I were hauling hay on Manning Creek. We had put a big load on the wagon and driven it out of the hay corral and closed the gate. All three of us climbed on the load to go home. Across a plowed field a jack rabbit was feeding. The ground had been plowed and a thin skim of snow covered everything. The old sage bunny was eating on a root turned up by the plough. Stull said, "Elmer, you cannot hit that rabbit with your old sixgun." I had the 1917 S. & W. with 1925 National match loads that day. I told them I would try. I laid down on my back and finally got into a comfortable position with my head and shoulders resting against the hay and my knees drawn up in front and used both hands. I emptied the gun, slowly walking the slugs toward that patient john rabbit and reloaded. With the eleventh shot I hit right under him. The slug ricocheted upwards and through his spine. Van jumped off the load and went over and put the rabbit out of his misery, then stepped the distance back to the wagon, a full 300 yards. That was the longest game shot I ever made with that 1917 S. & W.

During the depression of the thirties when a dollar looked as big as my hat, I stopped at a neighbor's one day. He made good moonshine in a little still cached away in the brush along the North Fork. His helper and his mother were there that day. Federal agents were constantly looking for stills in those days. He was very careful whom he offered a drink, but knowing me he asked me to come have one. After a round or two of his potent white mule, he asked me to see if I could hit a couple of woodchucks that used a rock ledge some 200 yards from his wood shed. I had the 6½ inch triple lock Target Smith & Wesson loaded with my 235 grain hollow base bullets and a moderate heavy load of 7.5 grains No. 5 with me that day. Resting my left shoulder against the wood shed and both arms over a log that projected out at one corner, I held the Call gold bead and part of the front sight up in the rear notch and perched the lower chuck on top of the front sight and slowly squeezed one off. The slug went right over the chuck, so I tried again using a trifle less front sight. Following the shot we heard the dull plunk of a hit and

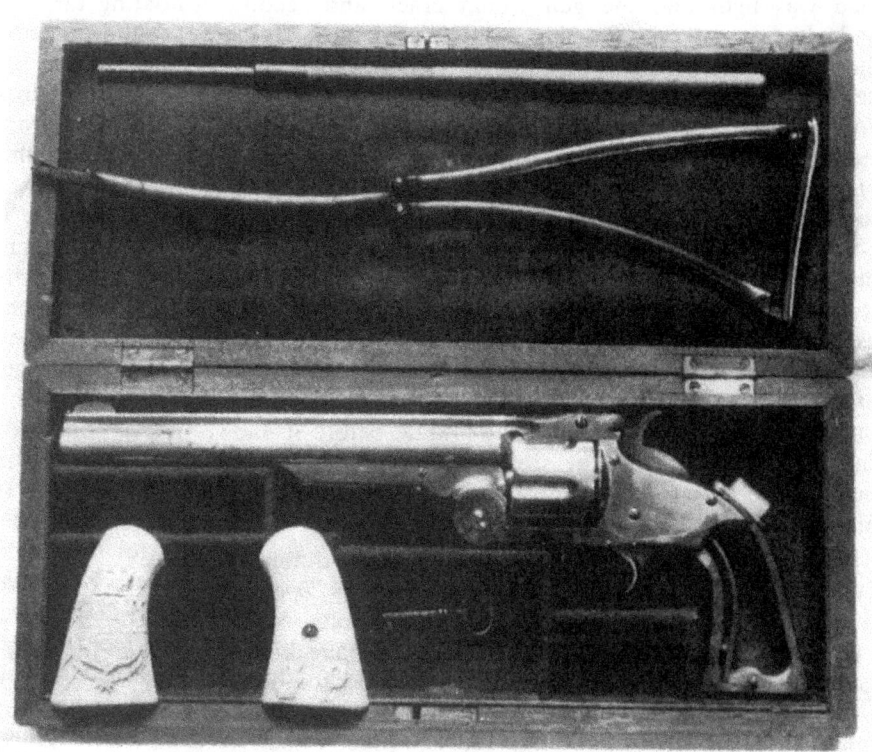

Cased .44 Smith & Wesson revolver.

the chuck's tail came up in the air, twitched a few times, and he rolled off the rock. I tried the same hold on the other chuck perched higher on the small ledge and after the gun recoiled we again heard that dull sodden plunk and this chuck also flattened out and his tail came up for a few seconds. Then he also rolled off the rock down the mountain. That was some of the best long range pistol shooting I ever did. The range stepped off was a full 200 yards.

One Sunday while the family and I were visiting Art Kirkpatrick's ranch on the North Fork, Art asked me to show his father my gun. I had had the old .44 Special 5½ inch S. A. Colt remodeled by Neal Houchins and flat-topped with a three leaf rear sight of my design. That day I was using my heavy .44 Special loads with Keith 235 grain hollow base bullets and 18.5 grains 2400. The gun is sighted for 50 yards with center notch, the rear leaf for 100 yards and the front folding leaf for 200 yards. Across the hay meadow and the North Fork of the Salmon, up the steep mountain was a rock some 18 inches high by two feet wide at what I estimated as 400 yards. After a big dinner, Art asked me to show his Dad how the gun would shoot. He said he would find some cans to shoot at but I told him I would try that rock across the river. "Hell!", he said, "That is a long rifle shot." I laid down on my back in the yard, while Art and his dad kept the kids out of the way, using my left hand for a head rest and with right leg drawn up and gun arm resting along it, I held up part of the front sight with the 200 yard rear leaf turned up and fired. The shot was low and the next shot just over. Then I proceeded to pound five straight slugs on the rock. Art would not believe his eyes and insisted on going over there even though it meant wading the cold North Fork. He did so and found the splash of my five hits on the rock. As nearly as he could tell by pacing the distance to the river and estimating its width and then pacing to the foot of the mountain, it was a full 400 yards to the rock.

These instances show what has been done and can be done by any good sixgun shot with a good gun and accurate ammunition and enough practice. If you wear the gun every day for thirty years and shoot a bit every day, you will become proficient.

Another time I was swapping work with Ned Gibbs. We had finished my job and were down on the island at Deadwater putting up Ned's hay. I had the 7½ inch S. A. Colt .44 Special with both my heavy loads and some factory loads. Ned, who was a six-gun nut, asked me to try the two loads on a rock about three feet square across the island and the river and the road. It was a long 400 yard shot. I alternated the factory 246 grain loads with my heavy hand loads of 250 grain Keith bullets backed by 18.5 grains 2400, in the cylinder. After a few ranging shots I found the rock from the back position with a head and shoulder rest against a big log. We were both amazed to find that the light factory load and the heavy hand load required exactly the same amount of front sight to hit that rock. The gun carries my long range front sight, so that holding up enough front sight is easy and exact, using the lower gold bar level with the top of rear sight. The factory load was light and the gun would crack and recoil, and after an interval the slug would knock dust from the rock. The heavy load with its vicious crack and heavy recoil required much less time to get to the rock and also threw up a lot more dust from the soft eroded stone, but the fact remains, I held the same amount of front sight for each shot and both loads hit the rock regularly for a couple of guns full. We decided that the much slower barrel time of the soft factory load allowed the barrel to raise higher in recoil before the slug exited from the muzzle than when the heavy hand load was used, thus giving the slow 740 foot second factory load enough elevation to arc onto the rock. The faster barrel time enabled the 250 grain slug, not withstanding the heavier recoil, to leave the muzzle before it had raised as high as with the slower factory load, hence both loads shot to the same elevation with the same amount of sight held up.

Since then I have tried this out with many different guns and calibers at long range, but the .44 Special is the only gun that has produced these results. With my short 4 inch .44 Special 1950 Target I have killed game at 60 to 125 yards with the same hold for both factory 246 grain and hand loads with 250 grain Keith bullet and 18.5 grains 2400 at a full 1200 feet velocity.

The .357 Magnum shoots to different elevation and also to one side or the other as a rule with widely different loads even when the same bullet is used and the .45 Colt seems to do the same. The .44 Special appears to shoot about the same with either the soft factory loads, which are only small varmint loads, or with my heavy hand loads which have killed about all the big game on this continent and a great deal of African game as well.

The best way to learn long range pistol shooting is with a .22 revolver or auto pistol. The ammunition is cheap and it is nearly as accurate at long range as a big sixgun. All that is required is either a lake or dry dusty ground to shoot over so the strike of the tiny pellet can be located to indicate the change in amount of front sight held up to be made for the next shot.

With good, greased, high speed ammunition you will be surprised to find your K-22 Smith & Wesson or your Colt or High-Standard or Ruger auto pistol or Colt Officer's model will shoot accurately enough to hit a man at 500 yards on still days. If a wind is blowing, you are out of luck with the .22 but on still days it will surprise the most skeptical if it is an accurate gun and you have the ammunition that fits it best.

Ed McGivern at one time did a lot of long range shooting with the 8⅜ inch Smith & Wesson .357 Magnum out to 600 yards and one friend of his was able, after some practice, to keep his shots on a man target *at that range from a rest position.*

There is nothing mysterious or mythical at all about long range sixgun shooting. It is the final test of gun and ammunition and the man behind the gun.

Get an accurate .22 long rifle target gun and put a floating target on a lake where you have a safe back ground and no possibility of ricocheting bullets getting into trouble. A can floating at about 150 yards is a good target to start on. Note the bullet splash. If low, hold more front sight up in the rear notch and sit the can on top the middle of the front sight and by all means squeeze the trigger slowly and carefully. If too high, hold up less front sight for the next shot and of course this can be done best from a steady rest position with both hands. Grip the gun normally in the shooting hand and then bring the other hand up loosely as a support. Make no attempt to use the other hand for gripping the gun at any point. Use it as a support for the shooting hand and to balance the weight of your hands on both sides of the gun so that it recoils naturally and freely. You do not have to grip the gun hard for this type of shooting with a revolver, but a firmer hold is necessary to properly control the auto pistol. For a time I used three Super .38 Colts for this work, but never liked them too well for long range work. They were very accurate and flat shooting, but the front sight was so low that I soon had it held up far enough to show the slide between the two sights and it was nearly impossible to keep the front sight in perfect alignment with the rear sight. Given high sights, the .45 and Super .38 would be much better for long range shooting. I had the King Gun Sight Company, now known as the Ricky Gun Sight Company, of San Francisco, fit higher front and rear sights to my old .45 Auto, and it then became much better for long range shooting but not as good as my old target sighted 1917 whose wide one-fourth inch front and rear sights were fitted by Neal Houchins of Philadelphia. A high front sight is necessary for long range shooting and my design of front sight, formerly made by King Gun Sight, is the best I have been able to evolve. The adjustable rear sight fitted to a few Colt single actions, in bygone years, was great for this work, as it was a tangent with long standard and about any range desired could be given it. The shoulder stocks as were once furnished for the Colt Dragoons, Navies and the .44 Army were a great help to long range pistol shooting. Now they are outlawed on modern guns by federal law but they were a real asset to long range pistol shooting.

At one time Smith & Wesson made some revolvers fitted with target sights, and extremely long barrels and detachable stocks such as the famous Buntline special S. A. Colt with long barrels and detachable shoulder stocks. These guns were capable of very small groups at 200 yards on still days and were used a lot for such work. I have never owned such an outfit, but do know it would be a great help in long range shooting. So much of my shooting has been done from the saddle, and the sixgun was short and handy; a shoulder stocked, long barrelled gun would have been just as unhandy as a rifle. I might as well have carried a carbine as such an outfit. However, they do show the accuracy possibilities of a good sixgun when properly held.

The first K-.22 Doug Wesson sent me had a bad chamber or two. I was not satisfied with its accuracy, so started shooting it at a stump in the snow at some 400 yards. The snow was wet and soft and I was able to trail up the ricocheting bullets and recover a number of them, proving cylinder and barrel alignment to be badly off. I sent Wesson the slugs and returned the gun. He sent me another that was superbly accurate with all six chambers at any range. At close range the first gun shot fair but with some indication of tipping bullets on the target. I was positive I was not getting all I was holding for. At long range the fault showed up instantly and the gun simply was not accurate. The second one he sent me was a peach. I later swapped it to Ed McGivern, plus a little cash, for a fine 6½ inch .44 Special Triple Lock Target. I hated to part with the K-.22 but wanted the .44 much more. I hope Ed had as much good service out of the K-.22, which he wanted for his wife, as I have had over the years with that super accurate old .44 Special Triple Lock.

After sighting in the second K-.22, Mrs. Keith and I were driving to North Fork for groceries one summer day and spotted an enormous woodchuck going up a trail on the side of the mountain at the Suydam ranch. We stopped the car and I started working on him with the K-.22 and Remington High speed ammunition. My first shots were all low, as the range was about 135 yards. The first shot and splash of dust below the chuck only hurried him up the straight path towards his cliff-home. On my fifth shot, however, we heard a dull plunk and he stopped and laid motionless in the trail. Pacing the distance proved him to be 185 long paces from the car. The tiny slug went into the back of his head and did not come out.

Another time I spotted a hawk eating something in the hay meadow above the Ranger Station on the North Fork. The range was around 150 yards. I had a .38/44 Smith & Wesson Outdoorsman and some Remington factory .38/44 loads. Resting both hands out of the car window I held up enough front sight, perched the hawk on top, and squeezed. I killed the hawk and was amazed to find it one of the little Kites. He was just finishing off a ruffed grouse and was so stuffed with meat I doubt if he could have gotten into the air. I split him open with my knife and there in his stomach was the breastbone of the grouse. How he ever stretched his mouth and neck enough to swallow it in one piece is beyond me, but there it was. That also taught me something of these so-called beneficial hawks. I have found all manner of so-called beneficial hawks full of grouse and quail. I am no longer impressed by their book reputations.

A friend asked me to sight a .30 caliber Luger carbine for him. It was a fine long-range gun. The barrel must have been 12 inches long and the shoulder stock was the holster and was easily attached to the grip. That outfit shot like a good rifle to 500 yards but is now illegal under Federal law. It was about as unhandy to pack as a rifle and I would prefer a good .30/30 or Mannlicher Schoenauer carbine with more power, but the fact remains it would shoot.

My .45 auto Colt made originally with shoulder stock holster, model 1905, is something else and the shoulder stock holster of this outfit is far too short.

Courtesy of Jack McPhee.

Trapping cabin and high caches on Alatna River, Alaska, 1940.

It is so short, in fact, one has to be very careful to keep from getting hit in the face with the slide when it is fired and for this reason it is an impractical outfit. Les than 100 of them were ever made, possibly around 80 all told, mostly for South American trade. They are now very rare collectors' items. I had it registered and put it in my Colt collection together with its plain model 1905 mate.

After you have become proficient with the .22 pistol at long range, graduate to larger guns. The .38/44 Outdoorsman and Colt Officer's models are fine guns for this work. Over average terrain the .44 Special is still better as its heavy slug will throw up dirt, dust, mud or snow when the lighter .22 and .38 bullets simply fade into the landscape. If you cannot see the strike of your bullet, you cannot walk them onto the target; so the big guns are best once one has mastered the art of long range pistol shooting.

Any difference in hold either of the grip or of the alignment of the sights shows up instantly at long range. Uniformity of grip and uniformity of sighting is of utmost importance and only through constant, steady practice can one acquire this consistency of grip and sighting so necessary if you would lob a sixgun slug on a distant target. Some call it straining the sixgun, but once mastered you can certainly astonish the amateurs wherever you go. True, hitting small objects or game, at long range with a pistol is in the nature of an accident, but if you shoot enough you will have an ever increasing number of such "accidents." Few people today realize the accuracy of a good sixgun at long range. They think long range accuracy can only be accomplished with a rifle. If they would stop to consider the artilleryman, they would see that a long barrel is not necessary to steer a bullet to a distant target. The artilleryman has a very short tube in comparison to the size of the projectile used, yet he can put it down a rain spout at several miles once he gets the range. A good gun crew with a 6 inch Howitzer can lob shells over a small mountain, land on a house or even smaller target, on the other side, at two or three miles range and never see their target. They have an accurate gun and an accurate projectile and the mathematics to hit any target within their range once it is clearly located on their map and their firing data figured.

I would liken the short barreled sixgun to the artillery piece. If it and its ammunition are accurate, you can hit a distant target if you can learn to hold and to aim with enough elevation to give you the necessary range. True, it is just a game, but a very interesting one and also one that can stand you in good stead if you get caught out in the open in a gun fight with no rifle for protection. In that case, as the Frenchman says, "You have to do with what you have to do with."

Editor's Note.

Judge Don Martin, a great friend and outdoor companion of Elmer Keith, adds an interesting explanatory thought to this chapter on long range shooting:

"Keith tells his stories honestly regardless of how they may sound. Frequently it would be to his advantage to tone them down to where they would sound more reasonable to the average reader. He will not do it. He does not exaggerate but he cannot help pin-pointing the dramatic as accurately as he does the bull's-eye. Keith knows that he is a good pistol shot but he has no idea that there is anything remarkable about it. He likes to play with high scoring pistol shots and compares his shooting with theirs. That there are people who cannot hit a wash tub at twenty yards with a hand gun is fully as incredible and astonishing to him as his stories may be to the wash tub missers."

Chapter VI

Game Shooting

OCTOBER 10, 1954, Clarence Negus and I drove up the Salmon river for an afternoon of steelhead fishing. As the deer and elk season was open, I took a .30/40 H. & H. Farquharson single shot rifle along in the car, just in case. We fished several holes with no luck, then parked and locked the car and walked to a hole a quarter mile from the road. I had sprained an ankle the previous week and it was still very painful. I was hobbling along the best I could on one good leg. The rifle was left in the car, but since I always carry a sixgun, the 4 inch 1950 Target .44 Special Smith & Wesson with my heavy 250 grain handloads went along.

We fished the lower end of the hole without success. Clarence got a few clams for bait. We moved toward the upper end and started fishing again. No game was in sight and the steelhead were not interested in anything we had to offer. My old dog, Stub, was working the brush for a bob cat or pheasant when he heard rocks roll across the river. Looking up stream we saw a big mule deer doe appear at the water's edge. She was across the river and upstream at about 125 yards, with the sun behind her and the reflection on the water making it difficult to see her. Stub started barking. Taking the short .44 in both hands and holding up some front sight over the top of the rear sight bar, I lined on her shoulders and fired. Clarence said: "You are high." I tried again but the sun glittering on the water made close aim impossible. My sights were simply a bright glare. The doe stood under a low cliff in dark shadow. My second shot also went high Clarence advised, but I did not see the strike of either. The old doe jumped into her peculiar, high bouncing gait along the river bank. She came to a cliff in the edge of the water and swam around. I was trying to see my sights clear enough to get lined up on her. As she emerged from the river in long bouncing jumps, I held ahead of her the length of one jump and held up the same amount of front sight and tried twice more. Both shots went low, splashing in the edge of the river, but the fourth one evidently ricocheted ahead of her, as she stopped. Still shooting from a standing position and trying to see through the sun glare over the water, I held up more front sight and set her head and neck over it and fired a fifth time. Clarence said, "She hunched up," but she was in the brush along the river's edge and out of my sight after the shot.

A few minutes later we saw her laboriously climbing a low ridge at 250 yards in the direction of a hay meadow. We could plainly see she was hard-hit and using but three legs. She stopped on the ridge and I dropped to a reclining back position and held up half of the front sight blade and placed the deer on top the middle of the front sight. I could see her better now. The sun's glare was not so bad, as she was well above the river, but as I was squeezing on the trigger, she hopped on over the ridge out of sight. I did not get the shot off. I asked Clarence to run up the river and try and keep her in sight. He did so while I hobbled along as fast as I could. For some minutes the deer was out of sight, then Clarence found her again some 400 yards away. We watched her walk into some heavy sage brush and climb up a steep slope 50 yards from the bottom, and lay down. How I wished for the rifle in the car But it was a quarter mile away. After satisfying ourselves the deer was down for the count we went to the car, drove up the river a mile to a bridge, crossed and drove back down through a ranch to within a few hundred yards of where the deer had bedded. We approached to 20 yards but she would not get up, so I shot her through the head. She proved to be a very big old doe and in good shape. The 250 grain Keith slug had passed through the right lung, and the right shoulder was broken. This was my ninth deer and eighth mule deer with a sixgun. Being crippled up to a slow and painful hobble this fall and with steep country hunting entirely out of the question, I can only conclude the good Lord was looking after my meat supply. We did not expect a deer at that steelhead hole or would have taken the rifle with us. Just another case of the sixgun coming in handy when needed. Range for the fifth shot, which bagged the doe, was around 150 yards. The heavy slug had cut a full caliber hole all the way. This was longer range than a short sixgun should ever be used on big game, but I wanted the venison badly. Had I

Keith shooting a sixgun at long range.

expected this opportunity, I would have taken one of my longer barreled guns.

In many sections of this country and Alaska, where deer are hunted in dense timber and thickets and the shooting is at close range, a good sixgun is a handier tool than a rifle. For one thing, you can get through the brush and timber with less noise if you have both hands to part the brush and both hands are often needed in packing out a kill. In dense cover the range may be no more than 20 to 40 yards and seldom will a deer be seen at all over 100 yards. For such hunting, a heavy sixgun will take small deer nicely if the hunter is a careful shot. When hunting cougar with dogs in deep snow, a rifle is simply out of the question most of the time. You are likely to need both hands and I have seen the time when I wished I had a long tail to hang on with when negotiating cliffs and snow covered steep slopes. Likewise, it is a man-killing job to keep in hearing of the dogs. The less weight one packs the better, so here again the heavy sixgun is the best tool.

Oscar Bohannon with another good buck killed by author.

Bob Hagel has tried the .357 Magnum, and killed two cougar with it. He has also tried a 1950 Smith & Wesson .45 Target with Keith 250 grain slugs and a light charge of Bullseye, but this light load did not have enough penetration to satisfy him. Had he used 7.5 grains of Unique, I believe he would have had better luck. He has also used extensively the .44 Special with my heavy loads for treed cougars and likes it best of all having killed several with the S.A. Colt, and more recently, with the Smith & Wesson 1950 Target which he prefers to all other guns.

The best way to pack a heavy gun in the winter is in a shoulder holster under the coat where it can be kept clean and dry and protected from the brush and limbs that constantly scrape your hips. You will also find it less in the way when negotiating cliffs and scrub mahogany. In wet, rainy country it is also the best position for the hunter to carry his sixgun.

When a rifle was available, except as above noted, I have always used it to hunt big game, as it is much surer if long range is involved. When back packing, fishing, prospecting or riding, the rifle is often in the way and too heavy to lug. Then is when the sixgun

A load of prime vension mule deer killed by the author with a sixgun.

A Fine Specimen of Oregon Brush Wolf.
Note the short wide, heavy head, short muzzle, and the width between the eyes and ears. It has rounded ears, heavy shoulders, a short tail, and is about one third larger than regular coyote.

comes into its own. You always have it and it is instantly available when needed. In making long circles when gathering cattle in the fall, the rifle would add extra weight on your horse; the sixgun is the tool. It will serve nicely for close range game shooting and adds little extra weight for an already overloaded horse to carry all day in steep country. At times I have hunted big game with a sixgun when no rifle was available, but I always strove to get as close as possible before shooting and then shot for a vital part of the animal.

One learns only from experience and I will relate enough of my own experiences in this chapter so the reader may profit by my mistakes, as well as successes. The .22 caliber handgun should be used only for very small game and target practice. I have known of a good many deer and bear being killed with a .22 caliber sixgun or auto pistol, but it is really the height of folly to shoot any big game animal with such an outfit. I had to learn the hard way. One time I walked out on a small cliff and when I peered over the edge there lay a big mule buck and a doe not over six yards away, perfectly oblivious of my presence. The season was open and we needed the meat. All I had was a K-22 Smith & Wesson and a box of .22 L.R. High speed solid bullet loads, as I was not hunting. I had been doing considerable double action aerial shooting with the little gun and knew it perfectly. Drawing the gun, I shot the buck in the back of the head and his head dropped. The doe jumped to her feet and I shot her in the back of the head and down she went. Then the buck jumped up and started to stagger around and I shot him in the back of the head again and he dropped again, then up came the doe and I again downed her. This was repeated until the gun was empty and I barely managed to

La Cole and guide. Bear is in trap, Old Mexico, fall of 1924. Easy sixgun shot.

A live coyote I brought home on a bucking horse.

reload the cylinder and close it before the buck again regained his feet and this time I shot him in the back of the neck killing him and he had no more than dropped than the doe was up and I finished her with a couple more in the back of the neck. The tiny bullets evidently did not have power enough to penetrate the heavy muscles back of the skull and then penetrate the skull as well from the rear. I swore, never again. When skinned out, I found the only two bullets that entered the brain did so from the neck

Jack McPhee of Fairbanks, Alaska, shooting a .44 Special S. & W.

Hacksaw Tom, right, with Mexican Javalinas.

shots where the skull joins onto the neck vertebrae, and in each case the killing slugs had gone down through this joint and into the back of the brain. Those that hit the back of the heads of both deer had merely flattened on the skull and a couple had skidded around under the skin on the side of the head.

Another time I had broken a big buck's shoulder low down below the brisket at 500 yards with the .30-06 while Jim Robbins and I were riding for cattle. We trailed the buck a half mile and jumped him and I got another shot at 300 yards running and hit him in the right flank ranging forward into the paunch. He soon sickened and bedded down out on an open sage brush covered mountain-side. We worked up to within 300 yards and waited for him to pass out, but he did not, so Jim suggested I take his .22 Colt Woodsman and finish the job. Not wanting to hit him again in the body with the rifle and not wishing to damage the head and cape, I followed his suggestion. I walked up to 50 yards and taking both hands planted the tiny slug in his forehead. He merely jumped up and ran past me and I poured the whole magazine full into his lungs as he went past on three legs. He soon bedded down again and I returned to Jim and we reloaded the little gun. This time when I approached he was too sick to get up and I proceeded to bounce most of that magazine full of standard .22 L.R. pills off his skull before one hit the small depression over the left eye and went into the brain. The rest of those bullets hit the sloping skull and glanced right out again and away. Those three deer were enough for me. I will never shoot another big game animal with a .22. It is simply a fool stunt.

With high speed, greased hollow points, the .22 auto pistol or sixgun is a fine little gun for killing small game such as rabbits, grouse, turtles, frogs, cottontails, squirrels, etc., including snakes, but by no stretch of the imagination is it fit for anything larger.

Sitka deer buck in easy pistol range. A sixgun is all that is needed for these deer.

Pair of mountain goats in sixgun range, Alaska.

Dressing an antelope killed by Keith.

One of the author's camps in the game country.

The spruce grouse or fool hen is always excellent eating. Photo by author.

A typical coyote ready for the sixgun slug. Photo by Lemuel C. Smelier.

The extreme bottom of the ear is the place to shoot to kill a grizzly with a sixgun.

Ted Keith at age 12, bringing in the meat from an elk hunt. Dressing an antelope killed by Keith.

I once watched Dr. Wilson L. DuComb try to kill a Gila Monster I had tied to a sage brush with a noose around his neck using a K-.22 and Western Super X copper coated L.R. ammunition. He hit that big tough lizzard five times about head and neck on an angle and each time the bullet would make a smear on his tough hide and howl away, until Doc walked around square with the side of his head. Then one penetrated the brain and killed it. Twenty-two L.R. ammunition does not have the velocity and power when fired from a short hand gun that it does when fired from a rifle with 18 inches or more of barrel. Even for small game shooting, I prefer the .32-20, .32 S. & W. Long, with flat pointed bullets or the .38 Special with flat point bullet, and this after many years experience with about all calibers on game.

The .22 W.R.F., known as the .22 Special, is a much better cartridge and a better killer on small game than the .22 L.R. It is a better cartridge for the woodsman to carry as all lubricant is enclosed in the case.

I have also had a hog's skull deflect .22 L.R. bullets many times when they were not struck squarely, but a heavily loaded .44 or .45 or .357 Magnum will do the trick nicely every time on deer, bear or hogs. In fact the skull may be well shattered on the smaller species.

In 1937 Westley Brown and I were hunting Stone sheep on the Musqua River in British Columbia. I had killed a couple of fine rams with the 300 Magnum and the last one had fallen on a ledge far above us. Westley said he would make the climb up that treacherous slope to see if the second ram was dead while I watched from below in case he was only wounded and got up. I would be in a position to knock him down again while anyone up in the ledges would lose sight of him in three jumps. When Westley got up to the ram he found the rest of the band, all young rams, still milling about, as I had killed the two leaders. They seemed completely unafraid of him and as he had a sheep license and a Colt Woodsman he proceeded to pink the best ram back of the shoulder with the little Colt. He planted most of the magazine of .22 L.R. in that ram behind the shoulder before one of the tiny bullets hit the spine and dropped the sheep, but whether it killed him, or the fall did so we never knew as the ram came end over end all the way down the steep slope to the grassy creek bottom and was dead when I approached him.

Of all the rim fire pistol cartridges, the one I liked best was the .25 Stevens long. This is a real small game cartridge and one I would like to see used today in K-22 and Colt Target revolvers as well as the Ruger Single Six. The cylinder would have to be a trifle longer, but the frames are long enough, and this would give the small game hunter a real load for all small game. I used it in a single shot Stevens pistol and it was a much better grouse load than any of the .22 rim fires. We have urged Ruger to chamber his Single Six for this fine cartridge. If Smith & Wesson, Colt, and Ruger would only make the guns, the ammunition companies would soon have a good supply of high speed ammunition available in both solid and hollow point. With its 65 grain slug in present loadings and the fact that the lubricant and bullet are covered by the case, it is an ideal small game cartridge for the trapper and hunter using a pistol and wanting factory loaded rim fire ammunition.

For big game shooting with a pistol we prefer .44 or .45 caliber guns, with flat point bullets loaded to as high velocity as the gun will safely handle.

A large entrance hole is just as important as a large exit hole; both let blood out of an animal and cold air in. Up to 50 yards we have seen just about as good results from such heavy loaded sixguns as from .30-30 class rifles. The .357 Magnum is good, but the heavier, larger .44 or .45 is much better, having about double the actual, if not the paper killing power. Ballistic tables are nice things to ponder over on a cold winter day by the fire, but they do not tell the whole tale, and often are very misleading. This thing we call life is something we do not yet under-

Guide Jack Johnstone with record goat.

This elk is getting mad; note that he is grinding his teeth. He charged photographer Andrew Erickson, but the latter, being on snow webs, easily ran away from him in the deep snow. Notice how the color of the elk matches that of tree bole.

stand. One man or animal will carry on with seemingly impossible wounds until literally shot to pieces and another will drop dead from a tiny .22 bullet. Placing the first shot is of vital importance in all game shooting or in a gun fight. Hit an animal right the first shot and the job is done, but wound him with a badly placed first shot and you can then literally cut the beast to pieces and unless brain or spine is hit he will carry on. The same has happened many times in battle and in gun fights where men were simply riddled yet continued to shoot back. The first slug delivers all the nervous shock the nervous system will stand or can absorb, after that you are merely destroying tissue, and the game dies from loss of blood unless you can hit the spine or brain and put them down. On the other hand if that first slug be properly placed, by the time the animal starts to recover from shock it is dead from hemorrhage or from suffocation if the slug has pierced the heart or lungs. If it hits the brain or the spinal cord the beast is down instantly and helpless if not dead. If the hit is a high lung shot, the lungs soon fill up with blood and the animal suffocates; if a low lung shot, the blood drains out and the beast may go a considerable distance, but he will leave a blood trail that is easily followed to the end. At sixgun and pistol velocities, all bullets should be flat pointed for best killing qualities. You cannot depend on upsettage or mushrooming unless bones are struck. If the bullet be properly shaped it will cut a full caliber hole which is what you want, and if it upsets, so much the better. We found this out the hard way, back in 1917.

We jumped a mountain goat, a tough old Billy and he started running nearly straight away from us. At 40 yards we landed a .45 caliber 250 grain Remington black powder slug in the seat of his pants, so to speak. This load caried full 40 grains of black powder and we later determined the slug went nearly the full length of that tough old Billy and broke the left shoulder where it lodged. The gun was a 5½ inch S. A. Colt. My second slug hit a granite boulder that got in the way as I followed the running goat with my sights. The dust and lead particles from this slug turned the goat up the mountain. My third shot caught him square through the lungs behind the shoulder. This turned him down the mountain and out of sight. I ran to the top of the ridge to keep above him and started along the ridge top. A big burn had

Mexican Ram. Photo by Keith.

Photo taken by Elmer Keith for a photo contest before testing a .45 on him. My hat slipped off for my trouble before I quit taking pictures of this one. Taken at only a few feet, it is the best photo I ever took of a cat out of about 50 I have photographed. Caught on ranch in Montana.

Croft and Keith, Durkee, Ore., August 1928.

covered the country that summer so that it lay deep in black and grey ash with plenty of black stumps and logs. Each sixgun slug that missed the goat threw up a cloud of ashes.

The old Billy came out in a little basin 300 yards below me. I dropped to a sitting position with back against a stump, holding the gun between my drawn up knees. After holding up most of the front sight and perching the moving goat on top of it, then sliding the sight over to the side of him to allow for his speed, I started shooting. I soon got the range and knocked him down twice with six shots. Reloading as the goat went out of sight, I followed along the top of the ridge, keeping above him. I must have followed him for over two miles, shooting only when I got a good rest position, as I was puffing from the run and high elevation until I could not hold steady in any other way. The heavy slugs were telling on the tough old animal also and I finally worked up to 30 yards of him and shot him through the heart broadside. This floored him but he was up in an instant and going again. Then I shot him through the neck, missing the bone of the spine. Again he dropped, but was up and going in a fraction of a second. In all, I fired 18 factory loaded Remington .45 Colt black powder hulls with their pointed bullets at that goat, and hit him with ten of them. He finally lay down behind a burned snag, and slipping up I finished him off with a blow of my belt axe on the back of the head. I had then just six cartridges left for my gun, and as it was good grizzly country I wanted to save them until I reached camp and could replenish my supply.

Only the first slug stayed in the goat, the other nine all going through him, punching very small holes. Two that struck him in the ribs at 300 yards had gone out the other side. Three slugs had gone through the heart, but they must have been among the last ones fired. A mountain goat is a very tough animal, and that one was no exception as we had to boil him at that high elevation for three days before we could eat him. But eat him we did, as we had been three months on frowsy bacon, running a township line along the Continental Divide in Montana. I back packed him to camp in two trips and tough as he was, he certainly made a very welcome change in our bill of fare.

Another time I jumped a big mule buck across a shallow draw. He ran broadside down the other side. My first .45 Colt landed right behind him—not enough lead—my second, which was aimed a bit further in front of his nose while he sailed along in his high bouncing gait, caught him behind the shoulders and through both lungs. He did not stagger or go down, but from the way he humped up I knew he was hit, and I followed him down the draw, over a low ridge

Keith in 1932 with mess of blue grouse killed with .38/44 Outdoorsman S.&W.

Live goat photographed by Keith at 12 feet. An easy six-gun shot.

Remains of mule deer fawn killed by coyotes. Beside it is one of the three coyotes I shot the next morning at 300 yards. Photo by Keith.

and across two more draws before I found him dead. Again the pointed Remington .45 Colt 250 grain slug had punched a very small hole. With a flat nosed bullet and the same hit, the deer would have bled out in a fraction of the distance. This shooting was at about 100 yards across the gulch. I could shoot a blue grouse through the body with that load and it would not damage much meat. Some that were shot squarely through the body with this heaviest of all .45 Colt factory loads even fluttered off the ground and sailed away down the mountain. That pointed bullet at sixgun velocities was not a killer, but it would surely penetrate. A big black bear with his paws on an old log facing me took one square in the center of the chest at 30 yards. It killed him almost instantly as it went back through the heart and then on an angle up through the spine and out of him on top of the rump. I think the shattered spine must have been the reason for his instant demise, as he simply slumped across the log and moved his head only a few times before giving his death call, not unlike the bawl of a calf. Again there was a very small wound channel until the slug hit the spine and was battered making a large exit hole.

After this I decided to do something about pointed bullets, so I got a .45/90 Winchester 300 grain mould and cast a few pounds of slugs with it, sized them down to .454 inches, and loaded them with 35 grains of F.F.G. black. This was a real killing load and trapped coyotes and bobcats and some small game soon proved its superiority in killing power over the pointed factory bullet. Many jack rabbits had run for a considerable distance with a factory .45 Colt through the lungs, but they did not go anywhere when slapped with the 300 grain flat point bullet.

My next chance at game came when I jumped a big buck, the following fall, on the brow of a ridge. He went straight away down the mountain, sailing out in long, high, bouncing jumps. He had jumped from almost under my feet and I instantly had the old gun on him, and as he reached nearly the height of a bound I shot. It hit him in the back of the head and the bullet came out between his eyes and he simply turned somersaults down the steep mountain. His skull was shattered for an area an inch in diameter.

Another big 300 pound mule buck I shot with that gun and load was also going down the mountain from me. The slug caught him between the shoulders breaking the spine and coming out of the lower front of his neck. He was killed instantly and rolled and slid nearly a quarter mile down the mountain in the snow. This load proved a very accurate one, a good killer, but with a terribly high trajectory as velocity could not have been much over 825 feet. I made several 6 inch groups with it at 100 yards, however, and it would

Record cougar killed in trap by Keith with .44 Special S.A. Colt.

Courtesy of Harold W. Johnson.
Alaskan brown bear with salmon. In good sixgun range.

always stay well within a foot circle at 100 yards which was good enough to kill plenty of game.

During the years about which I have been writing, I carried on a side-line business of breaking saddle broncs for the neighbors and the local cow outfits. I fancied myself as a "bronc stomper" and on several occasions rode a hundred miles to prove, to my own satisfaction, that some outlaw with a reputation for throwing all comers could be ridden. I usually had from half a dozen to ten or twelve wild cayuses around the place at a time. One day when I was riding a big outlaw that stood seventeen hands high at the withers, he put a foot in a badger hole while we were swinging along over the Montana prairie at an easy lope. We turned two somersaults and he came up running and kicking at me. My left spur had somehow gotten in front of the stirrup leather and I was hung hard and fast. He had knocked most of the wind out of me even though I flopped to the side and dodged his hips when they came over in each turn and let the cantle board and horn of the saddle protect my right leg, but I lost hold of the hackamore rope and he had a free head. The stirrup leather swung me so close to him he was kicking me with his hocks and my stern was bouncing over the frozen ground. The old .45 S. A. was still in its tight holster and I started shooting the instant I drew it. The first two slugs in his rear end only seemed to speed him up and I thought I was finished. The third angled upward and broke his back and again we went into a wild melee of somersaults. When we quit rolling I was out in front of the horse with that left stirrup leather stretched out toward me. He was trying to get up and was on his front feet but his back was broken. I planted the fourth slug in his brain.

I was really bunged up from that job and did no riding for several weeks thereafter. Only the .45 S. A. Colt and the heavy loads saved my life. The old gun was good for livestock owing to its penetration with either factory loads or my heavy 300 grain handloads.

Courtesy of Harold W. Johnson.
Sow Alaskan brownie with three two-year-olds. In pistol range.

One morning a neighbor called up saying the butcher was treed by a bull and asked if one of us would come over and kill the bull. It was 20 below zero. My partner and I had just gotten home from a 20 mile ride. We had danced all night and were pulling the blankets over us when the call came. Neither of us felt much like getting up to save the butcher, so we drew straws and as usual I was unlucky. I dressed, saddled up and rode over to the neighbor's ranch. The men were all away. The butcher had come to beef a big Durham bull. He had an old Colt Lightning .41. I never asked whether he had it loaded with shorts or longs. At any rate he was up a small quaking aspen that he had to hang onto and was about frozen. The bull walked around the tree butting it in an attempt to shake him out. When I rode up and stopped my cow horse the bull turned, took a look at me, and charged. I waited until he was only a couple jumps away and planted a 250 grain Remington black powder load from the old .45 S. A. in the center of his forehead. He dropped his nose to the ground, turned a somersault, and lay on his back with his tail toward me as my little cow horse jumped nimbly aside. I cut his throat as the butcher was too nearly frozen to do anything until he had gone to the house and thawed out.

Another time on the range while wearing that same old gun, I was roping cows which had gotten away from a bunch the boss had bought to brand. We were riding in pairs, roping, throwing and tying them, then building a little sage brush branding fire, rather than gathering all the cattle together in order to brand these few scattered strays. I roped a big old spotted cow with long sharp horns. I was riding a green colt with a hackamore and when the rope settled I flipped it over the cow's rump and spurred the horse ahead to throw the cow. He stopped short and went to fighting his head, then swapped ends when the rope hit his shoulder as the cow came to the end of it. They were big, heavy cows and I was tied hard and fast having a loop in the end of my rope and that passed under the front of the fork and up over the saddle horn. The cow fell but got up, turned and charged. I could not get that fool bronc to do anything but fight his head. One of those long horns caught him right behind the shoulder and went through his heart. He made a couple of buck jumps, swapped ends again, winding the rope around my legs until I could not get clear. He fell dead and pinned my left leg under him. The cow backed away, threw dirt over her shoulders with her front feet and came again. My partner could not get to me in time, so I shot her in the middle of the forehead with the old .45 and she did a somersault towards me. That mad cow would have then and there ended my career but for the old sixgun.

Another time I found a cow bogged down on the Missouri River. She evidently had not been in the mud long, because she was on the fight. I got a rope on her and pulled her out but her legs were numb and she would fall. I got my rope off and did it up, then went around behind her and tailed her up. The ungrateful old biddy whirled on me, caught one horn between my legs and threw me in the mud hole I had just pulled her out of. Then she came in after me. I drew fast and shot from the hip. The gun powder burned the hair on her forehead. I had to leave her dead in the bog hole. I was plastered with mud from head to foot and the only thing I accomplished was to save a mean cow from dying a slow lingering death. In those days we often rode mean horses and worked meaner cattle. I had to kill two more critters and one other horse to save my life at different times.

A few such experiences and a man might forget his breeches when he dressed in the morning but he certainly would not forget his sixgun. Over the years I tried everything in the sixgun line, but when punching cows, I did not find anything in a factory load for a sixgun that would beat the old Remington .45 Colt with a 250 grain slug and 40 grains of black powder for use on livestock, as it certainly would penetrate and only brain or spine shots would kill a horse or mad cow fast enough to save the shooter. My 300 grain bullet hand loads with 35 grains of black powder were just as good for the purpose, and opened much larger holes.

Finally a weak .45 Colt case head blew off with this load. The gas blew the loading gate off the gun, breaking its shank and cutting through the flesh of my trigger finger. From this experience I decided the bullet was a bit heavy for the thin cases and thin chamber walls of the cylinders. I cut one band and groove from the mould leaving it to cast a 260 grain flat point bullet. This worked very well with 40 grains of black powder. It was a very good game killer and flatter in its trajectory curve than the 300 grain slug with 35 grains of black. In 1925 I designed a bullet for the .45 Colt for Belding & Mull known as No. 454260. It proved a good close range bullet but did not seem accurate at long range, having a blunt nose like the old factory .41 Colt load. It punched a hole rather than cutting full caliber. I dropped it after ruining a barrel with some loads put up by F. C. Ness, then with B. & M., with 16.3 grains of No. 80 and this bullet of my design. The rear end of the barrel cracked in three places.

I later designed two copies of this bullet in .44 Special for Belding & Mull, one to weigh 260 grains and the other 280 grains. Both were very good at close range but neither seemed very accurate at long range. The very blunt, but round nose did not cut a large enough hole in game animals to suit me so I designed the Keith bullets for Lyman with a full groove diameter band in front of the crimping groove to cut a full caliber hole in meat or target and also so this band would cut down the jump from cylinder to barrel and true up the slug in the chamber before firing.

Bob Hagel killed eight treed cougar in one winter with these Keith bullets from a 4¾ inch .44 Special S. A. Colt. He used both my 235 grain hollow point and the 250 grain solid, finding the 250 grain solid bullet much the better for shoulder shots where he wanted to break the cat down, and the hollow point the best for lung shots behind the shoulder where he wanted to destroy a maximum amount of lung tissue with one shot. I killed one cougar, which placed third in world's records, with my No. 5 single action .44 Special and a light load of 9 grains Dupont shotgun and my 250 grain bullet. I was too hard up to buy pistol powder at the time, during the depression, and had to use the shotgun powder. The big cat had eaten over half of a mule buck I had killed for meat and I decided to trap him if possible. He came back and got two toes caught in my No. 14 Newhouse, then dragged it, a No. 4, and a small quaken aspen stick some four feet in length to which they were wired, down the canyon. He finally wound up the extra trap and light toggle in a snow brush. I found him there slowly tugging at the trap chain but when I broke a stick and he saw me, he stopped trying to get away and simply sat up and watched me like a gigantic house cat. I proceeded to take some pictures of him and he would open his big mouth and growl at me, then hiss, and when I stamped my foot in the snow he would really put on a show. But my camera had an indirect view finder and when I looked down in that crazy finder, the cat would close his mouth again so I could not catch him as I wanted him. I took a couple of shots anyway and when he then turned his back on me and laid down with head pointing up the gulch away from me, I thought, "If I could take one more step forward I would then be about six feet from him and would get a picture that would be all cat."

I had the No. 5 S.A. Colt .44 Special with 250 grain Keith slugs and a light grouse load of 9 grains Dupont shotgun cocked in my right hand and was tripping the camera shutter with my right thumb nail.

I started that one step forward but never finished it. The big cougar was in the air instantly, with left paw reaching for me, his mouth open and his tail sticking straight up in the air and his right paw dragging those traps and toggle. I flipped the .44 Special up and shot from the hip, hitting him square in the chest and jumped as far down the mountain side as I could. At the same time he flashed over my right shoulder and landed plop on his big belly in the snow. He could not move any of his four feet and his tail slowly came down to horizontal, but he could and did move his head and bit at every small quaking aspen he could reach, cutting off those of an inch or less in diameter. I dragged him out of the brush by his tail and took another photo of him as he died. That 250 grain slug removed most of the aorta from his heart and went up and lodged against the spine between the shoulders. Had it been backed by 18.5 grains of 2400 it would have shattered his spine. The skin, meat and entrails weighed an even 200 pounds and he was seven feet six inches from tip of nose to end of tail before skinning and tip of tail and tips of both ears were gone from fighting or freezing. Fooling with bear or big cats is poor business, and if I had not landed that slug perfectly, he would have made short work of me. A lighter gun, unless it hit and broke the spine, might have let me down in this instance.

My old friend Billy Bell, who built the Elk Summit Ranger Station between the Lochsa and Selway Rivers, was riding the trail one day when a grizzly jumped on his dog. Bear and dog rolled off below the trail on the steep mountain and Bill grabbed an 8 inch barrel 9 mm. Luger he was carrying at the time. He proceeded to pour the whole magazine into the bear's shoulders, shooting down hill, but the bear kept right on chewing the dog. Bill left in a hurry, mounted his horse and got out of there. He told me he was sure if he had carried his old .45 single action he could have dropped the bear and probably saved his dog.

Keith with 6 point bull elk, Oct. 19, 1919. Typical Montana elk country. This photo was taken by my hunting partner, Captain W. R. Strong, a brother of General George V. Strong who was head of G-2 in World War II. Two hours later Bill was shot and killed in front of me by Hans De Young, who was shooting at an elk. This elk was finally killed with a .38/40 S.A. Colt after nearly killing me.

Big game hunters' camp in the Idaho primitive area, north of Sun Valley, Idaho.
Courtesy of Union Pacific Railroad.

Charley O'Neil's small dog put something in a den in the spring of the year, and O'Neil, thinking he had a bobcat, took a P-.38 chambered for the 9mm. Luger cartridge and a flashlight and crawled into the den. He was surprised to find an old female black bear and two yearlings. The sow came for him and he killed her with a brain shot, then one yearling ran out of the den over the top of Oneil. The bear tore most of his clothes off on the way. Charley shot and killed the other yearling. His dog ran the first one back into the den and over the top of him again. He killed that one and heaved the three of them out of the den. He said he had a lot of respect for the penetration of the 9 mm. Luger cartridge but little for its shocking power.

In 1937 I had a ringside seat, so to speak, of a black bear charging unprovoked. We were cutting a trail through thick arctic birch, willow and scrub fir, from the Prophet to the Musqua River. Westley Brown was in the lead chopping these small trees and behind him Edgar Dopp was finishing clearing a trail for the twenty-three head of horses we had with us. Next came Dick Brown, followed by Doc Brown, both on their horses, then half the pack string, then myself with the last half of the pack string. Al Robinson, the cook, brought up the rear. A small, but old, male black bear got up out of his bed and charged Westley Brown. Westley ran back toward the pack train yelling "Look out for the bear," and trying to reach his horse and his .30/30 carbine. Seeing he could not make it, he whirled to the side of the trail he had cut and raised the four pound chopping axe high over his head. In the meantime Edgar Dopp had seen the play and caught the finger of his right glove with his teeth, pulled it off, then jerked out his .455 Smith and Wesson and using both hands, landed a heavy Belding & Mull slug in the bear's head, killing him instantly.

Momentum turned the bear in somersaults right to Brown's feet and his head landed on a stump Westley had previously cut off. Westley sunk the heavy chopping axe into the back of the bear's head up to the handle and asked, "How do you like that?" Edgar used a blunt point B. & M. bullet backed by a heavy charge of No. 80 and it did the job nicely. The bear proved to be an old boar, and why he charged Westley upwind of six men and 23 horses we never knew. Quick thinking and quick shooting on Dopp's part saved the day and a lot of trouble. If that bear ever got over Westley and into the pack string, there would have been some real excitement.

Another time Edgar Dopp was taking a pack string down the Halfway River in the spring and wallowing through snow slides when a grizzly charged one of the horses from above the trail. Edgar had a 9 mm. Luger and emptied it into the bear which charged across the trail, rolled into the river and sunk like a huge rock. The river was high and Edgar never saw the bear again.

Bull moose.

Cougar treed by Rood boys, an easy sixgun shot.

Jim Ross, an old guide living at Hudson's Hope, British Columbia, has many times killed his winter's supply of caribou or moose with a 4 inch barrel 9 mm. Luger, shooting them through the lungs. Personally we found both the 9 mm. Luger and the Super .38 sadly lacking in shock and opening far too small holes for use in big game hunting. I much prefer the old .45 Auto Colt with its high trajectory but heavier bullet and larger wound channel. Elmer Purcell also killed most of his meat with a 9 mm. Luger but worked in close and employed only brain shots for his big game killing.

We tried the .32/20 S.A. Colt and found it sadly lacking in killing power, even with the heaviest handloads. We killed three mule deer and one big cow elk with it, however, before giving up that cartridge. We did find that factory 115 grain soft point Winchester ammunition would expand nicely on a mule deer but would not expand at all in wood, either dry, hard lodgepole or green pine trees. In trees, the lead tip would smear off but the jacket would not rupture. The opposite was true when deer were struck with it. I emptied an S.A. Colt .32/20 at one deer, shooting at the right shoulder. Four of the slugs landed on the shoulder and two just behind it, all expanded very well, in fact some that hit the shoulder bone were expanded to the size of a nickel, and the jacket spread out almost in a sheet. The deer went on up the mountain while I reloaded. I hit a limb with the next shot and killed the animal with a spine shot the eighth. All three deer proved that the soft point would expand well if it hit bone and a little even when it did not. The elk, we killed with a brain shot that landed back of the right ear as she ran away from us. It went through the brain but lodged in the skull in front. It too, was well expanded.

In 1919 too much expansion and lack of penetration nearly cost my life when a .38/40 Remington soft point 180 grain factory bullet splattered out to the size of a quarter on a bull elk's skull without even knocking him down. I had dropped the huge old elk with a 220 grain soft point .30/06 in the side of the neck at 70 yards. He had slipped down hill and his head was under the snow which reached my hips in depth. I was standing in front of him, a foolish stunt, looking at his huge horns and decided to see if he was dead. I prodded him in the top of the withers with the muzzle of the Springfield. It was just like prodding dynamite, for he exploded out of the snow, all in one motion, and caught me on his brow tines, throwing me down the mountain. He knocked the wind out of me and I lost track of the rifle as I went end over end down the steep slope. I landed with my hips sunk through the crusted snow. My left arm and shoulder which hit a log, were numb. The sixgun belt was up under my arms. The old bull was buck jumping with feet bunched into the place where he had lain in the snow. Whether he was still stunned and not seeing well, or whether he thought I was under him in the deep snow, I will never know. However, when I cocked the sixgun he heard it, stopped and looked at me. I centered his forehead with the .38/40 S.A. Colt and fired. He simply shook his head and came for me. I shot him in the forehead again as he landed from his first jump. This dropped him and he slid up against me in the snow with his head and

Live billy goat photographed at 21 feet by Elmer Keith—an easy sixgun shot.

eyes buried as before. The first shot was one of the then new, tinned primer Remington .38/40 soft points. The second was one of my heavy handloads with a 210 grain cast .40/65 Winchester bullet backed by 40 grains of black powder. The Remington loads and my handloads were alternated in the chambers. The first slug had simply splattered out on his skull and not even broken the bone, while the handload had gone back into the jaws, but, as I later found out, too low for the brain.

I then hunted up my rifle and worked the snow out of my barrel with a tiny sapling, as it had landed muzzle first in the snow and only the butt stock showed above the crust. The only sensible thing I did was reload the sixgun and fasten the hold down strap around my right leg. After getting the rifle in working order, I went around behind the bull where he lay with his hind legs uphill and above the crusted snow and prodded him in the rump with the rifle muzzle, intending to shoot him if he moved. When the rifle touched him he lashed out with both hind feet, throwing me down the mountain again, jumped up and started running away with his head held high and horns thrown back over his rump. My back and hips again broke through the crusted snow with my feet high in front of me. I started shooting with the single action Colt before I had fully stopped rolling. The first slug went half way through the upright sword point on the left horn, the next two struck in the hams, and the fourth broke his back in front of the hips. He turned around with his front feet and started pulling himself back toward me with his hair all standing up on end along the back of his neck and grinding his teeth. I waited until he was close and centered the front of his neck. Luckily for me, it was one of my handloads and it broke the old boy's neck and ended the job. This shows just what a crazy kid can do to get himself in trouble. Why that bull charged me after throwing me down the mountain, then after getting up the second time, instead of finishing me, tried to run away, is something else I will never know. Had he turned on me then, I would not be writing this now. After this experience I quit the .38/40 forever and went back to the .45 Colt for more penetration and a heavier bullet. I used .45 Colts exclusively from then on until 1925 when I started experimenting with the .44 Special. After a few more years work with both the .44 Special and the .45 Colt, I decided the .44 Special in handloads was the best of all sixgun cartridges. In factory loads, the .45 Colt was superior, as it is today.

One morning while hunting horses and carrying a bridle and one halter, intending to pick up my saddle horse and lead a pack animal in hopes the bunch would follow him into camp, I jumped a big bull elk off to my left. He ran past me at 25 to 30 yards through the heavy timber. I jerked the Triple Lock Target I was carrying and slapped him behind the left shoulder before he got behind the trees. The gun was loaded with my 250 grain solid Lyman bullet and 18.5 grains 2400. Both slugs went clear through him and out on the other side. I waited and had a smoke, then trailed him down the slope into a creek bed, possibly 200 yards. There he had stopped and stamped around a bit. Then his lungs had filled with blood and he had suffocated and rolled into the creek.

A friend of mine shot a moose with this same .44 Special load, except it was before the advent of 2400 and I had loaded the cartridges with 12 grains of No. 80. He wanted him for his winter meat, as the bull was close to one of his trap line cabins. He shot him through the heart, a broadside shot. He said the bull humped up after the shot and walked slowly for about 100 yards, then laid down and died in his bed. That slug went through to the skin on the off shoulder.

About twenty years ago, I loaded several hundred Keith 250 grain solid .44 Specials, with 12 grains of No. 80 for Dr. James T. Maxwell of Omaha, Nebraska. He carried them and a 6½ inch .44 Special Smith & Wesson to Africa on a six weeks hunting trip. He kept 12 men supplied with antelope meat on the whole six weeks trip with that gun and my handloads and wrote me that it seemed to kill about as well as a rifle at the ranges he was shooting. Three years ago he wrote that the lot of ammunition I had loaded so long ago, still shot as well as ever.

The spring of '37 Dr. Wilson L. DuComb, of Carlyle, Illinois, and I were hunting down in Sonorra,

Mrs. Elmer Keith with a bobcat killed with .44 Special S.A. Colt, Dec. 1926.

Mexico. We decided to spend our last day hunting for the Mexican javalina or wild hogs. Charley Ren gave us a Mexican guide that day. He could speak no English and we no Spanish, so we had to get along with sign language. The guide's dogs gave tongue and started chasing several little wild hogs up a dry arroyo, choked with small desert trees, brush and tall saguarro cactus. The Mexican, a fine horseman, and I, also raised in the saddle, soon left Doc far behind. Finally the barking of the dogs was lost to us and we stopped to listen. Then we heard Doc yelling, so thinking he was in trouble, we whirled our horses and soon found him in front of a low cliff under which was a cave. He said, "I just saw some pecarries run into that cave."

The Mexican looked it over and said "No bueno" and started to leave, but we would have none of that. We had only that day and wanted a hog head apiece and knew these were in the hole, so decided to get them. Doc carried a Model 54 Winchester .30/06 and I had a Smith & Wesson .357 Magnum. In front of the cave was a very small amphitheatre clear of brush and surrounding it, tight on three sides, was tall cholla cactus, ripe and ready to shed its spines into anything that touched it. I crawled into the cave with my sixgun. The front part was large and I could see well, but then it choked down to about the diameter of my shoulders and went on back in the hill into another cave. When I crawled back into this bottle neck I could not see a thing in front of me, but could hear two sets of javalina tusks clashing like castinets. Next thing I knew I was hauled unceremoniously out of the cave on my belly. The Mexican had roped my feet and mounted his horse and dragged me out. He made slashing motions at his throat and repeated, "No bueno."

I guess he thought we were a very crazy pair of Americanos as we would not leave and I asked for some dry wood to smoke out those little devils. I believe all the wood we found had been dry long before the landing of Columbus, as it was easily set afire after we whittled a few shavings. I threw several of these limbs back into the inner cave and then bedded down in the sand in the front of the outer cave. Soon we could hear the little pigs coughing instead of clashing their tusks and finally I saw an apparition of grey bristles and flashing white tusks coming like the devil was after him. I planted a Keith 160 grain hollow point right in his face shooting double action, then jumped up and backwards to get out of his way as he tumbled end over end into that small arena.

The brain shattered pecarry would jump high in the air, a good six feet at times, just as a head shot rabbit will sometimes do, and he kicked up an awful lot of dust. Then the remaining hog came out and ran around in the dust clashing his teeth at me. I could see nothing of him, only the dead pig when he came up above the dust cloud in his death throes. Doc was pointing that .30/06 down into the melee from his perch on the cliff and I was more afraid of that rifle than the hogs. I backed into that wall of cholla, pronounced choya. My pronouncements are off the record. The live pig went back into the cave and when the dust settled we threw more burning wood into the cave and again smoked him out. I then had to spend the better part of an hour draped over an old log while Doc and the Mexican gleefully pulled cholla spines out of my back-side with knife and pliers. I never could understand why they were so happy about it, but we had our hog heads. That 160 grain .357 Magnum Keith hollow-point backed by 13.5 grains of 2400 so shattered the skulls that we had to piece them together again with plaster of Paris after cleaning.

Nasty little pigs; one of them almost slashed our dog's head off before I crawled into the cave. The Mexican sent him in on a half-inch rope to show us the fallacy of trying to get them out of a cave. He pulled the dog back out the instant the fight started but the old dog had one shoulder laid open to the bone from joint to near top of the back and a bad cut on the throat on the other side, and only a portion of one of the three strands of that half-inch rope was left, the rest severed as with a razor. After seeing what they did to the good old dog, I decided we would get them if it took all day.

Up to at least 50 yards a good heavy sixgun load seems to kill as well as most .30/30 rifles and opens a far better blood trail. It also penetrates much better owing to lack of expansion when solid bullets are used. A .44 or .45 caliber hole in game lets a lot of air inside and a lot of blood out of an animal and seems as effective as the 30 caliber rifle with its smaller entrance hole and much lighter bullet. One should, however, carefully study the anatomy of the game and its skeletal structure and know just where to hit any game animal to reach a vital part, or to hit the spine or brain, which puts them down to stay. I remember counting 1000 mule deer in one day from daybreak until two p.m. in the afternoon and could easily have loaded a big truck with sixgun killed deer that day. I never fired a shot but on all the close

Best coyote photo I ever made.

ones I figured out just where I would hit them if I wanted to kill them. A great many were less than 50 yards away. I saw three sets of bucks fighting before I had the horses in camp. You could walk to within twenty yards of them before they took notice.

The best shots on all meat animals to kill them with a sixgun, is through heart and lungs. The high lung shot is a faster killer than the heart or low lung shot, but neither is a quick stopper. On bear and cats the shoulder shot in line with the spine is better, as you have a chance of breaking the shoulder or hitting the spine and the latter is certain to put them down. I prefer to shoot deer and such meat animals through the lungs and let them go a distance. Put two slugs through the lungs for certainty. If possible, on bear or cats it is better to try and break them down in the spine or break the shoulder, or if close, like one black bear I shot in a garbage dump, simply drill the brain.

This fellow was so busy eating garbage he never saw me. I put a 250 grain .44 Special right on the base of his ear. It went through the brain and out the other side of his head and he never knew what hit him. I have seen many more bear at close range that I could have killed with equal ease but did not need them or want them at the time. It is of utmost importance to get as close as possible to any game animal, for a sixgun is harder to hold steady than a rifle. You should get close enough to be sure of placing your slug where you want it, or else forego the shot. Unless one needs the meat bady, long range shooting should not be indulged in with a sixgun. The first shot delivers all the shock which the animal's nervous system will stand and if it is not well placed, you can shoot them to hamburger without stopping them. Try to place that first shot right, then the job is done. It is well to follow up a good hit with another slug when shooting big game with a sixgun unless you are sure the first is enough. Be certain, play safe, shoot again.

A huge cougar which placed third in world records, trapped, photographed and killed with .44 Spl. by Keith when he jumped for him as described in one chap. No. 5 Colt used.

The following information is from a letter written by Bob Parrish of Corpus Christie, Texas. While hunting Texas whitetails, he stopped to eat his lunch. He sat down by a tree after leaning his rifle against another tree, out of reach. While eating, his eye caught a movement in the brush and cactus. Out walked a beautiful whitetail buck. Parrish was in plain sight, caught out in the open with no chance of reaching his rifle without scaring the deer. He had a 1950 .44 Special Target Smith & Wesson in his belt loaded with Keith 235 grain H.P. slugs on 18.5 grains of 2400. He slipped it out, then resting both elbows on his knees, held on the deer's ribs close behind the shoulders and carefully squeezed off the shot. The range was 90 yards. The buck humped up and was soon out of sight. He finished his lunch, then trailed him a short distance, finding him dead, and with lung cavity full of blood. Dressing him out proved that the slug had torn a hole from one to one-and-a-half inches in diameter through the lungs and the deer died as quickly as if shot with a rifle. The bullet expanded perfectly, and was found under the skin on the off side.

Chapter VII

Double Action Shooting

WILLIAM H. BONNY, alias Billy The Kid, was probably the first man to use double action extensively in combat. He carried a pair of 6 inch barreled Colt Lightnings in .41 long caliber. Only a couple of years ago one of these guns turned up in Butte, Montana, badly corroded, dirty and rusty and showing no evidence of having ever been taken apart. Yet when grips were removed for cleaning, one had "W. H. Bonney, New Mexico," and a date in the 1880's cut inside of it.

Ed McGivern of Montana, is the fastest and finest double action revolver shot that ever lived and probably ever will. He devoted a great many years to the study and the practice of the art of double action revolver shooting in all its phases, from trick shooting to defense work. His grouping of five shots on a playing card, from a .38 Smith & Wesson, in just $2/5$ of one second at eighteen feet is phenomenal speed and probably will never again be equaled by any other man. This was done on January 23rd, 1934, before plenty of reliable witnesses with the gun hooked up to an electric timer. For years McGivern advocated double action shooting for all police and law enforcement officers, in fact all who packed a double action gun, and he was right. However, his voice was just one among a multitude and was lost in the wilderness of target shooters. It is only in comparatively recent years that the F.B.I., the Border Patrol, and some police organizations have added double action shooting to the menu, and placed it on their regular training course. The National Match pistol course does not, at this writing, contain any double action shooting. We have long felt that all rapid fire revolver work, when fired with double action guns, should be fired double action. Ignorance is bliss. Today very few people realize the accuracy possibilities of the double action pistol when fired double action.

Our present rapid fire match course calls for such rapid cocking of the arm when used single action and requires so much training to master fast recovery and speed cocking that it is slightly absurd. Cockeyed hammers were developed by the old King Gun Sight Company to facilitate single action cocking. If the same amount of time was used in double action practice, the shooter would be making better scores and doing it easier. Double action shooting calls for training and lots of it, and for strong hands and trigger fingers. Once mastered, however, no one ever goes back to single action shooting for fast work or moving targets. Some twenty years ago I started double action shooting in earnest and worked at it steadily for several years. I soon found I could hit small objects tossed in the air easier shooting double action than single action and for really fast work the double action proved faster and more accurate than any auto loading pistol. Although I was raised on the single action Colt and went through all phases of single action shooting, even to developing my own modification of the John Newman slip hammer; using it exclusively a couple of years with trigger removed, hammer spur lowered and the hole for the trigger welded up solid, I learned and mastered slip shooting and found I could do as good work slow fire, even at distant targets, as with a trigger gun. But I also learned that it ruined me for trigger shooting as the two far different techniques do not combine. However, I substantiated John Newman's claims that the slip gun was a reliable weapon either for defense or game shooting. We could never develop a quick draw and hit with the slip hammer unless it was modified, as by J. E. Berns, with a separate spur at extreme top of the hammer for fast draw work out of a holster. That is for one hand use. Of course the regular S. A. Colt hammer can have the checking removed and by using two hands as our friend Walter Rogers does, the old single action can be drawn with one hand and the hammer slapped with the other to coordinate the action into a rather fast and deadly draw and hit at close range. This is known as fanning. More on this subject in a later chapter.

Getting back to double action shooting, with the advent of the .38/44 Smith & Wesson Heavy Duty, 5 inch .38 Special revolver, on the .45 frame, Charles J. Koehler of Saginaw, Michigan, sent me a new gun of this model and 500 rounds of factory ammunition. With the gun came the request that we practice with it and determine if Ed McGivern shooting double action had really put six shots through a can tossed in the air some 18 or 20 feet, by an assistant, before it fell back to the ground. We wrote Mr. Koehler at the time we never had any doubt that any claim made by Ed McGivern was true and that he had not only done the stunt before reliable witnesses and cameras, but also innumerable times, before he would even mention the fact. Just the same, wanting to really learn the double action game, I set to work and practiced all winter, shooting a few rounds and snapping innumerable times, on the empties, every day. I tossed my own gallon cans up, raising the gun with right hand as the left tossed the can in the air. By spring I had mastered the stunt. I made six hits five times straight running on the gallon can and threw it up in the air with left hand while shooting with the right. McGivern had his cans thrown for him, but as I practiced this one stunt all winter I naturally became proficient at it and proved beyond any shadow of doubt that fast, aimed, double action fire was not too difficult.

I had noticed many pictures of McGivern shooting with two guns and four or five aerial targets being shattered at one throw. It was exceptional shooting and never equaled as far as we knew. Many of those photos showed the guns below the line between McGivern's eyes and the target, though he insisted he used the sights. However, before our own winter's work at this stunt was completed I many times caught myself shooting by the feel of the gun and following and hitting the can without the use of sights, especially when a bullet had caught it on a corner and rolled it to one side. I still believe that McGivern could have, and did, hit many of his aerial targets in the same manner, by looking at the object to be hit and shooting as much by the feel of the gun as by aiming.

I also tried throwing the can with right hand and drawing from different type holsters, trying for as many hits as possible. Many different styles of holsters were used but the cross draw was the best we found for this stunt. After considerable practice I could toss the can up 18 to 20 feet, then slap that .38/44 from the cross draw holster and make three hits nicely and sometimes four. Once five hits were made, the last delivered when the can was about a foot from the ground. Most of the time, however, only three were managed. I found that the lighter the load used, the more hits could be made, as the gun was thrown out of line with the target less by recoil. We used the McGivern method exclusively, shooting very fast, with no hesitation in trigger pull and pulling the gun down out of recoil by the double action, poking it at the target, as the trigger was pressed.

This gun proved one of the fastest double action guns I ever owned. Seemingly the inertia of the heavy cylinder and the compact, heavy gun with light, smooth double action pull enabled our sub-conscious to take over. The gun was fired almost without conscious effort once it was lined up with the can in the air. Aim should always be at the bottom edge of any falling object and this type of shooting teaches you to stay with fast moving objects with a six gun and follow through.

It is also the best possible training for the gun fighter, as it teaches coordination and utmost speed. You are working against time, yet must maintain accuracy to make hits.

In 1931 Dee Vissing was a very good single action, one shot aerial shooter with a K-.22 Smith & Wesson and was expert on any small target tossed high in the air. He would hit marbles, empty cartridge cases, or small pebbles with a regularity that was monotonous. He did it all single action and one target at a time. He asked me to try it, but as I had been shooting double action, I soon found I could do better work that way than single action. Soon he had me hitting those small objects. I also found that sometimes when I missed I could whip in a second shot and hit. We shot at empty .30/06 cases a lot and they made excellent aerial targets. Sometimes a bullet would hit one squarely and send it sailing away. I never had the time or money to stay with this phase of the game as did McGivern and some of the men he trained, until they could split lead discs and small coins tossed up edgeways, or shoot through washers with tape pasted over their centers. I did do enough of this work to know that everything McGivern ever claimed was possible and many things he never mentioned.

Previously I had been breaking bottles, thrown in the air, with the Colt Woodsman and the .45 Colt auto and had become quite proficient at it, but the use of the double action was a revelation to me. I soon found I could do better with the double action than with the auto pistols after the first shot and in time chose to use a double action gun for this type of shooting in preference to any cocked single action. The heavy, smooth, double action pull seemed to aid me in following the fast moving object and pulling the gun down in line with it. After the first shot, there was no comparison. The double action was so far superior to the auto pistol as to leave no choice whatever.

The automatics seem to hop around. If you try fast aerial work such as hitting a can repeatedly, they seem to go off when you do not want them to, before you have recovered from the recoil and gotten back in line. After months of work and tests I concluded the double action revolver was much the faster for aimed hits than any auto loading pistol. For accurate delivery of six shots in the least possible time, I consider the double action revolver paramount.

Over thirty years ago I used to do good fast double action hip shooting with an old Colt Lightning .41 Long, and I still prefer its grip and action to the later side-swing Colts. The more recent Officer's models and New Service Target Colts have a pull that seems to increase the farther back the trigger is pulled, and this, combined with the lack of sufficient hump at the top of the grip, is not conducive to top double action shooting, on our part at least. There is no comparison between the smooth, effortless, pull of the Smith & Wesson double action as compared to the Colts, and the Smith & Wesson grip fitted our hands much the better of the two. The more pronounced hump at the top of the Smith & Wesson grip kept the gun from climbing or crawling in my hand. Many times with Colt's D. A. guns, I found before the gun was empty, that it had crawled low enough in my hand so that the hammer spur was striking the web between the first finger and thumb.

In the trigger action there can be no comparison, as the Smith & Wesson is far superior for double action shooting. When you pull past center with the Smith & Wesson it seems to follow through perfectly with very little disturbance of the aim, while Colt has a hitch at the end of the pull that jerks the sights to the side. Also the latter part of the Colt D. A. pull is the hardest, hence the greatest disturbance of aim, when the gun fires. The Colt D. A. grip does not fit my hand as well as the Smith & Wesson D. A. and the New Service Colt was always too large for my hands. Reach from trigger to back strap was too great for proper control in fast double action work. I have a fairly large hand, and wear 9½ to 10 gloves, but have short fingers entirely too short for trigger pull of the New Service Colt when fired double action.

We played the old game of trying to hit a gallon can six shots straight when tossed up with the left hand, using the Colt Officer's model .22 and the K-.22 Smith & Wesson. Neither gun was as speedy as the Outdoorsman or the Magnum Smith & Wesson. The K-.22 S. & W. proved the faster of the two. I many times made five hits and sometimes six, but rarely got over three with the tougher Colt D. A. pull. McGivern shot Colts and Smith & Wessons indiscriminately hitting small aerial targets with either, but his high speed groups were shot with Smith & Wesson guns. That is in line with my findings.

The foregoing paragraphs refer to the past. Colt double action pulls have been greatly improved in recent years. We have handled a few Colt guns, reworked by expert gunsmiths, with double action triggers as smooth and responsive as one could wish. I have yet to see a Colt or Smith & Wesson revolver, in factory condition, with a perfect double action pull. Some are good but none beyond improvement. Pistol makers hate to make changes—worse than Communists hate to make apologies. It has taken more than twenty years of insistent demand to get precision target sights on holster guns. It may take another two decades to get the ultimate in double actions from the factories. Epistles to Smith & Wesson and Colt, plainly written in four letter words, will speed the day.

In all fast double action shooting be sure to use the best ammunition possible and be sure of the primers. One misfire or hang fire will ruin your gun. If a load squibbs and drives the bullet part way up the barrel, or hang fires and goes off after you have turned it past the barrel with your next trigger pull, that gun is either in need of a new barrel or a junk pile. If it misfires, you are O.K., but if it squibbs and drives the slug part way up the barrel, your next shot is sure to ring the barrel. If it turns past center on a hang fire it will probably blow up the gun. Perfect ammunition is an absolute necessity for double action speed firing. You can't think fast enough to stop your finger if a cartridge fails.

In this connection it may not be amiss to say something of main spring tension. Smith & Wesson guns have a spring tension screw in the front of the grip. If this is backed out, relieving tension on the main spring, the double action trigger pull becomes softer and faster, but this can be overdone to the extent that you get hang fires and missfires and these are very dangerous, also a gun does not shoot accurately unless it has a full drive of the firing pin for normal indentation of the primer. Some guns have more main spring than needed but you must maintain adequate hammer fall not only for lock-time but also for certain, uniform firing of the primer or you will get in trouble sooner or later. Too light a hammer fall will never give good accuracy but will string the shots up and down on the target as the powder charge is not fired uniformly.

There is no mainspring adjustment on Colt double action guns. The only way to lighten the pull is by reduction in the width or thickness of the spring itself.

With hard primers such as are found in Government .45 auto ammunition, Colt and Smith & Wesson revolvers need all the main spring tension to surely kick them off. Try the two makes of guns in heavy calibers in fast double action shooting and you will soon see that the Colt tends to climb upward until the hammer spur hits the web of the hand, while the "hump" at the top of the Smith & Wesson grip keeps the gun in position. It is much easier to maintain a firm grasp of the Smith & Wesson. Next try the trigger pull, fast double action, while aiming at a target and you will see why you can easily keep the Smith & Wesson gun on the target as the hammer rises and falls. There is a decided twitch at the end of the Colt pull that tends to throw the sights out of line.

There are two schools of thought on the use of double action. One, best exemplified by our friend John Leppert, a former Lt. of the Saginaw, Michigan Police, is the delayed double action pull. John is a huge man, weighing over 300 pounds, and with very strong hands. He simply folds his huge mitt around a gun. He would pull the double action back until only a few ounces remained on the trigger pull and then hold, aim and squeeze off his shot exactly as in single action slow fire. This is really using the single action principle or, in other words, using the double action to cock the gun then squeezing off the shot as in slow fire. This is fine for men with long fingers or large powerful hands, but is not fast double action shooting as we know it. Our short fingers make it impossible, so we favor and use the McGivern system of smooth fast continued pull on the trigger until the sixgun fires. Many users of the Leppert system, including Bob Nichols, like the old long Smith & Wesson action the best and claim the new short action is no good for their purpose. We do not entirely agree with this theory as the new short action has proven almost as good for the McGivern system of continued pull. In fact the hammer does not come back as far and the lock time is faster. We believe a properly tuned up short action almost the equal to the old long double action pull for fast double action shooting. While it is true that the old actions usually came out as smooth as silk and very fast, the short action can be tuned up to do about the same thing and with increased speed of hammer fall, as it has a shorter travel distance.

Advocates of the Leppert school of thought, if they have the proper shaped hands and fingers for the job, can simply murder timed and rapid-fire with this system. They cock the gun with the double action pull and then have all the time in the world to squeeze off the shot. Not all of us are so blessed with long fingers and must use the McGivern system. We consider it the best anyway for any really fast work. The Leppert system is a much better method of shooting timed and rapid-fire matches, than by single cocking of the arm between shots, if you have the hands and fingers capable of the work. Many advocates of the Leppert system place the thumb on top of the cylinder latch as their long fingers permit complete control of the piece. We, however, find we do our best work with the McGivern grip on the gun, with the thumb curled downward just below the cylinder latch. McGivern fired his guns with the tips of his trigger fingers, as he had abnormally short trigger fingers. This in turn allowed him to contact the bottom of the trigger, giving utmost leverage on the trigger. We pull with the ball of the first joint of our trigger finger. It is wide enough to fill the hollow of the Smith & Wesson trigger.

A firm grip must be maintained in all double action shooting and, like the .45 auto Colt, one must grip the gun hard and firmly, but not hard enough to cause wrist tremor. If the hands are weak, a grip exerciser is a fine thing and is good for any pistol shooter to use daily. It improves the strength of the hand and the trigger finger and is a great help to forming correct habits in gripping the gun firmly without tremor. While you can do very fine slow-fire single action work with a lady-like grip on the gun, you will find you do your best work double action if you hold the gun firmly. There can be no movement of the gun in the hand during a string of shots if you would group them in a small space. Even, firm grip must be maintained or the gun will crawl or move in your hand and this is fatal to accuracy. The trigger finger should work independently of the grip on the gun and preferably touch only the trigger. A slight filler back of the trigger guard is an aid in this respect.

We do not favor oversize grips for fast quick-draw work. They are bulky and make the gun harder to conceal under a coat. Nevertheless, once the gun is in the hand, a large hand filling grip gives better control of the gun. The old Smith & Wesson grips that did not extend up to the top of the frame were inadequate and the recoil of the gun in heavy calibers pounded the web of the hand. But the Magna grip, which we urged long before it was brought out, is very good for fast double action shooting.

For me at least, the still larger Smith & Wesson Target grip, completely filling the hand with a filler back of the guard, and extending some three-eighths inch below the butt strap, is a still greater improvement for fast double action work. It fills the hand and gives one something to hang on to. It is wide enough to prevent any turning in the hand. The second finger also supports the gun with this grip and it is wider in the center to fill the hollow of the hand and flares out at the butt to give the best control. It's a big brute of a grip but seems the best of all for accurate placing of shots in fast double action shooting as it is a grip that does not move in the hand or crawl from heavy recoil. Once you close your hand on it and grip it, it stays put. Many years ago we sent Kearsarge, our ideas of the perfect sixgun grip for Smith & Wesson guns. They made us a couple of pair that fit perfectly. They come up to the top of the back strap and have a filler back of the guard, but do not have any wood in front of the front strap or over the butt strap of the gun. I found these grips best of all for fast draw and fast shooting for my hands. The Smith & Wesson Target stocks for the K models are smaller and fit me perfectly for quick draw work. In the big frame Smith & Wessons, I believe a slightly smaller grip better for our quick draw. For fast double action work, once the gun is in the hand, I prefer the Target grip on the .45 frame Smith & Wesson guns. We consider it about the best big target grip ever produced. It greatly cushions the recoil as it is spread over such a large area of the hand, in fact the whole hand, that the effect is minimized, all of which makes for better control of the gun in double action shooting. It tends to give smaller groups on the target.

To sum up the whole picture, I agree with McGivern and Nichols that the Smith & Wesson double action with the Magna or Target grip is the best possible choice for fast double action shooting. I favor Target guns with wide flat-top target sights as the best for the purpose. Width of the front sight should not be less than one-eighth inch, and one-fourth inch width is even better for the man with poor eyesight, and seems to do as well for those with good eyes. Rear sight notches should be wide enough to allow plenty of light on each side of the front sight with arm fully extended in regular shooting position.

We prefer flat-topped blade front sights. And if a

gold bead, the Call type, with flat face flush with the front sight or a gold insert even with the blade, in the Baughman front sight similar in size to the red plastic furnished to order on Smith & Wesson guns. McGivern developed a round faced gold bead which he prefers for all aerial and trick shooting. It does show up well against any background but I found that it tended to shoot away from the light as all round faced beads do for me. I do not object to a round bead but I want it flat across the face so it will not reflect side lights and tend to shoot away from the light.

If one were going in for very fast double action shooting such as several aerial targets at one throw, or five or six shot minimum time speed tests, the Smith & Wesson K model Masterpiece or 6 inch target gun in caliber .32 S. & W. long could well be the top gun, since it gives lighter recoil and faster recovery than the .38 Special or anything larger and also because the gun is quite heavy in proportion to its size. For all people with small or medium sized hands this would be the fastest gun, and, with the target grip, would fit men with larger hands. The gun is superbly accurate. With the light recoil of the .32 S. & W. long, one could get back on the target or shift to a second target faster than with a larger caliber. This is only for trick or exhibition shooting. For serious defense work the heavy calibers are much the best. You cannot recover from the recoil of a heavy load as fast as from that of a light load, but you do not need to make so many fast hits with a heavy gun. McGivern's five shot groups at exceptionally high speed are fine as tests of speed limits and would be hard on any man in a gun fight, but you need hit a man but once if the gun is heavy enough. We consider this very fast double action shooting fine for aerial targets or for stacking beer bottles one on top the other, shooting the bottom one, and breaking the others as they fall. For serious game or defense work we much prefer a heavy .44 or .45, or at least a .357 Magnum—something that can be depended on to stop any man or animal with one shot decently placed. You could have more than one opponent.

In a close encounter with a wounded grizzly or a mad bull, the big gun and heaviest safe load is the best by every standard and one big slug that will do the work of three to five small ones is so much the better. Do not expect to hit a can tossed in the air twenty feet double action, six times while it is falling, with a heavy .44 Special or .45 Colt load. It takes far too much time to recover from the heavy recoil and bring the gun back on the target.

Fast double action shooting requires a sort of poking motion of the gun hand. You fire when the sights come in correct relation to the target, and as the gun raises in recoil you start the double action pull for the next shot and poke the gun back at the target, striving to get on the target by the time the gun fires again. The heavy double action trigger pull helps get the gun down out of recoil and this poking motion helps bring the gun back on the target. Start by firing one double action shot at a single target, then firing two shots as fast as you can without hesitation in the trigger pull, finally graduating to three shot strings. When you can get off three shots in quick succession, start firing two strings of three shots. Just one, two, three, then one, two, three again. In time you learn to turn on all speed when you start aiming at a moving target and your trigger finger keeps right on going until the gun snaps on an empty case. This fast double action shooting is in the nature of a stunt, but once mastered, you can empty the gun quickly and make a good group on a stationary or moving target. It will help you no end in any phase of fast revolver shooting.

If you are practicing defense work, set up several man targets at twenty yards and see how fast you can slap a slug into each of them, shifting gun and aim to the next while it is recoiling from the last shot. This is practical sixgun shooting and will stand you in good stead in any tight place against either criminals or dangerous game.

Grip the gun high and hard, just leaving room for the hammer to come down without touching the web of the hand. The more you practice, the stronger will become your grip and the faster your trigger finger. It also helps a great deal in speeding up the mental impulse that first starts your finger in action. Practice with one hand and then with the other. To be a finished sixgun shot you should be able to use either hand. Get after that left hand if you are right handed and put it through its paces also. After you are good with either hand then start two gun work. If movements are synchronized so you do the same thing with each hand at the same time, it will come much easier for fast two gun double action work. I never got around to trying two guns on aerial targets, as McGivern and others have, but did a lot of two gun hip shooting, combined with quick draw. In spite of my best efforts, drawing and firing two guns was never as fast as with one gun alone, but with training you can get both guns in action very quickly. It is quite easy to shoot both guns at one target from the hip. If you try using two guns on two targets you will have trouble and you will have to work hard to ever master it. It would be useful in a gun fight against more than one adversary at close range, or to hammer a mad bear into submission, but one would be unlikely to have two guns with him except when demonstrating some such stunt. I have never seen a two gun man that was as fast for the first shot with two guns as he was with one gun, and I doubt if they ever get both hands up to quite the same speed as one. McGivern did his fastest double action shooting with one hand.

Shooting two guns at once, double action, is spectacular trick shooting and quite impressive to the audience. There is no end to the exhibitions that can be worked out for fast double action shooting. Throwing a gallon can out in front and drawing and firing two guns at once, double action, is good practice and will teach you control and speed. It takes a lot of practice to become proficient and more to keep in shape. Today, with the present cost of ammunition, it is only to be recommended to those wishing to become fast trick shots. I was once called on to demonstrate sixgun shooting for a C.C.C. Camp. I started off by doing long range shooting, then general target shooting, followed by mirror shooting and finally got to double action work. It must be remembered that you must do all slow fire, careful shooting, before you start fast double action shooting, as after a few double action shows you are never up to par on slow fire during the rest of that demonstration. I broke a lot of bottles thrown in the air, then made the six hits on a gallon can tossed up twenty feet with the left hand while I shot double action with a Smith & Wesson heavy duty .38/44 with the right hand, and lastly did some fast quick draw hip shooting, starting with one gun and then using two guns at once. I tossed a gallon can out in front, then drew two guns at once from Berns-Martin Speed holsters. The .38/44 Outdoorsman was used in the left hand and the heavier .44 Special Triple Lock in the right. I was lucky that day hitting the can with all twelve shots. It lay on a sloping gravel bar and the two heavy guns seemed to go off simultaneously each time and the can would bounce. Once when it was three feet off the ground I caught it with both guns, rolling it to the river's edge. At the start of this last exhibition the C.C.C. boys formed a wide V with the extreme wings out on either side, but after the two guns were empty, amid the noise and flying rocks and dirt, they formed an inverted V and the closest of the group were then standing right behind me while the wings were back behind on each side, a dubious reaction to what I thought was good shooting.

In all double action shooting, one cannot stress too often the importance of maintaining a firm, hard grip on the gun. It must be firm enough so that the gun will not move or creep in the hand from the recoil of successive shots and so the trigger finger will work independently and actuate the double action without twitching or moving the muzzle. Uniformity of grip is a prime desideratum, if small groups are to be made double action. While the grip on the gun should be independent of the trigger finger, nevertheless the trigger finger tip and thumb are squeezed toward each other, and for men with long fingers they may even touch at the tips. We favor McGivern's system of a continued pull with no hesitation. Speed comes with practice.

The old adage "Make Haste Slowly," applies to learning double action shooting. Learn to accurately place the first shot before trying for quick repeat shots even if it requires six months of practice. Once mastered try for two or three accurately placed shots, and so on until you learn to empty the gun and stay on the target. Stick to single targets and a single shot on each until you have mastered that phase. Then is time enough to try for two hits. Use large targets at the start. Place a slug in the center of a wash tub, if you wish, at ten yards, but shoot at something large enough to surely hit at the start of double action practice. As the groups grow smaller, graduate to smaller targets. At the start it is better to hit a gallon can at thirty feet than to miss a milk can at the same range. Hitting inspires confidence, and confidence inspires closer grouping and faster shooting. Strive first for accuracy of one shot double action fire, then for two shots with the same accuracy, and then three, and so on.

With the .38 Special there is some cumulative recoil when firing double action fast. One should sort of lean into it. This helps keep proper body balance which is very important if a moving object is to be hit. The gun and hand, arm and shoulder, should be firm and rigid and the body weight behind them, with the weight on the forward foot and the balance slightly forward. This greatly helps overcome the constant lift and pound of recoil and helps the hand, arm and body, poke the gun back on the target.

This is of utmost importance in any fast double action group shooting. Small groups cannot be fired double action, at high speed, without such gripping of gun and such forward balance of the body, if there is any recoil at all.

Once you have mastered shooting small groups with a sixgun, double action, and with fair speed, take up shooting at more than one object, shifting your aim from one target to the next and shooting one or two shots at each target. This is excellent combat practice and teaches you body and foot movement as well as gun and arm movements. The wider apart the targets are spaced the better. The standard man silhouette police targets placed several yards apart so one has to shift gun and body to line up on them are excellent. Go over three of these, placing two hits on each; then take six, starting at one end of the line and placing a slug in the chest of each as fast as you can aim and shoot. Such practice will stand you in good stead if you ever get into combat in either military or police duty. With heavy guns such as the .357 Magnum, the .44 Special and the .45, it takes more time to recover from recoil and get the gun back on the target. We believe practice with the heavy guns should incorporate shifting to different targets after every one or two shots.

On man targets one hit is all that is needed with the heavy gun and you are ready for another adversary. Men have been hit with five or six .38 Specials and then come on asking for more, too often to ignore. With the big gun you need hit a man but once, anywhere between the top of his pate and the pelvis bone, to take all the fight out of him. This is just one reason why we say that while group shooting, fast double action, is excellent gun training, it is more in the nature of an exhibition stunt and only useful in a gunfight if one uses a light caliber, inadequate gun.

You can certainly shoot the light gun much faster. It requires less time for a group of five or six shots double action. The heavier calibers have more recoil. For stunts such as punching six holes in a gallon can while it falls twenty feet, the small caliber with light recoil is the best choice. When shooting at a man who can shoot back, or at dangerous big game at close range, the ultra speed of the light gun is more than compensated for by the knock-down wallop of big slugs.

A railroad cop working down in the deep South wrote me of running into a gang breaking into a box car. When he ordered them to throw up their hands, one started shooting at him. He carried a 5 inch Triple Lock Smith & Wesson .44 Special with Keith 250 grain solid bullets backed by 18.5 grains 2400. He wrote, "I simply shot him twice in the chest with the .44, before he even started to fall, but he was all through shooting back after the first shot." The officer was a fast double action shot and punched two of my heavy slugs through the man before he thought to stop his trigger finger.

After a bit of practice at fast strings of double action shooting, it's hard to stop the finger until the gun is empty. It takes a certain amount of nervous energy and once turned on, it is not easily stopped. You are working at top speed and keyed up to the demands of speed. Then is when that forward body balance and firm grip on the gun are necessary. Then is when you need perfect ammunition, for it you get a squib or hang fire in the middle of a fast double action string, you are going to ruin a gun. You cannot stop that fast moving trigger finger until it has sent another slug to lodge against the first one and bulge the barrel. Several times when I have been shooting fast double action, and then shifted to cocked slow fire, I have had squibb loads kick a slug half way up the barrel and lodge there. Fortunately it has never happened in a fast double action string, but it could, and then one would need a new barrel, or a new gun, if heavy loads were used.

Smith & Wesson double action trigger pulls run from nine to eleven pounds, usually around ten or eleven. Their smoothness depends on many things. Hardened parts, polished to mirror-like surface, that will not wear from use, and fitted by changing parts until the correct pull is obtained rather than by stoning them down until the soft inner core is exposed to wear with use. The Smith & Wesson Main spring also gives a steady, even tension from start to finish of the pull, when the hammer falls without vibration, due to the tension being maintained on the trigger, even as the hammer falls. A free spinning cylinder is paramount. It must not bind or catch at any part of its cycle.

It must have enough clearance between its face and the rear end of barrel so it will never bind at this point from powder or lead fouling. It is fatal to any fast double action shooting and, in fact, may tie up the gun.

If the main spring tension screw is lightened by turning it outward to give less main spring tension, then the trigger return spring should also be lightened. With heavy caliber guns, .44 to .45, where recoil disturbs one for a fraction of a second and it takes longer to pull the gun back on the target, there is not the need for as fast a trigger return as when using lighter loads, with recovery so much faster. I doubt if much is to be gained by lightening the main spring to the point where the trigger return spring must also be lightened except on light caliber guns where fast double action work is contemplated. On big guns with heavy recoil it is permissable so long as these springs are not lightened beyond the speed of recovery. This much is positive: they should never be lightened to such extent as to cause inadequate hammer fall and uncertain ignition of the primer. To lighten the trigger pull until the hammer does not hit the primer a full, hard blow is fatal to accuracy, and can be downright dangerous if it causes hang fires.

I have one 1950 Target .44 Special whose action was worked over by Bob Christy. It is a very smooth, fast action. Bob told me at the time that he might have the return spring too weak for my trigger finger. We tried it out and while I could tie it up when it was empty I could not do so with full loads as the recoil delayed my trigger finger enough to allow the trigger return spring to function fully before the next pull. When snapping the piece empty I was too fast for its slightly sluggish trigger return. Since then I have had Smith & Wesson tune up two of these guns, one a .44 Special and one a .45 Target. After considerable shooting I fail to see where the lightened pull of the Christy job is any better. Christy, however, did make the pull much smoother than when it came from the factory.

The fact remains that Smith & Wesson can tune up a double action trigger pull until it is smooth and perfect from every angle and with full main spring tension.

Main springs must be kept at enough tension to surely indent the primer for certain firing, but excessive tension is detrimental to good shooting. You want enough tension to give the hammer a fast, snappy blow that will deeply indent the primer and make for certain ignition. You do not want more pressure on the main spring than is needed for fast hammer throw and certain ignition. The exact balance of main spring and trigger return spring tension is best adjusted at the factory and then left alone. The 1917 Smith & Wesson requires a harder pull and a stiffer main spring as a rule, also the 1950 .45 Target, than do other Smith & Wesson guns. This for the reason that they are often used with hard primer .45 auto Government ammunition. These hard government primers require a heavy blow to even dent them and certain ignition requires a much heavier blow than is common for other pistol primers. Guns are best ordered with a smooth, light double action pull from the factory letting their experts establish the correct tension ratio between the trigger return spring and the main spring. An extra pound or two in the trigger pull is far less a handicap than a jumpy or jerky pull. So long as it is smooth and clean, one can train his trigger finger to the weight of pull required.

As before stated, we have found the inertia of heavy cylinders seems to help fast double action shooting. The Smith & Wesson .38/44 Heavy Duty, the Outdoorsman and the .357 Magnum are the fastest of all double action guns, in my hands at least, though the K models are a very close second.

For fast accurate double action shooting, one should select a gun that suits the hand, as to fit and feel. While I can do good double action shooting with Mrs. Keith's small Smith & Wesson Kit Gun, I can do faster shooting with the larger K models and do still better with the big S frame .38 calibers. For men with large hands, the S. & W. target grip, which extends some three-eighths of an inch below the back strap and incorporates a good filler behind the guard, is a big help.

Smith & Wesson hammers and triggers are glass hard and are fitted at the factory by trying different combinations until the pull is just as desired. They are then matched and should never be changed. It is best to get a good pull from the factory rather than to have the case hardening stoned away by some gunsmith. Reduction of double action pull usually means reduction of single action pull as well. I like a 3 to 3¼ pound single action pull, rather light, for careful game shooting, and as light and smooth a double action pull as is possible with certain ignition, then leave the trigger pull absolutely alone.

I have not found the Smith & Wesson Centennial and Chief's Special models with coil main springs to give quite as smooth a double action pull as the larger guns with their long flat main spring, but these little guns can be adjusted as to weight of main and trigger return springs to give excellent double action pulls. One of the workmen in the Smith & Wesson plant showed us his pet Centennial. It had a perfectly smooth, and fairly light, double action pull.

Training of the hands and strengthening trigger fingers is the principal thing. Continued practice will soon strengthen the trigger fingers, also speed them up until you double action the gun with no effort and the subconscious takes over for fast double action shooting. You then concentrate on your aiming and bringing the sights back to bear on the target in the least possible time. Group shooting from the hip is something else again and will be taken up in the chapter on quick draw and hip shooting.

Remember to keep the weight on the balls of the feet with balance slightly forward. Lean into the gun so to speak. The hand and arm are fixed and rigid and you thus put some of your forward body weight back of the gun, which helps control recoil and to bring the gun back in alignment with the target in the smallest fraction of time. All things are relative. The heavier caliber gun has far heavier recoil, so do not expect to shoot as fast with the .44 or .45 as with the .32 and .38 calibers. It simply cannot be done. It is imperative to start practice with the small caliber first and to master it before graduating to the heavier calibers with more disturbing recoil. For exhibition shooting, the smaller, cheaper cartridges are just as good as the big ones and much faster to get off, but for serious work on man or game, the big guns and heavy slugs are in a class by themselves. Knock-down energy is more important than repeated hits with a smaller caliber weapon.

While straight slow fire target shooting requires a relaxed easy position, fast double action shooting requires body control. We are all individuals, all different, and a position that is right for one person may be all wrong for the next. Select a position and stance that suits you as an individual, bearing in mind the end result to be achieved. Find the position from which you can do your best work.

Double action shooting with modern revolvers is practical shooting. It is the system to use in all close range gun fights, if you carry a double action gun. When enforcing the law, or resisting hold-ups and bandits, the man who can deliver quick, accurate hits wins. This can best be done shooting double action. Speed of accurate fire may well mean the difference between life and death. Close range military combat by the soldier is the same thing. Hits on different targets can be made faster, by double action, than by any other method; hence it is the most practical. What you learn in aimed double action shooting, will stand you in good stead when you are forced to shoot in the dark by the feel of your gun, or in hip shooting where you have to beat an opponent, or lose both your life and the cause for which you are fighting.

In all double action shooting at objects tossed in the air, lean slightly forward and aim at the bottom edge of the target. Remember, it is falling. The shot must be aimed at the bottom to hit it. Also you are trying to follow it with your gun as in the case of repeated hits on a big tin can, so lean forward enough to facilitate pulling the gun down as it falls to earth. In time you will learn to lean farther forward as the can drops and you keep pulling and poking the gun back at the bottom edge of the falling object the while your trigger finger actuates the gun. This poking motion of the gun cannot be overemphasized. As the gun recoils the barrel whips upward and the gun and hand come back in recoil and you must poke or shove it forward again for the next shot in a sort of choppy motion of hand and arm. There is no sense in the fiction writer's tale of throwing down on anything. If you are going to work on aerial targets, bring the gun up in one hand as you raise the other hand to toss the object so that both target and gun come up together, perfectly synchronized, then start your double action shooting, aiming at the bottom of the can and striving to get off the first shot just as it reaches the height of the toss and sort of hangs in the air, before starting to fall. That is the time and place to hit bottles and all single objects in the air, just as they reach the top and hang for a fraction of a second before they gain falling speed.

I used to have a companion toss up bottles at the town dump and we would break them as long as we could find another one to shoot at. The helper should stand to one side and even with, or slightly in front of the shooter. He should toss the bottles or cans upward in a slow even swing of the arm so they raise to about the same spot in the air. If you toss them yourself it is easier, as you know where they will be at the height of their raise. Your gun should go up with them and be well aligned on the bottom edge when they settle and start to fall. In time you can learn to throw two cans, or two bottles and shift after one has been broken. Follow the other until you are at its bottom edge with the sights, and also hit it. With enough practice you can hit several objects thrown up in a group. Always work on the lower ones first. In 1952 at Camp Perry, I went out with a Remington trick shot and watched him demonstrate. He was very proficient with both rifle and pistol and I watched him shatter, with a pump gun, five clay targets that I threw up for him at one time, and again with a 28 gauge Remington auto shotgun. He insisted I could do the same thing. I did not believe him. He started by tossing up a single clay target. I dusted it. Then he tossed two and three until I was getting all. With that he shifted to throwing up five at once. After a few failures I managed to get all five targets three times straight with the 28 bore auto loader. It is much harder with a double action sixgun, but it can be learned and the procedure and coaching I was given that day applies to double action revolver shooting.

The main thing is timing, keeping the body and gun arm in correct relation to the falling objects, following them in their downward travel, while your trigger finger fires the gun each time the sights are in correct alignment. Hand, arm and body movement are as necessary and as important as trigger squeeze and the sight picture. It is a coordination of the whole body with the gun and the eyes in perfect timing.

Continued practice at targets double action and shooting as fast as the sights come on the target will surprise the most skeptical. You will soon find yourself shooting as well or better than if you cocked the gun and spent a lot of time aiming again. The Target should be big and the gun a .22 for the start. I know of nothing better than the K-.22 Masterpiece.

The police man-silhouette targets are excellent for this purpose and you will soon be hitting the small ring in the center of the target. Then is the time to increase the range. There is nothing mythical or impossible about double action shooting. The trigger is controlled and the shot squeezed off the same as in slow fire. Only you do it in a fraction of the time. There is no hesitation; you are working against time. The first aim is the best and the shot should go each time the sights lie right. "He who hesitates is lost," is a good adage for the double action shooter.

I am no Ed McGivern, but I did practice one of his stunts, namely the placing of six shots, double action, through a gallon can tossed twenty feet in the air. I went him one better and tossed the can with my left hand and kept at it, one winter, until I accomplished the feat five times straight before witnesses. It is simply a matter of intelligent practice, concentration, and conscientious hard work. In concluding this chapter, I urge all double action shooters to get a copy of Ed McGivern's great book, *Fast & Fancy Revolver Shooting*, and study the problems which he so well explains. Others can do what he has done if they will spend the time, the energy, and the money required.

New Smith & Wesson Main Spring and Wide Trigger

Since Smith & Wesson brought out the new U type main spring for their target arms and the new wide, finger contouring trigger I have installed sets of each in three 1950 target revolvers, two .44 Specials and one for the .45 Colt, all with 4 inch barrels, and have been testing them for fast double action work. They are a considerable improvement over the long flat main spring and trigger return lever spring. I have some very fine old long-action Smith & Wessons and have tried all Colts and these new U type S. & W. main springs combined with the new wide trigger and they have given me the best double action trigger pulls I have ever used, superior both to the old long-action Smith & Wesson and also to the recent short action trigger pulls. This new U type main spring retains the short action but is softer on the pull and has less jerk when the sear releases. With the wide trigger the pull feels lighter so the combination is a material aid to fast double action shooting and one can shoot double action almost as well as single action. We believe many peace and police officers, when they have this combination installed in their guns, will go to double action shooting for timed and rapid fire matches. One can shoot a double action gun, with perfect aiming and control, faster than he can an automatic pistol and this combination of new U type main spring and wide trigger will put the double action shooter on more equal footing with the .45 auto user in timed and rapid fire matches, if he will train his hand and finger a bit for double action.

The first three of the new springs sent me, still in the experimental stage, were a trifle too light to kick the trigger back as fast as we would like. Herb Bradley put one of them in my pet 4 inch .44 Special 1950 Target. I found I could tie up the gun in fast double action shooting as the trigger return spring and its centering pin was removed from the gun and only the front arm of the too weak U type main spring used to kick the trigger back to fire position. Bradley took a light trigger return spring that Bob Christy had fitted to this gun several years ago and cut it back a coil at a time until he removed five coils from it. He had enough tension which added to the feeble U spring, kicking the trigger back with certainty in fastest double action shooting, yet retaining the very soft double action trigger pull. This is the best double action pull I have ever known on any double action gun. Judge Don Martin and Paul Crowder, who have both tried this trigger pull, pronounce it the best yet achieved.

It eliminates all the jump at the end of the pull when the sear lets loose and one can shoot it like a single action. The next batch of U type springs sent to me from Smith & Wesson are slightly heavier and stronger and are now standardized. They still give a much smoother, softer, double action pull than the old flat main spring and eliminate the use of any trigger return spring whatever. I have been unable to tie the gun up in fast shooting. The new main springs will fit all new 1950 Target or later arms as well as the standard 1950 models. They should be fitted at the factory or by a competent gun smith to be sure the front lever does not quite touch the rear arm when the arm is at full cock single action. Hand polishing of all action parts helps further in producing the most perfect double action pull we have yet seen or used. I would have liked to have seen Ed McGivern use one of these guns when he was at his peak in fast double action shooting. It would have been something to remember.

The elimination of the trigger return lever spring and pin also makes for greater simplicity and we expect to see all later model Smith & Wesson guns made with this spring which eliminates the trigger return spring and pin, the main spring screw in the front strap and the main spring seat in the butt strap, all necessary with the old type main springs. The use of the new main spring will speed up production and cut cost of manufacture to the extent of a pin, a screw and return spring, as well as the main spring seat cut in the butt strap. It is a long step in the right direction.

Chapter VIII

Gun Rigs and Holsters

BACK IN THE 17TH CENTURY, hand guns, usually of the long flintlock variety, were carried shoved under a sash or waist belt. Small pocket pistols were hidden in the pockets of great coats and sometimes in pockets of capes. Military pistols, owned by officers in various armies, were usually found in holsters fastened over the pommel in pairs, with a big flint lock pistol on each side of the fork of the saddle. Heavy cavalry pistols of flint lock and percussion lock were often holstered in the same manner, as were the first Colt Walker revolvers.

The evolution of the gun man, and the displacement of the sword as the common personal weapon, came soon after the advent of the revolver, about the time of the war between Texas and Mexico. As the revolver replaced the sword, the belt holster replaced the saddle holster. The Colt Patterson five-shot revolvers were small neat weapons compared to the huge military flint and percussion army pistols. Cavalrymen and gun fighters of that era were not slow in developing holsters for these weapons that could be carried on the belt so that the gun would be instantly accessible. Fighting Mexicans and Indians, they often had horses shot out from under them and once in the clear could go on fighting on foot with their revolvers. In the war between the United States and Mexico our cavalry was often matched against Mexican Lancers. Later the Civil War evolved more changes in methods of carrying sixguns. While the Colt Walker sixgun, because of its weight, was best carried in saddle holsters, the lighter revolvers were more often carried on belt holsters. Early cavalry fighting soon indicated the need of carrying revolvers with the butt to the front so the gun could be grasped with either hand when the other held a saber or was engaged in managing the horse.

Percussion pistols needed to be protected from rain or snow to insure certain ignition and for that reason holsters of the period leading up to and following the Civil War were more often of the flap than open-top style. The open-top holster was developed in the Southwest in a dry, arid climate, where rain was mostly non-existent and where speed of gun handling was paramount.

Samuel H. Fletcher told me that when he enlisted as a trooper in the 2nd Illinois Cavalry at the start of the Civil War, they were given weeks of rigorous saber drill, mounted. They were made to swing a saber and saber dummies for countless hours each day until their wrists were hard and strong as steel. Later when they were embroiled in hot cavalry clashes, he said, they learned to depend on their .36 Navy Colts revolvers and their sabers rather than on the Spencer carbines with which they were also armed. They carried the guns in pairs, butts to the front, in covered flap holsters. Many men on the Southern side carried their guns the same way, but others who had experience on the frontier and in Indian fighting, often carried theirs in open-top holsters which were much faster. Many Confederate cavalrymen carried as many sixguns as they could lay hands on, often as many as four so they could keep up a continuous fire when necessary. They often carried extra loaded and capped cylinders in a pouch on the gun belt as well as in their pockets for a quick change when one cylinder ran dry in combat.

The many sanguinary conflicts of the Civil War and the constant Indian fighting on the plains, led to the development of the gun fighter. He in turn developed the belt holster to its highest degree of perfection. In many close range conflicts, the man who could draw and deliver accurate fire first, lived. Among civilians, many forms of holsters were developed, from the common Mexican belt type to the shoulder holster. In hot climates the belt holster was preferred, but gamblers and men living in colder climates often preferred the shoulder holster. Many gamblers and bar tenders simply carried their gun shoved in the front of their pants under their belts. Long coats were the order of the day, and these made concealment and protection of the weapon easy. After the Civil War, the Texas trail drives to the railroad in Kansas and the later drives of long-horns to Montana and Wyoming, saw the greatest development of the belt holster. The cow-puncher working cattle and often riding mean horses, soon found that the best possible way to carry his heavy sixgun was on a comfortable gun belt on the right or left side, depending on whether he was right or left handed.

The gun was carried butt to the rear, just the opposite of the Cavalry method. It is doubtful if a

When the sixgun should be carried under the coat in a shoulder holster.

better method of carrying a heavy sixgun on a horse will ever be evolved. Belts were usually two to three inches in width with 2½ inches being the most common and were often made of double oil grain chap leather to form a combination ammunition and money belt. Gold and silver was the usual medium of exchange and these heavy coins could be slipped in the gun belt out of the way and were then safe. The billet strap usually ran through a slit in the double chap leather at the buckle end, thus securing the coins in the circumference of the belt. The belt would also carry about 50 rounds of heavy .45 Colt ammunition. The riders walked as little as possible. The horse packed the weight.

Holsters were usually of the wide skirted Mexican-type, open-top and cut out a bit for the trigger, but many old ex-cavalrymen still carried their weapons butt to the front, so they could reach them with either hand, and in light neat holsters that snugly fitted the guns, with no extra weight in useless skirting leather on the holster. The professional gunmen, both on the side of the law and outlaws, soon developed gun fighting rigs that would permit them to perfect their individual style of quick draw. These took many forms, but there was not half as much variation then as later shown by the movies. Some slanted the butts of the gun ahead, the fastest method, while others preferred the butts slanted to the rear and the muzzles ahead. Hickock and Hardin often used a type of shoulder holster of their own design with both guns carried in a sort of vest with butts sloped to the front in easy reach of either hand. Dallas Stoudenmire, during his brief reign as marshal of El Paso, carried two 4¾ inch .45 S. A. Colts with butts to the front in leather lined hip pockets under the tails of his long coat—a very fast position when no belt or holster was worn, but an impossible one for the cowboy or horseman.

Sam Russell worked out his own design of hip pocket holster to carry a single 4¾ inch .45 S. A. in the right hip pocket with butt to the front. The back of the holster was a piece of heavy skirting and the form for the gun was lighter leather, and near the bottom on the opposite side from the barrel of the gun were loops for six rounds. This heavy almost square piece of skirting leather fitted snugly in his special made hip pocket so the holster would not work out of the pocket and the gun was held securely with butt to the front. Sam could stroll along the streets of any town with his right hand in right pants pocket and coat tail covering the gun, yet in a fraction of a second his hand could slide out of the side pants pocket, grasp the gun and draw it shooting. As the gun was drawn the muzzle was turned across his body to the front, or could be shot behind the back across the body at an adversary on his left side. It is still a very fast method of packing a 4¾ inch S. A. Colt and was used by many gamblers. I gave this holster to Charles J. Koehler of Saginaw, Michigan.

Texas Charley wore a pair of 4¾ inch .45 S. A. Colts in cross draw holster butts, sloped to the front. J. H. Fitzgerald of Colt also preferred the cross draw holster for all his quick draw stunts.

Many cow-punchers using a long barreled .45 S. A. Colt packed it in a belt holster, butt to the rear, and with the front of the holster cut low to allow the muzzle to clear in the least possible time, drawing with the gun hand and slapping the hammer with the palm of the other hand, fanning their shots in fast, short range gun fights. Walter Rogers still uses this kind of holster for his S. A. Colt and this method of drawing and hip shooting. A holster that suits one man may be slow for another. Each individual has to work out his own salvation in regards to type and style of holster.

When I was a boy, ladies went in for muffs rather than hand bags. When they carried pistols, it was usually a small short gun concealed in the muff. Some gamblers used Remington Double Derringers carried in holsters strapped to their wrists under their long coat sleeves. Some carried Derringers in their vest pockets.

Just before Christmas a friend escorted his five year old son into a local store to buy him a pair of cap pistols and holsters for Christmas. The little lad had already picked out the set he wanted—a small pair. His father remonstrated with him, asking if he would not rather have a large and very ornate pair of guns and holsters. "Nope," said the little lad. "Too big, don't want 'em, don't wike 'em, tant dwaw 'em fast enough."

I've seen many types of belts and holsters used on the range in my earlier days, but never did see one of those huge Buscadero corset outfits used, other than in the movies or by some trick shot in demonstrating two gun work. Likewise I never saw a real gunman that went in for those hugh Mexican type holsters with wide back skirt. Such rigs are like a square skirted saddle, just that much extra leather to cart around all day. The leather workers love them as they offer plenty of room for their fine leather carving and artistry, but they have no place on the range. They are hot and heavy and one is far better off with a comfortable belt of 2½ inch width and a small neat holster just large enough to carry the gun, with no surplus leather or weight. The extra weight might better be utilized in more cartridge loops and more ammunition. Likewise we could never see any horse sense in a lot of ornamental silver, nickel or brass studs on a gun belt or holster. A gun rig can be made neat and of best leather, hand carved if desired, with a nice silver buckle for the gun belt and that is ornamentation enough. Any more such ornaments only reflect sunlight and announce your presence far and wide on the range. I once acquired a gun belt and holster made by H. H. Heiser Company of Denver, Colorado. It was a very well-made outfit and came in a trade, but the whole belt and the big Mexican type holster was covered with little silver spots making the outfit as flashy as a canary-yellow Cadillac. We traded it off at the first opportunity. We never cared for nickel or silver plated guns for the same reason. During my life I have known many real gunmen but never knew one to own or use such an outfit outside of show business and never knew one to wear a glove on his shooting hand except in the coldest weather.

Today we have holsters and belts of many types and some of the finest workmanship that has ever been produced. Unless you are a uniformed officer who must, under orders, wear a Sam Browne belt outfit, you can have anything your needs or fancy dictates. Fine leather workers are legion in this country, but you will find as fine holsters and belts as are to be had made by the George Lawrence Company, 306 South First Street, Portland, Oregon; The S. D. Myres Saddle Company, El Paso, Texas; and the H. H. Heiser Company of Denver, Colorado. J. H. Martin, Calhoun City, Mississippi makes Berns-Martin holsters.

Let us look at the needs of the peace officer. If a uniformed police or state policeman is forced to wear a Sam Browne belt, there is nothing better, if as good, as the Myres No. 5 holster designed for wear on a Sam Browne belt. It tips the gun butt forward for quick draw work. This is a very fast reliable gun rig and one that won't let the officer down. If anything the safety strap should be ordered with long tab, so it can be folded around in back of the holster out of the way. When the Sam Browne belt is worn without a coat, it may be used also to hold the trousers, and the gun position is much better, lower and handier than if worn over a coat.

For the sheriff or plain clothesman who has prisoners to conduct from town to town, or to court, or from state to state, it is often advantageous to have the gun on the left side, especially if he must drive a car while escorting a prisoner. When the gun is worn on the left side, unless the officer be a south paw, it is well to wear it butt to the front so it can be reached and drawn with either hand. If the officer always wears a coat, the shoulder holster is also good. For the officer who is right handed, wearing his gun on the left side, the Lawrence Holster No. 86 is best for use on a Sam Browne belt, and for use on a waist belt the No. 405 Myers Holster is very good—also the Lawrence No. 30 Holster. An even better holster would be the Myres No. 5 made to hold the gun with butt to the front and straight up and down or slightly tipped forward, or the Lawrence No. 34 holster made to hold the gun vertical or with butt tipped slightly forward and butt to the front for left side wear.

For the officer wearing an automatic .45 or Super .38 or Smith & Wesson double action automatic, the Myres No. 116 holster is very good as it may be carried either as a shoulder holster, or slipped off the shoulder sling and carried on the waist belt on left side and butt to the front. It is fast and practical. When revolvers are carried in shoulder holsters, we prefer the Lawrence No. 7. It covers the gun except for the butt and protects it against perspiration. This is also the finest shoulder holster we know of for the hunter and trapper to carry his heavy sixgun while chasing cougar or trapping and wallowing through deep snow or brush and negotiating cliffs, etc. Worn under the coat the gun is perfectly protected yet instantly accessible.

For the plain clothesman carrying a two inch revolver, one of the fastest and best shoulder rigs is the Berns-Martin lightning holster, which carries the muzzle up and the butt down, on the right side, under the arm. This is also much the fastest shoulder holster made and the gun can be drawn with either hand. For all plain clothesmen who use short barrel light guns of .38 caliber this is the best holster for under coat wear. You can get it out and shoot across the body in very fast time, and if your right hand be occupied with a prisoner or with a car wheel, the gun can also be drawn easily with left hand and used in that way. Only the butt of the gun is left out of this spring, upside down, holster. The gun is protected against perspiration. It is also well concealed and the butt is to the rear.

These are all spring shoulder holsters. We do not favor a pouch shoulder holster of any kind. They are too slow and awkward to get into action. When an officer has to wear a heavy gun under an overcoat,

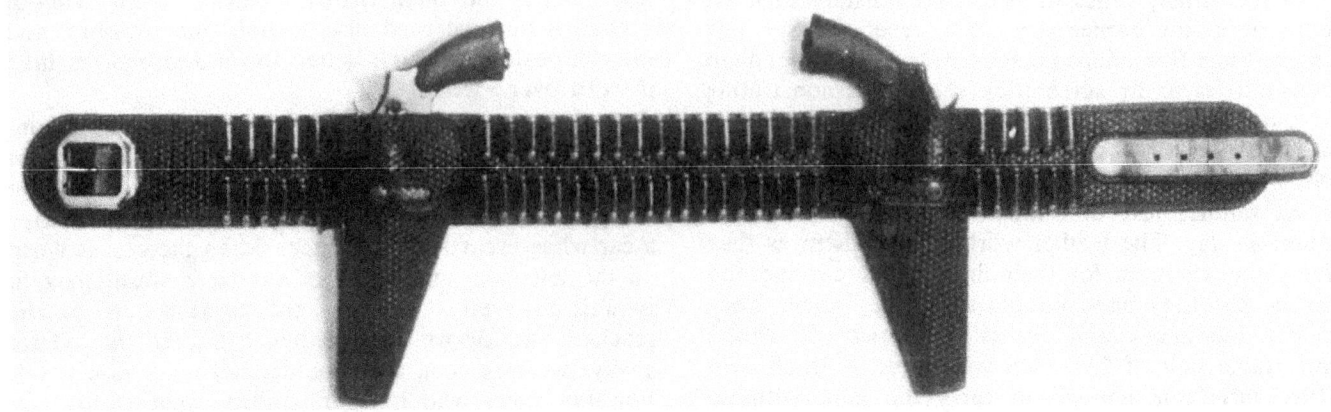

Keith Berns-Martin two gun outfit.

My Berns-Martin Speed outfit with 1917 guns in holsters.

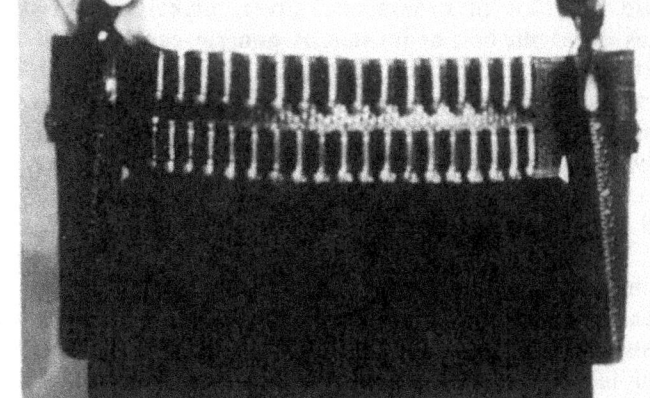

Berns-Martin Speed holster. Newman .45 Colt slip gun.

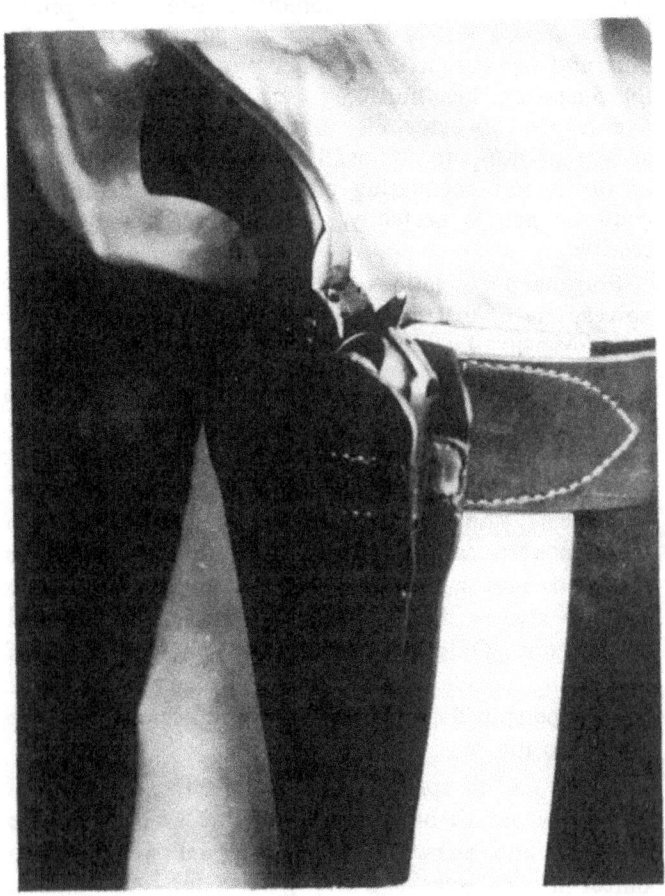

a shoulder holster such as the Lawrence No. 7 is probably as good as he can do, if waist coat and overcoat are left unbuttoned at the top so the gun is accessible. It is faster than trying to dig a gun out of a belt holster under heavy coats unless the coats are left fully open.

The Myres No. 405 cross draw holster, or the Lawrence No. 30, are both very fast under a coat on the left front of the body, for right handed men, or the reserve for south paws.

For the peace officer not using a Sam Browne belt and carrying his gun on either a waist belt, or a regular low hung gun belt, we believe the best revolver holster for double action guns to be the Keith pattern long safety strap Lawrence No. 34 Holster that tips the butt well forward. It can be made either right or left handed and leaves the hammer and trigger guard fully exposed and above the belt. The long tab safety strap can be folded back inside the trousers, if worn on a waist belt, or under the gun belt if any quick action is contemplated and when the officer is negotiating rough country or liable to lose the gun in a scuffle the safety strap can be used over the hammer. This is a very fine holster and carries any 4 inch or 5 inch or even longer double action gun in the best possible position for the fastest draw.

Myres also makes a similar holster, their No. 650 and 640 called the Tom Three Persons style, but with short safety strap. We believe it should be ordered with a longer tab below the button on the safety strap so it will be easier and handier to jerk free or to fold under the belt when not wanted. For the officer or civilian wanting to carry an automatic the same way, we have the Lawrence No. 31 holster and the Myres No. 511 or 507. Myres also makes their fine No. 987 holster in the same style for automatics.

Years ago we designed a holster for the Colt Single Action for the Lawrence Company known as the No. 120 holster. This carries the butt well forward for quick draw work, and has a long safety strap with heavy glove fastener to be used when working cattle or riding a bucking horse. The long strap can be folded down behind the belt when not needed. The belt loop extends down only far enough to be well stitched. This holster offers a minimum of weight and bulk and leaves the hammer and trigger guard clear and above the belt. It is our favorite holster for the S. A. Colt when worn either on a gun belt or waist belt, and can be made either right or left handed as desired.

Myres also has their famous Tom Three Persons design that is almost identical except that the belt loop is extended down to the bottom of the holster and sewed around the bottom. This is a slightly heavier holster and offers exactly the same perfect gun position. It is made either right or left hand and can be had with safety strap if desired. Myres also makes them with an extended top to protect the clothing from wear by the hammer but we do not favor this addition as it might slow one up with the single action gun. I know it would slow me up considerably with a single action, but is O.K. for the double action gun. Their No. 610 and 614 are typical examples of the excellent Tom Three Persons design. For those persons wanting elaborate, well ornamented holsters, for either single or double action of the old wide skirt Mexican pattern, there is nothing finer than the Myres No. 545 holster. We do not like the extra weight and bulk of this holster but it is a masterpiece of fine leather work.

The very elaborate Buscadero Hollywood Corsets for either one or two guns, especially for show work, are made by both Myres in their No. 50X and by Lawrence in their No. 50 outfits. They can be had as ornate with fine carving and silver work as desired. Holsters can be had that tip butts forward or back or vertically as desired, and while they offer good gun position for fast work, they are impractical. We never could see them outside a movie or on the stage.

There are several trick holsters on the market, or formerly were. The Audley with a spring that fitted into the trigger guard was one of them and at one time made for both revolvers and auto pistols. You pressed the trigger finger against this spring in drawing to free it from the trigger guard and the gun could not be drawn until this spring was pressed down. We also saw a motorcycle cop in Bay City, Michigan, with a sort of clam shell holster with a release inside the trigger guard. When you pressed the trigger finger against this spring trip, the whole outside of the holster sprung outward and ahead on hinges leaving the gun fully exposed. We never did favor either of these holsters as something might go wrong with the spring, or dirt or other foreign matter get lodged under it to prevent the spring being pushed down; then one would be in a bad fix, if in a gun fight. They both did possess one good quality, a gun could not be jerked out of the holster by an adversary unless he first pressed down on the spring inside the trigger guard.

A much better holster to our way of thinking is the Berns-Martin, designed by John Berns while in Alaska on a Naval radio station. Berns designed it to keep a long 7½ inch S. A. Colt up out of the snow and still be able to draw it fast when needed. He wrote me at the time and I advised having the idea patented. This holster is split down the entire front as shoulder holsters are split down the back. The spring encompasses the cylinder of the gun in much the same way but opens to the front. These fine belt holsters are probably the fastest holster of all for long barreled guns carried high on the waist belt under a coat. To draw, you push forward and down on the butt of the gun to clear the spring tension, then flip the muzzle up as you poke the gun toward the target. The trigger guard of the gun is completely enclosed and the gun cannot be jerked out of the holster from behind by an adversary. The gun is also well protected and no wear comes on the sights, which again is an advantage of the Berns-Martin Holster. J. Edgar Hoover's boys went for this holster in a big way and a great many of them still use it as it is a very fast rig. We do not find it as fast as the Lawrence No. 34 or 120 as some time is consumed pushing forward and down on the butt of the gun to clear the holster, but it is very speedy just the same. For short barreled guns we believe the Lawrence 34 or 120 and similar Myres Holsters No. 650 to 640 to be faster.

Many target shots use and like the Berns-Martin because after they smoke their sights the black will not be rubbed off in the holster. I used to do some exhibition work with two guns and the Berns-Martin two gun outfit proved very good for quick draw and hip shooting. For aerial work on tossed targets I did not like it at all, as the cross draw proved much the faster for this phase of trick shooting. This was due to the fact that the targets were thrown up and the gun should go up also. Having to push down and forward on the gun butt to clear it was moving it in the wrong direction for speed. Different stunts require different holsters for fastest time and one must study gun and target positions and then decide which type will best enable him to get the gun on said target by the shortest route and in the least possible time.

Individuals vary greatly in temperament, build, and

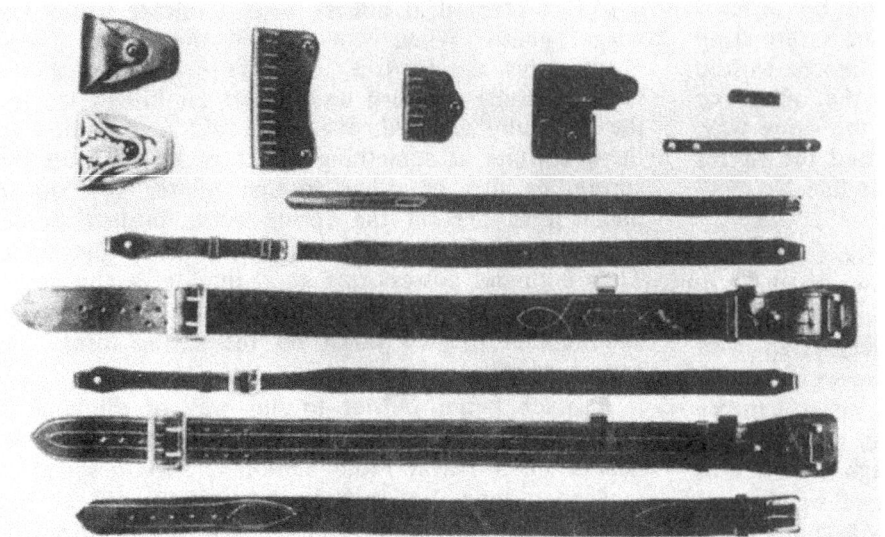

Group of Myres Sam Browne belts, cartridge loops, and handcuff cases.

Left, Myres number 8 Border Patrol Holster; right, Myres Jordan Holster.

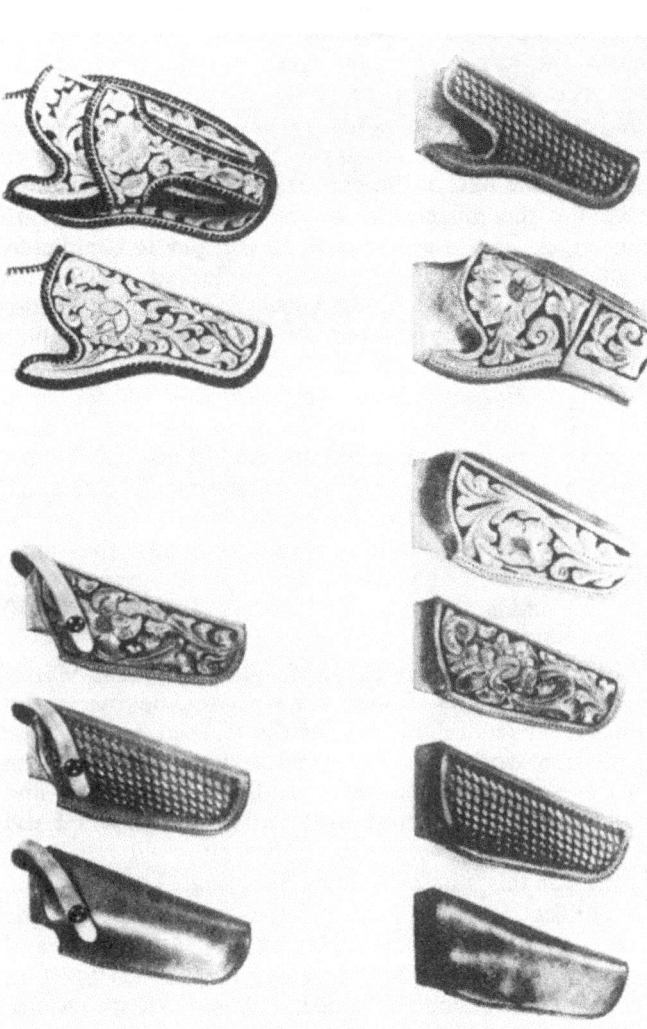

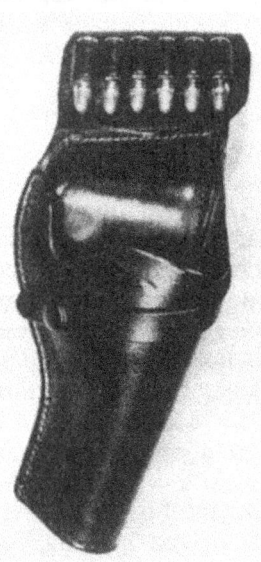

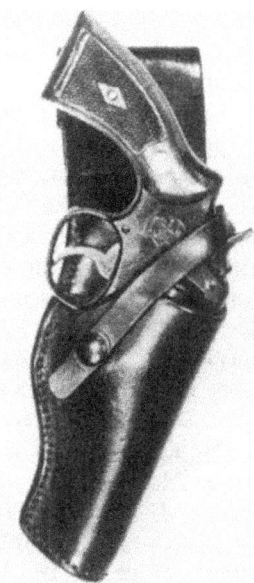

Group of S.D. Myres holsters. On left side are variations of the Tom Threepersons style holster for S.&W. and Colt revolvers, only. Three on top left have hammer protector.

general habits and each shooter will have to decide which type of holster fits him or her best and where and how it is to be worn. For the rider, it is doubtful if a better method was ever evolved to carry a heavy sixgun and its ammunition than on a comfortable gun belt. The butt of the gun should hang about halfway between wrist and elbow with the arm hanging naturally at the side. We have seen guns worn even lower but do not believe much time is gained in quick draw by having them lower. They are also more in the way and more apt to flop around with movement of the leg if worn in a lower position.

Many fat or big men prefer a cross draw holster and this also is very fast. It should be worn with the gun butt sloping toward the belt buckle and drawn and fired across the body with the side turned toward the target. This requires body movement as well as gun movement. I do not find it as fast for targets that the shooter squarely faces as the old cowboy hip draw.

Finely carved Myres leather holster and special belt. The holster is Mexican edge laced and lined with soft suede leather, and can be made for any style pistol.

I like the holster to fit the gun perfectly—rather snug and tight so that it will not fall out if you stoop over, or even fall down. The cow-puncher working rough country or riding mean horses needs his gun securely held in the holster or he may lose it. Riding a bucking horse will throw any gun out of its holster unless it fits perfectly and preferably has some sort of safety strap.

Capt. A. H. Hardy used to make some very fine holsters and while I did not particularly like the big skirts on them, they were set correctly as to angle and he evolved the best method we have yet seen for carrying six shells in the Colt single action safely and having the gun well secured in the holster. Inside the top front of the holster he sews a narrow strip of rather soft leather. With the gun cocked and fully down in holster, he brings this piece of leather over into the recess in the rear end of the frame where the hammer fits and lets the hammer down on it, marking the right spot with the firing pin. He then punches a hole to allow the firing pin to go through the strip of leather. With this simple holster attachment you can safely carry six cartridges in your single action because the strap inside the frame recess will not allow the firing pin to go down far enough to reach the primer even from a hard blow. The tension of the main spring on the hammer keeps the firing pin driven through its hole in the leather and the gun cannot be shaken out. You can have a horse roll over you and still have your gun fully loaded, and be safe. Any old single action man cocks his gun as he draws it. The gun comes out fast in quick draw work, with the cocking of the gun as you draw, the firing pin withdraws from the hole in the strap, thus freeing the gun. The idea is fool proof, and I have used it a lot. It is the best way of locking a single action gun in the holster and making it safe with six cartridges.

Unless this Hardy safety strip is used, we carry but five cartridges in a single action as any hard blow on the hammer can break the top of the sear or tear

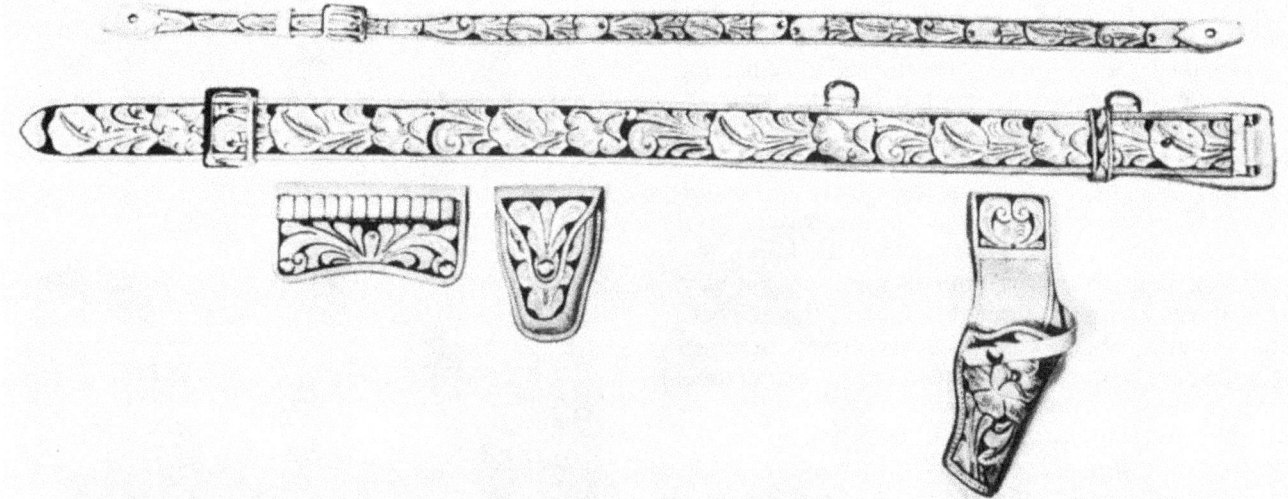

Carved Sam Browne belt, cartridge slide, cuff case, and Jordan holster by S.D. Myres Saddle Co. This holster was designed for Immigration Inspector Jordan, and has incorporated features of the number 5 Border Patrol holster plus the exposed trigger guard of the gun with an added plug behind the trigger guard to throw the butt of the gun further from the body.

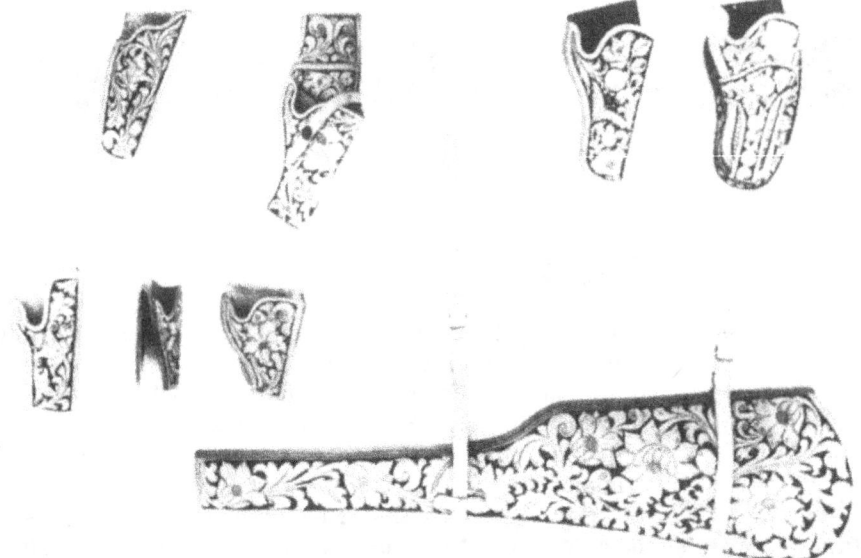

Some of the holsters manufactured by the S.D. Myres Saddle Company, El Paso, Texas.

Top—Left to right, Tom Threepersons style holster with extended hammer cover to protect clothing; hand carved Border Patrol holster; carved holsters with silver ornaments.

Center—Barton's Special holsters. The reverse flap will hold the holster in any easy drawing position, in the belt or pocket.

Bottom—Carved Telescope rifle scabbard.

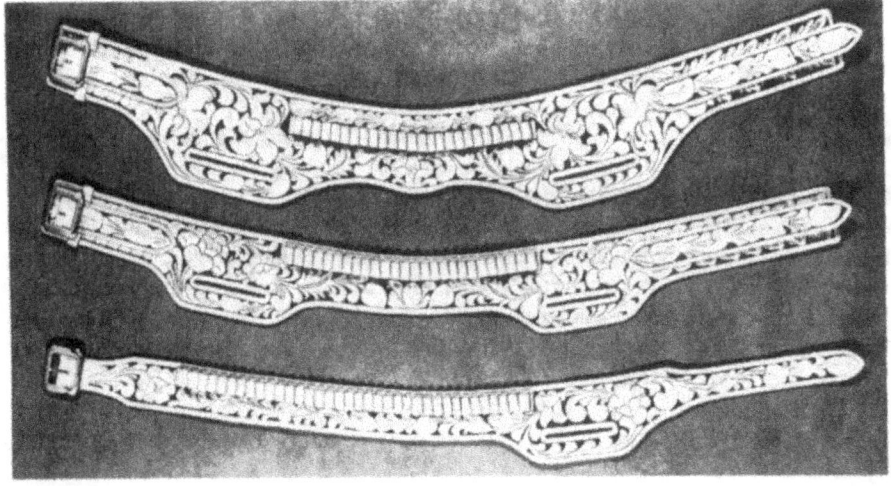

"Buscadero" belts made by the S.D. Myres Saddle Company.

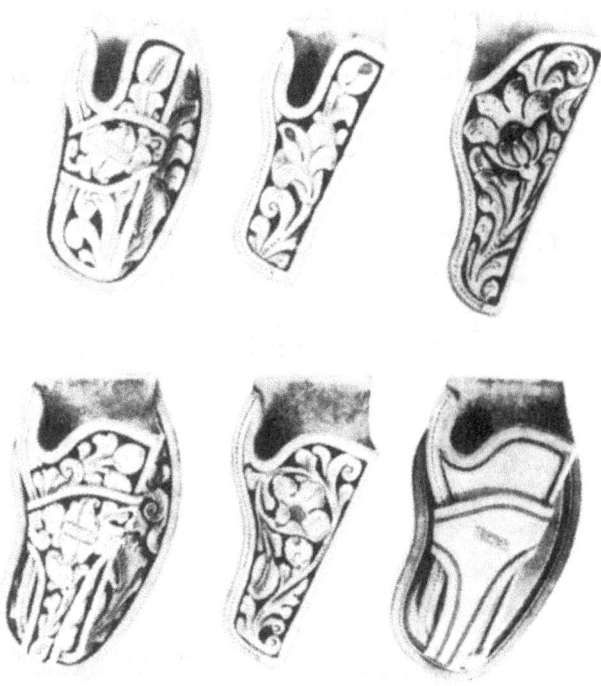

Myres Holsters
Top: Holsters for automatic pistols.
Bottom: Holsters for revolvers. All have pick draw effect.

out the safety notch in the hammer and fire the gun. We have known many old cow-pokes with a limp due to the fact that they carried six shells in their single action and something hit the hammer spur hard enough to fire it. Many were saddling their horses when it happened. They hung the stirrup on the horn and when they pulled upward on the latigo, cinching up, it would flop over and hit the hammer spur of their gun. Glenn Bradley of Salmon, Idaho, shot himself through the right leg this way with a .32-20 S. A. Colt. We have known many other victims of this kind of accident. If you want six cartridges in a single action gun, use the Hardy safety tab inside the top front of holster, and let your hammer all the way down with the firing pin through a hole in this leather.

Our remarks about Cap. Hardy's clever hammer strap gadget are entirely predicated on its being used with Colt single action pistols in the condition in which they left the factory. It is worse than useless to try to use it with Ruger and Great Western single actions which have retracting firing pins, and this also applies to all Colts rebuilt with firing pins in the frame. We have seen Colts fitted with over-hanging,

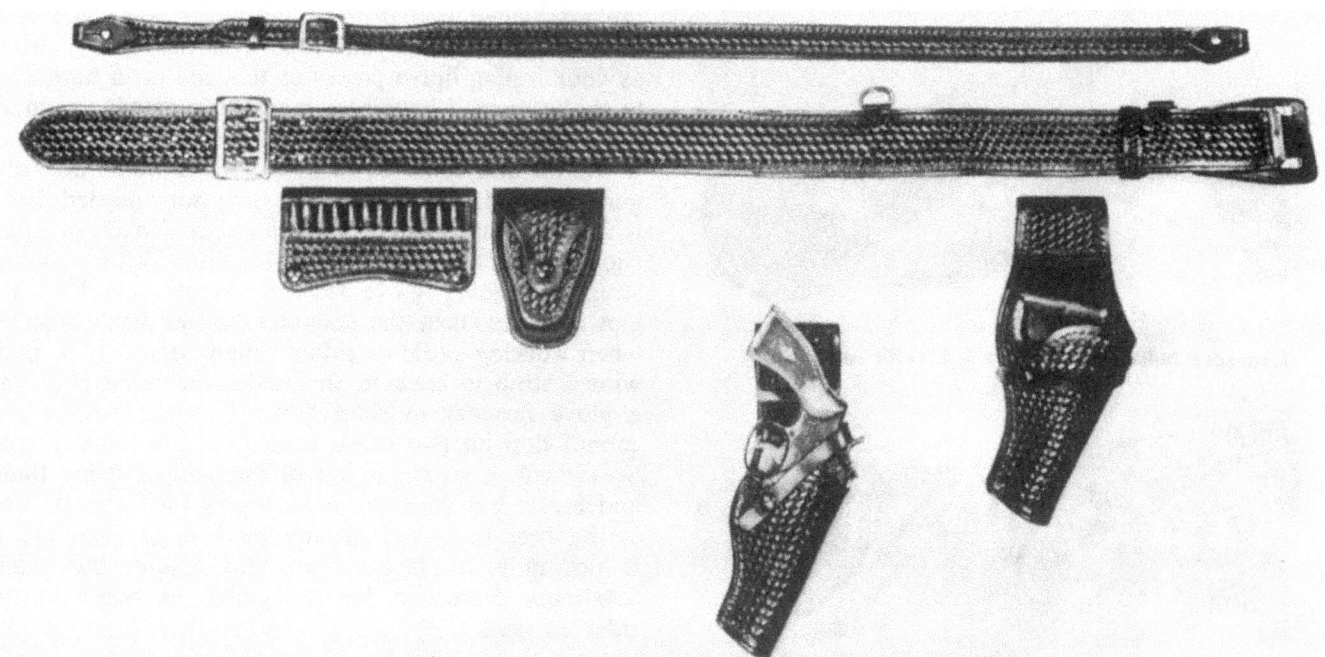

Sam Browne belt and holster combination in basket stamped leather by S.D. Myres Saddle Company. Bottom holster is Jordan style.

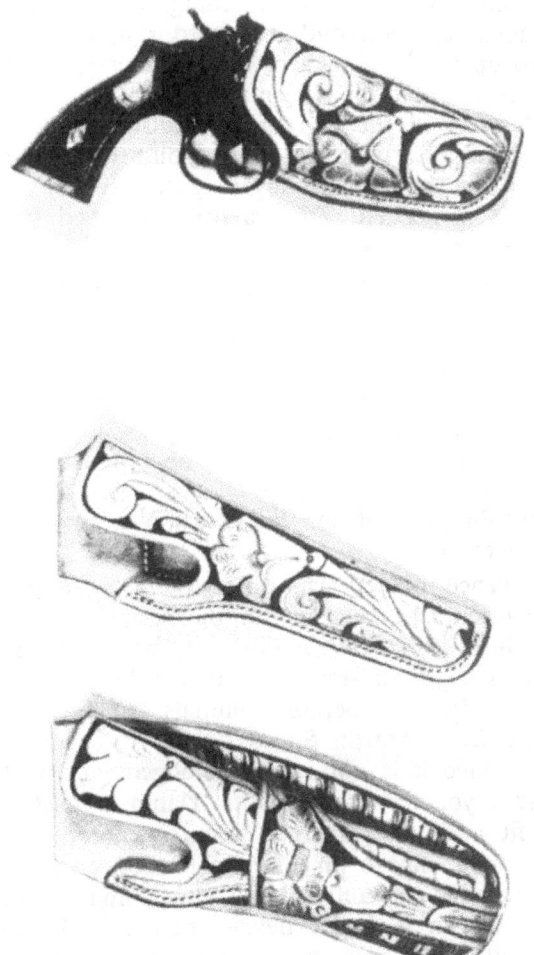

S. D. Myres holsters—the lower two for the Colt Woodsman or the Hi Standard; the one at the top for S&W and Colt revolvers only.

adjustable, rear sights that caused the hammer to lock and froze the gun in the holster. Used with a factory condition Colt, the holster does not have to be tight, as the hammer strap holds the gun securely; it must be loose around the cylinder to permit it to start revolving as the hammer is pulled back to release the strap.

For the hunter working rough or wet country on foot or the peace officer hauling prisoners in cars, the Lawrence No. 7 shoulder holster is a very good rig. The gun is completely covered except the butt; it cannot be accidently fired, and any prisoner attempting to get at it has to reach across the officer's body. This holster also fully protects the gun from rain or snow when worn under the coat, and about the only wear that comes on the gun is from the soft leather covered spring covering over the cylinder. Shoulder holsters are no good at all for riding broncs or working cattle. A good cow horse will drop his rump and stop from a hard run in two or three stiff-legged jumps and swap ends to take after a fast turning critter. Likewise a bucking horse will hit the ground as hard as he possibly can each jump, trying to throw his rider, and the shoulder holster will let the gun fly out of it the first time the pony comes down. I tried many such shoulder holsters when wearing a coat, as they kept the gun out of the way of the rope when roping, but none of them had spring tension to hold the gun when you stacked your horse out of a hard run for a quick turn after some fast dodging critter. The Lawrence No. 7 held the gun best of any we have tried. But even it would need a safety strap to hold the gun surely.

When roping cattle on the range, you should shift your gun to the opposite side so it will be out of

Lawrence holster number 34 L.F. with safety strap.

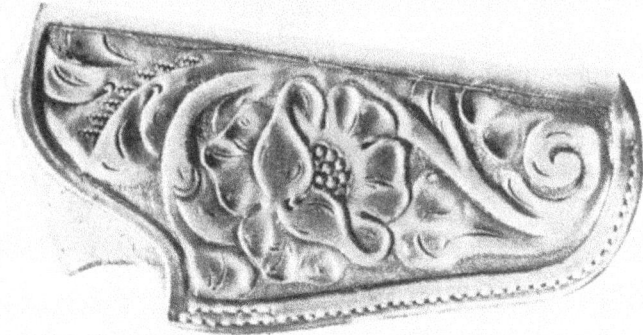

George Lawrence number 34 holster—my favorite for double action guns when made with safety straps.

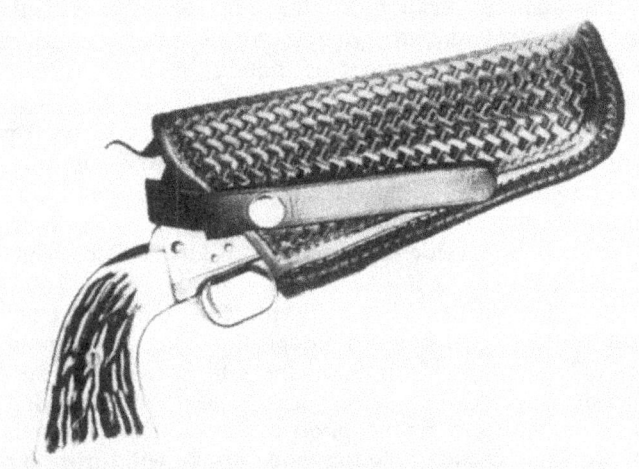

George Lawrence Keith design number 120 holster with Great Western S.A.

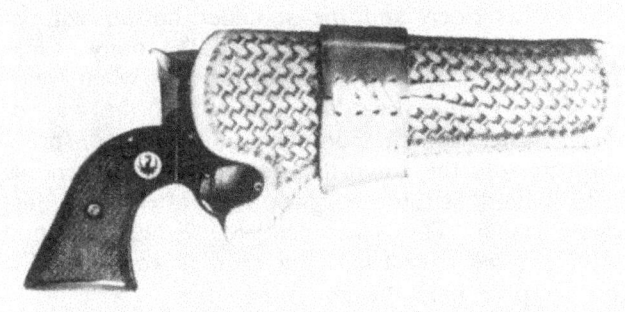

George Lawrence holster for Ruger Single Six.

the way when you drop a loop over some old wild critter, and then flip your rope over the hind quarters as your roping horse passes to the side on a hard run, to throw them. I have seen many sixguns caught under the rope as their owners busted a steer. They fly high in the air and come down in the rocks which does the gun no good. Likewise if the gun was needed later, it was far out of reach. The Lawrence No. 7, or other shoulder holsters, can often be fitted with a safety strap and heavy glove fastener to securely lock the gun in place, then the shoulder holster is satisfactory when working cattle or riding rough horses. It is made with a strap in back to slip under the waist belt, and a glove fastener to snap firmly in place so the gun cannot flop up and down each time the horse jumps. So carried, a sixgun is out of the way of flying limbs and brush and the rope when roping heavy stock, and is the best protected of any method of carrying. It is not quite as fast to get into action, but offers maximum protection for the gun, and safety to the rider as well.

When riding the range I used to have a leg strap for the bottom of our belt holsters that went around the leg and securely held the holster in place on the hip. When a horse started pitching, jumped a ditch, or made a fast turn out of a hard run, the gun did not flop up in the air where the hammer spur usually dead centers the elbow crazy bone. We also had a small snap in the end of the holster, and a ring on our chaps at just the right point to secure the holster. The gun then stayed put, and where we wanted it if needed. This precaution saved my life a couple times.

Many peace officers and movie stunt men want their holsters of stiff and hard material, and loose on the gun so it won't drag or pull when they draw fast. I prefer a holster to be fitted snug to the gun so that it requires some pull to clear the holster. In fast action I never could see where it slowed me down in the least if the holster was anchored by a leg strap or a snap in a chaps ring. At least the gun was still in place if the horse came a cropper and rolled over us.

The peace officer who engages in a rough and tumble often loses his gun in the scrimmage if it is carried in a loose holster. This may be fine for movie men working on a stage, but it can be fatal to the officer handling desperate criminals. In this respect the little Berns-Martin Speed holster is excellent for the gun since it is not easily dislodged, and will not fall out if you turn somersaults. Damn a holster that won't fit and hold the gun securely. Peace officers should never engage in a scuffle if they do not have to. They have the authority to stop a man, and that is what a gun is for. I never knew a real gunman who would risk breaking a knuckle in a fist fight. They talked slowly and softly but meant what they said and believed in using their gun rather than their fists. Only in Hollywood does the gunman also become a pugilist, and no movie seems complete unless the hero bulldogs a man off a horse and engages in a couple of good old Irish fist fights or free-for-alls. A real gunman would never think of taking the chance of damaging his gun hand.

Some civilians and plain clothesmen like and prefer small .38 caliber short barreled guns for their work in cities where, if the gun is needed, it will be at very close range. While many carry these two inch barrel jobs in the pocket, others prefer some sort of holster. For these the Berns-Martin Lightning, upside-down holster is excellent and both Myres and Lawrence furnish very small belt holsters such as the Myres No. 701, No. 45 and No. 38, or the Lawrence No. 20 and No. 22 holsters. Myres also makes wrist band spring holsters for the little Remington Double Derringers. These are handy and fast for real close range work if the coat sleeve is large enough to permit their moving down out of the sleeve, or reaching up under the sleeve cuff for them.

Police women usually carry their guns in their handbags with zipper or snap fastening, where they can get them quickly in an emergency. We have seen many couples traveling in a car who kept a ladies handbag laying between them. Inside was a short .357 magnum, .44 or .45, loaded and ready. If all States permitted law abiding citizens to thus carry a gun, there would be fewer holdups. This is a good method when two people are traveling together as either can get the gun in a second if they run into a stick-up artist. I have seen some good guns show up in a neat looking ladies handbag. The gun is there ready for instant use yet unsuspected. Myres makes a zipper bag of this sort for a short sixgun, either plain or fancy carved leather, with fleece lining and it can be had in about any desired shape with or without carrying strap.

Users of .22 caliber auto pistols can obtain anything they want, in belt or shoulder holsters, from one of the holster makers mentioned.

Good guns deserve good holsters. The new holster should be oiled, and the more it is used, the better it will fit the gun, and the softer and smoother it will become. Good neatsfoot oil is all that is required to soften and fit a holster to the gun. Sometimes a holster becomes loose after use and then a few stitches along the line of the bottom of the frame will take up the slack.

For gun belts we have a wide variety available. The most comfortable is usually a double, oil grain, chap leather in the form of a combination cartridge and money belt. Both Myres, and Lawrence and Heiser have excellent assortments of these. We like them in 2½ inch width. The holster loops should be ordered to fit a given width of belt. If you like carved leather, it can be had also. It is stiffer until oiled and used for a time. Cartridge loops should be tight and hold the cartridges firmly. Lawrence makes a belt with adjustable loops. The strip of calf skin that holds the

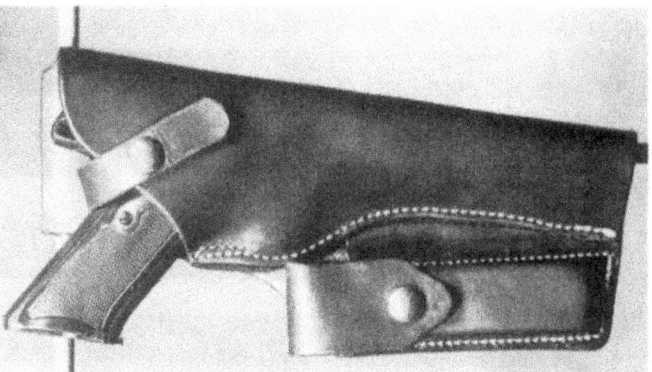

George Lawrence Holster with clip pocket for .22 auto.

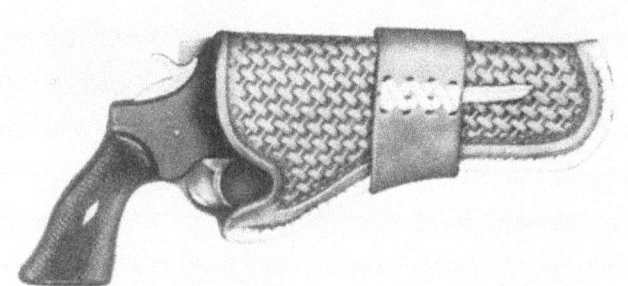

Lawrence holster for High Standard .22 caliber Sentinel.

Keith design number 120 George Lawrence holster for S.A. Colt or Great Western.

cartridges is threaded back and forth through slits cut in the face of the belt, if a double belt, or through the leather if a single belt. With a Marlin one can work it out to any desired caliber as the whole strip of loops is in one piece, and can be fitted over each round, and the surplus leather pulled out tight at the end of the belt. This makes a very fine gun belt and allows one to change calibers if he so desires, and still maintain a good fit. We much prefer them to sewed loops as the latter tend to loosen with use, and there is no way of taking up the slack except to run a shoe lace through them all.

I once had an old, chap leather belt of the money variety that carried two strips of loops on the left side opposite the gun and seemed to help balance it. It was a very comfortable rig. It came with an S. A. Colt holster made by A. W. Brill of Austin, Texas, on the Tom Three Person pattern. That old holster,

Waist Belts by George Lawrence.

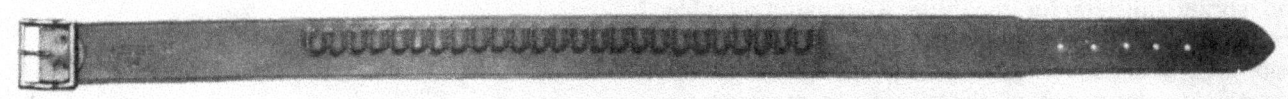

Plain Lawrence Cartridge Belt.

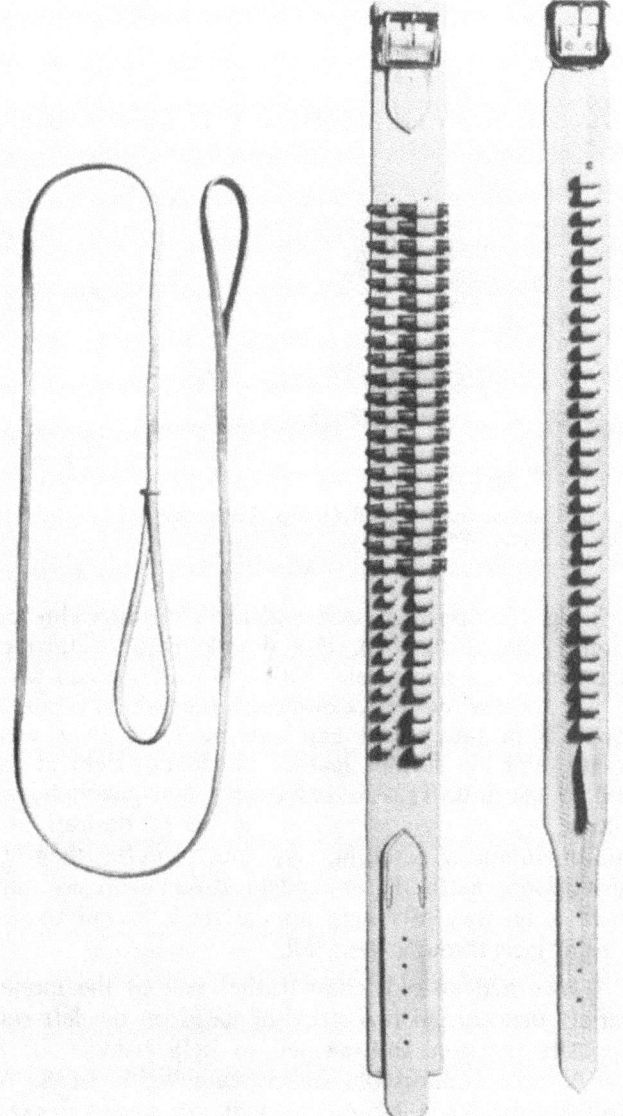

with oil grain chap leather on the back where it rubbed against the hip, was one of the lightest and neatest we have ever seen. The trigger guard and hammer were clear above the leather and the holster set at exactly the right angle for fast work. It was, and still is a good holster, though badly worn now. I believe in having more cartridge loops rather than a lot of extra leather in extra wide belts or fancy skirted holsters. I like a light, yet comfortable holster and belt that is neither bulky, nor heavy to wear. Breaking in a new belt and holster is a chore, and you will get your clothes well oiled in the process. But, it has to be done and can best be done in summer in warm weather, when the neatsfoot oil will easily penetrate the leather, and when you are wearing clothes that can be laundered readily. You are bound to get some oil on your pants and shirt when wearing a new holster and breaking it in. Once it becomes soft and polishes up from wear, it will not soil the clothing. Dust and dirt are best removed with saddle soap and water. Remember, oil will penetrate the leather better from the flesh side.

I have seen several types of swivel holsters; from the old army .45 holster with a flap of 1917 vintage to some made up for shooting through the holster without drawing the gun. Ed McGivern had such a pair made to go on studs on his belt so the gun and holster could be drawn off the belt together and fired without taking the gun out of the holster, or else could be swivelled on the belt and fired while still attached to the belt for the first shot. I never favored such outfits, as dirt or twigs could get wedged between gun and holster and prevent the cylinder from rotating, thus tying up the gun, which could easily be fatal. McGivern has probably done more work on this type

Lawrence Cartridge Belts.

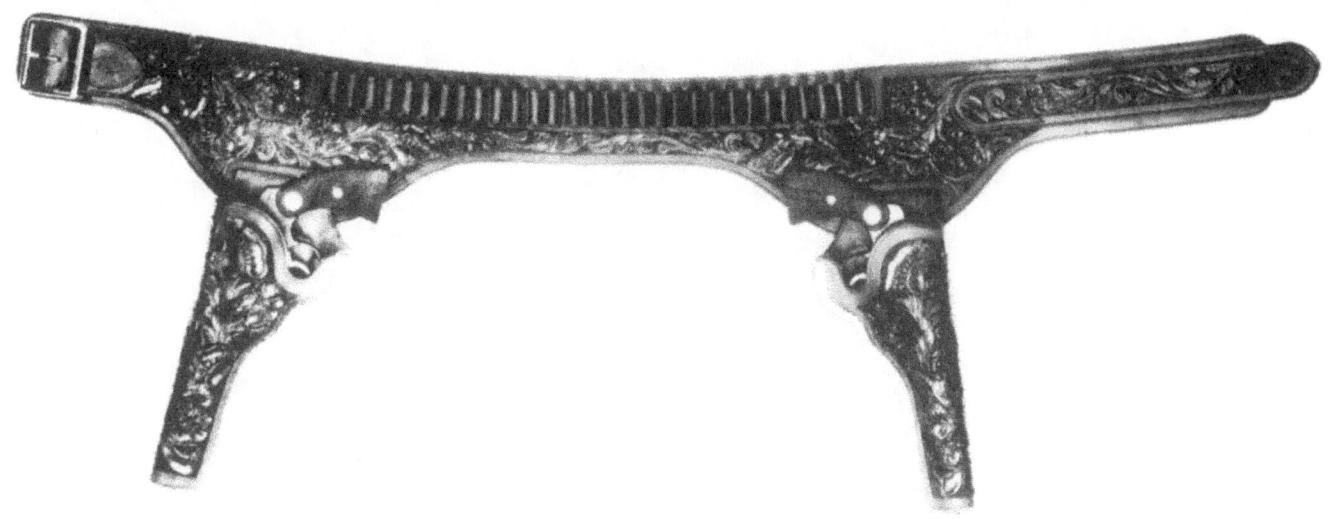

George Lawrence two gun outfit.

of swivel, drawless, holster than any other man, but I have not seen any of them in use recently. For one thing, if you would hit from the hip in fast quick draw shooting you should shove the gun toward the target as you would point your finger. If you try to hold the gun back against your body you cannot do an accurate job of gun pointing. Swivel holsters which can be fired from while the gun is still in the holster are more for movie stunts than for practical use.

The fastest sixgun rig I have ever seen or used—much faster than any holster—was developed by Jesse Thompson. It is not in production, and probably never will be as Jesse does not want it out. It is not a holster at all, but a stud screwed to the gun frame and a spring clip to receive it on the belt. I find that I can draw and shoot a .45 S. A. Colt with close range combat accuracy using this rig, faster than with any type of holster ever evolved. It is a practical outfit for under coat wear, but offers no protection to the gun. The spring clip can be used on a waist or gun belt as fancy dictates, but until Jesse Thompson gives the word to let it out, it will not be manufactured or sold. In fact, only a few peace officers and some of J. Edgar Hoover's boys have seen the rig. Jesse may be right, and the outfit best kept out of circulation. It is so much more practical and faster than a swivel holster that I, at one time, urged Thompson to patent and bring it out commercially, but he preferred to keep it out of the public eye.

Holsters should always be long enough to fully cover the gun muzzle, as any gun projecting through the holster will soon have one side of the muzzle worn away from rubbing on the saddle, and will cause the front sight to catch on the holster in quick draw work. It is well, however, for all holsters to have a small opening in the bottom so water can drain through and dirt sift out of them.

George Lawrence number 7 shoulder holster.

Chapter IX

Quick Draw and Hip Shooting

FAST GUN HANDLING is needed only for close range self defense work. Then, a person's ability to do fast accurate hip shooting may save his life. There is nothing magical or mythical about it. As an infant, you slowly learn the use of a spoon, then later the knife and fork. Your hand learns to find its way to your mouth with a laden spoon or fork as naturally and surely as a baby chick finds its food with its beak. Do anything long enough and you become proficient. You learned from practice just where your mouth is and not to stick your lips or tongue with the tines of the fork. The gunman carries his gun just so, and over a period of years his hand learns exactly where it is. Anyone with ordinary intelligence, and the use of his hands and arms, can learn quick draw and accurate hip shooting. It is only a case of practice and the practical application of the mental and physical abilities with which we are endowed. To a real gunman, hip shooting should be just as natural and sure as pointing the finger. You can point your finger accurately at anything you can see and you do not have to aim over it to do so. The sixgun should be an extension of your finger, and, if it fits you, point just as accurately. A typist learns the exact location of every key and does not have to look at the keyboard to hit the right letter (Elmer Keith excepted). The boy with his sling shot learns to lob rocks at stray cats surely and accurately by the feel of his weapon. The real archer can shoot an arrow quickly and accurately without perceptable aim, by concentrating his attention on what he wants to hit. So the finished sixgun shot can hit any reasonable sized object at close range by focusing his eyes on the target, and shooting by the feel of the gun, just as he would point his finger.

Human beings vary greatly in their mental processes and their ability to transmit a mental impulse from the brain to the hand. The Homo sapiens species varies greatly in the speed with which they think and act. Some are slow both mentally and physically, other think and act with the speed of light. Good drivers automatically do the right thing in an emergency, while poor ones fumble the job and cause wrecks. The person who can think quickly and puts his thoughts into instant execution, is the type who can best learn fast gun handling and instinctive gun pointing. Alert mental and physical processes are a necessity to fast hip shooting, and anyone so endowed can learn this phase of sixgun shooting with enough practice.

Study holsters and gun positions and select the one that is the handiest for you and with which you can get the gun out and in action with the least effort. Next, select the gun you like best, and which fits your hand best. Bear in mind in this gun selection to select a gun that points naturally and to the right elevation. Grip the gun naturally and concentrate on some target, close your eyes then open them and point the gun at it with a poking motion just as you would point your finger quickly. If the gun points low, it has too much angle of grip to frame, and should not be selected for this type of shooting. Usually the Bisley model S. A. Colt and the .45 auto point much too low for instinctive fast hip shooting. Lugers, the various Colt, Ruger, and High-Standard .22 autos point well and the old single action Colt, along with the new Great Western and Ruger Single Six point perfectly. The Smith & Wesson double action guns are good pointers and some Colt double actions as well. It is best to start with the .22 as you will have to burn up a tremendous amount of ammunition to become expert at this phase of the game. The fastest gun positions are the side hip draws, or the cross draw. For the hip draws, the butt of the gun should tip ahead, and for the cross draw the butt should tip toward the hand that will use it. With the side hip draws the butt of the gun is tipped forward and the muzzle tipped back to the rear, while with the cross draws the butt is tipped forward toward the belt buckle, and the muzzle pointed more to the side of the shooter. It makes no difference whether you are right or left handed, these are the fastest positions. With guns worn with the butt to the front, the butt should tip forward slightly and the muzzle to the rear; then in drawing they are turned across the body as you draw and poke them at the target.

Never try to do your best work by holding the gun close against the body. You can point it much more

Keith before the two gun draw. S. & W. guns, .38/44 Outdoorsman and .44 Special Triple Lock.

Hand to guns movement completed.

Both guns lifting and ready to fire.

Side view of both guns firing with heavy loads at a small rotten stump at a 10 yard range. The jar of guns and slight smoke hazes this picture somewhat.

Both guns still pounding the stump. Note bullets splash in snow beyond after complete penetration.

Both guns in recoil and bits of wood flying from the disintegrating stump. Note bits of wood in the air and blur of left hand gun in recoil. The 12 rounds demolished the stump.

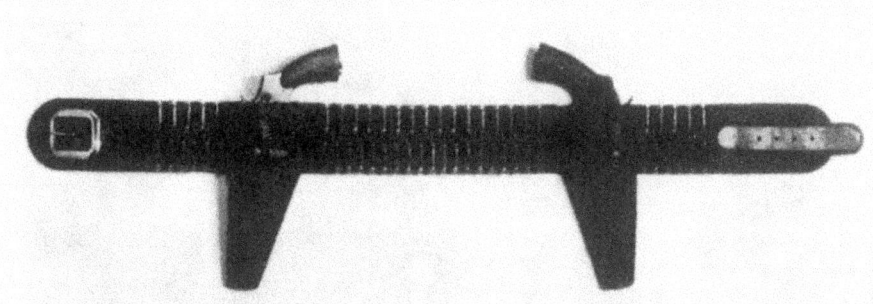

Elmer Keith's Berns-Martin two-gun speed outfit.

accurately if you throw or poke it toward the target. Fill the gun with empty cases to cushion the blow of the firing pin and practice drawing and poking the gun at the target as you press the trigger. Strive first for accuracy and not speed. Speed will come later with constant practice. Avoid all unnecessary hand or gun movements. The shortest distance between two points is always a straight line, and the same applies to your gun and the target. Jerk it out and flip up the muzzle toward the target as you press the trigger. There should be no hesitancy; simply throw your shot at the target in one smooth movement of hand and gun. Even timing and accuracy of gun pointing are paramount in importance. Speed will come later. Avoid any unnecessary gun spins as you would a pestilence.

We once knew a would-be tough lad who put a finger through the trigger guard of his 4½ inch New Service .38-40 and pulled upward with the finger, then spun the gun over and forward in line and shot with gun close to his body. That spinning the gun muzzle over from the rear cost him a good quarter of a second in his draw and he was never accurate in the placing of his shots. Such stunts may look well to the uninitiated in the movies but have no place in fast, sure, gun work. We have seen other quick draw artists, who started with the gun hand held along the bottom of the holster and brought the hand up and then forward in a sort of S movement. They were very smooth with this draw, and accurate, but lost time in that upward movement and the unnecessary hand movement. The shortest distance from your hand to the gun is the way to move your hand. It makes no difference if your hand is up or down, move the hand directly to the gun butt. Grasp the grip and hammer of a single action, or the grip and trigger of a double action. If a single action, you start cocking the hammer as the gun is drawn and poked toward the target; if a double action the pressure is started on the trigger as the gun is drawn and finished as the gun is poked toward the target. In time and with enough practice the subconscious takes over and you draw and shoot without any conscious mental effort. The mental impulse from the brain is all that is necessary to start and finish the draw and the shot. Many times spectators have asked me to draw and shoot slowly so they could see just how I did it. They said the hand moved so fast they could not see what happened. We tried but simply could not comply with their wishes as it spoiled both our timing and accuracy. A top flight quick draw artist will draw and shoot in about one-fourth second and hit anything the size of a man up to thirty feet. This either from the side hip draw or from the cross draw. With the side hip draw the best gun position we have found is with the butt about halfway between the wrist and the elbow with hands hung

Keith demonstrating his two hand game shooting position.

Keith demonstrating quick draw and hip shooting with No. 5 S.A. Colt from Lawrence No. 120 holster of Keith design.

Using 7½ inch S.A. Colt in Heiser holster.

loose at the sides. The gun is drawn or jerked out toward the target, the muzzle flipped up in line and fired, all in one split second motion.

With the cross draw, the gun is pulled across the body, and the muzzle swung up in line and fired all in one motion. J. H. Fitzgerald was an artist on the cross draw, and a fast man with a gun under any condition. His cross draw speed was phenomenal. He held his guns and wrists close in against the body and aimed by body movements, usually shooting at objects to one side or the other, depending on whether he used his right or left hand. He would always turn his side toward a target. Cross draw shooting across the body with revolvers, is hard on clothing as the cylinder barrel joint allows enough gas escapage to burn shirt fronts. But, it is a very speedy draw.

The only fast shoulder holster draw is the Berns-Martin lightning holster, and this draw, either right or left handed, ends in the gun firing across the body and the side turned toward the target. Cross draws were never as fast for us as the old cowboy hip draw, probably because we learned the latter first and practiced it a great deal. Likewise, we were always more accurate with the hip draw than with the cross draw. The gun is thrown directly at the target instead of having to either turn the body or stop the side swing of the gun if the target is in front of the shooter. Proficiency is a matter of practice in the style of draw you like best. I have seen some hand made shoulder holster rigs holding the guns rather low on each side with butts tipped well forward. These were very fast —much faster than any conventional shoulder holster —as the grip, hammer and trigger guard of the gun was fully exposed and the shooter could grip the gun naturally without having to bend his wrist. No such rigs have ever appeared on the market. When such a gun harness is properly made and fitted to the individual for wear under a loose coat, it is very fast. John Wesley Hardin is said to have used such an outfit. I have seen two or three of them worked out by individuals, and they were really fast.

During the War, while I was in charge of final inspection and proof firing of small arms at Ogden Arsenal, the officers of both Ogden Arsenal and also Hill Field were often given some training in pistol practice. At that time the army taught them to squat down facing their man silhouette targets and fire with gun held low in front of them, a sort of close range combat course. To an experienced gunman it was all wrong. In the first place, they were in a strained position and the .45 auto Colts with which they were trained all pointed low and also shot low. All they accomplished was to dig a furrow in front of themselves about halfway to the target with their magazine of slugs. We were often pulled off the job to keep the guns in order and to load magazines for them.

One day out of a clear sky, the Captain of the Arsenal guards picked up a megaphone and announced to all and sundry that Elmer Keith and Buck Lee would now demonstrate quick draw and hip shooting for the assemblage. I remonstrated, telling the Captain there was not a single decent quick draw rig on the Arsenal and that the .45 autos were not worth hell room for hip shooting, but that I would be glad to bring my guns and holsters into the arsenal and give him a demonstration at some later date. He, however, insisted that we shoot and Lee had been doing some elementary quick draw practice, so some of them evidently thought they had framed me. The captain said he had a Colt single action and also a .45 1917 Smith & Wesson with him, and that I could use either of them. I told him either would do but as there was not a single quick draw holster in the arsenal other than Buck Lee's, I would simply have to hold the gun down at arms length at my side until the signal was given. They agreed to this and we were each given a man's head and shoulder silhouette target at 15 yards range and stood up in front of all those officers. At the signal to go, I flipped that old 1917 up and out in line with the target and cut loose double action. I saw the first slug hit the one-by-four board on which the target was nailed, cutting into the very bottom of the target, so lifted the gun slightly and poured the other five all in the chest of the silhouette in a space I could cover with my hand. Then I unlatched the cylinder and let the gun spin on my finger as I turned and handed it to the guard captain with the cylinder open. Lee was still shooting and I saw dust raising between him and his target as I walked back to my bench in the rear to load more pistol magazines.

The Guard Captain again called me back and asked me to do the stunt over again. That time I knew the gun and when he gave the signal I flipped the 1917 up in line with the target and emptied it into the chest of the man silhouette. Again I unlatched the cylinder and allowed the butt of the gun to swing

Keith—start of two gun draw.

Keith demonstrating two gun hip shooting, S. & W. guns and Berns-Martin holsters.

forward on my finger and handed him the gun as I turned away from the target. Again I noticed Lee was still shooting and dirt was still bouncing up between him and his target. He used a .38 Special 4 inch barrel Smith & Wesson and had been coaching the Ogden police force. As I walked to the rear between the lines of benches on which the officers were seated I heard a Colonel tell a Major, "Major, we have just seen something." I was never again called on to load magazines at officer's practice, or to demonstrate hip shooting. Whoever framed me for that stunt wanted no repeat performance. The spread of my hand covered the last six shots from the good old 1917 Smith & Wesson, in the center of the chest on the silhouette target.

I was then shooting every day, testing guns, and was in good training. Lee had only recently taken up hip shooting and was green at it. I had many years experience behind me.

In 1925, while serving on the Idaho National Guard National Match .30 caliber team at Camp Perry, Ohio, the late Chauncey Thomas, who was there for *Outdoor Life* Magazine, arranged to give a talk on the Old West. He also wanted Fitzgerald of Colt and I to put on a quick draw contest on the stage for the benefit of the assemblage. I readily agreed. I was just a green kid of 26, had nothing to lose and thought I might learn something. Fitz, however, was working for Colt and had an important job to fill for the company. He told Thomas, "That damned cowpuncher is a snake with a single action. You will have to put us on separately for the demonstration." That was the way it was done and Chauncey Thomas would stand in front of one of us and make a break for his gun, then we would draw and snap on him with empty guns. The entire assemblage seemed to enjoy the show so I guess both Fitz and I got away with it O.K. We became fast and lifelong friends and I had my last good visit with him at Camp Perry in 1940 while serving on another .30 caliber National Match team, this time with the Idaho Civilians. He was a grand old man of the gun game and about as fast a double action sixgun shot as I have ever seen draw and hit. McGivern may have been able to shoot a double action gun faster once it was in his hand but I have yet to see any man get a double action gun in action any faster than Fitz. He was a big man, but quick as lightning. His cross draws were phenomenal in their speed as he moved the gun barely enough to clear the holster and shot across his body with the other hand and arm held back out of the way. I believe he was the fastest big man I have ever seen in action. An expert in all phases of disarmament of criminals, which he taught the various police organizations, Fitz would have made a top flight peace officer.

In practicing quick draw, avoid all strained or unnatural positions. Stand loosely but with the weight well balanced on both feet, and if anything, lean into your target slightly. In combat it is a good thing to move after the first shot and get down as low as possible so you will afford a smaller target for your adversary's fire. For that first shot, however, or when practicing on a target, stand naturally and loosely.

In 1940 Colonel George W. Busbey and I were visiting Don Martin at his ranch. We were doing some sixgun shooting and had set up a long line of bottles on a log. Then we placed the Colonel in the middle and decided to see which of us could get the most bottles starting at a given signal. Don winked at me and I knew what he wanted, so when the signal was given we started shooting as fast as we could recover from recoil and line up on another bottle. Soon the guns were empty, all bottles busted, and the Colonel trying to figure out what had happened, as each time he started to aim at a bottle it blew up in front of his sights and he did not get in a shot. That was a dirty trick we played on him as he is a fine pistol shot.

Learn to throw that first shot from whatever position you may be in. You may be lying on your belly drinking out of the creek, and have to roll to the side and shoot at the same time as a friend of mine once did who laid down beside a rattlesnake, not knowing it was there until too late. One should be able to throw a slug from any position he may be in, sitting, standing or lying down. After the first shot is time to move if necessary. In any gun fight in the dark, always move after or with every shot and change position as much as possible. An adversary will shoot at your gun flash.

Nothing will speed up your draw more than stepping on a big rattler. I remember one warm August morning when a partner and I were walking down an old cow trail in the sage brush looking for our hobbled horses. It was down on the old Staddler & Kauffman ranch on the Missouri river breaks in Montana, below Winston. I was in the lead and my attention focussed on the tracks of our mounts where they had slowly fed alongside the trail. Daylight was just breaking when I suddenly felt the powerful squirm of a big rattler under my right boot. My bridle was hung over the left shoulder. I still have no recollection of either drawing or shooting, but do remember the prickly sensation that flashed up the back of my neck. My partner claimed I went straight up three feet in the air, and shot once on the way up, once at the heighth of my jump and again as I hit the ground. The rattler was about as big as they come, coiled up tightly and made a big target. The heavy .45 Colt slugs made a mess of him as they went down through his coils and richochetted off the hard rocky ground. All I remember of its was the fact I had three empty shells in my gun and three clouds of black powder smoke were slowly drifting up the valley toward the first long rays of the rising sun. I was plenty scared

Keith demonstrating Jesse Thompson S.A. Colt belt clip before the draw, latest of all gun rigs.

Keith demonstrating S.A. Colt draw from belt clip, fastest of all gun rigs.

and my subconscious took over. Had my boots been loose, I would probably have left them right there in the trail when I went up.

Herb Bradley was climbing around the cliffs along the Middle Fork of the Salmon River while on a fishing trip when he had an even worse experience. A shoulder high ledge was in front of him. He just started to reach up for a hand hold when a warning whirr of a rattler sounded. As Herb recoiled and drew his Officer's Model Colt, the snake launched his whole body off the ledge at Herb. He shot from the hip, luckily shattering the snake's head just before it hit him in the chest. He said he was sick the rest of the day.

An old mountain trained gunman tells of walking down a lonely moonlit trail in mid-winter. He had seen the saucer shaped tracks of mountain lions several times and had them on his mind. As he passed under an over hanging limb he heard a squawl above him. In that instant it had but one meaning—lion. He says he blacked out and does not know what happened for a second or two. When he came to he was ten feet down the trail, turned around facing the tree and his cocked pistol was trained on a large hoot owl. Had there been a cat on the limb the gun would have been smoking.

After one has practiced getting a gun into action in a fraction of a second, enough years, all that is needed to start the fireworks is the realization of immediate necessity. The subconscious mind takes over and the shooting starts before another thought can register.

Play marbles with cyanide balls and juggle jugs of nitro-glycerine if you must have excitement, but never try to scare an old gunman. The results of success are likely to get your name sandblasted on a piece of white rock.

While taking a summer fishing party down the Salmon River by boat one summer, we camped at the mouth of the Cottonwood. Captain Guleke and the party fished while I elected to scout the goat country up the creek. I had a hunting party coming up for the fall run down the river and wanted to know where the goats were. I had climbed up a long steep ridge, then started working down through the cliffs. I got ledged up and had to pull off my loggers, hang them over my shoulder and slide down a crevice with the cold water of a spring running down the back of my neck while I hung on by side pressure with sock feet and hands to the slippery ledge on each side. Finally I came to a sheer drop off below me. I could not go back the way I had come down, but a goat trail worked around the top of the cliff and under another overhanging ledge. The trail was fairly wide up the creek, but I wanted to go down in the direction of camp. This way the trail was narrow. I soon came to a turn around a knife-edged ledge. The trail was barely eight inches wide and the rock hung out above it, crowding me off. I managed to sidle around this overhang and was hanging on to a projection with my left hand when I met a huge old yellow Billy Goat facing me at ten feet. He would have weighed a good 450 pounds, and knowing goats, I instantly had a cocked .45 S. A. Colt trained on his head, from the hip.

It was before the goat season and he was in summer pelage. I did not want him; neither did I want those long sharp black horns driven in my belly. Holding perfectly still I started talking to him in slow even tones. He would shake his head and look at me, plainly telling me to start something if I wished. I told him what I thought of his ancestry, as we both stood our ground, and I heartily wished I was back at the boat. Finally I said, "Bill, you ornery old devil, you can turn around and get off that ledge and I cannot, so it is either you or me and I am not going to jump." He took a long look at me, sat down and watched me awhile longer. He slipped one forefoot over his protruding hind leg and sat it down between the hindlegs, then the other front foot was moved over between his hind legs where they stuck out over the cliff. I encouraged him with slow even tones, telling him I did not want to kill him but would if I had to as I was caught where I could not turn around. He suddenly flipped his front feet the rest of the way around on the ledge, jerked his hind quarters up and started slowly away along the trail. He would stop and look back but I made no false move to follow him and waited a long time after he was out of sight before I too, followed around the ledge and to the safety of a big rock slide extending down to the creek far below. The goat was nowhere in sight when I got off that narrow trail around the cliff. I climbed the rock slide, then a side gulch and got back to the safety of the ridge which I followed back to camp. Out of respect for that old boy I never hunted that bunch of goats again.

If you want to really learn quick draw work and fast accurate hip shooting, first get yourself a good outfit. Get a comfortable belt and holster such as I have outlined in the chapter on holsters, that suits your own style best. Then get a .22 caliber gun for practice. If you like a single action, get the Ruger Single Six or the Great Western .22 caliber. If you like double action guns, get the Smith & Wesson K-.22, or Combat Masterpiece, the Colt Official Police or Officer's Model Match, in .22 caliber. Stand facing your target if a side hip draw is contemplated, or turn the side toward the target if you want to practice cross draw. See that the holster is tied down if the gun rides snug in it, or that the belt is low enough around the hips to hold it snugly in place if holster is loose on the gun.

Throw a big tin can or bucket out in front of you some 20 to 25 feet. Then focusing both eyes on the target, draw the gun and poke it at the target and shoot. Practice this over and over, thousands of times, not trying for speed but just teaching your hand exactly where the gun is and where the hammer spur is on the single action, and the trigger on the D. A. gun. If the shot goes low, lift the muzzle for the next shot and walk your shots onto the target, noting the dust spurt from each slug as it strikes the ground. Pay no attention to the gun; look only at your target.

Remember you are now striving only for accuracy and sure, smooth draw. Keep at it day after day, and week after week, and month after month, until you can hit that can every time and with eyes focussed only on the target. I find it helps to sort of bend over the gun after the first shot, with the weight of the body well forward. Grasp the butt of the gun and hammer or trigger exactly the same way each time. If it is a single action gun, you may elect to cock it with the ball of the thumb in which case a wide, sharply checkered Bisley type hammer spur is a great help, or you may elect to use the crook of the first joint on the thumb to cock the gun. We have seen both methods used, but prefer the ball of the thumb way ourselves. The trigger finger is extended straight down along the holster at the start of the draw, touching the side of the trigger guard, but never on the trigger nor putting any pressure on it until the barrel clears the holster and starts its forward upward swing toward the target. You don't want any fumbles or a slug through your leg, so practice slowly and carefully. This for the right or left hip draw, with the single action gun. If you have big hands it may be advantageous to hook the little finger under the butt of the gun. This gives better control in cocking the gun for repeat shots after it is out and the first shot fired. Learn to hook the thumb over the hammer spur even as the gun recoils upward, and when you bring it back on the target it is cocked for the next shot.

Steady constant practice, will make drawing and firing that single action, and hitting the can a certain thing, and it makes no difference if it requires three seconds for the draw and hit at the start. Keep at it, but only with the same sure, safe method. Speed will come in time. Don't attempt any speed stunts until after months of constant practice. You must first train your hand to throw your gun out pointing exactly at whatever object you focus your eyes on. The thumb must be taught to first cock the gun before the trigger finger takes over for the shot. The hand must be trained to bring the gun up in line with the target before the trigger finger fires the gun. This coordination of brain, eye, thumb, hand and trigger finger all requires steady practice. Strive always for accuracy first. Get your hits, as they are what counts. Speed will come if you practice long enough.

After you have mastered the draw and hit on one target, try two or more widely spaced targets, shifting the gun from one to the other as you cock it for the second and third shots. Remember, the recoil of the single action in heavy calibers always turns the gun up in your hand so that the hammer spur comes naturally under the thumb for cocking for the next shot. The little finger under the gun butt facilitates cocking for that next shot also if you have large hands. Next try throwing the can or bucket over your head or shoulder. Turn around as you draw and fix your eyes on the can for the shot. For shooting at two or three widely spaced targets, it is well to practice fanning as well. Draw the gun with a firm full grip with the gun hand, and as you poke it toward the target, slap the hammer with the other hand while you hold the trigger back firmly with the trigger finger. Then as you shift to another target, turn the body to do so. Only a short choppy slap of the left hand, if you are right handed, is necessary to bring the hammer spur back to full cock and let it slip firing the gun. The same is true for southpaws, but in reverse, of course.

In fanning you draw with the gun hand the same as in shooting with that hand alone, except the trigger is gripped hard at the start with the trigger finger, and the thumb is placed along the gun frame; as the gun muzzle comes up and is poked toward the target the palm of the other hand comes back along the top of the gun slapping the hammer back and letting it fire the gun. This is the fastest way of emptying a single action gun and good combat accuracy is also possible at close range if it is practiced long enough. Fanning is very hard on the hand, bolt and bolt spring, and you must expect some worn and broken parts in time that will have to be replaced. It is also hard on the bolt cuts on the cylinder, but is a fast practical way to use the single action at close range. It requires two hands, however, and one should never spend too much time practicing a stunt that requires the use of both hands as the fanning hand may be occupied elsewhere.

When you have trained one hand, get another holster for the left side and train the left hand, or vice versa. As you get more expert at quick drawing and hip shooting, increase the ranges used or decrease the size of the target. It is best to master the stunt with the .22 caliber and its cheap ammunition before turning to the larger calibers. The .22 short is just as good for practice as a heavier cartridge, and much cheaper, especially if bought in lots of ten thousand. When you have mastered the little gun, turn to the heavier more

Keith wearing George Lawrence belt and holster designed by Keith. S.A. Colt number 5.

practical calibers and you will find you are getting good results from the start.

Nearly all we have said about the hip draw with the single action applies to the double action gun except that with the latter, only the trigger finger is needed or used to fire the gun double action. Grasp the gun in a natural shooting position with thumb curled down alongside the gun frame in a firm double action grip, and train the finger to finish the double action pull only when the muzzle is in line with the target. It is no faster for the first shot than the single action for men equally well trained with either gun. The double action is much the faster after the first shot, for repeat hits, or for hitting different targets. The double action can be fired accurately much faster than by fanning a single action as the trigger finger alone can move faster than the whole arm and hand needed to fan a single action empty.

Cross draws do not work out as well with the single action as with the double action gun, unless the S. A. is fanned, for the reason that the hammer spur is not as well placed with relation to the position of the gun hand when drawn from a cross draw holster. Unless the butt of the gun is tipped well forward toward the belt buckle it is harder to reach the hammer spur with the thumb than when the gun is carried on the hip. Some become very expert at cross draw work with the single action, however, both by the thumb cocking method and also by fanning. Personally, I never favored fanning, as it is hard on guns and you might break a part in a critical situation and be left out in the cold, or six feet under. We prefer thumb cocking and fanning only after first shot if necessary.

John Newman used a still different technique. He

John Newman demonstrating two hand fast hip shooting.

John Newman with slip gun in left hand.

carried a pair of 2 inch barrel .45 S. A. Colts in his trousers pockets cut purposely large so he could point and shoot through the pockets if the case called for quick action. His wife usually wore a lot of very expensive jewelry, but no one wanted it when old John was strolling along with her as one or both hands were always in his pants pockets, and he could cock those slip guns with his thumbs and hold the hammer spurs back. If anyone had been fool enough to plug John he would have died, as the instant the pressure was released, holding back those stubby hammers, they would fall, firing the gun. When he packed a longer gun, it was usually in his waist band under the belt and he would draw it with his shooting hand cocking the slip hammer as he did so and bringing his other hand around to grasp the barrel at about the middle; then he pointed the gun at his target and slipped the hammer spur very rapidly with the thumb of his gun hand. It was a very fast and deadly system and he could slip a .45 slug into five different posts at ten to twenty feet in very short order.

John Newman was a finished gunman and as deadly in close range combat as they come. He had been in gun fights, knew the score, and always came out on top. I never could draw and shoot a slip gun as fast as I could a standard single action or one fitted with a wide sharply checkered Bisley-type hammer spur for the reason that the short stubby slip hammer must be cocked with the last joint of the thumb and this requires a different position of the gun than when carried in a holster. It is, however, excellent with a two inch barrel gun for shooting through coat or trousers pockets. Rough on clothes, but it might save your life. With your hands in your coat or trousers pockets, so long as the pockets are large enough, the gun with a short barrel can be grasped in a normal shooting position, and it is very fast to fire with a slip hammer. Newman also practiced drawing a long barrelled slip gun, holding it normally with the shooting hand, and slipping the hammer with the thumb of the other hand, another fast method of using the slip gun at close range. He was quite accurate as he had both hands to point the gun which was held about belt level in front of him while he watched only the target.

The cross draw is much better for double action than for the single action guns, as the gun comes out naturally and smoothly and pointed across the body

Quick Draw and Hip Shooting

at the target. For cross draw practice, stand with the side toward the target, and as you draw, throw the other arm around behind the back out of the way. The gun is pulled out of the holster toward the belt buckle and either fired in that position (very hard on clothes) or poked across the body toward the target just over the top of the holster with the arm held close across the body and pointed at different targets by turning the whole body. This is one method, the one favored by Fitzgerald and he was lightning fast and very accurate. The other method is to draw the gun in this manner and then poke it at any target in any direction, but more time is consumed where the gun is not pointing at the target as it clears the holster. With the cross-draw holster, if the time between starting the draw and a hole in the target is to be cut to an absolute minimum, the target must be to the left of the right handed shooter and to the right of the southpaw.

With the cross draw, the same as the hip draw, the .22 caliber is the gun to practice with. A few shooters practice the cross draw with both hands, notably Captain Sweet. He used to draw with his right hand, bringing the left hand up to grasp the frame of the gun between thumb and fingers with thumb on top. He fired small groups. This is not as fast for the first shot as when one hand is used. It is accurate and the gun so well controlled that very small groups can be fired in fast double action work. We prefer to use one hand only.

One should also practice getting and firing the gun upside down with the other hand. In other words if you wear a gun on the right hip let us say, you may get a hit in that hand or arm rendering it useless. If you have practiced the upside down draw with the other hand you may still save the day. If you are right handed and the gun in a right hip holster with butt to the rear, you can still reach it with the left hand, and if a double action gun, pull the trigger with the third finger of the left hand. The gun is drawn and pointed toward your target upside down. With a little practice it is not as slow or awkward as you would believe. Thus a gun can be drawn and fired double action with either hand when carried in conventional hip holsters with butt sloped to the front. This is another reason so many officers and old cavalry men carried their guns with butts to the front; so they could reach and use either gun with either hand.

However, when the gun is carried butt to the rear, the fastest of all positions for the hip draw, it is possible to reach it, draw it and fire it accurately upside down with bottom of grip held between thumb and first fingers while the third finger of the hand pulls the trigger double action. It can be practiced until the draw is both smooth and fast for close range combat work. With cross draw holsters either gun can be used with either hand by simply bending the wrist or reaching back under the butt of the gun with the fingers.

With the Berns-Martin Lightning holster, about all we have written on the cross draw holds true. You pull the coat back around the body out of the way with the left hand as you draw with the right. The butt of the gun is down and toward the rear, and you grasp it with an upward reach of the fingers. The front being split open and the spring holding the cylinder, the gun is simply wiped out of the holster across the body and fired across the body for close range, fast work. The gun level is higher than from holsters on the belt and this helps some in placing shots. The gun can also be reached with the left hand almost as well by simply turning the wrist with fingers next to the body and curved upward to seize the butt of the gun when it is drawn by a forward jerk toward the front of the body and levelled for the shot. This is the fastest shoulder holster now made. It also allows complete concealment of a small, short barreled gun.

A standard spring shoulder holster such as the Lawrence No. 7 holds the gun in a good position and securely enough for any but rough usage, but as the gun is covered to such an extent that the trigger guard and whole grip cannot be grasped when the hand goes for the gun and the grip must be shifted before the gun can be fired, it is a slower outfit than the Berns-Martin Lightning holster.

We have seen a few shoulder rigs for two guns, carrying them in almost the same position as the belt cross-draw holster, with the butts sloped to the front center and the barrels to the rear and about even with the lower rib. These guns could be reached with either hand and were in a good position. We understand that both Hickock and Hardin carried their single actions thus, and it is O.K. for either double or single action guns. They could be worn as outlined, under a loose, low cut vest or under an ordinary coat. The grips were presented in an easily grasped position much the same as the belt cross draw holsters, except that the guns were about six inches higher on the body. This rig has its merits for gamblers at card tables and for officers seated at the wheel of a car. The guns were up where they are easily reached and fired over a table or out the window of an automobile. The ones we saw were for two guns. The holsters were of light, rather soft, perfectly fitted leather and attached to a leather band buckled around the body just below the ribs, and sewn to the holsters; the guns were kept from swinging or flopping around regardless of the body position. A leather strap attached to each holster extended over the shoulder on each side and down to the band again. The weight of two heavy guns was well distributed on the shoulder straps. The butts of both guns were well presented for quick draw with the least possible movement by a man sitting at a car wheel or holding a deck of cards.

Some day I am going to have my own ideas of such a gun rig made up and try it out. It looks both fast and practical to me, as well as a comfortable way to carry two heavy guns. It could be made single just as well, but when two guns are carried, they balance the load, so to speak. The strap around from the holsters across the back keeps them in exact position and is sewn into the holsters about half the way down from the top. The straps over the shoulder are attached near the top of each holster but far enough back to be clear of the grip and hammers of the guns. The rig is practical for either single action or double action and would be the best of all holsters for a slip gun as the angle of the gun to the shooting hand is better than with any holsters I have seen on the market. In drawing, the guns were pulled across the body the same as in a cross draw, with the gun level six inches higher. Minimum hand movement is needed to clear the guns.

Over the years I have noticed that fast gunmen usually prefer their guns as near the usual position of their hands as possible so that the least possible movement is necessary to grasp the gun. The farther one has to reach for anything, the longer it takes to get it. There is a method in their madness.

Hip shooting, really instinctive pointing, is one phase of the pistol shooting game anyone can learn in time. Once mastered, along with quick draw, it will stay with you through life. You may get rusty and not as fast or certain as you were when you were in practice but you will always be able to do creditable work. Further, if you can see your target, you can hit it. We have seen individuals whose eyesight was very poor but who could still do good hip shooting. In all close range combat, where the man who lands the first slug is the one who wins, it is the only system to use. The knife thrower can throw a knife into anything he can see at close range. The trained gunman can place a slug with equal facility.

All quick draw instinctive pointing, is called hip shooting. Actually the gun is usually well up above hip level when fired. The gun is moved toward the target by the shortest route and fired before the gun movement is stopped. One should practice point shooting without the quick draw. It is well to master the art before attempting quick draw. This will familiarize you with the gun and how it points in the hand, whether high or low or on target. Some hold the guns level; some cant them to one side or the other and do equally good work. If it is more comfortable to the wrist to cant the guns out from the body, then do so. You will hit just as well. Canting the barrel and sights outward from the body enables one to align his gun higher with less wrist bend. With some guns having too much drop or angle from grip to barrel, it is an advantage to shoot them in this manner.

I do my most accurate work bent slightly forward, with eyes focussed on the object to be hit, paying no attention to the gun whatever. You must shoot where you can see the strike of your bullet so you can walk successive shots onto the target if the first one be high or low. Snow, water, dry dusty ground, or a big target frame are all good, but you must see where you are shooting to become proficient at this game. If practiced long enough it is surprising how accurate you can become. We have hit empty cartridge cases from the hip at 15 to 20 feet range with guns we were used to. You are not a master of a sixgun until you can do creditable hip shooting and quick draw work. It is not so different from knife throwing, archery, or even skeet shooting. Familiarize yourself with your gun until you know where the muzzle points as certainly as you can point your finger. Learn to instantly shift your point and walk your shots onto your target. If they first strike low, as they do with most beginners, lift the muzzle for the second shot; if high, lower it.

Dry, dusty ground and a tin can are about as good as anything for practice. You can see the dust spurt from each shot, and hold accordingly for the next shot. Just as a finished archer can whip an arrow back to the side of his jaw and loose it while he watches his target, so can the finished sixgun shot jerk his gun toward the target, fire and hit, all in one swift sure motion. It means hours of practice each week over long periods of time. The longer practiced, the more expert you become. We used to ride through the Montana sage brush, jumping an occasional jack rabbit and shooting at them just as fast as we could get the gun out of the holster with the horse in motion, either walking, trotting or in a lope.

Scoring results of some fast shooting.

We burned up a lot of ammunition, had a lot of fun and actually killed some of the big rabbits.

Shooting from a car is best done by using the sights, but you should also be able to hang onto a car with one hand and shoot with the other and hit reasonable sized targets at close range, by the feel of the gun alone.

A man may be able to punch little holes in the nine and ten ring all day with a sixgun at standard ranges and still not be a good combat shot. When the chips are down and your life is at stake, as happens very often in military action or may happen to the peace officer at any time, is when the months of practice will pay off and save your life. F.B.I., military combat teams and many police organizations now recognize this fact and have courses of fire closely simulating combat conditions. They have electrically moved and timed targets that flash up before the shooter and are gone again in an instant. The shooter must draw and hit in a brief fraction of time. They have simulated combat courses where two shooters walk along side by side and both draw and fire, speed-accuracy competition, striving each to beat the other's time. The electrically timed targets register which man landed his slug first and won the friendly gun fight—about the closest possible thing to actual combat.

For defense shooting, our present target courses offer only slow, timed and rapid fire, with no double action work and no quick draw work. They are not practical unless they also include quick draw and fast hip shooting. They are training their graduates to be target shots, not practical gun fighters.

If your gun is a double action, all close range quick draw and hip shooting should be done double action as that is what you will certainly use in an emergency. If a single action, you should master both one handed quick draw work as well as being able to fan the gun at close range. The more you practice, the more familiar you become with your gun. It becomes a part of you. In an emergency you will automatically do the right thing. Learn to draw and shoot from any position or while walking, riding a horse, or from a car. Also practice turning and firing at targets placed behind you in unknown positions. This speeds up ones mental impulses and reactions, helps keep you alert and on your toes and will pay dividends if you ever get in action. The police and peace officer never knows when he may be called on to use his gun to save not only his own life, but the lives of others it is his duty to protect. He owes it to his job to train himself as much as possible, so if the need ever arises he will not fail.

We have seen gunmen face a mirror and practice quick draw, snapping at their own reflected image. No doubt it helped them speed up and gave them a check on gun alignment. We have always preferred shooting at something to trying to outdraw the homely gunny in the looking glass.

The law enforcement officer is always at a disadvantage. The criminal usually has him spotted. The officer must wait until the criminal makes a break or fires the first shot unless he is a known desperado and badly wanted. For this reason the officer should train himself until he can draw and shoot with dispatch, should the occasion ever arise. Carrying a gun is very poor business unless you know how to use it. Never bluff with a gun or use it to intimidate

Toney scoring results of two Patrolmen on man targets.

Bill Toney demonstrating quick draw and fast hip shooting double action to class of Border patrolmen.

people. One tough in Helena nicknamed "Canuck" always carried a .38/40 New Service with 4½ inch barrel, and wanted to be thought a tough guy. One day he ran onto a group of small boys who had been hunting rabbits. A stormy day had driven them into an old, deserted mining building. They had built up a fire and were waiting out the storm when Canuck came along and joined them. Wanting to show how tough he was, he pulled his gun and started shooting around their feet, making them dance. After emptying his gun he reloaded it and one little lad of twelve years went over and sat down in the corner by his .22 rifle. He had enough of dancing. The next time Canuck pulled his gun and made another lad dance, the boy in the corner counted the shots and when the sixth one was fired, jumped up with his rifle, aimed at one of Canuck's feet and said, "Now, damn you, dance." Before Canuck could jump he plugged him through the right ankle with a hollow point high speed bullet, shattering the ankle joint, then reloading he kept his gun trained on Canuck until the boys all got out of the building, where they left Canuck to his own devices, reporting it when they got back to town. Needless to say, Canuck spent long weeks in the hospital and promptly left town when he was able. His days of intimidating people around Helena, Montana, were over.

The .22 caliber gun selected for quick draw and hip shooting practice should closely resemble the heavy gun to be later carried, so that all shooting with the light gun will apply to the larger gun, and you will experience no difference in the feel and pointing of the heavier caliber weapon.

If you choose a single action you can use the Ruger Single Six or the Great Western .22. The Single Six is a light gun but has a standard size S. A. grip exactly like the old Colt, and practice acquired with it will enable anyone to handle the Single Action Army or Great Western. The Great Western .22 Single Action is an exact duplicate in size of their heavier caliber weapons and handles and feels the same except it is the heaviest of all single actions.

Judge Don Martin, right, looks over the results of some of my sixgun shooting.

Once one has mastered it, however, the lighter guns of larger caliber will be even easier to draw and point.

If you are going to pack a double action gun, then the .22 caliber S. & W. Combat Masterpiece with 4 inch barrel or the K-.22 with 6 inch barrel will exactly duplicate the .38 Specials in these models. If you prefer a Colt, the Colt Official Police and Officer's Model Match with 4 or 6 inch barrels will exactly duplicate the fit and feel of the Colt .357 or Official Police or Officer's Model Match, or Marshal.

Training with either of these two makes of .22 calibers on their .38 and .41 frames will enable anyone to graduate to the .44 and .45 caliber double action guns, in either Smith & Wesson or Colt make.

If the shooter likes and employs auto pistols, then the Colt Ace or the Conversion unit is the best understudy for the Super .38 and .45 auto Colts or the Commander. Next is the High Standard; then the Ruger and Colt .22 auto pistols with 4½ inch barrels. Luger fanciers may be able to get the conversion unit for that pistol as we have seen some advertised. Once you master the job with the .22 you can shift to the big gun and do creditable work from the start, with no fumbles or lost motion.

Auto pistols should be carried cocked, with the safety on. Learn to throw the safety off as you draw. It can be done, but never seemed as fast to us as either the single or double action revolver. However, it can be mastered to the point where little time is actually consumed moving the safety.

Select the gun belt and holster, waist belt holster, or shoulder holster that suits you and your gun best, and feels most comfortable and permits most accessibility to your gun. Then stay with it both for the .22 and for the big service gun. Many like to carry their guns in the front waist band. It is not slow and with practice becomes a very good position with no extra weight carried, but whatever rig you decide on

Keith obliges E. D. Vissing, left, with some hip shooting.

as best fitting you for the .22 caliber, should also be used for the big gun so that all practice with the small caliber perfects your draw with the heavy gun.

The time may soon come when this country will desperately need every fighting man it can muster and an armed, and trained citizenry is the best possible insurance against invasion. For proof, look at little Switzerland. Neither Napoleon nor Hitler wanted any of it.

Chapter X

Gun Fighting

THE EARLY WEST developed a large number of trained and experienced gun fighters. The westward course of the Empire produced a breed of men unique in history. Life was cheap and killings commonplace. Outlaws preyed on the honest miners, citizens and early ranchers. About the only law was the town marshal and the early sheriffs. These men were hired or elected more for their ability with a gun than for their knowledge of the law. They had to try to control the toughest elements of society ever thrown together in one heterogenous mass of humanity.

Of these times and conditions the gun fighter was born. The menace of wild Indians and organized bands of outlaws preying on immigrants moving westward to the gold mines of California and the rich farm lands of Oregon was ever present. The law was confined to small communities backed by a gun fighting marshal, or was nonexistent. Over a goodly portion of this continent the law was a sixgun that was packed by each individual in six chapters. The age old law of nature, the survival of the fittest, ruled. Many outlaws and peace officers became very fast and deadly with a gun; they had to in order to survive. There are only two classes of gun fighters—the quick and the dead. Those on the side of the law, backed by honest citizenry, gradually shot some semblance of decency and order into each community. Many a Western town had a dead man to bury every morning. I saw the last of that era as a very small boy in Montana before the coming of the automobile.

Sheep and cattle wars, the Lincoln County War in New Mexico, the vigilantes of Montana, the numerous Indian wars, the Mormon migration, all had gunfighters in important roles.

Many outlaws became professional killers and for a fee would dry gulch anyone, or if necessary, provoke a gunfight and murder their man as surely as if they had shot him in the back. The killing of many an honest citizen was thus arranged and carried out for a price. While many of these professional killers ran up long lists of victims, either dry gulched or killed in so-called fair fights, they sooner or later met a peace officer, equally good with a gun and wound up in the cemetery. Usually nothing was done about such gun fights. If the killer had witnesses to swear the victim had an even break, he got away with it. A horse thief was considered beyond the pale and, if caught, was left dancing on air at the end of a rope.

John Newman told me of the death of Soapy Smith at Skaguay, Alaska. Soapy headed a gang that preyed on the returning miners and frequently relieved them of their pokes. A citizens' committee repaired to an old wharf storage house to deliberate on what was to be done with Soapy and his gang, leaving a guard behind. The guard's name was Reed. He was armed with a .38/40 single action Colt. When Soapy Smith heard of this, he picked up a .45/70 model '86 Winchester, and headed for the dock to break up the meeting. John Newman followed him but at some distance. Soapy turned around and yelled to get back or he would kill him. Newman had only his .45 Colt slip gun and the range was too great to risk starting a gunfight against a rifle. He continued to follow Soapy and was again cussed out and ordered to stop. Soapy again went on, Newman followed and was an eye witness to his demise. Smith came up to Reed and ordered him out of the way, then struck at him with the gun barrel. Reed grabbed the barrel with one hand as Soapy turned the rifle on him and fired, but as he went down his .38/40 single action shot Soapy through the heart. Smith's .45/70 slug hit Reed in the groin and he died shortly afterwards. Reed's gun snapped on a defective primer, or he might have saved his life. Soapy fired as Reed cocked his gun for a second try. The committee properly organized and cleaned up the rest of the gang, bringing law and order to Skaguay.

Another time Newman entered a saloon looking for a man who had sworn to kill him. The man raised a double barreled sawed-off shotgun, but Newman proved the faster and killed him with his .45 S. A. Colt slip gun.

Newman told me how he and two boy friends were once captured by a gunman and forced to work for him for nothing. Only Newman had a gun, a .45 S. A. Colt. The outlaw had taken all of Newman's ammunition but left him his gun. One day the boys found a

Smith & Wesson revolver, caliber .38 Special, 6½ inch barrel. No. 690. Cylinder rotates counter-clockwise. An early one.

loaded .38/40 cartridge. They had become well fed-up with working for nothing while the outlaw kept them under guard. They wrapped paper around the .38/40 hull, until it could just be driven into a chamber. It fitted tight enough so Newman knew it would stand the blow of the firing pin. At the first chance they jumped their boss and when he went for his gun, Newman let him have it at close range, the .38/40 bullet wobbling down the .45 caliber barrel. It did the business. They took a long chance but the 40 grains of black powder threw that 180 grain bullet hard enough to settle the outlaw's accounts.

Today, the F.B.I. is the best trained group of gun fighters in the world. Some army combat teams and some police organizations are quite well trained. All police and peace officers, as well as all officers of our armed services, should be trained gun fighters. Any man who carries a gun in the performance of duty should be well trained in every phase of its use. If he is not, he may fail in an emergency and lose his own life as well as the lives of those depending on him.

Not every man has the right temperament to become an expert gun fighter. Almost every day the papers carry accounts of how a criminal escaped after a running gun battle, or ran several road blocks before he was killed or captured. All too often good officers lose their lives in such encounters. These accounts show a lack of gun training on the part of the peace officers hired to uphold the laws. The officer should not only be adequately armed but should know when and how to use his gun. If he does not, he is not fulfilling his duty as an officer. Blunt words, but true.

In 1952, while staying in a Washington, D. C. hotel, I stepped outside for a walk around the block and some fresh air before retiring. I arrived in front of a theatre about a block from the hotel just in time to see a police officer jump from his car parked some twenty yards to my left. A black sedan drove past. The officer emptied a .38 Special revolver at the rear end of it. The car passed within 15 to 20 feet of me and I could never see where a single slug hit either the car or the driver. The cop might as well have been shooting blanks as far as results were concerned. Then he jumped in his car and turning on his red light and siren, took off after the black sedan as fast as he could drive. The street lights were excellent and any trained gunman would have ventilated the car and the driver too. Wild shooting such as I witnessed not only allows criminals to escape but endangers every one in the line of fire.

J. H. Fitzgerald told me of an incident he witnessed at the Chicago stock yards many years ago. A Negro cowpuncher had come east with a few car loads of steers from Colorado, and was standing by the heavy board fence looking inside at his charges. A cop came along, pulled a photograph from his pocket, made a brief comparison of it and the negro's back then pulled a .30 caliber Luger and started shooting the dusky cow-puncher in the back. Fitz said the big colored boy hooked one arm through the fence as he turned slowly around facing his adversary. When the Luger was empty the negro still hung onto the fence, then drew a 4¾ inch .45 S. A. Colt from his waist band and calmly asked, "Are you all through, white boy?" and shot the cop through the heart, killing him instantly. The Negro lived long enough to tell Fitz who he was and what ranch the cattle belonged to and to turn over his papers, before he too, took the long trail. A regretable incident, due to an untrained and trigger happy officer jumping to conclusions.

We can hardly avoid pointing out what a pip-squeak performance the Luger turned in. After the unfortunate negro had absorbed a magazine full of slugs he not only lived long enough to kill the officer, but to untangle his business affairs. Had he really been a desperado, and conditions been right, he could have loaded a fire truck with corpses after the first bullet hit him.

We witnessed a gun fight in Helena, Montana, that proved the .38 Special standard load a very poor man stopper. We had just ridden to town from the ranch when a cop friend named Martin waved us over to the corner of Sixth Ave. and Main St. He talked a few minutes as I sat on my cow pony, then pulled out a new six inch barrel Smith & Wesson M. & P. target revolver. He passed it over asking what I thought of it for a police gun. I told him then it was too small and if he ever got in a gun fight he might have to shoot a criminal more than once to stop him, or he might have to kill him with successive hits where one shoulder shot from a heavy gun could stop him cold. I had no more than returned the gun to the officer, than a small boy came running down Sixth Avenue and yelled at Martin, "There's a guy holding up the Chink Noodle Parlor." Martin remarked, "I guess this is it," and followed the boy back up the street, while I rode alongside. Arriving at the Noodle Parlor, Martin drew his gun and went in. The holdup was back near the rear end with a small nickel plated gun held on the Chinese owner, while he went through the cash register. At Martin's entrance he whirled around and

Author's Guns. Top—.357 S. & W. Magnum 6½ number 0139. Second—Triple Lock target .44 Special. Third—.44 Special 1950 Target, 4 inch barrel. Fourth—Early K-.22 Masterpiece. All are S. & W. guns. Kearsarge custom grips on top two guns.

shot at him. As no bullet came through the glass front I knew he had hit him. Martin shot fast, but planted all his slugs in the holdup's chest. Meanwhile, the holdup emptied his five shot .32 revolver. Two slugs came through the window. He threw his gun at Martin and it also came through the window into the street. A boy in one of the booths began to holler that he was shot, while the holdup hung onto the counter and slowly slid down to the floor. He died as he was being carried up the hospital steps. The boy had a .32 slug through the calf of his leg from one of the holdup's bullets and Martin had one through the left breast pocket of his blouse that went through a heavy note book and lodged in the bottom of the pocket. Had the gunman used a heavy gun he would have killed Martin the first shot. After this fight Martin procured a heavy gun. Officer Martin was later killed in a gun fight with an old class mate of mine but I never heard the details of their fight, or how it started.

Pink Simms told me of being in a gun fight once and being shot through the neck with a .32/20 and he never knew he was hit until the fight was over and he saw blood running down his shirt front. The bullet had missed both jugular vein and spine and he quickly recovered. In another gun fight between a friend of his and another man, Pink said a slug aimed at his partner missed him and hit Pink's saddle horn. It peeled the leather off the steel saddle horn then hit Simms on his heavy double chap and gun belts. He said it did not break the skin, but made him so sick he could not hang onto the saddle horn and fell off in the dust before the fight had ended. It was a 250 grain .45 Colt Slug that knocked him from his horse.

Another time Simms and a companion were ascend-

John Newman posing as an Arizona Marshal of 1879.

ing a flight of stairs in a hotel. The companion was just in front of him when a woman came out at the head of the stairs and aimed an old .45 Colt rod ejector double action at his companion and cut loose. The heavy slug cut a long groove in the staircase bannister then struck the man on the chaps belt. It brought him back on top of Pink, with a grunt, and they both tumbled to the bottom of the stairs. Simms always said he was an authority on the wallop of a .45.

Another friend of mine, Lt. Williamson of the Jacksonville Police Department, has had to kill four men in the line of duty. On one occasion he emptied his .38 Special into the chest of a crazed, razor wielding negro. The colored boy kept on coming saying, "I is gwin to git you, white boy." Williamson back pedaled as fast as he could, kicking the shells from his .38 and poking in one new round. This time he aimed between the colored man's eyes and killed him. I got a .44 Special for him. He had had enough of the .38.

For defense use we believe the holster gun should never be of less caliber and power than the .357 Smith & Wesson Magnum or the old 200 grain .41 Long Colt, and the .38/40, .44/40, .44 Special and .45 Colt or .45 auto are all much better stoppers. It takes a big heavy slug to knock the fight out of an insane man or one that is berserk with rage.

Another time Lt. Williamson and his partner received a call that a man had been shot over in the colored district, so they jumped in the prowl car and went to the address. When Williamson knocked, a darky came to the door. The officer inquired if a man had been shot there. "Yassa, Yassa," the darky informed them, "A boy done got shot here alright." The officers asked to see the body, but were informed there was no body yet. Then they asked who got shot and the polite colored lad said he was the man. Examination proved he had been shot through the abdomen twice with a .38 Special and was still on his feet, though his shoes were full of blood. They took him to the hospital where he soon recovered.

Another peace officer once wrote me years ago that he and a brother officer were called to subdue a huge negro who had gone berserk. He went for them and they each emptied a .38 Special revolver in him. The negro then got one down and had him about choked to death before his brother officer knocked the negro unconscious with his gun. They said that in spite of all the wounds through the chest and abdomen he recovered from the shooting.

Although most police organizations make it mandatory for their personnel to carry .38 Special weapons with standard or high speed loads, the above incidents prove the inadequacy of this cartridge when the chips are down.

I once saw Herb Bradley shoot a woodchuck through the neck at about ten yards with a Colt Officer's model and the standard .38 Special load. The chuck ran down his hole, came back up immediately and stuck his head out. We could plainly see the blood running out of the side of his neck before Herb shot again and hit the brain, this time killing him. I have seen many blue grouse and sage hens recover, take wing and fly off with .38 Specials through the chest cavity, if spine or wings were not broken. The small .356-357 caliber pointed bullet makes a very small hole with little shock effect, it seems. While the small, short barreled .38 and .41 calibers will do for hidden pocket guns as secondary battery or for the plain clothes man who cannot canceal a big gun in shirt sleeves, nevertheless, the officer should always select a more powerful arm for his main gun, or for the holster weapon. Criminals seldom travel singly and you may have more than one adversary. It is mandatory that you carry a holster gun powerful enough to floor an opponent, with one well placed hit.

I have two friends, both living, who have been shot with the .45 auto Colt. One of them, a Lieutenant in the Montana National Guard and a member of the 1924 National match team, had been shot through the right lung in a tavern in France. His right lung would collapse during the night and each morning he would get out of the tent and take several long breaths to inflate that injured lung. The other friend was hit in the stomach with a standard 230 grain jacketed bullet that first went through a heavy buffalo skin overcoat, his inside coat and clothing and lodged in his stomach. Surgeons removed the bullet, sewed him up and he was as good as ever in a few days.

Peace officers will find there is a lesson to be learned from each gun fight, if they will but study the details. Usually the cool head who uses his brains will win. I once had a cop friend in Helena, Montana, named Bill O'Connel. He was half Blackfoot Indian, a tall powerful man weighing over 200 pounds, over six feet in heighth, straight as an arrow and the best gun fighter on the city police force. Bill and I often hunted together Sundays.

I was a small youngster running a horseback paper route mornings before school. Each morning I arrived at the Helena Independent office, slung a couple of sacks of papers on my horse and took off. I used to roll the papers, kink them so they could be thrown and toss them at front doors as I trotted past. My first stop was always the Weise Cafe where I traded two extra papers for a cup of coffee and two doughnuts.

Bill was on night duty at the N. P. depot, inside the city limits but actually a mile from the main town. An indication of the liveliness of this part of town is that scarcely a porch post in front of the saloon and several eating houses had missed being gouged by a bullet in past gun battles.

After my coffee break I would meet Bill somewhere along his beat and give him a morning paper, then make my rounds, winding up at home to stable and feed my horse before breakfast. One morning Bill said, "There is something wrong in the saloon across the street," which was located some distance from the depot and near a big fur and hide house. The building was peculiarly shaped, a sort of wedge on the corner, or intersection of a side street. A door entered the tip of the wedge and a line of windows ran along the Helena Avenue side. On the side street was another door. While nothing was visible from the street, everything inside was plainly visible to a man on a horse looking over the curtained windows. I trotted by the place to see what was going on. Two gunmen had everyone lined up in front of the long bar that extended almost the full length of the east side of the building. At the end of this bar there was a break and a short bar against the back or north end of the building. One man held two guns on the small crowd while the other frisked them. Bill told me where he had a sawed off shotgun and a box of buckshot cached. He said, "I am going in." My orders were to keep the men in there with the shotgun, if possible, until help arrived if he failed.

As Bill went in the front door at the extreme tip of the wedged shaped building, one holdup whirled around and fired, then both bandits jumped over the bar. The others in the saloon dropped flat on the floor. The holdup's slug went through the transom over Bill's head. Bill had his .45 S. A. Colt cocked and waited. Soon one man's head popped up over the bar; as he fired Bill O'Connel's 250 grain slug hit him square between the eyes. The other holdup ran down the length of the back bar, keeping low out of Bill's vision, but when he attempted to cross the opening between the ends of the two bars at the corner he was exposed and Bill's second slug caught him squarely through both shoulders and he landed on his face kicking. No doubt he intended firing on Bill from the other bar, thinking Bill would still be watching the place where his partner had been killed.

One night while stationed on the uptown night beat, Bill had ordered a negro to halt in an alley. The negro turned and ran and Bill took after him. Finally Bill decided to stop him and drew his old .45 S. A. with its very light trigger pull. Just as he was going to shoot he tripped over a garbage can and fell headlong. The fall knocked all the wind out of him and the old gun went off. The negro stopped, then ran back and helped Bill to his feet, saying "Mista O'Connel, why did you shoot me? I knows I is killed." Bill took him to the station finding no bullet mark whatever on him, although the darky insisted he had been shot.

Bill O'Connel died in the Helena Hospital from flu and pneumonia, while I was flat on my back on another cot, downed by the same ailments. We used to send notes back and forth to each other by the nurses. One morning when I asked for Bill's note the nurse shook her head. I knew he had passed on. So died Bill O'Connel, a man without fear, a terror to evil doers and a friend of lost dogs, stray kids and everyone in trouble or need of help.

Sam Russell had been on old Faro dealer in the Southwest before moving to Helena, Montana, where he ran a one chair barber shop. Sam was a little man, but very fast with a sixgun and deadly with a .45 from the hip. He used to pull the shades down over his front window and instruct me in quick draw work, often shooting short Remington .45 squibb loads at the patterns in his linoleum floor covering. He had most of those small squares studded with the hollow base Remington slugs that had just power enough to drive them down about flush with the floor. If a cop came along and banged on the front door and wanted to know what was going on, Sam would say, "Go away. I am just giving a kid some pistol instruction.'"

While I was with a Government Survey crew in 1917, Sam got into trouble. He was seated at a back table in a saloon just above Broadway on the east side of Main Street. A big man came in and ordered a drink for the house. Sam evidently did not hear him or was not paying any attention to what he said. At any rate the big man then yelled at Sam, "Come on you little S.O.B. I said everyone up to the bar." Sam got up and remarked, "Say it with a smile, Mister, and I will be with you." The big man sneered and again called Sam a S.O.B. Sam told him, "Mister, I never took that name from no man and I will be back just as soon as I can get my gun." Sam went across the street to his barber shop. There he cocked one of his pearl stocked 4¾ inch .45 S. A. Colts and draped a big silk handkerchief over it muzzle and all, tucking the ends of the hanky back inside his coat sleeve while he held the cocked gun in his right hand.

The bar tender told the big man he was up against the real thing. He stood facing the front door where Sam had gone out. Everyone else in the saloon moved over to the back of the room out of line with either door. While the big man watched the front door Sam Russell came down the alley and kicked in the back door. The big man discovered his mistake too late and whirled to fire at Sam. Russell's .45 slug passed through his gun arm and thence through his body ending that fight in one shot. Sam was given three years in the State Penitentiary. The Judge confiscated his carved pearl stocked .45. Later when Sam got out, he had a friend steal the gun. I later swapped a .41 Rod Ejector to Sam for it and its mate and still have the old guns. Many an old time bar room killing began in similar manner. Some purposely provoked and some getting started almost accidentally.

Some years past, five acquaintances of mine were involved in a gunfight in a tavern operated by a woman and her son. It had been the scene of several other shootings and knifings under various managements. No one is satisfied that the exact cause of this affair has ever been brought to light. Three of the witnesses died.

Two men were sitting at the bar drinking beer. One was asleep on a lounge in the back of the room. Number four came in with a large turkey he had won at a shoot a few hours before with the presumed intention of giving it to the lady proprietor. What happened from here on has not been satisfactorily explained. An argument started. Number four pulled a gun, a Colt Officers .38 Spl., and shot one of the men at the bar twice. The other started for the door and was shot through the heart from behind being killed instantly. Both were unarmed. The proprietress ducked back of the bar. A fourth slug cut a deep groove in the top of the bar and clipped a lock of hair from her head. Her son, in the kitchen, picked up a .22 rifle and shot the killer high in the groin with a high speed hollow point bullet, getting a slug through the arm in return, but creating enough diversion to enable his mother to crawl on her hands and knees back of the bar to the kitchen where both escaped by the back door. *The chap on the couch never woke up. Being a sound sleeper probably saved his life.*

The killer hunted for the woman and her son for a while but his wound was making him sick and he went back to his car and drove a few miles, stopped beside the road, and was found there by the sheriff.

The first man shot, hit with two slugs, lived about two weeks. The killer died about a month after the affair. The boy with the .22 certainly saved his mother's life and quite possibly his own and that of the sound sleeper. Perhaps the truth of this senseless shooting is that the gunman was slightly deranged and a few drinks had thrown his mind wholly out of balance. The lesson is that no one can ever be certain that a criminal or insane person will not push him into a situation that has no answer except a gun. One psycopath managed to murder about twelve people in broad daylight in the business section of a New Jersey city a few years ago. He would have done well to get the third one in an Idaho or Montana town. New Jersey makes it a crime for respectable citizens to own guns. Idaho and Montana have no such laws.

Another bit of gunplay that occurred while we owned a ranch at Winston, Montana, showed the utter foolishness of anyone trying to hold up a town

Courtesy of U. S. Border Patrol.

such as Winston. At one time it had boasted several saloons, but at this time only one remained, along with a hotel, two stores, a rooming house, dance hall, and the N. P. depot.

An eastern gunman came to town and held up a Frenchman in his store, getting a few dollars. Then he started for the Depot to catch the next train out, but the Frenchman told Myers, who ran a store and the post office across the street. Myers phoned Taplin, the Depot Agent, and Taplin grabbed his old sawed off shotgun, loaded with buckshot, and ran out on the Depot platform to intercept the holdup. When he came in sight, Taplin gave him the contents of both barrels, one buckshot hitting him in the leg. He turned, ducked out of sight and made it back to the hotel where he climbed the stairs and barricaded himself in an upper corner room. The little town turned out en masse with their hunting rifles and proceeded to shoot that room full of holes—also the stick-up artist. I had ridden down to Winston, from the ranch, to get the mail when I heard the gunfire. Winston took the episode in its stride, in fact, laughed about it. When the room was broken into, the man, badly shot to pieces, was put on a stretcher and on the next train to Helena. He died en route. How anyone could be foolish enough to try to hold up a Western cow town is beyond me. He would never have a chance.

A few months ago the Sheriff, Jim Egge, called me one night to go with him to Patterson to investigate some trouble there. A drunk crazed miner had chased away his wife and family. A neighbor who knew him well had taken them in. Then the drunk got a knife, went over and demanded they come home or he would kill them all. The neighbor told him to go home and sleep it off, and let his family stay with them. Then the miner said, "I guess you want some of it too," and made for the neighbor with his knife. The man backed to his bedroom door and grabbed a .45 New Service Colt from its holster. He snapped three times at the drunk crazed knife wielder. Then, just in the nick of time, he realized the gun was empty and bopped him over the head, stunning him somewhat, then hit him a good one and floored him. He kicked him out and locked the door. When we arrived we found the drunk still dazed apparently from the two blows over the head with the heavy sixgun which had cut him badly and, incidentally, completely sobered him. He agreed to take his family the next day and leave the county, so we let him go as his wife would not prefer charges against him. The moral of that incident is never keep an empty gun around. His wife had unloaded the gun and it nearly cost him his life. Had he not been a very fast active man, the knife wielder would have gotten him.

Many times peace officers have to set up road blocks to apprehend dangerous criminals traveling in cars. When this is done, the road block should always be set up around a corner from the expected direction of arrival. This forces them to slow down as they come into the road block. Four officers and two cars form the ideal road block. One car should be stopped on each side of the highway and some thirty yards apart, leaving room for cars to pass through after inspection. The cars should be headed in opposite directions, so one car is in position to give immediate chase either way. See diagram. One officer from each car should stop approaching cars while the other two stay in the barrow pit, behind a wall, tree or any good cover, with a rifle. One rifleman disposed under cover on each side of the highway and one officer with each car to stop approaching cars and search them, forms the ideal road block.

Shotgun or pistol fire is not very effective against automobiles, but a good highpower rifle, preferably with armor piercing bullets, will stop them. The .30-06 with A. P. is a good rifle for the purpose, and the new Remington model .740 a good police and peace officer's rifle, if they prefer an auto loader. The officer approaching the car should always do so from the rear while his companion covers him. When a car comes to the stop, walk in from behind and on the driver's side, so you are behind him. See what or who may be in the back seat. If you want to yank him out of the car and you are behind him, you can do so with the least possible risk. Never trust a criminal. Never take your eyes off him for a second until he is frisked, disarmed and ironed.

Road blocks are tough jobs and many a good officer has been killed while manning them. Take every precaution. In disarming criminals, stand them facing a wall with their hands held high against it, or make them lay on their face spread eagled on the ground. One officer should keep them covered while the other officer frisks them thoroughly. Keep out of their reach as much as possible. They may be wrestlers; if they get their hands on you, they may well take command. Never prod a criminal with your gun. That is simply handing it to him if he is a well trained man. Keep your gun back out of his reach. Much as you may want to bop him with gun or fist, do not do it, keep clear. If a criminal jams an automatic against your body, press against it. The Colt

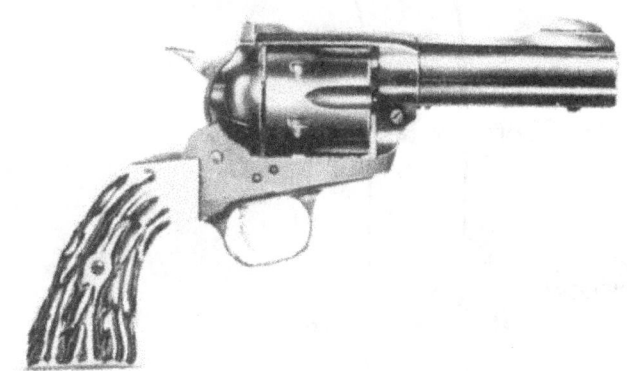

The New Great Western single action, The Deputy. Manufactured in .22 and .38 Special calibers, .357 Atomic, and .44 Special.

Service model and many other Browning patent auto pistols, may be pushed enough to move the slide back out of battery so the gun will not fire.

Disarming a criminal who has a gun poked in your ribs is very dangerous business. It can be frequently accomplished if the crook is not a gunman, but if he is, he will kill you. I have watched Fitzgerald disarm many men who were holding guns against his big tummy or back. He was very fast and would simply whirl around and press against the gun as he did so, thus turning the gun away from his body and at the same time his right hand shot down like the strike of a snake, grasping the gun. Then he would turn the gun back toward the top of the gunman's wrist, breaking his trigger finger if he resisted. If it is a case of your being shot anyway, might as well try it, as you may get away with it if you are fast enough. Fritz tried it on me four times; I had an empty gun and we both knew he would have been shot up every time. A real gunman never puts his gun in the reach of his adversary. If a revolver is not cocked, you can tie it up by grasping the cylinder, but if cocked it will fire.

If a car runs a road block and has to be stopped, the quickest way is for the rifleman to get the driver and it will go out of control. Tires can be punctured which will slow it down, but are hard to hit. Gas tanks are so well concealed that they are hard to find on a fast moving car. A heavy or high velocity rifle bullet will soon put a motor out of commission if you can get a side shot at it. But if a car gets past you then the surest way to stop it is to aim for the

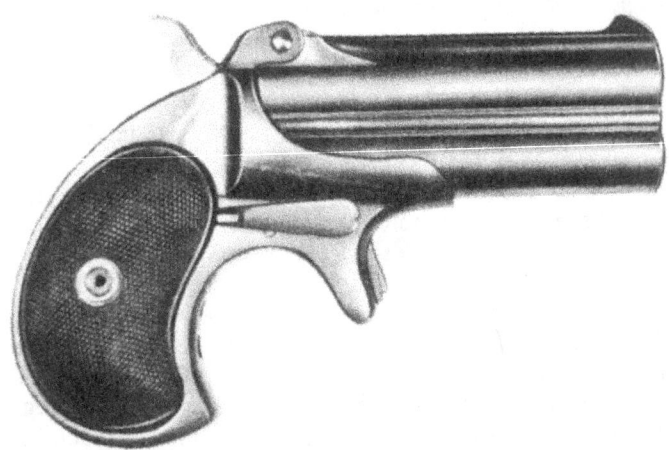

The New Great Western Double Barrel Derringer. Chambered for the .38 S. & W. cartridge.

driver through the left hand lower corner of the rear window. If a gunman's car is coming toward you, it can be stopped either by hitting the driver or by slugs through the lower part of the radiator in line with the fan and motor. No car will go far after a couple of bullets have gone through the lower radiator. If a rifle is used, it will probably ruin the motor. From the side the motor can be easily hit. Of course all officers want to apprehend criminals, not kill them, but there are times where it is foolhardy to take chances, and the officer had best shoot to kill. The County or City may send flowers to your funeral if you lose, but they will not support your family.

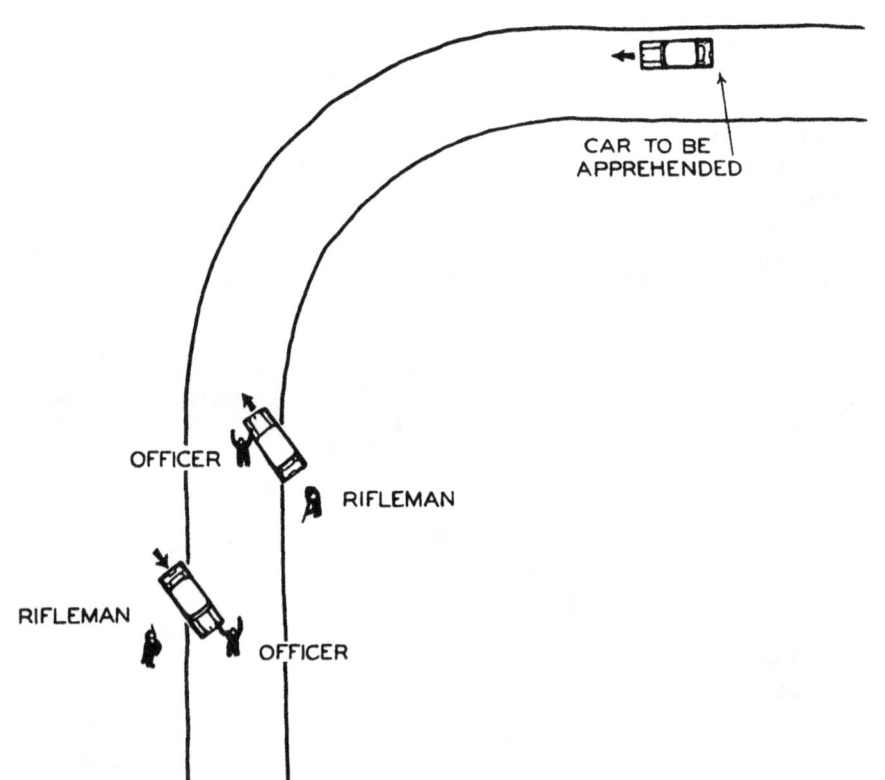

Rough sketch of ideal road block by two cars and four officers. Preferably set up with a sharp turn or curve between the car to be apprehended and the police cars. Criminals cannot see the road block until they have slowed down and turned the corner. From their view the road appears completely blocked, but cars can easily pass both police cars at low speed. If the car to be apprehended turns around and goes back, then the forward car is in position for hot pursuit. If he runs the road block, then the rear car is in position for hot pursuit. Both riflemen are preferably under cover in the ditch or side of the road where they both have, and can deliver effective fire without endangering brother officers.

Modern cars are poorly designed for police use as you cannot shoot out of the front of them. They should be made so an officer could shoot right over the car hood from the front seat, at a car he is chasing. In this respect, Jeeps are not so bad, but all present fast autos, never designed with this in mind, badly handicap an officer in a prowl car, as he has to lean out the door to the side to shoot. A little thought and effort on the part of the automobile industry, in the design of police cars would save many an officer's life and stop many a criminal who now makes a clean getaway.

A shotgun with buckshot is one of the most deadly gun fighting weapons up to thirty yards, Beyond that range it is problematical, and a good sixgun shot has the advantage. Likewise it is not much good against auto bodies unless slug loads are used, but if the officer will put a charge or two of buck on top and fill the bottom of the magazine with slugs, then he has a good and effective weapon that will ruin tires, open gas tanks or radiators, and shoot through car bodies as well. Pump or auto loading shotguns should be used with short barrels and five shot magazine capacity when fully loaded. It is best to carry them with three slugs down in the bottom of the magazine and two loads of O. O. buck on top, so the first two shots will be buck and then the heavy slugs for the rest of the magazine. At real close range the heavy caliber sixgun is faster and better than the shotgun and requires but one hand to get into action. If guarding prisoners with a shotgun, for Allah's sake, stay out of their reach.

Trying to bluff a criminal who is holding a gun on you is very poor business, and often leads you to soft music and the scent of lillies. If you are in reach of the man, that is one thing, and you have a chance, but if you are out of reach he has every advantage and it is best to go along with his ideas until such time as you may be lucky enough to get a break. Many good officers carry a small hidden gun in addition to their big holster weapon and this is good life insurance. If they are disarmed of their big gun and not thoroughly frisked, they may be able to keep their little gun hidden until such time as they get a chance to use it. Remember, hide-out guns are not restricted to officers.

Never bluff with a gun. If you are a trained gun fighter, then leave your gun alone until such time as you may need it. Leave it in the holster until you know you have to use it, and then shoot to kill or disable your adversary. Many police organizations teach their men to pull their guns before going up to cars they are stopping when trying to apprehend a criminal. This is good procedure for the tyro cop or the untrained man, but for the man who really knows his gun and how and when to use it, it is not necessary. If you know you have to use your gun, then do so and get it over, but do not threaten anyone with it until you are ready to use it. Criminals will respect you more if you talk to them and let them know the score and what they have to do, than if you wave a gun at them or prod them with it. Such actions put you down on even terms with them and they know it.

If you believe you have to use your gun, do not go into any fancy crouches or make any move whatever that will telegraph your intentions to your adversary. The man who starts first always has a big advantage. The best of the old gun fighters always made up their minds what they had to do, started first and usually came out on top. It takes time for the brain to telegraph a message to the gun hand and for the muscles to get into action. Some men react instantly and some are slow. If you do have to use your gun in a close range gun fight where speed of delivery of that first slug is paramount to the pursuit of life and happiness, then throw that slug from whatever position you may be in and then is the time to drop to a lower position or to take cover.

If the range is close, the shooting will be fast and from the hip, and if a double action gun, it should be used double action. If the fight is started at longer range, then there is plenty of time, and aimed fire is of utmost importance and the gun should be drawn and aimed and fired in one smooth even movement, not hurried and no time wasted, but be certain of the placing of the first shot. Then it is well to drop to the old back position and pull up one knee for a hand and arm rest from which you can shoot very accurately at considerable range. You then offer a much smaller target. If cover is available, it is well to jump behind it. Learn to shoot with either hand so you can shoot around a corner either right or left handed with least exposure of your body to return fire.

Never start a gun fight with a criminal beyond your effective range. A gambler in Salmon, Idaho, once called a cow-puncher some name and they repaired to Main Street to shoot it out. The gambler had a pair of Derringers and foolishly started the fight at fifty yards range. The cow-puncher simply took his time and centered him with his .45 and the fight was over.

For any but very close range work, the officer should raise his gun to eye level and use his sights. For any range over fifteen yards, sights had best be used even though the shooting is fast double action, and at any range over fifty yards, carefully aimed shots will pay dividends in any fight. The shots that hit are the only ones that count or do any good. At close range the sixgun is the best tool, but where ranges may be extended, a shotgun with buckshot or the tommy gun is a surer weapon for most officers and at still greater ranges the rifle is the best tool. A good sixgun shot is much more effective over fifty yards than a shotgun with buck or most tommy guns. A good rifleman by the same token can stop a car

Ted Keith, age 19, shooting long range with his 5" 1950 Target S&W .44 Special and Keith heavy loads. This is the best long range position.

that is far out of range of either sixgun, shotgun or tommy gun. In the apprehension of criminals, take as few chances as possible. The graveyards are full of brave sheriffs and police officers. The criminal with a list of murders and crimes to his credit will not give you any chance, so take as few with him as possible.

Any building harboring a criminal that has to be taken should be approached on a blind side if it has one—neither doors nor windows. Never go up in front of a door. If you knock or shake one, always do it from the side and expose as little of your body as possible. When a door is shaken by the night cop, to see if it is locked, the officer should always stand back to one side of it. Many a bullet has come through a door after a knock or shake of the door knob.

I once had a very good friend who was the night cop at Nampa, Idaho. One night he heard a noise in the Ford garage and presumably looked in through a window that had been broken out. They found him with a slug square between the eyes.

If you find a business house or other establishment has been broken into, with every chance of the burglar or criminal being in the place, it is best to keep out of sight and watch, and put in a call for help. If possible, cover every possible exit. The crook in the dark has every advantage against the officer outlined by street lights. Wait until he comes out or until daylight or help arrives. The desperate criminal will show the officer no quarter, so no undue chances should be taken with him. Police officers on their beat should never form any regular habits as to their time of arrival at any portion of their beat. They should never aproach from the same direction or make a habit of being at any place at any certain time. Spotters always watch an officer and make notes on his habits and if regular in his beat and habits, they will soon have him pegged and know when to pull a job. A good officer on night patrol should avoid being seen under bright lights. Keep to cover as much as possible and never, never form any regular habits of patrol.

If you get in a fight with a burglar in the dark, move after every shot if possible, for he will shoot back at your gun flash. Keep him guessing as to your whereabouts. If you can maneuver him into the light or where you can get a good shot at him, do so, but under no considerations should you barge in on a burglar, or expose yourself to his fire if it is possible to avoid it.

In arresting a wanted man, it is always best to approach him from the rear, if possible. Your voice will carry more authority if you do not try to manhandle him. The law is behind you and he knows it. Speak to him rather than trying to manhandle him. Get the cuffs on him and search him for weapons keeping his back turned to you while searching him. Make your search thorough but keep out of his reach as much as possible while so doing or have a brother officer watch him. When marching him off, it is safer to make him walk in front of you than to try to hang onto him. A good officer will tell them to run if they wish so he can shoot them and that usually keeps them on the straight and narrow path.

When feeding prisoners in jail, keep out of their reach at all times. Make them go to the other end of the cell while you set their tray down and stay there until you are back out and the door locked. Do not go into any room full of prisoners with a gun on you unless you back them to the far side where you can watch them. Never let a man approach close to you. He may have ideas. Let him know from the start you are taking no chances and he will respect you. If one officer must go into a crowded jail or with desperate criminals it is always best to have another watch outside with the guns.

Many an officer has had a criminal jump him while feeding him and has been locked up in his own pokey while the criminal took his gun and car and departed. Criminals with a possible death sentence, or a long prison term hanging over their heads will jump at any opportunity for escape, so take no chances with them.

To thoroughly search a prisoner, it is best to make him strip and then carefully examine his clothing and shoes. Often hacksaw blades, keys or weapons will be found between the layers of the shoe sole or in the seams of clothing. Sometimes such things are also concealed in the hair.

If you have to shoot it out with a criminal, shoot to kill and be done with it. If he is close and you have the time it is O.K. to take a shoulder or arm and disable and capture him, but if he is armed and shooting at you, better aim at the middle of him where your slugs will take the fight out of him in the least possible time. If he has jumped arrest and is running away, then the leg shot is the one to use, that will drop him and still keep him for the law. If he is armed and shooting at you, shoot to stop the return fire quick.

Wherever possible, police organizations should send their best man to the F.B.I. School for technical training and all phases of shooting. This officer can in turn, instruct the rest of their force. The expense of this training will pay big dividends over the years. He will be a finished gun fighter, know the tricks of disarming criminals, a great deal about investigation and securing evidence, and how to present it in court. He will also learn to put his individual mark on any weapon or other thing held as evidence so it can be positively identified in court.

Criminals like to mingle with a crowd to escape detection and arrest. It is then that they are hard to take. They won't hesitate to shoot at the officer even if innocent bystanders are in the line of fire, and the officer is badly handicaped. Time was when gun fire started, everyone dropped flat or dived into a doorway. It is not so common today, and people often stand and stare at the fight, taking chances of being hit themselves. One police lieutenant friend of mine had a winning way with known criminals if he could find them in a crowd. He was a big powerful man and if he ever got close to them they were his prisoner, for he simply banged them on the head with his sap and dragged them to his car. He always maintained the safest way to take a gunman in a crowd was to work in close to him and knock him so cold he would be hours coming to.

If a gunman has to be killed in a crowd, a hollow point expanding bullet that will not go through his body and hit a bystander is the best to use. If at all possible, it is best to tail him out of the crowd before trying to take him. Then if shooting starts you have him where you can use your gun safely as far as innocent people are concerned.

Many times officers are called on to search for burglars, in industrial buildings or big stores in the dark. This is a very dangerous and ticklish business. Keep away from windows where the criminal can cee you against the light, and keep down low. If you hear him and get his location, you can then throw some object on the other side of him or well away from you where the noise will attract his attention and possibly draw his fire while you work in on him. You must use your head, the same as if you were trailing a dangerous animal. Police and peace officers need to be competent, quick thinking men.

In securing evidence at the scene of a crime, be very thorough in your search; do not pass up any

U. S. Border Patrol practicing with Winchester model 1897 trench shotgun, the best alley cleaner of all.

possible clue. A bit of thread, a button, fragment of clothing, any blood stains, empty cartridge cases or bullets may all tell their tale under the scrutiny of carefully trained men. All fired cartridge cases and all fired bullets can easily be traced to the gun that fired them by marks on the primer and head of the case or any flaw in the chamber of the gun. The machining of the recoil plate will show on the primer as well as the individual firing pin. The fired bullet will always be easily identified if the striations on the sides are not completely eliminated by distortion or expansion. Every gun marks its bullets differently the same as finger prints differ, and a comparison microscope will show the suspect bullet along with another fired from the gun under suspicion to be the same, or else eliminate that as the suspect gun. Every bit of evidence should be collected with the utmost care and nothing handled to leave your own finger prints on it. Guns or empty cases can be picked up by inserting a pencil in the muzzle. Collect all possible finger prints for the finger print expert to lift and place on record. A Bible could be written on this phase of police work alone.

If an officer collects empty fired cases at the scene of the crime or bullets from bodies, they should be packed carefully in cotton in small boxes where they will not be damaged in the slightest, and if he is to be called to the witness stand to identify them as the cases or bullets used in the crime, he should mark them. Bullets can best be marked on the base and cartridge cases on a side. The mark should be small but positive so there can be no doubt as to their identity at the trial. He should have a brother officer who also knows his mark of identification. General Hatcher's great book, *Textbook—Firearms Investigation, Identification and Evidence,* is a very fine treatise on these and kindred subjects and is to be recommended to all officers.

Trouble usually comes at unexpected times and often from unexpected sources, so wear your gun so you can go into action in a fraction of a second should it ever be necessary. If you carry a gun at all, you should know how to use it, and when. Probably more good officers are lost each year approaching cars for some routine inspection or minor traffic violation than in any other phase of police work. They have no reason to suspect that the car in question harbors a wanted criminal and may not have even had a good look at the man when the car is approached. The criminal who is on the wanted list naturally thinks he has been spotted, so shoots first and then tries to get away in his car. Make it a habit to approach all such cars from the rear quarter where you can keep everyone under observation and have your gun ready for instant use. Car bodies are very thin and criminals can shoot through them without difficulty. The veteran peace officer, Bill Tilghman, was killed by a young punk when he approached a car for a minor traffic violation and had no reason to suspect a wanted man was in the car. Practice the safest rules of approach at all times; sooner or later the habit may save your life.

After you arrest a man, never take your eyes off him until he has been properly searched. Never under any consideration allow him to go into another room or into a car for a coat or a smoke or for any other of the innumerable excuses criminals will make up. Too often they are going for a gun. We had such a case happen here years ago that well illustrates the point. A man had been threatening people up the Lemhi River and a Deputy Sheriff was sent to arrest him. As he was usually armed, two young men were also deputized. They found him in a ranch house and arrested him. Then the Deputy, who should have been watching him, allowed the criminal to go into another room for a coat while he phoned the Sheriff's office

W. T. (Bill) Toney, Jr. demonstrating use of the sub-machine gun from the hip. He is U. S. Border Patrol instructor.

at Salmon. He told the Sheriff, "We have him and are bringing him in." Those were his last words as the criminal emerged from the bedroom with a .30/30 rifle and killed him, then each of the two young fellows who had been deputized. Later, with a big posse combing the hills and river bottoms for him, he was starved out and came in to a rancher he knew. The rancher took no chances and shot him on sight. He regretted it the rest of his life, but it was probably the best for all concerned.

Another case that happened in Montana before I left that State also tells its own tale of foolhardiness by the Sheriff. A man had gone beserk and killed his employer and the latter's wife on a ranch out of Manhattan. Taking a .30/30 rifle, he hid out in an old granary in a small basin. The Sheriff organized a large and adequate posse which surrounded the place and they should have kept out of sight until dark, then worked in on him with tear gas and shotguns or rifles. But instead, the Sheriff took a couple of deputies and boldly walked up to the granary, calling on the wanted man to come out and surrender. He had no intention of doing so and promptly shot the Sheriff and the deputies through the head, killing them all. The posse surrounded the place, then poured rifle fire through the granary from all angles, killing the man where he lay on some boards in the attic portion of the granary.

A few years ago an equally bad case occurred in Wyoming where some good officers were killed trying to cross open ground against a desperate man who was a good rifle shot. Then they called out the National Guard and brought up artillery and shelled the place after their man was long gone. His demise cost more lives before it was accomplished.

If you do get embroiled in a gun fight, remember your adversary is dangerous as long as he hangs onto his gun, so keep shooting until he drops the gun or goes down. If he keeps his grip on the gun after he falls, he is still potentially dangerous and should be shot again. Gun fighting is nasty business, but as long as we have a criminal element, or nations bent on mastery of the world, it will be necessary. The best possible defense against either is a trained citizenry of gun fighters who will keep and carry on the traditions of this great country for posterity.

We are sorry if this chapter has been a trifle lurid. We do not approve of gun fights any more than we approve of tornadoes and hydrogen hombs—but unfortunately we keep hearing about them.

The best way to keep from getting hurt in a gunfight is to keep from getting into a gunfight.

If you are in a position where you must risk gun battles, the surest way to keep them from starting is to take all reasonable precautions and to be fast enough and accurate enough so you can dominate the situation with self confidence.

An old time peace officer I know well, who for a dozen years took on all comers, usually alone, without trouble, gives us his rules:

Carry your gun in a cross-draw holster where you can get it quick, but keep it out of sight.

Never use one bit more force than is necessary to attain your legal objective.

Never rough up, abuse or humiliate a prisoner unnecessarily.

Tell the exact truth on the witness stand. If you are not sure what the truth is, say so. Never permit a prisoner to think you were a party to framing him.

Never arrest a stranger, however trivial the offense, without being tensed to get into action instantly. He may be crazy and he may be wanted for murder somewhere else.

We close this chapter with one more observation. No matter what the law reads or what the courts say, every adult citizen is entitled to own a gun for his personal protection. No anti-gun law ever disarmed a criminal; only respectable people are rendered helpless. The mounting crime statistics prove it.

Chapter XI

Revolver Versus Auto Pistol

IN THIS CHAPTER we will try to point out the good and bad points of both the revolver and the automatic pistol. Friends of each type will argue until doomsday as to the superiority of their chosen weapon. Each design has its own advantages. Each has its disadvantages. Every year I receive a great many letters asking my advice on this controversial subject. In the following pages I will attempt to fairly analyze both weapons.

The auto pistol is a more compact weapon, and, having no cylinder, thinner than the sixgun, especially in the larger calibers. For this reason it is less bulky and more easily concealed on the person. Fully loaded, it has the advantage of carrying more ammunition than the sixgun. It is totally dependent on perfect ammunition for certain operation. Jacketed bullets are almost a necessity to insure functioning and they must be either round nosed or a modification of my design if they are to feed freely from magazine to chamber. The auto pistol performs and feeds best with rimless cartridges and is less prone to jam with them than when rimmed cartridges are used. It has the advantage of seven to nine shot magazines which, with one cartridge in the chamber, makes it an eight to ten shot weapon. Only a single pull of the trigger is necessary for each shot after the first. With the P-.38, Sauer, Walther and the new Smith & Wesson double action auto pistol, the first shot can be fired by one double action pull. With all models and makes other than these the gun must be cocked or the safety thrown off before the first shot can be fired. Automatics must be chambered looser than revolvers to insure the cartridge feeding into the chamber with certainty. More tolerance is needed to insure the cartridge surely chambering and the action fully locking. Dirt on a cartridge may cause it to fail to chamber and jam the gun. Sand or mud thrown into the action of an auto pistol while open will surely jam it.

Most auto pistols headspace from the front end of the case to the face of the cartridge head, the 7.65 and 7.63 Mauser excepted. This headspace is critical and the cartridge case must be exactly the right length to insure certain ignition. Empty cases are thrown from the gun into mud, water, snow or brush and are hard to find under good conditions and impossible to recover under adverse conditions. The auto pistol is the poorest weapon for the hand loader. Ammunition is usually more expensive than for the revolver. Auto pistol ammunition is also less powerful than the heaviest loads in revolvers.

The lowered powered automatic actions are usually of the straight blow-back type; heavier guns are of the locked breech design with delayed unlocking and opening of the action. The most powerful of all automatic pistols is the Colt Model 1911 Service pistol loaded with a 230 grain bullet at between 800 and 900 feet velocity. The .38 Super-Speed automatic has approximately the same foot pound energy but much less knock-down power. Target loads with modified Keith type semi-wadcutter bullets running from 185 to 210 grains usually perform best at velocities around 870 feet. When these bullets are used, there seems to be a very critical relationship between velocity and accuracy. Regardless of ammunition, pistols made under the Browning patents must have closely fitted slides, links and barrel bushings, as well as match grade barrels and the snuggest possible chamber for match accuracy.

The Luger action is much different. The barrel and breech are integral. When fired, the whole assembly moves about a quarter of an inch to the rear at which point the bolt, so far kept in position by being hinged slightly below the line of thrust, is unlocked by the hinge pin running up a ramp, lifting the center connection which then folds together in the middle, letting the bolt-face come back far enough to eject the empty case and pick up a loaded round from the magazine as the bolt comes down to firing position.

Luger pistols have had more bad publicity than they are entitled too. This was caused first by the fact that the Luger was foreign-made and did not advertise in the United States. Gun writers, not permitted to call attention to the defects in advertised guns, could vent their spleen and establish their impartiality by pointing up Luger failures. They had a field day doing it in by-gone years. The rest of the Luger bad luck is due to the circumstance that vast numbers of these guns were made under wartime pres-

Keith on bronc with bobcat killed with .45 Colt 1920.

sure for German armies, and later peddled far and wide from salvage piles. It should not be forgotten, by way of keeping the record straight, that more nations chose the Luger as their military side arm than any other pistol, by far.

To have a chance in the highly competitive pistol market of today, the gun must be so designed as to lend itself to manufacturing short cuts. The Luger requires a great deal of machine work at close tolerances. It could hardly be made and sold in this country for less than $125.00. It appears unlikely that it will ever be made again. Our further remarks are based on the good guns made before and between the late wars.

The Luger is one of the most accurate of all auto loading pistols. It is also entitled to a high rating as a natural pointer. On Browning type automatic pistols the front and rear sights are on the slide and separate from the barrel. The Luger front sight (and that of the Walther P-.38) is a part of the barrel. As a rule the Luger has a hard creepy trigger pull and one that is very difficult to improve. Trigger finger pressure is exerted on springs as well as on the sear. Expert stoning of the complicated parts will result in a satisfactory trigger let-off, but few gunsmiths have mastered the knack. The Luger safety is badly positioned and very slow to release.

With one inconsequential exception all auto pistols are cursed with separate magazines, which may be an advantage to the military since a number of loaded magazines can be carried, but is often a source of trouble to the civilian, who may lose his magazine or drop it in mud, snow or water. Magazine catches can be accidently pressed while carrying the arm and the magazine be lost. They can also be unfastened and the magazine start out of the gun accidentally so when the gun is needed it becomes a single shot until the magazine is again jammed home and locked.

A jammed automatic pistol requires both hands to clear and get in action again. Magazine lips are prone to become bent or damaged until they do not function reliably. Sand, mud or snow will gum up all automatics. None made to date will function reliably in Arctic cold. In the humid tropics they will soon become hopelessly rusted and will balk unless kept well oiled and cleaned. The auto pistol has the advantage of holding more ammunition, but it cannot be shot as fast with accuracy, as a double action revolver.

Stocks stay put on the Browning type auto pistols, but tend to become loose on the Luger. The Luger is the best of all auto pistols for long range shooting. Its long sight radius, front sight mounted on the barrel and solidly joined breech and barrel, make a fine long range gun. For these reasons it is our choice of all auto pistols for long range work. Its unsatisfactory trigger pull however, usually makes it a two handed weapon for close shooting.

A few Lugers were made in the .45 Colt auto caliber but I have never seen one. The Colt .45 auto is the most powerful and the best man-stopper or game killer of all auto pistols. The Lugers 7.65 and 9 mm. and the Super .38 Colt have a much flatter trajectory with their high velocity ammunition, but deliver almost no stopping or killing power. Their light bullets slip through game or man with little shock effect and cause little hemorrhage. We have already told of one negro cow-puncher taking a gun full of Luger ammunition in the back and still being able to turn around and kill his murderer. We have also known of a treed cougar taking a gun full of Super .38's in the chest and still remain on the limb of a tree slowly bleeding out inside. One or two heavily loaded .44 Specials would have knocked him out, and the same will floor any man for the count.

On account of the empties being thrown from the gun and being hard to recover and the fact that all auto pistol ammunition must be perfectly resized and trimmed to exact length to function dependably, we have never favored reloading for the auto pistol. If the hand gun crank wants to roll his own ammunition, automatic pistols are not for him.

From a military standpoint the auto pistols have their advantage. Parts can be supplied and easily fitted in a few minutes with a minimum of tools. Extra loaded magazines can be carried and the emptied ones dropped out of the gun and fire sustained as long as the loaded magazines last. Time, and many a sanguinary conflict, has well proven that only a large caliber cartridge such as the .45 auto is a certain and reliable man-stopper. In spite of this, all of Europe has gone to the 9 mm. Luger round or some very similar cartridge of about the same power and the same caliber. We have always felt that infantry engaged as were our forces during the war with Japan and the later Korean conflict, where a great deal of close range night fighting took place, should be armed with a pistol of some sort. It need not be a long range weapon, but should have ample knockdown power. Only in the .45, of all pistol cartridges adapted to auto loading arms, has the bullet enough weight and caliber to be a certain man-stopper and even it does not compare with a heavy sixgun load.

As an automatic pistol for troops, always overloaded, the Colt Commander offers a light weight weapon using the same powerful .45 auto Colt cartridge, and would be a good arm for combat troops. Pistols were at a high premium in Korea and for a very good reason. A man in a dugout or foxhole with an enemy soldier has no chance to use a rifle and must depend on a knife or pistol for such hand to hand fighting.

The Army, for reasons perhaps known to themselves, but which are incomprehensible to me, has always belittled the pistol as a combat weapon. There is nothing in night fighting, or any close range melee, that comes as near double distilled purple poison as an expert pistol fighter. Thousands of American boys, who died in the island campaign against Japan and in Korea, would be home today if they had been given a pistol and taught the skills of pistol gun fighting.

The army is now experimenting with 9 mm. caliber weapons for service use. It seems we have to learn all over again what every war we have been in has clearly shown. The Philippine insurrection taught the Army that the .38 long Colt was no man-stopper and the 9 mm. Luger round is very little better, but we would not be surprised to see the Army adopt the 9 mm. as the standard military service pistol cartridge.

The best auto pistol in the 9 mm. caliber we have seen to date for combat use is the new Smith & Wesson. It is made in both single action and double action. With the single action model it must be cocked for the first shot, while with the double action model the first shot can be fired with a pull of the trigger the same as the Walther P-.38 and the double action revolver. We consider this a very great advantage and of utmost importance in any military or gun fighting weapon. The new Smith & Wesson, in the double action model, is the most practical auto pistol we have yet seen. It could be made in .45 auto caliber just as easily as in 9 mm., and if it were, would be an even finer military weapon than our time-tried Colt model 1911. It is a short compact weapon with ramp front sight of generous width and the S. & W. adjustable for windage rear target sight—the best sights yet put on an automatic pistol. While we like the gun very much we certainly would like to see it brought out in .45 caliber rather than the 9 mm. The doughboy would then have a short, powerful gun he could pack and get into action quickly in an emergency. Its double action feature for that vital first shot places it head and shoulders over the Colt model 1911 or the Colt Commander. When the Colts are carried in combat they should be cocked, and the side safety used. This can be thrown off quite fast, but is not as fast as a double action gun for the first shot.

While the New Smith & Wesson is about the same size as the Colt Commander, it has better sights either for military or civilian use. The fact that it can be had in double action for the first shot places it ahead of the Commander for defense. It has a 4⅛ inch barrel and is of the Browning type with locked breech, short recoil and dropping barrel action. Frame can be had in light alloy metal to reduce weight. This new Smith & Wesson, if made in .45 caliber, would be the ultimate in a compact, powerful, military auto loading pistol. The army is likely to adopt it if they go to the 9 mm. caliber. This caliber with its light ammunition, might be worthwhile for survival kits for airmen, but I think the fighting man on the ground should have it in .45 caliber. Smith & Wesson could make it in that caliber if the army insists. To be sure .45 ammunition is heavy, but one .45 slug will do the work of two or three 9 mm. slugs, and do it quicker. Only with brain or spine hits can the soldier be certain of stopping an enemy with the 9 mm. and they are not easy to make in combat. God forbid that our military drop the time proven .45 in favor of the 9 mm.

It is quite true that the .45 auto pistol is the hardest of all handguns to learn to shoot. Recoil is fairly heavy and the jar of the slide against the slide-stop contributes to the disturbance. Nevertheless, the .45 auto is a known and proven man-stopper. All large caliber automatics, with the exception of the Luger, point too low for fast hip shooting due to the fact that their grips are placed at too great an angle. Years ago the .45 Colt model 1911 was greatly improved in this respect with an arched housing, but it still points far lower than the Luger or a good revolver. One has to consciously pull the muzzle up to get it high enough to hit from the hip. The new Smith & Wesson, no exception to this rule, also points low, but it is better than others.

When we turn to the .22 caliber automatics, the story is different. Many are excellent pointers, but they are useful only for small game and target work. The Colt Match Target and Woodsman, the High Standard models and the Rugers all point well and are more on the line of the Luger, but our big caliber auto pistols have far too much drop for any instinctive gun throwing or night fighting where the sights cannot be seen. The .22 auto pistols are prone to jam, some more than others and far more than their larger cousins. The larger guns, if kept clean and oiled in warm climates, or clean and lubricated with graphite in colder countries, will function reliably most of the time except in extreme cold. Even then the old .45 auto will work far better than the .22 calibers. The grease on .22 caliber bullets becomes very hard at 20 to 60 below zero and they tend to stick in the magazine, and also fail to chamber. The dry bullets of the center fire calibers do better, but neither caliber can be depended on in extreme sub-zero temperatures.

Another fault of most automatics is a too long reach from the back of the grip to the trigger. Short fingered people cannot get a proper grip with wrist in line with the gun for this reason. The auto pistols possess one great advantage. The cartridge lies in the chamber of the barrel. There is no barrel and cylinder joint permitting gas to escape. The slug lies in the rifling throat and does not have to upset to fill a chamber throat, then jump forward a quarter to a half inch before engaging the rifling. For this reason the auto pistols are better suited to jacketed bullet ammunition than are most revolvers. Revolvers for jacketed bullet ammunition should be held to close tolerances as to chamber mouth with relation to groove diameter of the barrel. The chamber throat should be very close to groove diameter or gas will escape past the bullet in the throat before it reaches the rifling. Some gas is lost at the barrel and cylinder junction, but this is so slight as to be disregarded when we consider the fact that the cylinder gun will also handle much more powerful powder charges and longer, heavier bullets as well.

Auto pistol magazines are much slower and harder to load than are revolver cylinders, especially if the fingers are numb with cold. Extra loaded magazines, however, can be inserted in the auto pistol much faster and easier than the revolver can be reloaded. So both types of arm have their advantages and also their disadvantages. We have now covered the auto pistols, so let us look at the revolver.

The sixgun can be fired with one hand, either single action or double action. It is not critical as to its ammunition. It will fire shorts and light loads as well as the heaviest loads without any change or trouble. The recoil spring of the auto pistol is adjusted for one weight of bullet and pressure. A lighter load will fail to bring the slide back far enough to chamber a new cartridge and a jam will occur. If the ammunition is too powerful, undue slam of the slide is the result and it will soon be battered and useless. Not so the revolver. It will handle any velocity ammunition perfectly. If a cartridge snaps or fails to fire, you simply cock the gun again with single actions, or pull the trigger again with double actions. The sixgun, either double or single action, points much better from the hip, or in instinctive night shooting, than does any auto pistol with the exception of the Luger and most of the .22 calibers. About the only thing that can cause a jam is for a bullet to jump its crimp and project out in front of the cylinder. This will tie up any revolver until that bullet is pushed back inside the cylinder.

The revolver will function reliably in temperatures that will jam any automatic. It will also handle more mud, snow, dust or sand and keep on shooting than will any auto pistol. In either double action or single action, for men trained in its use, it is faster to get into action for the first shot than an auto. The cylinder gun is usually a bit more bulky to carry than the auto pistol, but in small guns it is nearly as compact and handy. The little Chief's Special or Centennial Smith & Wessons are lighter and more compact guns to carry in the pocket than is any comparably powerful auto pistol. These little guns will both handle .38 Special or .38/44 ammunition, and only the Super .38 compares with them in power. The clean high sights on target revolvers are much better for long range work than the low sights on nearly all automatics.

The revolver has the disadvantage that the chambers must lock in perfect alignment with the barrel. The revolver holds five or six rounds as compared to the larger magazine capacity of the auto pistol. The revolver, however, will handle much more powerful ammunition than is possible with any automatic pistol.

The sixgun is not critical of its ammunition either as to power or length of case. The sixgun is the tool for the handloader as he can load light target or practice loads or heavy hunting and defense loads and use them indiscriminately. The revolver usually has by far the best balance and hang, and will point more nearly right, and can be shot plenty good enough for close range combat accuracy in the dark. The double action revolver is the fastest of all hand guns for repeat hits.

The sixgun will fire 100,000 rounds of lead bullet ammunition, while the auto pistol will usually wear out a barrel in 5,000 rounds or less, if jacketed bullets are used. The empties are easily recovered for reloading from the sixgun while they have to be chased all over the country when kicked from an automatic. There is no separate magazine to get lost, or unlatched to tie up the gun. Poor ammunition can be fired in the sixgun that would not function in the auto pistol. As long as the slug gets out of the barrel the sixgun is still in action. The sights are held rigidly on barrel and frame and there is no movement of the sights and no slide to get worn and loose. There are no barrel bushings or links to become worn. The revolver can be chambered much closer than the auto pistol. Only one hand is needed to dump the empties from a modern double action revolver. One can push forward on the cylinder latch, swing the cylinder out and then bump the extractor against a knee and knock the empties from the gun. He can hold the gun between his knees and reload with one hand or stick the muzzle in the waist band and reload with one hand if the other is disabled. Try to reload an auto pistol magazine with one hand; you will find it a hopeless task. If you have extra loaded magazines for the auto pistol all is well and good. You can load the next magazine in the gun, press the slide stop down and get in action again. If you get a jam with the automatic you need two hands, and badly, to clear the jam.

The sixgun will handle any shaped bullet from a round ball to a wad cutter with equal insouciance. It will digest black powder or smokeless powder, and light squibbs or heavy service loads with accuracy. Chambering of the revolver can be much tighter than with the auto pistol and the rear end of the chamber does not have to be cut out at the bottom and a ramp sloped into it to properly feed the cartridges.

The .357 Magnum revolver will handle a 160 grain bullet to a full 1500 feet velocity. Forty-four Special and .45 Colt caliber revolvers will handle 250 grain bullets up to 1200 feet from the .44 Special, and 1000 feet from the .45 Colt. These are much more powerful loads than is possible with any auto pistol. Flat point bullets having maximum shocking effect can be used. Both types are safe in the hands of an educated gunman. The revolver is far safer in the hands of a tyro. One needs but a glance at the cylinder to tell whether a revolver is loaded or not. Only a few automatics have a loaded chamber indicator. When a revolver is cocked it is nearly impossible to not notice the fact. It is much easier to not notice the safety on an automatic. When a revolver cylinder is swung out, the gun is safe. When the magazine is removed from an automatic, there may still be a loaded round, out of sight, in the chamber and this fact has caused perhaps half of the automatic accidents.

When the magazine is lost from an automatic all that remains is a slow, clumsy single shot. There is nothing to lose from a revolver. If you have any of it you have it all.

Cartridge cases must be resized full length and trimmed to exact length for auto pistols, when reloaded. The sixgun will digest them perfectly whether resized or not, so long as they will go in the chambers and have enough crimp to withstand recoil.

The sixgun will fire when pressed hard against an adversary. Many automatics will be pushed back out of battery, from such pressure, and will not fire. In an emergency the sixgun will handle other loads than that for which it is chambered. the .32/20 will handle .32 S. & W. and .32 short or long, and the .45 Colt will chamber and fire .38/40 and .44/40 hulls. The .44 Special will fire .44 American, .44 Russian and any other .44 cartridge that can be gotten into the chamber. The 1917 revolvers will accept the .45 auto rim and the .45 auto round, with or without clips, except for a few early Colt New Service 1917's that were bored clear through the cylinder.

Not being critical of either pressure or velocity, the sixgun is the arm for the hand loader. It is also the gun for the man who has lost a hand or an arm.

The sixgun, as a rule, is the more accurate of the two types of arms except in .22 caliber. Good target sixguns will make 1½ inch 50 yard groups, and it takes a lot of work on any automatic pistol of large caliber, other than the Luger, to produce such accuracy. The new Smith & Wesson should prove quite an accurate arm with its fine sighting equipment. All told, we consider the automatic over .22 caliber as more of a military weapon, and not necessarily the best one at that. The sixgun is the weapon for the gun fighter, the police, the peace officer or civilian, and for all hand loaders. Auto pistols must be fitted looser to function than do revolvers, and a fine revolver can be fitted very close in every respect and still function perfectly. Trigger pulls are also easier to adjust on a revolver than on an auto pistol, and can be any weight from 2½ pounds upwards while auto pistols are not safe with a light trigger pull and may become worn until they will fire full automatic, when they are exceedingly dangerous.

Service caliber auto pistols are best left with a 3½ pound or heavier trigger pull for safety. The Luger has an abominable trigger pull and one that is very hard to adjust properly. Automatics require a firm, hard grip for best accuracy and men with strong hands do the best work with them, while sixguns can be shot accurately by anyone who can hold the gun properly.

In a gun fight one bad cartridge can jam the auto pistol and be fatal. The revolver will keep right on firing so long as a bullet does not jump its crimp or a squibb load leave a bullet in the barrel. Most automatics have safeties on the left side which are awkward for left handed persons. The sixgun is handled with equal facility in either right or left hand. A broken extractor will hopelessly gum up an automatic, or a broken ejector will cause the empty case to go back in the chamber and thus tie up the gun. When it comes to utter reliability under all conditions of service, our vote goes to the time-tried sixgun every time.

Chapter XII

Aerial and Trick Shooting

TO BECOME AN EXPERT aerial and trick shot requires the expenditure of a tremendous amount of ammunition. It also requires a lot of thought, study and hard work. Anyone with fair eyesight and the use of both hands can learn it, but it will require a lot of practice. It teaches fast gun handling, fast sighting, and perfect coordination between hand and eye. At one time I aspired to become a trick shot and did learn something of the game only to find the field well filled with better men. As there was a livelihood to be made, I reluctantly dropped out.

Unless you have access to free ammunition, trick shooting had best be mastered with the inexpensive .22 caliber ammunition. Twenty-two shorts are just as good as .22 long rifles for this work, for it is all close range shooting.

Many different stunts can be mastered by steady, conscientious practice and the more tricks one has in his repertoire, the better a showman he will be. We will cover some of them, and systems of practice in this chapter. Many more can be worked out, and the exhibition shot who develops new stunts from time to time will find a greater demand for his services.

Start with the .22 caliber and master all the stunts; then shift to the big gun for more spectacular results as seems advisable. Aerial shooting is but one phase of the work, but the toughest of all. Aerial shooting is difficult with one gun but when you try to use two guns it is something indeed. Ed McGivern shot two guns at aerial targets and broke as many as five targets thrown at one time, with the two guns. This requires the utmost in coordination and fast double action shooting. I believe the double action Smith & Wesson revolver to be the best gun for all aerial shooting, but many tricks can be mastered with single actions and automatics as well.

Start with a big target. Toss a gallon tin can up with the left hand and raise the gun hand as the left hand tosses the can in the air. Toss it fairly straight up, as it is much easier to hit this way than if tossed out to the front. Start by shooting once each toss until you hit it regularly. Toss it up ten or fifteen feet at the start and strive to bring the sights to bear on the bottom edge. Shoot just as it reaches the apex of its rise. After you master one hit with each throw, try for two, then for three. This will strengthen your trigger finger and gun hand and teach coordination between hand, eye and mind. When you acquire speed, then start tossing the can a bit higher—up to twenty feet. Strive for six hits, shooting as fast as you can work the gun and trying to keep the sights at the bottom edge of the falling can. If you toss it up straight enough, the can will fall toward you; less lead is required and it is easier to hit it. As you become proficient with the can falling directly toward you, try tossing it out farther from you until you master this more difficult phase. When you become expert on the gallon can and can make five or six hits while it is falling twenty feet, start on smaller targets. A tomato can is good and when you can hit it regularly, try smaller targets until finally you can hit marbles, empty cartridge cases or a small pebble or rock. When shooting at cans, many times you will hit one on a fold of the metal where there is more resistance and it will be thrown up again from the impact, giving you more time for repeat hits. Often, too, the can is spun off to one side from such hits and you have to follow it to keep working on it.

At all exhibitions you should keep the crowd well to the rear and any can that spins back over the audience had best be passed up. A good helper is of inestimable value and the tossing up of cans, bottles, and other objects becomes almost as much of an art as the actual shooting. For best results they have to be thrown about the same place, each time and it's simply a matter of timing. You know approximately where the target will be and you swing your gun up with it as it raises, and shoot as it reaches the top of the upward movement, if possible, when it seems to sort of hang in the air for a fraction of a second. This is the best time to hit all small objects and requires a lot of practice. Sight the guns point blank for 30 feet and leave the sights alone after that. Gun, arm and eye should remain as one rigid unit. Swing the body and shoulder to bring this unit to bear on the target. If practiced enough you can learn to hit very small objects tossed in the air, washers, small lead discs or coins. A spinning coin or washer makes

197

Long range shooting with a .357 S. & W. Magnum.

a fine and spectacular aerial target but one tossed up edgewise to the shooter is even more so. You can learn to hit the thin edge at close range if you practice long enough. Then is the time to try washers and washers with a piece of tape over the hole in the center. These should be tossed up with their full side presented to the shooter, who in turn attempts to hit the hole in the center. Such stunts are at very close range, usually six to eight feet, from the gun.

After you have mastered fast double action shooting and can keep your shots on a gallon can and two or three hits on a smaller can, then you can start practice on two objects thrown up at the same time. Again the targets should be thrown fairly straight up, well overhead, so that you are under them. Raise the gun as the targets go up, get your sights on one before it reaches the heighth of the throw, bust it and shift as fast as possible to the bottom edge of the second, now a falling target, and shoot. When you have mastered two targets thrown at the same time, then strive for three. This is very difficult. If you keep at it and have a good helper to toss the targets, you can get the knack. When you get three with fair regularity, try four or five.

When you can hit two or three separate targets thrown up at one time, you are getting good. Only continuous daily practice will ever get you to the stage where you can hit more than three tossed together. McGivern did this, shattering five targets at one throw. He did it with one gun and with two guns. We consider it more difficult using two guns. We learned in one afternoon to pulverize five clay pigeons thrown in a group, with a .28 gauge Remington automatic shotgun. Many of these stunts which look utterly impossible to the tyro are really not so difficult if you will stay with them day after day. When a big spread of targets is thrown up, it's best to concentrate on the lower ones first. This gives a fraction more time for the higher targets before they fall to the ground. One should endeavor to dust as many as possible while they are high in the air, as they gather momentum the farther they fall and are then harder to hit, as more lead is required. One must stand well balanced on his feet and with body forward, following the targets with the gun arm. When a target is over you, shoot at the middle of it, but if falling and out in front of you shoot always at the lower edge. If it is falling fast and near the ground, more forward allowance is necessary and you have to swing the gun arm very fast while you maintain a perfect sight picture.

Used light bulbs or even small camera flash bulbs make excellent aerial targets as do all bottles, but bottles must be broken well out in front or you risk being cut by sharp falling fragments. I have fractured many of them directly over head, then ducked my head and hoped a rear end or neck of said bottle with a sharp corner would not hit me on the head or hand and make a nasty gash. I am ashamed of myself for doing anything so lacking in common sense. Always toss bottles well out in front and shoot for the bottom edge of them. The .22s crack up glass objects and the big guns powder them, depending on velocity and where the hits are made.

When you have your degree in aerial shooting, a spectacular stunt is to toss a head of cabbage or a hard head of lettuce in the air and center it with a hollow point .357 Magnum or .44 Special heavy load. You will simply make salad of it and it can be done with a crowd around if you toss the head of cabbage or lettuce well up and shoot while it is at the top of its rise. An orange or apple also works very well for this stunt. A case of bad eggs can sometimes be had from a grocery store. They make excellent aerial targets, but like bottles, one should also shoot these well out in front. I have nicked some that were in the explosive stage themselves, and exploded on their own when hit. The aroma was not that of attar of roses.

A can of tomatoes is also spectacular. A high velocity revolver bullet will usually rupture it badly, often splitting it wide open and spraying the contents

Testing a sixgun at long range.

over a wide area. This stunt never fails to produce a howl of delight from the youngsters and looks of disapproval from the ladies.

In all aerial shooting, body balance is of utmost importance. One should lean forward into the gun, so to speak, and when following falling targets the body should bend forward as the target descends, keeping the gun hand and arm locked in rigid alignment with the shooting eye.

Shoot with both eyes open at all times, if possible. One can see more with two eyes than with one, and both eyes should be used. Shoot with the master eye at all times. You can determine the master eye by aiming at an object with the end of your thumb and one eye, and slowly opening the other to see if the aim moves. If the aim shifts, that eye is not the master and the other should be tried. One eye or the other is almost always the master, and when this is true one can aim his thumb tip at an object and then open the other eye and the aim is maintained while the eye last opened simply sees the target. The same is true with the sights of a gun. If both eyes are about the same and neither seems to be the master, then it is well to shoot with the right eye for right handers and the left with southpaws and slightly squint the other eye, opening it just enough to see a bit but not to take the aim off the sights. In this way and with practice you can soon train one eye to become the master, or shooting eye.

Some shooters may be handicapped with poor vision and for these we would recommend Dr. William Mitchell of the Mitchell Optical Company, Waynesville, Missouri. He has made an extensive study of grinding correct glasses for shooters. For the oldster like myself, whose arms are now growing too short to read as well as formerly, but whose vision is still perfect for anything beyond close reading or sighting distances, Mitchell can make a set of shooting glasses that will bring the sights in perfect sharp and black relation. The target will be slightly hazy. This is not as good as the keen vision of youth with rapid accommodation, but is better than not being able to see the sights clearly as a clear sight picture must be maintained for accurate shooting. With some of us the sights may be a trifle fuzzy or have grown whiskers, so to speak, but we can still keep a sight picture and do good shooting, seeing our target perfectly. For such shooters, glasses are not much help. When one's eyes reach a stage of far sightedness that blurs the sights into one indistinct lump, a set of shooting glasses is the only way to sharpen them up and retain a fair target picture.

For slow-fire work where there is plenty of time, the little Merit iris shutter disc that attaches over the lens of the shooting spectacles is a great help. One can step this aperture down until one gets a perfect picture of both sights and target, even when the eyes are far from normal. It is better for slow-fire shooting than corrected glasses, but the gadget is not practical for hunting, defense, or any fast work.

Dr. William Mitchell adjusting his special aperture on his shooting glasses for Keith.

It is useful only in slow-fire at fixed targets. However, it will enable many people with defective eyesight to see both sights and target much more clearly than otherwise. There is no rule against its use as it is fastened to the lens of the shooting glasses, is not a part of the gun, and only enables the shooter with faulty eyes to more clearly see his sights and target.

Some shooters are nearsighted and must have glasses corrected to see at a distance. They should then ask for glasses that will give them a good sight picture, yet enable them to see their targets as well. Bill Mitchell has worked on glasses for shooters so long that he thoroughly understands these conditions and can supply most shooters who have faulty vision with glasses that will be a big help. My eyes used to be as good as any man ever possessed and I still can read the finest line of letters on most visual acuity test charts, without glasses, but I have a little horizontal astigmatism and anything close to the eyes now becomes fuzzed a bit. Rear open sights on rifles are hazy. Sixgun sights, held farther from the eye, are still fairly clear, but not as sharp as when a set of Mitchell's corrected glasses are worn.

The rifleman has found an answer to blurring sights and targets. He mounts a hunting telescope sight with adjustable focus on his gun and sees sights and target as clearly as ever. Unfortunately there is no such perfect solution to failing eyesight available to the pistol shooter. We have studied the problem for years but have found no real remedy. Some shooters do best with sharp sights and whiskered targets; others with hazy sights and clearly defined targets. This much is certain—fuzzy sights are more susceptible to group shifts caused by side-lights and variations of light intensity, than are clear sights and indistinct targets. Father time takes his toll. These problems appear as one grows older. We hope we have not overemphasized

Dr. William Mitchell, left, and Elmer Keith aiming with special Mitchell shooting glasses with an aperture for right eye similar to Merit Iris shutter, but permanently affixed to the glasses. It greatly sharpens the vision and gives clear sights for the oldster.

the visional difficulties of elderly shooters. McGivern, greatest fast and fancy shot of all time, was at his best during middle age. Many of our shooting companions are past fifty and one will never see sixty again unless time reverses itself. Their instinctive pointing and hip shooting is as good as it ever was. In fact, they do not appear to have lost anything but a few points in competitive target shooting.

Many stunts can be worked out for the trick shot. Shooting with guns held upside down, pulling the trigger with the little finger, is one. Mirror shooting is another; the arms are folded across the chest with one hand holding the gun and the other the mirror. The arms should be locked solidly and the shooting eye moved until it sees the sights in perfect relation in the mirror, and the whole body moved until the sight picture is imposed on the target. The body and arms and gun and mirror must be locked together as one rigid unit and the whole moved until the sights bear on the target. It is not difficult at all. The firing should be single action. Automatic pistols are better for this stunt than revolvers, as revolvers may blacken or burn the coat sleeve, but either can be used. It takes practice to assume correct position of head, arms, gun and mirror quickly. Once found it is only a matter of moving the upper torso until the sights bear center and squeezing off the shot. We watched Colonel Walter Walsh in a hotel at San Francisco, using a lady's diamond ring for a mirror.

He had to hold his shooting eye very close to the stone but he broke all his targets nicely using only the diamond as a mirror. I never owned a big diamond or even had the loan of one. All practice in this stunt has been with small hand mirrors.

Splitting playing cards turned edgewise to the shooter is another nice stunt, to be done at close range, of course. The pistol or revolver must be perfectly sighted for line. Place the card as far away as you can clearly see the sharp edge. This can be done either single or double action, but is easiest single action. Wad cutter bullets, or bullets of the Keith design with a square shoulder are best, as they cut the card cleanly while a pointed or round nose bullet will not do so well unless it hits dead center.

Driving corks down bottles is another good trick and not so difficult if the gun is perfectly sighted for this close range work, which should not be attempted at more than 15 to 20 feet. I have accomplished the stunt at 30 feet, but it is far more certain at the shorter ranges. Last spring, while sighting in a 1950 Target .44 Special Smith & Wesson, my partner drained the last drop from a fifth of Scotch. We wedged the bottle neck tightly in the crotch of a willow at 20 feet. The bottle had a big cork covering the whole neck. We centered it, split the wooden top and drove the cork proper down the neck of the bottle. Only the neck was left, the rest shattered and thrown away by the impact, but the edge of the bottle neck had a slight splash of lead, showing that we did not get the big slug exactly centered.

Another stunt is to shoot at the center of a white square of paper nailed or tacked over the end of a block of wood that will stop the bullets. This also must be done at close range. Shoot one shot in the center of the paper then empty the gun in the same hole. If there are some who doubt that you hit after the first shot, even though at close range the hole will usually enlarge, you can split the block and show them all the slugs welded together in a lump. Five to seven yards is far enough for this stunt.

Another excellent and very spectacular stunt is to stand three tall bottles on end, one on top of the other. Beer bottles are excellent. This also is a close range stunt as are most trick shots. Start at the bottom bottle double action and smash it shooting again as fast as you possibly can, aiming in the same place and busting each bottle as it falls. The crash of each bottle momentarily slows the fall of the next, but you have to be a fast double action shot to master this. It can only be done with loads having light recoil, as heavy recoil lifts the muzzle and you cannot get back in time to crack the next bottle. Properly done, this stunt is very interesting but it requires a fast double action gun, an exceptionally good double action shot, and light loads. Grip the gun hard, lock the arm in position when you start, shoot the first bottle, then pour successive shots in the same place. I have seen bottles thus stacked up, simply explode as they reach the ground. It can also be done nicely with .22 auto loading rifles.

Tin cans may be placed on rocks that slope upward behind the can and a shot placed just under them to throw them up in the air and a hit made on them when they reach the top of their raise. This is not always easily accomplished and one must have a clear background behind the targets for a long dis-

Six shots off hand at 10 yards by Elmer Keith on December 9, 1930—6½ grains Bullseye, Keith 250 .44 Special.

tance. Sometimes the cans will be bounced quite high making excellent aerial targets. In this way you throw your can with the bullet and then strive to hit it, and it may go at any angle. I have seen tough composition balls thrown fairly high in this way, making excellent aerial targets. As the first shot at the bottom edge is fired at close range, they can be made to raise almost straight up.

Rolling cans down the road is another easy and spectacular stunt. Merely aim at the bottom of the can, so the slugs strike the ground just under it, and you can easily keep one bouncing along the ground. This stunt can be done nicely with any type of sixgun or auto pistol as plenty of time is to be had for each successive shot. The faster you can hit under the can when it comes to the ground, the better, keeping it moving. Twenty-two caliber guns will roll or bounce it along but heavy caliber sixguns will throw the can high in the air giving one plenty of time to double action the gun or cock it again before the can comes

down for the next hit. Try always to keep the slugs just barely under the can so the strike is slightly on your side of the center of the can.

Shooting at two objects at once with two guns is a very difficult stunt and the farther these two objects are apart the more difficult it becomes. They can be hit even with guns extended at each side with practice but you must have perfect body control. To do this stunt you aim one gun and lock the muscles of that hand and arm, aim the other gun and then fire both together. It requires a tremendous lot of practice. Shooting at two objects in front with two guns at the same time is not so difficult. You aim one gun and hold it, and when the aim is right on the other gun you fire both together.

Two gun hip shooting with a different target for each gun is very difficult, but two gun work on one object, from the hip, is quite easy and very spectacular as two heavy guns create quite a disturbance.

Snuffing candles, shooting ashes off cigars, etc., requires accurate guns and loads perfectly sighted for the short ranges involved. Guns sighted for normal ranges shoot low at close ranges so must be resighted for such stunts. While spectacular, we never did like shooting toward a person as a defective bullet or a hang fire might injure the fellow holding the cigar or what have you. The candle trick is excellent or standing a cigar or cigarette up, and knocking the ashes from it, but we refuse to shoot the ashes from a cigar while held in someone's mouth. Often bits of tobacco

Ned Gibbs shooting .357 Magnum S. & W.

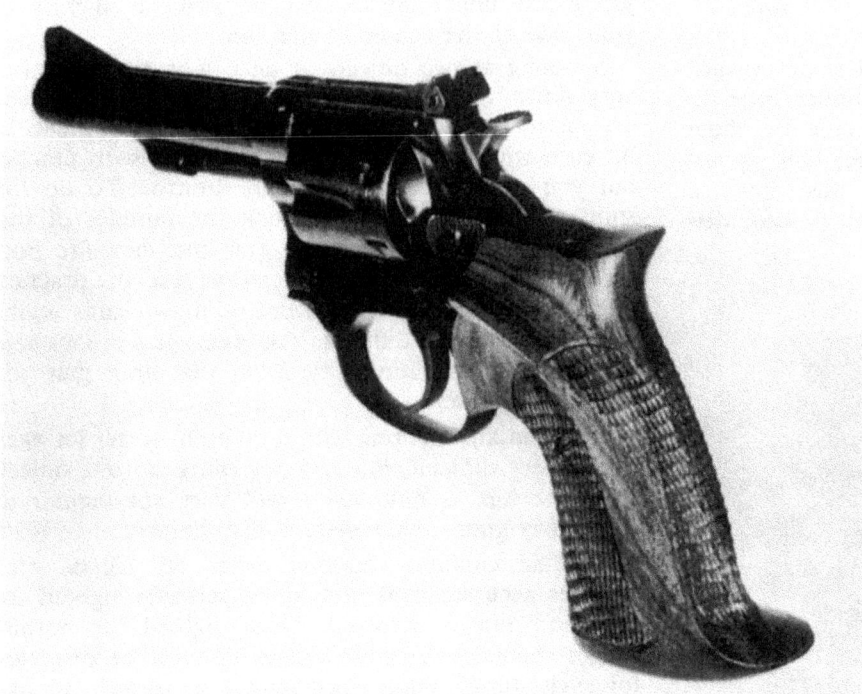

Herters Custom Tailored Pistol Stocks.

will be thrown in the eyes of the holder, if nothing worse, unless they are closed. The same accuracy of aim and fire is shown if the cigarette, candle or cigar is placed on some inanimate object rather than held in the fingers or teeth, and is a lot safer. The stunt of shooting apples off someone's head classifies the participants as ready for the insane asylum. You never know when you may get a weak primer or a slight hang fire. A gun recoils straight back and the barrel raises less when a cartridge squibbs and the slug hits lower. There is no sense in any dangerous stunts. If carried on long enough, like Russian roulette, a fatal accident will result.

Drawing pictures with bullets from sixguns is done the same as when rifles are used. The .22 automatic pistols with a box of extra magazines are best for this stunt. It requires some artistic ability as well as perfect holding. Plenty of ammunition and time is all that is required to make a bullet hole artist. Sketch the Indian head or rabbit or whatnot on a piece of cardboard the same size you will use for your shooting. Sketch it often enough and you will have a mental picture. It will be quite easy then to place your bullets as you did your lines in the pencil or crayon sketches.

Shooting at swinging targets is another stunt that is not too difficult if enough time is spent at it. You can hit them easiest at the end of their swing by aiming where they are going to be and shooting there. They have to stop an instant before going back. It is a matter of timing. Busting them at the bottom of the swing is the hardest as they are then at maximum speed and require considerable lead.

Targets simulating running rabbits can be arranged on wires the same as running deer and running man targets and are very practical as they teach swing and lead which, once mastered, greatly improves practical shooting ability. I prefer live running jack rabbits for real fun, however, and wherever you have the black tail jack rabbit, always a pest, one can have plenty of fun walking them up and when they jump, drawing the gun and shooting at them as they run away. In time you will hit a few of them and enjoy more real sport than you have ever known with a sixgun. This kind of

Herter's Custom Pistol Stocks.

shooting is vastly different from assassinating varmints with a 'scope sighted, high-powered bull gun from a dead rest.

One evening Judge Don Martin and I were driving down a lane in the Pahsimeroi valley when we ran into a horde of these pest jack rabbits coming out of George Santee's alfalfa meadow. We stopped the old Buick, turned off the switch, and taking Don's 1917 .45 S. & W. and a handful of three shot clips, proceeded to lay fifteen John rabbits low. They were all moving, but not fast, just hopping across the road in front of the car. I had the barrow pit full of dead ones before I gave the gun to Don. They kept on coming in a seemingly endless stream. Judge Martin ran up a good score before the big bunnies stopped coming out of the fence corner and we drove on toward home.

Running Jack shooting, like trick shooting, teaches one fast gun handling and fast double or single action fire as well as lead and swing. Enough of it will make a practical gunman of just about any shooter.

When shooting for a crowd, keep up a running fire of remarks. When not actually shooting talk to them about what you are doing or are going to do. Jokes and wise cracks help. It holds their attention and prevents them from losing interest while guns are being loaded and during possible delays. The program should be arranged so all the slow fire events, such as splitting cards, snuffing candles, mirror shooting and long range shooting, if any, come first, followed by bullet hole pictures. One shot aerial exhibitions are best next. After these put on the rapid fire aerial tricks with two or three larger objects thrown at one time by an assistant. Work up from slow shooting to rapid fire and end with something like two guns bouncing a can. You can move from slow accurate fire to speed events without losing anything, but you cannot do your best slow fire accurate shooting after rapid fire without a rest between. Your slow fire shooting perhaps requires the most skill, but it is the less spectacular. By saving the rapid fire for the last you can gradually increase the tempo of your show and end it with rapid double action stunts.

It takes years of unremitting effort and thousands of dollars worth of ammunition to become a first class exhibition shot. There are endless ways to put on a bogus show and only a few people in an audience

Anita Hays throwing can and Ted Keith hitting it double action with S&W Kit gun.

will know the difference. These are the reasons why there are so few really great exhibition shots. But if you become a little better than just good, one of the great ammunition companies may give you a life job demonstrating their product. Actually, it just about takes a big ammunition company to keep an all around exhibition shot in practice.

Chapter XIII

Slip Shooting, Fanning, Cavalry Guns

BY THE ELIMINATION of the trigger, the trigger half of the bolt spring, reduction in length of the bolt cam on the hammer and lowering the spur on the back of the hammer, the S. A. Colt and Great Western single actions are made into slip guns. This automatically eliminates many parts of an S. A. gun that can break. Many old gun fighters simply removed the trigger from their single action, making it a slip gun and eliminating the sear and hammer notches, both liable to breakage. The trigger half of the bolt spring also became inactive. They shot with their thumbs or fanned their guns, using them primarily as close range fighting weapons.

If the little tapered stud on the hammer that actuates the bolt is filed down in length until only the width of the bolt arm is left, it greatly reduces the amount that the bolt arm has to bend to pass over it, and thus greatly reduces amount of strain on the bolt arm. Then when the sear and hammer notches are not used there is very little to go wrong with an S. A. Colt or Great Western revolver. If a coiled bolt spring is substituted for the usual flat spring, another weakness is eliminated and the single action becomes the most simple and reliable weapon known.

John Newman went even farther by cutting off the regular hammer spur and putting a shorter, smaller, smooth hammer spur about half way down the back of the hammer. This became the true slip gun. While the old gunman used to stone off the checkering on the hammer spur to facilitate fanning the weapon, he was never as accurate with his gun as when it was shot with one hand and the hammer spur slipped from under the thumb, but he was very fast.

Not so, the true Newman slip gun, for fine accuracy is possible with this method. The gun is gripped hard, preferably with the little finger curled under the butt of the gun. The short stubby hammer spur is gripped under the last joint of the thumb and held there while you simply press the side of the thumb against the side of the frame or, if you have long fingers, press the tip of the thumb against the tip of the trigger finger to fire the gun. This pressure will release the short stubby hammer spur as slowly and deliberately as you would squeeze the trigger on a conventional gun. Different sized and shaped hands require slight modifications in the position and length of the slip hammer spur. J. D. O'Meara required a longer spur, and I required one of a length between those used by Newman and O'Meara and slightly higher than Newman's hammer spurs. Once worked out and practiced with for a period of months, slip shooting is just as accurate as trigger shooting, and much faster for the single action gun. However, be it understood, if you practice to become a good slip gun shot, you have to unlearn all you have learned of trigger squeeze and using a trigger. The two guns are entirely different and require entirely different techniques in their manipulation. I played with the slip gun for a year or more to the exclusion of all trigger guns and became a master of it. I found I could kill game just as well with the slip gun as with trigger guns, but I could not go back to the trigger gun and do good work. Likewise the trigger shot cannot do the best work with the slip gun. To become good with the slip gun, you have to forget trigger guns and shoot slip guns exclusively. Being a gun crank I would not do it, and finally gave up the slip gun for that reason. I had one trigger guard welded up with no hole for a trigger and still have my old slip hammer and this guard.

There can be no question but that the slip gun properly mastered becomes one of the best gun fighting weapons of all time. There are very few parts left in the gun to break and it is utterly reliable Once you learn that hard, firm grip on the gun, with little finger under butt and with the stubby hammer held down under the rear joint of the thumb, you can then squeeze off a shot as deliberately as you would with a trigger. The grip must be hard, however, so there will be no jerk when the slip hammer leaves its position under the thumb joint. I never could grasp that short hammer spur in quick draw work and get the gun in action as fast as a conventional hammer or a Bisley-type hammer. For quick draw work with a slip gun, the best method is to draw the gun with the shooting hand and then slip the hammer with the thumb of the left, or non-shooting hand, as Newman did. Even then I seemed slower than when using a conventional hammer and fanning it with the palm of the left hand.

J. E. Berns finally worked out a hammer for the slip gun that could be drawn and fired as fast for the first shot as any single action, and yet could be used as a slip gun. Berns has long slim fingers. He left the trigger in the gun and fitted a small, short checkered spur at the extreme tip of the hammer for fast cocking as the gun was drawn for the first shot; then as recoil threw the gun up he went to straight slip shooting using the short stubby hammer spur and holding the trigger back. I tried all systems and used the straight slip hammer gun with no trigger for some time, killing a lot of small game, owls, jack rabbits, chucks, snakes, a few eagles and bobcats and one running coyote at 400 yards, but finally decided I would have to drop the system if I were to keep my hand in with other guns. For the gun fighter using but the one type of gun, the S. A. slip gun is a good one, but he will have to stick to that one type of weapon. It is not as fast for the first shot as conventional trigger guns unless fitted with the Berns hammer spur and a trigger, which must be held back after the first shot. I found that for me, the best system of using the slip gun was to fit the hammer with a second extended pin at the extreme top of the hammer, high enough for regular fanning for the first shot and then to shift to one handed slip shooting with the lower hammer spur gripped by the last joint of the thumb. It worked out very well, was fast, eliminated the trigger and sear, and made the trigger half of the bolt spring inactive. It gave me a regular S. A. Colt without trigger for conventional fanning while the lower spur could be used for accurately aimed slip hammer fire. It was practical and worked well, but it so seriously handicapped me when using conventional trigger guns that I was regretfully forced to give it up.

John Newman would have nothing else and used .22 caliber S. A. Colts for practice and the .45 Colt for serious business. He was a mighty competent gun fighter, accurate and deadly with the .45 slip guns which he always carried in pairs.

The movies have done much to make fanning popular. The great picture, Shane, depicted the star fanning a long 7½ inch S. A. Colt.

In fanning a single action, the gun is drawn and poked at the target just the same as you would throw a standard single action at a target with one hand, but instead of cocking the gun, the gun hand merely grasps the gun and draws and pokes it at the target while the other hand comes back over the top of the gun in a quick slapping motion, the palm catching the hammer spur and pulling it back to full cock and releasing it, the trigger finger holding the trigger back at the same time. The single action can be emptied faster this way than by any other known method and the accuracy well trained men attain is surprising at close range. I have seen several advocates of this type of shooting good enough to cut a man in two up to ten or fifteen yards with that burst of fire, and do it every time.

Fanners never could do the fine shooting so often depicted in the movies, but they could salivate an adversary, if near, very quickly. Although fast for those who have practiced it long enough, it definitely is not as fast for the first shot as a single action, drawn and shot with one hand only. Ed McGivern practiced fanning for a considerable time, finding that the truth lay somewhere in between the two extremes. It was not as fast as his double action draws for the first shot, and not nearly as accurate, but it was fast and accurate enough for a short range man killing job. Fanning a single action requires two hands, and if one hand is otherwise engaged or has been hit with a bullet, it would be out of the question. Likewise two hand work is not as fast as the lightning swift draw of one well trained hand. The trigger must be held back, removed from the gun or taped back against the rear of the trigger guard. The hard slapping blow on the hammer jerks the cylinder around to place and is hard on both the ratchet and the tip of the hand. It is also hard on the bolt, bolt cuts in the cylinder and the bolt spring, as well as the bolt arm.

Keith in Montana with bobcat killed with .45 Colt 1917.

Parts will break from this hard useage and the bolt cuts will soon fit the bolt loosely. I would never allow anyone to fan a single action of my own that I cared anything about. Walter Rogers uses this method for his first shot draw, shooting from the hip. If the trigger is removed and the sear and hammer notches eliminated, there is not so much to go wrong with the gun but it must be understood, fanning is hard on any gun.

One old Texas gun fighter told me of having to trail up and kill an outlaw who always fanned his single action which had no trigger. The fight started at about 60 yards. He said he drew, used both hands, aimed and fired once and killed him, but he was nicked twice and said the air seemed full of slugs while he aimed and fired that one shot from his .45.

Fanning a single action will produce more broken and worn parts than any other method of shooting we know of, and we do not recommend it.

The single action Colt is one of the safest guns ever invented for the cavalryman or horseman. Just one shot can be fired with each pull of the trigger and another pull on the trigger cannot fire a second shot until the arm is manually cocked again. For this reason, it is a safe gun for the man who may have to manage a bad horse at the same time. Often horses hit in gun fights began to pitch and the rider is better off with a single action than a double action or automatic which he might fire accidentally in the scrimmage. The old single action points so naturally, it is an easy gun to use from a fast moving horse when hits must be made. Shooting from a running horse is fast becoming a lost art. The rider should lean forward and throw the gun toward the target in a sort of chopping motion, shooting at the end of it. More hits will be made by this method than any other from a fast moving horse traversing rough country. We have run down enough coyotes to know. One is lost trying to aim a sixgun from a hard running horse, as there is enough jar and motion to keep the gun bouncing up and down, but one can swing his arm and gun toward the target and throw a slug into it quite easily at close range.

I once had a little cow horse in Montana that dearly loved to chase coyotes or jack rabbits. He was very fast and if we could get within 200 yards of a coyote and have half a mile to go he would usually catch up with him. We would sail over a four strand barbed wire fence like a bird and when he got close to a coyote or I hit the yellow sage wolf with a slug, that little devil of a horse would strike at him as we went over him. He was wicked with his front feet and if he could hit a coyote he would roll him every time. Several times when I had emptied the gun at one and had hit him once, the little horse would finish the job with his forefeet.

One day Father borrowed him to ride to Winston for the mail. Though he had pitched with me every

Fanning the S.A. Colt .44/40, Ed McGivern shooting.

time I rode him for over a year, he had finally decided to quit bucking. I used only a hackamore on him and never allowed anyone to ride him, but weakened this day. As Father rode slowly across a big hay meadow, a coyote jumped out of a deep irrigation ditch. The little horse took after him and Father could not hold him with the hackamore. Coming to a barbed wire fence the coyote went under and the horse and father sailed over the top. He ran him another quarter mile across another hay meadow and was striking at the coyote with his front feet when it dived into a grove of quaking aspens. Dad never asked to ride Snake again after that experience.

Given a half mile of smooth running, Snake would catch a big Montana jack rabbit. Many a time we let him out after one and would kill it with the sixgun when we got close and the rabbit had laid his ears back and started to dodge from one side to the other. The horse would swing his head to one side as I shot, but never lost sight of his quarry and seemingly enjoyed the chase as much as did the crazy cow-poke who broke and rode him. I tried all manner of ways of shooting from a running horse. I tried pointing the gun and aiming, usually missing, and the old cow-punchers method of simply throwing a slug the same as throwing a rock, by a sort of chopping motion. Then business picked up. We also ran wild horses in those days, and many times I have turned a bunch that were getting away by throwing heavy .45 slugs in front of them, kicking up the dust and turning them in the direction we wanted them to go.

The Civil War and the Indian campaigns produced many cavalrymen who could do very creditable shooting from the back of a running horse. I was lucky enough when I was a boy to witness several demonstrations by these old troopers. They would gallop past a rock, tree or fence post and "throw down" on it, as we have described in the coyote shooting paragraphs. They were good, make no mistake on that score, and seldom missed a man sized target. It was these veterans of many a now forgotten skirmish who taught me to shoot from a horse in motion.

Sometimes we had to kill a wild scrub stallion that was stealing mares from the ranches for his harem. A horse is hard to kill. You can stop him only with a slug along the line of the spine or a brain hit and you have to be fairly close to do so with a sixgun. A couple bullets through the lungs will slow him down in time until you can get close enough to make a killing shot. The best method we ever found of hitting anything from a fast moving horse is the old cowboy-cavalry style of throwing slugs with that chopping motion and the arm fully extended toward the target. It is really a pointing motion, bringing the gun down in line with the target, and works where every other method fails.

When I was a boy, I let off steam by running a bunch of broncs in the corral and roping and riding everything that looked mean, or by chasing coyotes with horses and killing them with sixguns or trying to rope them. Today boys get their fun by fast driving in modern autos, causing too many needless wrecks, or by driving slowly up and down the streets, whistling at the girls. I believe the old Western recreations produced more real men than the modern trend does.

To an old cow-puncher there is nothing quite like getting up before daylight, eating a big steak and dutch oven biscuits with strong coffee. Then, as the horse herd comes in, roping a mount and saddling him, stepping in a good fitting saddle and feeling the lithe, bone jarring jumps of the bronc as he lets you know he is ready to buck you off or start his day's work. Then riding through the sage-scented high mountain air and watching the sun break over the eastern mountains, as you start the day's long circle. I would not trade the memories of that life for anything we now have to offer youngsters.

Single actions are slow to load from a moving horse as you have to open the loading gate, pull the hammer to half cock, or hold it in that position if you have filed away the safety and half cock notches, while you poke out the empties with the ejector rod and catch and pocket them if you reload. Then you have to pull cartridges from your gun belt, fill the five chambers and let the hammer down on the empty one. With the side-swing modern double actions you merely unlatch the cylinder and knock all empties out with a blow from the palm of the hand, refill the chambers and latch the cylinder. With the auto pistol you can drop out the clip, pocket it, slip in a new clip, pull the slide, let it go forward and push up the safety, and you are reloaded. Just the same, the old single action is the safest gun to use while riding a mean or high spirited horse.

Most horses are gun shy at first. We used to rope and throw them, then sit on their heads while we engaged in target practice. We would shoot from them at every jack rabbit we could jump until they would merely swing their heads away from the blast when they saw or sensed the gun coming out of the holster. Never shoot right over or past a horse's ears if it can be avoided as it will, in time, deafen him. Treat him with due consideration as a partner, and you will have a pal for the rest of his life. I have had several shooting horses that enjoyed hunting as much as I did. Horses are intelligent and you must have at least as much mentality at they possess to properly train them to become shooting horses. I have had horses almost trample me out of my bed when a grizzly came near camp. They came to me for protection, believing the guns I carried would take care of any situation.

Chapter XIV

Loading and Management of Cap and Ball Sixguns

DURING THE HEY DAY of the percussion revolver, paper cartridges were furnished in little wooden containers with a space for each. The box was milled from solid wood and split, and a paper wrapper was glued over it with a thread at the joint which could be pulled, thus separating the two halves and opening the six shot cartridge box. Conical Colt bullets were used in these paper cartridges with a rebated heel, leaving room to glue the tip of the paper cylinder to the base of the bullet. The powder charge was poured in the other end of the rolled paper cylinder which was folded over a couple times to seal it, the bullet was dipped in melted wax or tallow and the cartridge was complete. These conical pointed bullets gave more range and penetration than round balls, but never were as accurate in our guns, nor did they kill game as well as the round ball. The pointed bullets seemingly slipped through game with a very small wound channel while the blunt round ball at fairly high volocity, tore a good wound channel all the way.

One can still make paper cartridges for any caliber cap and ball sixgun today by this method, but I much prefer to load round balls and powder from a flask with a proper charger. The most accurate method of loading these guns is to use a round ball of pure lead, backed by a heavy charge of black powder and a greased felt wad between powder and the ball. I have tried many types of conical bullets but the round ball seemed to always beat them for groups. The guns were for the most part, cut with a gain twist, which certainly is right for any revolver and would, I believe, be a big improvement on modern revolvers. The bullets jump straight forward from their seat in the chamber and are going straight ahead when they take the rifling, so it is only reasonable that the rifling should also start straight and gradually increase in pitch as it nears the muzzle or steering end of the barrel. In this way the balls or bullets are perfectly engraved with the rifling without any slippage or skidding. They then make a perfect gas seal and leave the muzzle in more accurate form.

I would like to see modern revolvers cut with a gain twist. Of course, to use a gain twist, the projectile must have a short bearing surface like a round ball or have a set of narrow rotating bands to take the rifling so the pitch can change without skidding or slippage. The usual grooved modern revolver bullet with its several groove diameter rotating bands, not unlike an artillery shell, is ideal for gain twist rifling. In this respect the old percussion pistols were superior in design to modern guns but gain twists are slow and hard to cut, and for this reason went into the discard along with the old guns. Long ungrooved bullets would not work well in a gain twist barrel, since the front would be trying to turn faster than the base, and one end or the other would have to slip or skid to get the slug through the bore. Round balls with their short bearing or bullets with cannellures and several groove diameter bands will work much better in gain twist than in conventional barrels.

Caliber markings on cap and ball guns are seldom correct. The various .36 Navies run from .38 to .40 caliber. The .44's usually run a full .454 or larger. I have one Colt .28 caliber and one Colt .30 caliber in my collection.

The old guns should be thoroughly checked to see that the chambers are in good condition and not deeply pitted. I have known of some cylinders that were rusted throught between the chambers and when fired all the charges would go at once. This is very dangerous. If the chambers are clean, the nipples also in good condition and the key holding the barrel and frame together tight and snug, you are all set to use the gun. Pitted barrels foul faster and are seldom as accurate as good barrels, but do not prevent use of the arm. A powder flask with a charge cup on the end of it is almost a necessity, both to carry the powder and also to dispense it in proper charges. Without a proper powder flask, a small bottle can be used with an empty pistol cartridge case for a charger.

Nipples vary in size and percussion caps from 9 to 12 will fit about any size sixgun nipples. The No. 12 I have is marked Colt, and it fits a big Dragoon revolver. One should select a cap size that is a snug push fit on the nipples, but not tight enough to prevent their seating fully down on the nipple. A couple times I have had muzzle loading rifles fire when I pressed the cap down too hard on the nipple. The

Keith at Work.

the gun. I once had the bottom chamber of a .36 Navy go off and drive the ball into the recess in the rammer, expanding it until it was next to impossible to remove and had to be turned down again before it would work. Multiple discharge must be avoided at all costs as it is not conducive to longevity, nor will it leave the guns in good shape for posterity.

If the nipples are in bad shape with cracked, chipped, rusted, or badly battered edges, they should be replaced before the gun is used. Sometimes they are very hard to remove, even with a nipple wrench. If Penetrene or soaking in coal oil fails to loosen them, then heat must be applied to the cylinder to break up the rust scale. E. M. Farris & Sons, Portsmouth, Ohio, and other firms usually carry supplies of pistol nipples. Any good gunsmith can make them. They should be examined to see that the hole is not too large from the cap seat down to the power chamber. Usually all that is needed is a good funnel at the rear end of nipple to carry the flash, and squirt it through a very small orifice into the powder chamber. If the center and forward portion of the nipple carries a small hole, so much the better as less powder gas comes back from the discharge. Too large a flash hole all the way through the nipples means a lot of gas to the rear; the caps are blown to pieces, and sometimes the hammer is partly raised from the pressure. Once you determine that the nipples are in good shape and find caps that fit them correctly, you are then ready to proceed with the loading of your cap and ball sixgun.

Cast the round balls of pure lead, preferably in a mould of exactly the same size as the original moulds furnished with the pistols, or with the originals. The balls should be slightly oversize to make a perfect seal and also to afford a slightly longer bearing surface for the rifling. The mouths of the chambers are chambered slightly larger than the bore and a round ball of correct size should only start in the chamber mouth with hard thumb pressure. It is best to seat them with the sprue cut forward so the base will be unmarred and true in shape.

Next take an old felt hat, a thick heavy one, or similar heavy felt material an eighth inch thick, if you can find it, and soak it in a mixture of melted tallow and beeswax. If you do not have the wax, then deer, elk, beef or mutton tallow will do. When cold and hard, take a slightly oversize wad cutter and cut wads. You can get wad cutters, also moulds, from the Lyman Gunsight Corp., Middlefield, Connecticut, for any caliber cap and ball gun. The wad should be slightly larger than the chamber bore.

The wads can be packed in empty cap boxes or typewriter ribbon cans and the bullets carried in old Civil War bullet pouches, any sack or container, or loose in the pocket.

Now we are ready to load. First see that all nipples are clear, either with a long pin or by blowing through

caps were a bit small and I forced them down, splitting them. Each time they fired from this pressure with the ball of my thumb, they raised instantly a healthy blister. So be careful to get caps that will fit snug and tight, but which will also seat easily. Never try to use a Percussion sixgun with loose caps as recoil of one charge will jar the cap on another chamber; the flash may get into it and fire a second or third chamber at the same time. I have had it happen. Also I have had caps that were too small and did not seat fully, fire the charge of other chambers from recoil which threw them back against the frame of them. Hold the muzzle up with the gun at half-cock so the cylinder will revolve freely. Pour in the powder charge (it should almost fill the chamber) leaving room only for the greased felt wad. Place a single greased wad on top the powder, start the round ball down in the cylinder mouth with the ball of the thumb, then turn it under the rammer and ram it home so the powder is tightly compressed and the ball seated just below the mouth of the chamber. The ball will be upset somewhat in the process and this helps make a certain seal at the front end of the load against flash back from the discharge of other chambers. Repeat the procedure until all six chambers are fully loaded, then latch up the rammer, turn the muzzle away from you and cap each nipple, being sure they are fully down in place on the nipples. Let the hammer down between nipples on the safety pin provided for the tiny notch in the center of the bottom tip of the hammer or, if this is gone, just let the hammer rest between nipples and your cap and ball sixgun is ready for action.

If unable to get heavy felt for the greased wads, use a double thickness of lighter felt. If you wish to play with something less than the maximum load, place a dry wad or two under the greased wads. In any event, the powder charge must be compressed. The charge should always stop the loading lever before it comes to the end of its movement.

Powder should be the best black powder in shiny black granulations, free from dust and dirt and size F.F.F.G., for the very small calibers such as .28 and .31, and F.F.G., for the .36 and .44 caliber guns. A percussion sixgun thus loaded will shoot clean all day if you blow your breath through the bore a few times after each six rounds are fired. It will also shoot very accurately if it is a good gun.

Under no circumstances should you ever load a percussion pistol with anything but black powder. Don't even think of trying bulk smokeless shotgun powder. This and the pistol and rifle smokeless powders in common use are certain to wreck the gun. These guns were made decades before smokeless powder was thought of. They will not take it. There are no exceptions to the rule. It is final.

I had one .36 Navy Colt that had a pitted barrel, but with the above load it would cut clover leaves for its six shots, at 20 yards, all day with seated back and head rest and two hands used between the knees to further holding. It was my first good sixgun and the good Lord only knows how many grouse and rabbits and other small game I killed with the gun. Finally Maurice C. Clark, a friend from Bozeman, Montana, had to have a .36 Navy to fill an order and offered me a brand new Army Colt .38 Special for it and we swapped. I have regretted it the rest of my life. The modern Colt never did shoot as well as the old Navy.

Cap and ball guns will collect fouling in the action after repeated firing. The best way to clean them is to remove the barrel by driving out the wedge key with a hardwood drift thus removing the barrel and cylinder. Heat a pan of water until it boils and soak both barrel and cylinder in this, then scrub them out with a bristle brush and let them dry by their own heat. If the action is badly fouled it is best to remove stocks and straps and the internal parts, the hand, bolt, trigger and bolt spring and carefully clean them with hot water and dry them. Then oil and put them back together. Oil the chambers and barrel or wipe them with a rag dampened with solvent and then a dry rag inside the chambers. Coat the base pin, on which the cylinder revolves, with a heavy cup or gun grease, and replace cylinder, barrel and key. Next reload your gun and it is again ready for action. The loads may remain in the gun for years and still fire perfectly if the loading has been done as above directed.

Sut Ellis of Winston, Montana, an old buffalo hunter, once told me of having a running fight with a band of horse stealing Indians on the north side of the Missouri below Winston. He and a band of hunters lost some horses to the Indians during the night and took up their trail at daylight. During the day they caught up with the band and engaged in a running fight. They shot a horse from under one Indian and he took to the rocks. He killed one of the whites before they got him through the head with a sixgun slug. Sut said they picked up their fallen buddy and buried him but never did bother to bury the Indian or even look him over as they again hurriedly took up the trail. He said he thought he could still find the place even though many years had elapsed and that he was going back over the scene of the fight that summer.

I told him to get the Indian's gun if he could find it. A month later when I went to town for my mail, Sut gave me an Indian's skull with a .45 slug hole through it and an old Colt .36 caliber revolving rifle, with the stock in two pieces at the grip from weathering and a possible fracture when he dropped it. Three of the chambers were still fully loaded. He said the gun, the skull and most of the bones were still there wedged between some big rocks. Mother did not like that gruesome memento of the fight laying around the house so I gave both the gun and the skull to Will H. Everson of Bozeman, Montana. The old Colt revolving rifle was, as one would expect, a hopelessly rusted wreck.

For its size and weight nothing is so deadly as the round ball of pure lead when driven at fairly good velocity. Maximum loads give these slugs fairly high velocity from a 7½ inch barrel gun. Both Major R. E. Stratton and Samuel H. Fletcher told me the .36 Navy with full loads was a far better man killer than any .38 Special they had ever seen used in gun fights.

The barrel must be kept tight on the frame and

Left to right: Ted Keith, Anita Hays, and Lorraine Keith having some informal tin can practice.

if the long slot in the base pin becomes worn, sometimes it is necessary to cut out the hole in the frame slightly so that the wedge key will surely pull the barrel and frame tightly together. Also at times a new key must be made to properly draw them together. Frame pins can be replaced if worn, and the holes below the rammer can be drilled out and trued up for larger pins if necessary.

The so-called .44 caliber guns were really .45's, and quite powerful weapons when fully loaded. Many a buffalo was killed from horseback with the heavy Colt Dragoons using the round ball and 50 grains of F.F.G. black powder. The big guns would drive the ball well through the lungs of a running buffalo at a few feet range. I had one old Dragoon at one time that had killed a number of the big California grizzlies. The owner used to bait them and sit up in a tree above the bait on moonlight nights and shoot down into the back of their heads.

Remington, Starr and some other percussion revolvers had a top strap and a groove for a rear sight and usually were fairly well sighted except that practically all percussion sixguns shot high. They were designed as man killing weapons and sighted high purposely so that one would have a longer effective point blank range on a man target. Nearly all of them must be resighted for game or target shooting. The Colts, Manhattans and some others had no strap over the chamber and usually carried the rear sight in the nose of the hammer. I have seen a few of them that shot just right to this sighting, but on most of them the hammer notch rear sight was off to one side or the other when they were at full cock, and the front sight was nearly always too low, and they shot too high for any practical purpose other than gun fighting.

Resighting hurts their value to collectors, but is necessary if you would do good shooting with them. The best way to do it is to fit a small dovetail front and rear sight to the barrel alone. Then the front sight can be filed down until it is exactly right at 20 yards, or 50 yards as you may prefer, and the rear sight notch cut out to suit the individual preference as to shape and width. So sighted, the old guns will do very fine work. For years I carried a solid ivory stocked .31 caliber 1849 Pocket Colt in a saddle pocket in order to shoot trapped bobcats, coyotes, skunks, eagles, etc. A .31 round ball driven into the front of the chest, or the butt of the ear, did not damage the skin, and when placed right, killed very quickly and saved possible escape of many animals whose toes were so nearly worn off from fighting the trap that one good pull would have freed them.

A Montana friend trapped a big golden eagle and, as he had a sale for a live eagle, he worked a gunny sack over the bird and tied him on behind the cantle of his saddle and started back to Winston with him. Several of us who were in the town that day were amazed to see Bert's old mule come pitching down the street, bucking for all it was worth, with the saddle under its belly, but with a gunny sack extending from the saddle strings up to the mule's back. There was no sign of the rider and we could not imagine what had happened. We roped the mule and threw her, then hog tied her to keep her flying feet in place while we uncinched the saddle. Then we saw one corner of the sack extending up to the mule's back and long talons were sunk in around the back bone. I put a couple .45's through the sack to sort of limber up whatever was in it. Then we slit the sack with a knife and found the big golden eagle. The claws were sunk into the mule right around the vertebrae in a death grip and we had to unjoint the leg and pull the tendons to retract those long claws from the mule. Bert was mad as the devil when he came limping into town for he had not only been thrown into a patch of cactus but also had his eagle killed in the deal. No doubt the poor mule was glad to get rid of both riders. He said the eagle must have worked one foot around until it straddled the mule's back behind the saddle skirts and then he clamped down. The mule had gone crazy and threw Bert high, and into a big patch of prickly pear. I would have enjoyed seeing that ride.

One trapper at Winston said he never used a gun on trapped bobcats but always killed them with a club. I did not like a big blood clot on the top of the scalp when I skinned mine so usually shot them through the heart from the front. One day this lad came into Winston nearly dead from loss of blood. The meat was all torn from his ribs on one side, and his face was badly chewed. His clothes were almost non-existent. He said he had trapped a big cat down Beaver Creek and had picked up a big black birch stick for a club. Black birch, laying on the ground, rots very quickly. When he hit the cat over the head the club broke and the cat was on him in a flash. The old Victor No. 3 trap came apart at the first lunge and the cat raised merry hell with the lad, biting him in the cheek and shoulder and arm the while he played a tattoo on his ribs with his terrible ripping hind feet. The cat finally desisted probably thinking him dead, and left. We prefer to sixgun trapped bobcats.

A lot of fun and good shooting can be had from muzzle loading sixguns. True, they are dirty and throw a big cloud of smoke, but that same smoke cloud or screen was often an advantage to the old gun fighter as he could see through his own gun smoke much better than an adversary some distance away could, and for this reason many of the old timers preferred black powder for a sixgun. In a low ceilinged room, a few shots from a black powder sixgun lays down such a smoke screen that you can only see when you are down next to the floor. At night the blast of the first shot would put out all the kerosene lamps from concussion.

If one or more chambers of a cap and ball pistol have been fired, never start to recharge them without first removing the live caps from the nipples behind the unfired chambers. This is not merely a safety precaution; it is a life saver. You place the gun at half cock to freely revolve the cylinder for loading and are holding a loaded, cocked gun pointing at you. Do you see why the caps must come off first?

Percussion pistols in good working condition are not just century old relics; they are very deadly weapons. Great grand dad was far from being disarmed or helpless with a cap and ball pistol, fully loaded and capped, swinging from his hip.

Chapter XV

Repairs, Remodeling, Resighting

MANY SECOND HAND or used guns are bought or traded each year and the buyer should know how to properly examine them before purchase. In the old cap and ball Colts, which often run into considerable value, one cannot be too careful as there are a great many frauds. Many Walkers, Dragoons, Wells Fargo and 1848 Pocket Colts have been faked or used to make fakes, such as using two Dragoons to make up a Walker Colt. X-Ray pictures of these guns may be very enlightening. They will show welds where no weld should be and one can see how the deceit has been accomplished. Sections of two Dragoon cylinders have been welded or silver soldered together, and the lug spliced out to Walker length by addition of another section of Dragoon lug. Barrel lugs have been bored out to receive nine inch sections of Colt rifle barrels and new barrels, with lugs, have been made, machined to shape and rifled, some with gain twist as in the original. All collectors and students of old guns naturally frown on counterfeiting rare arms, but it has been done, and in quantity. Some good looking and apparently genuine Walker Colts have turned up with a certain serial number and later another was located with the same serial, or company number, proving one to be an imposter. Walkers were numbered by Companies, and the serial is very short as a rule, usually under the number 200 and preceded by the Company letter, A.B.C.D.E.F. etc.

I once owned A. Co. No. 90, a cut off, badly rusted, then polished and reblued wreck. I traded it to a man in Vermont, getting nicely stung in the deal. The next time I heard of A. Company No. 90 Walker was from F. Theodore Dexter, who wrote me for the dope on it and its condition when I owned it. Naturally I told him the truth. The gun, as I shipped it, had the barrel cut back to 6½ inches and had been buffed and blued until the Company number, A 90, was very shallow and in places obliterated. When Mr. Dexter purchased the weapon it was in new condition with a nine inch barrel, complete in every respect. The markings were sharp and clear including U. S. 1847 over the latch. On the face, it was a good specimen but he did not try to sell it as he easily could have. He promptly exposed the fake.

I cannot condone such reworking of an old wreck to make it appear to be a valuable, new condition specimen. Many Walker and Dragoon parts such as frames, straps, cylinders and possibly a few barrels were in storage in the government arsenals and these have been bought up and used to rebuild and imitate original Company numbered guns.

Other gunsmiths have made Walkers from scratch and given them a false Company number. I have seen some that were not made at the Colt factory, yet appeared to have been, and have also seen S. A. Colts machined from solid steel that were identical with the original execpt for methods of manufacture. This is where the Colt expert can tell the fake from the original. Methods of rusting and ageing have also been developed until it requires the services of an expert to tell the real from the bogus. One should never buy a rare Colt without having it carefully examined by an expert and preferably by two or three.

The Wells Fargo Colt is rare and the 1848 Model pocket Colt is even harder to find. The 1849 Pocket Colt, which may be roughly described as an improved version of the two models just mentioned, is comparatively numerous and consequently much lower in price. Quite a few 1849 guns have had the rammer removed, the rammer hole filled, the barrel cut back and a pin from sight installed and have been otherwise tinkered up to resemble the more valuable previous models. The 1848 carries a square back trigger guard, round bolt stops on the cylinder, a very short curved trigger, and no roller in the hammer. The Wells Fargo is also made without a rammer but with larger trigger guard, round in shape, and with long trigger and square stops. Patterson Colts have been faked but the job is much more difficult and time consuming and is seldom attempted. A Colt authority can tell the frauds at a glance, almost, by the difference in machine marks.

Recently in Washington, D. C., I saw a gold brick Target S. A. Colt. It had been welded up and sights installed to represent the original flat-top target Colt S. A. Army, and with a strictly dishonest intent.

Back in the Twenties and before S. A. Colt guns became collectors' items, Harold Croft and the writer

Colt 1855 Root model cased with accessories.

had many Colts remodeled into flat-top target guns with the idea of improving the guns. Our guns were so different as to leave no doubt that they were made up to improve them and not to, in any way, imitate a factory model. The work was done by Houchins, Sedgley and O'Meara, and the guns flat-topped for Croft and me bear little resemblance to the original flat-top target S. A. Army and Bisley Colts. The frame was extended back further, different sights installed, and tops of the hammers cut off. They cannot be confused with the original flat top target models valued by collectors today, but are collectors' items in their own right. They were written up in *The American Rifleman* and other magazines and no informed person will mistake them for original models. However, unscrupulous gunsmiths have turned out many fake copies of the originals in the rarer models. Anyone who has made an imitation gun should plainly mark it with his name, the date of manufacture and leave it so the world will know it is a hand made model and not an original. The trouble starts when such models fall into the hands of rascally dealers who will make them appear as of original Colt manufacture. Even the Colt shoulder stocks have been made from scratch and numbered to correspond with an original Colt cut for the stock, and the stock screws added.

It is a curious fact that these counterfeiting gunsmiths could have made more money doing honest work than by engaging in disreputable business, but some mental twist prevents them from seeing it. As it is they have made gun collecting difficult and risky. The beginner should only buy from reputable dealers, not forgetting that they too, may have been deceived. If possible, before putting important money on the line, get the opinion of an experienced collector.

While this faking of rare Colts is common knowledge among Colt collectors and dealers, it is not generally known by the tyro Colt collector, and as more men take up the collection of Colts each year, it is only fair that they be warned of what to expect. I have seen little in print on the subject outside Collectors' magazines with small circulations. In buying any old Colt for a collection, look it over carefully as to serials and see that all are alike, as guns with like serials are of course, much more valuable than guns made up from scattered parts with different serials.

When purchasing a modern used gun, the gun should be carefully examined. If it is an auto pistol it should be checked for fit of slide on frame and for barrel wear especially in the throat; the barrel bushing and link should be examined if it is a Colt Government model. Barrel wear comes first in the throat of the barrel just forward of the chamber, and if the grooves are blackened here from escaping gas and the lands worn down flat, it should be either rejected or rebarreled. Check it for function firing to see that everything works right, and for accuracy.

Great Western double Derringer, this pilot model made from an original Remington. Note old firing pin cuts welded up and new center fire pins added.

In buying a used revolver, check it for cylinder alignment. With most guns if the light can be thrown just right, you can tell if barrel and cylinder line up and lock in line by looking down the muzzle of the piece. The piece should be fired and all fired cases carefully checked to see if they are normal in size for expanded cases and show no bulges or scratches. The chambers should also be carefully examined under a glass to see if there are any bulged bolt cuts. Barrel and cylinder clearance should be carefully checked; also the fit of the bolt in the bolt cuts on the cylinder. The chamber throats should be miked inside with an inside mike, or by upsetting a soft slug in them and then mikeing it for size, and the same should be done with the barrel by upsetting and driving a soft slug through the bore with a hard wood rod for a drift, then mikeing it for groove diameter and for comparison with chamber throats. Firing pins and recoil plates should be examined for pitting or cracks. Barrel and cylinder clearance should be checked and should go from .002 inches to not over .005 inches in most guns. Some good guns have up to .010 inches but that is more than needed. When barrel and cylinder clearance goes as much as .020 inches they should be rebarreled.

Barrel throats should be examined for wear or erosion and the full length of the barrel carefully examined for bulges caused by having a bullet stuck in the barrel and another slug fired on top of it, which will always ring or bulge the barrel. If you slug the bore, you will find the slug jumps when it comes to such an enlarged portion. Check the alignment of frame and barrel carefully. With the old cap and ball Colts and other percussion arms without top strap, it is very common to find them bent at the joint of the barrel lug and frame and the barrel pointing off toward Mother Jones' place. If they were dropped and a horse stepped on them, it would be easily done. I have seen new Officer's Model Colts with frame and barrel that did not line up right, requiring the rear sight to be moved well to one side before they would shoot in line. Turn down any such gun as it can never be as accurate as one whose barrel and cylinder properly line up. Cap and ball, and also late model guns have been ruined by banging some crook over the head. Hitting a man's skull with a sixgun is poor business and often causes bent barrels. Many S. A. Colt and Colt cap and ball sixguns have their stock straps badly sprung out of alignment from having been used to hit a man on the head with the butt, or from using the butt of the gun as a hammer. It is common in movies to see a sheriff nailing up wanted notices with the butt of his gun. I even saw one movie of a cow-poke pulling staples with his front sight, then walking his horse across the wire and driving the staples back in the post with the butt of his gun. Some of the guns we have examined must have been used by such nincompoops.

With single action guns, it is best to take them apart and examine the sear or the top of the trigger and the safety, and the half and full cock notches in the hamer to see if they are original or have been torn out and new ones filed in the hammer. Check the front sight for vertical alignment over the bore. If it projects up at an angle over the bore, better reject the gun. Many barrels are not correctly fitted and are turned either too far or not far enough, and for this reason the sight is not vertical over the bore and then has to be bent to make the gun shoot in line. Reject any gun with too light a trigger pull, or one that does not always want to stand cocked. Such arms are dangerous and need new sears or hammers. With swing-out cylinder double action guns check the fit and locking of the crane. It should latch up solid and tight, and if loose at the front end, as many old Colt guns are, it should be rejected. Smiths & Wessons seldom get loose in the crane due to their front cylinder lock. Check the base pin or extractor for straightness when the cylinder is revolved. Many Colt base pins, or extractors, have been bent by hitting a man over the head with the gun. Incidentally, if you have to hit a man with your gun, always retain your regular grip on the revolver butt and hit him with the front bottom of the frame and even then you may bend or spring a barrel. Never reverse the gun and hit with the butt as he may grab it and shoot you.

Always retain your proper grip on the gun so it can be used as a gun, if it becomes necessary.

Check the base pin bushing on Colt and Great Western single actions. It should be the full length of the frame so the cylinder has no end play. If the cylinder can be moved back and forth, then a new base pin bushing is necessary. The base pin fit itself should be examined, and if the holes through the front and rear of the frame are worn, a larger base pine should be turned up to fit snugly. Base pin latches should also be checked; this can best be done by firing a few heavy loads. If the base pin kicks out of its seat and moves ahead from recoil, you need a stronger base pin catch spring or a new base pin, or both. The old screw front base pin catch was much the stronger and the best, but required a screw driver to loosen so the base pin could be extracted and the cylinder removed.

All end play should also be checked on double action revolver cylinders. Reject any gun with end play of the cylinder. If possible, shoot the gun for group as many revolvers of older manufacture and some not so old, have one or more chambers that do not properly line up with the barrel. These can be checked by firing groups with each chamber, marking the outside with a crayon until you determine if all chambers shoot to the same sighting. If one or more are out of alignment, which may be caused either by improperly positioned bolt cuts or by the boring not being exactly in proper alignment, it will usually show up, not only in the grouping but also by spitting and by a greater lead deposit on one side of the chamber mouth and barrel throat than on the other. A bullet cannot turn a corner and be delivered in its true form into the barrel, and any gun that tries to do it should be rejected. If fired cases eject hard, either singly or six simultaneously, the arm almost certainly has damaged or rough chambers, either from careless machining or rust, or it was swelled by excessive loads. All empty cases should extract freely and easily.

Check the bores and remember, a pitted or rough

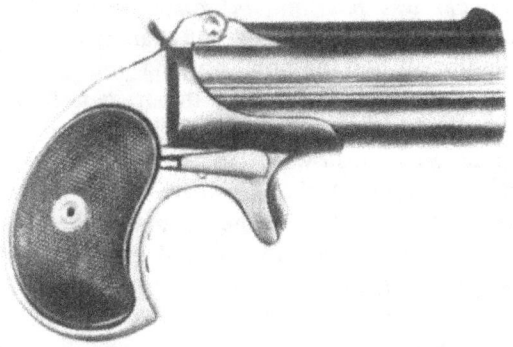

Great Western double Derringer in .38 caliber made by remodelling the Remington .41 Rim fire. This one is in .41 center fire, but new gun will be in .38 caliber. Note extra heavy lump at hinge joint. This gun to be in production in 90 days and 500 are to be made in first lot. Should make nice ladies' handbag gun.

barrel will lead much more easily than a smooth bore. Guns with too great a discrepancy between chamber throat diameter and barrel groove diameter should be rejected. Excessive resizing of a bullet in the barrel throat is not conducive to accuracy. Carefully examine the rear end of all revolver barrels to see if they have been bulged or cracked from excessively heavy loads. A crack here may indicate a chamber out of line or a cylinder with side play. Also check the muzzle of the barrel as that is the steering end, and if it has been burred or battered it will have to be recrowned or replaced. In conclusion, do not waste money on cheap imitations of Spanish, German, or other foreign manufacture. Buy only the best American makes in used guns, and only after careful examination and a test on the target.

Used guns are best repaired at the factory where they were made—another reason for buying standard American makes. The next best way is a competent pistolsmith who thoroughly understands the work.

Whenever a hand, bolt, trigger, or hammer becomes worn or the sear notches cracked or broken, it is best to have new ones installed. The same is true of all vital parts in either revolver or auto pistol. Replace with new parts rather than by welding and refitting old parts. Sometimes it is impossible to obtain new parts, as with many early Colts, and they must be made by hand. Christy Gun Works, 875 57th, Sacramento, California, has made hand fitted parts for many guns for a long time. Pachmayr Gun Works, 1220 So. Grand Ave., Los Angeles, California, has done a great deal of this work. We also have many pistolsmiths scattered over the country who do such work and are fine workmen. When the factory has the parts and will accept the job, they are usually the best bet, but when they do not have the parts one must find a pistolsmith or a firm specializing in gun repair.

The Colt single action is prone to break several small parts; the bolt and bolt spring in particular, and the sear or top of the trigger, and the hammer notches. The bolt itself is weak. Much breakage is due to careless handling or mistreatment of the gun such as fanning or pulling the hammer partly back and letting it fall without holding the trigger back. In this case either the top of the trigger, that is—the sear, or the hammer notches usually suffered. The Colt single action bolt, however, is frail and cut out square at the rear end. If the arms are both tapered from the rear solid portion to the tips, and the square cut in the middle changed to a round cut, the chances of breakage are greatly lessened. Also if the cam stud on the right side of the hammer is cut down to about half of its original length, leaving just the width of the bolt arm, it does not put as much strain on the bolt arm when it cams up over the stud, and will greatly lessen the likelihood of fracturing the bolt arm. The bolt spring itself is stamped out of spring steel, and if both the trigger and bolt arms of this spring are tapered in thickness from their rounded base to their tips, they will stand a great deal more use without breaking. The cut in their middle should also be filed round instead of square.

Bill Ruger eliminated all the flat springs from the Ruger Single Six and fitted it with coil springs. At an N.R.A. meeting in Washington, D. C., he had a machine powered by an electric motor which cocked and snapped a Ruger Single Six all day long just as fast as the gun would operate for the full seven days of the exhibit. It was a notable demonstration of the reliability which perfect design and expert engineering produces. I seriously doubt if any other make of single action revolver would have lasted through that thoroughly exhaustive test. Ruger's improvements clearly show what can be done with single action guns to make them almost unbreakable. Sedgley once built a single action, with all coil springs, from an old Colt, and Ralph Pike of Kalispell, Montana, makes a bolt spring for the S. A. Colt of the coil variety that is unbreakable. The same spring can be made to handle both the bolt and trigger, and has been done by Herb Bradley of Salmon, Idaho. It eliminates all breakage of the bolt and trigger spring. Great Western is now experimenting with further improvement of their springs, and the elimination or improvement of all parts likely to break under continued usage.

When it comes to the hammer notches and sear in a single action, not much can be done, as the trigger half, or sear, is small and narrow and thin, and is liable to breakage. Great Western uses beryllium copper for their bolts, triggers and hands as they have found it much more shock resistant and less liable to metallic fatigue. The safety and full cock notches can be removed from the hammer. It makes the gun much harder to load or unload, as you must hold it manually at half cock, but it does eliminate most of the chances of breakage. A hammer with both safety and half cock notches removed is fool proof as there is no place for the sear to engage except at full cock. There is no chance of breaking off the sear top of the trigger or breaking out the safety and half cock notches, as they are non-existant. Such treatment of the S. A. complicates loading and ejecting empties, but certainly removes most of the chance of sear breakage. Great Western now has a new design of sear hammer and trigger that are not so delicate as the old Colt.

With the later single action Colts having the spring plunger base pin catch, the base pin is likely to kick ahead under the recoil of heavy loads. The other style frame, where a simple set screw locked the base pin in place, was much the best. When the new type base pin catch is used, one must often replace the spring with a stronger spring to be sure of enough tension to hold the base pin. Croft and the writer remodeled one single action with a turning cross bolt or lever that locked securely in the cut in the base pin, absolutely preventing its ever kicking ahead, and the arm of the lever was in turn locked by a small spring plunger like that of the breech block lever pin on the old Sharps side hammer. It has worked the best of any base pin catch we have ever seen and is a great improvement over the existing Colt and Great Western, or Ruger base pin catches.

In the eighties Colt made an excellent flat-top target single action in both the Army and Bisley models. Why they ever dropped production of these great guns is an unsolved mystery. While a great improvement over the standard models, there was still room for improvement and Harold Croft and I did do considerable modernization of the single action along the lines of the flat-top Frontier and Bisley models. We extended the flat-top frame farther to the rear and cut off the top of the hammer spur so it would go under it and fitted adjustable rear sights for windage in the extreme rear of the frame. We also fitted front sights in barrel bands with the first of the sloping or ramp type of front sights, later to be called the Baughman front sight. We had front sights both fixed, and with elevation incorporated in them similiar to the old Officer's model Colt, and I had one made up with a three leaf folding rear sight for various ranges. Though we offered Colt a loan of the lot of them, to study our improvements with a view to improving and modernizing the old gun, they never took us up on our offer, and allowed the gun to slowly die out for lack of advertising and improvements in its basic design, essentially that of 1847.

We further improved the gun by cutting off the Bisley hammer spurs and dovetailing and brazing them into S. A. Army hammers to give a much lower and nicer shaped hammer spur well below the line of sights. We also had wide triggers made that exactly contoured and fitted the trigger finger. In addition we tried a three point main spring which greatly speeded up lock time, and we drilled holes through the hammer to lighten it where it would not in any way weaken the hammer. Our flat-top target models with extended sight radius, wide trigger and Bisley-type hammer, improved base pin catch, main spring and bolt spring, greatly improved the old gun. Herbert Bradley made the first coil bolt springs we tried. Had the old gun been changed at the Colt factory at that time to our design, and properly advertised, it would still be one of the best selling guns they ever turned out.

Today Bill Ruger, still behind on orders for his Single Six .22 caliber, has developed the best target single action we have seen. This first one is in .357 magnum caliber, but other calibers will follow. Ruger has brought out the new gun along the lines of our design, and has dropped the micro rear sight down flush with the top of the flat-top frame and fitted a Micro ramp type front of one-eighth inch width. He still has not improved the hammer spur, nor fitted a wide trigger. But his all coil spring action leaves little to be desired as it is practically unbreakable. We will soon see in production a Ruger single action chambered for the most useful big calibers. It will be a fine target sighted accurate gun and a great improvement over the old Colt.

The Great Western Arms Company of California is now turning out better finished and fitted single actions than any we have seen from Colt. Arms making was a new venture with this company and they had a lot to learn about it. Their first arms were not properly timed, adjusted or fitted, but all the late production I have examined have been satisfactorily fitted and timed and extremely well polished and blued.

Great Western supplies their single action in all the barrel lengths and calibers that were formerly produced by Colt, and some new ones such as the Hornet, the .30 Carbine and the .357 Atomic. They use the finest of steels so the present Great Western is a stronger arm than the original Colt and will take higher pressures before the cylinder or rear end of the barrel will rupture. They have made many tests to find out exactly what their product will stand, and today it will safely take as heavy pressures as any sixgun ever produced.

The Great Western Target single action uses Micro sights both front and rear. The top of the frame is milled off flat, and the rear sight installed with two screws through the top strap. The front ramp is fitted to the barrel about one-fourth inch back from the muzzle, giving the shooter excellent adjustable target sights, but rather high ones. Target sighted models may be had in 4¾ inch, 5½ inch, and 7½ inch barrel lengths, and the fixed sight model resembling the Colt in appearance is made in 3½ inch without the ejector rod and in the three standard lengths of barrel as well.

Colt people are now thinking seriously of going back to Colt single action production, and in fact, put on a straw vote for all members on whether they desired the gun to be produced again or not, at an N.R.A. meeting in Washington. The shooters voted for it and the collectors against it. Had Colt been willing to up-date the single action as many of us asked them to, instead of scrapping it, they could have still had a monopoly. What they can do today against such vigorous competition as Ruger and Great Western are sure to give them, is an open question. Their obvious advantage is the romance of the old name.

Many outfits now advertise for repairing and refinishing various auto pistols and sixguns. Christy Gun Works, and Colt both do a beautiful job on the single action and the Gun Reblue Company, Biltmore, North Carolina, have long specialized in refinishing and repairing any and all hand guns. They are a highly specialized outfit and can deliver the most beautiful and ornately finished hand gun, either auto or revolver. They reblue and recase-harden frames and parts and plate in silver, nickel, gold or chrome, as desired. They also do most superior engraving and fit the finest carved pearl and ivory stocks we have ever seen from any source since the early cap and ball Colt arms. If you want the fanciest finish, or the finest in carved ivory or pearl stocks or plating, then Don Gowan of the Gun Reblue Company can do the job to your exact specifications. He has a staff of experts on all phases of this work. Old ivory grips that are chipped can be repaired, or new ones made and frames reblued or case-hardened in colors. This is an old, well established, firm to whom we have referred customers for nearly twenty years and have as yet to hear a single complaint. They do restoration work on the older arms as well as engraving and ornamenting the most modern.

We believe all sixguns and auto pistols should have ajustable sights. The only exception to this is the short barreled pocket guns intended only for close range hip shooting. The best type of adjustable rear sight we have found to resight any fixed sighted revolver, either single or double action, is the Smith & Wesson Micrometer Click rear sight with both windage and elevation incorporated in it.

All that is necessary to fit this sight is to mill out a channel for it full length of the top of the frame where the usual hog wallow rear sight is, and a slight cut at the extreme rear of the frame for the sight proper to bed down in. The sight is easily installed with screws and weakens the frame little, if any. This gives a much lower sight line and a lower front sight than any installation possible with the excellent Micro rear sight. We much prefer it to the Micro for revolvers. Bill Ruger, with his new .357 Magnum Black Hawk, is the only one who has been able to use the Micro rear sight and keep his sight line fairly low. He took an unfair advantage of the older guns by designing the .357 with Micro sights in mind. Not only did he achieve a good sight line but built an unusual amount of rugged strength in the top of the frame.

When guns with fixed sights are to be sighted, we

Target sighted 1917 Smith & Wesson with front sight filed down to the base and this split and a blade front fitted and pinned in place. Rear sight dovetailed in rear end of frame.

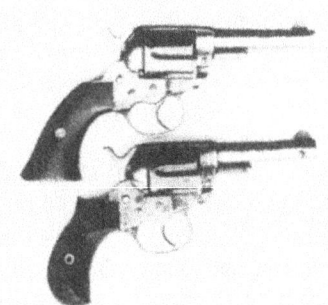

Two views of Colt Lightning .38. Top gun remodelled as to grip by Herb Bradley. Lower gun Standard .38 Colt Lightning.

consider the Smith & Wesson type sight much the best. The King Gun Sight Corp. formerly fitted a sight of this type. This firm has been taken over by the Rickey Gunsight Company of Burlingame, California, which carries on the old King traditions and fits their own version of the S. & W. micrometer rear sight to both single and double action arms. They also offer a wide variety of front sights with white, gold or red beads, or bars, on the top of the front sight post, and have fitted luminous sights for night shooting. Usually with an S. & W. or King-Rickey rear target sight, one must fit a front sight either on a ramp attached to the barrel or to a barrel band, to hold the front sight blade. Some ramps fit over the old front sight stud and are tinned in place, and some are simply sweated to the barrel and the sight blade pinned in a groove on top. Usually a higher than normal front sight is required and this is the best way to accomplish it, though we have seen barrels bedded down in a tray of water and the front sight built up higher with a torch, reshaped and filed down to exact height. This makes a good job if done right and the barrel is kept immersed so the steel is not damaged by the heat of the welding torch. Smith & Wesson front sights may be filed down to the stud, then a slot milled in the stud and a blade front of any desired shape filled with a cross pin through the bottom of the blade and the stud. This makes an excellent job.

The Rickey and S. & W. type rear sight gives maximum sight radius when used with a ramp-type front that slopes upward toward the muzzle with the highest, or sighting point of the front sight blade almost flush with the muzzle of the gun.

Auto pistols are usually easier to target-sight than revolvers as the slide offers an excellent place for the dovetail of the rear sight, and the Micro sight is the best we have seen as an auto pistol badly needs a higher set of sights, and this arrangement gives one a higher sighting line and a higher front sight. With Lugers and their dovetail front sight, no problem is involved as a new sight of the dovetail pattern can be made up with a good target width blade and driven into the slot. The Micro sight can be installed on most worthwhile auto pistols. The Colt Government models with the front sight riveted to the top of the slide have the bad habit of shaking that sight off with continuous usage. We believe the sight should have a longer base screwed to the top of the slide as well as the tiny lug riveted on the inside of the slide.

One of the finest jobs of target sighting a .45 Auto Colt that we have seen was done by Johnny Giles, Clearwater, Florida. He had a solid rib extending from one end of the slide to the other and permanently fixed to the slide with the target rear sight on the rear end and an excellent target blade in the front end of the rib, thus making a very rigid, permanent installation of the best in target sights. C. R. McCashland, Hinton, West Virginia, prefers to fit the S. & W. type micrometer rear target sight to all revolvers, and does a very nice job. He also does accuracy jobs on the Colt .45 Auto.

Frank Pachmayr, who originated the accuracy jobs on Colt .45 autos, still does as nice a job on them as anyone. The Pachmayr Gun Works, 1220 South Grand Ave., Los Angeles, California, specializes in these .45 Government model accuracy jobs and the fitting of any type of target sights to them. Pachmayr also first developed coil main springs in the target revolvers, and fitted one of them in my .357 Magnum, along with his short action and Bisley-type wide hammer spur and finger fitting wide trigger. This is the finest target action I have ever seen on a double action gun from any custom gunsmith. Hammer fall is very short and snappy and with practically no jar. The coiled spring gives the easiest cocking and the wide hammer is perfectly and sharply checkered for fast cocking. The wide full curved trigger perfectly contours the whole front of the trigger finger giving one perfect control at all times. The Pachmayr Gun Works are also expert at restocking, alteration and timing of any revolver or auto pistol as they pioneered it and can hold their own with all comers for fine work. We have a checkered and carved one-piece rosewood stock for the S. A. Colt made by Pachmayr that is a work of art.

They also make cockeyed hammers as does the Rickey Gun Sight Company of Burlingame, California. These are a help in rapid fire as they allow free and easy cocking of the arm with slightly less thumb movement. However, for all else but highly specialized timed and rapid fire work, which we feel should be shot double action, they are an eye-sore to us. Pachmayr can make and fit as nice a low wide hammer spur as anyone can desire to any arm, either double or single action, and has made some of the best Bisley-type hammer spurs we have seen for the single action.

The Rickey Gun Sight Company also carries on the old traditional King short action for both double and single action revolvers. We have a couple of single actions with the King short action, wide Bisley-type hammer spur set lower than the conventional hammer spur and a wide, well curved trigger. They are a pleasure to use and are the single actions I prefer to use in demonstrations of quick draw work as their actions are so short, smooth and fast, as well as easy cocking. I can get best speed with them. The wide, deeply checkered hammer spurs do not slip under the thumb and the hammers are positive in their short action.

The King and Pachmayr short actions give faster hammer travel, less jar and a shorter hammer throw than the conventional long actions, and are more like the new Smith & Wesson short actions in their lock time. This all makes for faster lock and ignition time from the time the trigger releases the sear until the bullet is on its way and makes for higher scores or better game or defense shooting.

Single action base pins can be greatly improved by fitting them with a larger head that one can grasp easily for removal. They must be cut out on two sides to allow the barrel and extractor housing clearance, but still offer a large well knurled hold for the fingers, and are much nicer than the tiny head of the usual S. A. base pin. All too often these get stuck in place and someone uses pliers with the result that both the base pin and the barrel are badly scarred. Skeletonizing of the S. A. hammer helps lock time some, but improved coil main springs or three point suspension-type springs help even more to eliminate the heavy jar of the old hammer in its fall. While it would surely knock off any primer regardless of how thick the cup, and was very reliable, it was detrimental to the best shooting. Smith & Wesson have now developed a new three point main spring which we intend to test before this work is finished and on the press. Mr. Hellstorm tells us it greatly improves the double action trigger pull of Smith & Wesson guns. I hope it will put the new Smith & Wesson short action back into the same class as the old long hammer throw Smith & Wesson for smoothness and lightness of double action pull, and possibly improve on both the old long and the new short action trigger pulls. There can be no question but the short action offers the fastest lock time, and if the double action pull can be improved to equal or better the old long action Smith & Wesson D. A. pull, we will have arrived.

Recently I checked a new Colt Target .38 Special or .357 Magnum on the Officer's model frame. It had a lug running full length under the barrel and the extractor rod was recessed into it for a heavy muzzle weight balance. This particular gun had a very fine double action trigger pull, the best I have ever seen on a Colt, and was marked "the Python." If they would also incorporate a yoke or front base pin lock along with the encased ejector, it would be the finest Colt double action so far. From briefly checking it over, we liked this gun better than any Colt D. A. Target arm we can remember.

Recently Christy Gun Works has developed a low heat silver solder that appears to be the best material for affixing front ramps to barrels of any I have tried. It seems much stronger than regular silver solder. Yesterday we watched Herb Bradley face up and polish two pieces of key stock, then put the flux between them and clamp them together. He brought them up to a low heat, merely enough to flow the new silver and barely touched one side of the junction of the two pieces of steel.

We put the soldered strips in a heavy vice, he purposely left one end project, and used a wrecking bar to tear the two pieces apart. They finally broke loose but only after nearly tearing the heavy bench and vice from the wall. The new solder had only flowed over half of the surface; had it all been covered I doubt if it could have been pulled apart. Such solder is of ample strength for any front sight or ramp.

Revolver grips may be changed to suit the individual and some auto pistol grips as well but the latter usually involve external changes rather than basic strap changes as the frame also houses the magazine. With revolvers, however, you can change the grip to suit you as to size, angle in most cases, and also length of grip. Croft and I developed the No. 3 S. A. grip, as we called it. He first developed it and I added some slight modifications, giving the bottom rear of the stock a greater flare. With this stock we took the regular Bisley back strap, cut it off for length and changed the angle to about the same as that of the S. A. Army and incorporated with it an S. A. Army trigger guard. The hammer had also to be altered of course, to conform to the high back strap of Bisley pattern. Altogether it makes the finest of all S. A. grips. The back strap comes up over the rear stock strap screws on the back of the frame adding greatly to the height of the stock and thus fills the top of the hand, yet retains the same old fine angle of the S. A. Army stock. It is not too difficult a job for a good metal worker, but requires a Bisley back strap which is not easy to come by these days, but one could be cut out by hand.

Another method of lengthening and improving the S. A. grip for men with extremely large hands is to take the stocks and straps off a Colt 1860 .44 Army cap and ball and fit them to the S. A. Colt. This makes a very nice long grip for the man with extra large hands, and many S. A. Colts were so fitted. The regular straps can have pieces of metal added which are welded or silver soldered and spliced out to desired length. The new Christy Silver Solder, while it is flowed and worked at a low heat, will safely stand the heat of hot blueing solutions making it ideal for such work where you do not want to weld. We have also seen the regular S. A. Army straps and stocks cut down shorter and smaller to fit a man with abnormally small hands. He uses my heavy .44 Special loads incidentally, and wanted the grip of the gun to fit his hand.

Bradley once changed the grip of a Colt lightning to that of the S. A. Army. We have seen some of them changed to give the same shaped grip as the Colt S. A., about the same size as the smaller cap and ball guns, but still retaining the hump at the top of the grip for fast double action shooting. These made very nice handling guns. The big Colt D. A. Frontier can also be altered in this way to give the S. A. type and shape of grip or with the hump at the top of stock left on for better control of the gun in double action firing. Of course the gun must be restocked. Such working over of the old guns destroys their value to collectors but does make for a better fit of the gun to individual shooters. Standard S. A. Army Colt, Great Western and Ruger single action all have a rather short grip and personally I usually use them with the little finger curled under the butt of the stock. This gives better control of the arm for fast cocking when it raises in recoil. A longer grip would fill and fit my hand better. The Croft No. 3 grip is the best fit I have yet attained with a modern single action. The old Colt Walkers and Dragoons had a most perfect grip and one that fits my hand perfectly, but the straps are a bit too large to fit the small S. A. Army frame.

The late Frank Frisbie altered a fine Triple Lock Target .44 Special for a pocket gun. He cut out the front of the trigger guard, an alteration I do not approve of at all. He removed the hammer spur so it could not catch on the clothing or pocket in fast work and he changed the back strap to about the same shape and angle as the S. A. Colt so the gun would roll upward in the hand and cushion recoil of my heavy loads. He liked the over all job with barrel cut off at the end of the ejector housing leaving it with a length of 3¼ inches. It was a splendid arm for its purpose but I would have much preferred the regular S. & W. grip with its hump. I find I need that hump. For me at least, it is a necessity for fast double action fire. Without it the gun will crawl downward in my hand until the hammer spur hits the web between thumb and finger and ties up the gun. The Frisbie Triple Lock S. & W. did, however, point wonderfully well. My personal preference leans toward the Smith & Wesson .44 Special or .357 Magnum with a 4 inch barrel carried in a holster, and with no alterations on the guard or straps. In my book they are about perfect as they come from the factory.

Good metal workers can, however, alter a sixgun to nearly any desired shape as to stocks and hammer spur or trigger and sights, and for the shooter these are often a great help. We find the wide trigger gives better control; the pull seems lighter than it actually is and makes for a better let off. Wide Bisley-type hammer spurs are a great advantage on S. A. guns. For one thing, they are slightly lower and faster to cock with one hand and infinitely faster for any one-handed quick draw work where the ball of the thumb hits their sharp checkered surface and cocks the arm as it is drawn from the holster. They are next to impossible to fan, but who, aside from the movies, wants to fan a fine gun. Target sights on an S. A. gun prevent fanning, in any event.

Many shooters like ribs on the barrels of their guns full length, as was first started by the King Gun Sight Company, and is now carried on by the Rickey Gunsight Company. These were ventilated, and while they give the gun a bizarre appearance and add some weight to the muzzle, they also leave holes for dirt, difficult to remove, in which to collect. If a revolver barrel is to be ribbed, I prefer a solid rib as is on the new S. & W. guns. Smith & Wesson control the weight of their barrels by the width of the full length top rib and can give you a set of K models matched for weight in .22, .32 and .38 Special. Their new 1955 model Smith & Wesson Target .45 chambered for the .45 auto cartridge or the .45 auto rim is an example. This arm has a wide heavy full length rib to add weight to the muzzle for steadiness in holding when shooting long target strings. It has the Smith & Wesson large and wide target hammer spur and the wider trigger. The gun comes fitted with the hand filling Smith & Wesson Target grips. All told, it is hard to conceive of a better designed, finished, or fitted target gun for any big cartridge.

The Pachmayr Gun Works used to alter many target guns along the same lines and fit them with wide hammer spurs, special stocks, heavy ribs if desired, and any type of sights. Colt's new .38 Target arms incorporate a barrel with a heavy lug full length under the barrel proper to act as an extra weight, and also to serve as a housing for the extractor rod. Weight can be added to a sixgun by any of these methods, and stocks of solid silver or ivory can be added for more weight in the butt to change the balance.

Front sights that are too low, causing the gun to shoot too high can easily be built up either by welding or by soldering with this new Christy silver solder, and then filing to shape and exactly the right height as you shoot them in. By the same token, rear sights that are too low can also be built up higher if desired, by welding or by silver soldering on a piece of metal and then cutting a new rear sight notch. Most hammer spurs can be altered in shape by forging and hand filing, and we have seen many S. A. Army hammer spurs changed into excellent Bisley-type spurs by forging and filing the original spur into this shape. Both Pachmayr and Rickey do an excellent job of altering single action hammer spurs.

Croft and I had a good many S. A. Colts flat-topped. This was accomplished by laying on a flat strip of metal and welding it solid to the top strap. Flat-topping a frame is a job for only the most expert metal welders, as the inside of the frame must be blocked solid from every angle or it will twist and warp. While it made a beautiful job when properly done it was expensive and not particularly superior

Another of John Newman's pet slip guns, with back strap cut in two and a piece riveted underneath so as to lower the hammer spur the maximum amount.

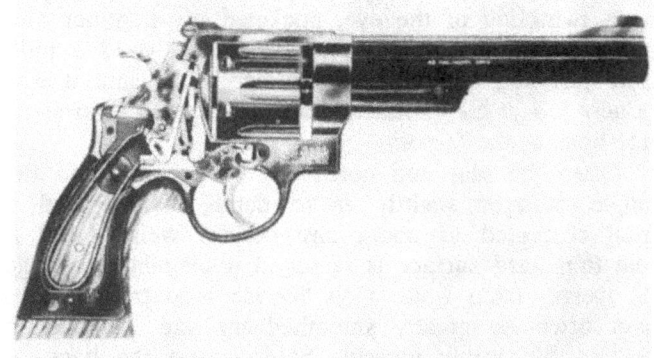

Smith & Wesson .45 model 1955, with side plate removed, showing target hammer, target trigger, target stock, and the new U-type main spring.

to fitting a target King or Smith & Wesson rear sight to the frame. J. D. O'Meara did several of these jobs and even welded a new flat-top on a gun that blew up in my hand. The top strap left for parts unknown along with the top three chambers of that old .45 S. A. when it let go, but O'Meara welded it up into a beautiful flat-top target frame, supplied a new cylinder, and sent it to me to test with my heavy loads. It shot perfectly and withstood the heavy loads with no sign of damage. J. D. O'Meara was a wonderful workman, even though he had but one hand to work with.

Some shooters like the trigger guard spur as on the old Smith & Wesson Russian. We have seen many of these added to the trigger guards of modern arms. They can be fitted either by welding, or by using the new Silver solder and give the shooter a firm grip for the second finger. They change one's grip, however, more to that of the free pistol than the sixgun.

Revolver trigger pulls can be cut to about any desired weight and still be safe if the work is properly done. Where plenty of hammers and sears are available at the factory, the best way to adjust a trigger pull is to switch sears and hammers until a combination is found in factory parts that will give the perfect let off of desired weight. Smith & Wesson use glass hard parts and it is far better to switch parts until the right combination is found than to stone them. The hardened surface is retained and the trigger pull will never change. Cutting down or increasing a trigger pull is best done by changing the angle of the sear bite slightly. Johnny Lindner of Helena, long gone to his reward, used to change all revolver and auto pistol trigger pulls by using a small and very sharp center or prick punch and throwing up a slight burr on each side of the hammer that prevented the sear from falling into the notch to its full depth. This worked out perfectly on the Colt S. A. and also on the .45 auto. He fixed the pull on a .45 auto for me at three pounds. It never changed nor malfunctioned, but when my friend Fitzgerald of Colt tried it at Camp Perry, he had the gun apart in a twinkling of the eye, pocketed my hammer and fitted a new one that never did give as good a pull. Fitz just had to have the hammer as he said it was a new job in his experience and he wanted it to show the boys at the factory.

Often the sear and notch can be polished and the angle changed slightly as to depth of bite and a pull corrected to about any desired weight, but if the thin hard surface is removed it may later change in weight from wear. Colt Service auto trigger pulls can often be greatly smoothed up and lessened in weight by simply pressing hard against the back of the cocked hammer while you pull the trigger. It is a burnishing action and will often reduce the pull by a pound or two as well as to smooth it up. Fitzgerald always employed this system after a few strokes on the full cock notch with his fine cut file.

Abnormally heavy main springs such as used to be furnished in some of the older Colt single actions, and also on the first Great Western revolvers caused very heavy, hard, trigger pulls. These could be greatly lessened by reduction in the strength of the main spring. The width of the spring can be reduced by filing, but the cuts should be lengthwise of the spring as any cross cut will often cause it to fracture crossways. Springs can also be ground sparingly on the flat side if the grinding is from end to end and care is exercised to keep the cutting uniform and the spring of uniform thickness, then polished until no marks appear on the flat surface. Usually it is best to work on the sides of the spring and reduce its total width to cut tension.

We found another way to lessen main spring energy in Colt and Great Western single actions without changing the spring. We cut a tiny piece of fairly heavy cardboard so that it would fit under the bottom tip of the main spring, between the spring and the guard strap and below the main spring screw, then tightened up the screw on this piece of cardboard which not only cushioned the main spring, but also lessened its angle, thereby greatly reducing its tension. There is no necessity for a main spring that is heavy enough to give the hammer an extremely heavy jar when it falls. A lighter spring will always give better accuracy so long as it imparts a heavy enough blow on the firing pin to insure certain and uniform ignition of the primer.

Smith & Wesson guns have tension screws on all the models with flat main springs, and these can be backed out a turn or two with no ill effect if the spring is unnecessarily strong. If much tension is removed, however, the sear spring must also be cut off and reduced to properly balance the assembly. Main spring tension screws should never be backed out to the extent that the blow of the firing pin is weakened enough to inhibit uniform and certain ignition. Modern primers are remarkable for consistant reliability. A single misfire is reason for suspecting the gun is at fault; usually not enough main spring tension, though it could be several other things. Two misfires in a day are proof. Unreliable and faulty ignition cannot be tolerated. Primer flashes of varying intensity produce uneven chamber pressures which spread groups vertically. Weak primer ignition may cause a cartridge to squib with just enough power to drive the bullet into the barrel. If another comes in behind it, a ringed barrel is the least that can result. Most of the crimes committed against main springs today come from trying to lighten the double action pull. If you are tempted to this type of tinkering remember, it is better to have a little more hammer energy than you need than to have not quite enough.

Quite a few old guns have atrocious trigger pulls and jarring hammer falls due to excessively stiff main springs. They should be overhauled by a competent gunsmith. The pistols turned out at this writing by Ruger, Colt, Smith & Wesson and Great Western are quite carefully balanced as to tensions in the factory, and altering spring action is more likely to produce bad results than improvements. At least, it is decidedly not a job for an amateur to take on.

James V. Howe, in his excellent two volume *Modern Gunsmithing*, thoroughly covers all trigger pull alterations, and with sketches graphically portraying the exact methods of adjusting trigger pulls.

Strikers or firing pins should be kept round and smooth on their surface. A few pierced primers may cause them to be pitted and sharp and they will then pierce more primers and let more gas to the rear to do further damage to the pin and the recoil plate. If pitted, they should be stoned to an even round contour and polished again. Length of the firing pin is also critical. They should be long enough for a certain, deep indentation but not long enough to pierce primers.

Cylinders can be shortened and cut back to give less jump for the bullet in calibers with short cases. C. R. McCashland, Hinton, West Virginia, does this job on New Service and Smith & Wesson 1917 revolvers. By fitting a special barrel back through the frame to the end of the cylinder he can cut down

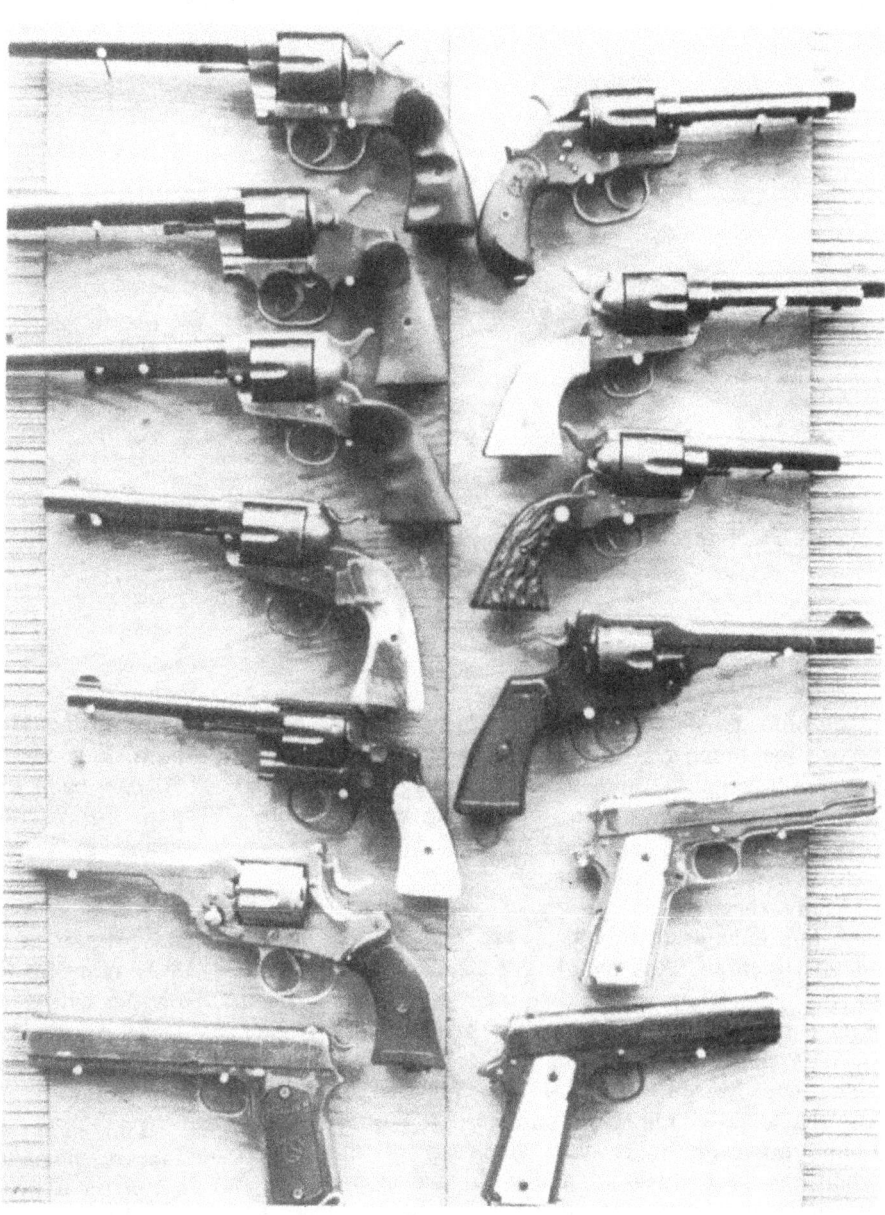

A. M. Hughel's sixguns, many of them remodeled.

the length of the cylinder until the .45 caliber 230 grain jacketed slug has very little jump from chamber throat to barrel throat, and he claims a great increase in accuracy by this alteration. We have also seen a few caliber .38 S. & W. guns with cylinders cut back for a shorter jump of the bullet and improved accuracy. The gun thus converted has an odd appearance with its short cylinder and barrel projecting back through the frame, but the target shooter wants the last possible point he can score so he perhaps, finds it worthwhile.

All better manufacturers now lap pistol barrels and we heartily approve. It pretty well whips the leading problem, and ultimate accuracy is not the offspring of a lead splotched barrel.

Aside from the change of sights and the adjusting of the pistol for finest accuracy, auto pistols do not lend themselves much to alteration. The back strap can be altered and added to in order to give the grip more of an angle in relation to the frame, but even here you are limited by the fact that the stock straps house the magazine so not much change of angle can be had except by the addition of more metal at the bottom of the back strap as in the arched housing improvement for the .45 Auto Colt.

Ruger Single Six loading gates are inadequate and hard to catch with the thumbnail. I have had mine altered to about the same shape as the S. A. Colt. Don Gowan of The Gun Reblue Company alters these Ruger loading gates to S. A. Colt shape before he engraves and finishes them, thus making a more practical and far more attractive job.

With all such jobs the work can be done and the gun repolished so the final job appears as neat and clean as the original. You can blue only as well as you can polish, so remember, if you want a satin

Slip guns by J. D. O'Meara.

Top—.45 Colt with extra .45 auto cylinder.

Bottom—Rebushed gun, caliber .22 L.R.

black-blue finish, you must attain a perfect polish before the blueing is started. Great Western revolvers of recent manufacture are beautifully polished and blued; in fact their finish and blueing compares very favorably with the finest old Smith & Wesson pre-war high bright blue finish, though darker.

Many shooters like a trigger stop on a sixgun to end the backward travel of the trigger just as the sear is released, thus avoiding a twitch by the muzzle of the gun from the release of the trigger tension. Ruger has his trigger spring in back of the trigger, so it is under tension from the rear and this spring being compressed when the sear releases, eliminates any back lash. On Colt and Great Western S. A. Guns, however, there is a backslap of the trigger when the sear releases, and a trigger stop screw is an advantage for fine shooting. Usually these are fitted through the back of the trigger guard and can be adjusted to just touch the trigger when the sear releases, eliminating the trouble.

Separate rebounding firing pins are also an advantage on S. A. guns, particularly for the high velocity calibers such as the .357 magnum, the .22 Hornet and the .30 Carbine round. H. W. Bradley of Salmon, made and fitted the first of these we ever saw over twenty years ago, and they worked splendidly. Later Christy Gun Works developed one on very similar lines that has given excellent service. Great Western used the Christy firing pin for a time, then developed a larger and stronger one for their guns. Colt is also using them in their double action .357 magnum, and S. & W. have long used them in their .22 calibers. Many other firms have used them in .22 caliber arms. In the high pressure numbers such as the Hornet, .30 Carbine and the .357 Magnum, they are a necessity to prevent the primer from flowing back into the firing pin hole and tying up the gun. Firing pin holes in revolver recoil plates are prone to wear, particularly with the tapered large diameter firing pin featured by the S. A. Colt, especially if it is snapped much empty in practice. In time the primers of hot loads will set back into this enlarged hole tying up the gun; this in turn places undue strain on the cylinder hand and either it or the ratchet will wear or break in time. All sixguns chambering hot cartridges should have a rebounding firing pin in the frame.

Time was when you bought a sixgun just as the factory made it, and liked it, or had extra work done on it by a private smith. Today about all companies building revolvers and auto pistols are trying to improve them in every possible way so that now the sixgun crank can get about anything he desires direct from the factory. This is a healthy attitude for the industry, and will cause more and more shooters to take up the handgun. In this country we have far more pistol shooters than ever before, and as the legislators become educated to the necessity for training our youth before they enter the army, the demand for good side arms will increase. Years ago only a few of us cranks plugged for better arms. Today there is enough compeitition in the industry to keep them on their toes, and the payoff is—better guns. It is a healthy condition. An armed and trained citizenry is the best defense any country ever had, not only from foreign enemies, but from criminals and subversion at home.

Chapter XVI

A Bullet Chapter

Selection of Bullets

Now let us take up the actual work of reloading our sixgun cartridge. First, we may as well select the shape, weight and design of the bullet needed for our purpose or which best suits our individual fancy. If it is for short range target practice and a light load needed, as well as a light powder charge wanted on account of absence of recoil and light report, then the shooter may as well select a bullet of normal weight, or somewhat lighter than normal if it be equally accurate. Bullets with a square front band or shoulder should always be selected for serious target work as they cut clean holes which aid in the scoring, as well as often giving the shooter the benefit of the full caliber of his gun on a close shot. The true wad cutters, with an absolutely square face, are seldom accurate beyond close range and I do not favor their use as much as the bullet having a longer point.

All revolver bullets should have an adequate crimp groove for properly crimping the bullet in the case, not only to hold it against the shock of recoil, but also to assist in perfect powder combustion. A great many revolver bullets listed by our different mould makers do not have such a crimp groove and must be seated friction tight, using a very light powder charge, or else crimped over the shoulder of the front band. I think it well to avoid such bullets Select those having a deep, bevelled crimp groove that will aid in forcing the front edge of the case into an adequate, sure crimp. Nothing is more exasperating or more conducive to the creation of a cloud of blue smoke than to have a sixgun bullet jump its crimp from the recoil of the gun and project out past the front end of the cylinder, thus tying up the arm completely for the time being. Such things can be very dangerous if the gun be used for protection, and they will hopelessly spoil a rapid-fire string at the target.

Modern smokeless powders require a heavy, uniform crimp to hold the bullet against the initial ignition of the charge, in order to insure its proper ignition and combustion. Some powders, such as Bullseye, are easily ignited and are not so sensitive to crimp resistance, while others, such as #2400, require the maximum in heavy crimp to burn at all, let alone burn completely, or as they should for normal results. As the flash from the primer spits into the powder it starts the ignition of the charge, building up some gas pressure at the same time. If the crimp is weak and uneven, this initial ignition may alone be sufficient to shove the bullet out of the case before all the powder is properly ignited, thus causing squibs, hang-fires or similar troubles. Often such squibs are blamed on the primer, whereas the real cause is a crimp insufficient to properly hold the bullet in the case against this initial pressure until that powder charge has been properly ignited. As the bullet moves into the barrel from such a poorly ignited charge, the pressure becomes less and less, often dropping to a point too low to even burn up the powder.

With black powder we have no such trouble, it ignites very easily and thoroughly, "exploding" at once and burning completely if loaded in the proper charge. Many smokeless powders are not only hard to ignite, but harder still to "keep going" properly and such brands require heavy crimps, and often heavy bullets as well, in order to set up sufficient resistance at the initial stage of ignition to insure uniform and complete combustion. Unless the crimp be heavy and the brass case firm and sound, that crimp cannot hold long enough for such powder to be uniformly or properly ignited. Unless so ignited, that charge cannot burn completely, and it may not burn at all but only drive the bullet up in the bore of the gun or just barely out of the barrel, leaving the bore, and often part of the action, covered with unburned powder grains.

I like a wide, bevelled crimp groove and do not care for these narrow, cannelure-type of lines which some bullets carry on their front band. A bevel slanting towards the base, is necessary for best results. To get power out of any sixgun load, it must have a strong and heavy crimp, as I have explained above, and this crimp can best be formed by considerable restriction of as much of the edge of the case as possible; the wider the groove and its bevel, the more brass we are able to "crimp" into it. When the cartridge is fired, this crimp must be forced open. That part of the front band in back of the crimp must do this forcing, and it has a lot of work to do in opening out the crimp completely and evenly. A bevel here is of considerable help in opening the crimp to the full diameter of the case mouth while not tearing off the rear edge of the front band or the edges of the rear band which follows, which could possibly reduce its diameter and cause gas cutting. Experience has proved to me that small, narrow grease grooves (generally with no crimp groove) with correspondingly narrow bands are not nearly so well suited to properly forcing the crimp of a heavy sixgun case, without in turn deforming the base and other bands on the bullet, all of which is an argument for the need of bands as wide and as strong as you can possibly get on your bullet. You need adequate lubrication, of course, but you do not need bullets so short and decorated with such a multitude of grooves that they are hard to cast, offering little resistance to gas cutting, and also giving little bearing surface for the lands of the gun to work on and spin the bullet in its passage through the bore.

For illustration, take the old .38 Special Ideal bullet #358311. This bullet has a perfect crimp groove, as well as a good lubrication groove, with wide, heavy bands. It is not a killer in any sense of the word, but is superbly accurate, and where maximum penetration is wanted from cast bullets in .38 caliber, this bullet, cast very hard and used with a good dose of Hercules #2400 in heavy frame guns, will surely deliver the goods. All round nose bullets tend to glance more on bone, if not struck squarely, than do flat point ones. Most of the light weight bullets do not have good crimp grooves, but must be crimped over their front shoulder. With some very fast burning, easily ignited powder like Bullseye, they give good results for close range shooting. But for any serious target work at 50

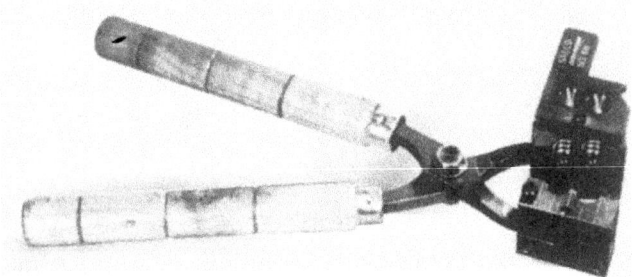

Seco two cavity mould.

yards, or for hunting or defense work where good stiff charges are used, the bullet should by all means have a good crimp groove and be tightly crimped in the case. No front band whose forward edge must be crimped over with the mouth of a strong brass case, can be perfectly square after forcing out that crimp, and thus cannot be in best condition to perform its wad cutting or full diameter hole punching properties.

I have had Remington, .45 Colt black powder loads jump their crimp and tie up the gun on many occasions, and have had considerable trouble from this source with some of my own reloads in the .38/40. Many times I have had bullets recede into the case where the shell was not full-length resized. A sufficient crimp groove is also a necessity in keeping the bullets from being shoved back into the case when pushing the cartridges out from belt loops. This is another reason why the handloader should select only bullets which have a good deep, adequately bevelled, crimping groove. All Keith bullets have properly designed crimp grooves for the above reasons. In utilizing them, be sure that your crimp is uniform, strong and heavy.

The base band to your bullet had also better be a wide and strong one. I have had much trouble with narrow banded bullets gas-cutting through their base band from a fast or hot burning powder. Also, lubricant easily leaks past a narrow base band and if loaded cartridges are stored away during a hot spell, it may get into the powder charge, where it does no good. I want a wide, full diameter base band to my bullet, which will help eliminate both fusion from the hot gasses and the hazard of a squib load from lubricant leaking into the powder charge.

Another reason I prefer all the width possible to both base and forward bands on my bullets, particularly in .38 and .44 calibers, is to eliminate the squirting of lubricant past the bands and the consequent messing up of the entire bullet while lubricating and sizing it. Most of these small band, multiple groove bullets are extremely hard to lubricate without grease squeezing past their sides and getting all over both base and point of the bullet. I have found that a single, wide and deep lubricating groove will come the nearest to eliminating these faults, yet still carry sufficient lubricant for the purpose intended. Furthermore, some of the shallow grooved bullets cannot be sized down

Seco Thermostatically controlled electric furnace and melting pot.

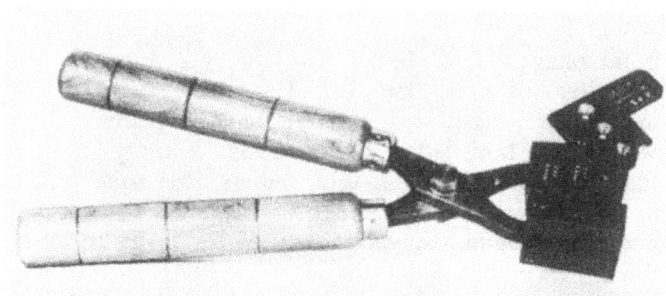

Seco three cavity mould.

more than a thousandth or so, whereas with a deep grooved bullet you can take off a few thousandths and at times thus use the bullet in guns of different bore dimensions. In designing my .45 Auto and .45 Colt bullets, I could not get their bands as wide as I wished, due to the over-all length of the bullet being limited by its maximum weight specifications; still, they seem to work out all right, but I do not like them as well as the wider bands permissible on my .38 and .44 Special designs.

Many years ago I began to look about for the ideal shape of sixgun bullet to suit my own ideas and needs. I was in search of a bullet that would not jump its crimp from recoil and which would also give the revolver its maximum killing powder. With all this in mind, I first designed the Belding & Mull #454260 bullet, which proved a very good missile for the .45 Colt. My objection to this design was that I could not get as good long range accuracy with it as I wished. Later, I worked out a similar design in .44 Special, of 260 grains weight. Harold Croft and I together then worked out still another variation of this .44 bullet which weighed 280 grains, and retained the Belding & Mull blunt, round nose. On all three we had a good crimp groove and also one large, deep lubrication groove. Croft paid for the cherries for these last two bullets. We used these for some time, but the crimping grooves proved hardly deep enough. By that time I believed that I could greatly improve on their design, both in accuracy and killing power, so I worked out the first of my bullets for the Lyman Gun Sight Corporation.

I wanted this new bullet to seat out of the case as far as length of the cylinder would permit, the same as I had done with the Belding & Mull bullets, but I also wanted a wide, heavy band in front of the crimp groove to help true up the cartridge in the cylinder and so keep the bullet in perfect alignment with the bore while firing. This band would also act as a wad cutter for target and game shooting. But I wanted the front band of my bullet to finish the work of its flat point and to cut full wad cutter holes in anything it struck, and with its square shoulder it does just that. At the same time, I wanted a long, flat pointed bullet which would be better balanced for long range accuracy, yet give maximum killing power, and cut full sized holes in anything it struck. At that time (1928) Harold Croft was visiting me and we spent a month, all told, experimenting with the .44 Specials. He did not think much of my design then, as he watched me make a rough sketch of it. The Lyman folks decided the bullet had good possibilities, and their Mr. Pickering had the steel model turned out and sent to me for examination. This first Lyman-Keith bullet was in 250 grain weight and is listed in the catalog as #429421.

Tests with #421 on jack rabbits and similar game soon showed that it was the best killer we had so far tried; that it would not jump its crimp, and was the most destructive bullet we had then used on game. Next, I had Lyman make up another bullet exactly like it, but with a hollow base to weigh but 230 grains. Mr. Pickering again worked out this model for the new bullet from my own crude drawings. This lighter weight permitted the use of still heavier charges of #80 powder and, owing to its higher velocity and flatter trajectory, proved an even better bullet for long-range game shooting. It is catalogued as #429422 in the Lyman Hand Book. Later, when these bullets had proved to be exactly what I wanted, I sent Lyman similar designs for the .45 Auto Rim and .45 Colt, both in solid, flat-base type to weigh 240 and 250 grains #452423 and #454424 respectively. The illustrations of these

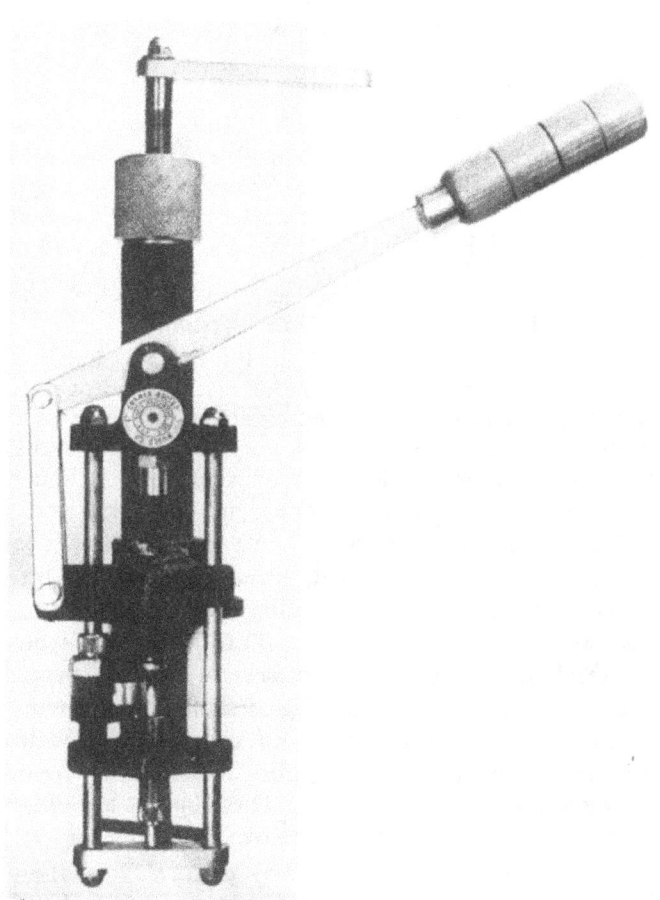

Seco bullet sizer and lubricator made by Cramer.

bullets in the #31 through #39 Ideal Hand Books are transposed.

These two .45 bullets proved to be so very good in their respective calibers that I determined to finish the job and design a similar bullet in .38 Special. I had first worked out the design of this bullet in 1929, but did not send it to Lyman until some years later. This bullet weighed 173 grains in solid form, but was too heavy to group-in with the sighting of several guns which I tried it in, usually shooting so high it was necessary to add height to the front sight or cut down the rear sight. It shot to about right elevation with the S & W heavy duty .45 frame gun, but altogether too high in my Outdoorsman. Don Martin used it exclusively and still swears by it in his target S & W Military and Police Model.

I asked Lyman to make up another bullet exactly the same, but with a hollow base to weigh 160 grains, which they did. My friend, Charles B. Keller, was working on a similar design, but when he saw this one, he said it was exactly what he wanted and was about the same thing as his design. This bullet proved to be very accurate, a good killer, and entirely satisfactory in every way.

When I first worked out this design of sixgun bullets, I believed that the flat point combined with the groove diameter front band would give killing power enough for any purpose, but I wrote Lyman that if anyone wanted even more shock, they could get it by adding a hollow point to the flat-base models. The late Capt. Frank Frisbie and Harold Croft ordered the first .38 Special mould of Lyman's with a hollow point, working out the plug size with Mr. Pickering. This proved to be the most destructive .38 caliber bullet I have ever used on game. It expanded readily with heavy loads of powder, and when cast as soft as one to twenty, expanded perfectly if given a velocity of 1000 feet. This bullet is catalogued as Ideal #358429, and as #358431 in the hollow-base version.

The hollow-point seems to be the more popular of the two. With heavy loads of powder, it is altogether too destructive for grouse and similar table game as it blows them to pieces, but it is very suitable for pests, for long shots on heavier game or where not too much penetration is required, I believe it would kill more quickly than the hollow-base 160 grain bullet. This 160 grain Keith hollow-point, ahead of a heavy charge of powder, is the only .38 caliber bullet I have used that would kill a porcupine "dead" with one shot when hit through the paunch. I shot several of them out of big pine trees with such placing of shots and it seemed to kill instantly in all cases. Of course, the powder charge was heavy, and was used in heavy .45 frame Colt and Smith & Wesson guns. These bullets expanded to such an extent that they tore two inch holes at exit.

The uniformily excellent killing performed by these hollow-point bullets in .38 caliber prompted us to try them in the larger calibers as well, so we had Lyman hollow-point some moulds in both .44 Special and in .45 Colt. In the former, the regular Lyman hollow-point plug gave the bullet a weight of 235 grains, and by using this same size plug in the 250 grain .45 Colt mould, its weight was also cut to 235 grains. These weights are both better suited to high velocity loadings than were the 250 grain solid bullets. The solid bullets in all four calibers will penetrate more deeply, but will not tear such unbelievably large holes in game as do the hollowpoints. Since the .45 Colt bullet is the longest of the two in this caliber, I decided it would work out the best in hollow-point shape for both .45 Auto Rim and .45 Colt. The shooting by both Dickey and myself, as well as many others we have handloaded it for, proved it to be the most destructive of all .45 bullets. A good many years ago a doctor from Michigan, I believe, whose address I cannot remember, sent me samples of a .45 Colt hollow-point bullet he had used for years with black powder loads and with which he had obtained very fine results. The cavity was very large, and although he used 40 grains of black powder, it expanded perfectly, even on snowshoe rabbits. His bullet was of a round point style. I cannot remember its weight. His experiments proved that any sixgun bullet can be made to expand very reliably at over 900 feet velocity with the proper size hollow-point and correct temper to the alloy.

My designs of sixgun bullets have been so widely used all over this country and Canada, and have proved so uniformly popular, that I honestly believe they will give as good or better results than any design obtainable today. They were designed for normal and heavy loads and not for light, practice loads; still they have been used very successfully by several fine target shots for gallery use with light powder charges. Dr. Murphy of the Winnipeg Revolver Club made the possible score with my flat-base, 250 grain .44 Special bullet. They cut holes in target paper just as clean and full as do the commercial wad cutters, and at the same time have long, well-ballanced points which will shoot accurately to 500 yards, whereas most true, square-fronted wad cutters begin to fall off in accuracy at any range over 50 yards and often will show tipping on the target at not much more than this. Other mould makers have copied the design, and some individuals have tried to revamp and rename the bullet by shortening its point or changing the size of the hollow-point cavity, but so far I have not seen any improvement on the original. Winchester and Major Wesson used this design in working out the .357 Magnum. Their design is simply another variation on this bullet. My bullet is not the first with a flat point and square shoulder. Harry Pope used the same type of flat point and wad-cutting forward band many years ago. However, the Keith bullet was the first one to incorporate a flat point; a wide, groove diameter band extending in front of the cartridge case; an adequate crimping groove; a wide, deep lubrication groove; a good and sufficient

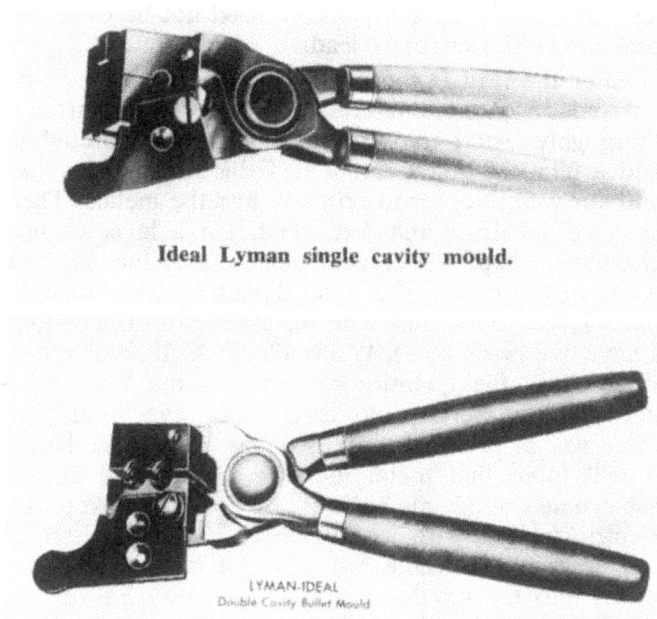

Ideal Lyman single cavity mould.

LYMAN-IDEAL
Double Cavity Bullet Mould

Many shooters want to load the lightest possible bullet for extremely short range shooting, and for such purpose select the "collar button" bullets or a round ball. The latter worked best in the old percussion guns, which were cut with a slow gain twist, and where the ball could be flattened out with the rammer to fill the cylinder. They may also be loaded in modern revolvers with very light charges of some really quick powder, like Bullseye. They are not as accurate as the collar button type and neither one is as good as a longer and heavier bullet for any purpose whatsoever. Frank Waterman loaded round balls a great deal for his .45 Colt. These loads shoot quite accurately and are very cheap, but I for one, prefer the longer, heavier weight. These light bullets and round balls, when used with extremely low charges, have a bad habit of bouncing

width of base band, and a dirt scraper-wad cutter, all on the one bullet.

Anyone who will take the time to recover his fired revolver bullets from snow, oiled sawdust, cotton waste or similar mediums which do not mutilate them, will immediately see that the greatest strains on the bearing bands of a sixgun bullet come on the front band. Look at the illustrations of fired bullets in General Hatcher's excellent book on firearms identification. The bullet, traveling at high speed as it leaves the cylinder, jumps straight ahead into the barrel throat proper. There it skids about until it is gripped by the lands and forced to spin and rotate through the bore by them. Most of this skidding and slippage is taken up by the front band. The grooves left on it by the lands are generally always about twice as wide as normal, showing clearly that the bullet does strip this front band a bit before enough of its bearing surface has entered the barrel to hold it securely to the lands. By having a wide, groove diameter front band located in front of the crimp groove, we can cut this stripping and skidding to a minimum. Owing to the sharp, square shoulders and bands of these Keith bullets, they do not always drop from the mould cavity as easily as may those bullets with rounded bands and grooves but those sharp shoulders are well worth the slight added work in casting; for one thing they will better scrape out the fouling left in the bore at each shot, a point much apprepciated by the man using black powder.

The short, very blunt bullets usually do not work so well at long ranges as the longer ones, but even length can be overdone, as weight must be kept down to around the standard for that caliber for suitable long range accuracy. Too heavy a bullet raises pressures to such an extent that velocity must be kept very low, this in turn limits one's ability to hit relatively small objects at the longer ranges, due to the high trajectory.

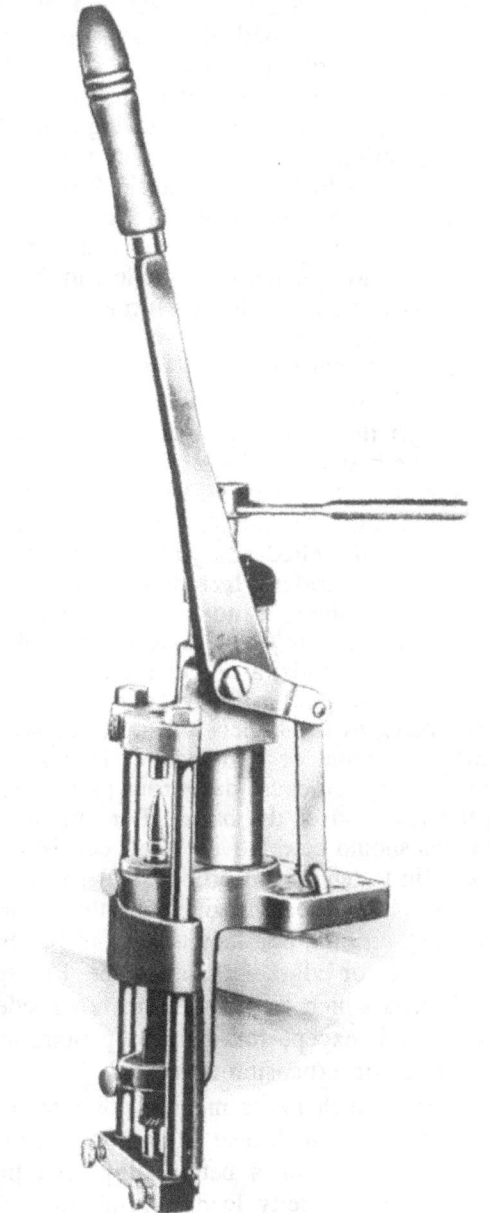

Ideal bullet lubricator and sizer (Lyman).

back from any hard surface, or even a green tree trunk, for that matter, a situation which is not favorable with me. Whenever I get down to this extreme "light" load stage, I generally go back to the ranch and break out one of my .22 handguns, which are much less expensive to shoot and far less trouble to fix up with the most satisfactory sort of a light load.

The catalogues of the different bullet mould manufacturers in this country offer about every conceivable size and shape of revolver bullet, and even the crankiest shooter should be able to find something which suits him. My own design suits me better than anything I have ever seen or used, but it may not suit another individual at all. As the Irishman said, "I believe in letting every man scratch his fleas in his own way."

Bullet Casting

After deciding upon the weight and design of the bullet you wish to reload, the next step is to cast up an ample supply of that particular bullet. To obtain anything like proper results, it is necessary to possess a good melting pot and a dipper having a nozzle shaped to fit the pouring hole in the gate of your mould. The metal is best melted in an electric furnace and next best over a gas range, although very good work can be done with the kitchen stove; and I must admit having cast a great many more bullets in this way than over any gas range or electric furnace. We have also used a gasoline blast furnace for bullet casting. It is at best, a hot, hard job and one that few reloaders really care to perform.

The larger the melting pot, up to say twenty pounds capacity, the better, as a large pot will hold more metal and maintain a more uniform heat than is the case with a smaller quantity of metal. First, melt the lead and when that is all melted add your tin or antimony. For most revolver cartridges, including all light and normal pressure loads, there is no use in having the bullets harder than one part tin to sixteen parts of lead, and for really heavy loads, a one to fifteen mixture is hard enough. A very soft alloy is dangerous with over-normal loads, as the bullets will upset or swage out in the cylinder throat or barrel cone. This squashed-out, over-sized slug can cause dangerous pressures, and may split the rear end of the barrel. For automatic pistols, the bullets should be relatively hard, consisting of about one part tin to ten parts lead, in order for them to slide up easily out of the magazine into the chamber. The harder they are, the less they are apt to batter or catch on the corner or edge of the chamber. But such "very hard" bullets which are brittle, are not needed in any revolver load, except for extreme penetration, where no upsettage or expansion is wanted.

Tin has a much lower melting point than lead, but will not stand as much heat as antimony. For this reason antimony is often a better alloy than tin for use with very high velocity loads. A mixture of part tin and part antimony works very well for some heavy loads. Hollow point bullets with velocities up to 1000 feet, to insure proper expansion, need not be over one part tin to sixteen parts lead.

After the lead is thoroughly melted, add the tin or tin and antimony mixture and let it melt and mix thoroughly. After the mixture has melted thoroughly, add a lump of tallow about half the size of a walnut and stir well in order to properly flux the metals. Then skim off all dross and dirt. Next, put a layer of fine charcoal on top; this prevents unnecessary burning and waste of the metal. The Ideal dipper works very well, but a larger dipper made on the same pattern is better. I have one made by H. W. Bradley, which holds about three times the quantity of metal as the Ideal, and does the best work of any ladle I have ever used. The more weight of metal there is in the dipper, the better it will force that metal into the mould, and at the same time exclude air bubbles. By the same token, the electric furnace with its still larger pot is the best of all, because the whole pot of metal is used to force metal into the mould. Much finer quality bullets are obtained as a result of the process. The ladle must be kept very hot. I have found it advantageous to have a small stool or box set between myself and the gas furnace, and on a level with the top of the melting pot. After casting a bullet, the ladle handle can be laid down upon the box, with the hot bowl projecting over the pot of the metal. In this way the handle of the dipper stays comparatively cool.

It is best to warm up the moulds a bit at the side of the furnace or stove until they are comparatively hot, but still not hot enough for good work. Then add the final heating only by casting bullets. When the mould becomes hot enough to do really good work, it will usually require a few seconds for the metal to solidify in the sprue cutter. With hollow base or hollow point moulds, care will have to be exercised to allow them to cool longer than the solid bullets, or else the plug may tear out one side of the bullet if the moulds are jerked open too soon after pouring the metal. Use a wooden stick or light mallet with which to strike the gate, and never allow any hard object to come in contact with the face of the mould. Special care must be taken not to use anything harder than the mould itself to cut off the sprue. Never allow anyone to dig a bullet out of the mould when it sticks in one of the halves. Tap the blocks gently with a soft stick until that bullet drops out. When a mould gets hot enough to do proper work, the bullets will generally drop out when it is opened suddenly. I have found that bronze moulds usually cast easier than iron moulds. Why, I do not know. Bronze moulds also are simpler to care for, and do not require greasing after using to protect from rusting.

In casting the bullet, hold the mould in the left hand, rotate it a quarter turn to the right so that the bullet cavity lies horizontal, then raise the dipper from the melting pot as nearly full of metal as practical, fit the nozzle to the cavity in the gate of the mould and slowly rotate both mould and ladle back to the left to a vertical plane. Now hold the mould and dipper in this position for a few seconds to allow plenty of time for the cavity in the mould to be filled completely before placing the dipper back over the pot. With an electric furnace, hold the mould firmly against the nozzle for a few seconds, before cutting off the flow of metal.

The main cause of uneven, partly filled bullets is the result of removing the dipper from the mould too soon and thus not allowing sufficient time for the cavity to fill. Remember, that after the cavity of the mould is filled, the metal shrinks as it hardens; therefore, the dipper should still be in place to allow the shrinking and cooling bullet to draw enough metal from the dipper or nozzle for a few seconds to insure even, full weight bullets. Removing the dipper too soon from the nozzle or the mould will often cause the base band of the bullet to have uneven, partly filled, or rounded edges. To obtain accuracy, it is absolutely essential that all bands on the bullet be perfectly filled and sharp. In casting some 566 grain bullets for my old Buffalo Sharps, I must of necessity hold the ladle over the mould for a long time before removing it, or else the big slugs will have a rounded edge, and quite often, an air hole in the base.

With large caliber, heavy, sixgun bullets, if the moulds are hot (as they should be) and the sprue is still in a molten condition when the dipper is removed, it is well to add a little more metal to the "puddle" in the cavity of the gate, thus insuring perfect, evenly filled and full weight bullets. Many people think all that is necessary to cast bullets is to melt the lead in any kind of a ladle, then take an iron spoon and pour some metal in the mould until it is full. Although our ancestors did just this in running round balls for old percussion and flint lock rifles, it is next to impossible to secure perfect, modern revolver bullets from such methods.

Mould handles should always be long and cool. The most disagreeable bullet moulds of all to cast with are the short Colt, double ball, iron moulds furnished for old percussion or cap and ball guns. The early, round ball rifle moulds also usually had very short metal handles, and as soon as the moulds were hot enough to cast perfectly, they were too hot to hold in the bare hands. The old Ideal No. 4 with its bullet mould in the end of the loading tool and handles of metal is another type that soon gets too hot to hold. The reason for the Ideal No. 4, and all these very early light moulds, was to cut down weight as much as possible. In that day transportation was a serious problem and the less weight it would take to do the job, the better, as those men were often gone for months with all their possessions on their back. If any additional weight was tolerated, it was wanted in more powder and lead, not in long, cool, but bulky and heavy bullet moulds. Many of these short, all metal moulds can be fitted with detachable handles that will afford adequate length and comfort

Western metal piercing bullets .357 magnum and .45 auto.

in bullet casting. A pair of heavy cloth gloves is also a necessity at times, although I do most of this work bare-handed. Still and all, I acquire fewer burns when I wear cotton gloves while casting bullets.

When casting over a kitchen range, the heat from the stove necessary to maintain an even temperature of the bullet metal, usually makes for very hot work. Generally, the women have asbestos mats of various sizes on which to place hot pans. (These can usually be obtained at any hardware store). I have found it advantageous to procure a number of these and stack them up all around the melting pot in order to keep as much surplus heat as possible from rising up in my face. This also helps maintain a more even temperature in the melting pot by holding the heat where it is most wanted. When casting over a kitchen range, the work should be done in the cool of early morning or evening, or better still, on cold winter days. The firewood should be perfectly dry and split sufficiently fine to keep up a steady blaze. With coal to burn, the problem is easier once a good fire is going, but with some coal, such as that we get in the West, it is very hard to get a fire at all, let alone one sufficiently hot enough for bullet casting. The metal should never be too hot, as it then burns away and forms too much dross. It should, however, be hot enough—metal, dipper and mould so that when a bullet is run it will require a few seconds for the sprue to solidify. Too hot a metal takes too long to solidify, often imparting a sort of galvanized or frosted finish to the bullet, and is also more apt to oxidize the mould inside until it will no longer cast good, smooth bullets. The electric furnace, preferably with thermostat control, will insure uniform heat.

The metal should be stirred from time to time, dipping deep in the pot and a little tallow added occasionally to flux. This of course, does not always produce family harmony, as the good wife is very apt to wish that both yourself and that accursed smoking pot of metal were elsewhere. However, this is necessary for best results in bullet casting. Always dip the ladle or dipper down deep in the pot, as this helps to keep the metal evenly mixed. All bullet mixtures tend to change in temper as the metal is used up, so it is very hard to maintain the same proportion throughout an evening's bullet casting.

The tin, antimony and lead should be carefully weighed and not merely guessed at.

The charcoal over the top helps to keep the metal clean and free from dross. Any dross in the dipper or on the nozzle of the electric furnace will often be deposited on the sides or base of the bullet, causing it to be unevenly balanced. This kind of bullet should be discarded. When the melting pot gets too hot, the metal usually turns a blue color. The heat should then be cut down somewhat, as it will only oxidize and burn up the metal. Extreme heat also tends to change the temper of the alloy to some extent.

Where electricity is available, the best system for bullet casting is an electric furnace. I have used both the Potter and the Saeco. The little Potter will run out a tremendous lot of bullets and as it is small, it does not heat up the whole room, but the metal supply must be replenished often owing to its small capacity. The Potter may also be had in a larger size and is a better buy if you do much bullet casting or use a gang mould.

The best electric furnace I have used is the thermostatically controlled Saeco, made by the Santa Anita Engineering Company of Pasadena, California. This has a large pot, holding considerable metal, and is controlled by a thermostat at any degree of heat desired. While the Potter may be operated at two different temperatures, the Saeco has a wider range and can be turned up for melting, and when the metal has reached the right temperature for perfect bullets, can be turned to exactly the right temperature to maintain even, full cast bullets. Both outfits are very good and a great improvement over the old kitchen range, Ideal pot, ring and dipper we used to use. Sometimes the nozzles of electric pots become tinned and coated with sprue; rub the end of a tallow candle on them; this will grease them enough so the dross and metal will no longer adhere.

Another thing to watch out for is that the pouring nozzles of electric furnaces are quite large in diameter, and many moulds have the screw and lock washer holding the sprue cutter very close to the pouring hole. I have, on occasion, had to file away one side of the screw and lock washer before the nozzle of the electric furnace would bed down fully in the pouring hole on top of the mould. If it does not seat fully, a splash of melted metal, often quite a stream, will run out to the side and cover the side of the mould and the floor or work bench. The nozzle must seat fully in the pouring hole of the mould before you raise the lever lifting the cut off in the bottom of the pot. The weight of metal in the pot all works to fill the mould perfectly and is many times better than even the largest hand dippers, as instead of a few ounces, you have fifteen to twenty pounds of molten metal forcing the mould to full capacity.

The lever on the furnace or melting pot should be raised for a couple seconds to be sure it forces the mould full and the mould held firmly against the nozzle, for a second or two after the cut off lever is closed. If this is done, very little sprue will accumulate and perfect bullets will result.

Many moulds will become cranky during casting. The sprue cutters will function perfectly for a time, then get tight or bind and one must loosen the lock screw to allow the sprue cutting plate to move freely. This is due to expansion of the metal of the mould. If the sprue cutter or top of the mould blocks becomes tinned, rub a tallow candle over them quickly and cast until you burn off the surplus grease. They will usually stay clean and free of tinning for some time. A dip of the candle in the molten metal of the pot occasionally and a stir with the dipper will keep the metal fluxed and mixed and in best condition for casting perfect bullets.

Since I loaded my first pistol cartridges with black powder, using nut cracker tools, there have been many advances in handloading machinery, not the least of which is the electric furnace. I have no hesitancy in recommending the Potter and Saeco. They eliminate most of the unpleasant features of bullet making; they make better bullets possible, and they save time. In my opinion, emphatically, an electric pot is the bullet caster's best friend.

A new mould is often quite a task to break in; the one best way to do it is to keep on casting bullets. At times, it is well to grease the mould inside with a little tallow when hot and then continue casting until the bullets begin to drop out on opening the mould. Of course, after greasing, the mould will cast only wrinkled bullets until all traces of the grease are burned out of the blocks, but when this is accomplished, it will often cast much better. Occasionally the addition of a little lump of grease to the mixture and a thorough stirring of the metal, also helps make the casting of perfect bullets an easier task, as well as keeping the metals better mixed.

Great care must be exercised in not allowing water or moisture to collect about a bullet mould or melting pot while casting, as water in a pot of molten metal acts like fire to a giant powder cap, and will explode hot lead all over the surrounding scenery. Caution must be used in adding odd bits of metal to the pot, especially old lead pipe in the winter time, as it may contain some ice inside. All such old metal should first be heated up or preferably put in the pot while the latter is cold so that both pot and metal will be brought to the right temperature together. Another sure-fire way of producing excitement, to say nothing of bad burns, is to drop a loaded cartridge in the melting pot along with a quantity of recovered bullets that you wish to melt up, as Lemuel Smelzer once did while working with me at Durkee, Oregon. My face, hands, arms and shirt front were completely covered with melted metal, as well as Mrs. Keith's cookstove and the walls of the kitchen. Both of my eyes burned, and it was some time before I could see at all. Needless to say, I got hot under the collar in more ways than one.

Some moulds are very cranky and it may take considerable steady casting before they will throw good bullets, then again they may suddenly begin to throw imperfect bullets after having cast perfect ones for hours. Sometimes the trouble will result from the metal being too hot or too cool. Other times, it seems to be nothing but pure unadulterated cussedness on the part of the mould, and one will simply have to keep working along until the mould again casts properly. At such times, I often grease the mould inside, and then cast until the grease burns out completely, a process which often starts the mould casting good bullets again.

There may be times, after a mould has been used a great deal or has been heated too greatly from continuous casting when the metal was entirely too hot, that the cavity will become oxidized and will cast rough looking bullets, the points or an edge of the bands of which will not fill out at all. In mild cases, this is usually cured by dropping a small bit of tallow in the mould, then casting continued until the mould has burned out all of the grease. This procedure is usually successful. In aggravated cases this will sometimes fail to do the trick. The mould will then have to be repolished inside to remove the oxidization. Most printers use Putch's Pomade for mould polishing, but this is often very difficult if not quite impossible to obtain, particularly by those individuals living back on the ragged edges of civilization. We have found that powdered pumice stone works about as well, cutting out the oxidization quickly and repolishing the mould cavity.

The safest way to do this is to take a full and sharp bullet—one which perfectly fits the mould—place it in the cavity and grip the handles until it is held firmly. After doing this, take a small punch and mark it in the exact center. Now take a small breast drill and drill down in the center about half the length of the bullet, being very careful to hold the drill vertically. While a friend checks one side, you check from the other angle. Next take a small machine screw, turn it down into the cavity in the bullet thus formed and you have a real "polishing head." This can be rotated or turned by a screw driver twirled between the palms of the hands, but it is best to cut off the head of the screw and chuck it in the breast drill. Then coat the bullet with light oil and some powdered pumice stone, and while a friend or helper holds the mould halves together with a steady, even tension, but not tight enough to bind the bullet and prevent its rotating, spin the bullet around and around until the mould is thoroughly polished. This will usually require but a few minutes, and after the mould has been used enough to burn out the oil, it will again cast perfectly. Of course, the mould should be thoroughly cleaned after the polishing, before again casting. This can be best done with gasoline.

Sometimes a mould may refuse to do good work because of trapped air imprisoned in the cavity when the metal is poured into it. In this case, the mould will have to be vented. Very few workmen can properly vent a mould as could Harry Pope and others of the fine old Scheutzen rifle makers, most of whom are now dead. However, there are ways of accomplishing this yourself. Remember, there are always two ways to skin a cat. The mould, if for a solid bullet, can be vented by merely making a very slight scratch on the face of one block back about one-eighth to one-fourth inch from the cavity, and as near as possible to that portion of the cavity that refused to fill out properly. The slight burr thrown up by a tiny knife cut or scratch will usually allow the imprisoned air to escape and the mould to still cast perfectly. With hollow point moulds, the best system I have found is to take a pair of small ordinary pliers, and with the rear portion of the jaws, (used for small wire cutting) grip the plug down next to its handle so that the point to be cut or marred will be about half way between the mould cavity and the outside of the mould. Holding the pliers fairly tight on this hollow point plug stem, rotate it with the fingers and thus make a small cut around it. This will throw up a slight burr, which spreads the mould just enough to allow the air to escape, but not enough, however, to allow the molten metal to flow out between the mould faces and make an angel out of your bullet. The above stunts will usually cure any balky mould, but they must be done carefully or the mould can be ruined very easily.

Some folks think that a mould can be used as a pair of pliers. I have had some thoughtless individuals use my moulds to pull nails, etc., when I was not at home. Such practices come under the same classification as the cow-puncher who uses the front sight of his sixgun to pull staples and then, after leading his nag over the wire while he stands on it, drives them in again with the butt of the gun. Such people use the top of their heads merely as a hat rack, possessing nothing but solid ivory above the ears.

Use as light a pine stick as possible to strike the gate and cut the sprue off the bullet, as many moulds have too light and too thin a swinging gate (including the Lyman) which sooner or later will not be struck perfectly square and will bend, with the result that your bullet will turn into an angel and have wings on the base. Sometimes the gate or sprue cutting plate will warp from the heat. When this happens, they must then be placed on a perfectly flat surface plate and trued up again, a job which is at best difficult unless one is properly equipped to do it.

Where possible to do so, bullet casting should be

done during the cold of winter, as it is then a much more pleasant job than on a hot summer day. The work table or bench should be handy to the worker, so that he can drop the bullets out without having to move about too much. The top of the table or bench should be covered with several thicknesses of cloth, burlap or old blankets to cushion the bullets when they fall, as they are very easily upset or battered for different bullets, yet with their new type moulds, needs but the one set of handles.

After the cast bullets are thoroughly cool, go over them and select the perfect ones for use and throw the imperfect bullets back in the pot for remelting. All told, this bullet casting is by far the hardest job of hand reloading. As we have pointed out, an electric bullet pot will take away much of the grief, and

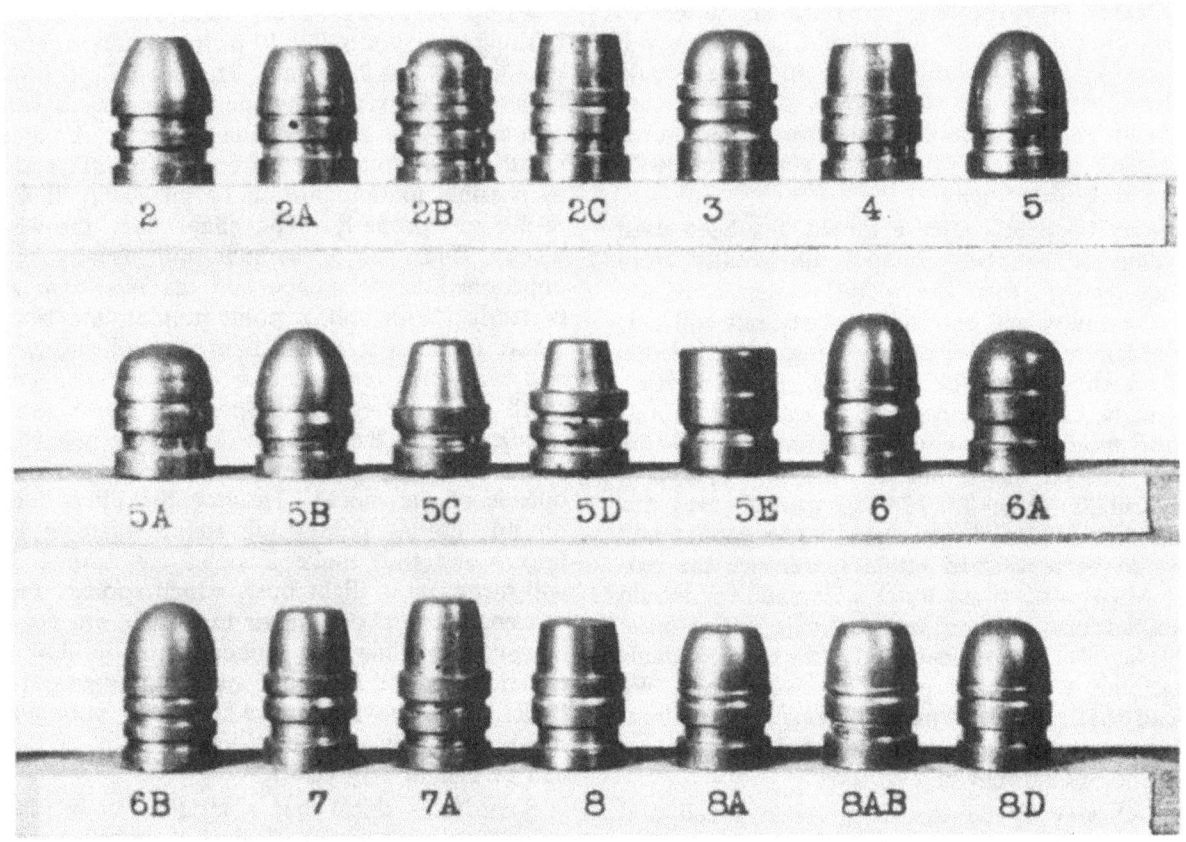

Seco revolver bullets Numbers 2, 4, 7, and 8 Keith designs.

when they come hot from the mould, being very soft and not thoroughly hardened.

When through casting with an iron mould, it should always be greased while still hot, and the best way to do this is to leave the last bullet in the cavity and drop some grease on the base of the said bullet, or point, if it is a point cut-off mould. Belding & Mull made moulds of solid nickel, while the Yankee Specialty Company made theirs of bronze. These latter bronze moulds are very good and cast fine bullets with the least effort of any I have used. They also had a 255 grain bullet for the .44 Special that gave wonderful accuracy for me at extreme ranges, although being a round nose bullet, it has little stopping power. The Lyman system affords the reloader a great many different moulds with one set of handles. It takes but a few minutes time to change blocks, so that the handloader can purchase several sets of mould blocks if it isn't a hobby, and does not have a recreational value, there isn't much point in doing it. If you are interested you will enjoy making your own slugs, and if you are not interested you just won't do it at all. It is as simple as that.

Bullet Sizing and Lubrication

Now that we have a plentiful supply of bullets cast up for use during the next few months' shooting, we can proceed with the operations of sizing and lubricating. First of all though, it may be wise to examine the bore of the sixgun which these bullets will be fired through and ascertain beyond the shadow of a doubt just what its cylinder and groove dimensions happen to be. I know of many shooters who have been using all sorts of revolvers for years, yet who have never yet taken the trouble to determine this most vital point.

A BULLET CHAPTER

Clamp your sixgun vertically into a vise which has its jaws suitably padded to prevent marring the gun. Now take a soft lead bullet, start it point first down the muzzle of the gun and tap it on into the bore, using a small stick of hardwood as a drift, and tapping that with a mallet or hammer. Be careful to drive it in as straight with the axis of the bore as possible. After it goes down flush with the muzzle of the gun it may upset or flare out at the base. Pay no attention to this, but take a hardwood cleaning rod and drive that bullet on through the barrel, having first opened the cylinder or removed it from the gun. If you do not happen to have a suitable vise around, you can hold the gun in your hand or between your knees while the bullet is being forced through. As the bullet emerges, catch it with the fingers or on some folds of cloth laid in the cylinder recess of the frame.

Now we have a bullet which, if it has been properly driven through the bore, will give us the exact groove diameter of that particular barrel, which is what we are interested in. Hold the bullet in your left hand by its point and turn your micrometer up on its base and middle bands, using only the ratchet with which to turn. Any Colt gun will be easy to mike, as they have six grooves and lands. Remember that the "lands" on that bullet are the groove diameter of your barrel. Mike both base and front or middle bands, being sure to take the reading from the widest part of the bullet. In other words, make certain your micrometer is bearing on the center of the band on each side. With Smith & Wesson guns and their five groove barrels, this is a harder job, as one must mike from the edge or corner of one land across to the edge of the corner opposite. If done carefully, they can be miked all right, but they are harder to do than the Colt barrels.

It might be advisable to repeat the slugging operation and shove another soft bullet through the gun, then check against the first readings. After having ascertained this groove dimension beyond any doubt, it might also be well to repeat the process and determine the diameter of the cylinder throats. This is not so important as the groove diameters, but it is well to know for certain that these throats are not smaller than the barrel grooves, a situation which I have often known to be the case with the older .45 Colt single actions. Take a full-sized bullet, as it comes from the mould, and make certain it can be pushed through the cylinder throats without any difficulty; or, if you want to "slug" them properly, upset a soft bullet in each throat and then mike these accurately.

Now we are ready to proceed with the sizing of the bullet, and possibly its lubrication at the same time. With light loads and comparatively light, short bullets, the diameter of the sized bullet can be as much as .003 of an inch over groove diameter of your barrel, but with normal and heavy loads I much prefer that those bullets be sized to not more than .001 of an inch over our groove diameter. This .001 of an inch is the diameter over groove measurements, which I prefer for most sixgun loads, although as elsewhere stated, for large caliber guns of .44 and .45 caliber, a difference of .001 of an inch is not so important as in the smaller .38 caliber guns. Thus, in the .44 Special and .45 Colt you can get by with a diameter of .002 of an inch over groove diameter easier than you can in a .38 Special or smaller caliber. Even a diameter of but .001 of an inch over groove diameter seems to shoot with extreme accuracy, and I prefer such a sizing of bullets for maximum or magnum loads, especially in the heavy frame .38 caliber guns. My S. & W. Magnum measures .357 of an inch groove diameter and I size my bullets for it to .358 of an inch, a sizing to exact groove diameter alleviates pressures and seems to work just as well.

Most of the Smith & Wesson .44 Special guns I have slugged and miked, ran .430 of an inch groove diameter, and I size all bullets for these guns to .431 of an inch. Many late 1950 Target S. & W. .44 Special guns run only .428 inch groove diameter, and for these .429 is the best sizing. Most of the Colt guns I have tried, and there have been a great many, have shown groove diameters of .4265 of an inch to .4286 of an inch and for these guns I generally size the bullets to .429 of an inch. With some early .44/40 Colts which have since been fitted with .44 Special cylinders, I have found the groove diameters to run as small as .423 to .424 of an inch, and for such the bullets should be sized down to .425 or .426 of an inch and any larger diameter should never be tolerated. There is no "hoss-sense" whatever in trying to resize your lead bullets ahead of some 15,000 to 25,000 pounds pressure in the thin walled cylinders of your revolver. Furthermore, I have seldom seen any accuracy obtained from the use of bullets greatly in excess of the groove diameter of the gun.

As I said before, care should be taken to see that your sized bullet will always shove through the throat of the cylinder chambers of the gun by hand and using but little effort. Many .45 guns, especially the older, very early production, will be found with barrels having groove diameters of only .450 to .452 of an inch and the chambers will be found correspondingly small, while with other guns, especially those assembled from old parts (and there are thousands of these assembled guns floating around), the cylinder throats may mike only .450 of an inch while the bore may be as much as .454 or even .455. Such a combination is hopeless for accuracy until you have had those chamber throats reamed out to .001 of an inch over groove diameter. I have had some Colt guns which had a cylinder throat measurement of .457 and a groove diameter of .452. Such a combination cannot give proper results, and the best cure for such cases is a new

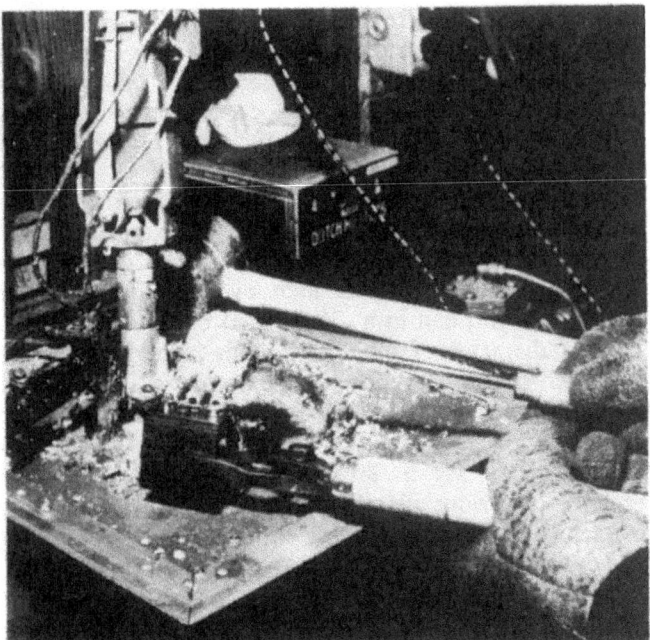

J. W. McPhillips, custom loader, casting revolver bullets in a three cavity mould in his shop at 285 Mastic Ave., San Bruno, California.

cylinder. Any cylinder having extremely large chamber mouth measurements is also mighty apt to be chambered oversize. This extreme variation amongst the .45 Colt clan, as well as the fact that similar variations seemed to exist in most loading tools made for it, was one of the reasons why I quit the .45 caliber in favor of the .44 Special as my heavy caliber cartridge.

The late J. D. O'Meara was an exceptionally skillful workman on .45 Colt guns, as he thoroughly understood all of these facts. He reamed out several .45 Colt cylinders for me and also fitted new barrels to some of the guns. Some of the finest shooting .45 Colts in existence in the West today are those which that fine old scout worked over and fitted up. The men now owning those guns should be proud of them. He had but one hand to work with, and how he ever turned out such good work with only that one "mitt" has always been a mystery to me.

Now that we have figured out the exact diameter to which our bullet must be sized, we can get along to the actual performance of the job itself. By far the best method, and the cheapest in the long run, is to obtain one of the Lyman Ideal, the Modern Bond, or Saeco bullet sizers and lubricators. These machines are splendid and there is nothing that can quite take their place for doing the combined job of sizing and lubricating, which they do at the one operation. Any of these firms can furnish you with extra dies for any caliber, or to any measurement you may desire, as well as supply you with an exceptionally good grade of stick lubricant in proper size to fit their machines. I cannot recommend too strongly that the handloader obtain one of these sizing and lubricating machines. There is nothing to equal them as a time and labor saver, or to do as perfect a job, provided the proper dies and punches are arranged and properly regulated in the machine. Get one of these machines by all means, so that you may avoid a lot of trouble.

If the beginner cannot afford one of these machines, then fairly good results can be obtained with the Ideal or Belding & Mull small, hand bullet sizers. The Ideal should be obtained in the base-first type which screws into their #3 or similar loading tool in place of the loading chamber. These dies may be had in any diameter, all very accurate, but the bullet must first be lubricated by hand before it can be sized. For this lubricating, about the best method I have found is to take a very shallow pan or pot and in it melt up enough lubricant for the job. Use either a prepared lubricant like the Ideal Banana, or a home-brew article of beeswax and tallow, or even pure beef tallow can be made to do.

Take a pair of fairly long tweezers or pliers and gently grasp the point of the bullet, then immerse its base into the melted lubricant as deeply as necessary, at least deep enough to cover all its lubrication grooves. Lift it out and stand it on its base on a clean, planed board. A still better method, is to stand all your bullets on their bases in the shallow pan and then pour melted lubricant around them until

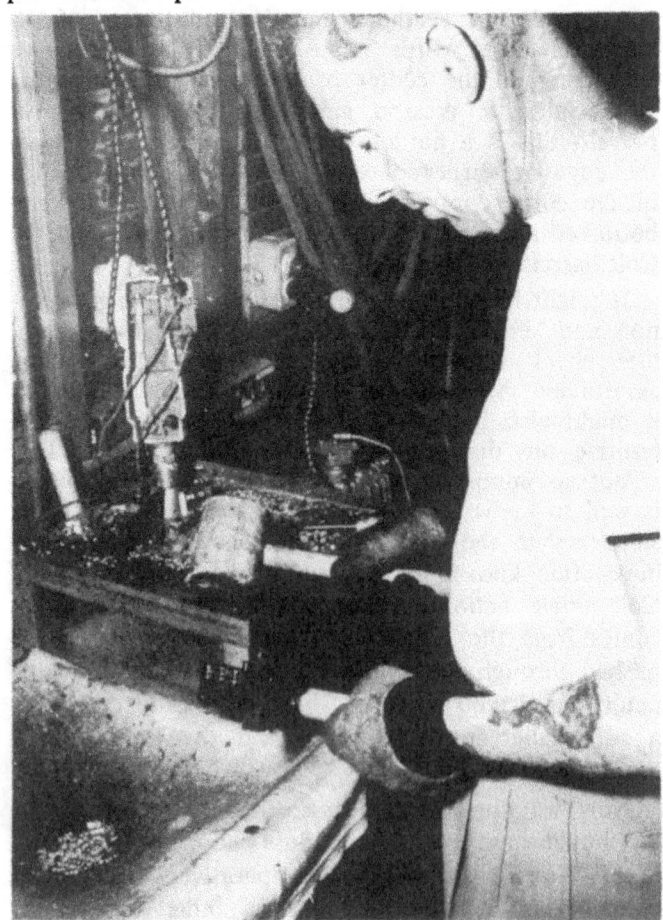

McPhillips, dropping the bullets from the moulds.

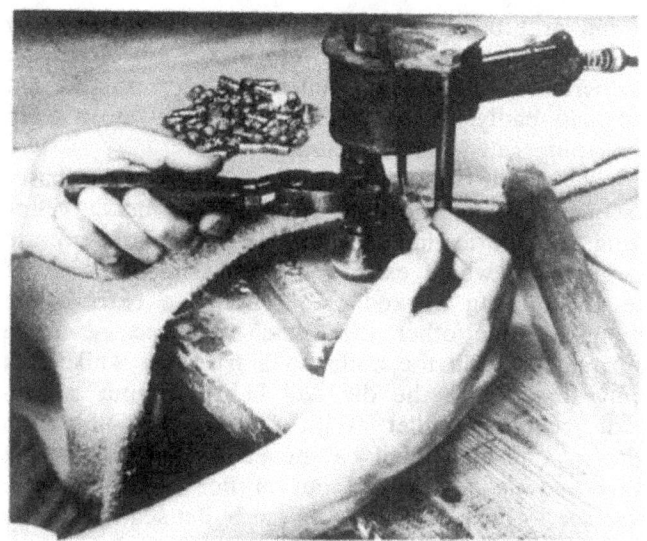

Courtesy of Moody's Reloading Service.
Photo by George Gresh.

Bullet casting operation showing Potter electric furnace and Ideal mould for Keith 235 gr. H. P. bullet for .44 Sp. (#429421). Portion of old axe handle serves well as sprue cutter.

it is above the level of the top groove, or as deep as you want it. After the lubricant has hardened, take an Ideal Kake Kutter, or similar gadget made at home by cutting the head off a suitable rifle cartridge and expanding its neck until it will just slip over the base of the bullet, and thrust it down over the point of each bullet, one after another, until the "slicked off" bullets work out the top of the tool.

They are now ready to be put through the base-first handsizing die. After this is done, all surplus grease should be carefully wiped off the points of the bullets, as well as from their bases. Take the time to do this last, because it may affect the powder charge or cause a squib. Any grease left on the point of the bullet will only gum up the loading chamber of the tool or cause trouble from seating it and the following bullets at too great a depth in the case. After cleaning, pack your finished bullets away neatly, using some small covered box or similar container and standing them all base down and against each other so that their lubricant will not spread all over adjoining bullets, and so they will be protected from dirt and grit, elements which promptly adhere to the greased bullet and stay there.

While on this subject of bullet sizing, I want to say a word or two regarding those old Ideal tools which had a hole drilled through their lower handle with a swinging punch in the upper handle, for the alleged purpose of sizing bullets. I have never yet found one of these tools with a sizing hole which was round; also that punch invariably strikes the bullet base off-center, badly upsetting, and in many cases, bending the bullet while forcing it through that hole. Such tools are a joke and will only ruin already excellent bullets, which almost always shoot more accurately just as they come from the mould than they do after being shoved through any such excuse for a bullet sizer. If you have such a tool, get a separate bullet sizer of the base-first type, or if your tool has the double-adjustable, removable chamber, order the base-first sizing die and chamber to fit it and good results will be obtained. Never attempt to correctly size bullets through one of those makeshift sizing holes in an old combination tool. During World War I, every Ideal tool I was able to procure had an oval shaped bullet sizing hole. For serious revolver shooting, all bullets must be accurately and perfectly sized to fit the individual gun.

The price of the Ideal, Seco, Hollywood or Bond machine will soon be justified by the saving in time, as well as by the added convenience and accuracy of its use, and the elimination of all surplus grease from the bullet and hands. When lubricating bullets by hand, I always get some of the grease on my clothes as well, and my nose never fails to itch just about the time my hands get greased well and good—everything manages to get well lubricated by the time the job is finished.

Leading of sixgun barrels is usually caused by too hot a powder, by an oversized or an undersized bullet, or by too heavy a charge of powder. With the heavy loads of #2400 Hercules powder that I have mentioned, some leading will occur at times in perfect and well polished barrels. Such charges are bound to be fairly hot, as the bullet is driven up the bore at such high speed that the friction alone may cause some leading. Plenty of good, graphite impregnated lubricant is usually sufficient to stop this. But I remember one time, when using very heavy charges of Bullseye in an old S. A. Colt .32/20, that the gun

Courtesy of Moody's Reloading Service.
Photo by George Gresh.

Bullet sizing and lubricating operation using the efficient Meepos Speedlube. Bullets in foreground are all Keith design as follows: (L. to R.) 235 gr. H. P. for .45 Long Colt; 240 gr. solid for .45 Auto Rim; 225 gr. H. P. for .45 Auto Rim; 235 gr. H. P. for .44 Sp.; 160 gr. H. P. for .38 Sp. and .357 Mag.; 173 gr. solid for .38 Sp. and .357 Mag.

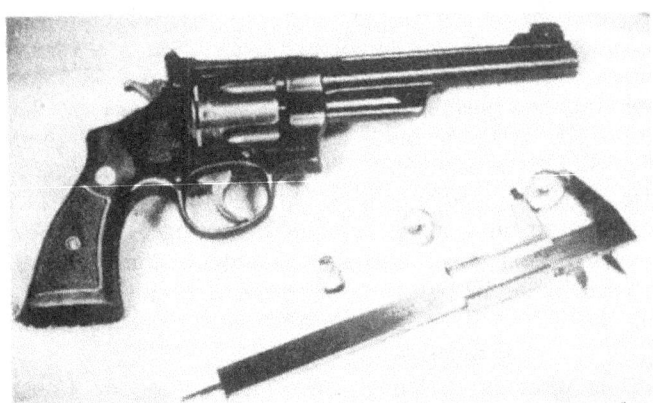

Courtesy of Moody's Reloading Service.
Photo by George Gresh.

A .44 Sp. S. & W. Model 1926 Target with King red bead reflector front and white outline rear sights. Middle bullet was recovered from deep snow bank after passing broadside through jackrabbit. Bullet on right expanded to diameter of .865 inch on passing broadside through upper part of deer and lodging just under hide on opposite side. Distance of shot was 70 yards. Keith hollow point 235 gr., 18.5 gr. of 2400.

leaded badly with either hard or soft bullets, due to the extremely hot powder fusing their bases.

I discovered that even #5 is too hot for heavy doses. I sent Major Wesson a 230 grain Keith hollow base bullet fired from my S. & W., triple lock, .44 Special that went lengthwise through a coyote at 50 yards with 7.5 grains #5. The yellow dog turned around with a yelp when that bullet struck him in the chest and then piled up. I recovered the bullet from a snow bank in back of the coyote. That bullet still showed the base band badly fused on the outside, and this in spite of its hollow base which, some would have us believe, always spreads or swages out to completely fill up the bore.

Most bullet moulds are cut large enough to throw an oversized bullet and thus insure its working properly through the sizing die; hence almost any bullet as cast will be oversized for the average sixgun barrel; therefore there is a necessity for sizing tools or machines to swage or size down bullets to the proper diameter. Some bullets might come from the mould in proper size to lubricate and use. Many of the Schuetzen rifle bullets are made this way and need only to be lubricated. However, it is much the best to resize all revolver bullets. Any mould which casts an undersized bullet should be promptly returned to the factory or thrown away, for it cannot be properly resized or lubricated, as the grease will squeeze out along the sides and make a very messy job of things. Furthermore, undersized bullets are apt to gas cut and lead badly. This condition prohibits them from developing satisfactory accuracy.

With all the bullet sizing dies, whether the base-first accessory of the tong tools, or the much better sizing and lubricating machines, it is essential to use a top punch which exactly fits the point or nose of the bullet being worked. Do not try to extemporize or make some other top punch do, because these top punches hold the bullet in a true line while it is being forced into the die and help turn out a perfectly centered bullet. With improperly fitting top punches, the bullet will be shoved to one side or the other and its axis forced out of line with the base. Also see to it that the base of the bullet seats squarely in the die, so that it will not be upset and the bullet ruined. Keep both the inside of the top punch and the top of the base punch wiped clean of surplus grease, and be sure to adjust the seating depth of the machine so that the bullet will be shoved clear down into its sizing die and will have all of its bands properly sized, particularly the front band. Do not have any lubricant ahead of the front band.

Too much care cannot be exercised in the preparation of your bullets. Regardless of how much care and skill you employ in loading the cartridge, you will not get accuracy unless you have perfect bullets which are the correct diameter for your individual gun.

For practice shooting, one can shoot into large blocks of wood or better still into one of these patented bullet stops with target holder attached, and thus save all your lead for remelting. Use of these will greatly cut down the cost of such shooting. For the last twenty years I have been using a Koehler Brothers bullet stop, both for target practice and for sighting in guns for folks who come here for a visit or to get their gun sighted up. This excellent back stop catches all the lead, and it is surprising the amount of bullet metal I take out of it during a year's time and save for future use. It is also much more handy to clip a target on the front of this Koehler backstop than to mess around hunting up tacks and using a block of wood. Furthermore, the back may be removed from this bullet stop in a very few minutes and the bullet metal easily taken out.

Chapter XVII

Cartridge Reloading

Revolver Powders

We have today, quite a variety of satisfactory revolver powders to select from and the handloader can obtain almost any velocity he desires by using the proper brand. For light to normal charges, Bullseye is a splendid powder. It is especially useful in very light, gallery or practice loads where only a pinch is required. Its charges run so light and the load bulks up so small in the case that it is one of the cheapest of all pistol powders to use. It is exceptionally accurate, even in very light charges, and best of all, it ignites easily. No matter how much air space remains in the case or how poor or irregular the crimp is, just as long as a good smokeless primer is used, Bullseye will do its stuff. It is a very fast burning, hot powder, and will burn completely and cleanly in very short barrels. Pressures are highly uniform if care is used in loading. Bullseye is not a good powder for any but light to normal loads, as it is too hot and will fuse the base of the bullet, if extreme charges are attempted. The base band will melt badly before the maximum pressure is arrived at.

Undoubtedly the greatest handicap in using Bullseye is the ease with which two charges can be loaded into the same case. The powder is so condensed, and so little is required for even normal loads that a double charge can readily be thrown and the bullet seated with no trouble—the trouble only comes when that double charge is fired. Bullseye has a balance point around 9000 pounds pressure, with a satisfactory working range extending some 4000 to 5000 pounds below, and only some 3000 pounds above this point. It has what might be termed a medium working range, and is so dense a powder that extreme care should always be used in its loading. It is a very accurate, reliable powder and is extremely stable.

Du Pont Pistol Powder #5 or #5066, its successor is a bit better powder for average loads than Bullseye. It bulks up somewhat better in the case and a double charge is more easily detected. In any case, however, extreme care must be exercised in loading any of the dense pistol powders in order to avoid this trouble. Being a nitrocellulose powder, #5, or #5066, is not quite as hot burning as Bullseye, but it does not possess the ease of ignition of Bullseye. It has a wider working range and a balance point of about 10,000 pounds. It works well in light loads, probably in not quite as small charges as Bullseye, but it can be used in charges slightly over normal without running into too great trouble. Still, it is too hot and quick burning for heavy loads and will fuse bullet bases before the maximum safe pressure can be reached in the heavy frame guns.

Du Pont #6 is a very accurate powder for normal loads but no better than the much later #5066 and with about the same working pressure.

The above three brands are the smokeless powders which the beginner should start off with—after he has had a bit of experience with black powder. Carelessness must not be tolerated when the charges are being thrown in the cases, and a close inspection should be made of each block full of charged cases before the bullets are seated. Use only the proper smokeless primers and don't attempt any "cocktail" loads or fancy black-powder-priming stunts until you have gotten the hang and swing of things. After, say six months or a year of such loading and shooting, you will be qualified to take up the loading of the following powders:

Hercules Unique is a fine powder for loads slightly above normal on up to the full pressures the arm will safely stand. It is not nearly as good for magnum revolver loads as their #2400, but is a fine powder up to 15,000 or 16,000 pounds, giving very good velocities for the pressures developed. I consider it a much better powder than obsolete Du Pont #80 for heavy and medium heavy revolver loads but it has a narrow working range and is also a very hot, nitroglycerin powder like Bullseye; accordingly, one must load carefully with a close check on pressures. Unique is a fine powder for loads around 1000 feet velocity, getting close to 1100 feet in some cases with normal weight bullets. The magnum loads are not obtained with it as well as with #2400, as its heat fuses the bases when overloaded. I do not consider it a suitable powder for light loads.

Unique best takes the place of #80 powder, giving about the same velocities that may be obtained with the

See Publisher's Note at end of chapter.

241

New Service Colt .455 rechambered to .45 Colt. Blown up with an overload of 40 grains 2400 with Keith-type soft oversize bullet. This compressed charge of 2400 must have detonated as the bullet did not have time to enter the barrel and shaved the part out on top of same as cylinder and top strap left the gun. A 40 grain black powder measure must have been used as the charge almost filled the cartridge case. Five loads were pulled for a check on the one that blew the gun.

latter, but with less pressure, and with less variation in pressures. In some cases it will give results better than are obtainable with any other powder. I like it very well for loads in the .45 Auto Rim. Unique has a balance point around 13,000 pounds, with a working range of about 4000 pounds above this, but very little below. It is a very accurate and thoroughly stable powder and a reliable brand to use if the charge is properly fitted to the cartridge and due care is exercised in its loading.

For a good many years Du Pont #80 powder was our best bet for heavy revolver loads, in spite of criticisms by many handloaders. Properly loaded, it will give very fine accuracy at comparatively high velocity. I do not like it as well as Unique for many loads, mainly on account of its being affected by moisture or extremes in temperature. It will dry out if stored in a hot place. Also, the permissible charge may vary as much as two grains in different lots of this powder, this being a big variation for some cartridges.

Cartridges loaded with #80 and stored in a hot and dry climate may in a short time so increase in pressure that they are decidedly unsafe, hence this powder should be loaded for immediate use and not stored away. This fact, that it will dry out and greatly increase in power and pressure under some storage conditions, makes it an unsafe powder for revolvers under all conditions of loading. At times, loads worked out and carefully checked at low temperatures become altogether too strong for use in hot weather. I consider it now obsolete.

Du Pont #80 has a balance point around 16,000 pounds, which is above the safety line for many revolver cartridges, yet well within the limits of safety of our better made, heavy frame .44 Special revolvers or in .38 Special guns on .45 frames. It does not burn well unless loaded to near the maximum safe pressure and will squib badly at times in lighter charges. But, properly loaded, for near or immediate use in heavy charges, with these charges properly worked up and the loading carefully controlled, it will give a good account of itself. Unless loaded in full charges, there will be considerable unburned powder left in the bore of the gun and even in maximum loads it does not burn any too completely. It will not give as good velocities as will Hercules #2400 in magnum and maximum charges in such cartridges as the .38 Special, .357, .44 Special and .45 Colt, yet it works well in all these calibers and is very good in the .45 Auto Rim. The .32/20, .38/40 and .44/40 take well to it, but higher velocities, with the same or less pressure, can be obtained with #2400.

I know of several good Officer's Model Colts being blown up with a charge of 11 grains of #80 behind the standard 158 grain bullet. In order to find out the pressure this load developed, I loaded some and used them in my S. & W. Outdoorsman with fine accuracy and great killing power. Knowing them to be greatly in excess of maximum safe loads for the .41 frame guns, I sent some to Peters for test and my friend Colonel Tewes reported an average pressure of 42,000 pounds. It was no wonder that those Officer's Models let go. I do not consider #80 a safe powder or a good one for any light frame revolver. In the .45 Colt it will work well up to a charge of 15 grains with my 250 grain Lyman bullet, provided the bullet diameter is carefully checked and the bullet properly and well crimped in the crimp groove. Over this charge, I am off #80 in the .45 Colt and with good reason, because with 16.3 grains and my 260 grain Belding & Mull .45 Colt bullet, I cracked the rear end of the barrel in three places.

My friend Ashley Haines has obtained wonderful results with #80 in both the .45 Colt and the .44/40 Single Action. However, he is a very careful handloader who thoroughly knows what it is all about. I had good results with this powder in the .38/40. But recent shooting has shown me that with less velocity it will expand the cases more than does #2400. Since the advent of this later Hercules powder, I am through with #80 in revolvers.

Hercules #2400 is the powder used by Winchester in working up the .357 Magnum cartridge, and to my notion it is the best of all powders for extreme or

K-38 S. & W. Target blown up by faulty hand load—too much fast powder.

maximum loads in heavy frame, thick cylindered revolvers. This powder will not work well in anything but heavy loads and if these loads are crowded too much it will fuse the bullet somewhat, causing leading; still I believe most of the leading one obtains from this powder is due to friction from the greatly increased velocity. Number #2400 does not develop as high pressures for the same velocity as does #80 and seems to be a much more suitable powder. Certain results may be obtained in the .38 Special, .357 Magnum, .44 Special and .45 Colt which cannot be equalled with any other powder I know of.

This #2400 is no powder for the novice to use in reloading pistol ammunition. Very fine high velocity loads however, may be worked up by the experienced handloader, and with it maximum killing and stopping power will be developed. For use in the .38 Special cartridge to be fired only in guns like the .45 frame Colt or heavy S. & W., we load a charge of 13.5 grains of #2400 with the 160 grain Keith Lyman hollow point or 173 grain solid bullet and get killing results that are not to be obtained with any other combination in this cartridge. In the .44 Special we load 18.5 grains with my 235 grain hollow point, or 250 grain solid in the old web cases, or 17.5 grains in the new solid head cases, and with the .45 Colt we use the Keith 235 grain hollow point and 18.5 grains of #2400. Loads such as these should only be put up in new, heavy cases in perfect condition. They will at any rate, give you the maximum power in these calibers. In the .357 Magnum S. & W. revolver we load 15 grains of #2400 and the 160 grain Keith Lyman bullet, or 14.5 with the 173 grain solid. With all the loads listed in this paragraph, the bullet diameter is fixed at .001 of an inch over groove diameter and cast to a temper of one part tin to sixteen parts lead, or a mixture of half tin and half antimony in the same formula. A sizing of exact groove diameters works equally well.

I have tried to work out a good load in the .45 Auto Rim case with #2400, but have not been successful, the powder seemingly developing the maximum permissible pressure long before it reaches a clean burning stage. This #2400 powder seems to work best in the longer revolver cases and the .45 Colt charges I' have mentioned throughout this book are intended for the standard, long Colt shell and not any of those short, Remington squib cases. The .45 Colt charge also works well in the new 1950 Target S. & W. with Keith 250 grain bullet seated to crimp barely over the front based and sized .454 inches for this .457 barrel.

With all revolver loads, it must be kept in mind that you are working with pressures which must be held under a certain definite point, and when you go over such pressures the gun may go to pieces. You do not have the margin of safety such as exists in loading rifle cartridges, where a grain or so too much may mean only a pierced or blown out primer with possibly a spurt of gas in the face; in the sixgun such action would probably wreck the arm. The powder charges

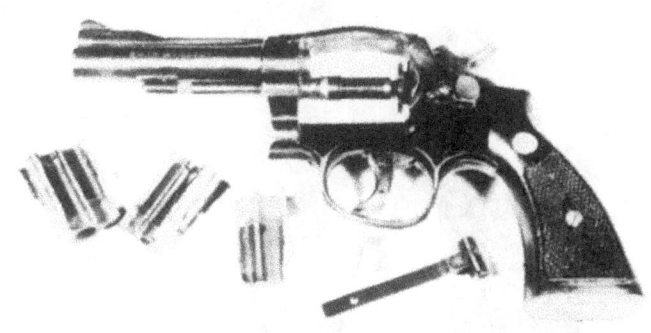

Smith & Wessen Combat Masterpiece blown up with a faulty hand load.

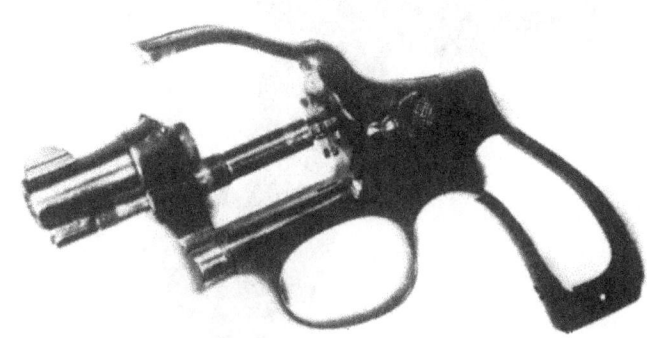

Smith & Wesson Chief's Special blown up with a too heavy hand load.

Smith & Wesson .44 Special target blown up with faulty hand load. These guns, including the Colt New Service, all show detonations caused by far too heavy hand loads by careless hand loaders. Usually two charges of powerful pistol powder will turn the trick nicely.

in a revolver cartridge are small in proportion to modern rifle charges, consequently an increase of a fraction of a grain in the handgun may raise pressures much more in proportion than would a two grain increase in the rifle. Therefore, act accordingly.

In preparing light or normal cartridges, the charges may be loaded very satisfactorily by using Belding & Mull, Lyman, Saeco, Hollywood, or similar powder measures, first carefully checking the measure settings

Pacific Gun Sight Company Standard Model reloading tool without automatic priming device.

bullet and still get about 900 feet velocity from his relic.

For most revolver cartridges, black powder should be secured in the F. F. g granulation, but for the smaller .32 cartridges the F. F. F. g will give a bit more velocity. It is peculiarly well adapted for use by the chap who cannot afford more than the very minimum in tools at the outset, and who must also purchase the very lowest priced tools obtainable.

After a "course of sprouts" with black powder, the amateur reloader will be ready to obtain a powder measure and scales and start in on smokeless powders. By first sticking to light and then normal smokeless powder loads, checking his settings with reliable scales, he will have no trouble. I advise against the use of scoop measures with any present day smokeless powder.

With all modern smokeless powders, full length case resizing is necessary to hold the bullet friction tight and to keep it at its proper place while the crimp is being formed in the loading chamber, as well as to help prevent its receding into the case after being loaded. Never fire a smokeless powder cartridge when its bullet has receded into the case to any degree. Some smokeless powders require a certain amount of air space for proper combustion and any decrease or

with an accurate scale. Don't put too much faith in the corner or village drug store scales for this or any other powder weighing. I have seen several druggist's balances which were far better adapted to weighing brickbats than small powder charges. A Fairbanks assay scale, the Troemner, Redding or other standard balances, or the Pacific powder scales are to be relied on. All heavy loads should be weighed.

For the average beginner in handloading, there is nothing quite so safe as black powder, True, it is dirty, and smokey, and fouls bore and cases badly until both have to be cleaned with hot water or solvent, but a lot of fun, satisfaction and experience can safely be obtained by its use. You can cram in all the black powder the case will hold, force the bullet on top of it, crimp it any old way that holds the bullet from jumping forward and that load will go off properly and its pressures be safe. Weigh black powder, measure it, scoop it up or just fill the case and strike off with a knife blade and you will still be safe. With all its faults, it is the only powder for the novice to start off with and I recommend his sticking to it until the fundamentals of the reloading game have been thoroughly learned. For the chap who shoots one of those old assembled, junk-pile .45 Colts, it is the one brand to stick to, because with it he can use the 250 grain lead

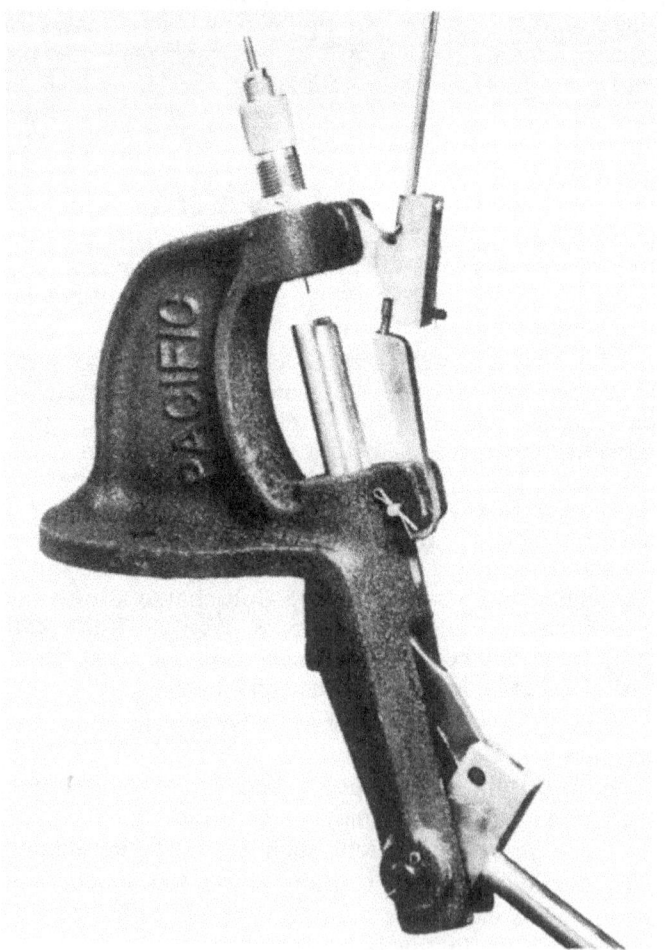

Pacific Gun Sight Company Super Model reloading tool with automatic priming device.

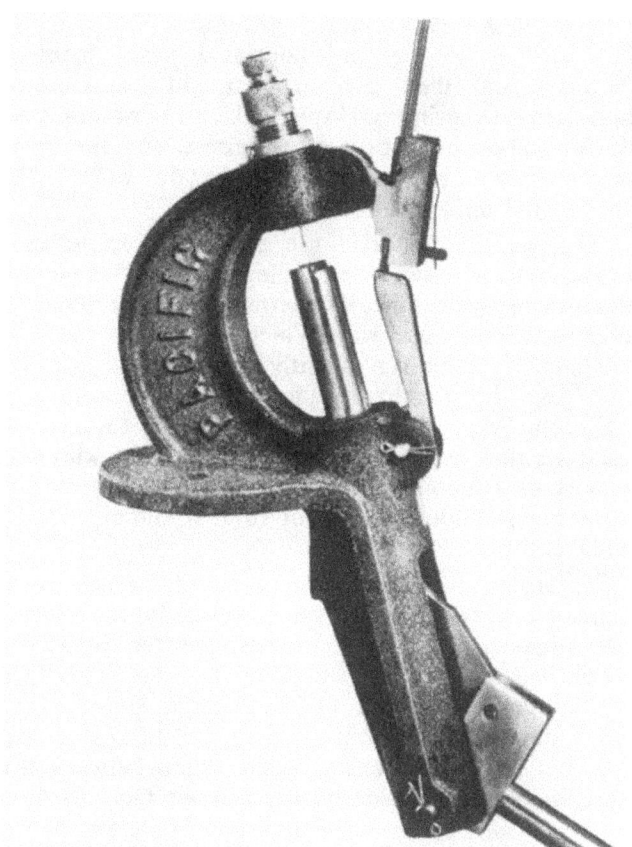

Pacific Gun Sight Company Standard Model, reloading tool with automatic priming device.

change in the seating depth may prove disastrous, as the pressures are sure to increase.

I am not going to pad this chapter with pages of lengthy tabulations of loads for the various sixguns, but prefer to insist that the reader obtain the very latest lists of such recommended charges direct from the Lyman Gun Sight Corp., Belding & Mull or other makers of loading tools. These companies have them available for distribution at all times and are continually bringing out new and more up-to-date lists with full data on any recent developments in either cartridges or bullets. They are also constantly checking and rechecking their recommendations for pressure and velocity every time a new lot of powder is placed on the market. As they have the very finest equipment possible for such testing and experimentation, their recommendations can always be relied on and anyone adhering to the tool makers lists should never run up serious pressures or encounter risk or accident if he first obtains a good working knowledge of the necessary essentials of handloading. I would particularly stress the importance of the shooter carefully checking his bullet diameter against the groove and cylinder throat dimensions of his guns. Also stick to the use of pistol primers in pistol cartridges; do not substitute rifle primers. One rifle primer may wreck your gun. If these things are carefully adhered to, any man with even a limited amount of gray matter can safely handload his sixgun ammunition.

Your stock of revolver powders should be stored in a cool and dry place, preferably where the temperature is never over 70 degrees Fahrenheit. I have had both rifle and pistol powders dry out and become noticeably stronger after being exposed to the extreme heat of a hot dry summer. The permissible charges then had to be cut down a grain or two. Once I had to cut a heavy rifle load as much as three grains. Care should be taken that the labels pasted around the canisters do not become displaced or lost. And if such should happen, see that no mistake be made when that powder is again identified and labelled. It is well to scribe the number and lot of the powder on the bottom of its canister as soon as received; then there should be no trouble in case a label gets lost or is eaten off by insects.

Again, I wish to stress the necessity and importance for beginners to adhere strictly to the powder company's or loading tool company's loads for a good many moons, or until the basic essentials of handloading and ballistics are thoroughly mastered. Also, considerable knowledge should be obtained from the action of smokeless powder, as well as some knowledge of pressure indications. Nothing is quite so safe or suitable as black powder to start off with, but there is no necessity of always using soft coal in your guns. No one should attempt to handload the heavy charges I have listed or mentioned for use with my bullets until he possesses a thorough knowledge of all angles of the loading game, and this knowledge should first be obtained by loading and firing a great many normal loads. Even then, such loads should be worked up with extreme caution, starting in with a couple grains less powder than I advise and carefully working up to what I have recommended. Go slowly—about the same way a three-legged coyote would approach a dead yearling that he had reason to believe is surrounded with well concealed steel traps. If this is done, we will have no trouble or accidents from handloading.

There are some individuals who will read over the powder or loading tool company charges or my recommended loads, and then say, "Well, this guy Keith used 18.5 grains of this new #2400 powder behind his 235 grain bullet, eh? Hell, he probably cut the charge a grain or two, in writing about it, to make it safe for everyone, so I'll just add two grains for a starter and get his real load." Anyone proceeding along this line of reasoning WILL get a real load—probably a new gun also. Handloading is NOT for such logical minded jaspers, and such have no business shooting anything but factory loads. I once encountered a fellow who measured his charges of #5 Du Pont powder by pouring them in little piles on a piece of white paper—said he could tell by the eye just the right sized pile of powder to make the correct charge. But he had better eyesight than I have.

Pacific Gun Sight Company Inside Ironer, cut-away view.

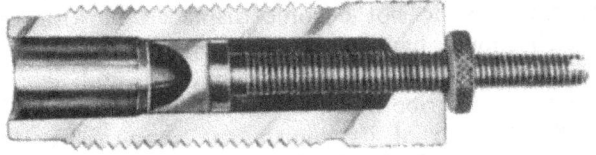

Cut-away View of Pacific Gun Sight Company pistol and revolver seating die with built in crimper (parts J. and K.).

Cases For Reloading

The next thing on our list of components necessary for the reloading of revolver cartridges will be the cases. Right here will be a good place to caution against the reloading of any or all makes of factory cartridges which have been fired with mercuric priming. Externally, such cases may look all right, but the structure of the brass has become so rotten that in resizing, the heads very often pull completely off from the body. And if there is one mean job to perform, it is to remove such a headless case from the loading chamber of a tool, generally scratching the die in so doing. Such rotten cases may be very dangerous to fire if reloaded, although in sizes such as .38 Special they may stand some few loadings. I once tried to resize a bunch of fired .45 Colt Western cases in an old Ideal full length die. They stood driving into the die splendidly, but when I tried driving them out, the head came off nearly every one, leaving the brass cylinder in the die, from which it was extremely hard to remove. I have often got as far as the crimping operation with such shells in the Pacific tool and then had the heads pull off in extracting the finished cartridge, spilling powder in the dies and causing no end of trouble.

I have finally come to the conclusion that the only fired, factory loaded cases which may be reloaded satisfactorily are the Remington Kleanbore or those Winchester and Western cases which are primed with their non-mercuric, non-corrosive primer. I have reloaded a great many Winchester .357 Magnum cartridges and have had no trouble whatever with them, but with some other calibers, particularly the .45 Colt, the heads nearly all pulled off. Therefore, if the shooter desires to buy factory ammunition and save his empties for reloading, he had better stick to the Remington Kleanbore or the Winchester with non-mercuric priming. The one best bet will be to buy new-unprimed cases from the factories and then use only straight non-mercuric, non-corrosive primers. Any make of new cases will do for reloading, if ordered unprimed and the proper primers used exclusively. When you order them, specify the uncannelured case.

The various factories use different thicknesses of brass in their cases, some being thin and some quite thick in the walls. The Westerns seem to be about the thickest I have used, with Winchesters about the same. Remington cases run slightly thinner, but are very fine cases for the handloader and give absolute satisfaction. Most of the Peters and U. S. cases I have used seemed to be the thinnest of all, and with some makes of reloading tools they were so thin that the crimping shoulder would not form a sufficient, or an even crimp on the bullet.

Naturally, there is considerable difference in the capacity of the various cases. Usually the Western and Winchester have the smallest powder capacity, as would be expected from their thick walls. This factor has quite an influence on the charge and the pressures developed, not only due to the density of loading, but also to the effect of the crimp between thick and thin cases. Naturally, the heavier the case brass,

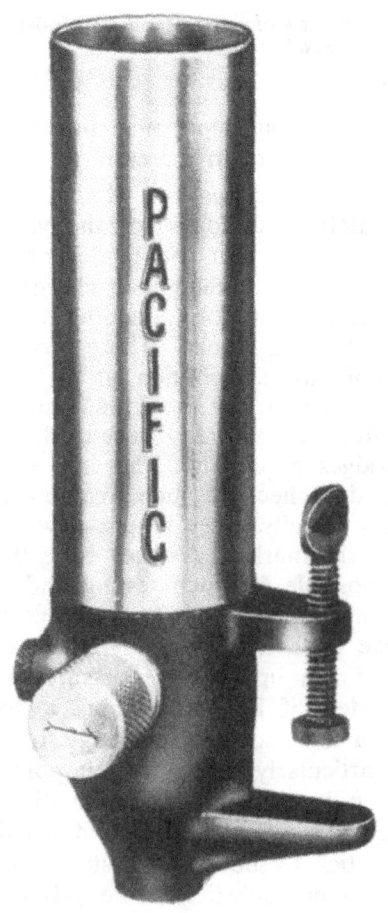

Pacific Gun Sight Company Powder Measure.

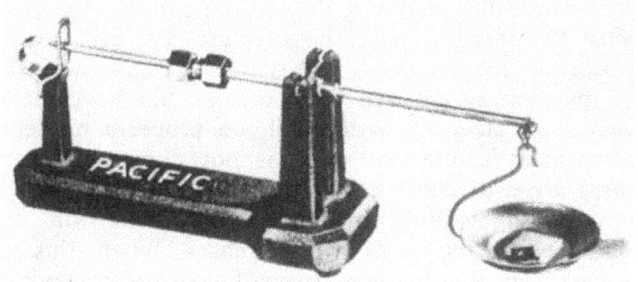

Pacific Gun Sight Company Powder Scale.

the more resistance necessary to force the bullet from its crimp. This difference in case thickness and powder capacity between the various makes is not generally understood and often leads to trouble. It is one reason why I dislike to recommend or list maximum loads in certain calibers. Take for instance, the .45 Auto Rim case. This caliber comes in two distinct types of case, the older style having a primer pocket protruding into the powder chamber and known as the "semi-balloon" or "folded head" type, and the modern style, developed for extreme pressures such as we encounter in the .357 Magnum where there is a heavy brass bottom or "web" to the case, the entire primer pocket being in back of this solid brass wall with its flash hole leading to the powder chamber. There is a great difference in the powder capacity between these two types of cases, and the handloader should know exactly what he is doing before reloading them. The older semi-balloon type case will hold more powder but will not withstand pressures as the more modern, heavier based case does. However it usually develops higher velocity for less pressures than does the new solid head case with its smaller capacity. Furthermore, I have had both .38 and .44 Special cartridges which were reloaded a few times, blow out the entire front part of the semi-balloon pocket, finishing the case for any further use.

Most of the present day revolver cases for smokeless powder come with a cannellure scored around the body, against which rests the base of the bullet. Most of the factory loads are put up in these cannellured cases. I have never been able to figure out their reasons for this. With new cases, or cases full length resized that hold the bullet friction tight anyway, there is no real need for such a cannellure. Possibly this cannellure aids in the mechanical operations back at the factory by preventing the receding of the bullet while it is being crimped; probably it assists in water-proofing the cartridge or is an added safeguard against receding bullets, or lubricant leaking into the powder charge.

From the standpoint of the handloader, this cannellure is a damn nuisance. When such cases are fired, they invariably flatten out the ridge of metal until it becomes a mere line on the case. This in turn lengthens the fired case, when it is full length resized, to a greater

Pacific Gun Sight Company Rifle Dies, cadmium plated.

length than new factory uncannellured cases. Even if not resized, this case will be of greater length than before firing, because the metal, which is flattened or forced out of that groove from the pressures of discharge, must of necessity go into increased length. Such lengthening makes it necessary to keep those cases segregated, loaded and crimped together, so that the one readjustment of the loading tool will keep the crimp in its proper place.

Light loads will not expand the cannellured case as much as will heavier loads, hence the heavier loaded, new, cannellured cases will stretch the most upon being fired. Another bad feature of the cannellured case is that if you wish to seat a bullet which is longer than the factory standard, or to seat it deeper in the case, as in some light target loads, you have trouble in getting it below that cannellure. If you force it past, the cannellure only swages down the base, making it under-size and somewhat boat-tailed. Either of these only furthers gas cutting and is no help in obtaining accuracy, or the case may bulge so it cannot be slipped into the chamber. When those cases are reloaded without full length or neck resizing, then, and only then

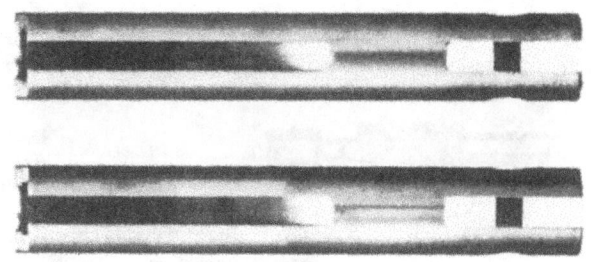

Pacific Gun Sight Company Shell Holders.

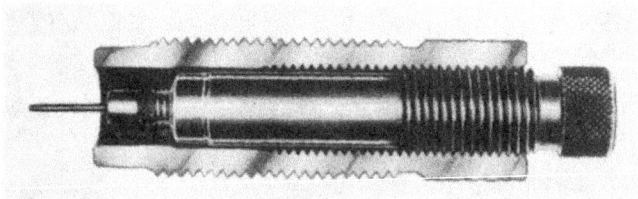

Cut-away view of Pacific Gun Sight Company pistol and revolver Sizing Die (parts C. and D.).

does that cannellure prove of help, as it prevents that bullet from receding in the case too deeply and crowding the powder charge. I, for one, prefer to get uncannellured cases whenever possible.

In resizing fired cases, they should always be first brushed out with a good stiff bristle, or better still, a soft brass wire brush to remove any dirt or grit from the inside. Fired cases which have been laid aside for any length of time may have a sort of gritty scale formed over the inside. This flakes off and scores the dies badly. After this brushing out they should be slightly oiled before resizing, and the inside of the case should also be oiled if the case mouth is going to be expanded up to a definite size after the body has been resized. A bit of practical experience is advisable here, as this oiling operation must not be overdone or the case will wrinkle in the die. Just use enough very light oil to reduce friction and die wear somewhat, but not enough to "feel" the oil when the case is handled. Don't get the idea that the oil may be dispensed with though, for if you have ever driven a dry case into a resizing die and then tried to get it out, you will understand what I mean.

Before oiling or being driven into the die, the cases must be clean, because the slightest dirt, grit or corrosion on their outsides will scar or scratch the inside of the resizing die. All these dies should be made of very hard steel, or better still, be properly hardened after manufacture, but such is not always the case, for I have to continually lap out my Pacific dies to remove slight burrs in the surface, which in turn scratches up the outside of the cases. Where this grit comes from is a mystery to me, but it always finds its way into the die in some manner or other. The new hard chrome plated dies are best.

The actual resizing of the fired cases may be either a comparatively easy or tough bit of work, depending upon the equipment used and the way you go about it. With the various bench tools, such as the Schmitt, Pacific, R.C.B.S., or Hollywood, it is not much of a job, provided the dies are kept clean and the cases properly oiled. These short pistol hulls are not nearly as hard to resize as the longer rifle cases, some of which are quite a problem to get in and out of the dies. With most of the sixgun cartridges, the various hand resizing dies may be used with perfect satisfaction. The most important thing is to make certain the die is resting on some solid, substantial backing. An anvil is ideal, or a piece of heavy steel rail—even a solid stump will do. Avoid pounding cases into a die resting on a light table or bench. Use a heavy hammer for the job. Place the grain end of a short billet of hardwood against the head of the case and drive it on into the die. With the proper dies and layout you should be able to drive it in with one hearty "sock". In driving the case out of the die, use the correst sized

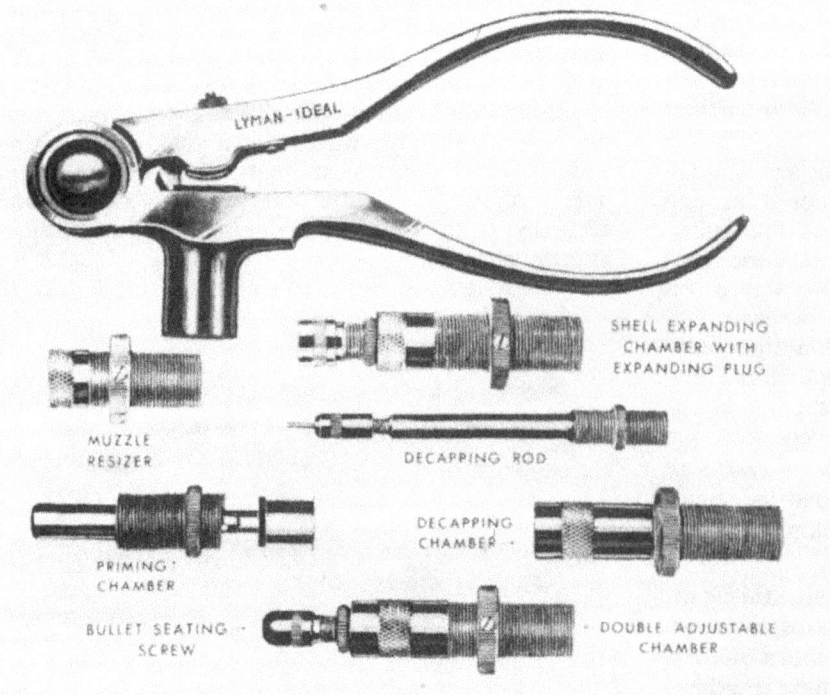

Lyman Ideal Reloading Tool No. 310 for rifle, pistol, and revolver cartridges.

drift, one large enough to barely go into the case mouth and with a recess in its base to fit over the protruding primer pocket. Do not use a smaller punch or a nail; you may only bulge out the head of the case. Most of these hand resizing dies are cheap makeshifts anyway. I know of only one which is really fit for the job, and it is not on the market. Wilson, of Cashmere, Washington, makes it on the same order as the chamber of your rifle, with the drift fitting down into the tool where it strikes against a shoulder. With this you cannot drive the case too far, neither can you batter up its head. A vise is even better for resizing than the hammer and drift method. A bench reloading tool is best of all.

After being sized, the cases should be wiped dry inside, provided they have also been oiled there. Nothing is quite so good for this purpose as the proper

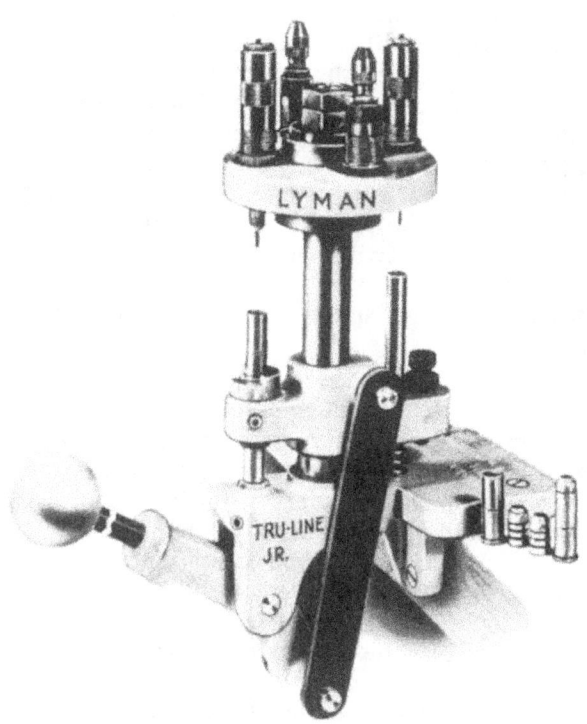

Ideal Tru-line Jr. to handle 310 dies in a bench tool.

size wooden cleaning rod with a knob type tip, on which is tied a bit of cotton flannel.

This continued resizing of the cases is generally harder on them than the actual strain of firing; each working of the cold brass makes it more brittle until finally the case will split, usually at the neck. Some fired cases may have had a flaw in the brass or may have been fired with a mercuric primer, their next reloading causing a ruptured case. If it gets past the reloading stage, the body is apt to crack open or the head blow off when fired. Hence, all such split necks or cracked body cases should be discarded the moment they are noticed.

Often, after a cartridge case has been fired and reloaded, particularly if it has been resized and the neck expanded a few times, the case will stretch, and then when a bullet is crimped with the loading chamber at its normal setting, that crimp will be deeper and heavier than if the case were of standard length. This can cause high pressures, with some danger from the heavier loads. Consequently, all cases should be checked for over-all length after a few loadings and those overlength from the standard should be filed or trimmed. There are now several splendid tools made for this purpose which every serious handloader should possess. Occasionally, new cases for the same cartridge will be found to vary in length slightly, especially different makes, and if the loading chamber is adjusted for the shorter length, it will buckle the longer case or force on it too deep and heavy a crimp.

Before reloading fired cases, always sort them out into groups of each separate make. Better still, keep

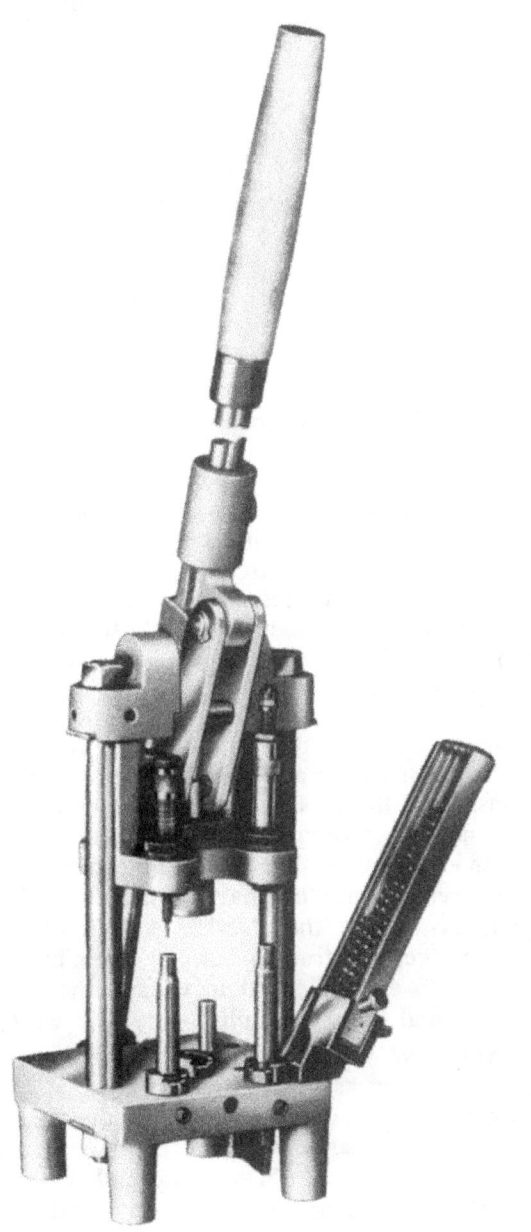

Tru-line Lyman Ideal bench reloading tool.

them segregated and use each for the load which experience has proved best adapted to that make of case. When this is done, the differences in length, wall thickness and powder capacity will not cause trouble. Accuracy is absolutely dependent on perfect uniformity, and uniformity cannot be obtained by mixing up a batch of cases from different makes and then expecting them to hold, handle and fire the same charge with any semblance of uniformity. It would be just as logical to seat different weight bullets into our batch of cartridges and expect them to shoot into the same hole.

Cases which have been fired and reloaded many times usually become much harder than new cases, due to the working of their brass in resizing and expanding. Such cases may take or hold a heavier and stronger crimp than new brass. In time, from firing or working, these old cases usually crack at the neck and are discarded. Generally you lose a case or two every time you put the batch of empties "through the mill". Do not replace these losses with new cases, with the view of "keeping the box full", as such a mixture of old and new brass cannot possibly give uniformity. New cases, especially those with cannellures, hold less

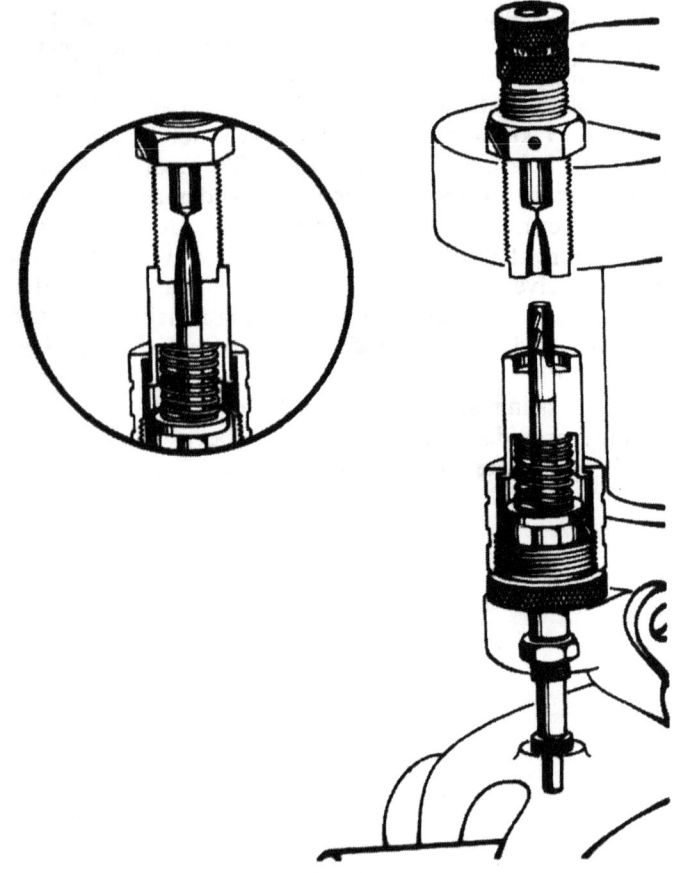

Hollywood tool dies.

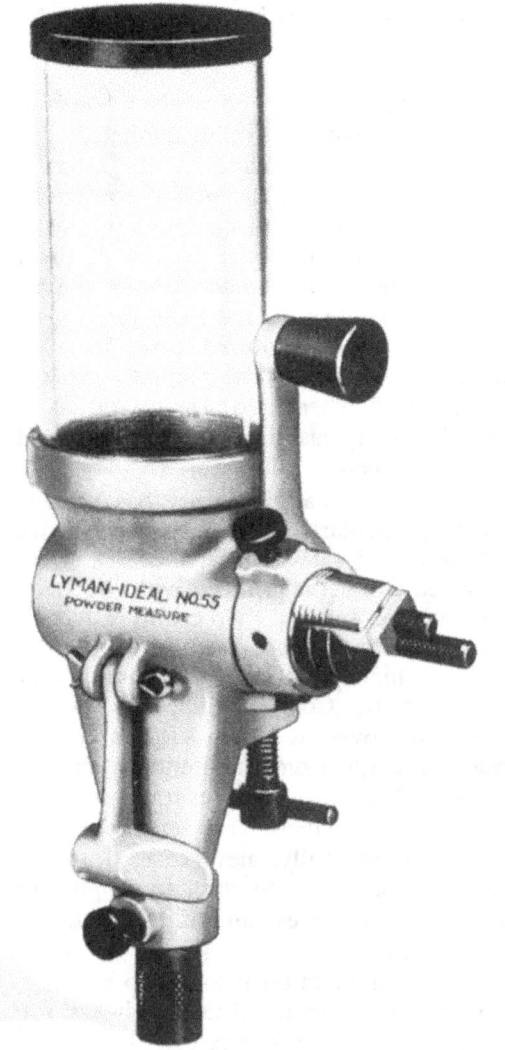

powder, than will be the case after they have been fired a few times, flattening out that groove, and the brass wall as well, and stretching somewhat.

One feature I particularly like about new Remington cases is the manner in which they chamfer the mouth of the case. All I have ever purchased from the factory came with the mouth carefully chamfered. They loaded slick as grease, even with the smaller Lyman tools. With the other makes, it is necessary to take a sharp knife and peel off a slight shaving from the inside of the mouth before loading them for the first time. On subsequent loadings, the case mouths must be expanded or flared out a mite so that the bullet can be seated without shaving off some of its base edging. As this is the steering end of the bullet, it should be kept as true as humanly possible. R.C.B.S. furnishes an extra die just to expand the case mouth properly, and these acomplish very fine work.

If you have used black powder, the cases must be cleaned as soon as possible after firing. A can or jar of water comes in very handy on the target range. Drop the fired cases into this container as soon as ejected from the gun. Then decap and wash them out in a strong, boiling soda solution, rinse in boiling water and dry as rapidly as possible without heating them too much. Black powder residue corrodes very soon and will eat away the brass if left unchecked, completely ruining the cases for future use.

I do not particularly care about cleaning cases fired with smokeless powder, as it is seldom necessary. Cases can be cleaned perfectly with the cyanide solution recommended in Mattern's book, but there is an element of danger to it unless great care is used, and I for one do not recommend it. I have reloaded six-gun cases fired more than fifty times with smokeless powder, and they were often stored for several months without any cleaning, except the brushing out and slight oiling necessary to prevent their getting so gummed up with dirt and residue that they will no longer chamber in the dies or cylinder of the gun.

The new Winchester solid head cases in .44 Special and .45 Colt hold at least two grains less powder and heavy loads must be cut down somewhat from those used in the old semi-balloon type primer pocket case. In the .44 Special they are not as efficient as the old balloon primer case, for they give higher pressure for comparable velocities.

Primers and Priming

The modern small arms primer is such an ordinary looking bit of apparatus and can be put into place so readily with simple tools, that the average handloader is apt to get a bit careless when it comes to the easy, but important operation of repriming. As a matter of fact, in my early days, I knocked out many a fired primer with a small nail and then shoved the new one in place with a homemade punch. Strange to say, these primers all worked nicely, after a fashion, but then they generally do this anyhow. To me, one of the

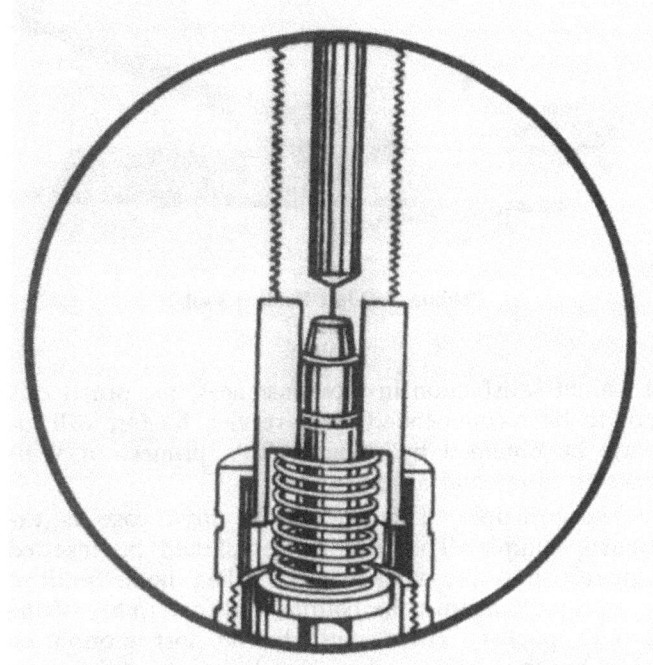

Hollywood pistol bullet seating die.

mysteries of this present day is how the primer will stand the abuse and misuse commonly given it and go off prematurely, yet pop so surely every time the firing pin strikes it.

There is a great deal more to this vital operation of repriming than appears on the surface or is to be found printed on the box in which they are packed. First off, use pistol primers in pistol cartridges. Rifle primers are much too powerful for pistol use—they will detonate the charge, and usually ruin the gun.

It is much the best to use the pistol primer of the same make as the cases being loaded; in other words, follow the manufacturer's advice, and when using his cases, prime them with the primer he made and intended to be used in the distinctive primer pocket which may be formed only in his make of cartridge. There may be slight, but appreciable differences between the various makers' product of the same case. I have found some in which the inner edge of the primer pocket was rounded, while in others, it ran out to a square edge. The primer intended for use in the former pocket had a rounded front edge and if inserted into the square edged pocket of the latter would seat too deeply, possibly having to be "squashed" a mite to grip properly. This compression does not do the pellet a bit of good either. Furthermore, some makes of primer are designed with a convex or fully rounded face, while others are appreciably flattened on this outer surface. The protrusion of your hammer nose may not be quite sufficient to reach the latter type if loaded into the wrong cases.

While it is true the average handloader indulges in rather indiscriminate substitution in this matter of using one maker's primer in another make of case, and with

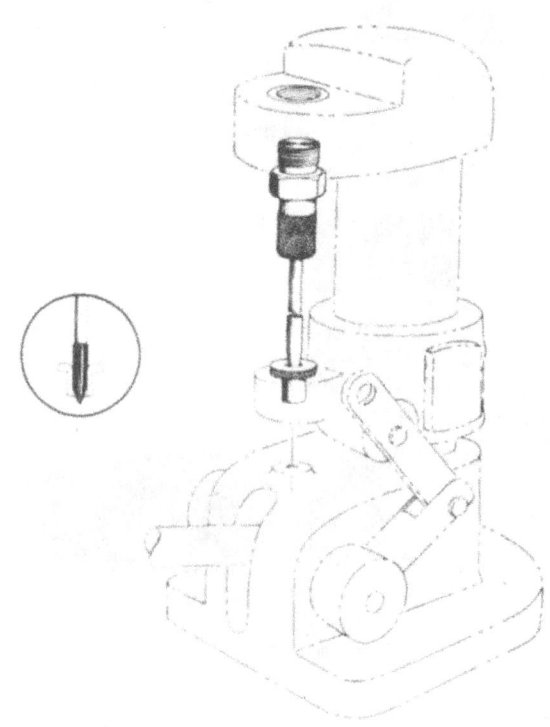

Hollywood tool.

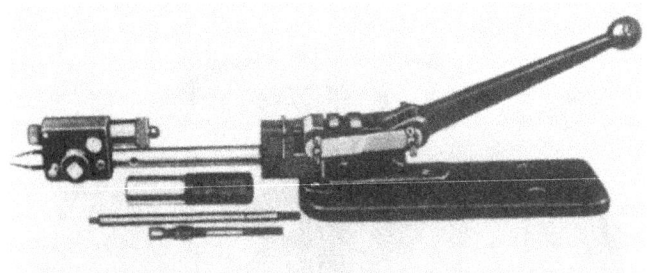

Belding & Mull loading tool.

apparent satisfaction in most instances, the practice is not to be recommended. Best results, by far, will always be obtained by using W.R.A. primers in Winchester cases, and so on.

The principle of repriming the fired case is extremely simple. The new primer should be inserted squarely into the pocket and pushed home until it bears solidly against the bottom wall (or "web") of the primer pocket. There must be no lost motion or play by the primer when struck by the firing pin, detonation should be instantaneous, and the full flame from the priming compound should "spit" through the flash hole into the powder charge. In performing this exceedingly simple operation, the greatest of care must be observed to avoid disturbing the priming compound, or "pellet" as some call it. This composition should not be mashed, pulverized or displaced in the least, this being pretty apt to occur if the primer is shoved in cockeyed, or flattened too much in an attempt to make certain it is properly bearing against the web of the case.

Formerly, some of our loading tool manufacturers treated priming as if it were a sort of by-pass to more essential operations, and arranged their tool accordingly. Take the old Ideal tong tools for example. These came equipped with the early "nut cracker" type of priming arrangement, where the primer is squeezed into the case by hand pressure, with no method of guidance or stop gauge to indicate when seated enough. This worked very well with black powder, for which the tool was designed, as this old soft coal only needs the suggestion of a flame to start it off right. The main thing to remember in priming with these tong tools

Hollywood Universal loading tool.

Hollywood micrometer powder measure.

Cartridge Reloading 253

Hollywood loading press.

is to start the primer in squarely, and to stop the pressure in time and not flatten the cup or pulverize the compound. When a primer slips in easily, there is a tendency to mash it out a bit so it will "fit" better. In any event, it is hard to properly gauge this seating operation by the "feel", which we are obliged to do with this type of tool. A much better method is to knock off that useless bullet push-rod intended for sizing, then insert a suitable stop gauge (made in tee or rivet shape) into the allegedly round sizing die. With a bit of experimenting, this stop gauge can be filed down until the handles can be closed only the exact amount necessary to properly seat the primer Another good point is that it finally lets the owner make some good use of that fool sizing hole. This stunt permits very accurate seating of the primers with these tong tools, but it remains a hard matter to start some of them into the pocket squarely as they will smash sideways or become badly distorted. Still, the smaller sized pistol primers work very well with some calibers and makes of cases.

Another trouble often encountered is that the primer seating punch may not be ground down smoothly or to proper contour, or it may be off center in some tools. I have owned many old Ideal tools in which the seating punch would mar and distort the primer, often leaving lines scored across it which could not help but favor the piercing of the primer if pressures got a bit high. Any deformation of the primer such as this is very apt to break up and powder the "pellet" of priming mixture inside the cup. Being then in a powdered form instead of the hard cake intended, it cannot offer the proper resistance between the cup and anvil necessary for instant and uniform ignition. Do not put up with any distortion or marking of the primer cup with any make of tool.

The old Ideal #2 Re- and Decapping tool is a much better arrangement for priming, and when you get hold of one properly assembled and adjusted (not all of them are), you have a pretty accurate hand tool—about as good as could be desired. With this #2 tool, the primer can be dropped into the carriage, all slack taken up, and the case then given a twirl with the fingers which will automatically square-up the primer and start it into the pocket accurately. Then, if the seating punch was adjusted correctly at the factory which it may not be), that primer will be seated to exactly the correct depth until it bears properly against the web, by which time the handle is past dead-center and you cannot smash or distort the pellet in the least. Occasionally, I have purchased one in which everything clicked just right, and it is a most pleasing, efficient and rapid tool to use when so properly adjusted. To be really worthwhile, there should be some method by which the seating punch can be reversed—one end used for round-faced primers and other for flat ones. The middle of this seating punch also should be threaded, so it may be accurately adjusted for seating depth.

Most of the larger hand and bench tools come

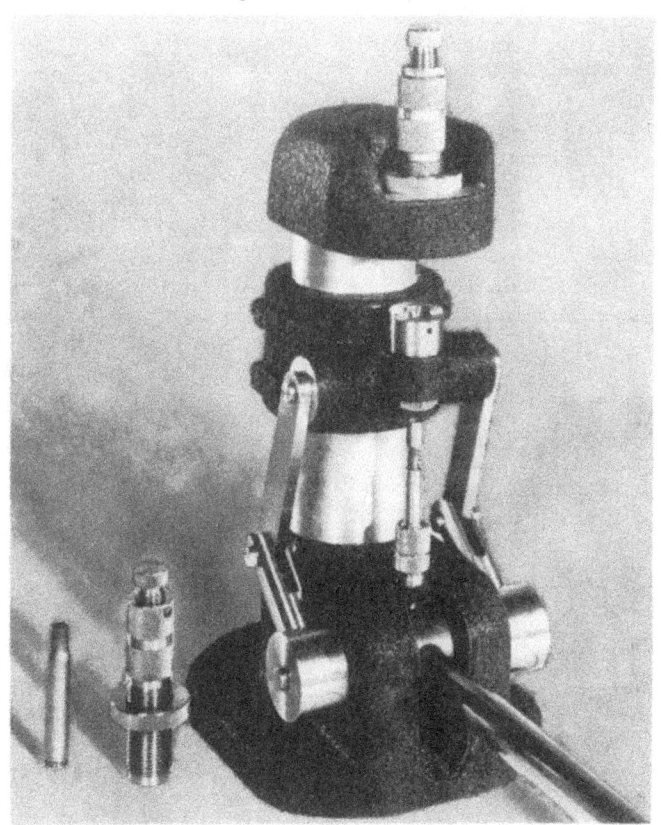

Hollywood loading press.

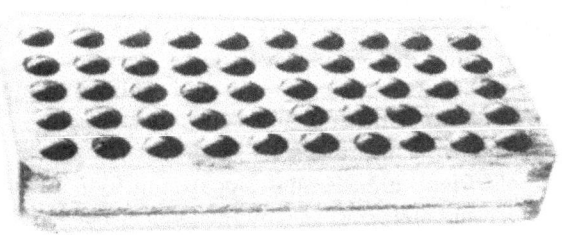

Belding & Mull loading blocks.

equipped with a priming arrangement which is entirely O.K. The Belding & Mull is an exceptionally good one when properly adjusted. The Schmitt, Pacific, R.C.B.S. and Hollywood are also good, and perform the de- and recapping of the case along with other operations, permitting good time to be made, yet doing precision work also. Most of them can be had with automatic primer feed that is both fast and reliable.

In seating, it is imperative that the primer be forced slightly below the base of the case and not left flush or protruding. Any protruding primer is dangerous, whether fired in rifle or sixgun; such is also the cause with an occasional misfire. It may project so far out of the case as to rub across the recoil shield of the gun and fire prematurely or else put undue stress on the hand which revolves the cylinder, which at times may tie up the arm. Such friction is fatal to fast double action work and could be very serious if you are in a jam.

When priming with the hand tools, it is a good idea to place each primed case mouth down into a suitable loading block. When finished, pick up this filled loading block, hold it about level with the eyes with the cases all slanting one way, then cock your shooting eye across those bases and make certain every primer is

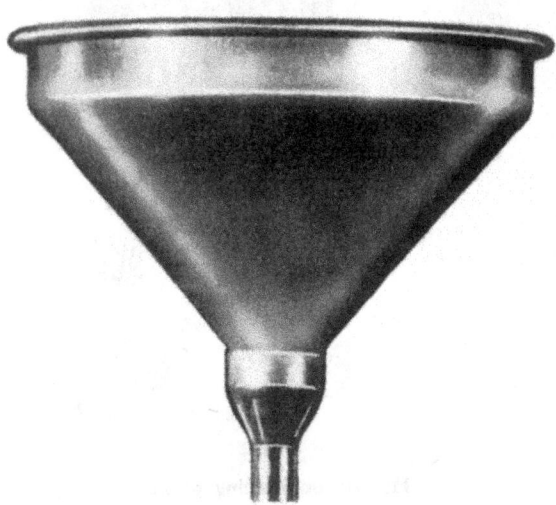

Pacific Gun Sight Company Powder Funnel.

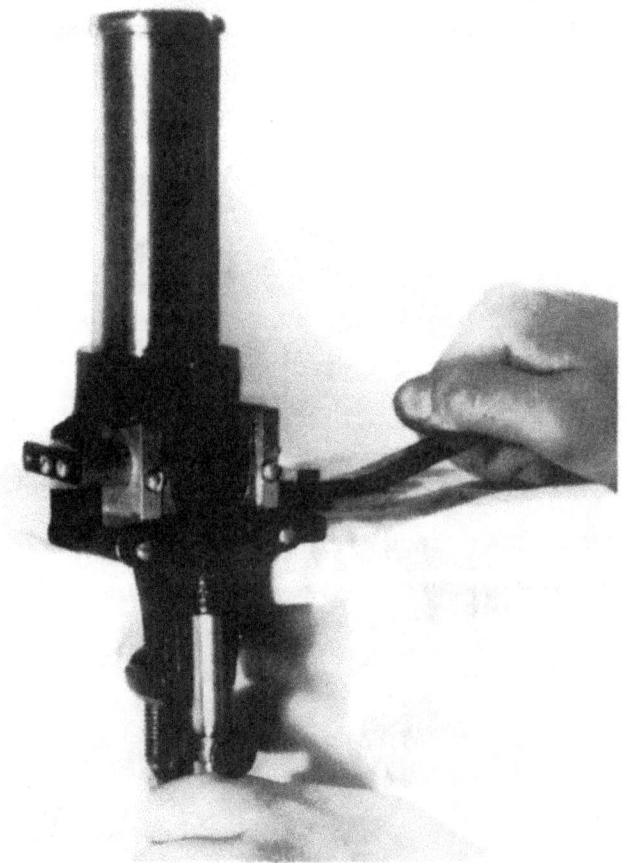

Belding & Mull powder measure.

seated slightly below the level of the head of the case. With a little practice, any protruding primer will be instantly spotted by this method. In my opinion, this check-up is almost as necessary as the same operation performed later on at the other end of the case with a view to detecting double powder charges.

Misfires seldom happen if even ordinary care is taken in the priming operation, but they can occur however, from a protruding primer, as the hammer blow may merely seat it deeper in the case pocket and yet not mash the pellet. They can also occur through the primer cup being mashed so badly in insertion that its detonating compound is pulverized and displaced from between the cup and its anvil. For certain instantaneous operation, the primer depends upon this pellet being undisturbed until it is mashed between the primer cup and anvil by the indentation of the firing pin. See that your priming operations and handling are conducted in accordance with these principles.

The stability of small arms primers is amazing. I have often loaded some whose age I knew to be around twenty-five years, yet they functioned perfectly when fired. We remember seeing the primer situation somewhat upset by the introduction of all the various non-corrosive, non-mercuric, types of primer composition, some of which were not yet out of the experimental

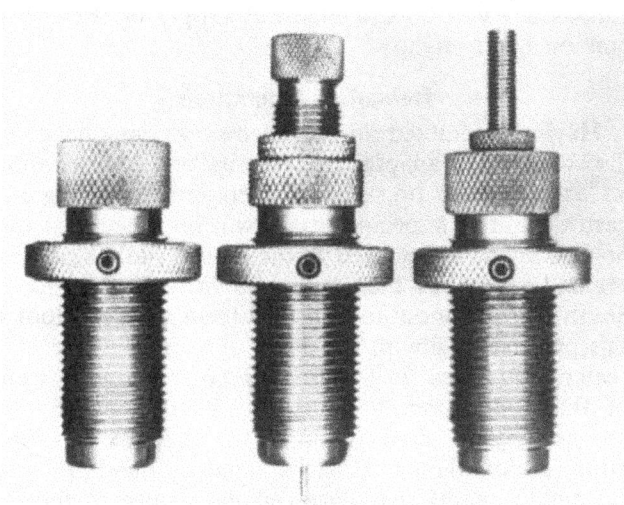

Three Die pistol set, R.C.B.S.

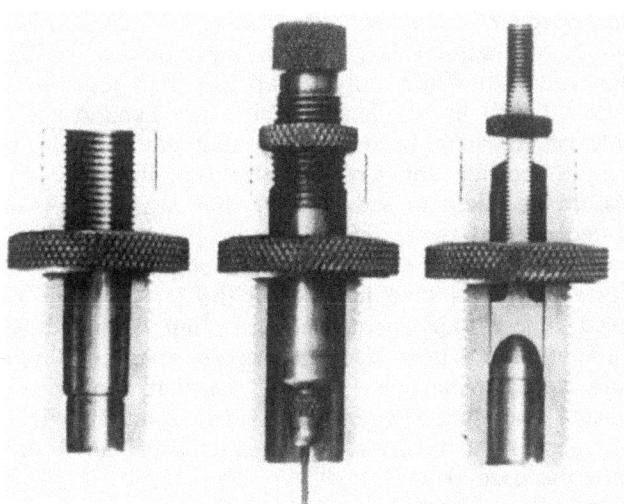

Cut-a-way three die R.C.B.S. pistol set.

Occasionally one hears of handloaders who consider it necessary to ream out the flash hole of the case to a larger diameter. This is unnecessary and dangerous in the extreme. The manufacturers have already made that flash hole as large as necessary with due regard to the danger of back pressure from the charge. Let it alone. If it were possible to safely have it any larger, they would have made it so. Each manufacturer has his own ideas as to just what diameter this flash hole should be when used with HIS primer; another argument for using only that primer in his case.

Expelling the fired primer, or decapping, as it is commonly called, is an operation which is not likely to cause trouble if the right tool is used and the old primer has not been permitted to corrode in the case pocket. The various bench type tools generally do this along with one or two other operations, so it is not much of a problem with them. With some makes of tools, their decapping pin bushing will be found to be much smaller than the inside diameter of the case, especially with the Belding & Mull. This is quite a nuisance as one must fish about for the flash hole with the point of the decapping pin, then when located, insert the pin on into the flash hole and hold it there

R.C.B.S. powder measure.

stage when put on the market. A few proved to be reliable and somewhat in keeping with the claims made by their manufacturers, while several others did not. I would strongly advise using only the Remington and Winchester, non-mercuric and non-corrosive types, or the Frankford Arsenal non-mercuric, all of which have proved dependable for me.

There are two sizes of primers manufactured for revolver cartridges, and in some calibers it is possible to obtain cases made for either. The larger sized primer is usually the more powerful. The powder charge which is maximum for the case with the smaller primer may prove a little on the dangerous side if loaded into a case taking the larger one. Follow the recommendations very closely in such matters, or else cut the charge a trifle and again work up slowly to the full load in instances where the large primer case must be used. The smaller size primer will handle heavier pressures in .38 caliber cases than the larger size.

until the pressure of the hand lever takes up all slack and punches the old primer out. All decapping pin bushings should be made almost the full inside diameter of the case neck for accurate centering and prompt and convenient expulsion of the fired primer—but some are not.

Generally, it pays to expel the primer from the case pocket shortly after the cartridge is fired. Do not allow your empty cases to stand around until those old, fired primers have become corroded. At times, where cases are apt to be laid aside for several months before being used again, it is advisable to do this single operation by itself. This is a job to which almost any old cow-poke who drops in for the day can be safely put at; he is not apt to do much harm other than break off a decapping pin or two, and any experienced handloader will have a plentiful supply of these extra pins on hand anyhow.

Reloading Operations

Having assembled all our necessary components and discussed their adaptability, merits and shortcomings, let us now take up, step by step, the reloading of a cartridge. If new primed cases will be used, they must first be lightly chamfered at the mouth (unless of Remington make) and then belled slightly. Years ago, the Smith & Wesson outfit used to furnish a special tool for this purpose, made on the order of a straight-line bullet seater. This was well worth its cost and the trouble of that extra operation. If present day bench tools are used, they come equipped to perform this operation; if not, then it must be done by hand. Be careful not to chamfer or flare out the mouth of the case to too great an extent. R.C.B.S. furnish a special die for this purpose and it is very efficient.

If fired cases are to be reloaded, they must first be decapped. With the Schmitt, Pacific, R.C.B.S., Hollywood, and similar large bench tools this is a simple operation, they not only decap but also reprime the case, as well as full length resize and expand the inside of its neck to a uniform diameter—all in one simple opertion and with one stroke of the lever. Care should be taken to see that the dies are carefully adjusted so that the cases will be properly belled at the mouth and the new primer seated completely into the pocket with its face just below the level of the case head. These tools mentioned are often equipped with an automatic primer feed, the primers first being loaded into a magazine. One should see that they are all turned the same way and loaded into the primer charger in the position which seats them anvil down into the case pocket.

With the combination type of hand tools the primer must first be started into the pocket with the fingers and then forced into place, gently but firmly, until fully seated. I much prefer to use the Ideal #2 tool for this purpose, when hand tools are used, because it does the two operations of decapping and repriming at one handling, and if properly adjusted at the factory, will prime the case very accurately and satisfactorily. Any tool or seating punch which distorts the primer, mars its face, or smashes it in the least should be discarded as it does not further accuracy to have the priming compound broken or displaced.

I am greatly in favor of using the more expensive, heavier bench types of reloading tools. It is true they cost much more, but in the long run they prove to be the least expensive and are far more satisfactory. With most of the hand tools, it takes so many more operations to put an empty, fired case in shape to reload. If your time is worth anything, it is much the best to purchase the heavier, speedier bench tools which will accomplish several of these necessary operations with one motion of the operating lever. Not only will they do these operations in much less time, they are capable

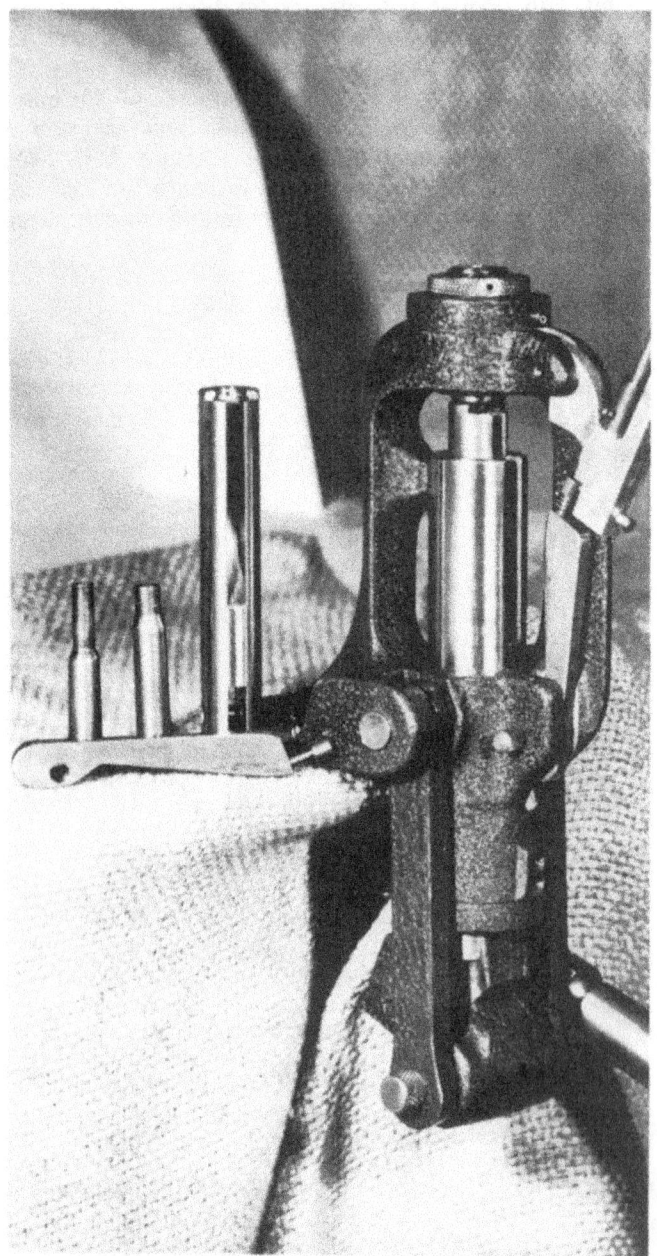

New Small Model B. press takes Pacific-type holders and primer arms.

of greater precision with closer adjustment, and the work is done with far less effort on the part of the operator.

The greatest weakness of the hand tool becomes apparent in full-length resizing of the fired case, or even in neck resizing with some cartridges. In many instances the case may be reloaded and fired several times in close chambered guns, without this full length resizing, but by far the best results will be obtained if this operation is always performed. I know of no tong type of tool which will do even neck resizing with ease or accuracy, although this operation is comparatively easy with the bench tools. When it comes to full length resizing of the fired case, the heavy bench tool is in its element. To do this operation with a hand resizing die, the latter must be placed on a heavy, solid foundation, then the oiled case is started into the resizing chamber and a section of hardwood used as a drift. One must strike the drift a direct blow with a heavy hammer or mallet until the case is driven entirely in with its head flush or rim against the face of the die. The operation should be performed with a minimum of hammering, accomplished with as few blows as possible so the case will not become expanded before it enters the die. With the proper layout and skill most revolver cartridges can be driven in with one good tap. I have found that a heavy hammer works better than a mallet for such work, as one hits more nearly center and in line with it than with the bigger mallet. Always drive the case out of the die with the proper punch usually provided with the tool. Where the case must be resized with hand tools, the operation is best done first, before decapping and repriming. A vise is a much better method when available. A heavy bench tool is still better.

After this resizing operation, the case will usually be too small at the mouth to allow the bullet to enter properly, so must be slightly belled. Some tools have made provision for this operation by providing an expanding plug, such as the lower end of the loading chamber on the Lyman, or the rod end of the Belding & Mull. With such tools, care must be taken to bell the case mouth but slightly, just enough to permit the bullet to enter, and no more, because excessive flaring may split or prevent it from entering the loading chamber.

The smaller hand tools, such as the Lyman, B. & M. or Bond, will resize only the neck of the case. Examine such resized cases carefully and make certain that the die and operation leaves the neck in perfect alignment with the body of the case; I have seen many which would not do so. If the tool neck resizes one side of the case more than the other, discard or return it to the factory, for accurate ammunition cannot be turned out from such a tool. Again, full length resizing in heavy bench tools is best.

The combination of components you have selected may not be entirely suited to the dimensions of the hand tools being used, and it may be necessary to expand the inside of the neck after the case had been resized. Cases vary in thickness, you know, and an extra thick case will mean greater restriction, with consequent less inside diameter at the neck, than those made of thinner brass. This, in turn, means more bullet pull and can cause a variation in pressure which is not conducive to accuracy, or even safety, for that matter. In fact, with some heavy cases the inside neck diameter may be such that the bullet cannot be seated without distortion. The Belding & Mull hand tool expands the neck of the case to uniform inside diameter, as all tools should do. This operation is often another argument for the much better bench tools, which all have expanding plugs.

I believe all fired cases should at least be neck resized before being again reloaded, but better results will be obtained under almost all conditions if they are full length resized and the inside of the neck then expanded to the proper uniform diameter.

After the fired case has been reworked into proper shape, we come to the powder charging. This is a relatively simple, yet important operation, upon which much depends and from which serious trouble may

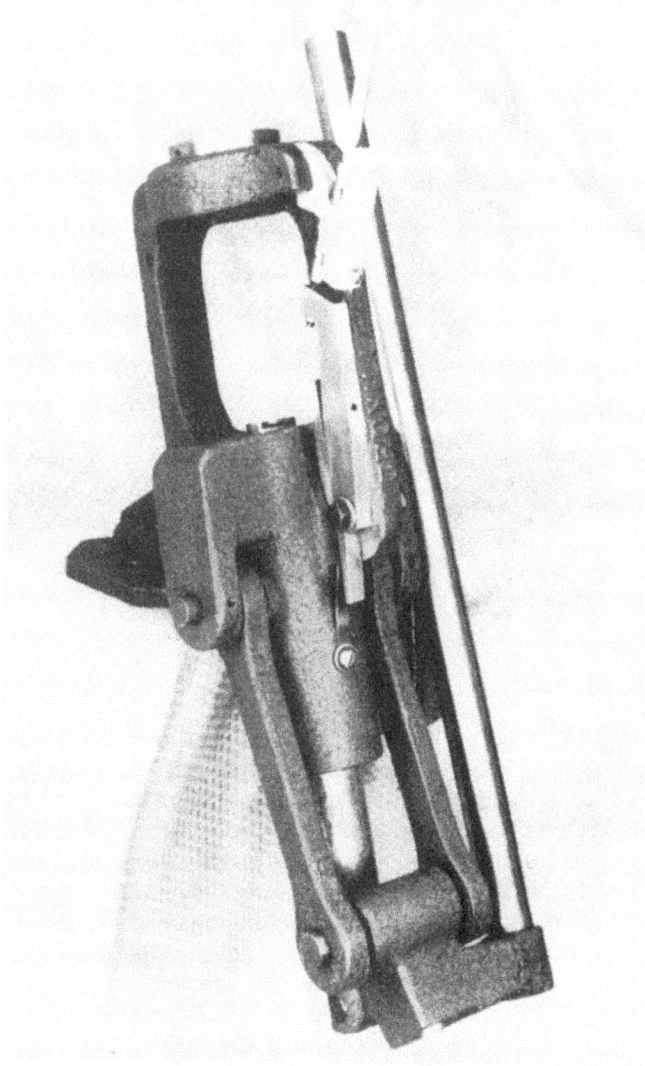

R.C.B.S. loading press, large size.

occur if done improperly. For light to normal charges, there is nothing quite so handy or safe as the Lyman, B. & M., Hollywood, R.C.B.S., Saeco, or similar gravity powder measures used in conjunction with an accurate scale or balance and kept in necessary working order by frequent inspection and cleaning. An accurate scale weighing to one-tenth grain is necessary to check up any powder measure—and they should be checked frequently. Before setting the measure for the charge desired, go over it carefully and clean it

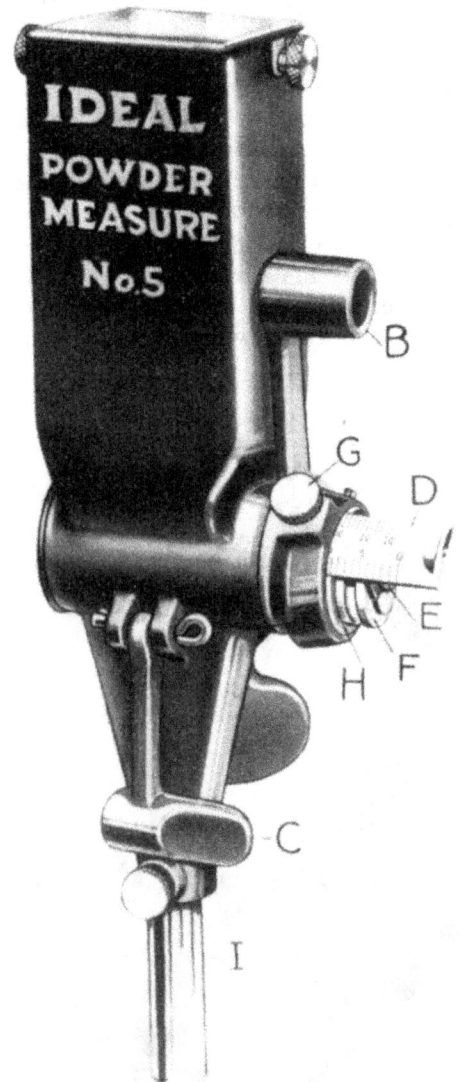

up a bit, making sure that there is no dirt or cobwebs in the drop tube which might hold up part of a charge. See to it that this tube is seated fully up into its socket and securely clamped. No parts should be gummed up or oily. Once the proper setting is obtained, the locking nut or set screw should be turned up tightly enough to hold the setting against any possibility of movement, yet not so tight as to strip the threads. We particularly like the micrometer adjustment of the Hollywood and R.C.B.S. powder measures. Make periodic checks with the scales to see that the setting remains undisturbed. Weigh all heavy loads.

The hopper should be kept at least half full of powder at all times. Leave the cover off in order to see that it does not run too low. The Belding & Mull is supposed to be the exception to this rule, as it has a charging chamber separate from the big hopper. However, I prefer to keep even this measure over half full, although it will throw accurate charges as long as the lower, glassed-in compartment is filled with powder. With this B. & M., which is known as the visible powder measure, owing to the glass front over its lower reservoir, the charge drops into a small tube and is then cut off exactly and uniformly at each throw of the operating lever. The charge must then be poured, by means of a funnel, into the cases. In using the Ideal measure, the empty case is held under the mouth of the drop tube and the charge thrown directly into it. Various sized tubes may be obtained for all calibers. An up-and-down stroke is made with the operating lever, then the little knocker at the side is given a flip with the forefinger to jar out all the powder, and the job is done. If the drop tube is kept clean and tightly clamped in place and the operations done uniformly, this is a very accurate and reliable powder measure. I prefer the R.C.B.S. or Hollywood, but the Saeco is equally accurate. All have transparent plastic hoppers.

For hand weighed loads, I like the Belding & Mull measure, as it can be set just under the charge wanted, this allowing the under-charge to be thrown on the scale pan, where one can then add the necessary few grains to balance. An empty case can be used in a similar manner with the Ideal or other measures, and it really works about as well, except for the fact that you do not have as convenient a tube to hold in the hand. However, a most satisfactory sort of tube may readily be improvised from some of the larger caliber, straight rifle cases.

If you do not happen to own an accurate balance, assay or gold scale, borrow one from some friend, or cut down the load if you cannot get it. Use the friend's scale to check measure settings also, and while over there for this purpose you had better accurately mark the setting with a scribe, then it can be kept to that mark. All the various measure manufacturers print tables in their catalog showing the settings of the measure slides, but such are only approximate. These measures should never be used for normal or heavy charges of smokeless powder unless checked by means of accurate scales and then closely watched and kept at that setting. All heavy loads should be weighed. With black powder, these tables and slide settings can be used safely, but with all smokeless powders I advise a close check with the scales and then a periodic check and double check.

The charging of cases should always be done in conjunction with a loading block, which may be purchased from any tool-maker or easily made by the shooter. It pays to have several of these blocks on hand, of a thickness and size suitable to the various caliber car-

The beginner's outfit, capable of producing excellent ammunition.

tridges being loaded. The holes should be sufficiently large to take the head of the case without crowding, and deep enough to hold the case securely, yet permit it to be gripped with the fingers when removing. Make them to take 50 or even 100 cases, and large enough not to be tipped over.

After the charges have all been thrown, and charged cases placed in the loading block, it is a wise precaution to take the block to where the light is good and there go over every case with the eye and make certain none has received a double charge. Do not neglect this precaution when using the denser smokeless powder such as Bullseye or #5066. Some powders, such as #80 or #2400, bulk up so well that it would be very hard, if not impossible, to throw two charges into the same case, while with some of the condensed powders such as Bullseye, this would not be noticeable unless closely scrutinized.

When loading black powder into some of the heavier walled cases, it may be a hard matter to get the charge in without unduly crushing it in seating the bullet. The answer to this is to pour the charge slowly into the case through a long tube and allow each grain to settle properly, which it cannot do if dumped rapidly into a funnel. The Lyman outfit sells these long tubes for such purposes. By using one and turning the crank slowly, the charge will have time to settle much better than it would with any amount of jarring and thumping. In loading some of the larger black powder rifle cartridges, I have often been obliged to use a long tube and then tap the case considerably while pressing a length of steel rod on top of the charge.

Charging the cases is an operation best performed while alone; if a friend or assistant should be around, all hands must attend strictly to their own business while the charges are being thrown. The person operating the powder measure should attain a regular cadence and sequence and keep his mind on the job.

Do it "by the numbers" as they say in the army. Both the measuring or weighing of powder charges should be done with the greatest of care and attention to details, with no careless or slipshod methods allowed. The better the equipment used for this operation, the nearer perfect the results, and the more satisfactory will be the finished ammunition. Personally, I prefer to use the double block system, keeping to my left one block in which are the primed cases, mouth down as they were positioned when inspected for protruding primers. I take out one of these empty cases with my left hand, charge it properly and accurately, and then place it mouth up into another block placed to my right. And I don't like to be bothered while shifting these cases.

Now that we have the cases correctly charged with powder, our next step will be to adjust the loading tool properly in order to accurately seat and crimp the bullet. All loading chambers should be double adjustable, that is, adjustable for case length, and the degree of crimp given, and also adjustable for bullet seating depth, so as to seat the bullet and crimp it exactly where desired. With such a chamber, the tool may be adjusted to crimp or not, as desired. Any tools which do not provide adjustments such as these should be discarded, as they will not permit the proper assembly of various makes of components or allow any variation whatsoever in the bullet used.

When adjusting any tool for a new cartridge or combination of components, it is best to first slightly unscrew the case length and crimp adjustment. Then take an empty case, similar to those being used, and placing it in the loading chamber, so adjust the length of crimp that the case will not go completely into the die, but will project out about a thirty-second of an inch. That is, it should lack that much of seating flush into the die. If plenty of old cases are on hand, they can be utilized for such adjustments; in fact,

View of one end of shop set up for sixgun work.

it pays to keep a supply on hand for just this purpose. Once the crimp adjustment is correct, clamp it up tightly with the set collar provided. It has been my experience that the one set collar with which the tong type tools are provided is not enough for the purpose. It pays to obtain an extra supply of these collars so that you can fit two to every loading chamber and bullet seating punch. Once the correct adjustment is obtained and these two collars set up tightly, that adjustment stays correct.

Next comes the adjustment for bullet seating depth. Take the bullet seating screw, or punch, and screw it back until it is well out from its proper adjustment. Place a bullet in the mouth of the case, insert it in the chamber, and close the tool until you feel the first sign of pressure, then remove and examine for position of bullet. Adjust accordingly and repeat this operation until the bullet is seated correctly and with a suitable crimp forming in its crimping groove. Here is where a few more old cases can be used. Load them up as dummies and keep a supply around for speedy and accurate use as tool adjusting gauges. Adjust your tool so that it will form an accurate and heavy crimp in the crimp groove, yet not so heavy that it will buckle or distort the case.

After the tool is properly adjusted, with its lock screws or collars turned up tightly so that they will stay that way, take your primed and powder charged case and start the base of the bullet into the case mouth with the fingers, assuming of course, that you have cleaned all traces of grease or lubricant from the bullet base. Align that bullet as correctly as you can with the axis of the cartridge, and seat it sufficiently to stay that way while it is being inserted into the tool. Slip it into the loading chamber and repeat the seating and crimping operation. Examine the first few cartridges closely for crimp adjustment, for a too heavy or improperly positioned crimp may bulge the case just in back of its mouth. Once the tool is properly adjusted and securely clamped, there should be no further trouble as long as the same make of cases are used, and no difficulty should be experienced in completing the loading of that batch of ammunition.

The charged cases, with bullets seated in their mouths, should always be inserted upwards into the loading chamber of the tong type tools to avoid any possibility of a spill. Any surplus grease should be removed from the bullet points in order to prevent the front of the loading chamber from becoming gummed up with it and seating improperly. To the uninitiated, it might seem that the tool has changed its adjustment, whereas it really needs to be cleaned out. If the loading chamber should become gummed up with sur-

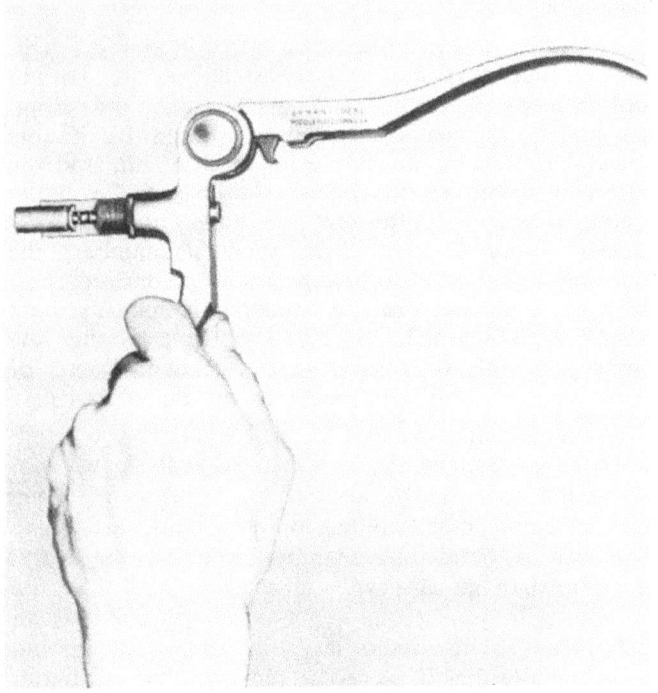

Seating primer Lyman 310 tong tool.

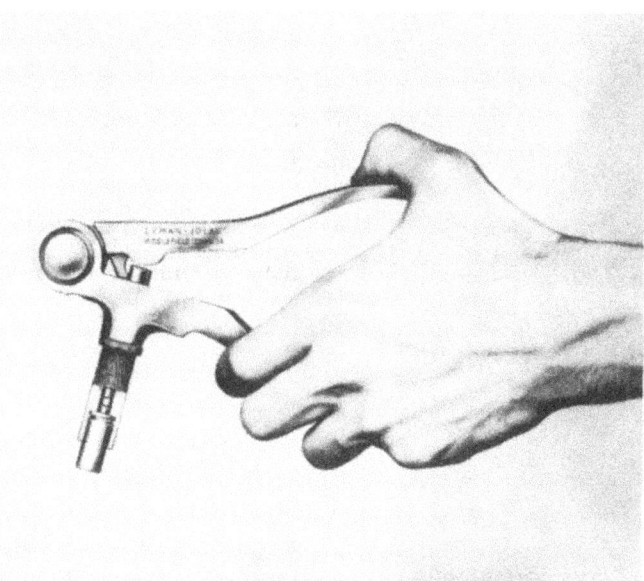

Ready to start the primer in the pocket.

plus lubricant, stop and remove all such dirt with a cloth on the end of a small stick.

In seating the bullets and crimping the case on them, do so slowly and with a minimum of effort. Do not try to force things; if it should require undue exertion to form the crimp on a certain cartridge, you had better stop and see what is wrong. Nothing is more troublesome or exasperating than to buckle a case in the loading chamber. This generally calls for the complete dismounting of the tool in order to remove the cartridge, and a consequent complete readjustment of everything. There are times when an extra long cartridge case can cause an unbelievable amount of trouble in tying up the loading tool.

Certain sixgun cartridges may be particularly hard to reload at times. I refer to the .32/20, .38/40 and .44/40. For some reason or other, these three calibers seem to be made of thinner brass than the other sizes, and often when one comes to putting a crimp on the cartridge, their bottlenecked construction causes the case walls to collapse easily. With some lots of cases or types of bullets it is practically impossible to do a proper job, as so many cases will buckle in the loading chamber of the tool. It is often the usual thing to lose six or seven cases out of each lot being reloaded. I had a lot of this trouble in loading for my .38/40, and it was one of the reasons why I went to the straight .45 Colt case. At times the trouble may be remedied by making two or three operations out of the bullet seating and crimping; screw out the loading chamber so the tool will not crimp, run the lot of cartridges through the tool, and seat the bullets properly, but do not put any crimp whatever on the case. Then adjust for crimp only, make another run through to crimp the cartridges. It may be necessary to make two distinct operations of this crimp, setting the tool for a light crimp the first time, and then increasing this crimp on a second attempt. There can be combinations with which it is almost, if not actually impossible, to turn out a satisfactory job with one of these calibers.

It may be well here to say a few words about the different types of bullet seaters and loading chambers. For loading metal cased bullets in rifle cartridges, the straight line "die-and-plunger" sets like the Niedner, Dubiel, Belding & Mull are very fine tools, and will do a perfectly satisfactory job when properly made. Notice I say "when properly made"; very few of them are. Much talk about "precision", "accuracy", "close dimensions", etc. is heard from the various makers of these tools, yet the sad fact is that most of them are made to about as close tolerances as are used by the tinsmiths in turning out rain-spouts. To be worth some of the prices paid, and to give satisfaction to the user, any precision, straight line bullet seater should be made to about the dimensions of a maximum rifle chamber. The "bore" of the tool should fit the bullet so closely that it can be seated down into the neck of the case without its base edge touching the mouth of the case, assuming that there is a slight chamfer to the latter, which there should be. Any bullet loaded in a tool properly made as I have described, will be truly seated in a "straight line", and what is more important its base will remain as perfect as it was when it left the factory, not having a segment of the base edge scraped off by one side of the case mouth. Exceedingly few of the hand tools will do this.

However, whether properly made or not, I do not like this type of bullet seating chamber in the least for loading revolver cartridges for the following reasons: The case is placed in the chamber of the die and the latter fitted into the safety base in order to prevent any metal coming in contact with the primer while the bullet is being seated. Then the bullet is dropped down the bore of the die, and "dropped" is right, be-

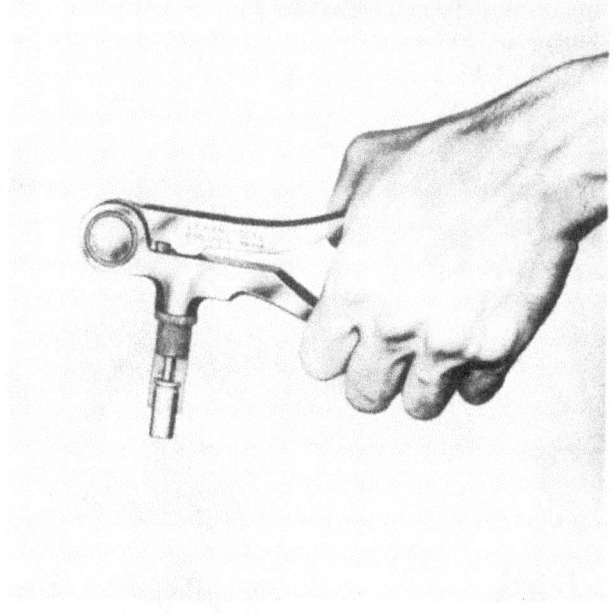

Final seating of the primer.

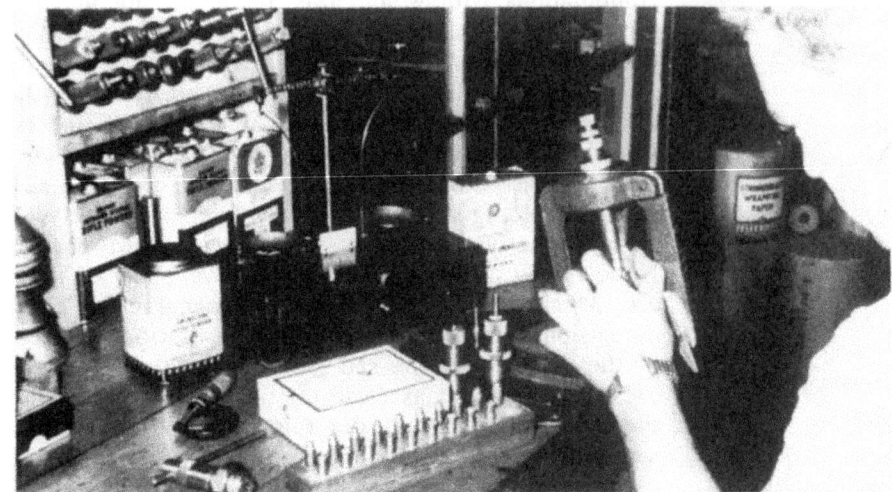

Loading .357 Magnums in the shop of Fred Huntington, R.C.B.S. Gun and Die Shop at Oroville, California. Priming the case R.C.B.S. tool.

cause it invariably falls down until it strikes the mouth of the case, whereas it should be necessary, with a properly made tool, to shove it lightly down by hand with almost enough pressure to amount to what a machinist would term a "push" fit—at any rate the bullet should fit closely to the bore of the die, which it seldom does with the average specimen of straight line tool. Upon dropping in the bullet, the seating plunger is slipped on top of it, after which there is struck a sharp blow on the top of the plunger to seat the bullet to its proper depth, and also to form the crimp with some tools. These latter tools do not permit any adjustment to form the proper degree of crimp or to allow for slight differences in length which may exist between different lots of cases.

Also, and worst of all, unless very closely chambered (which most are not, as I have said before), this blow on the bullet necessary to seat the bullet or form the crimp is pretty apt to have some upsetting effect upon a soft, lead revolver bullet. At times this upsets the larger calibered bullets until they are no longer of correct diameter for the gun in which they are to be fired. I may be wrong in this contention, but from my experience and from my findings in the case of one .45 Colt gun blown up when this type of loading tool was used, I believe that revolver bullets should be seated and the cartridge crimped with a steady, even push or pressure and not by any blow from a hammer or mallet. There is too great a tendency for that soft bullet to upset, or "slug up" as the ballasticians express it.

Many years ago, I learned in loading muzzle loading rifles—both the old heavy-slug muzzle loaders and the Pope, Schoyen, Petersen and Ballard breech-muzzle loaders—that in order to properly seat the bullet down through the false-muzzle, it must be done with one sharp, heavy blow struck with the palm of the hand. If several successive, light blows were struck, that bullet would be greatly upset, and as a result was then hard to push on down with the loading rod to its proper seating depth ahead of the chamber. It is obvious that no one strikes as hard a blow with the palm of his hand to these bullet starters as is applied with a mallet when seating a revolver bullet into a case having its neck resized to hold that bullet friction tight, and then to form a deep and uniform crimp in a heavy and stiff brass case. To me, the principle is all wrong and I consider it highly dangerous if used with car-

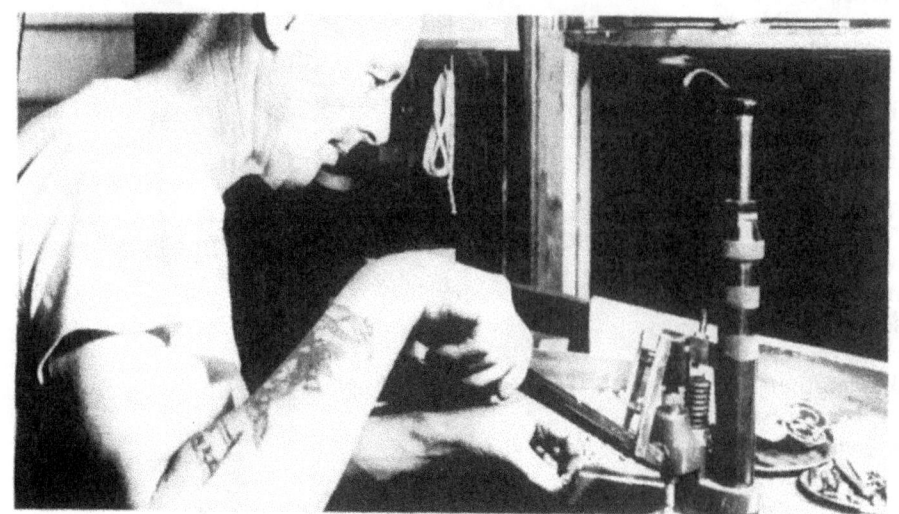

McPhillips sizing and lubricating Keith revolver bullets.

McPhillips re- and decapping and resizing revolver cases.

tools—the Schmitt and R.C.B.S. are the only tools in which I have not encountered this trouble at times—is having too large a diameter in the loading chamber or sizing dies. This fault can generally be seen at a glance, as the finished cartridge will come from the chamber with a well-formed crimp on one side and only a slight one on the other. This trouble may also be caused by having cases which are too thin walled. If the chamber will not form a perfect crimp with at least one make of case, send it back to its maker for correction. This will mean a new loading chamber. As I have previously stated, different makes of cases vary greatly in thickness, and where one make may be too thin to form a proper crimp in your tool, another make of the same case may work perfectly. The ammunition companies are improving their product all the time, and we can look for an even greater improvement and standardization in the future.

Some oversize loading chambers will often seat and crimp a bullet out of line with the axis of its case. Such improperly seated bullets cannot shoot accurately, even in the finest gun ever made. This may occur with the tong and hand tools or even with the straight line, custom made bullet seaters if the latter are not made to proper close tolerances. All seating or loading dies, whether for rifle or revolver cartridges, must hold the bullet in a straight line with the axis of the case before the bullet seating plunger is forced home; otherwise the bullet will be started into the case out of

tridges developing maximum or magnum ballistics; I shall stick to this contention until I am shown otherwise.

For metal patched rifle loads such bullet seaters are very fine indeed, but then these loads are seldom crimped. Also the hard metal patch bullet resists such deformation and upsettage much better than the relatively soft, lead revolver bullet. For seating the .32/20, .38/40 and .44/40 metal patched bullets for use in revolver cartridges, this type of bullet seater will prove to be all right, but I do not favor it for seating or crimping any soft lead bullet.

Some of the loading tool makers are rather careless about a few thousandths of an inch in the tolerances of their tools and dies. It is best for the purchaser to specify exactly what he wants in the thousandths of an inch when it comes to bullet sizing dies. Then it would be well when they are received to size down a few bullets and take a micrometer and make certain that they will do the work as specified, checking not only for diameter across one way, but also going all around that sized bullet, to make certain it is true. If it comes from the die with one reading greater than the other, and is obviously out of round, or its diameter is different from that ordered, send it back for correction. Make certain that you know how to handle the micrometer first, because not everyone can do this properly.

Another fault to watch out for in some makes of

McPhillips charging the cases with powder.

McPhillips, seating the bullet and crimping the case on same.

line, its base and sides will be shaved in places and it is very likely to be crimped tightly in that crooked position, whereupon the fault can no longer be seen with the naked eye. There you have one cartridge which cannot possibly shoot accurately.

The better and more complete your loading equipment, the better and safer will be the cartridges you produce, provided that the old brain is also used in their production. Regardless of how well a reloading tool is made, it cannot perform its operations properly unless some gray matter is also used in the handling of this tool. Reloading tools do not have college educations.

Most of the revolver charges recommended in the Ideal and other hand books are safe, conservative loads and are listed there for that very good reason. The beginner therefore, will do well to stick to such loads until he has acquired plenty of actual, practical experience with them; then he may safely venture a bit further and use more powerful charges. Do not try to assemble heavy loads with no equipment other than a cheap combination, hand, or tong type tool. It takes a proper assortment of adjustable, precision tools and their accessories to tackle such loads with safety and confidence.

I have never used a finer precision tool than the Schmitt or the R.C.B.S., while the Pacific and Hollywood are very close seconds. The R.C.B.S. seems to be the most powerful press of them all. The Pacific at times is slightly faster than the Schmitt, as the loaded cases are inserted mouth up into its loading die to seat and crimp the bullet. This facilitates handling without danger of spilling the powder. Still, the Schmitt has certain advantages not possessed by the other; the bullet can be started in the case with the fingers, the case set down on the workbench and the die placed over it, whereupon the assembly is held friction tight and then placed in the tool and its lever operated. No tool will produce finer ammunition than the Schmitt, but the Pacific, R.C.B.S. and Hollywood are also very good, and as I have said before, they are the faster of the two types. The Hollywood, and R.C.B.S., are both very fast precision tools as is the Pacific. I do not like any progressive loading tool.

I have had no experience with the more elaborate automatic type of bench reloading machine suitable for military and police organizations or the larger clubs. These tools are very costly and the men who operate them are generally old shooters and experienced reloaders—men who do not need to be told what to do or how to do it. Such tools do the complete reloading operation with a minimum of adjustment and operation; in fact they are miniature factory loading machines, and are far beyond the reach of the average shooter. I have used the Lyman, and the older Ideal

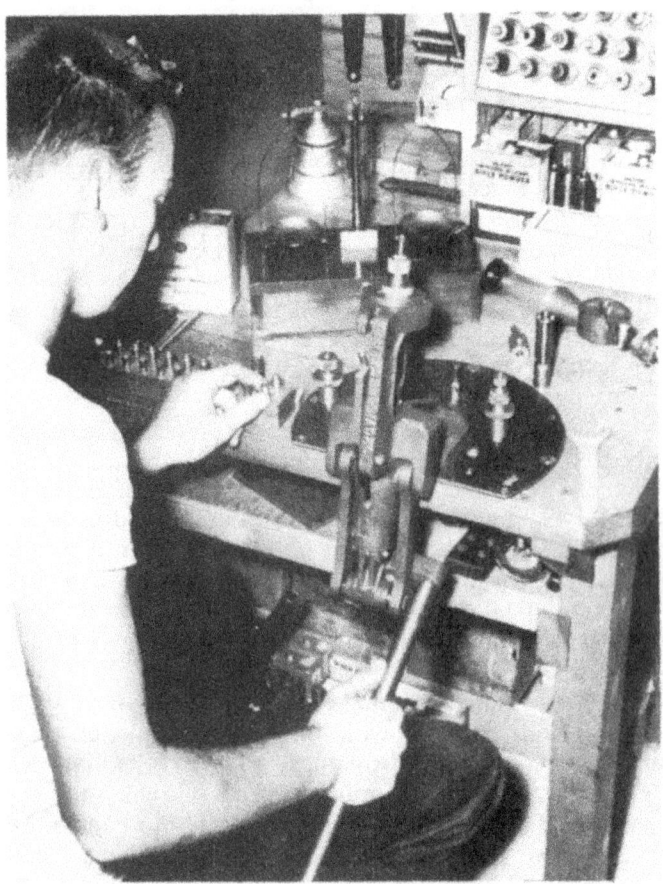

Expanding and decapping in the shop of the R.C.B.S. Gun & Die Works, Oroville, California, with R.C.B.S. tools.

Priming with R.C.B.S. tool .38 Special reloading. R.C.B.S. Gun & Die Shop, Oroville, California.

tools for a great many years, and although much has been said against this type of tong tool, when they are properly handled they will produce splendid ammunition and very good results may be secured with them. Also, they are small, light, easily moved about, and they do not break a man because of their cost. But I strongly believe in buying the Schmitt or Pacific, R. C. B. S. or Hollywood tools in every case where the handloader can afford them, particularly if his time is valuable, as they will do so many operations at one stroke of the operating lever that a great deal more ammunition can be loaded than in the same time with the cheaper type of hand tool.

The finally loaded cartridges should always be wiped clean of all excess dirt and lubricant and carefully packed in proper boxes. Those boxes had best be labeled as to the primer, powder charge, bullet weight, shape and temper used. The date of loading is also advisable. A good plan is to have a quantity of gummed labels made up in the form of a pad, having these details printed thereon and blank spaces left to be properly filled in for each load. Space for bullet diameter can also be useful. It is well to keep a record of all loadings, their performances, accuracy, pressure indications, etc. for future reference. Otherwise your reloads will soon become so badly mixed up that it will be impossible to tell which is which or for what purpose it was loaded. It does not pay to have too great a variety of small lots of cartridges lying about. Often it is well to adopt some distinguishing mark for the nose of the bullet; then if you travel about with a cartridge belt filled with both grouse and big game reloads, you can distinguish the one from the other at a glance—possibly at a touch also.

With all bullet seaters, a bullet seating punch that exactly fits the nose of the bullet must be used to insure perfect bullet seating and prevent any distorting of the bullet. Order seating punches to fit the bullet used.

Avoid any progressive loading machines that throw the powder charge in a sequence of operations. The jar of other operations can increase the powder charge and such progressive loading machines have blown up many a fine revolver.

Pressures, Primer Flattening and Case Expansion

While handloading his revolver ammunition, the average shooter has no elaborate pressure gun available to promptly advise him when he is running into dangerous pressures, and he probably would know nothing of its proper use if he did possess such intricate equipment. He is obliged to determine his pressures by more simple and practical, if far less accurate means. It has become the custom amongst shooters to observe the set-back and flattening of the primer in their fired cases and use this indication as a means of judging pressures. To my mind, this is a very uncertain manner of determination and this method should not be carried too far.

Primers, as made by the different ammunition companies and the Government arsenal, vary so much in thickness and composition of the metal cup, as well as in the power of their priming compositions, that they alone are no reliable indication of pressures. I have come to almost disregard primer flattening, as long as those primers are not pierced or do not protrude back into the firing pin hole in the recoil shield of the gun. However, with my most frequently used primer, the thick Remington nonmercuric, which is a very stout affair, I observe this flattening as one sign of pressure, but only to a limited extent. Other makes of primer are not so considered, owing to difference in construction. The new Winchester seems to be the thinnest of all, and even regular factory loads often show these primers

.38 Special cases, left to right, resized and primed in R.C.B.S. tool and dies, middle case mouth opened in No. 2 die to prevent shaving of case. Right, the finished cartridge with bullet seated and crimped without shaving of the bullet. R.C.B.S. Gun & Die Shop.

flattened out and apparently flowing to the extreme edge of the cup, yet the pressures developed are only normal for the load. The primer may be badly flattened and yet the load be a normal one and entirely safe to use.

You can fire an empty case with primer alone, and the chances are that it will be flattened as badly as if a good load of powder were used, and it also will probably be driven back and partially out of the case. This is because all revolvers must have considerable head space to insure rotation of the cylinder (and cases should be full length resized so they will fit rather loosely and freely in the chambers for this same reason). When you fire a loaded cartridge in a revolver, its primer starts to back out of the pocket, but the pressure of the load throws the head of the case back against the recoil shield, reseating the primer (General Hatcher has this very well illustrated in his big book). Fire this same case with primer alone in it and there is no set back given the case, which can reseat the protruding primer, and it is therefore permitted to protrude and flatten out, possibly to a greater degree than if fired in the normally loaded cartridge.

In the cartridge case itself, and its expansion, we have the most reliable "practical" gauge to go by outside of the factory pressure gun. Whenever a fired revolver case extracts hard, then that powder charge, or combination of components, is altogether too powerful for safety. The load should immediately be cut down at least two grains in weight and no more cartridges of that assembly should be fired. In double action, simultaneous ejection arms, the entire cylinder full of fired cases should at all times extract easily and freely, by a punch on the extractor rod from the palm of the hand. This is assuming of course, that clean cases are used and they are not gummed or corroded in the chambers. If your cases expand to such an extent that it takes several blows and considerable effort to drive the extractor rod back and eject all six of those fired cases at once, then you are getting into heavy and dangerous pressures, and the load should be cut down or its components changed or modified.

This may not call for a reduction in the powder charge, for that might not be the trouble at all. An oversized or too soft a bullet may be what is raising those pressures; but at any rate, whenever such signs of dangerous pressures are encountered, stop shooting that load right then and go over all its components until you have determined what is causing the trouble. Of course, good judgment dictates that the powder charge promptly be cut down a grain at least, until the cause of the trouble has been determined. Nothing is to be gained by dangerous pressures; on the contrary, much is to be lost, including a good gun. Usually, velocities do not increase in proportion to the increase in pressures, and with almost all powders, both rifle and revolver, after a certain "balance point" is reached in the load any further increase to the charge is usually detrimental to accuracy and the slight additional velocity gained is not worth other sacrifices. One had better stick to what is known to be a safe combination and get the increased power from a new and improved powder when the manufacturers have released it and recommended it for higher velocities.

With the Colt, Great Western, or Ruger single actions, where the cases are ejected singly, any signs of tight cases should be heeded at once. In these guns the bolt cuts, which stop the cylinder from revolving and align it for firing, are directly over the center of each chamber, and any undue pressure may bulge out these cuts and form a depression on the inside of the chamber into which case walls will expand. This will cause extraction troubles on all future loads, even light or normal charges. I have seen many of the older .45 Colt single action guns which had these bolt cuts bulged out from the firing of only heavy, black powder loads. At any rate, remember that the fired case is about your best safety gauge, watch extraction accordingly and be guided by it, with the flattening and other primer indications as a supplementary guide.

With well known primers which have been used considerably, you have a mental picture of just how they look after the different loads have been fired and one can often use these primers (and the old bean) as an additional indication of pressures developed. The indentation of the firing pin itself on the primer should always be watched. Any pierced primer due to too much hammer-nose protrusion, extreme pressures, a rough, sharp or corroded firing pin, allows gas to be driven back into the works. This will in time cause corrosion of these parts; also minute particles of the copper cup will be blown back into the works and may jam the action. Very heavy pressures will also blow the firing pin indentation back into the firing pin hole and will thus tie up the gun so that it is very hard to revolve or open the cylinder of a double-action arm. Such things as these are always to be watched for and avoided at all costs. When the pressure raises to such an extent that it is too heavy for safe and certain results, it may cause leading or you may wake up, as I did once, and find only the grip, barrel and half the cylinder of your gun remaining in your hand and you will be lucky if some of the flying parts have not struck you, or worse still, hit some friend standing nearby. I spent a good many years finding out just what a sixgun would and would not stand, and as a result of experience, I now have a great deal more respect for some of the cautions and "Don'ts" placed in the catalogs and handbooks on reloading. Never, never use a rifle primer in a revolver or pistol load. They are much too powerful.

There is one other indication of pressures, which, although a simple one, can be followed with a considerable amount of safe judgment. I refer to the sound of the cartridge upon being fired. Any experienced hand loader or shooter can tell rather closely by the sound of his gun whether the load is a safe one or not. A certain caliber sounds quite distinctive upon being

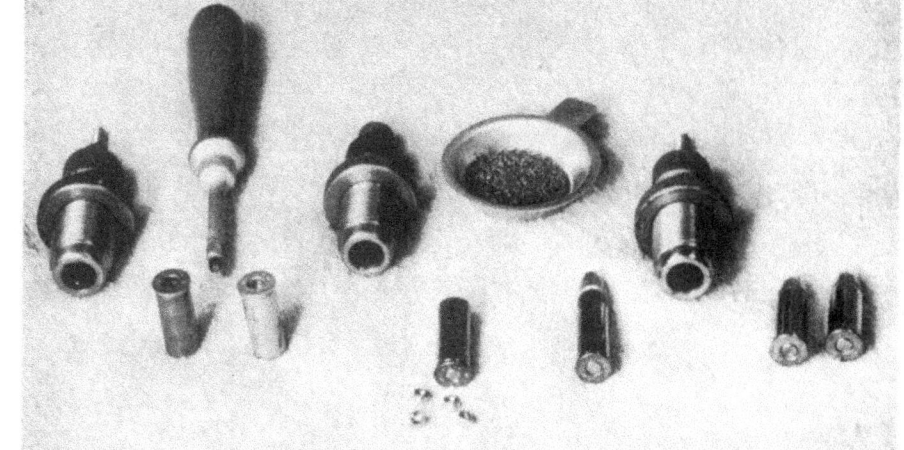

Shows steps in reloading operation: (1) sizing and decapping die, (2) cleaning primer pocket with hand tool, (3) expanding die also gives slight bell to mouth of case and primers are seated with this operation, (4) powder charge weighed and funneled into case, (5) seating die seats bullet to desired depth with crimp.

*Courtesy of Moody's Reloading Service.
Photo by George Gresh.*

fired with standard cartridges. If the load is light, it has a different report than a normal load, and if heavy, still a different sound. When it begins to reach the dangerous stage, it has a still different, ear-splitting, sharp crack. With a bit of practice one can accustom his ears to the sound of normal and safe reports, and the beginner should fire enough different makes of factory loads to become accustomed to the sound of what he knows to be safe, satisfactory ammunition for that caliber gun. The loads which are not heavy enough to fire cleanly, give off quite a hollow "plunk" which can instantly be detected by the ear as being too light. In the same way, the old-timers could instantly tell when a muzzle loading, cap-and-ball rifle was properly loaded; if the charge was rammed down by some dub, the report sounded quite prolonged and "spongy," while the same load put down the muzzle by an expert would crack like a blacksnake whip.

I do not claim that pressures may be judged by the report of the gun, but I do maintain that an experienced shooter can obtain a very close idea as to the safety of his loads by the sound of their report, and that beginners should train their ears to such indication. Also, in shooting a handgun, one should observe the indication of smoke given off when the cartridge is fired and should stop the moment any peculiarly colored or unduly large amount of smoke is seen. I was once shooting some factory loaded .38 Specials and fired a shot which gave off a most peculiar, reddish smoke from the rear end of the barrel. I stopped shooting, looked into the matter and discovered a bullet stuck half way up the bore. Any improperly burning powder charge gives off an excessive amount of smoke and will probably also fill the barrel and action with unburned powder grains. Watch out for such shots.

For most purposes a heavy revolver load is undesirable and not needed. Most practice shooting should be done with light or normal charges. There are times however, for game shooting, or defense purposes, or long range practice, when very powerful loads are needed, and for these purposes the hand loader should select the heaviest brass procurable.

For most calibers and heavy loads, select only the solid headed case, if possible to obtain such in the caliber cartridge you are using.

If the bore of your revolver becomes badly leaded from excessive pressures, or from too heavy a charge of too hot a powder which fuses the base of the bullets, it may then raise the pressure of all succeeding loads fired through it until that lead is removed. Accuracy will suffer too. A good, stiff brass bristle brush is about the best thing to use to remove this lead. A special lead removing kit is also sold by Gun Specialties, 327 College Park, Georgia that does a splendid job of removing lead from all pistols. At times, you may encounter leading for no apparent reason; sometimes it is due to a rough or pitted barrel, or one with tight and loose places in it.

Throughout this book, I have constantly stressed the importance of some heavy loads being safe only in heavy .45 frame guns. Perhaps I had better state exactly what models of guns come under this classification; then there will be no mistake made by a beginner who might otherwise have a light framed gun blown up with a load which is only safe in a heavy framed model.

In Smith & Wesson make, the following models come under my classification of heavy framed guns: The Heavy Duty, encased ejector, 5 inch police revolver in .38/44 caliber; the Outdoorsman .38/44 caliber with 6½ inch barrel and target sights; the .44 caliber Military and Police models, which also take in the old Triple Lock S. & W. in .44 Special and other calibers. Lastly, the .357 S. & W. Magnum revolver. All these guns in the various calibers are built on heavy frames and are suitable for loads such as I have mentioned. The Highway Patrolman is also suitable.

In Colt make, the Single Action and Bisley models come under the classication of heavy framed guns. The Colt New Service, in both plain and target models and the Shooting Master are all made on the .45 frame and are safe with heavy loads. The D.A. Colt Frontier with solid frame is another. The Colt Officer's Model is made on a .41 caliber frame, and I do not consider it

Showing first operation on Pacific tool. Cases, after being coated lightly with heavy lubricant, are sized and decapped. Cases need not be lubricated when using the rather expensive Lifetyme die shown leaning against frame of tool.

*Courtesy of Moody's Reloading Service.
Photo by George Gresh.*

suitable or safe with the heavier .38 Special loads I have mentioned and listed, except guns of late manufacture or their .357. The Ruger Black Hawk and the Great Western are both heavy .45 frame guns.

Never attempt to reload any sort of cartridges for the cheaply made revolver. Only Smith & Wesson, Colt, G. W. or Ruger guns should be used with reloaded ammunition. I remember one time a boy chum of mine obtained an old, nickel plated, break frame revolver for the .38 S. & W. cartridge, it was Iver Johnson or H. & R. make, and with it he got a box of old U.M.C. cartridges. We repaired to an old lime kiln near Helena, Montana to do a bit of shooting. Harold Garret decided that I, having had more experience than he, should do the shooting, so we proceeded along that line. I picked out a rock about the size of my hat and started shooting at it at a range of about twenty yards. My first shot went over the rock, the second went low, so I then told Harold I would hit it at the next shot. I did hit it too, but the top strap blew off the gun at its junction with the ribbed barrel, and went whizzing back through my hat, parting my hair and giving me a small scalp wound at the same time. The top of one chamber was blown out and the barrel slowly flopped over until it pointed at my feet. I looked at the gun, felt my head, and then chucked that bit of pot metal as far down the gulch as I could. We found the piece of top strap at the base of the old kiln, badly battered against the rocks, so it must have had some velocity itself. From that day on, neither of us have ever monkeyed with another such cheap handgun.

Never, under any circumstances reload cartridges to be used in one of these European imitations of our American handguns. Some good handguns are made in Europe, but they are not imitations of anything. I particularly refer to the Spanish junk, advertised and stamped as "made for the Smith & Wesson cartridge." These weapons are bad enough when used with standard factory ammunition; many of them split the barrel or blow out the top of a cylinder even with it. So if you own one of these contraptions, don't reload for it, and don't try to trade it to some other unsuspecting sucker—throw it away where it cannot be recovered. Many of the handloads I recommend and use safely in Smith & Wesson and Colt arms would blow these imitations to pieces at the first shot, and although the metal of their cylinders is too soft and weak to hold any real sixgun pressures, it is plenty hard enough to cut a hole in your skull if a piece strikes you when the gun lets go.

It is well never to allow anyone to stand at one side of a sixgun while it is being fired, especially with experimental loads. This also applies to normal loads, particularly if the cylinder is not fitted closely to the rear end of the barrel and has excessive clearance here, or if it is a gun which shaves the bullets in the least. Even with the best of guns this is poor business, as the cylinder might not be locked in perfect alignment. Small particles of flying lead can strike a person in the face or eye with disastrous results. A bursting gun cylinder would be extremely dangerous to bystanders. With the old percussion guns this is particularly bad business as fragments of the fired and bursting caps often fly out at right angles to the line of fire and many shooters have received bad eye injuries from this cause alone. Many of these old relics are badly rusted, or have been in that condition and restored, so extreme caution should be used when they are "tried out." They

Courtesy of Moody's Reloading Service.
Photo by George Gresh.

Set up for 18.5 gr. of 2400 in .44 Sp. using Ideal No. 55 powder measure and checking on sensitive Redding scale.

should always be shot out at arm's length. Don't try any hip shooting or other fool stunts, as the nipples may be badly rusted and permit considerable gas and cap fragments to fly outwards and up into the shooter's face if held close against the body. Such guns may easily put out one's eye.

Working Up Special Loads

In working up special loads for any revolver or cartridge, always start with a charge which you know will be light and gradually increase its weight by not more than half a grain at a time, even when the case and primer show no signs whatever of pressure. Whenever the primer begins to flatten out and the case shows any expansion or signs of pressure, then it is best to make any further increase by about one-tenth of a grain at a time, stopping when a good safe, satisfactory load is reached, and always below the stage where the cases show the least signs of extracting hard, even when six are ejected simultaneously.

First, check the groove diameter of your gun if you do not already know it. Then check your bullet diameter, also noting in what manner it may possibly differ from the standard bullet. If it has a deeper seating depth, cut the first charge very much lower than that recommended by the tables. I have stressed the importance of checking the seating depth of various bullets, the difference in powder capacity with various bullets, and also the difference in powder capacity of the various makes of case for the same cartridge. Remember always that a deeper seating depth, other things being equal, will give higher pressures and a quicker and more complete combustion of the powder charge. A smaller powder chamber, due to thicker case walls, will do the same thing. A heavier crimp, whether due to cases longer than standard, or stretched and hardened by continued resizing, will also increase pressures. Too soft a bullet temper may also increase pressures, this being due to excessive upsettage in the cylinder throat or barrel cone. Remember that all hot powders, especially those like Bullseye, and #5, #6, #5066 or Unique, are not suitable for extreme or heavy loads, as they are much too fast and hot and may fuse the base of the bullet before they show signs of much pressure, leading the gun badly with consequent inaccurate results.

It is best to keep even heavy loads within the limits of safety as shown by case expansion and primer flattening to a lesser degree. Nothing is to be gained by going above the safety line with any load, as after that point is reached any increase in the powder charge seldom adds anything appreciable to velocity; on the contrary, it generally decreases the accuracy and even two-tenths of a grain increase may raise the pressures as much as three thousand pounds after the maximum safe figure is reached. It is well to stay within the safety margin, but by this I do not mean the 15,000 pounds pressure limit arbitrarily imposed by the loading companies for most revolver loads. This figure is necessitated by the fact that most, in fact, practically all, of the factory revolver cartridges loaded today must be safe if loaded into and fired from a revolver of their caliber made back in the '70's or '80's. The .357 Smith & Wesson Magnum is the first revolver cartridge developed since about 1908 with the exception of the .45 auto rim; think of that in this day when an automobile or radio three years old is an antique. What a bunch of saps we shooters are to swallow all this advertising patter about "modern" handgun cartridges.

With any of our lighter framed handguns, even with the .38 Military and Police and Official Police models in Smith & Wesson and Colt arms, it is safest to always stay around this 15,000 pounds limit. But with the thicker walled cylinder and barrels of the Smith &

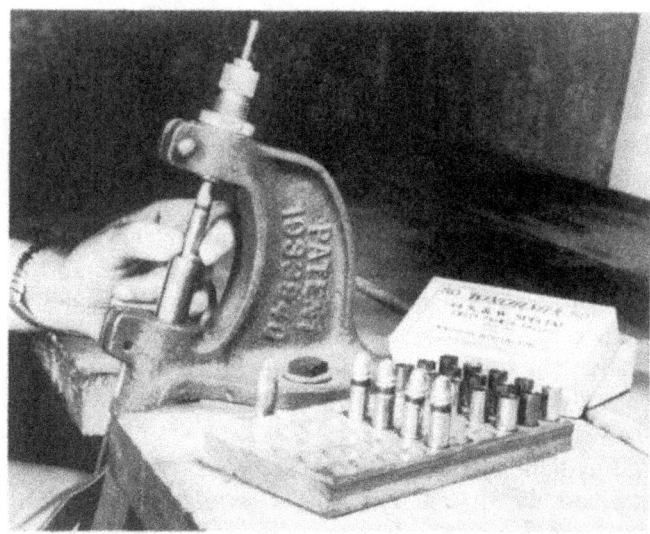

Courtesy of Moody's Reloading Service.
Photo by George Gresh.

Bullet seating operation with Pacific tool. Close inspection will show how case necks have been expanded by use of R.C.B.S. third die. Bullets start readily in cases and eliminate shaving of bullet metal. Keith 235 gr. hollow point .44 Spl.

Wesson Heavy Duty Police revolver, the Outdoorsman, the .357 Magnum, and the Highway Patrolman, and with the Colt Single Action and New Service frame guns in the medium calibers, also the Great Western and Ruger single actions, pressures can be raised to around double this limit. I know of one Heavy Duty Smith & Wesson gun which I myself used for a long time, in which one thousand loads were fired developing up to 42,000 pounds pressure; also two Single Action Colts handled the same heavy charges of #80 powder for a similar long series of shots with no damage whatever. I am not recommending that such charges be duplicated or used. I am merely stating an actual occurrence. I have also used powder charges for years in my .44 Special Colt and Smith & Wesson guns which developed an average of 20,000 pounds pressure, with no trouble whatever from either hard extraction or damage to the guns. But such charges cannot be used as a steady diet in the .45 caliber cartridges, or in light frame .38 caliber arms, or in the .38/40 and .44/40 guns, as trouble is sure to develop sooner or later. Until the advent of the .357 Magnum, the .38 Colt Automatic cartridge was, if I remember right, our highest pressure handgun cartridge, its maximum running from 25,000 to 28,000 pounds. Yet guns made back around 1908 are considered entirely safe at these figures. My heavy .44 Special load of 250 grains Keith bullet and 18.5 grains 2400 in old web cases or 16.5 grains in the new solid head Winchester cases gives over 1200 feet velocity with just 20,000 pounds pressure for the old cases and 20,000 for the new solid cases.

For target shooting, nothing heavier than standard velocity is needed, certainly nothing over 900 feet with standard weight bullets. It is well to practice with such velocities, or even lighter loads. The latter will be far more pleasant to shoot and much more can be learned by their use. In the .38 Special, loads as light as 2½ to 3 grains of Bullseye with the standard weight bullet are plenty fast enough for twenty yard revolver work, whether in practice or serious competition. The longer fifty yard work usually requires more powerful charges, the standard velocity being about right at this range. In working up satisfactory light loads, trouble may be encountered in getting the powder charge burning right; keep in mind that a heavy crimp can improve ignition, as can a heavier bullet, or seating the bullet deeper in the case. Bullseye is the best powder for really light and moderate loads. It takes an exceedingly fast powder which will burn at low pressures to do the trick.

For hunting, the load should be heavier than most stardard cartridges. The bullets should by all means be of the flat point, sharp shoulder design or else with hollow points, even for small game shooting. If anything larger than small game is to be shot with the handgun, the shooter will need the most powerful handloads that his gun will safely handle with correctly shaped bullets, the most powerful combination he can shoot with accuracy.

Self defense work calls for the same ticket and most men of experience prefer heavy calibered guns for both hunting and defense, calibers such as the .357 Magnum, .38/40, .44/40, .44 Special and the various full loads in .45 caliber. Caliber has a great deal to do with actual killing power and the larger the hole you open in anything, the quicker you will kill it, other things such as penetration being equal. For this reason alone, if for no others, a properly loaded .44 Special will prove a more deadly killer than anything smaller; or larger either, with our present model guns. The smaller calibers will not cut such large holes and will not throw as much weight of lead. The present .45 guns are too thin in their cylinder walls to safely stand the pressures of the .44 Special heavy hand loads. And when it comes to using factory loads, this is another and a much sadder story.

Some authorities claim that any revolver load which is heavier than the normal factory cartridge is not accurate. I cannot agree with this contention, as all of my best long range game shooting has been accomplished with heavy loads in the .32/20, .38/44, .357 Magnum, .44 Special and .45 Colt arms. It is true that some men cannot shoot heavy loads with the same accuracy and effect that they can the lighter and more pleasant charges, due to the heavier recoil and report of the former. In practice work or fine target competition, there is nothing to be gained and much to be lost by trying to hold down loads giving a heavy recoil and sharp muzzle blast, but in game or defense shooting, which never consists of firing a long string of shots, then these heavy loads are well worth while.

Some cartridges have a most ear splitting report when heavily loaded, the .32/20 being a particularly bad offender in this respect. Some shooters do not mind this at all, while with others it will in time develop a tendency to flinch and pull off the shots. The .357 Magnum cartridge gives quite a muzzle blast and report, especially when firing with the shorter barrels. Such noise, blast and recoil are absolutely unavoidable in shooting heavy loads, and one will simply have to become accustomed to them. Do not use such loads for your practice shooting; fire lighter charges in the gun for this so that you will not develop any bad habits. Under the excitement of defense work or in most game shooting, the report and recoil will never be noticed. In fact, the gun is apt to both feel and sound like a .22 caliber. I know this from experience. The few shots fired for such purposes will not interfere with anyone's nervous system to the extent of causing missing or flinching.

Many shooters will be desirous of working up a hand load which will shoot correctly with the fixed sights their gun is equipped with. At times this becomes quite a problem. Usually a slow, heavy bullet load will strike the target the highest of any, while very heavy, high velocity loads will generally strike lower—often

Courtesy of Moody's Reloading Service.
Photo by George Gresh.

Various Keith bullets and loads. From left to right: 225 gr. H. P. in .45 Auto Rim cartridge; 235 gr. H. P. in .45 Auto Rim cartridge; 235 gr. H. P. in .45 Long Colt; 235 gr. H. P. in .44 Sp.; 160 gr. H. P. in .38 Sp. and on right, seated deep in .357 Magnum with crimp at front of forward band.

low and left—so much so at times, that without adjustable sights it becomes quite a problem to hit with such loads. In most cases, this is due to the change in barrel time; the slow and heavy bullet has a much longer barrel time, hence the barrel raises higher in recoil before that bullet emerges from the muzzle. With a high velocity load in the same gun there is less barrel time and the bullet gets out of the barrel before it has raised so high from recoil. I took this matter up with Major Wesson many years ago, and he found that a higher rear sight was necessary for their .357 Magnum revolver when the standard .38 Special cartridge was used in the gun. Quite often, a lighter bullet at the same velocity will cause the gun to group to the left of its regular sighting.

The larger the caliber of the gun in proportion to its weight, the more uniform must be the shooter's grip on the gun butt to obtain equal accuracy and grouping on the target. Usually the very finest target accuracy will be obtained with normal to slightly over normal velocities. Some bullets shoot with uncanny accuracy at very high velocities, particularly those which were designed with this in mind. Others will not do so well if the standard velocity is increased.

By judicious examination and selection of the bullet weight and powder charge, it is often possible to have the gun with fixed sights shoot exactly to the point of aim. More often such guns will shoot too high, too low, or to one side or the other with the load the shooter particularly wishes to use. In general, the hand loader is best fitted with a target gun having adjustable sights, so that he may adjust it to shoot exactly right with his pet loads. Different revolver loads show just as much variation in their point of impact as do rifle loads, and adjustable sights are of equal importance if the shooter wants to hit anything. Anyone soon becomes plumb disgusted with a gun he cannot hit with. Only the .44 Special seems to shoot both light and heavy loads with the same weight bullet to the same point of aim.

In testing your handloads for accuracy, remember that quite often a load and bullet which shoots well and groups closely on the target at short range, may not carry well at all at long range. Really long range work with the revolver is the finest test of all for ammunition. I have seen ammunition used with considerable success in fast target competition which would have been hopeless for long range work. Long range work soon shows whether or not a bullet design is accurate. With too

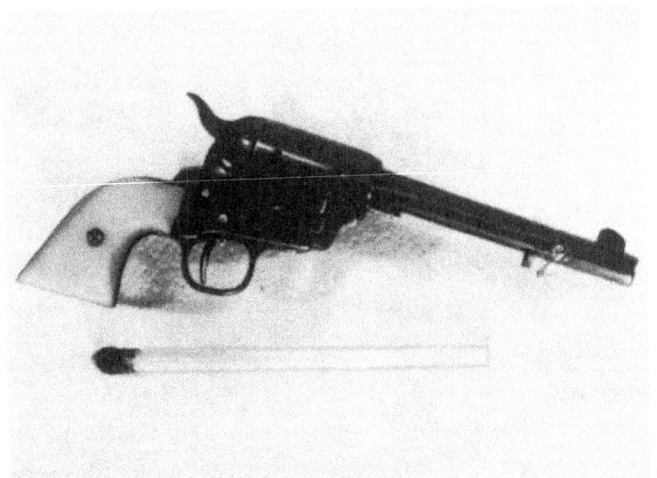

Smallest miniature single action shown with common match for comparison—it can be fired and is complete in all details.

blunt a point it soon loses its accuracy. These true wad-cutter shapes lose out very fast after the fifty yard mark is passed, or if the wind is blowing, whereas the longer pointed, better balanced bullets will retain their fine grouping qualities out to extreme range.

In testing for shocking or killing power, remember that soap, wood and similar penetration or upsettage tests may mean very little. Bullets, even soft points from .32/20, .38/40 and .44/40 which may not expand in the least when fired into wood, merely smearing back the exposed lead tip, will nearly always expand perfectly on meat and bone. The real test of any such bullet is to kill game or livestock with it, then you find out quickly just what it will and will not do. Living flesh, filled with blood, tissue and fluids, acts differently on bullet metal than any other medium. These soap and other substitute tests really mean very little in comparison.

If you want to catch your fired bullets in an undamaged condition to see how they are taking the rifling of the gun, one of the very best methods I know of is to shoot into soft snow drifts. Snow, unless packed very hard, will not expand or mark a bullet in the least, and the fired bullets may be recovered in the Spring or when the snow melts. I will admit that this may be a rather long, drawn out test, but I have seen heavily loaded, hollow point bullets shot through a great deal of snow without deforming in the least. Yet that same bullet would expand and turn wrong side out when shot through a jack rabbit. It is only by such hand loading and experimenting that we learn. Most of the few present improvements in revolver loads are directly due to the efforts of the individual experimenters.

I will close this chapter with a few of the heavy, maximum loads I have personally used. These cartridges are intended to be assembled by skilled and experienced shooters, from new, factory components, powder charges carefully weighed. Always start in with about two grains under the charge recommended and gradually work up. If the first one or two shots from a lot show signs of excessive pressure when fired, STOP RIGHT THERE and either pull down, or destroy the remainder of those loads. Then, starting with a lighter charge, again start working up, but be more gradual about it and check over all the components once more. Never be in a hurry when loading ammunition. Make haste slowly, and good and safe results will be obtained—also ammunition that cannot be purchased over the counter.

.38/44 Special. Keith 160 grain hollow point, or hollow base bullet sized .357 to .358. Hercules #2400 powder. Charge 13.5 grains with either of the Ideal catalog numbers of this bullet: #358429 or #358431, the bullets being crimped in their crimp groove. Remington .38/44 cases and primers.

.357 Magnum Smith & Wesson. The two Keith bullets listed in preceding paragraph. Maximum charge 15 grains Hercules #2400 for the 160 grain bullet and 14.5 grains for the 173 grain solid bullet. Bullet diameter .358 of an inch.

.44 Smith & Wesson Special. Keith Lyman 250 grain flat base and 235 grain hollow point and hollow base. Ideal #429421 and #429422, use 18.5 grains in old web cases and 17.5 grains in new solid head cases.

.45 Colt, long case. Keith Lyman 250 grain flat base, and 235 grain hollow point Ideal #454424 bullets. Use 18.5 grains 2400 in either old web cases or new solid head cases. Hercules #2400 with bullets sized .452 or .002 of an inch over groove diameter in old guns running .450 of an inch groove diameter and sized .454 of an inch for newer guns with larger bore diameter. This charge can be used with all three bullets, but it is maximum. This charge may also be used in the new 1950 target S. & W. for the .45 Colt cartridge by crimping barely over the front barrel and sizing the bullets .454 inches in either old or new solid head cases.

.45 Auto Rim. Bullets sized .452 of an inch. The best heavy load for the .45 Auto Rim revolver is the Keith-Ideal 240 grain #452423 or the Keith-Ideal #454424 cast one to sixteen tin and lead, and sized .451 of an inch and loaded with 7.5 grains of Unique with good stiff crimp. A charge of 7.5 grains of Unique with any of the three Keith bullets is also a very nice load in the .44 Special, giving around 900 feet.

BUT—remember, Brother, I assume the risk and consequences of only such of the above loads as I myself assemble.

Reloading Auto Pistol Cartridges

First select a bullet that has either a round nose or one of the wad cutter type that will allow seating of all bands inside the case.

Next cast your bullets of one to ten or even harder mixture of tin and lead. Resize all auto pistol cases full length and then trim them to exact overall length of the factory new cases. Seat the bullets friction tight and be sure they are resized small enough to hold said bullets friction tight in their proper place. Remember automatic pistols have headspace from the head of the case to the front shoulder of the case, so do not put any crimp on the case whatever. All auto pistols are regulated for a given bullet weight and pressure of the load and all loads must strictly adhere to this pressure for proper functioning of the arm. The bullet nose must have enough taper and be hard enough to feed up on the ramp and into the chamber with certainty, and the cartridge case must be exact as to length and with the front of the case perfectly square so it will head-space against the shoulder at the front end of the chamber.

Any change to a lighter load will also necessitate a reduction in the strength of the recoil spring. Any increase in the normal pressure and velocity of a given weight bullet will increase the velocity of the slide to the rear and will soon batter up the slide and cause worn and broken parts, so stick to standard velocity and standard bullet weights as much as possible or a heavier bullet with reduced powder charge to give same pressures. A lighter bullet can also be used with a slightly increased powder charge to again give standard pressures and cause certain functioning of the arm. Jacketed factory bullets can also be reloaded perfectly and will give factory ammunition results. The auto loader throws its cases away where they are hard to find, so for this reason we do not consider it the best arm for the reloader.

PUBLISHER'S NOTE:
Loading ammunition is a most exacting procedure. Great care and accurate measurements are safety essentials. Elmer Keith possesses a broad knowledge of the subject and has conducted many experiments over a long period of time. Maximum loads based on theory and research have been developed. His findings are included in the above chapter. The publisher assumes no responsibility for either the handloader's care with powder and his ability to make accurate measurements or with the exacting recommendations of the respected author.

Roy Weatherby and Elmer Keith.

Chapter XVIII

Selection of Cartridges

OVER THE YEARS a great many pistol and revolver cartridges have been manufactured for use in a wide variety of guns. Many of the old arms are still present, and there is some demand for ammunition for them. Pistol and revolver ammunition, like shotgun gauges, is becoming more standardized and will become even more so in the future. The less the number of calibers and loads that have to be carried in stock and still give the shooter a cartridge for every need, the better, as it allows greater perfection and economy in manufacture of those loads still on the list.

The more experiment and the more rounds loaded of any certain caliber, the greater the improvement. This is clearly shown in the 30/06 rifle cartridge and has been also proven in the .22 L. R., the .38 Special and the .45 Auto, in hand gun loads.

Let us go through the list of handgun cartridges. While a great many sizes and loads have been produced to date, most of them are now obsolete and need be given little consideration. Colt and Smith & Wesson each listed identical cartridges, but with different bullet shapes for years. This did not promote standardization, and standardization and perfection of the few best loads is what is needed. If the big ammunition companies carry a smaller number of pistol and revolver loads, they can do more research on each, which leads to better and more accurate ammunition. Nothing new in sixgun cartridges has appeared over the horizon in the last fifty years, except the .357 Magnum S. & W. True. We have had many improvements in various existing cartridges, but the ammunition companies have not brought out a single new pistol or revolver cartridge. Were it not for the thousands of serviceable arms on hand, many numbers now carried could be scrapped and the shooting fraternity would not lose a thing. Many of these sizes would have been dropped, were it not for the thousands of arms manufactured in Europe and brought into this country after World War I. Collectors create a demand for many of the older hulls, which has forced the companies to retain a longer list than they otherwise would.

Let us go through the catalog of pistol and revolver cartridges, selecting the best, and eliminating the poorer loads that sooner or later will become obsolete.

In rim fires we need but two, only one of which is now in current use in hand guns. These are the .22 L. R. and the .25 Stevens long. The .22 L. R. is a very useful cartridge for practice and for some small game, as well as match work. The .25 Stevens, now almost off the market, is a far better rim fire cartridge for small game hunting, and should be retained. Some of our more modern revolvers ought to be chambered for this excellent cartridge. With its inside lubrication, it can be carried loose in the pocket without picking up grit and dirt. It is amply accurate, and has about twice the killing power of the .22 L. R. We would like to see the Smith & Wesson K Models chambered for this cartridge, also the Ruger Single Six and the High Standard Sentinel. It is just about ideal for small game if loaded with 60 grain bullets in plain and hollow point style and to a velocity of 1100 to 1300 feet from the hand gun. The old Stevens Lord Model was chambered for this excellent small game cartridge and all who used it, preferred it to the .22 rim fires, even for squirrel shooting. It will kill the larger grouse cleanly with good bullet placement using hollow points. It has enough penetration for brain shots in livestock, and to kill trapped animals. This is one old cartridge that should be rejuvenated and brought back. If one good revolver was chambered for it, the demand would soon put it on a permanent basis among our pistol and revolver loads.

Next we have the old .30 and .32 caliber rim fires, both long obsolete and best left that way as they did not offer anything over the .32 center fires. Of the .32 center fire cartridges, only two are worth consideration; they are the .32 S. & W. long and the .32/20. The .32 S. & W. long is a wonderfully accurate target cartridge and useful for that purpose, but in factory loadings is a very poor game cartridge. Properly hand loaded with a bullet like Ideal 313445 and four grains of Unique, for a velocity of 1000 feet, it is a wonderful small game cartridge. With lighter loads such as the same bullet backed by 2.5 grains of Bullseye it is a superior target cartridge capable of close competition with the larger .38 Special. It must be remembered however, that in center fire revolver cartridges it is easier to load an accurate load in a .38 caliber than in a .32

Elmer Keith answering gun questions at the 1955 N.R.A. Annual Meeting in Washington, D. C.

caliber. This for the reason that cases and bullets in .32 caliber must be held to far closer tolerances as to diameter than in .38 caliber and the same applies to the .38 caliber as compared to the .44 caliber. The .32 S. & W. long should be kept on the active list as it is an excellent small cartridge.

The .32/20 has always been a good small game cartridge in either the rifle or revolver, and properly loaded in heavy .45 frame guns, is an excellent high speed revolver load as the 100 to 115 grain bullet can be given up to 1500 feet velocity with 10 grains of No. 2400 powder. Such loads have an ear splitting crack, but are superbly accurate if properly loaded and are very effective if properly placed on all small game up to coyotes and bobcats. They are a bit on the destructive side in full loads for small game animals such as rabbits and birds, but for the man wanting a small caliber high velocity load of magnum-type in the revolver of .45 frame, the .32/20 is the one best bet. I killed three mule deer and an elk with the load from a S. A. Colt and the Lord only knows how much small game in the many years I packed that caliber gun as a boy. For the hand loader who wants a flat shooting accurate small bore, the .32/20 is it.

Many custom jobs have been built on the S. A. Colt and some on the New Service Colt for the .22 Hornet, .25/20 and the .30 carbine, but we never could see much use in a caliber under .32 for a center fire revolver cartridge. There is some excuse for the .30 carbine cartridge in the .45 frame sixguns for use by army personnel who have access to plenty of that ammunition for practice and small game shooting, but the .30 carbine is not a good killer in the army pointed full patch bullet and not nearly the equal of a good flat point 115 grain bullet from the .32/20 at 1500 feet. The .32/20 case is almost a straight taper, reloads easily and well and resizes well with any heavy bench tool. The best bullet for the cartridge is the Ideal 311316 with flat base to weight just over 115 grains. This bullet is regularly made for a gas check, but a gas check is a mistake in a revolver and the plain base form is the better.

I cannot fully underwrite the .32/20 cartridge as pistol fodder unless handloaded as outlined. It was originally designed for rifles and taken up later by Colt and Smith & Wesson. As long as black powder loads prevailed all was smooth sailing. When smokeless powder arrived, trouble came with it. The cartridge was loaded down to be safe in light pistols, and lost its reputation as a rifle load. It was frequently loaded with too slow a powder for best pistol results and gained a bad reputation for bullets sticking in pistol barrels. Later a special high pressure load for rifles was placed on the market with a plain, and often ignored warning on the carton not to use them in pistols. Just what the over all .32/20 factory ammunition situation may be today, I do not know, and know still less about what it may be if you read this book several years after publication. All I stand on is that the .32/20, used in a heavy cylinder revolver, can be handloaded into a fast and effective cartridge.

For my part, the small pocket pistol calibers such as the .25 Colt auto, the .32 Colt auto, .32 S. & W. and the .380 Colt auto can all be thrown in the discard pile. They were made for a myriad of small pocket defense pistols, yet are too small to be adequate as defense weapons. Both guns and loads are off the active list as far as I am concerned.

The .30 Luger will no doubt be with us, also the .30 Mauser, as long as we have guns for their use, but both are inferior to the 9 mm. Luger and the Super .38 Colt auto cartridge for auto pistol usage. They are in about the same category as the revolver made for the .30 carbine cartridge, accurate flat shooting loads, but short bullet weight for deep penetration, and lacking in caliber either for defense or larger game shooting. Both the Luger and the Mauser are slow weapons to get in action and are at their best for game shooting. They must be used with soft pointed bullets for expansion if they are to kill well, and these are no longer loaded commercially. It would be a mistake to bring out a new gun for either hull.

This brings us up to the various so-called .38 calibers which are in reality .35 and .36 calibers. The old

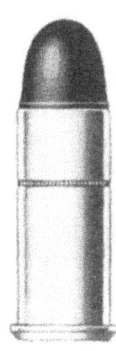

.44 S. & W. Special.

.38 long and short Colt are now obsolete and were made for arms with .360 of an inch groove diameter and depended on upsettage of the slug to fill the bore. They were lacking in both accuracy and killing power. With the passing of the old Colt Lightning, the .38 Army Colt and S. & W. guns, these cartridges are fast becoming obsolete. The army found during the Philippino insurrection that the .38 Long hollow base bullet was neither a stopper nor a killer and lost many fine officers who emptied their .38 army colts into a Moro's chest only to have him keep on coming and clip off their head with one swipe of his bolo. These loads will soon drop from the active list. The .38 Smith & Wesson is a superbly accurate cartridge and during the last war received a great rejuvenation by being adopted by the British for their service cartridge with a 200 grain bullet. They were known as the .38/200. The British are noted for going back to and adopting obsolete cartridges, and this is no exception to the rule. The cartridge is not powerful enough for a certain man-stopper and must be placed fairly well to offer much in this line. The British should at least have adopted the .38 Special which is also too small for a man-stopper or service cartridge. Smith & Wesson made a great many arms in this caliber for the British load, and these today are being peddled all over this country. I have received literally hundreds of letters asking if they can be rechambered to .38 Special. The answer is, of course, "NO." These arms have a .360 of an inch groove diameter. The .38 S. & W. cartridge is also larger in diameter than the .38 Special, so it cannot be rechambered and the bore of the barrel is too large for .38 Special bullets. The only conversion of these arms to .38 Special is by fitting both a new barrel and a new cylinder in that caliber.

The .38 S. & W. is very accurate and we once had an old break top three inch barrel S. & W. gun that would consistently hit a ground squirrel up to 60 yards if you held all the front sight up in the rear notch. I cleaned up most of the old Montana National Guard in pistol matches with the little gun, shooting against the army 1917 revolvers and .45 auto Colts, but it was a pip squeek load, and accuracy was about its only virtue. I look for the British to soon throw it and their .38/200 grain bullet service load in the discard pile and adopt a more powerful weapon. The Smith & Wesson Company also gave the load a further boost when they chambered their little five shot Terrier, on the .32 frame for it as a very light ladies' pocket gun. The load, however, is due to be discarded even though it will be in strong demand for many years to come, because of the many guns now in existence chambered for it.

.45 wad cutter.

For years many would-be ballisticians labored under the delusion that a short case was best for maximum velocities and accuracy in pistol and revolver loads; nothing could be further from the truth. While short cases will handle fast powders like Bullseye to best advantage, they will not hold a proper load of a slower burning powder like 2400. With the short case, the internal pressure is exerted over a small area of the cylinder and bursting pressures are very soon reached, while with a longer case like the .38 Special in comparison with the .38 S. & W., or the .44 Special in comparison with the short .44 Russian, the pressure is spread over the entire length of the cylinder. This allows much higher velocities with normal pressures than is possible with the short cases. For this reason the .32/20, .38 Special, .44 Special and the .45 Colt are our best cartridge cases for high velocity loading of full weight heavy bullets in revolver calibers.

This brings us to the .38 Special cartridge, the accepted standard for target and police work. While a wonderful target cartridge, it has proven inadequate as a man-stopper in so many cases as to need no further comment here on that score. As a Police cartridge it probably was at its commercial best in the Western 200 grain Super Police loading. This heavy bullet was better suited to the .38/44 Heavy Duty Smith & Wesson than other lighter .38 Special arms, because of its tendency to shoot too high for the sighting of standard .38 Special arms. The .38/44 Remington load was the first high velocity load with a standard 158 grain bullet at 1100 feet, and was and is a very fine long range load for the cartridge. It was brought out for the Heavy Duty .45 frame S. & W. gun and is better suited to that gun than to lighter models.

In standard round nose 158 grain at a velocity of around 870 feet, it is not a good killer, even on jack rabbits, big grouse or chucks and they must be hit just right for a clean kill. I have also seen it fail, even on big fox squirrels, if they were hit too far back. It is at its best as a game killer with the Keith 160 grain hollow point backed by 5.3 grains Unique in light framed guns or 13.5 grains 2400 in heavy .45 frame guns for use on all light game. For deep penetration, combined with full caliber holes there is the Keith 173 grain solid backed by five grains Unique in the standard weight guns and 13.5 grains 2400 in the .45 frame guns.

The cartridge is very versatile in that it will handle most any load accurately from heavy defense and game loads down to the lightest target load with bullets of 105 to 112 grains propelled by 2 to 2.5 grains of Bullseye for 50 foot gallery work. More matches have been won with the .38 Special than any other center fire cartridge, but also more .38 Special guns have been used than any other caliber. It is no more accurate than the .44 Special, if as accurate, but more men can shoot the light .38 Special load than the heavier .44 Special. A very nice cartridge for target and small game shooting, also for light pocket defense guns. As a holster weapon we maintain it is not as good as a larger caliber for defense or military use.

For timed and rapid fire target shooting where the arm is cocked for each shot, the .38 Special with light loads is a very hard cartridge to beat, giving very little recoil, so that it is fast to cock and get back on the target.

The cartridge in the old Remington .38/44 load with solid head case and a metal tipped swaged lead bullet gave excellent penetration, and in the new high speed jacketed bullet loadings will give extreme penetration, but very little shock. It will penetrate the brain of a big grizzly or a domestic bull but has to be placed right to do so.

Next we have the various .38 caliber auto loading cartridges, the old .38 Colt auto, now about obsolete, the later Super .38 auto Colt and the well known 9 mm. Luger. The .38 Colt auto developed 1070 feet with a 130 grain jacketed bullet and the newer Colt Super .38 auto raised the ante to 1300 feet with the same 130 grain jacketed bullets. Both loads are excellent for penetration but have little shock. I have shot a lot of small game, and some game not so small with them, and found them inferior in shock effect in every case to the .45 Colt auto cartridge. They would shoot much flatter over unknown ranges and penetrate a great deal better than the 230 grain .45 auto punkin. On small game the .45 auto was by all odds the best killer and also on body shots on deer and similar game, but for brain penetration the two .38 auto cartridges are superior to the .45 auto. The old model 1901 Colt auto and its variations should be used only with the standard Colt .38 auto cartridge. The later Super .38 and Commander will safely handle the higher velocity loading of the Super .38.

The 9 mm. Luger carries a 124 grain bullet at 1150 feet in standard loading and is not as powerful as the Super .38, but is a wonderfully accurate flat shooting auto pistol load. A great many foreign countries use it as their standard military load. It does well over unknown ranges, but lacks wallop, and while it will penetrate very well, it must be placed exactly to kill anything of any size. We have shot a great many grouse and similar sized game with all three of these loads and also the high speed loading in the .38 Special and find little difference, but what there is, is in favor of the high speed .38 Special with 158 grain lead bullet from the .38/44 or other .38 Special guns suitable for high speed loads.

Many hand loaders have used the Keith 160 grain hollow point in all three of these auto pistol cartridges and some of the 160 grain Keith hollow base bullets. They seat all bands down in the case friction tight and use three grains of Bullseye in the 9 mm. Luger and claim perfect functioning and excellent small game killing. The same bullets have been used in the Super .38 with 5 grains of Unique with excellent results, the Keith bullet cutting a full caliber hole in solid form and expanding well in hollow point.

Formerly the cartridge companies used to load .38 and 9 mm. auto pistol cartridges with jacketed soft point bullets. They expanded considerably on game of any size and were much more effective than present day full patch round nose bullets. Why the practice was dropped I do not know; they should be no more expensive to manufacture or load. These three auto pistol cartridges are all excellent target cartridges, but they, one and all, throw their empties away in the brush or weeds or dirt where they are difficult to recover. The ammunition is also much more expensive than rimmed revolver cartridges of corresponding power. For the handloader they are never as good in a sixgun, as cases must be not only full length resized but also kept trimmed to exact length so they will headspace properly and bullets must be of my design with all bands seated down in the case or standard shape, and must be cast very hard to function properly. They are the best small caliber auto pistol loads for any defense work, but never the equal of the .45 auto for such usage, except for brain shots on a bull or similar animal.

Next we have the .357 magnum Smith & Wesson cartridge. I worked with Doug Wesson on this development and sent him the first Keith bullets used in developing the load. We also put 1000 rounds of 173 grain Keith solids backed by 11 grains No. 80 through a .38/44 heavy duty S. & W. revolver just to see if it would take them or blow up. They developed an average of 42,000 pounds and the gun held them with no danger. At the time we wanted to modernize the .44 Special (and still do for that matter), but Mr. Wesson was determined to bring out a high velocity load and did so in his .357 magnum. The first factory cartridges were loaded with 15.3 grains 2400 and a modification of my bullet design to weight 158 grains from the 8⅜ inch barrel, with a velocity of 1510 feet. Since then the loads have been greatly changed and some we tested after the last war were little, if any better except in the shape of the bullet, than the .38/44. Some late loads with ball powder are very hot and lead the gun badly.

This is the only .38 caliber cartridge, really .357 of an inch, that we consider an adequate man stopper under all conditions. It is also effective for game shooting. Doug Wesson killed moose, elk, and grizzly with it as well as mule deer and antelope and often at good rifle ranges. My own Smith & Wesson Magnum No. 0139 has killed deer, cougar and all lesser game, but it does not compare in actual killing power with a heavy loaded .44 Special or .45 Colt. Most present loadings seem to run around 1300 to not over 1400 feet with 158 grain bullet. With the metal piercing load they give wonderful penetration, and with the modified Keith bullet they give excellent killing effect on either game or man but they can never equal a larger caliber throwing a heavier slug at comparable high velocities.

When Doug Wesson and Mert Robinson of Winchester redesigned my bullet for use in this cartridge, they eliminated the forward band and added a second grease groove and crimped over the front shoulder. This was a mistake, and accuracy suffered. They designed the case one-tenth inch longer than the .38 Special, to, they said, prevent its use in .38 Special guns, but over-looked the old swing out cylinder .38 Long Colt army gun that will accept and fire .357 magnum ammunition. Today we notice Winchester and Western are going back to a forward band in front of the case, more like our original bullet design but with a much narrower band because of the short nose of the bullet exposed in front of the case. The .357 magnum is one so-called .38 caliber cartridge that is adequate for man stopping and is a far better police weapon than any .38 Special but requires a fairly heavy gun to handle the load comfortably. Colt has developed their .357 magnum on the old .41 Officer's Model frame and we would not be surprised to see Smith & Wesson bring it out in the K model frame with an encased ejector lug on the barrel and possibly some changes in cylinder and frame to handle the more powerful ammunition. Personally, I think the .41 frame light enough and the load is more comfortable to use from the .45 frame guns than the .41 frame. The .357 is the one modern revolver load we have today and the first high velocity load after the .38/44 Remington production.

We obtained best accuracy from the solid head Remington .38/44 cases loaded with Keith 160 grain hollow point or 173 grain solid, and backed by 13.5 grains 2400 in .45 frame guns and obtained the most powerful loads with the Keith 173 grain solid crimped barely over the front band with 14.5 grains 2400. In the .38/44 cases we crimped in the regular bevelled crimping groove. With the Keith hollow point or hollow base we used 15 grains 2400 and crimped barely over the front shoulder with the magnum case.

Dick Tinker shot the long range targets for Ed McGivern's book with the Keith hollow point backed by 13.5 grains 2400 in .38 Special cases. Testing the gun for The American Rifleman story, when it first came out, I found that at ranges over 125 yards we could not hit jack rabbits nearly as well with the factory loads as with home grown loads with the 160 grain Keith bullet in .38 Special cases backed by 13.5 grains 2400, with the forward band to help true up the slug in the chamber, and which apparently greatly improved long range accuracy. We killed 125 jacks in three days and the longest shot was at one standing on his hindlegs at 180 yards, taken offhand, both hands used, with the long 8⅜ inch magnum S. & W Distance was measured by Julius Maelzer, an old surveyor.

The .357 has one advantage over larger calibers in that you can also use .38 Specials for light shooting or practice. For its caliber of .357 of an inch it is an excellent and most modern cartridge. It develops more foot pound energy than any other factory load, but when handloads in the larger calibers are considered, then the .357 magnum falls far behind a heavy .44 Special or .45 Colt load in actual killing power.

This brings us to the .41 caliber. The old Remington double derringer and many another derringer and the Colt house pistols chambered for the .41 short rim fire were primarily surprise weapons for very close range. The load has little power and will not even penetrate a tin can unless it hits it squarely, owing to its low velocity.

The little guns were very popular, and still are, as hide away weapons or vest pocket guns but have little actual stopping power. Their power is as much psychological as anything else, for anyone hit with one is in immediate need of surgery. They will drive a greased pointed slug into a man, but very seldom if ever with complete penetration and they must then be dug out by a surgeon. They carry a lot of dirt, lint, etc., into the wound and like the .22 Long Rifle or other .22 rim fires, are very apt to cause infection. For this reason real gun men fear getting hit with one of these little guns far more than a more powerful cartridge that leaves a clean wound. We look for their popularity to decline sharply when the new Great Western Derringers of similar shape and design appear on the market for the .38 S. & W. and .38 Special cartridges.

The .41 short and long Colt center fire are better cartridges and the .41 long with its blunt nosed 200 grain bullet is an excellent man-stopper, far better than any loading of the .38 Special. It was Billy The Kid's favorite. He packed two rod ejector Colt Lightnings for the .41 Long Colt cartridge. This was also the gambler's favorite cartridge. It is a short range cartridge but one giving considerable wallop. The Colt lightning, the S. A. Colt and the old Army Special double action Colt all were chambered for it and in all cases were bored over size in the groove diameter depending on upsettage of the inside lubricated slug to fill the grooves. Early loads were with a shorter case and outside lubricated heel type bullet. Had the guns been bored and rifled to correct diameter for the bullet, they would have been much more accurate and a cartridge that would have been more popular. Today this is about the only field left open for a new modern revolver cartridge.

Many experimenters have worked with the caliber and one of the first of the .40 specials was sent to me to test by a man in Oregon, in 1927. He used the .401 Winchester rifle case cut off to proper length with a 200 grain slug, and obtained excellent results on everything. The bore is .401 of an inch groove diameter, and if a proper solid head case was brought out that would take the bullet in full groove diameter inside the case, and if it was loaded to around 1000 to 1200 feet velocity, it would make one of the best of all police cartridges. Given a bullet of my design of 200 grains weight at 1200 feet, it would be a good killer on anything, superior even to the .357 Magnum.

The cartridge case should be the same length as the .44 Special and thus capable of handling a long 200 grain slug of my design, a copy of my .38 and .44 special bullets and with No. 2400 powder would easily give 1200 feet velocity. It would be the perfect medium bore revolver load for .45 frame guns, but would be too large for lighter frame guns and I would not favor its use in the Colt Officer's .41 frame as the chamber walls are too thin and the rear end of the barrel too light for such a powerful cartridge. It could be named the .40 Special or .41 Special. Many experimenters have already developed and used the load on game and target, but until a gun and cartridge are brought out for it, it will remain just a dream of old sixgun cranks.

The .41 Long Colt today is at its best when hand-loaded with the 200 grain hollow base Lyman Ideal bullet No. 386178 and a charge of 5 grains Unique for 880 feet. It's a good load. It is no target or long range load, but is a reliable defense load, and a good man-stopper.

This brings us to the .38/40 and .44/40 rifle cartridges for which countless Colt, S. & W., Hopkins & Allen and other arms have been chambered. In the day when the cartridge was a popular one in models '73 and '92 Winchester, it made a very handy combination to have both rifle and sixgun handle the same loads. Most of the old Colt guns were chambered long in the cylinder and the fired cases expanded almost to the mouth leaving only a fraction of their original neck. This necessitated excessive resizing of the cases to bring the neck back to the cannellure. It resulted in short case life. The body of the case is large, almost the same as the .45 Colt, leaving thin chamber walls. This limits pressures. The case is too long for a maximum weight bullet in either caliber without very deep seating of the bullet. Long bullets must be seated with their base back into the powder chamber in order to keep them in permissible length. We tried every possible combination in the .38/40 and used it on everything including deer and elk, nearly getting killed by one bull elk. A factory Remington soft point .38/40 expanded on his frontal skull plate and failed to reach the brain.

I used 210 grain Winchester bullets and 260 grain .40/82 Winchester cast bullets sized to fit, and heavy charges of No. 80 powder. We obtained very fine accuracy and plenty of power, but the bottleneck cases expanded excessively with heavy loads and caused not only resizing, but also extraction troubles. All told, I found the .38/40 and .44/40 cases to be stinkers to reload with anything but standard length bullets. These bullets did not have a good crimp groove, in fact no crimping groove at all, and depended on friction fit and crimping over the front band. With a thin case they would often recede in the case due to insufficient grip by the case neck. They worked well with 40 grains of Black, but I never did like them for smokeless powder and longer than standard bullets. With 12 grains of No. 80 we once drove a 260 grain .40/82 bullet through a six point bull elk behind the shoulder and killed him. Today these cartridges are used only in the old guns and a few S. A. Colts fitted up by the Christy Gun Works, and some new ones by Great Western. The bullets are short and stubby in proportion to their caliber, and while accurate, will not penetrate on livestock or heavy game as well as the longer bullets of greater weight from the .44 Special or .45 Colt.

If you have a .38/40 or .44/40 in good condition, the best loads are the 180 grain bullet for the .38/40, and the 200 or 210 grain cast bullet for the .44/40, backed by 18.5 grains 2400. Both are more powerful and better killers than the .357 magnum. The .38/40 is really a .40 caliber, and anyone owning a .41 Colt S. A. or a .38/40 can interchange cylinders for the two cartridges.

The .44/40 was Ashley A. Haines' favorite and he did exceptionally fine work with it often getting 1½ inch groups at 50 yards with his heavy hand loads. Of the two cartridges, I consider the .44/40 much the better of the two as it will handle 210 grain bullets to 1200 feet velocity nicely, and is an excellent killer. I do not believe either Colt or Smith & Wesson will ever again chamber a gun for these two loads, so for revolver use they are going into the discard and should not be considered for a new gun. The Model '92 Winchester, especially the little carbine, is an excellent weapon and if you own one of these and want loads for both rifle and revolver, the .44/40 has its place. No new rifles or pistols are now chambered for either cartridge.

The chamber walls being almost as thin as those of the .45 Colt, the .38/40 and .44/40 cannot be safely loaded to heavier pressures than can that caliber. Both cartridges were designed for black powder and both are on the road to obsolescence, with the .38/40 in the lead. Neither will do anything the .44 Special will not do better. It would be a mistake to buy a gun chambered for either of these old timers today.

Next we have the various old outside lubricated .44 calibers, and the .44 Henry Rim fire for which some Colt S. A. guns were chambered. These are all now obsolete as well as the .44 Smith & Wesson American, and ammunition is very hard to obtain for any of them. They are now relics. The old .44 long Colt outside lubricated cartridge comes in the same category, and need not be considered further.

The .44 Russian was, and is, a superb target cartridge with a 246 grain slug at 770 feet; today's factory .44 Specials are loaded to exactly the same velocity with the same bullet weight. The .44 Russian shoots well in .44 Specials. No new guns are chambered especially for the .44 Russian. It must be considered a thing of the past except for those owning guns chambered for it. It established a great many records in the past, but will not do anything the .44 Special will not do, and the latter is also capable of handling much more powerful loads with its longer case.

Of all existing revolver cartridges, we consider the .44 Special to be the best. It is the most accurate revolver load in existence and is easier to hand load accurately than is any smaller cartridge. Fully loaded, it is the most powerful hand gun cartridge in existence. It will handle all weight bullets from the old Anderton 210 grain to the Belding & Mull, Keith Design 280 grain, and handle them accurately. It will make the smallest groups with light squibb loads or heavy defense and game loads. The chamber walls are thick enough to handle pressure much more safely than will the .45 Colt, the .38/40 or the .44/40. The rear end of barrel, where it projects through the frame, is also heavy enough to take pressure without belling or splitting.

The .44 Special is the only load we have found that will shoot to the same sighting with light or heavy powder charges so long as the bullets are of the same weight. In thirty years of hand loading the cartridge I have never had any trouble from case heads blowing off or pulling off in the resizing dies. In fact, case life has been long, some cases having been reloaded twenty times, or more, with heavy loads. The straight case gives even, uniform friction fit to the bullet when properly resized and crimps well in the bevelled crimping groove, giving uniform combustion and pressures. It handles either light charges of bullseye for target work or heavy charges of 2400 for game, defense, or long range work, with equal accuracy. A discrepancy of .001 of an inch in a .44 Special bullet is not as important as the same in a .38 Special slug, and it's far easier to load accurate ammunition for the .44 Special than any other revolver cartridge I have used.

1. Standard .44 Special bullet. 2. Loaded round. 3. Keith 260 grain .44 Special Belding & Mull bullet. 4. Loaded round, Keith design.

The cartridge has been badly handicapped all its life by being sadly underloaded. The factory load of a 246 grain slug at 770 feet is no more than a light target load and a disgrace to so fine a cartridge. There is no earthly reason why the loading companies cannot load this cartridge to at least 1000 feet in factory loads. All guns chambered for the .44 Special, including the old Triple Lock Smith & Wesson, will safely handle it, and even heavier loads. The straight case resizes easily, and while there has been a demand for solid head cases, for many years, we have seen no need of them as we have never had any trouble with the old ballon primer cases in .44 Special caliber.

Today Winchester and Western have brought out excellent heavy, solid head cases for the .44 Special, so that gripe is now water under the bridge. They have the cases, but still refuse to give us an effective load.

The cartridge, with either light or heavy loads, will consistently group into 1½ inches at 50 yards with correctly sized bullets. Ammunition companies, having squibb loaded the .44 Special since its inception, have given the shooting world an erronious opinion of its possibilities. As commercially loaded, it is a satisfactory target and small game cartridge, slightly superior to the .38 Special for defense, but well under the .357 magnum or the .45 Colt. Handloaded for maximum performance, the .44 Special exceeds them all in knock-down stopping power and long range accuracy. In 1927 I designed a blunt, round nosed bullet at 260 grains which was brought out by Belding & Mull. Later Harold Croft and I designed another bullet along the same lines, but weighing 280 grains.

These bullets did well enough at close range, but proved inaccurate at longer distances. I dropped the Belding & Mull style, and starting from the ground floor designed an entirely new bullet for the Lyman Gun Sight Company, now sold as Ideal No. 429421, in 250 grains. I also added a hollow point and a hollow base to the design, bringing these bullets down to 235 grains each, moulds for which are also supplied by Lyman. The weights are based on one part tin to sixteen parts lead. I worked up a load of 12 grains of No. 80 and used it for years, finding it the ultimate, at that time, in a long range revolver load. Later when Hercules No. 2400 became available, I switched to that powder, using as much as 20 grains, but as the cases showed signs of excess pressure, I dropped back to 18.5, which is my present standard, proven by years of use. The late J. Bushnell Smith chronographed the load, finding it to be well over 1200 feet in velocity with the 250 grain solid bullet and slightly faster in the 235 grain types. The working pressure is around 20,000.

I custom loaded these bullets for many years and shipped them all over the world. They have killed about all American and much African game, and have been used by officers of the Border Patrol in numerous gunfights, with telling effect. Many chaps, wanting their names in the funny papers, have made copies of the Keith-Lyman bullet, slightly changing the shape of the nose or the width of the bands, but with no improvement on the original. Dr. Murphy of the Winnipeg Revolver Club made several 20 yard possibles with the Keith-Lyman 250 grain .44 Special bullet in actual competition, with 6.5 grains of No. 6 powder. Another doctor from Omaha carried my heavy hand loads with him to Africa and wrote that he had no trouble keeping the whole safari supplied with antelope meat with these loads and his 6½ inch Smith & Wesson. We have successfully used the load here on about everything including elk, moose, bear, mule deer, mountain sheep and mountain goats. Last fall I killed my mule deer with it from a 4 inch Smith & Wesson while on a fishing trip, being too badly crippled with a broken ankle to think of hunting.

When the new solid head cases came out, I purchased a quantity of Winchester make and worked up the load with them finding that 17.5 grains of 2400 seemed to duplicate the 18.5 grain load in the old cases, with the 250 grain bullet. We tried both 17.5 grains of 2400 for an average pressure of around 25,000 pounds and 18.5 grains 2400 with same 250 grain bullet for an average of around 28,000 pounds pressure, but settled on 17.5 grains 2400 at around 25,000 pounds pressure as the best load. Velocities do not increase proportionally to the great increase in chamber pressure built up by the heavier loads. The best heavy load is 18.5 grains 2400 with the Keith 250 grain bullet, in the old balloon primer pocket cases, or 17.5 grains 2400 in the new solid head cases.

For a light target load, I use 4 grains of Bullseye in the new solid head cases or 5 grains in the old balloon primer pocket cases. It is very accurate and shoots to the same sighting at any range, believe it or not, as does the heavy 2400 load. The slow loads require more time interval at long range, but the barrel time is also slower and the barrel recoils higher before the bullet exits so that both loads go to the same sighting. This is something we have never attained with any other revolver load. We use and recommend the same powder charges for the 235 grain Keith-Lyman hollow point or hollow base bullets.

There is no reason why the loading companies could not bring out this load and bullet design. We would then have the finest of all powerful revolver loads available in any sport shop. It is a safe load in any gun we know of, chambered for the .44 Special cartridge, including the old New Century or Triple Lock S. & W., if the bullets are sized to exact groove diameter or not over .001 of an inch larger, and are cast one to sixteen tin and lead, or harder.

G. E. Murphy, 40 Willard Street, San Francisco, California, has been furnishing Keith 250 grain bullets plain cast or copper coated, sized and lubricated and known as the Mar-Mur Bullets. The Wilser Western Arms Co., 205 Second Street, San Francisco, California, lists them for sale. They are excellent bullets for the man who does not wish to cast and size his own. Moody's Reloading Service, 1016 North Warren Street, Helena, Montana, has been carrying on a custom loading business and specializes in these loads since the death of Dick Tinker and J. Bushnell Smith who formerly loaded Keith-Ideal bullets to order. J. W. McPhillips, 285 Mastic Ave., San Bruno, California, also loads these heavy .44 Special Keith loads.

For extreme penetration, combined with good disruptive qualities, we like the 250 grain solid Keith slug best of all, but when more destruction is wanted, or for use on chucks, jack rabbits, coyotes and bob-

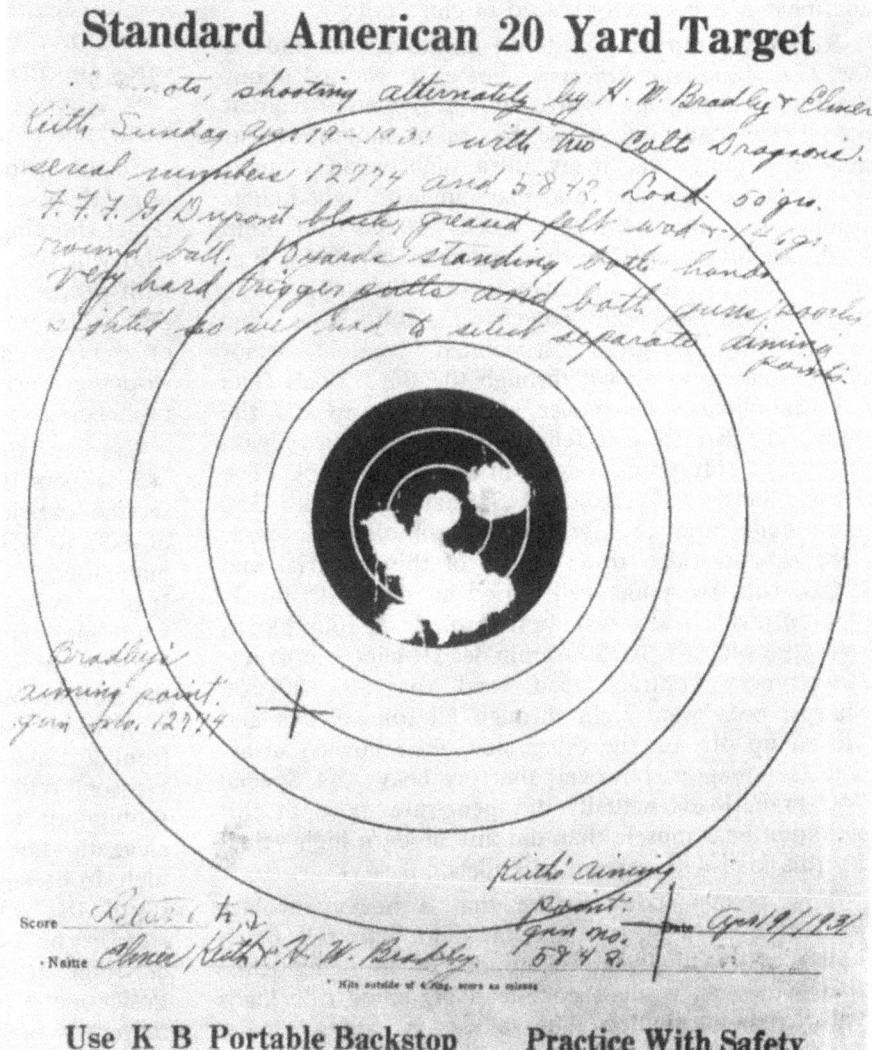

Twelve shots, shooting alternately by H. W. Bradley and Elmer Keith, Sunday, April 19, 1931 with two Colt Dragoons, serial numbers 12774 and 5842—load, 50 grains F.F.F.G. DuPont black, greased felt wad and 146 grain round ball, 10 yards standing, both hands. Very hard trigger pulls and both guns poorly sighted so we had to select separate aiming points.

cats, the 235 grain hollow point will be found even more deadly as it will expand and tear holes the size of a dollar in tough game, and will simply explode jack rabbits with most of the animal being blown away. Jacks shot in the chest with the 235 grain Keith hollow point backed by the heavy 2400 loads will usually have the head and front legs intact and the rest of the body gone with possibly a hindleg hanging from a strip of skin. If shot in the rump, usually the whole front half of the big bunny is gone, with possibly an ear or a foreleg hanging from a strip of skin. They are certain stoppers on coyotes or bob-cats, and also on lung shots from the side on deer, black bear or any similar size game.

If you want a light indoor gallery load, you can use the 210 grain Anderton bullet with a charge of 3 grains of Bullseye and have a fine shooting accurate load, and one that has very little recoil for fast timed and rapid fire work. Outdoors in the wind, a heavier load is advisable. The light bullet will require a different sighting, but as long as you use the full weight bullets or close thereto, you need not change your sights for either light or the most powerful loads.

The heavy loads penetrate much better with 250 grain Keith-Ideal bullet than does the standard .357 magnum and the wound channels are much larger even when solid bullets of my design are used in both calibers.

The cartridge is accurate to extreme long range as I once demonstrated to Harold Croft, by dropping three or four slugs from each cylinder full, into a 4 by 4 foot target at 700 yards, shooting from a seated back and head rest position with both hands holding the gun between the drawn up knees. The flame of burning powder gas at the cylinder-barrel junction was hard on my Levis, but this position enabled me to lobb the slugs into the target.

If you want the ultimate in a big revolver load for either target, defense or game shooting, the .44 Special is the one best cartridge. You can kill small game, cottontails, grouse or squirrels with the factory load or its equivalent, without mutilation for table use, or you can use a heavy load that will kill any game on this continent if it is exactly placed at close range.

Recently I ran some tests on imitation bear muscle for *The American Rifleman*. The stuff was of about the same consistency as live rubber. We fired a great many rifle loads into those blocks of imitation bear muscle, finding that many ultra high velocity loads including the .270 and .300 magnum with light bullets would blow up in the first block. .30/06 180 grain loads usually stopped in the second block of this material, between four and five inches thick. The .375 magnum with 300 grain lodged in the third block. The .30/40 Krag 220 grain soft pointed "corelokt" Remington load went almost through the third block. The 6.5 Mannlicher Schoenauer with 160 grains did the same. The British 400 Jeffery elephant cartridge with 400 grain soft point lodged in the third block. The 4 inch Smith & Wesson .44 Special with Keith 250 grain bullet and 18.5 grains 2400 in old style cases went right through three blocks of this material and lodged with the point well buried in the fourth block. The only rifle loads that went through all four blocks were the old .45/70/500 grain lead bullet, smokeless Government contract load, and the .45/120/566 Sharps; both went right through all four blocks and kicked up dirt on the other side, then howled away. The fact remains however, that my heavy .44 Special 250 grain loads actually did penetrate more of this imitation bear muscle than did any modern high velocity rifle load with expanding bullets.

Few people today realize that a heavy revolver load or even a Super .38 Colt auto with full patch bullets will actually penetrate deeper in living game than will most modern American big game rifle loads with expanding bullets. The velocity is so much lower for the handgun that its bullets are not expanded and blown to pieces as happens in any tough substance with expanding high velocity rifle bullets.

Years ago, a revolver club in Kentucky used to hold 300 yard turkey shoots using mostly .44 Special Smith & Wesson and Colt revolvers with a high rear sight set for 300 yards. Many of the members hit a silhouette of a turkey actual life size two to three shots out of five off-hand at that range.

The .44 Special is perhaps our most accurate target cartridge. The late Nate Spering of Philadelphia made several five shot 25 yard groups with my No. 5 single action Colt with factory Remington loads that cut just one ragged hole. He was a wonderful pistol shot. Groups were shot off-hand in standard target position. For the man who is strong enough to hold the big gun, it will deliver the very finest target accuracy. Fast rapid fire matches however, are harder with the .44 Special because the gun has more recoil, raises higher in recoil, and more time is required to get it back on the target. The large bullet hole is easily spotted—too easy in fact. After you see three or four go in the same place, you are apt to tighten up and throw a wild one. Just the same, it gives you all you are entitled to in any slow fire match and it is doubtful if any other revolver cartridge will equal its fine accuracy. One time I put four straight in one ragged hole at 20 yards, in the center of the ten ring, then foolishly took a look at that group. It's too bad I tried too hard, and pulled an eight for the fifth shot.

So much for the .44 Special. I consider it the finest large revolver cartridge we have, either for straight target shooting or for the handloader, or game shooter who will reload or buy custom hand loads. It is also, with proper loads, one of the finest cartridges for the peace officer, and with heavy loads will do as good or a better job than any other cartridge, either in stopping a criminal or for car body penetration in apprehending criminals.

Climbing the caliber ladder, we come to the various .45 calibers. In the auto pistol our old .45 Colt auto service cartridge with 230 grain bullet at velocities of 800 to 850, and some near 900 feet, is the best man-stopper of all the auto loading pistol cartridges. It is an exceptionally accurate load as well. Trajectory, while high, is not too high for close range shooting, or for straight target shooting. I used to shoot a lot of the stuff and used up a case of 2000 rounds every two months on jack rabbits from the .45 auto, and also from a super accurate target sighted 1917 Smith & Wesson. With the latter arm I killed a great many jack rabbits up to 200 yards, and one at 300 on the eleventh shot. This of course, from the 1917 with its high front sight. For the man who prefers the auto pistol, the .45 auto will deliver the goods as a man-stopper or on game, better than any smaller auto cartridge. It is at its best for penetration with the new Police metal piercing load which actually goes through more car body material than does the .357 magnum with a standard flat point bullet, and seems to equal or beat the metal piercing .357 magnum as well.

In the 1950 Target Smith & Wesson with suitable barrel length, it makes an excellent police and peace officer's gun as one can carry the gun full of auto rim reloads with my 240 or 250 grain .45 caliber bullet sized to .451 and backed by 7.5 grains or Unique, a really powerful load with those heavy flat point bullets. He can carry some extra clips of the three shot variety loaded with .45 auto ammunition for the quickest of all revolver reloading. This makes it a very good combat weapon. For straight target shooting, the new semi-wad cutter factory loads such as Remington 185 grain, and the Western 210 grain are best as they give less recoil and cut clean holes in the paper as well as being superbly accurate. The most accurate service type .45 ammo I have ever fired was 1925 Government National Match, but I have shot a lot of Western that was not far, if any behind in extreme accuracy. The cartridge is too short to take well to No. 2400 powder, and we have had the best luck with heavy loads using Unique, better suited to the short case. So loaded, the cartridge is a good close range game cartridge with heavy loads and kills very well, it seems to beat the old .45 Colt when the latter is used with a standard factory pointed bullet ammunition.

Both Colt and Smith & Wesson guns are cut with six narrow and shallow lands especially for jacketed bullet ammunition. Groove diameter is usually .450 of an inch for S. & W. guns and around .452 of an inch for Colts. For this reason these revolvers do their best work with a fairly hard bullet of around one to ten tin and lead mixture.

Wad cutter type bullets of 185 to 200 grains are very accurate in these revolvers when cast hard and sized to .451 of an inch, and backed with from 3.5 to 4.5 grains of Bullseye. For timed and rapid fire work, where revolvers are used, the light loads pay dividends in lighter recoil and faster recovery and cocking. For target work I especially like Ideal Bullet 200 grain No. 452460 for both the .45 auto, and the .45 auto rim for a light load. These short bullets seem more accurate in the .45 auto than in the 1917 and 1950 revolvers. This due to the very long jump from the short .45 auto or auto rim case before they hit the barrel throat. For this reason I have had better accuracy from the Keith design 240 grain .45 auto rim and 250 grain .45 Colt bullets sized down to .451 from the 1917 and 1950 target revolvers, than I have obtained from the short bullets intended for the .45 auto pistol. The forward band on my bullets trues up the slug in the chamber throat and greatly improves accuracy.

In the .45 Auto Pistol, many of these short wad cutter type slugs work wonderfully well with as little as 3 grains of Bullseye, but the recoil spring must be cut down if the gun is to function reliably with such light powder charges. They give very light recoil and rapid return to the target and are one reason why so many shoot the .45 auto in preference to the revolver in .45 caliber matches. For slow fire, the revolver is much the better tool, but in rapid fire the auto pistol wins hands down. If full power ammunition is used with full weight bullets, the 1950 Target Smith & Wesson will do wonderfully well, either with the jacketed bullet ammunition or with .45 auto rim with Keith bullets cast hard for the shallow rifling and sized to .451 of an inch. But the fact remains, these guns do not shoot quite as well with short bullets of light weight, and heavy bullets mean more recoil and for that reason are slower in rapid fire matches. These .45 auto rim revolvers are made and rifled for jacketed bullets and the reloader must use bullets of comparable length and weight for best accuracy, and cast them hard enough to hold the shallow rifling. Many boxes of lead bullet .45 auto rim ammo we have tried were not accurate at all and simply would not stay in my hat at 50 yards. The bullets were too soft and would not hold the rifling but the same guns were superbly accurate with match .45 auto ammunition with jacketed bullets, or with my hand loads with Keith design slug cast hard and correctly sized and crimped in auto rim cases.

My friend Rizzola of the Navy Pistol Team does very well with the 1950 Target Smith & Wesson. He uses hard cast bullets to hold the rifling and sizes them .452 of an inch. My own guns will not accommodate the .452 of an inch sizing in the chamber throats when the Keith bullet is used. I had to size to .451 before the forward band would enter the chamber throat without undue pressure on the case head.

C. H. McCashland has cut down the cylinder of the 1917 guns to the right length for the .45 auto cartridge and fitted a new barrel extending back through the frame to meet the shortened cylinder. While it is truly an odd looking gun, he reports a great increase in accuracy due to cutting down the bullet jump from cartridge case to barrel throat. This free jump in chamber throats was the reason for the forward band of full groove diameter on my bullets to be loaded out in front of the case and crimp. It has given me better accuracy than any other shape of cast bullet in revolvers, for that reason.

A short barreled 1917 or 1950 Target Model makes an excellent police gun with good knock-down power and a speedy reloading feature if the three cartridge 1917 clips are used. For match shooting, use the Keith-Ideal bullet No. 452423 cast hard, at least one part tin to ten lead or use jacketed bullets. These guns are all rifled for jacketed bullets. The 1917 revolver was brought out during World War I because we did not have machinery to build Colt .45 automatics fast enough to supply the troops. It is a sort of hybrid afterthought, and is not equal to a gun chambered for the regular .45 Colt cartridge. The long cylinder jump the bullet must make is bad engineering, even if it was smart emergency engineering. The .44 special is a far better gun for all purposes, and especially for match shooting. If they were allowed in .45 matches, revolvers using the automatic cartridge would soon be as scarce as W.C.T.U. members at a distillers' convention.

The old .45 Smith & Wesson cartridge with its short case has long been obsolete and also the short Remington cartridge for the .45 Colt. Today we often hear the .45 Colt Peacemaker cartridge referred to as the .45 Long Colt. Some newcomers to the game claim there is no such animal, but if they had shot the short variety that Remington turned out in such profusion before, during, and after World War I, they would see there was some basis in referring to the .45 Colt as the .45 Long. These short .45 Remington cartridges for the .45 Colt were never very accurate due to the long bullet jump and the only thing that was standard about them was a 250 grain bullet. They were soundly cussed out in all the sporting magazines of the time and all old sixgun cranks deplored their use if either accuracy, or power was wanted. They were a disgrace to the .45 Colt gun. I never tried them, but believe

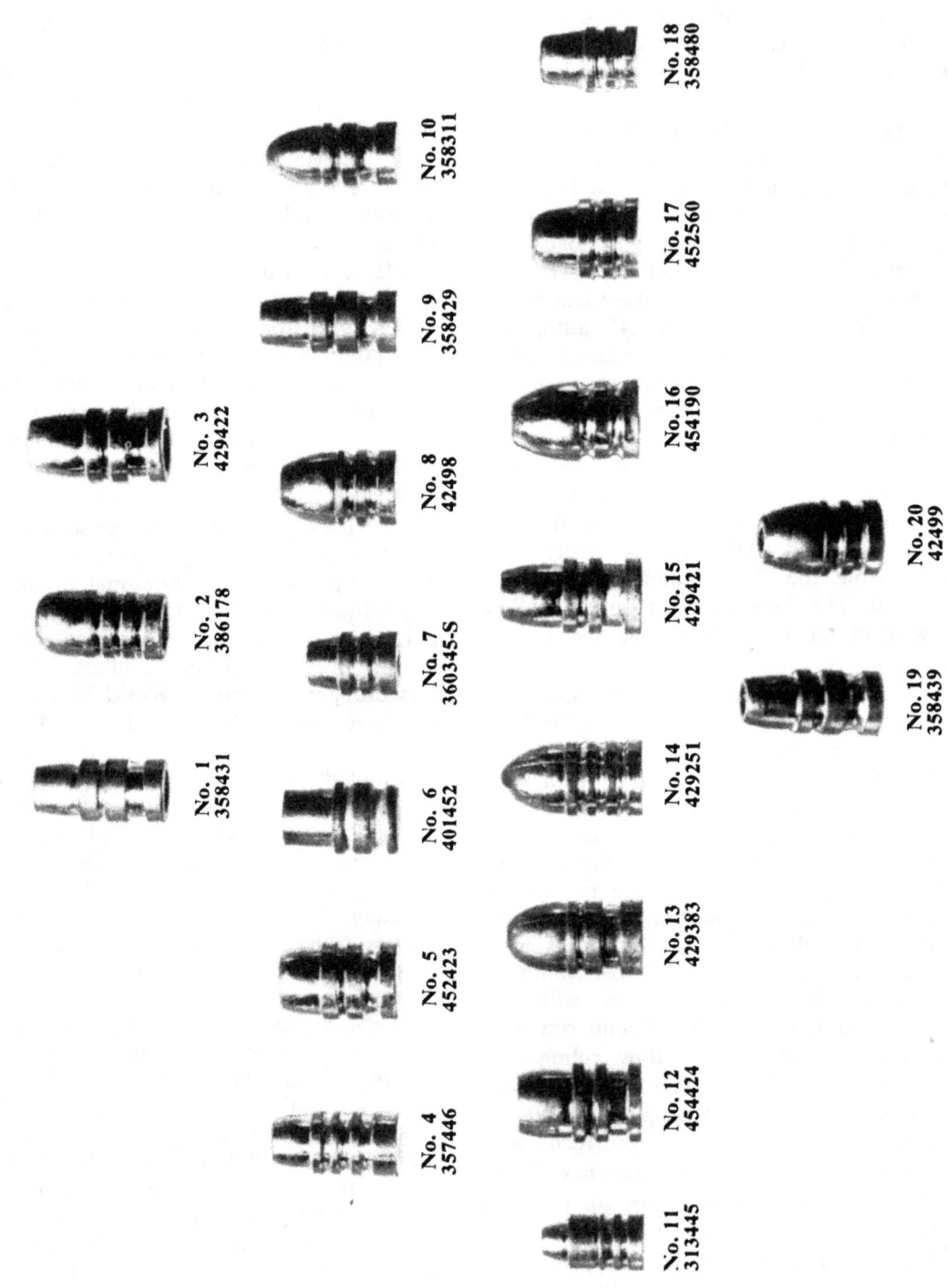

SELECTION OF CARTRIDGES

KEITH DESIGN IDEAL BULLETS

No. 1	No. 2	No. 3	No. 4	No. 5	No. 6	No. 7	No. 8
358431	386178	429422	357446	452423	401452	360345-S	42498

No. 9	No. 10	No. 11	No. 12	No. 13	No. 14	No. 15	No. 16
358429	358311	313445	454424	429383	429251	429421	454190

No. 17	No. 18	No. 19	No. 20
452560	358480	358439	42499

No. 1. Keith bullet 358431, 160 grain hollow base.

No. 2. Hollow base .41 Long Colt bullet of 200 grains.

No. 3. Keith 235 grain hollow base .44 Special bullet.

No. 4. Lyman Bullet for the .357 Magnum, weight 156 grains.

No. 5. Keith .45 Auto Rim solid bullet, weight 240 grains.

No. 6. Gordon Boser copy of Keith bullet for .41 Special and .38/40, weight 206 grains. A very good .40 caliber for a Special cartridge.

No. 7. Lyman target bullet for light target loads for .38 Special or .38 S. & W. designed by J. B. Crabtree. Weight 115 grains.

No. 8. Lyman standard bullet for .44/40, weight 210 grains.

No. 9. Keith bullet No. 358429, 173 grain solid for the .38 Special and .357 Magnum cartridges. Best heavy .38 caliber bullet.

No. 10. Lyman 358311 standard round nose bullet for .38 Special and a very accurate bullet.

No. 11. 313445 Lyman bullet for the .32 S. & W. long and .32/20. A very good bullet.

No. 12. Keith .45 Colt bullet 250 grains, No. 454224. Best .45 Colt bullet, is equally good in .45 Auto Rim when sized to .452.

No. 13. Lyman .44 Special round nose bullet No. 429383, for .44 Russian and .44 Special weight, 244 grains. Designed by H. D. Frisbee.

No. 14. Lyman standard .44 Russian and .44 Special bullet, weight 253 grains. No. 429251.

No. 15. Keith design 250 grain bullet No. 429421. The best .44 Special bullet, very accurate at all ranges and with light to very heavy loads.

No. 16. Lyman standard .45 Colt bullet No. 454190, weight 255 grains.

No. 17. Lyman 200 grain wad cutter bullet, No. 452460 for .45 auto and .45 Auto Rim. A fine target bullet.

No. 18. No. 358480 Lyman target bullet for the .38 auto, 9 mm. and Super .38.

No. 19. Keith design 160 grain hollow point for the .38 Special and .357 Magnum. One of the most accurate .38 caliber bullets.

No. 20. No. 42499 Lyman Hollow point bullet, weight 200 grains for the .44/40.

they would have worked in the old .45 break top Smith & Wesson guns, and that may have been the reason for their existence.

The standard .45 Colt, like the .45/70 in rifles, simply will not die out. The demand is still strong for it, and will be for many years to come. It is a good, accurate, and lethal cartridge, and one that has well served the American sixgun man for eighty years.

The old Remington loading of the standard .45 Colt case with black powder was a 40 grain charge with a 250 grain bullet; it was a 900 foot second load, accurate and dependable. The Remington smokeless load of the time was put up in the short case and was a light squibb affair good only for small game shooting and hardly accurate enough for that. Today the cartridge companies no longer load the old 40 grain black powder charge but it was, and it still is, a good and safe load in the old guns. We have seen it penetrate eight inches of pine, time and time again. It also went through deer, mountain goat and black bear for me, but owing to its pointed bullet it does not tear a very large wound channel.

Today the .45 Colt is well standardized with a 250 to 255 grain pointed bullet at 870 feet velocity, with smokeless powder, and in this loading is safe in the old guns and performs well in the most modern guns, the new 1950 Target Smith & Wesson chambered and bored for the .45 Colt and the Great Western Single Action. It is a good load, extremely accurate in good guns, and one I prefer to the smaller, higher velocity .357 magnum for a defense gun. Properly handloaded with the Keith 250 grain bullet and 18.5 grains 2400 powder in either the old or new solid head cases, it is a killer, and far exceeds the .357 magnum in actual killing power on anything. My heavy load gives around 1100 feet velocity to the Keith 250 grain flat pointed bullet, and its square front band cuts full caliber holes in anything. The cartridge is far from obsolete. The thin chamber walls and thin rear end of barrel will not permit as heavy pressure loading as will the .44 Special, but just the same the old .45 Colt is still a whale of a good cartridge when reloaded with my heavy load, and not bad at all with factory smokeless loads. It is accurate to a half mile and I have done very good shooting with it at small objects at one-fourth mile, many times with 4¾ inch single actions with target sights, and lately with the new 4 inch 1950 Target Smith & Wesson. As one grows older and his hair starts to turn grey, his respect for this grand old load increases. If I had to shoot only factory ammunition the rest of my life, I would take the .45 Colt as my game and defense cartridge.

The most powerful safe load I know for the old cartridge is the Keith 250 grain Lyman bullet cast one to sixteen tin and lead, and sized to not exceed .001 of an inch over groove diameter, and backed by 18.5 grains 2400 with a good crimp in the bevelled crimping groove. In the Smith & Wesson 1950 Target and the old Triple Locks made during or before World War I for this load, the barrels were cut with a .457 of an inch groove diameter. Smith & Wesson cylinders are shorter than are Colt's and for this reason the Keith bullet must be seated with all bands inside the .45 Colt case. This cuts down the powder space, but owing to the oversize groove diameter this deeper seating still seems to work perfectly in the .45 Colt chambered Smith & Wesson guns.

Accuracy is excellent, even with all bands seated in the case and crimped barely over the shoulder of the front band, and this gives us the right over all length for the short S. & W. cylinder. I tested the new solid head cases so loaded with bullets sized to .454 of an inch or .003 of an inch under groove diameter. They upset and filled perfectly and shot very accurately and with excellent velocity. Evidently the oversize groove diameter alleviated pressures of the deeper seating making the use of the full 18.5 grains 2400 possible. And the five wide heavy lands displace a lot of bullet metal and help no end in upsetting the 250 grain slug to perfectly fill the grooves. Recovered bullets show no sign of gas cutting or stripping except the usual short skid on the front band common to all bullets fired from revolvers. We would never use this short seating of our bullet on a full load of 18.5 grains 2400 in the tighter bored Colt revolvers or the Great Western. Their cylinders are amply long for standard loading of my bullet, but the deep seating expedient with the short S. & W. cylinders works out perfectly.

A great many Smith & Wesson, Colt and Webley 455 revolvers have been rechambered for the .45 Colt cartridge lately since Britain has been dumping them on our markets at low prices. The Colts are usually bored about the same as for the .45 Colt and work out perfectly for the .45 Colt load but the Webleys and Smith & Wessons have shorter cylinders and usually .457 of an inch groove diameter. There are two ways to load for them. One, as above, by deep seating of the Keith bullet with all bands inside the case. The other is to cut the cases shorter with a case trimmer until they are correct over-all length for the Keith bullet crimped in the regular bevelled crimping groove. This is the better procedure, but also entails more work in trimming down the cases to shorter length. As long as the bullets are held to a sizing of not over .454 of an inch, they seem to work perfectly with no heavy pressure developing from the deeper seating in these guns with .457 of an inch groove diameter. So much for the .45 Colt. It is a grand old load, is still with us, and will be for many years to come. In hand loads it is inferior to the .44 Special but with its heavier slugs, it far exceeds the power of the hand loaded .357 magnum, the .38/40 or .44/40.

This brings us to the old .455 British service cartridge. This is a short case, heavy bullet, low velocity load. The bullet, even though pointed in shape, has so much weight and caliber it has well served as a man-stopper for a great many years. This country is flooded with these arms today, and Canada loads a 260 grain load for them. The British loading was very light as to powder charge, and we have actually seen the big slug in flight many times when shooting up against the sky at some object in a tree, but its weight and caliber give it good stopping power. It is good on small game as the low velocity causes very little mutilation.

It is obsolete today and hard to get in this country as our loading companies have all dropped it. It is at its best in a reload with the Lyman 290 grain hollow base slug Ideal No. 457196, backed by 5 grains Unique for a velocity of 700 feet. This is a very lethal man-killer, but has high trajectory and is for this reason a short range load. These various .455 revolvers with the above load, however, are perfectly adequate for any defense work at close range against man targets, and are far superior to any loads in the .38 Special for this purpose.

The best conversion of these .455's is to the .45 Colt as they are overbored for the .45 auto cartridge and allow much gas escapage in Webley and Smith & Wesson make if rebuilt for the .45 auto cartridge. They can be used, however, with the .45 auto rim case with mouth expanded to take a full caliber bullet, or the Keith bullet at .454 of an inch, and work very well. They should never be altered for the .45 auto or auto rim with jacketed .450 of an inch bullets. The .476 is a big British cartridge formerly used in their service revolvers and with which we have had no experience. Some Webley revolvers were made to handle both the .455 and the .476 British service cartridges, and some Colts were made in New Service and S. A. Army models for the big load. It has long been obsolete, and like the old Remington single shot 50 caliber navy cartridge, is today only a relic for the collector.

In concluding this chapter, I venture the opinion that we could do very well with a great many less cartridges than are listed. In rim fire the only three we really have use for are the .22 L. R. and .22 short for close range practice, and the .25 Stevens as a small game cartridge. We could dispense with all the .32 calibers except the .32 S. & W. long and perhaps the .32/20. The .30 Carbine can be loaded to do the same work as the .32/20 for use in modern single action revolvers of Great Western make or Christy rebarreled (and recylindered) S. A. Colts.

In .38 caliber we need only the .38 Special, .38 S. & W. and .357 magnum in rimmed variety, and the 9mm. luger and the Super .38 in the automatic line.

Unless some hand gun manufacturer brings out a genuine .41 Special with a full power modern factory cartridge, this caliber will go in the discard. There is no reason to believe the .41 Long Colt can keep it on the shelves. In automatic fodder we should keep the 9 mm., the .38 A. C. P. and the .45 A. C. P. Worth retaining in centerfire rimmed revolver ammunition are the .32 long Colt, the .32/20 (perhaps), the .38 special, .38 S. & W., the .357, the .44 special, the .45 autorim and the .45 Colt. We do desperately need a modern, up-to-date, full powered factory loaded .44 special—the king of all handgun cartridges.

Chapter XIX

Ornamentation, Barrel Lengths, Balance, Velocities

NO FIREARM BETTER LENDS ITSELF to ornamentation than does the sixgun or auto pistol. The finest work of this nature ever done in this country to my knowledge was by Kornbrath, but we have many excellent gun engravers today, some of whom were pupils of the old master. Many have taken it up as a hobby, and some have developed until they went into the work commercially. Some do etching, some hand chiseling and some inlay work, and a few do both. I prefer engraving, and a small amount of fine tastefully applied engraving to a full coverage of coarse, crude work. A gun looks better plain than with coarse or gaudy ornamentation.

With a blued finish, either gold or silver inlay work stands out in sharp contrast, but yellow gold is the most beautiful treatment for inlays. I have seen many sixguns ornamented with silver inlays; some carried a few neat small figures or animals and were very nice. Some were about half covered with inlaid silver and resembled a pinto horse. To my way of thinking they were too gaudy and not nearly as beautiful as the same gun would have been with a few small neat inlays. Silver, while more contrasting in color with blued steel, does not give the rich appearance the gold inlays do. To my way of thinking nothing is better than base relief work in yellow gold of small figures or animals perfectly executed. A limited amount of such work combined with fine scroll or floral engraving, gives a sixgun or auto pistol the most beautiful and tasteful appearance that can be applied. I would far rather have a few small perfectly executed panels of fine scroll than a full coverage of the gun with any coarse engraving.

Deep hand chiseling is to be preferred to acid etching and a gun well engraved remains a thing of beauty throughout its existence. Even when worn bright from the holster, the engraving is enhanced in beauty and an engraved gun can take a lot of hard knocks and not show it as a plain highly polished blued gun will. Engraving will hide and cover up a lot of scratches, and even when an engraved gun is well worn from hard service, it still has the appearance of an aristocrat.

Many go in for glitter: silver and gold, as well as nickel and chrome plating. I once saw a copper plated gun, a .44/40 S. A. Colt, which I bought and later let Ben Comfort have. Hacksaw Tom, an old western character who lived for years in the Salmon River Canyon, had the gun when I first saw it. Hacksaw had wintered in Arizona the year before. When he came to Salmon, he brought along a red haired woman and took her down the river with him. Captain Harry Guleke and I were then running parties down the Salmon on summer sight-seeing and fishing and fall hunting trips, and we stopped at one of Hacksaw's camps. He had the red haired lady with him then. A couple weeks later we came along on another of our boat trips and again stopped for a visit with Hacksaw. This time he had no red headed lady, so I asked him what became of her. "Oh," says Tom, "You did not know about it, but I made a hell of a good trade. A fellow that lives down below me a few miles offered me a good .44/40 single action for her, straight across, and I swapped." He produced the copper plated .44/40. I gave him $25.00 for it.

That copper plating was really nice. It had turned almost jet black every place except where the holster rubbed, and there it was, of course, bright copper finish. On the whole it made a rather pleasing treatment and one that could not rust in any climate. Plated guns have their inning in damp humid climates. As long as the plating remains intact, they will not rust, whereas a plain blued gun will from the moisture on one's hands or from the air, and must be kept coated with oil or grease at all times to keep them from rusting. This is especially true of guns carried or used near salt water. For very hot humid climates or damp salt sea air, the plated gun is very useful and is perhaps the best finish to be had if you would keep your gun in perfect condition.

They all appear gaudy to me and while they look big after dark, and some police officers prefer them for use in the dark, they also reflect sunlight in daytime and that is not conducive to good shooting. They have their psychological effect when used to stand up a criminal after dark. By and large we do not like their appearance or their reflection of light, as sun reflecting on a bright plated gun will show for

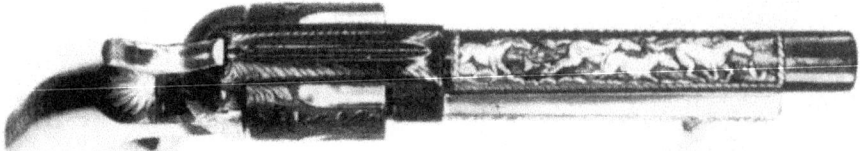

Gold relief work and engraving by "Woodie" Ward, 4225 College Street, Beaumont, Texas. Engraved for F. B. Fletcher (Fletcher Oil Co.) Bay City, Michigan. Photo by R. G. Dixon.

Engraving by "Woodie" Ward. Photo by R. G. Dixon.

Engraving by "Woodie" Ward. Photo by R. G. Dixon.

Engraving by "Woodie" Ward. This work is in relief and was taken from one of the old S. & W. posters of years gone by. It shows rider and horse running from Indians in creek (background) who were giving close chase but, gave up in creek—in very close detail. Photo by R. G. Dixon.

Ornamentation, Barrel Lengths, Balance, Velocities

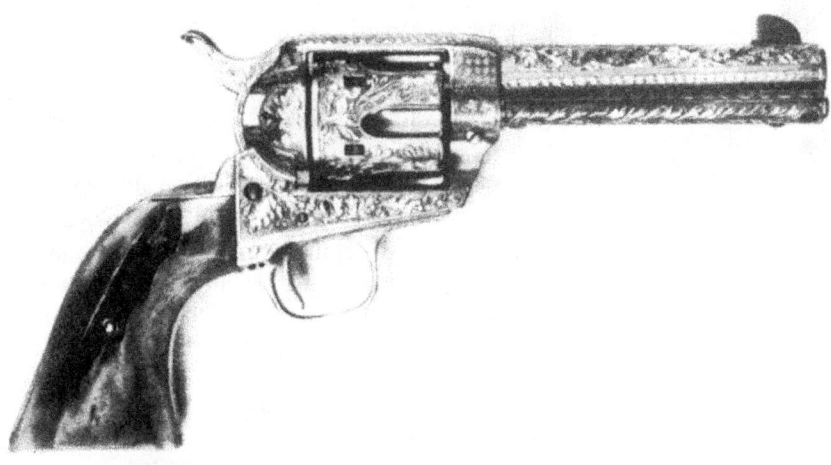

Engraving by "Woodie" Ward.
Photo by R. G. Dixon.

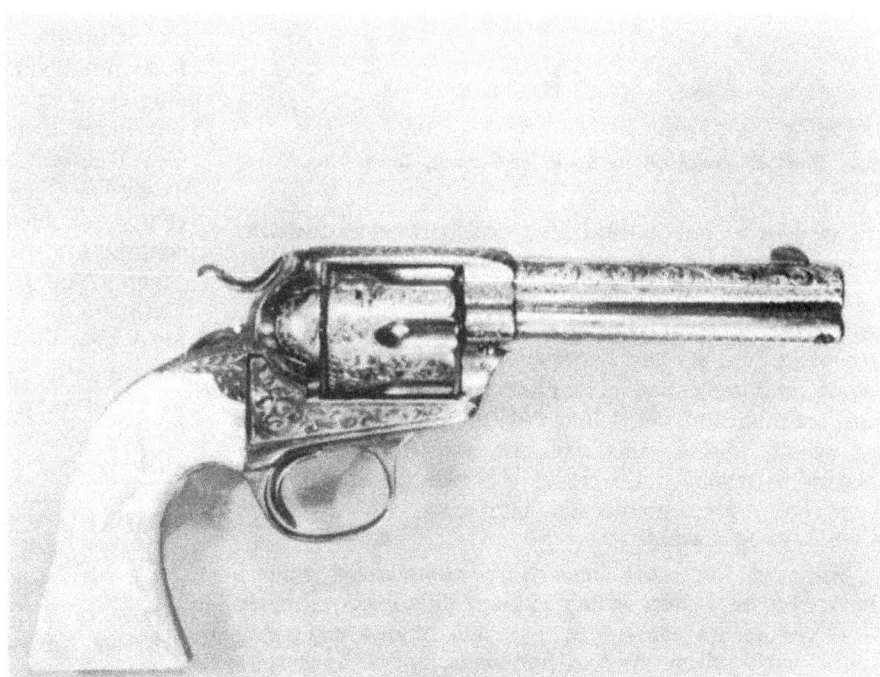

Fancy 4¾-inch barrel Bisley with pearl carved stocks.

Fine engraved and ivory stocked third model Dragoon.

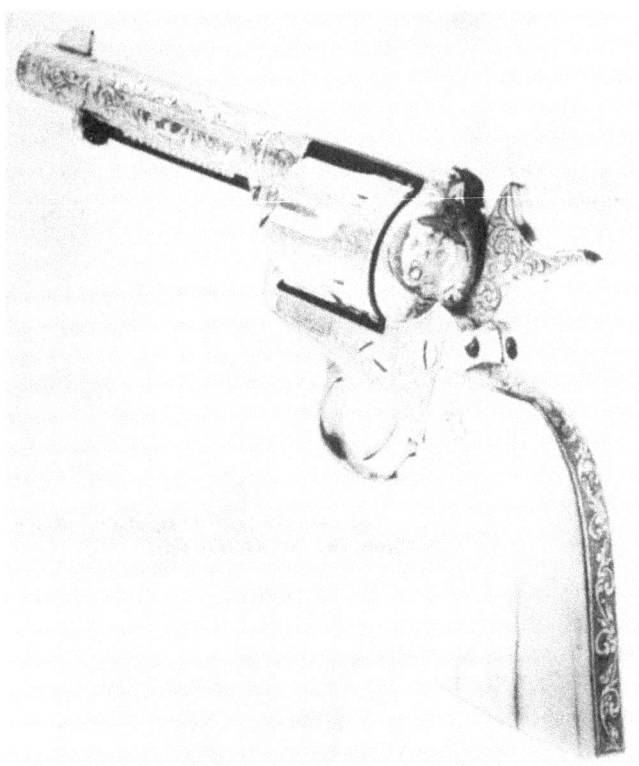

S.A. Colt .45 engraved by John R. Rohner, Iowa City, Iowa.

miles, like a mirror, and give your presence away to either a man or the game you may be hunting.

I have seen many guns lately in most modern design with different plating treatments; some had gold cylinders, triggers and hammers and the rest of the gun blued, and some had gold plated cylinders and trigger and hammer and the balance of the gun silver, chrome or nickel. Plated guns will not rust so long as the plating is intact, but I never did like their looks except the above mentioned coppered .44/40 S. A. Colt I once owned.

Some of the most beautifully ornamented guns I have ever seen were either ancient flint locks or early Colt percussion arms with very fine filigree engraving inlaid with yellow gold in fine lines, and I have seen some S. & W. guns with the same treatment. These are beautiful examples of the gun making art and the photos tell the story far better than any word picture. Kornbrath and others went in for fine engraving and gold inlaid animals or men in action, and these are superb masterpieces of the engraver's art and are absolute tops in ornamentation, for the work is so fine it resembles an oil painting and so perfectly executed that one never tires of looking at such scenes in raised base relief with yellow gold in contrast with finely polished blued steel.

The Gun Reblue Company, Biltmore, North Carolina, does a lot of this engraving and fancy plating. Engraving, I always felt, was lost on a plated gun as it does not show up well, while on a blued gun it shows up better, and as the blueing wears off the gun is still well ornamented and shows up the engraving to better advantage.

Woody Ward of Beaumont, Texas, has a unique and beautiful treatment of pistols and revolvers by overlaying small figures and scroll designs in yellow gold. His work is neat and nice, and beautiful and rich, but not gaudy or coarse in any way. His ornamented guns stand out as perfect examples of sixgun overlay work in precious metals. Gerald Averill of Missoula, Montana, also does some nice work.

Engraved, inlaid or plated guns are usually stocked in pearl, ivory or fine woods. Of all materials, I prefer well seasoned elephant or mastodon ivory. It colors with age and has beautiful grain in many pieces, is hard, and wears better than wood, and even in smooth finish, it is not slick. A beautiful gun with good colored ivory stocks is a thing of beauty anywhere. I do not like checkering on ivory stocks—better plain than checkered. Carving in base relief is the best treatment for ivory or pearl stocks. Some inlays like gold medallions, coins or presentation shields are appropriate on the inside stock; the outside stock should be carved. I do not want any crude carving; either the best examples of raised animal's heads or eagles or else keep the plain beauty of the natural smooth ivory. The Gun Reblue Company now turns out some of the finest examples of carved ivory stocks I have seen. They recently executed an American spread-eagle to our design and also a long horn steer head on S. & W. Magna type grips and that is the best treatment I have yet seen for the big Smith & Wessons. On the steer head one horn is extended to the top of the grip and the other to the bottom of the rear end of grip. This makes a very nice job as the raised under-cut horns fill the crease in ones hand at the fold and give a most perfect grip as well as a beautiful job of ivory carving. Usually the human hand has a hollow in the palm when it is closed around a sixgun or pistol grip and for this reason, raised base relief carving of ivory, pearl or wood, of a design that will fill the hollow in the palm of the hand is beneficial to a good, uniform grip on the gun. It not only enhances the beauty of the stock and gun, if well executed, but also is helpful in getting a firm grip on the gun, and best of all it makes one take the same exact grip each time, which is one of the secrets of accuracy. Carved designs should be designed and executed with utility in mind as well as beauty of design, each complimenting the other.

Many of the old percussion Colts had one piece ivory stocks like the wood stocks for the same and earlier percussion models. These are the best stocks to be had on any single action gun, but cannot be used on a Ruger because its straps are cast in one piece. The glued wood center ivory stocks seem just as good as far as service is concerned, and are much easier to make and cheaper, and in addition not so much ivory is required for the two slabs as if the whole stock were made in one piece and cut out for the straps and main spring.

Pearl is an excellent material for all plated guns and seems to go well with a gaudy gun, but I do not like it as well as ivory. It is flashy in appearance but I prefer the dull beauty of old ivory showing grain and contrast, and which has aged enough to take on a rich creamy color. Carved pearl is beautiful stuff if well executed, but the carving does not seem to show up as well, either in photos or on the gun, and does not show the contrast between the plain and carved surfaces as well as does ivory. When the pearl is thick enough to make a perfectly shaped stock, it is nice, but I do not like any of the thin skimpy stocks formerly furnished in pearl, as they do not offer a good secure grip on the gun. Pearl is always slicker than ivory. Engraved or gold inlaid and blued steel with carved ivory, and possibly a gold inlay in the ivory, is the most beautiful treatment one can have accorded a fine sixgun or auto pistol.

Next to ivory and pearl, I prefer rosewood or Macassar ebony in contrasting colors for stocks. Differences of opinion, however, make Presidential elecitons and horse races, so everyone is entitled to his or her own preference as to ornamentation. I have found that hard dense rosewood or Macassar ebony wears almost as well as ivory and holds its checkering beautifully. Checkering with a bit of carved border or fence around it makes a wonderful sixgun grip and can be made to any style and to fit any hand. I have a very fine S. A. Colt one-piece stock made of rosewood by Frank Pachmayr that has neatly checkered designs surrounded by small, neat floral carvings. It is a masterpiece in a wood stock. I also have two pairs of carved stocks in Circassian walnut by the man who once made the Kearsarge stocks. He even reproduced my signature on the outside of the stocks of this pair of S. & W. Magnum-type grips to fit right and left hand guns. I have never seen a finer made or finished pair of sixgun stocks. They are beauties and fit perfectly. Smith & Wesson recently made me, to order, a couple of pairs of plain clothes type, rounded butt, magna grips of figured rosewood checkered. These are among the best grips I have seen for fast double action work and also look very well on a gun.

Barrel lengths effect the balance and velocity of the pistol. With the automatic pistol we have to take about what is offered by the factories except in the Luger with 4 inch or 8 inch barrel, the 6 inch Navy model and the .22 caliber auto pistols which are furnished by Colt and High Standard usually with choice of 4½ inch or 6 or 6¾ inch length. On sixguns, however, we can have about anything that our fancy dictates.

I have seen old gun fighters pack an S. A. .45 Colt with no barrel at all, as a hidden close range surprise weapon. Just grip, frame, cylinder and mechanical parts. The big slugs upset to fill the chamber mouths on firing and then went straight enough for a gun fight at six to ten feet. It offered the shortest possible gun for carrying in the pocket and could be shot through the coat pocket when necessary. They were wicked weapons at close range, but did not burn nearly all of the powder charge. The slug was apt to land crosswise on the targets, which made no difference to the man using them. Better velocities and more power are secured with a short barrel from 2 inch to 3 inch in length and can be fitted with sights and are accurate as well. For the pocket gun to be carried in pants side pocket or coat pockets, two inch guns are excellent. For carrying in the hip pocket, however, there is no need of ever going below a 4 inch barrel. I

Left to right, Colonel Tod Sloan, represenative of the N.R.A.; the late Major General Merritt A. Edson, Executive Director of the N.R.A., and Elmer Keith.

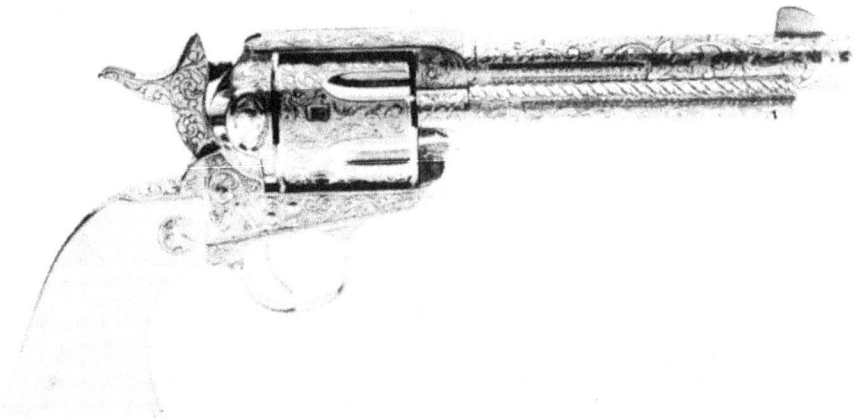

S.A. Colt .45 engraved by John R. Rohner.

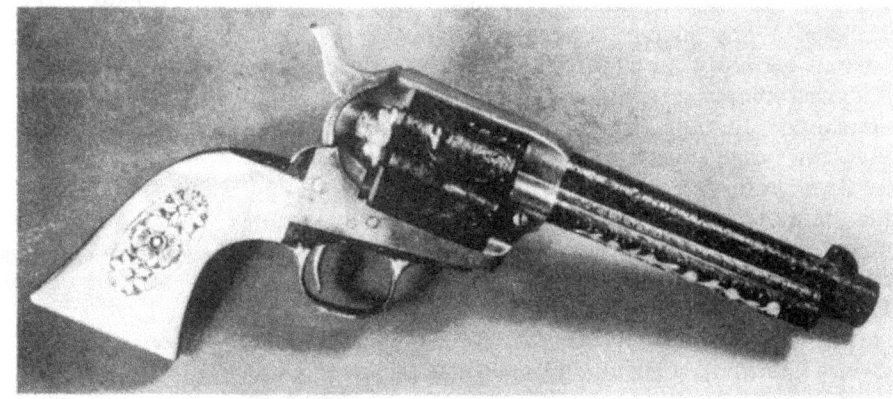

Engraved by E. Averill.

used to carry a 4¾ inch single action in Sam Russell's hip pocket holster very comfortably with butt to the front. This for street wear of course, as it was impossible for the saddle. Short 2 inch barrel jobs are best for pocket use, but do not give as good accuracy as a longer barrel, particularly if high speed or hollow base bullets are used, because the muzzle blast is very severe at the end of a two inch barrel and will distort the base of the bullet causing tippers and keyholes on the target.

Bullets fired from the cylinder without a barrel usually show the base of the slug badly mushroomed and larger than the middle or front bearing surface of the bullet. For this reason barrels under 4 inches are a mistake for any holster weapon, as they are not as accurate as longer barreled guns unless low velocity is used as well as a flat-base hard bullet that will not deform from muzzle blast. Such short barreled guns are fast and if used at a few feet for fast hip shooting, are excellent, but they usually come in .38 Special or smaller calibers, and for this reason are never as effective, when the chips are down, as a heavier holster weapon.

I never could see much sense in cutting a heavy caliber gun, .357 magnum to .45 Colt, below 4 inches. It is too bulky and heavy for a pocket gun, and while

Don Gowan, manager of the Gun Re-Blue Company shows the Berns-Martin Lightning holster in position but with his arm under the gun to better show the holster, also a fancy single action.

ORNAMENTATION, BARREL LENGTHS, BALANCE, VELOCITIES 297

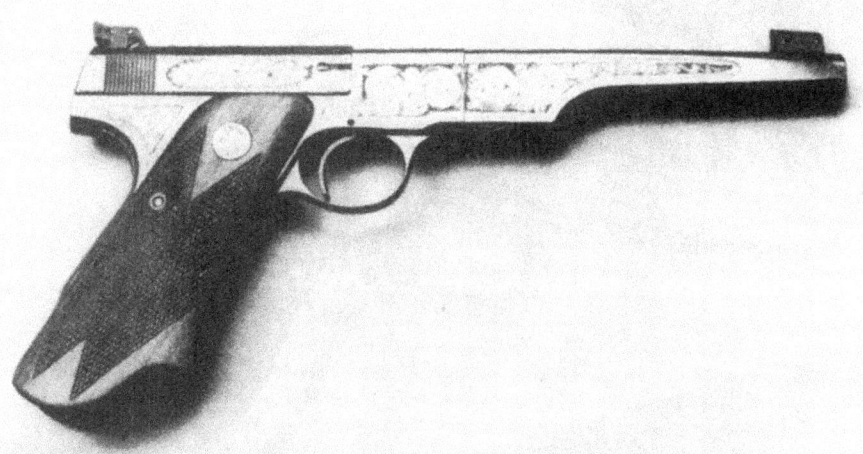

Engraved by E. Averill, Rt. 3, Miller Creek Road, Missoula, Montana.

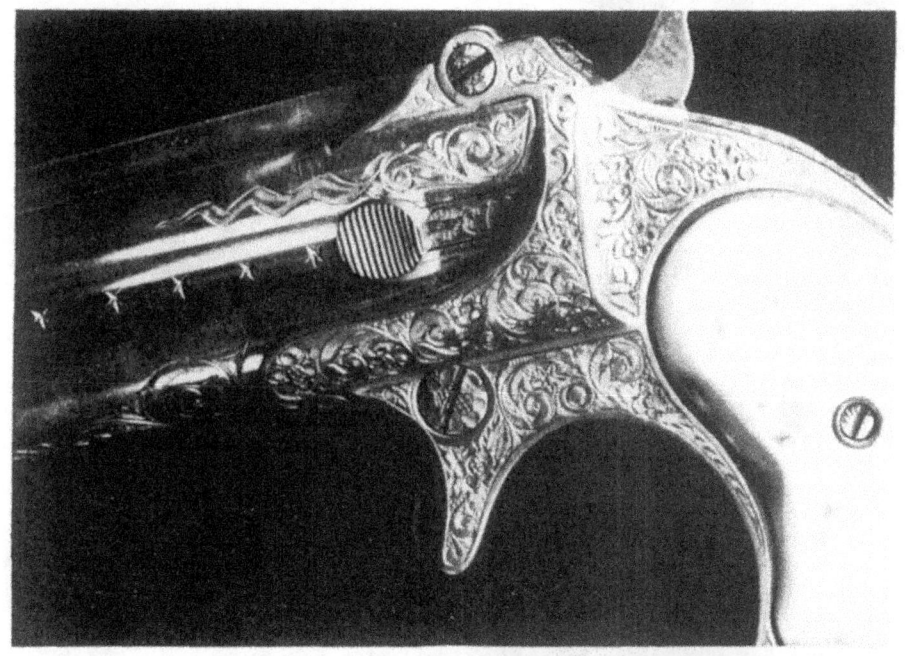

Engraving on a .41 Remington Double Derringer.

Smith & Wesson light weight Chief's Special .38 caliber revolver engraved by Gun Re-Blue Company.

Colt Commander engraved and with plated slide, side safety and trigger by Gun Re-Blue Company.

Group of pearl, ivory and stag fancy grips made by The Gun Re-Blue Company.

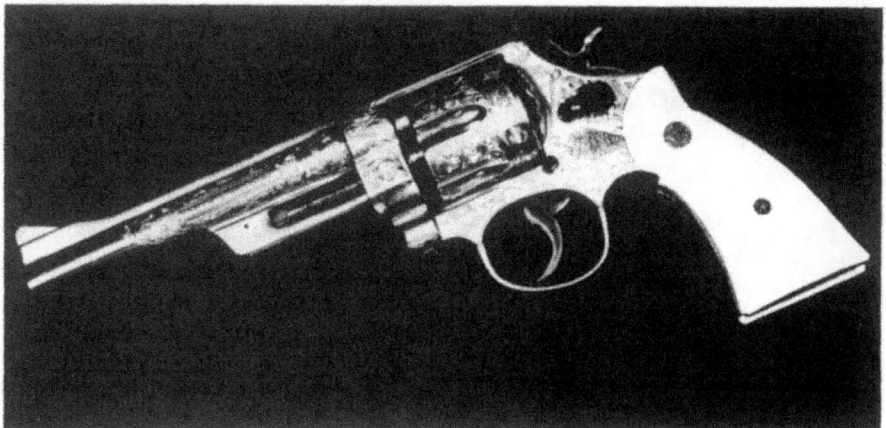

6½ inch Smith & Wesson Magnum with ramp front sight and engraved and plain ivory stocked by the Gun Re-Blue Company—Magna-type stocks of good elephant ivory.

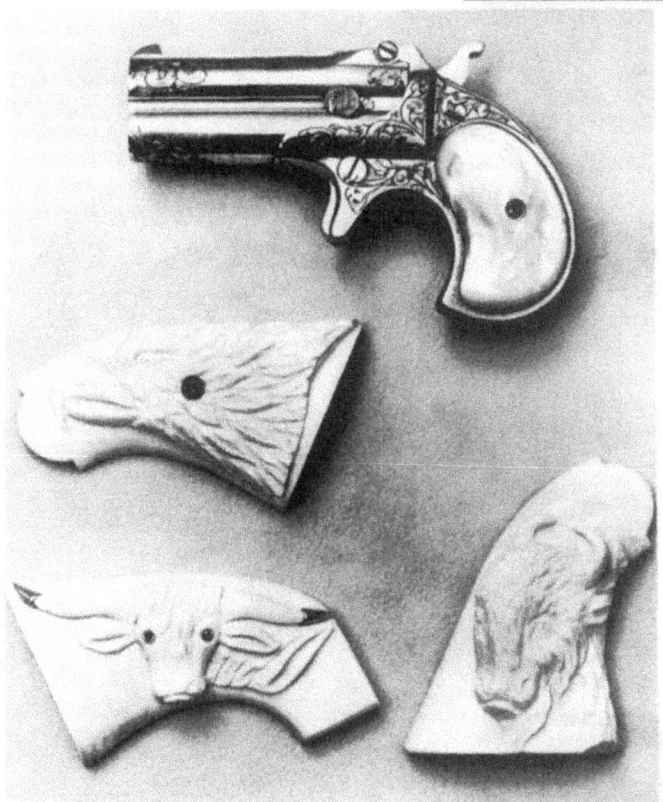

The famous old Remington .41 rim fire Double Derringer engraved and with plain pearl grips. Also two fine sets of carved ivory grips for the double action gun and one set of ox head carved ivory with jewelled eyes and gold tipped horns for the single action, Colt, Ruger or Great Western by the Gun Re-Blue Company.

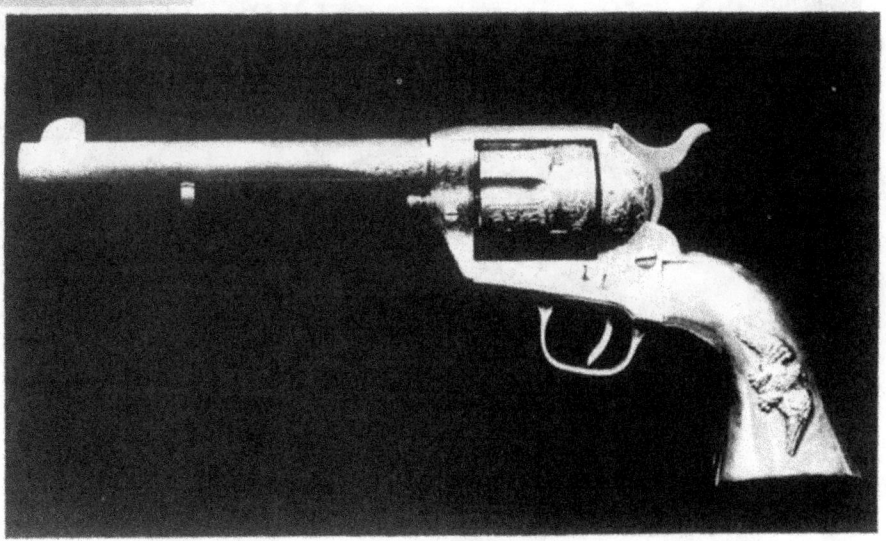

A very fine S.A. Colt with sterling silver solid grips.

8⅜ inch barrel Smith & Wesson .357 Magnum engraved and fitted with stag grips by the Gun Re-Blue Company.

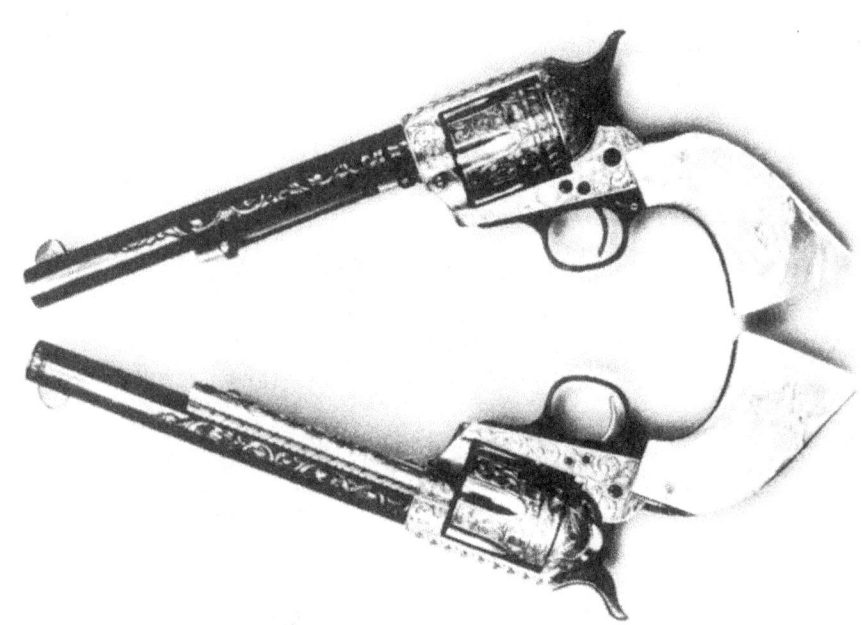

Pair of 7½ inch Colt single actions engraved and with gold plated straps, frame, extractor housing and hammer by Gun Re-Blue Company, fitted with bear's head carved pearl grips. A very ornate pair.

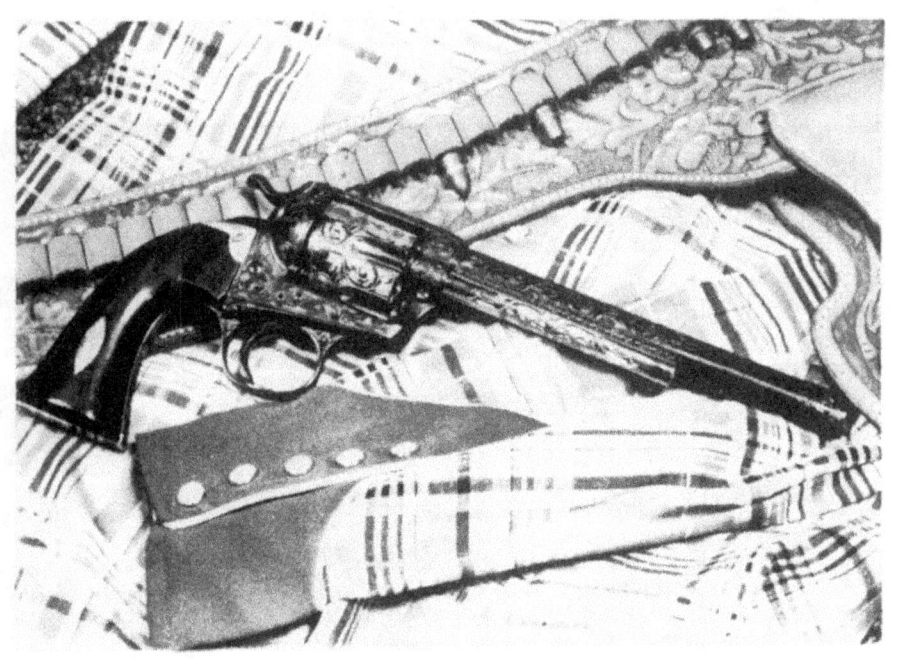

Engraved and stocked Bisley Colt by Gun Re-Blue Company, Biltmore, N. C.

Ornamentation, Barrel Lengths, Balance, Velocities 301

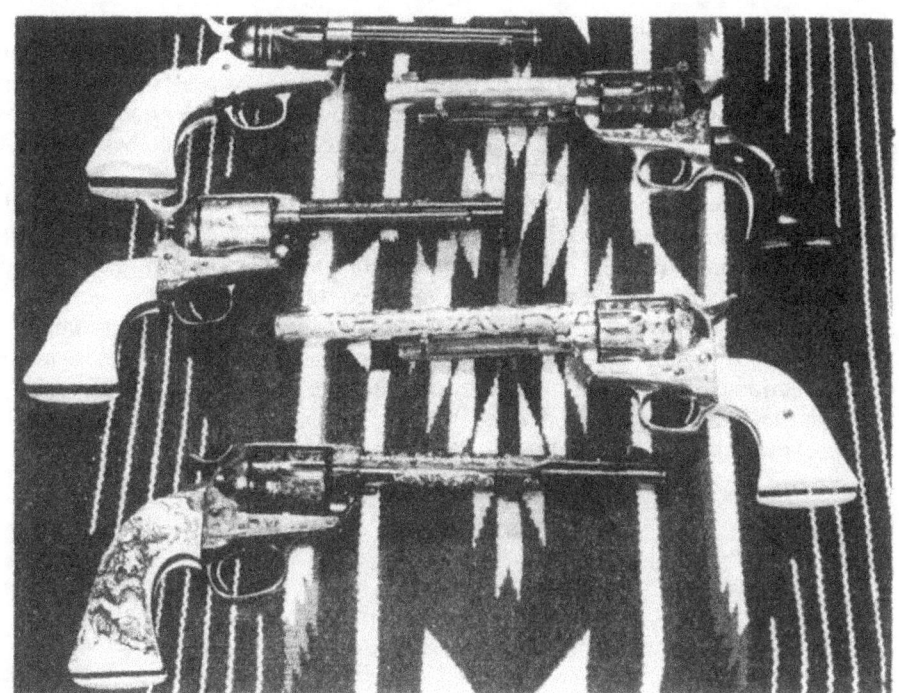

Fancy guns engraved and stocked by Gun Re-Blue Company.

Engraving by "Woodie" Ward.

S. & W. Magnum engraved and stocked by Gun Re-Blue Company.

such a short barreled heavy caliber gun can be used in a coat pocket, especially a top coat, or with the single action in specially made large pants pockets, as John Newman used to pack them, I believe most men are better fitted with a 4 inch barrel job, on the waist belt, in a quick draw holster.

For the plain colthesman, the 4 inch double action gun is about right, or the 4¾ inch single action carried on a holster on the waist belt. It rides high enough; it does not hit the seat of a chair or car when seated, and is comfortable and yet a very fast and deadly weapon for the gun fighter. The 4 inch in the big double action Colt or Smith & Wesson and the 4¾ inch in the Colt, Ruger, or Great Western single actions gives one the best balanced guns on earth for fast hip shooting. The weight of the gun seems to lie right in the hand, and with the single actions, rests on the second finger as it should. The same effect can be had with double action by a grip with a slight filler behind the trigger guard or by use of the smallest of the patented Pachmayr grip adapters. Men with large hands seldom need the grip adapter, but those with small hands often find it advantageous.

In the big .45 frame guns, we find the 4 inch for double actions to 4¾ inch for single actions to be the best length for balance and fast handling. Good balance is absolutely essential to fast accurate hip shooting as you throw the gun toward the target, and if it does not balance right you may hit higher or lower than desired. The perfectly balanced gun, however,

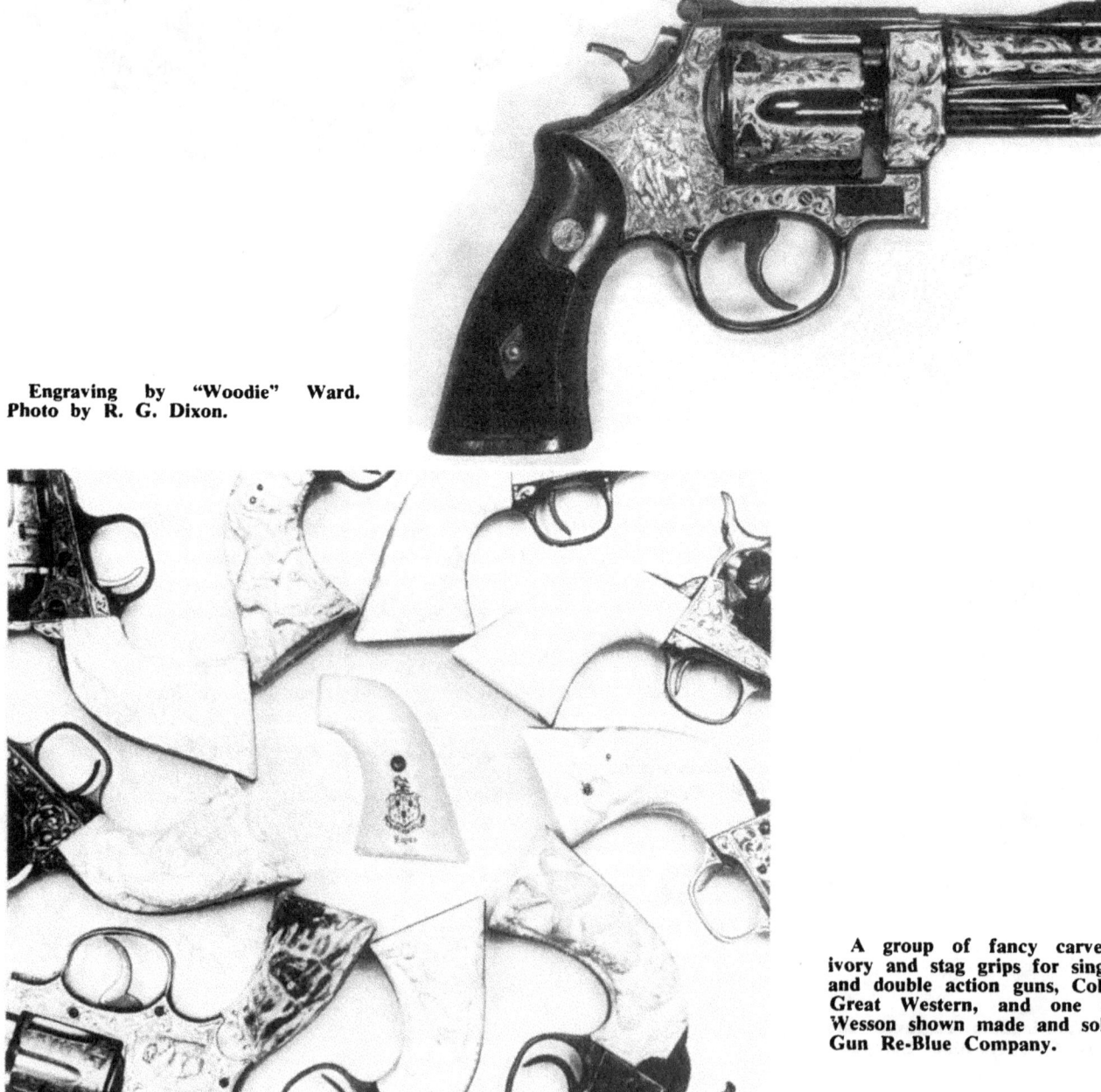

Engraving by "Woodie" Ward. Photo by R. G. Dixon.

A group of fancy carved, pearl, ivory and stag grips for single action and double action guns, Colt, Ruger, Great Western, and one Smith & Wesson shown made and sold by the Gun Re-Blue Company.

throws its slugs right where you point and points as naturally as your finger. Big men, six feet or over, with large hips can carry a 5 inch gun just as easily as small men can a 4 inch job on the waist belt without it punching the car or chair seat and then pushing the waist-belt upward. For these bigger chaps, the longer 5 inch barrel is perfectly acceptable. The balance of the piece suffers for fast work as the barrel lengthens over 5 inches, and I believe the best barrel lengths for the gun fighter to be 4 to 5 inches. For such purposes I prefer the 4 inch Smith & Wesson double action .44 Special, the 4¾ inch single action of same caliber, or the new Great Western "Deputy" with 4 inch barrel—this is a very fine S. A. for the gun fighter.

Long barrels are for deliberate target, long-range shooting, but are more cumbersome to carry and slower to get into action than short barreled guns. I never could swallow the yarns told of Wyatt Earp being lightening fast with a Buntline special. It is a physical impossibility for him, or any man, to handle a long 12 inch barreled gun as fast as a short barreled one. Bat Masterson and Bill Tilghman, we do know, preferred and used 4¾ inch .45 S. A. Colts and with good reason. Both were experienced peace officers and came through on their feet in many a desperate gun fight. For the hills, game shooting or straight target shooting, the longer barrels have merit as they give longer sight radius, higher velocity and greater bullet energy.

For use in the hills or from horseback, the 6 to 7½ inch barrels are fine, but the 7½ inch single actions and the 8⅜ inch Magnum S. & W. will usually ride against the saddle skirts. This is the reason so many .44 Army 1860 Model Colts, Colt Navies and the huge Dragoons had one side of the muzzle worn away. They rubbed a hole through their holsters, then rubbed against the saddle skirts until one side of the muzzle was often worn to the bore. They do not balance as well as the shorter weapons, but are superior in power and sight radius and one can better place his shots with them on game, or for long range work. The 8⅜ inch magnum is so muzzle-heavy it takes a tremendous amount of practice to toughen the hand, wrist and arm muscles to hold it steadily for long strings with one hand. This great length of barrel is better suited to deliberate two handed game shooting than anything else.

Next let us look at velocities. Under 4 inches of barrel length in revolvers, a great deal is lost in velocity for each inch removed and it may be as much as forty feet or more with some loads and powders. Fast hot powders such as Western's new ball-pistol powder or Bullseye which burns in the first few inches of cylinder and barrel are by all odds the best for use in two inch or three inch barrel jobs. These fast powders give good velocities in short barrel guns, but may distort the base of a soft bullet and for this reason give some keyholing on the target. Up to 4 inches barrel length on revolvers, considerable muzzle velocity and energy is lost for each inch removed. Over 4 inches not so much is lost, as a cylinder plus a 4 inch barrel will burn nicely about all the powder with most fast pistol powders. With some powders and loads a gain of only seven to ten feet may be added for each additional inch in barrel length over 4 inches. For instance, a recent chronograph test of the .357 magnum with a 6 inch barrel

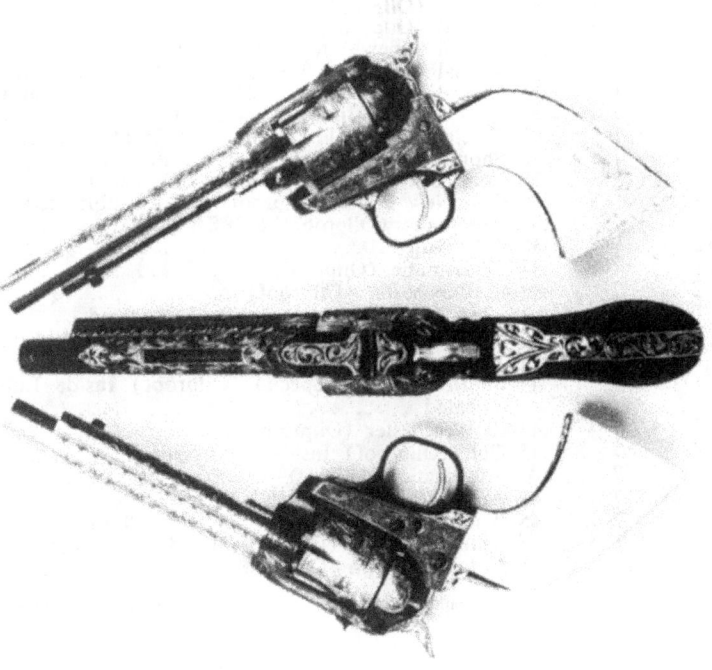

Three Ruger Single Sixes, with real loading gates, engraved and also plated barrels and cylinders and spread eagle carved pearl grips on two of them by Gun Re-Blue Company.

WESTERN PISTOL AND REVOLVER CARTRIDGES—SPECIFICATIONS AND BALLISTICS
ALL CARTRIDGES OTHER THAN BLANKS LOADED WITH SMOKELESS POWDER

LOAD No.	PRIMER No.	CARTRIDGE	BULLET Wgt. Grs.	Type	BARREL LENGTH	MUZZLE VELOCITY Feet per Second	MUZZLE ENERGY Foot Lbs.	PENETRATION 7/8 Soft Pine Boards at 15 Ft.
K1208R	....	.22 Short SUPER-X Wax Coated	29	Lubaloy	6"	1,035	69	....
K1262R	....	.22 Short XPERT Greased	29	Lead	6"	865	48	....
K1203R	....	.22 Short (Blank) Black Powder	...	No Bullet	....	.....	....	....
K1216R	....	.22 Long SUPER-X Wax Coated	29	Lubaloy	6"	1,095	77	....
K1225R	....	.22 Long Rifle SUPER-X Wax Coated	40	Lubaloy	6"	1,125	112	....
K1264R	....	.22 Long Rifle XPERT Greased	40	Lead	6"	950	80	....
K1267R	....	.22 Long Rifle SUPER-MATCH MARK II Greased	40	Lead	6"	950	80	....
K1302T	1½	.25 Automatic (Oilproof)	50	Metal Case	2"	820	75	3
K1310T	1½	.30 Mauser (7.63 m/m) (Oilproof)	86	Metal Case	5½"	1,420	385	11
K1312T	1½	.30 Luger (7.65 m/m) (Oilproof)	93	Metal Case	4½"	1,250	323	11
K1314T	1½	.32 Automatic (Oilproof)	71	Metal Case	4"	980	158	5
K1316T	1½B	.32 Smith & Wesson Blank (Black Powder)	...	No Bullet	....	.....	....	....
K1317T	1½	.32 Smith & Wesson (Oilproof) Inside Lubricated	85	Lubaloy	3"	720	98	3
K1320T	1½	.32 Smith & Wesson Long (Oilproof) Inside Lubricated	98	Lubaloy	4¼"	820	146	4
K1384T	1½	.32 Smith & Wesson Long Super-Match Clean-Cutting (Oilproof) Inside Lubricated	98	Lead	6"	770	129	....
K1323T	1½	.32 Short Colt (Oilproof) Greased	80	Lubaloy	4"	800	114	3
K1325T	1½	.32 Long Colt (Oilproof) Inside Lubricated	82	Lubaloy	4"	800	117	3
K3249T	108	.32 Colt New Police (Oilproof) Inside Lubricated	98	Lead	4"	795	138	3
K1390C	6½	.32-20 Winchester (Oilproof) Inside Lubricated	100	Lubaloy	6"	1,030	271	6
K3214C	108	.32-20 Winchester (Oilproof)	100	Full Patch	6"	1,030	271	6
K1391C	6½	.32-20 Winchester (Oilproof)	100	Soft Point	6"	1,030	271	6
K1381T	1½	.357 Magnum (Oilproof) SUPER-X Inside Lubricated	158	Lubaloy	8⅜"	1,450	738	12
K1382T	1½	.357 Magnum Met. Pierc. (Oilproof) SUPER-X Inside Lubricated, Lead Bearing	158	Metal Point	8⅜"	1,450	738	12
K9004T*	108	9 m/m Luger (Parabellum) (Oilproof)	115	Full Patch	4"	1,150	365	10
K1336T	1½B	.38 Smith & Wesson Blank (Black Powder)	...	No Bullet	....	.....	....	....
K1337T	1½	.38 Smith & Wesson (Oilproof) Inside Lubricated	145	Lubaloy	4"	745	179	....
K3867T*†	108	.38 Smith & Wesson (Oilproof) Inside Lubricated	200	Lead	4"	630	176	5
K1379T	1½	.38 Special Met. Pierc. (Oilproof) SUPER-X Inside Lubricated, Lead Bearing	150	Metal Point	5"	1,175	460	11
K1380T	1½	.38 Special (Oilproof) SUPER-X Inside Lubricated	150	Lubaloy	5"	1,175	460	9
K1341T	1½	.38 Special (Oilproof) Inside Lubricated	158	Lubaloy	6"	870	266	7
K1346T	1½	.38 Special Super-Match (Oilproof) Inside Lubricated	158	Lead	6"	845	251	7
K1342T	1½	.38 Special (Oilproof) Inside Lubricated, Lead Bearing	158	Metal Point	6"	870	266	7.5
K1343T	1½	.38 Special Super-Match Mid-Range Clean-Cutting (Oilproof) Inside Lubricated	148	Lead	6"	770	195	....
K1345T	1½	.38 Special Super-Police (Oilproof) Inside Lubricated	200	Lubaloy	6"	745	247	7.5
K1348T	1½	.38 Short Colt (Oilproof) Greased	130	Lubaloy	6"	770	171	4
K1350T	1½	.38 Long Colt (Oilproof) Inside Lubricated	150	Lubaloy	6"	785	205	6
K3849T*	108	.38 Colt New Police (Oilproof) Inside Lubricated	150	Lead	4"	695	161	4
K1353T	1½	.38 Automatic (Oilproof) SUPER-X	130	Metal Case	5"	1,300	488	10
K1389T	1½	.38 Automatic	130	Metal Case	4½"	1,070	331	9
K1354T	1½	.380 Automatic (Oilproof)	95	Metal Case	3¾"	970	199	5.5
K1357C	7	.38-40 Winchester (Oilproof)	180	Soft Point	5"	975	380	6
K1361T	1½	.41 Long Colt (Oilproof) Inside Lubricated	200	Lubaloy	6"	745	247	3
K4474T*	111	.44 Smith & Wesson Russian (Oilproof) Inside Lubricated	246	Lead	6½"	770	324	4
K4484T*	111	.44 Smith & Wesson Special (Oilproof) Inside Lubricated	246	Lead	6½"	770	324	7.5
K1372C	7	.44-40 Winchester (Oilproof)	200	Soft Point	7½"	975	422	6
K1374T	7	.45 Colt (Oilproof) Inside Lubricated	255	Lubaloy	5½"	870	429	6
K1375T	7	.45 Automatic (Oilproof)	230	Metal Case	5"	860	378	6
K1376T	7	.45 Automatic Super-Match	230	Metal Case	5"	710	257	5
K1383T	7	.45 Automatic Met. Pierc. (Oilproof) SUPER-X	230	Metal Case	5"	940	450	11
K4553T*	111	.45 Automatic Rim (Oilproof) Inside Lubricated	230	Lead	5½"	820	343	6
K4554T*†	111	.45 Automatic Rim (Oilproof)	230	Full Patch	5½"	820	343	6

*Supplied in Winchester brand only. †Discontinued. Will be supplied until stock is exhausted.

Courtesy of Western Cartridge Company

showed an average velocity of 1270 feet while the same load in an 8⅜ inch barrel showed an average of 1328 feet or a total of 58 feet for the 2⅜ inch addition to the 6 inch barrel. The same .357 magnum load in a 2 inch barrel gave only 1093 feet, while in a 4 inch barrel it did an average of 1206 feet. This was a gain from 2 inches to 4 inches barrel length of 113 feet, a very material gain in velocity or 57½ feet per inch. In the 4 inch barrel at 1206 feet as against a 6 inch barrel, we find it averaging 1270 feet, a gain of 64 feet per second or an addition of 32 feet per inch. This high velocity .357 magnum loading can be taken as representative of what happens when the barrel is shortened below 4 inches, also what is gained when it is increased to 6 inches or to the extreme of 8⅜ inches. The ballistic figures we have just quoted were taken from a commercially loaded cartridge and are not final. When ammunition is hand-loaded for maximum velocity, we would expect Bullseye to give the best results with light bullets and short barrels and something slightly slower, such as No. 2400, with long barrels and heavy bullets. Maximum handiness and effectiveness are reached at barrel lengths between 4 and 6 inches and it would seem that the 4 inch gun is not so far behind the 6 inch in actual performance.

The fact remains that where the long barrel can be carried with ease, barrels up to 6 inches or even 7½ inches are slightly better than shorter barreled guns, both for velocity and energy, and also for sight radius. In the long barrels we have to pay for these gains by having poorer balance and a slower gun for defensive work as well as a longer more unhandy gun to pack. Probably the 4¾ inch single action and 4 to 5 inch double action is the best compromise, all things considered. I personally prefer the 4 inch in a double action for a defense gun, or in single action, the 4¾ inch. I once saw a single action with a cut down extractor rod and housing in .45 Colt caliber, owned by the late General Schwartz, that had a 4 inch barrel and it was a mighty handy defense gun, yet it would extract its empties.

For holster use, I cannot see a gun of under 4 inch barrel; and for fast quick draw work, I do not like one with over a 5 inch barrel; but for game shooting in the hills, the long barrels are slightly better, and especially for two handed game shooting. They offer the ultimate in velocity, energy and sight radius. In making a selection, decide what the gun will be most used for and make your choice accordingly.

Chapter XX

Care and Cleaning

A GUN IS A TOOL; treat it as such. Automatic pistols and sixguns are easy to keep in perfect condition. A good workman takes care of his tools; a gunman does the same with his pistol or revolver. In dry climates very little care is necessary, but in damp, humid areas or near the sea where the air is always charged with salt, one must take every precaution to keep his gun in good shape.

After firing the gun, clean it; regardless of whether modern non-corrosive ammunition is used or not, clean it anyway. It takes but a few minutes to run a swab through the bore and chambers saturated with Hoppes No. 9, Bore-Kleen, or any of the various other good solvents on the market. Wipe off the outside of the gun. With revolvers, clean the front and sides of the cylinder, the rear end of the barrel and recesses in the frame; cock the gun and swab the firing pin and hammer. If lead appears in the throat or the bore, push a stiff brass bristle brush through it a few times followed by the solvent swab. The muzzle and around the front sight should also be swabbed with solvent, but with this caution, some solvents are hard on gold beads. If the outer surface of the gun is then wiped off with a slightly oiled rag, the gun will stay in perfect condition for a long time in a dry climate, but if in a very damp, wet one or along the seacoast, it is well to coat it with a heavier grease, such as Rig, which has body enough to stick to bore, chambers and outside. Salt air will attack any exposed steel surface. A few drops of oil should be used in the mechanism, and this can usually be applied by dropping it behind the trigger and when the hammer is cocked.

In dry climates it is well to have a gunsmith, with perfect fitting screw drivers, dismantle a gun every few years and clean all parts with solvent and oil and replace them, especially if the gun is carried on a horse or in a car where dust will sift into the works and accumulate and in time gum up everything with old dried oil and dirt. Never try to dismantle a gun if you are not thoroughly familiar with the procedure, as you may damage or ruin parts, or have springs jump away from you and become lost. The lads who just must see what makes a gun work should get a job in a gun factory.

More guns are ruined every year by neglect, or by some curious soul wanting to see what makes them tick, than are ever worn out by actual shooting. Dismantling fine guns with ill fitting screw drivers is a crime. When a gun really needs disassembly, cleaning and oiling, it should be done by a competent gunsmith, never by an inexperienced tyro.

Modern revolvers and pistols fired with smokeless ammunition are very easy to clean and need little attention; usually only a patch saturated with solvent, or better still, one of the wool swabs Smith & Wesson formerly furnished with their guns, and a few minutes work is all that is required.

When black power is used the story is different. The powder fouling must be removed, either with an aqueous solvent solution or just plain water, on a patch, and the gun thoroughly dried and swabbed with oil or solvent. When fired with old corrosive primers, solvent or water is the safest method of removing all primer salts. Cap and ball guns must be dismounted occasionally to get the fragments of broken caps out of the action and to wash the parts, oil, and replace them. A good solvent is excellent for this purpose and if it is not available, nothing is better than clean boiling water. The parts will dry of their own heat and can then be lightly oiled.

With all cartridge single actions, the cylinder, base pin and bushing, should be removed and cleaned and oiled. Colt and Great Western base pin bushings should be kept well oiled so they will not gum up and get stuck in place. Also the holes in the frame for the base pin. Cap and ball base pins should always be coated with a heavy grease like Rig or Winchester gun grease or some other heavy grease that will stay in place. The base pin is usually cannellured most of its length to hold such a grease. With swing-out, cylinder, modern revolvers, the base pin latch in the rear of the frame should be kept oiled, and also the front latch with S. & W. guns, and the triple lock should have all three latches well oiled.

With auto pistols, one should insert the swab

through the magazine port with the slide back and action open and swab off the face of the breech block and the entire inside of the magazine well, and the ramp from magazine to barrel chamber. Seldom is it necessary to dismantle them unless they become caked with dust. More auto pistols are ruined through loss of parts from being dismantled by inexperienced persons than are worn out by actual use.

All guns, if you use them daily, will become worn in places and the finish will be polished away; and they are bound to accumulate a few scratches, but they should show only normal use and not abuse. Never use a gun for a hammer or a club if you care anything about it. The average western movie thriller certainly does not teach the youngster proper care of a good sixgun. You will see the movie sheriff nailing wanted notices to buildings with the butt of his gun and you may also see some movie cow-poke pulling staples in the fence with the front sight of his gun and then driving them in again with the butt after leading his horse across the wire. I have examined many guns that had been so used, and all were ruined: stocks broken and chipped and dented, frames badly scarred and front sights bent or battered out of shape and stock straps sprung until the stock no longer fitted the gun. The carpenter does not throw his saws and tools on the floor or drop them on the ground or abuse them; neither should a gunman so treat his sixgun.

The movies also show guns being dropped in sand, dirt, or even in the rocks, and while it may have to happen that way sometimes, it is always detrimental to the gun.

Many guns are wrecked or damaged by tyros practicing quick draw. If they do not thoroughly understand the single action, they will often partly cock the hammer on the draw and let it slip with full main spring tension. The sear, which is the top of the trigger, will fall into the safety or half-cock notch and either tear out the notch or break the top of the sear. Guns are scarred by a tyro fumbling his draw and dropping the gun in the dirt, rocks or on a hard cement floor. Quick draw should be practiced slowly until all the mechanics are fully mastered and no slip occurs. Make speed follow proficiency.

Spinning guns on the finger and all such stunts come under the same heading as Russian Roulette. They have about as much relation to fast gun handling, or gun fighting, as spinning a rope has to roping calves. Both are for show and have no practical application.

Treat a gun as you would your watch; it will get enough scars if you accord it every care, but it will still be a good gun, clean and trustworthy when you need it. You can tell a good workman by his tools and, by the same token, you can judge a gunman's ability by the gun he carries. I have seen many an old cow-poke's gun with the grips worn away from the steel at the edges of the strap, both wood and ivory, but the gun was clean, oiled and as deadly as a coiled rattlesnake, and ready for business. Constant contact with brush and clothing and saddles may have worn the sights and the muzzle on one side. The ivory or wood of the stocks was polished away from the steel; the gun showed use but not abuse. At times it is hard to properly clean and care for a gun, particularly on long cow drives or pack trips, when you are traveling every day from morning until night. I used to pack a small tin box in my pocket with a leather thong large and stiff enough to poke down the bore of my gun and a bunch of solvent soaked patches in the can. The leather thong had a slit in one end and patches were threaded through this and pulled through the bore and chambers and the gun wiped off. It has enabled me to carry guns all my life under every conceivable condition and yet keep them in first class shooting order. Being carried behind a big trail drive is about the worst thing that can happen to a gun, as it becomes caked with dust. Most automatics will jam and quit you cold after such treatment if not kept properly cleaned and oiled.

In hard rains one can usually keep his gun under a coat or slicker, but if none is available and the gun becomes soaked, it should be dried out as soon as possible and oiled to prevent rust. A shoulder holster under a waterproof coat is the best place for a gun when you are out all day in steady rain or wet snow. River-boat traveling is perhaps the hardest of all on a gun, and unless watched and oiled very often it will soon rust as everything in the boat soon becomes saturated with moisture. A bed roll becomes so damp that it will rust any gun rolled in it during the day. Sheep skin lined pouch holsters, wonderful dust covers in a car in dry countries, will absorb so much moisture they will rust any gun in boat travel. Some such wool lined holsters are now treated with a special rust resisting compound and guns carried in them are safe.

Hand guns should never be thrown loose in the glove compartment of cars as they rattle around and become scratched and scarred and accumulate dust that sifts down into the mechanism and will soon put them out of commission. It is also the first place a crook will look for them if he breaks into your car, and more sixguns are stolen from glove lockers in cars than from any other source each year. They are far safer in a holster under the seat, if not carried on the person. Many clamps are now sold commercially to hold a gun on the dash or steering wheel of the car. It is in sight for officer's inspection and where you can get it if it is needed. Some states prohibit the carrying of any gun in a car without permit.

Many a gun has been lost or damaged by being hung over a saddle horn and the horse left to graze. He may decide his back itches and roll on the gun in the dirt, mud or rocks to the detriment of the gun. When you leave a horse, take your gun with you, whether a rifle or sixgun.

Small children should never be allowed to play with a gun if it has any value, as they will surely ruin it, either by taking it apart, using it as a hammer or by subjecting it to other abuse. It is also dangerous if it can be loaded and fired at all. They should be taught that guns should be left alone. It is only natural for children to want to play with guns, and their education should start early in life so they will grow up with due respect for a deadly but useful tool.

When hunting or carrying a gun in bad weather, the shoulder holster under the coat is the best and safest place for the gun. If negotiating rough country or climbing around ledges or cliffs, a belt holster while handy for quick work, exposes your gun to many scratches and hard knocks. One should shift his gun around where it won't get damaged in such country, or else carry it in a shoulder holster inside the shirt or coat.

When working cattle, running wild horses or riding colts or mean horses, all shoulder holsters of the spring variety and all belt holsters of the spring variety, like the Berns-Martin, are out, unless they have a safety strap with heavy glove fastener. Many times I have seen sixguns fly high in the air and come down in the rocks, dirt or mud, always to the detriment of the gun. The best outfit for carrying a gun on a horse is a belt holster with a safety strap.

Guns to be stored over long periods of time should be cleaned thoroughly, the mechanism oiled with a light oil and the inside of the barrel and chambers greased with a fairly heavy grease, such as Rig, and the outside thoroughly covered with the same, and wrapped, preferably in heavy oiled paper or some of the patent rust preventative paper, and stored in a clean cardboard box. They will then keep in perfect condition for many years. Never put any heavy gummy grease inside the mechanism of a gun, it will harden in time and gum it up hopelessly. A little care before a gun is put away will pay dividends over the years.

This chapter concludes this work of many months. I advise every shooter of the handgun to become a member of The National Rifle Association of America. This is the only organization in the world actively fighting for our heritage, the right to own and bear arms, the free, untrammeled and patriotic possession of sixguns for ourselves and posterity. Sixguns helped materially to settle this country. May they help to keep it a nation of free men and women. Only the National Rifle Association of America carries the fight into the halls of Congress for safe and sane gun laws, and it well merits the support of everyone who burns powder in this country today. Only by its support and perpetuation, can the shooters of America hope to continue the free use of the sixgun.

It occurs to me that many students of ballistic tables, and paper experts may find faults with what I have written in this book. More power to them. I will not quarrel with anyone interested in handguns. What I have set forth did not come from books, greatly as we admire nearly all we have read. It came from personal experience, from thousands of conversations with cow-punchers, backwoods gun packers, gun fighters on both sides of the law, and the reminiscences of battle experienced veterans of all our wars from the Civil War on. Add to this an endless correspondence with these same people, with police officers, sportsmen and pistol cranks from all over the world outside the Iron Curtain, and you have the background for our expressions.

That I could be wrong is an eventuality that has not escaped me. I just painted the pictures as I saw them. I do not know how to do anything else.

www.ingramcontent.com/pod-product-compliance
Lightning Source LLC
Chambersburg PA
CBHW080531170426
43195CB00016B/2532